Sta Monica, CA

The Collected Works Of
HAL LINDSEY

The Collected Works Of
HAL LINDSEY

THE LATE GREAT PLANET EARTH

SATAN IS ALIVE AND WELL ON PLANET EARTH

THE LIBERATION OF PLANET EARTH

INSPIRATIONAL PRESS

Published in 1992 by

Inspirational Press
A division of LDAP, Inc.
386 Park Avenue South
New York, New York 10016

Inspirational Press is a registered trademark of LDAP, Inc.

Published by arrangement with Zondervan Publishing House

Library of Congress Catalog Card Number: 92-72503

ISBN 0-88486-067-1

Designed by Hannah Lerner

Printed in the United States of America.

CONTENTS

THE

LATE GREAT

PLANET EARTH

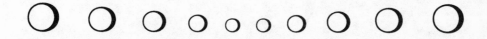

CONTENTS

ACKNOWLEDGMENTS

Grateful appreciation is extended to the following for permission to quote from their copyrighted materials:

LIFE Magazine: From *Reminiscences*, by General Douglas MacArthur, *Life* Magazine, © 1964 Time Inc.

THE LOCKMAN FOUNDATION. For Scriptures from *The New American Standard Bible, New Testament*. © 1960, 1962, 1963 by The Lockman Foundation.

NATIONAL COUNCIL OF THE CHURCHES OF CHRIST. For Scriptures from *The Revised Standard Version of the Bible*. © 1952, 1956 by The Division of Christian Education, National Council of Churches of Christ in the United States of America.

SIMON & SCHUSTER, INC. For quote from *Has Man a Future?* by Bertrand Russell. © 1962 by Simon & Schuster, Inc.

VAN NOSTRAND REINHOLD CO. For quotes from *China: Emerging World Power* by Victor Petrov. © 1967 by Litton Educational Publishing, Inc., by permission of Van Nostrand Reinhold Co.

ZONDERVAN PUBLISHING HOUSE. For Scriptures from *The Amplified Bible: The Amplified Old Testament* © 1962, 1964 by Zondervan Publishing House. *The Amplified New Testament* © 1958 by The Lockman Foundation.

INTRODUCTION

THIS IS A book about prophecy—Bible prophecy. If you have no interest in the future, this isn't for you. If you have no curiosity about a subject that some consider controversial, you might as well stop now.

For the past thirteen years I have been giving messages on Bible prophecy throughout the United States, Canada and Mexico. The interest in this aspect of Bible study has been amazing, particularly in the past few years. People who are confronted with the state of the world today are eager to learn what the Best Seller has to say about the future. As a traveling speaker for Campus Crusade for Christ I had the opportunity to give messages on prophecy to thousands of people. These messages have consistently proven to be popular with every age group.

This is not a complex theological treatise, but a direct account of the most thrilling, optimistic view of what the future could hold for any individual. I make no claim of knowing exactly when the world is going to end. In fact, I have never taken to the hills with my possessions and loved ones to await Doomsday. I believe in a hope for the future.

We have been described as the "searching generation." We need so many answers—answers to the larger problems of the world, answers to the conditions in our nation, and most of all, answers for ourselves.

How do we know in what direction we should go? How can we separate truth from opinion? In whom can we trust?

On one side we hear that the answer to our dilemma is education. Build bigger and better schools, hire more teachers, develop a smarter generation. Has the academic community found the answers? There are many students who are dissatisfied with being told that the sole purpose of education is to develop inquiring minds. They want to find some of the answers to their questions—solid answers, a certain direction.

What do the politicians say? "We have the solutions to the problems. Elect us and we'll prove it to you."

I am not downgrading the importance of electing honest, intelligent men to positions of leadership. This is important, terribly important, but are they able to provide the answers to the basic and visceral questions of man?

Throughout history we have seen impressive strides taken by men who were stepping ahead of their time. We have seen reforms advanced from ideas generated by men of vision. And yet governments change, men falter and fall, great ideas are sometimes rejected by the shortsightedness of other men. Are we able to say that the answer is in the realm of political action?

There are other places men search for answers: philosophy, meditation, changing environment, science. Please don't misunderstand me, all of these are good if used properly. However, if we are to be absolutely honest, if we are to use our intellectual integrity, let's give God a chance to present His views.

In this book I am attempting to step aside and let the prophets speak. If my readers care to listen, they are given the freedom to accept or reject the conclusions.

Hal Lindsey

1 ○ Future Tense

We believe whatever we want to believe. DEMOSTHENES, 348 B.C.

IT WAS A perfect night for a party. In the warm California evening the lemon trees perfumed the patio and the flickering Tiki torches cast shadows over a lavish table. The aroma of steaks sizzling on the barbecue grill was tantalizing and we were wishing someone would give the signal to eat.

To our dismay we discovered that no one else was outside. We were alone . . . with our appetites.

Crushed in a tight circle in the overheated living room were most of the guests, waiting rather impatiently for the fortune teller to read their palms. One by one they would eagerly hold out their hands, knowing they would hear flatteries, but hoping there would be some half-truth about themselves which would give them a mental uplift—an egobuilder to tell the boys at the office or the girls at the bridge table.

And so it has been from the beginning of time. People have been obsessed with the desire to know what is going to happen in the future.

From kings and rulers to servants and slaves, rich, poor, lowly and mighty people have called upon wizards, prophets, seers, magicians, the stars and the moon for powers and signs beyond the understanding of the human mind.

Astrology originated in ancient Chaldea, in the region around the Persian Gulf. All the proud kings of Chaldea, and later Babylon, had staff astrologers to advise them concerning the future.

The Greek father of historians, Herodotus, speaks of the incredible city of Babylon and mentions the enormous ziggurat from which the astrologers tracked the stars. The ruins of several of these "observatories" called ziggurats have been uncovered in the area of ancient Babylon by twentieth-century archaeologists. Obviously astrologers were VIP's in Babylon.

The Pharaohs of Egypt imported the knowledge of astrology and magic from Babylon. Some scholars have said that the Pharaohs constructed certain parts of the pyramids to line up with the stars.

The importance or position of a man has nothing to do with his superstitious concerns. Julius Caesar was the greatest of Roman leaders, and yet depended upon "augurs" for prophetic advice. An augur is a soothsayer or fortuneteller. In ancient Rome there was an official high-ranking government group, probably similar to our State Department, which was called the "Board of Augurs." The great Roman orator, Cicero, was a member of this board. However, it has been said that although Cicero took his duties seriously since he was a man of great loyalty to his country, he privately considered some of the augurs' prophecies to be absurd.

Caesar depended upon "signs in the sky" to conduct affairs of state and rule the mighty Roman empire. As the leader of the people, he set the example for his fellow Romans to become obsessed with horoscopes.

Many strange customs have been followed in determining the course of people and nations. Decisions of marriage and journeys, wars and alliances, have sometimes been made because special court seers read certain signs of omens from the entrails of a chicken!

Starry Eyed

Many people today are discovering astrology again. Popping up on the newsstands are so many pamphlets and books about the stars that one would almost think it was a new phenomenon. The hippy musical, *Hair*, has its own staff astrologer to advise the cast on personal matters and make sure the circumstances are right for business. One of the most popular songs of the moment is "Aquarius."

Astrology is having the greatest boom in its history. All you have to do is look in almost any newspaper to find out from one of the syndicated star-gazers what your forecast is for the day. Columns on the subject now run in 1,220 of the 1,750 dailies in the United States.[1]

Writers have taken astrology and applied it to almost everything one can imagine. There is *Astrology Made Practical*, *Astrology Made Easy*, *Astrology for Everyday Living*, *Astrology Guide to Health and Diet*, and even *Astrology Guide to Your Sex Life*.

A few years ago Bing Crosby starred in a movie in which one of his songs contained the words, "Have you heard . . . it's in the stars . . .?" There was something prophetic about that song!

Astrologers frequently guard their trade by predicting in generalities. However, sometimes they venture beyond vagaries and are explicit in attempting to foretell exact happenings. The result may be acute embarrassment for the astrologer.

For instance, in a national publication of 1968 an article was featured that quoted a "renowned astrologer" in her predictions about the upcoming elections in November of that year. By reading the stars this astrologer said that Rockefeller would be the next president of the United States, and either Ronald Reagan or John Lindsey would be vice-president. As for Hubert

Humphrey, she stated, "I've studied his chart very carefully and do not believe he will be considered as a serious contender even for the second slot on the Democratic ticket."[2]

These political gentlemen may or may not have been disappointed by the outcome of the elections of 1968, but the astrologer was probably a bit chagrined.

On Prophecy

Two hundred years ago a distinguished English statesman, Horace Walpole, said, "The wisest prophets make sure of the event first."

Many people would probably dispute that statement and draw attention to some of our famous contemporary prophets. There was Edgar Cayce, for instance, who was called America's "sleeping clairvoyant." Cayce spoke of future events while in a self-imposed hypnotic trance. He gave personal readings to guide the vocations and health and personal relationships of hundreds of persons. However, he went beyond individuals and prophesied the reversal in Japan's attitude of friendship for the U.S. before World War II, certain battles which would take place during that war, and the increase in racial tension in America.

However, Cayce's special contribution to the realm of psychic phenomena extended beyond mere prophecy. He advised others on how to develop this psychic ability, how to interpret dreams, where to find peace, and many other subjects. His telepathic statements, made during this hypnotic sleep-state, have been indexed, catalogued, and preserved by a special research society in Virginia. Although he has been dead for more than twenty years, when we called the local library to locate some of his books we were told that they were all checked out and we would have to be put on a waiting list.

What about the popularity of Jeane Dixon? Her books and articles have become national best-sellers. She has fascinated and astounded heads of nations with her uncanny skills of perception.

President Franklin Delano Roosevelt consulted Mrs. Dixon. At the height of his concern over the world crises, and plagued by his own ill health, he sought her advice. In the company of other national leaders of the past, Roosevelt sought to find out what the future would be from someone who possessed special uncanny ability to prophesy.

Jeane Dixon told President Roosevelt that eventually the U.S. would be allied with Russia against Red China. However, she warned FDR not to give Russia anything that wasn't ours to give. The president, however, evidently did not heed this advice, for it was not long afterward that the Yalta conference was held and FDR concluded a secret agreement with Russia to give the USSR certain territory which has remained under her domination ever since.

Mrs. Dixon has made some predictions which have had striking fulfillments. She sent word, it is reported, to the late President Kennedy prior to his trip to Dallas, warning him that he would be killed there. She also predicted several years ago that we would have a Republican president elected in 1968.

By her own admission, however, Mrs. Dixon says she is not infallible. For instance, she predicted that Red China would plunge the world into war over Quemoy and Matsu in October of 1958. (If you can't remember that far back, this did not happen.) She thought Walter Reuther would actively seek the presidency in 1964. (He didn't.)

High Spirits

Spiritualism and mysticism are weaving their spells among all age groups. We saw a handsomely illustrated magazine recently that featured "Prophecy, ESP news, psychic experiences, and spiritual healing." Provocative advertising included "Communications from the Sun World," and a new book which reveals "how they live in another dimension that is only an instant away from rapport with Earth."

It is a mystic time. Famous movie stars and wealthy socialites are traveling to the countries of the Far East to consult with "holy men." The influence of spiritualism in our popular songs, jewelry, and even clothing, is obvious. We received an invitation recently from an Indian spiritualist who says she "advises on all affairs of life." She also has a guarantee (money back?) to remove evil influences and bad luck from anyone who consults her.

The spirits are running in religious circles, also. A famous bishop, now deceased, stimulated interest in psychic phenomena by his communications with his dead son.

In churches and on college campuses mediums are receiving speaking invitations. The writer of a religious column in a Los Angeles paper recently reported, "Suffering from religious persecution and occasions of fakery in the ranks since its beginnings in the mid-1800s, the spiritualist movement in America is gaining new confidence today."[3]

In the field of higher education there are more than forty colleges which now conduct psychic research under the title of parapsychology. The interest in these subjects is growing in proportion to the increase in astrology and prophecy.

C'est la Vie

"The future" is big business. Frenchmen, for instance, spend more than a billion dollars a year on clairvoyants, gypsies, faith healers, seers and prophets. In Paris there is "one charlatan for every 120 Parisians, compared with one doctor for every 514 citizens and one priest for every 5,000."[4]

If you want to hear what the future has in store for you, perhaps you should see your travel agent for the fastest way to France. But try to avoid the need for a doctor or a priest—their services are rather scarce.

Escape

We were on the campus of a large university talking with some students in the comfortable lounge of one of the dormitories when we noticed a very attractive girl hesitate in the doorway. She stood for a few moments, her eyes glancing vacantly around the room, and then darted out as if she were being chased by demons. "What on earth do you think was wrong with her?" I asked my companions.

"Probably her vibrations were wrong," answered one young man. "She might have thought there was someone or something in here that was a threat. Who knows?"

Vibrations, spirits, stars, prophets—what an absorbing interest we have today in the unknown, the unseen and the future.

In our imaginations we long to step out of our humdrum existence and into worlds beyond. Take science fiction as an example. It fascinates us. We read books from the serious to the comic about men with miraculous powers of vision or perception. We sit with fascination before our television sets as we are transported out of the present and into the tomorrows.

Tell It Like It Will Be

In talking with thousands of persons, particularly college students, from every background and religious or irreligious upbringing, this writer found that most people want reassurance about the future. For many of them their hopes, ambitions, and plans are permeated with the subconscious fear that perhaps there will be no future at all for mankind.

This is a natural and prevalent attitude. Looking at the world today, it seems to be on a collision course. As the headline expressed it in a recent news magazine—"The World in a Mess."

People are searching for answers to basic questions. It is like the two young men who went into a book store and asked for "a book on the philosophy of truth." The clerk was flustered and very apologetic. She didn't want to discourage them, but she said they were asking for the impossible.

I wish I had been in that book store. It would have been so simple to walk over to a rather prominent display and pull out the Book that generations of readers have believed contains the "philosophy of truth." It not only contains truth, but also the great themes of peace, love, and hope, which are the desires of this and every other generation.

However, compared to the speculation of most that is called prophetic today, the Bible contains clear and unmistakable prophetic signs. We are able to see right now in this Best Seller predictions made centuries ago being fulfilled before our eyes.

The Bible makes fantastic claims; but these claims are no more startling than those of present day astrologers, prophets and seers. Furthermore, the claims of the Bible have a greater basis in historical evidence and fact. Bible prophecy can become a sure foundation upon which your faith can grow—and there is no need to shelve your intellect while finding this faith.

We believe there is a hope for the future, in spite of the way the world looks today. We believe that a person can be given a secure and yet exciting view of his destiny by making an honest investigation of the tested truths of Bible prophecy.

2 ∘ When is a Prophet a Prophet?

Men's curiosity searches past and future.— T. S. ELIOT

WHAT WOULD YOU think of prophets today who would be willing to stake their lives on the absolute truth of their claims? They could not allow themselves errors in judgment or mistakes in the smallest detail.

There were such prophets. They were daring men, sure of the source of their faith and strong in their belief. There is a book which boldly documents the statements of these men.

They are known as the prophets of Israel and their writings have been miraculously preserved in the Bible.

Passing the Test

Are we able to trust these old prophets? What were their credentials? In a book of the Old Testament, Deuteronomy, Moses predicted that there would be many prophets who would come to the Jewish people, culminating in the final and greatest of all prophets, the Messiah.

Moses anticipated a problem. How would people know whether a prophet who claimed to speak God's message was a true prophet? A question was asked of Moses which is still being asked today. "How may we know the word which the LORD has not spoken?" (Deuteronomy 18:21).

And Moses gave the answer—the true test of a prophet: "When a prophet speaks in the name of the LORD, if the word does not come to pass or come true, that is a word which the LORD has not spoken" (Deuteronomy 18:22).

Failure to pass the test of a true prophet was a bit severe. The only grade allowed was one of 100 percent accuracy. Anything less would doom the prophet to death by stoning, which was the method of capital punishment in those days (Deuteronomy 13:1-11).

A Greek proverb says that the best guesser is the best prophet. If the prophets of Israel had been simply "guessers," they would have had to take the cruel consequences—a slow and torturous death inflicted by flying stones.

The prophets of Israel also pointed out to their people causes of current problems. This is never very popular; true prophets would not be likely to win the "Most Beloved Citizen" award in their home town.

They not only made short-range predictions which would be fulfilled during their lifetimes, but also projected long-range predictions about events far in the future. Often they didn't understand the significance of their own prophecies (I Peter 1:10-12). However, many of these prophecies are predictions of exact historical happenings which will lead to the end of history as we know it.

The astonishing thing to those of us who have studied the prophetic Scriptures is that we are watching the fulfillment of these prophecies in our time. Some of the future events that were predicted hundreds of years ago read like today's newspaper.

Let's examine some selected Bible prophecies and apply the test of truth to them.

Accurate Short-range Prophecy

Jeremiah, a prophet of Israel, was not vague in his prophecies. He told his people that Judah, the southern kingdom of Israel, would be invaded and destroyed by Nebuchadnezzar, the King of Babylon. It was not a very cheerful prophecy, and Jeremiah probably didn't receive a standing ovation.

He said that King Nebuchadnezzar would destroy the land, that it would be desolate (Jeremiah 25:9). Jeremiah was not the type to soft pedal; he prophesied that the capital city, Jerusalem, would be destroyed and that its people would lose their capacity to laugh.

After he presented this miserable picture, Jeremiah foretold that any Jewish survivors would be carried off to Babylon as slaves. To compound the complexity of these predictions, he said that the Israelites would be Babylonian slaves for precisely seventy years (Jeremiah 25:11).

At this point Jeremiah would probably have won a contest for "The Man Least Likely to Succeed" in Israel. In fact, he made Pashur, one of the religious leaders of the time, so furious that Pashur beat him and put him in stocks (Jeremiah 20:2).

Archaeology and ancient history confirm the fulfillment of Jeremiah's prophecy. Jerusalem was destroyed, Judah was laid waste, and her people were taken captive in Babylon for seventy years.

Why did the Jewish people preserve the messages of Jeremiah? These messages which foretold of their defeat and captivity were an indictment against them. It was because Jeremiah passed the test of a prophet which was established by Moses. As despised as Jeremiah was by his contemporaries, they did not dare destroy what they believed were God's words.

Jeremiah was such a bearer of sad tidings that even today we speak of complaints as "jeremiads."

An Arrow in the Armor

One of the lesser-known men of God who achieved a straight "A" in prophetic marksmanship was Micaiah. However, this was not a time when such perfection was awarded with a gold pin and guard, or a seal on Micaiah's diploma. On the contrary, he was thrown into prison and fed bread and water. What did he do to deserve such treatment?

Micaiah lived at a time when a good king, Jehoshaphat, was reigning in the southern kingdom of Judah. In the northern kingdom of Israel ruled Ahab, a wicked king.

For some reason Jehoshaphat visited Ahab, who immediately tried to persuade him to join forces against a troublesome Syrian enemy from an area called Ramoth-Gilead.

Ahab gathered his own special prophets together—we might call them members of his Inner Security Council—and asked them whether he should go to battle against Ramoth-gilead or not. The 400 prophets were so soothing to Ahab that they should be called the "soothsayers" of his kingdom. They all agreed, without dissenting opinions, that Ahab should go into battle and that God would bring him through triumphantly.

But Jehoshaphat was not satisfied with the advice of these "prophets" in spite of their unanimous agreement. He said, "Is there not here another prophet of the LORD (Israel's God) of whom we may inquire?" (I Kings 22:7).

We can imagine how petulant Ahab must have been when he replied, "There is yet one man by whom we may inquire of the LORD, Micaiah the son of Imlah; but I hate him, for he never prophesies good concerning me, but evil" (I Kings 22:8).

Jehoshaphat insisted that Micaiah be consulted, so an officer was sent to bring him in. When the officer found him he tried to persuade the prophet to be a good fellow and go along with Ahab's "Inner Security Council" and tell the king what he wanted to hear. But Micaiah replied, "As the LORD lives, what the LORD says to me, that I will speak" (I Kings 22:14).

He realized as he said this that he was putting his life on the line.

When Micaiah was brought before the two kings, Ahab asked him if they should attack Ramoth-gilead. Micaiah answered in what must have been a tongue-in-cheek manner, "Sure, go on and win . . . the Lord will give it into your hands."

Ahab knew he was being ridiculed and commanded the prophet to say what was really on his mind. In answering, Micaiah showed the boldness that characterized a true prophet. First, he labeled all of the 400 "court prophets" as liars. Then he predicted that Ahab would be killed in the battle and that the Israeli army would be routed.

The chief of the false prophets—Ahab's "Chairman of the Security Council"—walked up and slugged Micaiah, probably with the same premonition of fear that made Pashur, the Israeli religious leader, take a whack at Jeremiah.

So Micaiah went to jail and Ahab went to battle. But first Micaiah challenged all the people to witness his grade on the test of a prophet. He said, "If you (meaning Ahab) return in peace, the LORD has not spoken by me" (I Kings 22:28).

Ahab wasn't going to take any chances with this pessimistic prophet, Micaiah, so he disguised himself during the big battle. But one of the enemy archers shot an arrow labeled "to whom it may concern" and in the most amazing and coincidental manner it struck Ahab in one small exposed place in his armor and killed him.

Micaiah passed the test of a true prophet. Ahab and all of his "yes men" flunked.

What Do You Say, Isaiah?

One of the most astounding prophets of all time was Isaiah, the son of Amoz. His brilliant, eloquent, even poetical predictions were made over a sixty-year span (740-680 B.C.) during the reign of four successive Judaean kings.

Isaiah proved himself a prophet by Moses' test many times. One striking incident was during the reign of King Hezekiah. In about 710 B.C. a mighty Assyrian army, numbering in the thousands and commanded by the vicious King Sennacherib besieged Jerusalem (Isaiah 36:1, 2).

(If you stumble over some of these unpronounceable ancient names, glance at your daily newspaper and notice the tongue twisters assigned to people today.)

Sennacherib was a crafty fellow. He sent his eloquent "mouthpiece," a fellow named Rabshakeh, to the people of Jerusalem with a powerful propaganda speech. Rabshakeh, an ancient "Minister of Misinformation," told the people of all the defeats suffered by neighboring countries. This was brainwashing in the craftiest sense. The techniques used were intended to induce the besieged citizens of Jerusalem to surrender without a fight.

When King Hezekiah heard how his people were being intimidated, he sent a delegation to Isaiah to plead with him to pray to Jehovah, the God of Israel. Isaiah then made some short-range predictions. He said that a rumor would reach King Sennacherib of internal trouble in his kingdom and that he would return without attacking Jerusalem. Furthermore, he said that Sennacherib would be assassinated in his own land.

It happened just as Isaiah predicted. Jerusalem was spared a certain defeat and King Sennacherib was killed by his own sons (Isaiah 37:36-38).

Isaiah Predicts One Hundred Years in the Future

Isaiah also predicted that Babylon would completely destroy Judah and carry away all the treasures of Israel. He foretold that the surviving sons of the royal family would be eunuchs in the palace of Babylon. This occurred just a little over one hundred years later (Isaiah 39:5-7).

One Hundred and Fifty Years in the Future

Isaiah gave an incredible prediction when he foretold that the mighty invincible Babylonians would be conquered and so completely destroyed by the Medes that Babylon would never be inhabited again (Isaiah 13:17-22).

This was an astonishing prediction at that time since the city of Babylon became one of the seven wonders of the ancient world and was considered impregnable. Yet approximately 150 years after Isaiah's prediction the Medes and Persians besieged the towering walls of Babylon. This was no small feat. Those walls were 150 feet high and so thick that five chariots could run abreast around the top.

The Medes and Persians were cunning. They dammed the Euphrates River which ran under the Babylonian wall and through the city. While Babylon was celebrating at a drunken royal ball, the Median army marched along the dry river bed under the wall and conquered the city. This was the very night that "the handwriting on the wall" appeared to the arrogant Babylonian king. It read, "Mene, mene, tekel, upharsin." Daniel, the prophet, deciphered it to the drunken mob as follows: "Your kingdom has been weighed in the balance and found wanting. It is divided and given to the Medes and Persians." That night the Babylonian kingdom fell (Daniel 5:1-31).

Two Hundred Years in the Future

Isaiah predicted that a certain king named Cyrus would see that Jerusalem and the Temple were rebuilt by allowing those who wished to do this work to return to the land of their ancestors (Isaiah 44:28—45:4).

Almost 200 years after this prediction a certain Persian king also named Cyrus, granted royal favor to the Jewish captives left over from Babylon and sent them to Jerusalem with a requisition for materials to rebuild the city (Ezra 1:1-11).

The Prophet Preserved

Many so-called Biblical scholars today try to "late date" such predictions as Isaiah's to make his prophecies seem to be after the fact. To do this not only violates the consistent witness of the history of those times, but also makes the Jewish people religious charlatans and deceivers. The Jews would have had no reason to keep for posterity those writings of the prophets if they were a fraud.

The Israeli prophets were not popular, as we have shown. In the times of Jeremiah, Micaiah, Isaiah, and the others, the odds were against anything they wrote or said being accepted. Yet they were preserved above all the other writings of their day.

What made these prophets so special? The answer lies in the test of a true prophet which Moses gave—their prophecies must all come true. They could not be ignored. We cannot ignore them. They passed the test—summa cum laude.

3 ○ Do We Really Live and Learn?

History teaches us that man learns nothing from history.   HEGEL

I T'S IRONIC THAT man never seems to learn from past mistakes, especially when they relate to major catastrophes. World War I was called the war to end all wars, yet within a generation World War II was fought in basically the same arena. We are now running around the world desperately seeking to put out fuses which could explode into what might be the last war on earth.

Through the grim pages of history we see the record of man's constant struggle to live with his fellow man. Families fight against families, tribes against tribes, and nations against nations. Most people hate war, and yet since recorded time the world has seldom seen peace.

General Douglas MacArthur said, "Men since the beginning of time have sought peace... military alliances, balances of power, leagues of nations, all in turn failed, leaving the only path to be by way of the crucible of war. The utter destructiveness of war now blots out this alternative."[1]

Mankind has not learned the futility of war from history. However, as tragic as this is, there is another lesson, even more tragic, which has not been heeded. This involves a people whose most cherished hope had been the coming of their great Deliverer, called the Messiah.

The central theme of the Jewish prophets was that "the Messiah" would come and fulfill the promises given to their forefathers, Abraham, Isaac, and Jacob. In these promises Israel is to be the leading nation of the world under the reign of the Messiah who would bring universal peace, prosperity, and harmony among all peoples of the earth.

The paradox is that there has come a Jew who claimed to be the Messiah. He fulfilled many of the ancient predictions, but was rejected by those who should have recognized Him first. The question is this: If He was truly the long-awaited Messiah, as millions have believed, why didn't the majority of the religious leaders of His day believe His claims? These religious leaders, after all, knew the Messianic predictions. Ignorance was not their excuse. The reasons they didn't believe Him are fascinating and extremely relevant to this hour of history in which we live.

Two Portraits

Two completely different portraits of a coming Messiah were described by the Old Testament prophets. The portraits, painted by the sure hand of God, were placed on the same canvas, framed in one picture.

For those who lived prior to the birth of Jesus of Nazareth, the perspective of these two portraits of the Messiah was difficult to understand.

Imagine a man looking at a range of mountains. He is able to see the peak of one mountain, and beyond it the peak of another. However, from this vantage point, he cannot see the valley which separates these two mountains.

Men viewed the two portraits of the Messiah in the same manner. They saw two different persons, but missed the connection. They did not perceive that there could be just one Messiah, coming in two different roles, and separated by the valley of time.

One portrait of the Messiah depicts Him as a humble servant who would suffer for others and be rejected by His own countrymen. This portrait we may call "the Suffering Messiah." (Look into the prophecies of Isaiah 53 for the perfect picture of this Messiah.)

The other portrait shows the Messiah as a conquering king with unlimited power, who comes suddenly to earth at the height of a global war and saves men from self-destruction. He places the Israelites who believe in Him as the spiritual and secular leaders of the world and brings in an age free of prejudice and injustice. It's easy to see why this would be the most popular portrait.

We may call this second picture "the Reigning Messiah." We find this description in such prophecies as Zechariah 14 and Isaiah 9:6, 7.

These two portraits of the Messiah presented such a paradox that the rabbis at least a century before Jesus of Nazareth was born theorized that there would be two messiahs. They could not see how both portraits could be true of the same person. Their misunderstanding led them to believe that the suffering one would deliver the people from their sins by bearing the penalty of death for them. He would be primarily a "Spiritual Deliverer." The reigning king would conquer Israel's enemies and bring world peace. He would be primarily a "Political Deliverer."

The Big Question

Why did the majority of the Jewish people, who knew the teachings of their prophets, reject Jesus of Nazareth as their Messiah when He came? Why did they ignore the portraits of the suffering Messiah? Jesus Himself pointed out to them Old Testament predictions concerning His life and ministry which were being fulfilled in His life.

First of all, the Jews didn't take their prophets literally as far as this suffering Messiah was concerned. They took very literally the portrait of the Messiah who would come as the reigning King. However, they had degenerated in their own religious convictions to the point where they didn't believe they were sinful. They believed they were keeping the law of Moses; therefore, they saw no need for a suffering Messiah to deliver them from their sins.

The Jewish religious leaders had built up a tradition of interpretation which made keeping God's laws merely an external thing (Mark 7:1-15). Jesus, however, pointed out the true meaning of God's law in the Sermon on the Mount. He showed that murder was not just refraining from actually killing someone, but that it was being angry with your neighbor without just cause (Matthew 5:21, 22). He also pointed out that adultery in God's sight was merely looking at a woman with lust (Matthew 5:27-32).

He expounded the real meaning of "love your neighbor as yourself" as applying to your enemies as well (Matthew 5:43-48).

With each commandment Jesus emphasized the false interpretation of the religious leaders and contrasted it with the true meaning which God had always intended. He showed that God looks upon the heart and not just upon the outward performance of man.

I am sure that if you took the previous paragraph seriously you may feel a little uncomfortable right now. You may be saying to yourself what I said some years ago when the true meaning of the Ten Commandments was first pointed out to me. "Who in the world can be accepted by God if he is going to have to keep the law in his thoughts and motives?"

If this is what you are thinking, congratulations! You have just discovered the whole purpose for the law of Moses. The commandments were never intended to be used to work our way to God. The commandments were primarily given to show us how perfect we would have to be in order to earn acceptance with God by our own good deeds. This is why God says to us, "Whoever keeps the whole law and yet stumbles in one point, he has become guilty of all" (James 2:10 NASB).

It is easy to see in the light of this why the Bible says, "... by the works of the Law no flesh (man) will be justified in His (God's) sight" (Romans 3:20 NASB).

The law was given to show mankind why it needed a "suffering Messiah" who alone could make man acceptable to God. Any person who hasn't come to see that his most basic problem is an inner spiritual one prefers a political deliverer to a spiritual one. It is not difficult, therefore, to understand the basic attitude which rationalized away the prophetic portrait of the suffering Messiah.

Jesus presented His credentials as the suffering Messiah, but many rejected Him because they were looking for a great conqueror. They were looking for that political leader who would deliver them from the Roman oppression. In their blindness they discounted more than *300 specific predictions* in their own sacred writings about this Messiah.

The second reason why the Jewish people rejected the Messiah was one of indifference—an indifference to their spiritual need. They couldn't be bothered. They were too busy. They had a chariot race or a party to attend. Caught in the treadmill of daily existence, the deeper needs of the inner self weren't important.

In addition, they didn't bother to do any investigation for themselves. Many knew there was something unusual about this carpenter from Nazareth, but their religious leaders rejected Him and they took their opinions instead of searching for the truth themselves.

It was because people will not do their own research that Jesus made an astounding statement on the signs of the times. He showed simply and clearly how prophecies were being fulfilled by His life. And yet, to the sorrow of many, He was ignored.

Signs of the Times

The religious leaders of His day were the number one skeptics. They came to Jesus and asked Him to show them a sign from heaven. They wanted some sensational miracle which would give them proof that Jesus was their promised Messiah. They wanted Him to suddenly step out of the sky as the conquering Messiah (as He is revealed in Zechariah 14) and take over all the kingdoms of the world and defeat the Roman empire.

Jesus had already given them important signs to prove who He was. He had healed many persons and had raised at least one from the dead. But they didn't consider this sufficient evidence to prove His claim of being the Messiah.

Jesus answered these religious leaders by saying: "When it is evening, you say, 'It will be fair weather, for the sky is red.' And in the morning, 'It will be stormy today, for the sky is red and threatening.' You know how to interpret the appearance of the sky, but you cannot interpret the signs of the times" (Matthew 16:2, 3).

The signs of the times. It is important to see what Jesus was driving at. People in Palestine, even today, indulge in being amateur weather forecasters. Weather conditions are such that the particular signs given here are fair indications of what the weather will be.

Jesus said that the signs leading up to His coming were just as clear as the face of the sky. Let's examine these signs, these credentials. Let's look at specific predictions of how this man Jesus would come to fulfill the role of the Messiah, of how He would fit into the first portrait of the suffering Messiah.

The first theme of predictions relates to the circumstances of His birth. These were His credentials.

Birth Credentials: His Family

God revealed to Abraham, the father of all Jews, that he would have a direct descendant who would be a blessing to all the peoples of the earth (Genesis 12:1-3).

Furthermore, God revealed to Jacob, who was one of the descendants of Abraham, that the Messiah would come through one specific tribal state—the tribal state of Judah. The Jews established states in the land of Palestine after they took it over, and they were divided according to twelve families. These families originated from the twelve sons of Jacob (Genesis 49:10).

His family credentials were narrowed even more, from the tribe of Judah to the family of David. The prediction was given to David, the great king in the history of Israel, by the prophet, Nathan.

Nathan said, "Thus says the Lord of hosts. . . I will raise up your offspring after you, one of your own sons, and I will establish his kingdom. He shall build Me a house, and I will establish his throne for ever. I will be his father, and he shall be My Son. . ." (I Chronicles 17:11-13 Amplified).

King David was promised at least two exciting things here. First, one of his direct descendants would reign forever. Secondly, this person would not only be one of his direct descendants, but in a mysterious way He would be uniquely the Son of God.

Rabbinic tradition ascribed this to be a prediction of the Messiah. Consequently, one of the most common Messianic titles is "the Son of David."

Birth Credentials: The Place

The prophet Micah lived seven hundred years before the birth of Christ. He was a contemporary of the great prophet, Isaiah. It was revealed to Micah that the Messiah would be born in Bethlehem.

"But thou, Bethlehem Ephratah, though thou be little among the thousands of Judah, yet out of thee shall he come forth unto me that is to be ruler in Israel; whose goings forth have been from of old, from everlasting" (Micah 5:2 KJV).

This was a prophecy of the Messiah which was unmistakable because it referred to His eternal pre-existence. . . "whose goings forth have been from of old, from everlasting."

This was no ordinary man, but a supernatural person who would invade history from Bethlehem.

This prophecy is quoted in the New Testament in Matthew, in answer to Herod's question to the Hebrew theologians about where the Messiah would be born. They answered him: "In Bethlehem of Judea, for so it is written by the prophet" (Matthew 2:5).

How remarkable it is that century after century the Hebrew people handed down these detailed prophecies. They had to be revelations from God, otherwise they would not have been preserved in such a consistent manner.

Birth Credentials: The General Time

We have examined the prophecies concerning the family line of the Messiah and the place of His birth. Let's look at the time factor.

The prophet Daniel, while in captivity in Babylon, was given a precise timetable and sequence relating to the future events of the people of Israel. Daniel was told that there would be a certain number of years which would transpire between the time a proclamation was given which allowed the Jewish people to return from their Babylonian captivity back to Israel and the coming of the Messiah.

This proclamation can be established according to Scriptural history in Nehemiah 2:1-10. Also, archaeologists have uncovered evidence of this same proclamation in the ancient Persian archives.

From the time permission was given to return and rebuild the city of Jerusalem and the Temple until the Messiah would come as the Prince, the heir-apparent to the throne of David, would be 483 years (69 weeks of years—483 years). Sir Robert Anderson of Scotland Yard spent many years of his life verifying and validating the details of this prophecy. He wrote a comprehensive book of his study called, *The Coming Prince*.

Not only was Daniel given specific years, but also a sequence of major historical events which cannot be denied.

First of all, there was the proclamation given to the Jews to return from captivity and rebuild the Temple.

After that, the Messiah would come as the Prince.

Then the Messiah would be "cut off," which is an idiom for being killed.

After the Messiah was killed an army would sweep in and destroy the city and the Temple which was rebuilt previously by the returned Babylonian exiles (Daniel 9).

Daniel's prophecy shows that whoever the Messiah was He had to appear before the city and the Temple were destroyed in A.D. 70 by Titus of Rome.

There was only one person who was taken seriously as the Messiah before A.D. 70. We have the logical candidate for that role in the carpenter from Nazareth.

Credentials Relating to His Ministry

We have considered a panorama of Jesus' birth credentials to verify His claim as the Jewish Messiah. To pile proof upon proof, consider the prophecies relating to the deeds Jesus would do upon earth—prophecies about His own ministry.

The prophet Isaiah presented a vivid description of the coming Messiah when he said: "Say to those who are of a fearful heart, 'Be strong, fear not! Behold, your God will come with vengeance, with the recompense of God. He will come and save you.' Then the eyes of the blind shall be opened, and the ears of the deaf unstopped; then shall the lame man leap like a hart, and the tongue of the dumb sing for joy. For waters shall break forth in the wilderness, and streams in the desert" (Isaiah 35:4-6).

Jesus knew the Old Testament prophets. He quoted this exact prophecy from Isaiah when John the Baptist seemed to have some doubts about Him. John was the herald who announced the coming of Jesus as the Messiah, and yet even John could not reconcile the two portraits of the Messiah. When he was taken prisoner he sent some messengers to Jesus to ask, "Are You the Coming One, or shall we look for someone else?" (Matthew 11:3 NASB).

Jesus answered by quoting the predictions of the miracles He would perform. "Go and report to John the things which you hear and see: the blind receive sight and the lame walk, the lepers are cleansed and the deaf hear, and the dead are raised up, and the poor have the gospel preached to them" (Matthew 11:4, 5 NASB).

The fact that Jesus was performing these very miracles were His credentials to substantiate His claim that He was the Messiah.

Credentials Relating to His Rejection and Suffering

Probably the most phenomenal predictions relating to the suffering Messiah's portrait are the prophecies that show His rejection and suffering. One of the great passages on His rejection is Isaiah 53. This is called the "bad conscience of the synagogues" because it is no longer read in the temples on holy days, as it once was.

In Isaiah 52 there is a general look at this One who is called the servant of God. It is obvious here that the prophet is not talking about Israel, which in some passages is called the servant of God, but about one who would save Israel. "Behold, my servant, (Christ) shall prosper, he shall be exalted and lifted up, and shall be very high. As many were astonished at him— his appearance was so marred, beyond human semblance, and his form beyond that of the sons of men" (Isaiah 52:13, 14).

This was a reference to what happened at the trials of Jesus when He was repeatedly hit in the face. "So shall he startle many nations; kings shall shut their mouths because of him; for that which has not been told them they shall see, and that which they have not heard they shall understand" (Isaiah 52:15).

In this passage the prophet is saying that He would startle, or astound nations (meaning the non-Jews) and that they would see things they had never seen. The Gentiles, in other words, would begin to understand the ways of God.

However, Isaiah speaks of His rejection by the Jews, which in itself was remarkable since Isaiah was a Jewish prophet who wrote at least 700 years before Christ was born. Isaiah predicted that his people would reject the very one for whom they looked (Isaiah 53:1-3).

Notice an interesting fact. The prophet writes of this event in the past tense, which was a common literary device of the Jewish writers. . . ("many were astonished. . . his appearance was so marred"). When they wished to emphasize the certainty of a prophecy they would put it in this tense, which is called the prophetic perfect tense in Hebrew.

It was further prophesied here that the Jews would reject this Man because He didn't have the royal splendor they desired. Isaiah said He would be "despised and rejected," which is precisely what happened.

In this part of the prediction the credentials of the Messiah as a person who would be a substitute for the iniquity, or wickedness, of man are presented: "Surely he has borne our griefs and carried our sorrows; yet we esteemed him stricken, smitten by God, and afflicted. But he was wounded for our transgressions, he was bruised for our iniquities; upon him was the chastisement that made us whole, and with his stripes we are healed. All we like sheep have gone astray; we have turned every one to his own way; and the LORD has laid on him the iniquity of us all" (Isaiah 53:4-6).

Rabbis since the birth and death of Jesus of Nazareth have reinterpreted this passage to say that the third person singular pronoun does not refer to a personal Messiah, but to the nation of Israel. However, the passage speaks of this person as bearing the consequences of the transgressions of Israel. Israel could not be a substitute for itself, since the passage clearly states that the Lord hath laid on *Him* the iniquity of *us*.

Isaiah 53 continues to say that this person would not receive the true justice of the Jewish law. This, of course, was true during the trials of Jesus. They were astounded that He didn't try to defend Himself. . . "He was oppressed. . . yet he opened not his mouth" (Isaiah 53:7).

Again there is a clear prediction that the Messiah would die for the transgressions of Isaiah's people, as well, of course, as for the whole world. ". . . he was cut off (killed) out of the land of the living, stricken for the transgression of my people" (Isaiah 53:8b).

The details of prophecy relating to this portrait of the Messiah are exact. Isaiah says that He will die beside criminals. "And they made his grave with the wicked." His grave would be with the rich: "And with a rich man in his death" (Isaiah 53:9).

Did it happen? Of course. Jesus was crucified between two thieves. After His death one of the rich Pharisees, Joseph of Arimathaea, took pity on Him and buried Him in his own tomb. Joseph was the rich man predicted here.

We can picture Isaiah, standing at Calvary, looking at the panoramic view that Jesus saw and experienced on the cross. However, Isaiah saw this 700 years before Jesus was born!

To continue in this remarkable passage, Isaiah speaks of the fact that men could be declared righteous and acceptable to God because He bore their sins. In Biblical vernacular, this is the meaning of "justified."

Isaiah said that He "made intercession for the transgressors" (Isaiah 53:12). Most persons with only a slight exposure to Christian teaching will remember the words of Jesus from the cross when He said, "Father, forgive them; for they know not what they do."

Thirty Pieces of Silver

Another Old Testament prophet was Zechariah, who wrote almost 500 years before Jesus lived. In his book he gave another specific and minute prediction which could only refer to one person. He wrote: "And I said unto them, If ye think good, give me my price; and if not, forbear. So they weighed for my price thirty pieces of silver. And the LORD said unto me, Cast it unto the potter: a goodly price that I was prised at of them. And I took the thirty pieces of silver, and cast them to the potter in the house of the LORD" (Zechariah 11:12, 13 KJV).

Notice the three specific trends in this passage. First, there would be a time when the people would estimate their own God's worth at thirty pieces of silver. Then, these thirty pieces would be cast down in the house of the Lord, which is the Temple. Finally, the money would be given to the potter for the graves of the poor people.

Do you suppose any present-day "prophets" would dare make such an exact prediction?

It happened exactly as told. Matthew records this when he tells of Judas going to the chief priests who were plotting to murder Jesus and saying, "What will you give me if I deliver Jesus to you?" And the priests decided they would give thirty pieces of silver for the betrayal (Matthew 26:14, 15).

After Jesus was betrayed and Judas saw that Jesus was condemned to death, which was more severe than Judas had anticipated, he regretted what he had done. He went to the priests and tried to return the money, but the priests insulted him. Judas became infuriated. He threw the money down in the Temple (Matthew 27:3-5). (Prediction fulfilled.)

The priests took the money and piously said it wasn't proper to return to the treasury the price of the betrayal, so they decided to give it to the potter to buy a potter's field (Matthew 27:6-10). (Trying to ease their consciences, no doubt.)

Notice one very important point. Jesus had no control over this prophecy. It had to be fulfilled without any interference on His part. This fact explodes the major premise of a book which has gained some popularity, called *The Passover Plot*. While the writer of this book does a service by accepting the historical reality of Jesus, he claims that Jesus deliberately plotted to fulfill the predictions of the Messiah given in the Old Testament. This theory could not be valid because there is no way to explain how many predictions, such as the one about the thirty pieces of silver, could be fulfilled when the circumstances were out of Jesus' hands.

Predictions Relating to the Crucifixion

Jesus told His disciples that there were predictions of His suffering in the Psalms (Luke 24:44-46).

One of the clearest prophecies is found in Psalm 22, which was written by King David more than 1000 years before Christ. David describes events which could not have happened to himself since they were beyond the scope of his own experience.

The Psalms were accepted as the word of God and David was speaking "in the Spirit," as the ancient rabbinical schools recognized. The psalmist gives a detailed and precise prediction of a person being crucified. He speaks of the suffering of the Messiah as if he were on the cross with Him, feeling His pain, seeing the people and events around him. Speaking in the spirit of the Messiah, David says, "I am poured out like water"—he is speaking of the profuse perspiration of one hanging in the intense sun. "And all my bones are out of joint"—this is one of the most excruciating aspects of crucifixion. The ligaments stretch and the bones pop out of joint.

He tells of the intense thirst—"and my tongue cleaveth to my jaws." Jesus said on the cross, "I thirst."

"For dogs have compassed me: the assembly of the wicked have enclosed me: they pierced my hands and my feet. I may tell all my bones: they look and stare upon me. They part my garments among them, and cast lots upon my vesture" (Psalm 22:16-18 KJV).

"Dog" was a common slang expression the Jews used for the Gentiles—Jesus was surrounded by Gentiles at the crucifixion. He was crucified in the nude; this passage speaks of the shame of it. At the foot of the cross the soldiers gambled (or cast lots) for His robe.

As perfect as this passage is in its prophetic accuracy, it gains additional importance when we realize that crucifixion as a way of punishment was not known at the time David wrote this. The Jews of that time executed by stoning. It was not until about 200 B.C. when the Romans adopted this cruel practice that crucifixion was widely used—800 years after this prophecy.

Guaranteed Accuracy

If there is one thing that guarantees the historical accuracy of what the New Testament authors wrote it is the animosity of the Jewish people who crucified Jesus. The message of these prophecy fulfillments was spread by word of mouth all over the Palestinian area starting fifty days after these events happened.

If those who crucified Jesus could have disproved any of the historical realities of these events they would have done so and destroyed the whole movement from the beginning. But they didn't bring up any refutation of the facts of fulfilled prophecy; instead they put to death the persons who were proclaiming these facts.

That generation did not take seriously the credentials of the suffering Messiah. Jesus predicted the destruction of those who put Him on the cross. "For the days shall come upon you when your enemies will throw up a bank before you, and surround you, and hem you in on every side, and will level you to the ground and your children within you, and they will not leave in you one stone upon another, because you did not recognize the time of your visitation" (Luke 19:43, 44 NASB).

Was this prophecy fulfilled? As previously mentioned, Titus and the Roman legions swept down upon Jerusalem and destroyed it in A.D. 70.

Will We Learn?

Will we repeat history? Will we fail to take the prophets literally and seriously? Will we be indifferent? Will we allow those who claim to be religious leaders to explain these things away and not investigate for ourselves?

There are many more predictions about the reigning Messiah who is *yet to come* than there were about the suffering Messiah. Will we fail to weigh these prophecies for ourselves, in spite of what others may say?

The remainder of this book will present the prophecies which are related to the specific pattern of world events which are precisely predicted as coming together shortly before the coming of the Messiah the second time—coming in power to rule the earth.

Many of these predictions were in the same paragraphs as those relating to the first coming of the Messiah. Do we dare allegorize away the meaning of these?

Will these predictions be fulfilled just as certainly and graphically as those of the first coming?

This writer says positively, "Yes."

4 ○ Israel,
O Israel

There are few countries which have played so central a role in world history as the Land of Israel.   DAVID BEN GURION, 1965

SOME TIME IN the future there will be a seven-year period climaxed by the visible return of Jesus Christ.

Most prophecies which have not yet been fulfilled concern events which will develop shortly before the beginning of and during this seven-year countdown.

The general time of this seven-year period couldn't begin until the Jewish people re-established their nation in their ancient homeland of Palestine.

Keys to the Prophetic Puzzle

A definite international realignment of nations into four spheres of political power had to occur in the same era as this rebirth of Israel. Each sphere of power had to be led by a certain predicted nation and allied with certain other nations. The relationships of all these factors to each other is easily determined by the following clues: first, each one of the four spheres of political power is said to be present and vitally involved with the reborn state of Israel.

Secondly, each one of these spheres of power is a major factor in the final great war called "Armageddon," which is to be triggered by an invasion of the new state of Israel.

Third, each one of these spheres of power will be judged and destroyed for invading the new state of Israel, by the personal return of the Jewish Messiah, Jesus Christ.

It should be obvious that these predicted movements of history are inter-related in their general time of beginning and ending. This is why the prophecies can be pieced together to make a coherent picture, even though the pieces are scattered in small bits throughout the Old and New Testaments.

Raised Eyebrows

Many Bible students in recent years tried to fit the events of World War I and II to the prophetic signs which would herald the imminent return of Christ. Their failure discredited prophecy.

The people who have fled to the mountains to await the end of the world haven't had the faintest idea about the truths in Bible prophecy.

It is because of these unscriptural attempts at calculating dates that some eyebrows rise when we speak of Bible prophecy today.

Dream and Reality

The one event which many Bible students in the past overlooked was this paramount prophetic sign: Israel had to be a nation again in the land of its forefathers.

Israel a nation—a dream for so many years, made a reality on 14 May 1948 when David Ben-Gurion read the Declaration of Independence announcing the establishment of a Jewish nation to be known as the State of Israel.

In 1949, Prime Minister Ben-Gurion said that Israel's policy "consists of bringing all Jews to Israel . . . we are still at the beginning."[1]

What Countdown?

This seven-year period we have called the "countdown" is a period of unique events. There is more prophecy concerning this period than any other era the Bible describes.

The apostle John counted out seven years for this period when he spoke of the second half being forty-two months (i.e., 3½ years), and the first half being 1260 days (i.e., 3½ x 360 days, which is the Biblical year) (Revelation 11:2, 3).

The prophet Jeremiah spoke of the time when God would return His people of Israel and Judah from a great captivity and dispersion. He calls this period "the time of Jacob's trouble."

As Christ told of the world conditions that would immediately precede His coming, He said, "For then there will be great tribulation [affliction, distress and oppression] such as has not been from the beginning of the world until now, no, and never will be. And if those days had not been shortened, no human being would be saved" (Matthew 24:21, 22).

In other words, this period will be marked by the greatest devastation that man has ever brought upon himself. Mankind will be on the brink of self-annihilation when Christ suddenly returns to put an end to the war of wars called Armageddon.

Israel, the Fuse of Armageddon

What has happened and what is happening right now to Israel is significant in the entire prophetic picture. Men who have studied events that were to occur shortly before the great holocaust known as Armageddon are amazed as they see them happening before their eyes.

Too few Biblical scholars pay any serious attention to the proven prophetic content of Scripture. Dr. William F. Albright, eminent archaeologist and professor of Semitic Languages, noted this fact after he had verified many historic fulfillments of Bible prophecy. He said, "That the prophets were not only dedicated men, but also predictors of the future, is fully recognized in Biblical tradition but has been under-emphasized by modern Biblical scholars. . . ."[2]

The nation of Israel cannot be ignored; we see the Jews as a miracle of history. Even the casual observer is amazed how the descendants of Abraham, Isaac, and Jacob have survived as a distinct race in spite of the most formidable odds. What other people can trace their continuous unity back nearly 4,000 years?

Twice the Jews have been destroyed as a nation and dragged away as slaves under inhuman circumstances; twice the Jews returned to their ancient homeland and reestablished their nation.

What other people have preserved a distinct and separate national identity in spite of a total of some 2600 years of being scattered—years of dispersion, as it is called? During all these years these men and women without a country have suffered the most insane and unjust persecutions ever endured by any collection of people or nationalities.

Jewish survival is a phenomenon. However, Jewish history, with all of its tragedies and triumphs, has been accurately foretold.

Setting the Stage

History may be dry bones to some, but the history of how the stage was set for the rebirth of Israel is fascinating. This history also serves as a standard to test how reliable future prophecy concerning Israel will be. Let's look at the record of past prophecy fulfilled concerning Israel.

God's Woodshed

Some 3500 years ago, at a time when the Jewish people were enroute from Egypt to possess the Promised Land of Palestine, Moses predicted that they would be chastened, or disciplined, twice, as a nation, for not believing their God and rejecting His ways. The first stage of this disciplinary action came from Babylon.

Misery in Babylon

Moses predicted that a mighty nation would invade and destroy Israel. The invaders would be so fierce that they would have no respect for either the very old or the very young. Civilians would be massacred and property completely destroyed. The survivors would be taken as slaves.

As previously noted, the prophet Isaiah added details to what Moses predicted, about 150 years before it occurred. Isaiah said to a king of Judah, named Hezekiah: "Behold, the days are coming when all that is in your house, and that which your predecessors have stored up till this day, shall be carried to Babylon. Nothing shall be left, says the Lord" (Isaiah 39:6 Amplified).

The prophet Jeremiah, several years before it happened, predicted how long the Babylonian captivity would last: "And this whole land shall be a waste and an astonishment, and these nations shall serve the king of Babylon seventy years" (Jeremiah 25:11 Amplified).

Precisely as predicted, the Babylonians swept into the southern kingdom of Israel and Jerusalem and destroyed it. Those who survived the holocaust were carried off to Babylon as slaves where they remained for seventy years (II Chronicles 36:15-21).

At the end of this period of enslavement the Persian king, Cyrus, released some of the Jewish people to return and rebuild the Temple in Jerusalem (II Chronicles 36:22, 23). You will recall that this king had been predicted by name some 200 years before by Isaiah (Isaiah 44:28; 45:4).

The Winds of Rome

In the same prophecy in which he predicted the first stage of divine discipline, Moses also predicted the second stage. He said that because of continued disbelief and rejection of their God, Israel would be destroyed as a nation a second time. This time the survivors would be scattered throughout the world in every nation. They would be relentlessly persecuted—men without a country. Moses gives a graphic portrayal of the history of the Jews when he says that they will be scattered among all the people of the earth, where they "shall find no ease." The Jews will find no rest for their feet, their very lives shall "hang in doubt" (Deuteronomy 28:64-68).

Many other prophets, such as Isaiah, Jeremiah, Ezekiel, and Amos to name a few, all predicted the great world-wide exile of the Jewish people and the destruction of the Jewish nation.

Just before His arrest and crucifixion, Jesus said, ". . . for there will be a great distress upon the land, and wrath to this people, and they will fall by the edge of the sword, and will be led captive into *all the nations* . . ." (Luke 21:23, 24 NASB).

It's very important to note that this great theme of prophecy concerning the global dispersion was predicted by Jesus as occurring to the same generation that crucified Him. He said, "Truly I say to you, all these things shall come upon this generation" (Matthew 23:36 NASB).

History verifies the accuracy of these prophecies. Just as predicted by Jesus, less than forty years after His death Titus and the Roman legions destroyed Jerusalem and the nation, slaughtering hundreds of thousands. Those who survived were shipped off to the slave markets in Egypt. Soon the supply exceeded the demand and they were worthless, even as lowly slaves.

For almost 2000 years the sons of Abraham, Isaac, and Jacob have wandered around the earth with no country of their own, in constant fear of persecution and death. I am sure that they have asked the question millions of times, why all this evil for us? The true Christian has looked on with amazement and compassion, while the Jew has become a phenomenon to the world. It is no wonder that Moses wrote concerning their sufferings and punishment, "They (i.e. the judgments) shall be upon you for a sign [of warning to other nations] and for a wonder, and upon your descendants for ever" (Deuteronomy 28:46 Amplified).

Israel's history of misery which has exactly fulfilled prophetic warnings should be a sign to the whole world—a sign which among other things should teach that God means what He says, and says what He means.

Israel Reborn

The same prophets who predicted the world-wide exile and persecution of the Jews also predicted their restoration as a nation. It is surprising that many could not see the obvious: since the first part of these prophecies came true we should have anticipated that the second part would come true, also. This restoration was to come about in the general time of the climactic seven-year countdown and its finale—the personal appearance of the Messiah to deliver the new state from destruction.

Set the Record Straight

Right here a careful distinction must be made between "the physical restoration" to the land of Palestine as a nation, which clearly occurs shortly
before the Messiah's coming and the "spiritual restoration" of all Jews who
have believed in the Messiah just after His return to this earth.

The "physical restoration" is accomplished by unbelieving Jews through
their human effort. As a matter of fact, the great catastrophic events which
are to happen to this nation during "the tribulation" are primarily designed
to shock the people into believing in their true Messiah (Ezekiel 38; 39).

The Scoffers

For many years prior to 1948 some Christian scholars denied the possibility of accepting the prophecies concerning the restoration of Israel as a
nation in Palestine. As a matter of fact, many Bible teachers taught that all
prophecy relating to Israel's future was fulfilled in Israel's past. Others
taught that the promises made to Israel must be applied to the Church (since
Israel rejected her Messiah.) Some theologians of the liberal school still insist
that prophecy has no literal meaning for today and that it cannot be taken
seriously. It is difficult to understand this view if one carefully weighs the
case of Israel's rebirth as a nation.

Truth From Dusty Books

There has been down through history a group of men who diligently studied the prophetic content of the Bible and took it both seriously and literally. This writer searched through many commentaries on the subject dating back to A.D. 1611 and found that many scholars clearly understood that
the Jews would return to Palestine and re-establish their nation before the
Messiah would come. These men held this position in spite of mocking and
ridicule on the part of the majority of Christendom.

The certainty of Israel's physical rebirth as a nation and restoration to Palestine was seen by Dr. John Cumming in 1864. Thumb through his fascinating
old book, over a hundred years old, and you'll read: "How comes it to pass
that as a nation they have been dispersed over every land, yet insulated, separated, and alone amid the nations? The predictions of their restoration are in
words as definite only not yet fulfilled. As a nation they were cut off and dispersed, and it is *as a nation that they shall be gathered and restored.*

"But one closing act in this great dramatic history of an extraordinary people is yet wanting to complete the whole. Their restoration is predicted and demanded. Who will stretch out his hand to move the scene and call forth the actors."[3]

Was this man a prophet or a student of the prophets of God?

The fact that the Jews had to be restored as a nation before Christ could return was seen by James Grant, an English Bible scholar writing in 1866.

"The personal coming of Christ, to establish His millennial reign on earth, will not take place *until the Jews are restored to their own land,* and the enemies of Christ and the Jews have gathered together their armies from all parts of the world, and have commenced the siege of Jerusalem . . . now the return of the Jews to the Holy Land, and the mustering and marshalling of these mighty armies, with a view to capturing Jerusalem, must require a *considerable time yet.*"[4]

(This was written eighty-two years before Israel was made a nation.)

Increase Mather, a famous minister in the early colonies of America, wrote a book published in 1669 entitled, *The Mystery of Israel's Salvation.* In this book he developed many of the crucial prophecies of Israel's restoration. He, too, showed that the Jews would return to Palestine and become a nation before their spiritual conversion and the return of the Messiah, Jesus Christ.

The great contribution of these men who stood against the prevailing religious opinion of their day is obvious. They prove that these prophetic passages are clear and could be understood if taken literally. A hundred or more years ago the prospect of the nation of Israel seemed impossible. Their faith in these passages in the Bible has been verified before our eyes!

These men used what may be called the golden rule of interpretation which the Biblical record of fulfilled prophecy indicates is correct.

"When the plain sense of Scripture makes common sense, seek no other sense; therefore, take every word at its primary, ordinary, usual, literal meaning unless the facts of the immediate context, studied in the light of related passages and axiomatic and fundamental truths, indicate clearly otherwise."[5]

This is the method which this writer has diligently sought to follow.

Three Important Events

To be specific about Israel's great significance as a sign of the time, there are three things that were to happen. First, the Jewish nation would be reborn in the land of Palestine. Secondly, the Jews would repossess old

Jerusalem and the sacred sites. Thirdly, they would rebuild their ancient temple of worship upon its historic site.

The Nation Born in a Day

Some 2600 years ago Ezekiel showed that the Jewish nation would be reborn after a long world-wide dispersion, but before the coming of the Messiah to judge a great enemy who would rise up against the new nation. Here is Ezekiel—speaking prophetically to this great enemy of the revived state—"After many days you shall be visited *and* mustered for service; in the latter years you shall go against the land that is restored from the ravages of the sword, where people are gathered out of many nations upon the mountains of Israel, which had been a continual waste; but its *people* are brought forth out of the nations . . ." (Ezekiel 38:8 Amplified).

The Time of This Prophecy's Fulfillment

There are several clues in Ezekiel's words which make it possible to pinpoint the time of this restoration.

Clue one: "The latter years" is the first. Dr. Kac, a Jewish medical doctor and noted Bible scholar, sums it up this way: "The phrase 'latter days' always refers in the Old Testament to the time of Israel's final and complete national restoration and spiritual redemption."[6]

Clue two: This restoration is clearly after a long-term desolation of the land of Israel. Note the following statements in the context: "the land that is restored from the ravages of the sword . . ." And, ". . . the mountains of Israel, which had been a continual waste. . . ."

Clue three: It is also a time when the Jewish people are being returned from exile "out of many nations." Ezekiel 37 is part of this context and details the miracle of the physical restoration of the Jews to their own land, then afterward their spiritual conversion. This was predicted to occur at a time when the world would be saying, "Behold, they say, Our bones are dried up, and our hope is lost; we are completely cut off" (Ezekiel 37:11 Amplified).

Clue four: The crux of the case is that this physical restoration to the land is directly associated with triggering the hostility which brings about a great judgment upon all nations and the Messiah's return to set up God's Kingdom. In other words, it is the presence of this reborn nation of Israel, flourishing in prosperity, that excites a great enemy from the uttermost north of

Palestine to launch an attack upon them which sets off the last war of the world. This war is to be ended with such a display of divine intervention that a great many of the surviving Gentiles and Jews put their whole trust in the true Messiah, Jesus Christ.

It cannot be emphasized enough. This restoration would take place after a world-wide dispersion and long-term desolation of the land of Israel. However, it would occur shortly before the events which will culminate with the personal, visible return of the Messiah, Jesus Christ, to set up an everlasting Kingdom and bring about the spiritual conversion of Israel.

Jesus the Prophet

Jesus Christ also pinpointed the general time of His return when His disciples asked Him two important questions. "What will be the sign of your coming?" they wanted to know. And "What will be the sign of the end of the age?"

The "coming" referred to in the question above is commonly referred to as the second advent of Christ. It was only natural that they wanted to know what signs would indicate His return to set up God's promised Kingdom.

In answer Jesus gave many general signs involving world conditions which he called "birth pangs." He said that these signs, such as religious apostasy, wars, national revolutions, earthquakes, famines, etc., would increase in frequency and intensity just like birth pangs before a child is born.

One of the great signs He predicted, however, is often overlooked. He speaks of the Jewish people being in the land of Palestine as a nation at the time of His return. He speaks of "those who are in Judea" fleeing to the mountains to escape the great battles that immediately precede His return (Matthew 24:16).

Another statement of Jesus demands a national existence with even their ancient worship restored. "Pray that your flight may not be . . . on a Sabbath" (Matthew 24:20). This indicates that the ancient traditions regarding travel on the Sabbath would be in force again, thus hindering a rapid escape from the predicted invasion.

Even the Temple has to be rebuilt according to the sign given in Matthew 24:15. (More will be said about this shortly.)

Jesus' predictions regarding the nation restored to the land are extremely significant when we recall that He predicted a world-wide dispersion and complete destruction of the nation which would begin with the generation which crucified Him (Luke 21:22, 23; Matthew 23:36).

Yet when Jesus looks into the future and describes the conditions which would prevail at His coming, He puts the Jews back in the land as a nation.

It is in this context that Jesus predicts an extremely important time clue. He says: "Now learn the parable from the fig tree: when its branch has already become tender, and puts forth its leaves, you know that summer is near; even so you too, when you see all these things, recognize that He is near, right at the door" (Matthew 24:32, 33 NASB).

Perfect Parable

When the signs just given begin to multiply and increase in scope it's similar to the certainty of leaves coming on the fig tree. But the most important sign in Matthew has to be the restoration of the Jews to the land in the rebirth of Israel. Even the figure of speech "fig tree" has been a historic symbol of national Israel. When the Jewish people, after nearly 2,000 years of exile, under relentless persecution, became a nation again on 14 May 1948 the "fig tree" put forth its first leaves.

Jesus said that this would indicate that He was "at the door," ready to return. Then He said, "Truly I say to you, *this generation* will not pass away until all these things take place" (Matthew 24:34 NASB).

What generation? Obviously, in context, the generation that would see the signs—chief among them the rebirth of Israel. A generation in the Bible is something like forty years. If this is a correct deduction, then within forty years or so of 1948, all these things could take place. Many scholars who have studied Bible prophecy all their lives believe that this is so.

The Repossession of Jerusalem

Another important event that had to take place before the stage would be fully set for the "seven-year countdown" was the repossession of ancient Jerusalem. Much of what is to happen to the Jewish people at the return of the Messiah is to occur in the vicinity of the ancient city.

Zechariah some 2500 years ago predicted the great invasion against the Jewish people who would dwell near ancient Jerusalem at the time of the Messiah's second coming. Chapters 12 through 14 of Zechariah graphically describe the events in sequence.

Here is an outline of these crucial chapters:

1. The siege of Jerusalem by all nations (12:1-3).
2. A description of the battle in and around Jerusalem (12:4–9).

3. The personal revelation of Jesus Christ as Messiah to a remnant of Jews in Jerusalem (12:10).
4. The repentance and faith which occurs at this personal revelation (12:11–14).
5. The opening of the fountain of forgiveness to repentant Israel (13:1).
6. The triumphant return of the Messiah (14:1-21).

It is clear in these chapters that the Jews would have to be dwelling in and have possession of the ancient city of Jerusalem at the time of the Messiah's triumphant advent.

Jesus Christ also predicted this situation in His last great public message before His arrest. He warned the Jews who would be living in Judea to look for "the abomination of desolation," which was spoken of by Daniel, the prophet, standing in the "holy place" (Matthew 24:15).

"The abomination of desolation" has a technical Jewish meaning which is to desecrate the Temple by bringing a Gentile or an unholy thing into the holy place (a consecrated compartment where only an authorized priest is to enter). An "abomination of desolation" happened once before in Jewish history when in 165 B.C. an invading king named Antiochus Epiphanes slaughtered a pig in the holy place.

The point is this, in order for there to be a Temple, there would have to be a repossession of the Temple site in ancient Jerusalem.

In March and April of 1967 I was lecturing on this subject at many college campuses on the West coast. I said that if this was the time that I thought it was, then somehow the Jews were going to have to repossess old Jerusalem. Many chuckled about that statement.

Then came the war of June, 1967—the phenomenal Israeli six-day blitz. I was personally puzzled as to the significance of it all until the third day of fighting when Moshe Dayan, the ingenious Israeli general, marched to the wailing wall, the last remnant of the Old Temple, and said, "We have returned to our holiest of holy places, never to leave her again."

Needless to say, I received quite a few phone calls after that. Again, against incredible odds, the Jews had unwittingly further set up the stage for their final hour of trial and conversion.

The Third Temple

There remains but one more event to completely set the stage for Israel's part in the last great act of her historical drama. This is to rebuild the ancient Temple of worship upon its old site. There is only one place that this Temple can be built, according to the Law of Moses. This is upon Mount Moriah. It is there that two previous Temples were built: the first was built by Solomon 3000 years ago. The second was built by the returning Babylonian exiles 2400 years ago. This one was completely refurbished by Herod the Great later on in an effort to win the favor and acceptance of the Jews. The second Temple was totally destroyed by Titus and the Roman Legions in A.D. 70.

There is one major problem barring the construction of a third Temple. That obstacle is the second holiest place of the Moslem faith, the Dome of the Rock. This is believed to be built squarely in the middle of the old temple site.

Obstacle or no obstacle, it is certain that the Temple will be rebuilt. Prophecy demands it.

Jesus Christ predicted an event which would trigger a time of unparalleled catastrophe for the Jewish nation shortly before His second coming. This "abomination of desolation" or desecration of the inner sanctum of the Temple would occur at the midway point of God's last seven years of dealing with the Jewish people before setting up the long-awaited Kingdom of God (Daniel 9:27).

Daniel's prediction also indicates that a prince would rise up from among the people who destroyed the second Temple (who were the Romans in A.D. 70) and that he "would make a firm covenant" with the Jewish people. This treaty would guarantee the religious freedom to reinstitute the old "sacrifices and oblations" of the Law of Moses.

This "prince" must be from a revived form of the ancient Roman Empire. (More about this in a later chapter.)

The apostle Paul predicts the activities of this Roman prince in great detail and gives us insight into the act that is called "the abomination of desolation." Paul speaks of this person as one who "opposes and exalts himself above every so-called god or object of worship, so that he takes his seat in the temple of God, displaying himself as being God" (II Thessalonians 2:4 NASB). By this act, the Roman prince, who is also called "the Lawless One" and "the Antichrist," breaks his covenant with the Jewish people and causes the Jewish temple worship, according to the law of Moses, to cease (Daniel 9:27).

Tie It All Together

The main points are these: first, there will be a reinstitution of the Jewish worship according to the Law of Moses with sacrifices and oblations in the general time of Christ's return; secondly, there is to be a desecration of the Jewish Temple in the time immediately preceding Christ's return.

We must conclude that a third Temple will be rebuilt upon its ancient site in old Jerusalem.

If this is the time that this writer believes it is, there will soon begin the construction of this Temple. Are there any evidences of such intentions in Israel?

In a fascinating article written shortly after the recapture of old Jerusalem, a reporter interviewed a famous Israeli historian, Israel Eldad. In answer to the question, "Do your people intend to rebuild the Temple?" Eldad said, "From the time that King David first conquered Jerusalem until Solomon built the Temple, just one generation passed. So will it be with us."

The reporter was so startled by that answer that he asked, "What about the Dome of the Rock which now stands on the temple site?"

Eldad replied, "It is, of course, an open question. Who knows, maybe there will be an earthquake."

The hope of rebuilding the Temple that is present in the hearts of devout Jews, some of whom are in powerful positions in the Israeli government, was clearly reflected here.

With the Jewish nation reborn in the land of Palestine, ancient Jerusalem once again under total Jewish control for the first time in 2600 years, and talk of rebuilding the great Temple, the most important prophetic sign of Jesus Christ's soon coming is before us. This has now set the stage for the other predicted signs to develop in history. It is like the key piece of a jig-saw puzzle being found and then having the many adjacent pieces rapidly fall into place.

For all those who trust in Jesus Christ, it is a time of electrifying excitement.

5 ○ Russia is a Gog

The next war will not be with the Arabs, but with the Russians.

GENERAL MOSHE DAYAN, 1968

. . . and come from your place out of the uttermost parts of the north, you and many peoples with you, all of them riding on horses, a great host, a mighty army; you will come up against my people Israel, like a cloud covering the land. In the latter days I will bring you against my land, that the nations may know me, when through you, O Gog, I vindicate my holiness before their eyes.

EZEKIEL 38:15-16, 650 B.C.

THE NEW STATE of Israel will be plagued by a certain pattern of events which has been clearly forecasted.

Shortly after the restoration of the Jews in the land of Israel, an incredible enemy will arise to its "uttermost north." This enemy will be composed of one great nation which will gather around it a number of allies. It is this "Northern Confederacy" that is destined to plunge the world into its final great war which Christ will return to end.

When I was a teenager watching the end of World War II, facing the continued fear of another war, I wondered then how it would all end. I once heard a radio program with a minister saying that the Bible indicated that the last war of the world would be fought between nations symbolized by an eagle and a bear. That was interesting to me, but he didn't back up his remarks with any definite proof. Even though I wasn't religious or interested in the Bible, I still spent many hours in bull sessions about this subject with other men who were as irreligious as myself. Little did I realize at that time how definite the Bible is about who the nations will be that play the major roles in the last drama. There is certainly more revealed than the vague symbols of an eagle and a bear.

There are three major prophecies on this northern sphere of political power which are to be found in Ezekiel 38; 39; Daniel 11:40-45; and Joel 2:20. It is of paramount importance to identify the time to which these prophecies apply, who the leading nation of the confederacy is, and who the allies are.

Then we shall see what this Northern Confederacy will do and how it will end.

What Time Is It?

There are several clues in Ezekiel's prophecy which establish the time to which it applies.

First, several times in the prophecy it is ascribed to "the latter years" (Ezekiel 38:8) and "the latter days," which have been previously noted (Ezekiel 38:16) . These are definite terms which denote the time just preceding and including the events which will be climaxed by the second advent of Jesus Christ, who will come this time as the "reigning Messiah" to set up God's promised Kingdom.

Second, this prediction is found in a context with a definite chronological sequence of events.

Ezekiel 36 and 37 speak of the final restoration of the Jews to the land of Palestine, a restoration from which they will never be scattered again. This restoration has two distinctions which show that it couldn't be speaking of the time when the Jews returned from the Babylonian exile.

The first distinction is that they are to return from a long world-wide dispersion. (The Babylonian dispersion wasn't very long nor was it world-wide.) The second distinction is that this restoration is immediately prior to and connected with the period of tribulation. This period brings about a great spiritual rebirth of the nation and the return of Jesus the Messiah to rescue them from their enemies.

Ezekiel speaks of the physical restoration of the nation when he says: "But you, O mountains of Israel, shall shoot forth your branches and yield your fruit to My people Israel; for they are soon to come home" (Ezekiel 36:8 Amplified).

And again from Ezekiel, "For I will take you from among the nations, and gather you out of all countries, and bring you into your own land" (Ezekiel 36:24 Amplified).

Ezekiel then foretells the spiritual regeneration of the people at some point *after* they are restored as a nation when he says, "Then will I sprinkle clean water upon you, and you shall be clean from all your uncleanness, and from all your idols will I cleanse you. A new heart will I give you, and a new spirit will I put within you: and I will take away the stony heart out of your flesh and give you a heart of flesh. And I will put my Spirit within you and cause you to walk in My statutes . . ." (Ezekiel 36:25-27 Amplified).

The parable of Ezekiel 37 describes these same events in this sequence: first, the physical restoration as a nation in the land and then the spiritual rebirth of the people. Ezekiel explains the prophetic vision, indicating the dry bones as "the whole house of Israel" hopelessly scattered throughout the nations of the world (Ezekiel 37:11). The bones coming together and sinews and flesh being put upon them is explained as meaning the regathering of the people into a physical restoration of a national existence in Palestine. Isn't it fascinating how graphic this physical analogy is?

Ezekiel's vision, however, goes beyond the purely physical. It says ". . . but there was no breath or spirit in them" (Ezekiel 37:8 Amplified). This indicates that the real spiritual life would come with the rebirth of the people after the restoration.

This restoration and spiritual rebirth of the nation is to be the beginning of the everlasting kingdom which the Messiah is promised to bring. Ezekiel says, "I will make a covenant of peace with them; it shall be an everlasting covenant with them . . . I will set My sanctuary in the midst of them for evermore" (Ezekiel 37:26 Amplified).

Study Ezekiel 38 and 39. The most significant part of this chain of events is established here. These chapters indicate with certainty that after the physical restoration of the nation, but before the spiritual rebirth, the great northern enemy will invade Israel (Ezekiel 38:8, 16). Then God will supernaturally judge the northern invaders, and this is the very act which will impel the Israeli people to know and believe in their true Messiah, Jesus Christ (Ezekiel 39:6-8).

Zechariah beautifully described this scene when he quotes God as saying, "And I will pour out upon the house of David and the inhabitants of Jerusalem a spirit of compassion and supplication, so that, when they look on him whom they have pierced, they shall mourn for him, as one mourns for an only child . . ." (Zechariah 12:10).

Ezekiel speaks in chapters 40 through 48 of a new worship pattern which will be established after the Messiah, Jesus Christ, comes to reign on earth over the Kingdom of God.

Since the restoration of Israel as a nation in 1948, we have lived in the most significant period of prophetic history. We are living in the times which Ezekiel predicted in chapters 38 and 39.

In 1854 a scholar named Chamberlain summed up the crux of what has just been said. In commenting on Ezekiel 38, he observed, "From all which I should infer, the coming restoration of Israel will at first be gradual and pacific; a restoration permitted, if not assisted and encouraged or protected. They will return to occupy the whole land, both cities and villages; they will be settled there, become prosperous and increasing in wealth, before this great confederacy of northern people will be formed against them."[1]

Consider that Chamberlain wrote this over one hundred years ago—long before Israel was a nation "assisted and encouraged" by other countries.

Who Is the Northern Commander?

For centuries, long before the current events could have influenced the interpreter's ideas, men have recognized that Ezekiel's prophecy about the northern commander referred to Russia.

Dr. John Cumming, writing in 1864, said, "This king of the North I conceive to be the autocrat of Russia . . . that Russia occupies a place, and a very momentous place, in the prophetic word has been admitted by almost all expositors."[2]

What's the Evidence?

Ezekiel describes this northern commander as "Gog, of the land of Magog, the chief prince (or ruler) of Rosh, of Meschech and Tubal" (Ezekiel 38:2 Amplified). This gives the ethnic background of this commander and his people.

In other words, the prophet gives the family tree of this northern commander so that we can trace the migrations of these tribes to the modern nation that we know.

Gog is the symbolic name of the nation's leader and Magog is his land. He is also the prince of the ancient people who were called Rosh, Meshech, and Tubal.

In the Biblical chapter commonly called the "Table of Nations" by scholars these names are mentioned. (See Genesis 10.) They are described as the grandsons of Noah through his son Japheth, with the exception of Rosh (Genesis 10:1, 2). Magog is the second son; Tubal is the fifth son; and Meshech is the sixth son.

You must be all excited about Magog, Meshech, and Tubal by this time! You are probably saying, "What in the world do these crusty relics of fiction have to do with Russia?" Let this writer assure you, these names are not fiction, but they have turned up in many archaeological discoveries in very early accounts of ancient history. One reason for this is that the families of these forefathers adopted their names as "tribal names." The family descended from Magog became known as the tribe of Magog, etc.

Dead Men Do Tell Tales!

It is necessary on the next few pages to establish some documentation from ancient history. Some people find this subject "a little dull," to say the least. If this is your case, you may wish to skim over the high points. For others, it will prove to be rewarding to check carefully the grounds upon which the historical case is built.

Herodotus, the fifth century B.C. Greek philosopher, is quoted as mentioning Meshech and Tubal. He identified them with a people named the Samaritans and Muschovites who lived at that time in the ancient province of Pontus in northern Asia Minor.³

Josephus, a Jewish historian of the first century, says that the people of his day known as the Moschevi and Thobelites were founded by Meshech and Tubal respectively. He said, ". . . Magog is called the Scythians by the Greeks." He continued by saying that these people lived in the northern regions above the Caucasus mountains.⁴

Pliny, a noted Roman writer of early Christian times, said, "Hierapolis, taken by the Scythians, was afterward called Magog."⁵ In this he shows that the dreaded barbaric people called the Scythians were identified with their ancient tribal name. Any good history book of ancient times traces the Scythians to be a principle part of the people who make up modern Russia.

Wilhelm Gesenius, a great Hebrew scholar of the early nineteenth century, discusses these words in his unsurpassed Hebrew Lexicon. "Meshech," he says, "was founder of the Moschi, a barbarous people, who dwelt in the Moschian mountains."⁶

This scholar went on to say that the Greek name, "Moschi," derived from the Hebrew name Meshech is the source of the name for *the city of Moscow*. In discussing Tubal he said, "Tubal is the son of Rapheth, founder of the Tibereni, a people dwelling on the Black Sea to the west of the Moschi."

Gesenius concludes by saying that these people undoubtedly make up the modern Russian people.

There is one more name to consider in this line of evidence. It is the Hebrew word, "Rosh," translated "chief" in Ezekiel 38:2, 3 of the King James and Revised Standard Versions. The word literally means in Hebrew the "top" or "head" of something. According to most scholars, this word is used in the sense of a proper name, not as a descriptive noun qualifying the word "prince."

The German scholar, Dr. Keil, says after a careful grammatical analysis that it should be translated as a proper name, i.e., Rosh. He says, "The Byzantine and Arabic writers frequently mention a people called Rôs and Rûs, dwelling in the country of Taurus, and reckoned among the Scythian tribes."⁷

Dr. Gesenius in his Hebrew Lexicon says, ". . . Rosh was a designation for the tribes then north of the Taurus Mountains, dwelling in the neighborhood of the Volga."⁸

He concluded that in this name and tribe we have the first historical trace of the Russ or Russian nation.

In the light of the abundant evidence, it is no wonder that men long before Russia rose to its present state of power foresaw its role in history. Bishop Lowth of England was one of these men. He wrote in 1710, "Rosh, taken as a proper name, in Ezekiel signifies the inhabitants of Scythia, from whom the modern Russians derive their name."[9]

In the eighteenth and nineteenth centuries, such men as Bishop Lowth, Dr. Cumming, and Rev. Chamberlain, were ridiculed by many of their contemporaries. After all, who could have imagined then what we now see in modern communist Russia—a country founded upon atheism?

Where Is the Uttermost North?

The final evidence for identifying this northern commander lies in its geographical location from Israel.

Ezekiel puts great stress on this by saying three times that this great enemy of Israel would come from their "uttermost north." It is mentioned in 38:6 and 15, and 39:2. The King James Version doesn't translate this accurately, but the Revised Standard and Amplified Versions of the Bible do. The Hebrew word that qualifies "north" means either "uttermost" or "extreme."

You need only to take a globe to verify this exact geographical fix. There is only one nation to the "uttermost north" of Israel—the U.S.S.R.

"Thus says the Lord God: Are you he of whom I have spoken in olden times by My servants the prophets of Israel, who prophesied in those days for years that I would bring you, *Gog*, against them?" (Ezekiel 38:17 Amplified). The answer to this challenging question thrown down by God through Ezekiel centuries ago is now rather obvious, wouldn't you say?

General Dayan's statement that "The next war will not be with the Arabs but with the Russians" has a considerably deeper significance, doesn't it?

Final Exam

Just think for a moment how incredible a thing we are considering here. How could Ezekiel 2600 years ago have forecast so accurately the rise of Russia to its current military might and its direct and obvious designs upon the Middle East, not to mention the fact that it is now an implacable enemy of the new state of Israel? How could men like Chamberlain and Cumming, for that matter, one hundred years ago have so clearly seen the future rise of Russia to its present world-threatening position?

The answer is again, it seems to this writer, obvious. Ezekiel once again passes "the test of a prophet." He was guided by the Spirit of the living God. In the apostle Peter's final letter, written as he faced certain and imminent death, he stated the source of the prophets' wisdom and insight. Peter first states where prophecy did not originate; "But know this first of all, that no prophecy of Scripture is a matter of one's own interpretation" (II Peter 1:20 NASB). In other words, the prophets did not dream up their own interpretation of life and history.

Then Peter declares where prophecy did originate, ". . . for no prophecy was ever made by an act of human will, but men moved by the Holy Spirit spoke from God" (II Peter 1:21 NASB).

When a man knows that he is about to die, he usually gets around to saying the things he considers to be most important. Peter considered the certainty and relevance of the prophetic word to be the most important thing. He even warned that in "the latter times" men posing as religious leaders would rise from within the Church and deny, even ridicule, the prophetic word (II Peter 2:1-3; 3:1-18).

If you pass this book around to many ministers you'll find how true this prediction has become.

Who Are the Allies?

Ezekiel partially catalogs the ancient names of the peoples and nations who would be confederates of Russia in 38:5 and 6.

Persia

All authorities agree on who Persia is today. It is modern Iran. This is significant because it is being wooed to join the United Arab Republic in its hostility against Israel. The Russians are at this moment seeking to gain footholds in Iran by various overtures of aid. In order to mount the large-scale invasion predicted by Ezekiel, Russia would need Iran as an ally. It would be much more difficult to move a large land army across the Caucasus Mountains that border Turkey, than the Elburz Mountains that border Iran. Iran's general terrain is also much easier to cross than Turkey's. Transportation, however, will be needed through both countries.

Watch the actions of Iran in relation to Russia and the United Arab Republic. This writer believes that significant things will soon be happening there.

Ethiopia or Cush (Black African Nations)

Ethiopia is a translation of the Hebrew word, *Cush*. Cush was the first son of Ham, one of the sons of Noah.

Moses mentions "the land of Cush" as originally being adjacent to an area near the Tigris and Euphrates rivers (Genesis 2:13).

After examining many authorities on the subject, the writer discovered once again why Dr. Gesenius is recognized as one of the great scholars of history. Gesenius summarized all of the evidence as follows: (1) The Cushites were black men. (2) They migrated first to the Arabian peninsula and then across the Red Sea to the area south of Egypt. (3) All the black people of Africa are descended from Cush.

Gesenius observes, "Indeed all the nations sprung from Cush and enumerated in Genesis 10:7, are to be sought in Africa."[10]

Cush is translated "Ethiopia" twenty-one times in the King James Version, which is somewhat misleading. It is certain that the ancient Ethiopians (modern Abyssinia) are made up of Cushites, but they do not represent all of them, according to history.

The sobering conclusion is this: many of the African nations will be united and allied with the Russians in the invasion of Israel. This is in accord with Daniel's graphic description of this invasion (Daniel 11:36-45).

The Russian force is called "the King of the North" and the sphere of power which the African (Cush) force will be a part of is called "the King of the South."

One of the most active areas of evangelism for the Communist "gospel" is in Africa. As we see further developments in this area in the future, we realize that it will become converted to Communism.

Libya or Put (Arabic African Nations)

Libya is the translation of the original Hebrew word, *Put*. We have the same problem pinpointing these people as with Cush. Put was the third son of Ham (Genesis 10:6). The descendants of Put migrated to the land west of Egypt and became the source of the North African Arab nations, such as Libya, Algeria, Tunisia, and Morocco. The first settlement of Put was called Libya by the ancient historians, Josephus and Pliny.[11] The Greek translation of the Hebrew Old Testament, called the Septuagint, translates Put as Libya in about 165 B.C.

The conclusion is that Russia's ally, Put, certainly included more than what is now called Libya. Once again there are current events to show the beginning of this alliance.

The territory of Northern Africa is becoming solidly pro-Soviet.[12] Algeria appears to be already Communist and allied with Russia.

As we watch this area in the next few years we shall see indications that it is destined to join the southern sphere of power which will attack Israel along with the "King of the North."

Gomer and All Its Hordes (Iron Curtain Countries)

Gomer was the eldest son of Japheth, and the father of Ashkenaz, Riphath, and Togarmah. These people make up an extremely important part of the future Russian invasion force.

Dr. Young, citing the best of the most recent archaeological finds, says of Gomer and his hordes, "They settled on the north of the Black Sea, and then spread themselves southward and westward to the extremities of Europe."[13]

Gesenius speaks of part of Gomer's "hordes" as being Ashkenaz . . . "the proper name of a region and a nation in northern Asia, sprung from the Cimmerians who are the ancient people of Gomer. The modern Jews understand it to be Germany, and call that country by this Hebrew name. . . ."[14]

Josephus called the sons of Ashkenaz, "The Rheginians" and a map of the ancient Roman Empire places them in the area of modern Poland, Czechoslovakia, and East Germany to the banks of the Danube River. The modern Jewish Talmud confirms the same geographical picture.

The conclusion is that Gomer and its hordes are a part of the vast area of modern Eastern Europe which is totally behind the Iron Curtain. This includes East Germany and the Slovak countries.

Togarmah and All Its Hordes
(Southern Russia and the Cossacks)

In Ezekiel 38:6 "the house of Togarmah, and all its hordes" are specifically pointed out as being from "the uttermost north." Gesenius says that "they are a northern nation and country sprung from Gomer abounding in horses and mules." Some of the sons of Togarmah founded Armenia, according to their own claim today, Gesenius continued.

Dr. Bauman traces evidence of some of the sons of Togarmah to the Turkoman tribes of Central Asia. This would explain the statement, ". . . of the uttermost north, and all its hordes."

The conclusion is that Togarmah is part of modern Southern Russia and is probably the origin of the Cossacks and other people of the Eastern part of Russia. It is interesting to note that the Cossacks have always loved horses and have been recognized as producing the finest army of cavalry in the world. Today they are reported to have several divisions of cavalry. It is believed by some military men that cavalry will actually be used in the invasion of the Middle East just as Ezekiel and other prophets literally predicted. During the Korean War the Red Chinese proved that in rugged mountainous terrain, horses are still the fastest means of moving a large attacking force into battle zones.

Isn't it a coincidence that such terrain stands between Russia and the Israeli?

Ezekiel indicates that he hasn't given a complete list of allies. Enough is given, however, to make this writer amazed by the number of people and nations which will be involved.

Gog, Take Command

Ezekiel, prophetically addressing the Russian ruler, commands him to, ". . . be prepared; yes prepare yourself, you and all your companies that are assembled about you, and you be a guard *and* a commander for them" (Ezekiel 38:7 Amplified).

In other words, the Russian ruler is to equip his confederates with arms and to assume command.

If you have doubts about all that has been said in this chapter, isn't it a bit unnerving to note that almost all of the countries predicted as part of this great army are already armed with weapons created and manufactured in Russia?

What's Your Game, Gog?

We have seen that Russia will arm and equip a vast confederacy. This powerful group of allies will lead an attack on restored Israel. However, Russia and her confederates will be destroyed completely by an act that

Israel will acknowledge as being from their God. This act will bring many in Israel to believe in their true Messiah (Ezekiel 38:15 ff.).

The attack upon the Russian confederacy and the resulting conflict will escalate into the last war of the world, involving all nations.

Then it will happen. Christ will return to prevent the annihilation of all mankind.

6 ○ Sheik to Sheik

Our basic aim will be to destroy Israel.   NASSER OF EGYPT, MAY, 1967

They have said, Come, and let us wipe them out as a nation; let the name of Israel be in remembrance no more.   PSALM 83:4 (Amplified) prophesied about 1000 B.C.

WHEN THE PHONE rings and it's the person we have just mentioned in conversation, inevitably we say, "What a coincidence, we were just talking about you." Or when we open the mail and find the check that we needed to pay an urgent bill, we enjoy the timely coincidence.

However, in writing this book too many pieces and events have fallen into place for us to believe they could all be "coincidence." This is why we believe what one vague religionist has called "the divine hand from somewhere" set the stage the week we began this chapter.

In the last chapter some of the confederates of a future Russian invasion force were documented from Biblical prophecy. The confederates who are relevant to this chapter are the Arabic nations. The Bible says that Egypt, the Arabic nations, and countries of black Africa will form an alliance, a sphere of power which will be called the King of the South. Allied with Russia, the King of the North, this formidable confederacy will rise up against the restored state of Israel.

So where is the coincidence?

As we were researching the current status of the leading Arabic nation, Egypt, we discovered that on the campus of a large university, less than ten minutes away, it was Arab Week. Obviously they must have planned it to coincide with our study.

With echos of Scheherazade humming in our subconscious, we made our way. . . .

On Campus

We found an exotic mixture of West and Middle East along the shaded walks of the beautiful university. Some students were wearing head-coverings, Arab-fashion, to indicate where their allegiance was. The vision was not quite like Lawrence of Arabia galloping across endless stretches of white sand, but the effect was striking.

Tables were everywhere around the Student Union. We were deluged with printed materials concerning the rightness of the Arab cause against Israel and their determination to liberate Palestine.

In a short while we were supplied with documents which substantiated the alliance of the Arabs and the Russians, a bond both present and actual, but also a fact which was prophesied approximately 2600 years ago!

The purpose of "Arab Week" at the university was to rally support for the Palestinian Revolution. According to the literature which was being distributed, "the Palestine Revolution draws moral support from the revolutionary movements of the world. The Arab student movement has given the revolution their total support. Arab intellectuals, joined by many world-thinkers have given their support."

This "revolutionary movement" is part of the Communist movement which has supported "wars of liberation" in countries around the world.

From the standpoint of this study of alliances which make up the King of the South we saw a valuable link in the alignment of several black African nations with the Arabs in their determined plan to "liberate" Palestine from Israel. This is another confirmation of prophecy as we have seen from Old Testament prophets.

Egypt: Leading Actor

We speak of "Arab," and yet it is obvious that the real leader in the Arabic world is Egypt. This country is in a strategic spot in the prophetic landscape, which is the reason we should follow the events in the Middle East with great interest.

Egypt is located at the southern end of "the land bridge" which connects the continents of Europe, Asia and Africa. The value of this important piece of real estate, which has been established by centuries of fighting will play an important part in events which we will show in the chapter on World War III. Conveniently for Egypt, it has an ideal location for its role of leadership in the Afro-Arab world.

"Egypt's geographical size, large population, 150,000 man military establishment, advanced industrialization, and President Gamal Abdel Nasser's military Arab nationalism make it the political, intellectual, and cultural center of the Arab world, as well as much of Africa."[1]

What about Nasser? He has become the symbol of leadership for both African and Arabic "wars of liberation from Western imperialism." Nasser's manifesto, "Philosophy of the Revolution," provides us with insight into the future direction which we can expect of the Arab and African situation.

"Nasser views the world as a stage, with Egypt as one of the principal actors. This role is three-dimensional, described in Nasser's language in terms of circles. The first of these is the Arab area with Arab unity as the main plot. Beyond this circle lies Africa, which Nasser envisages as the seat of struggle between white 'imperialists' and the indigenous Negroes for possession of its riches. Encompassing these two circles is the world of Islam, also threatened by 'imperialism.' In the past few years, Nasser appears to have expanded this conception of the third circle to include all non-Western and underdeveloped Western countries."[2]

Nasser has not swerved from his written goal to bring about a kind of "Arab Socialism." He has repeatedly said that kings, sheiks, sultans, and capitalism must all be obliterated. This has appealed to the common Arab who has been oppressed for centuries. Using the "Gospel of Materialism," plus the common bond of Arabic race identity, wedded with the Moslem religious ties, Nasser believes that he can unite the Arabs to lead the resurrection of all underprivileged nations into a mighty third world force. He envisions himself as the one to lead the nations of Africa, black and Arab, to unity.

Somehow the aims, ambitions, and worldly directions of dictators past and present never seem to change. There has never been a benevolent dictator.

How to Make Enemies and Influence People

Nasser has fallen into a trap which has ensnared all Arab leaders. It would appear that the only way to remain a popular leader in the Arab world today is to keep the flames of hatred toward the state of Israel fanned to a fever pitch. The one who can make the most elaborate and gory promises of Israel's destruction is number one on the hit parade. Whenever an Arab leader senses his popularity waning, he whips up a propaganda program about the need to liberate Palestine, according to Middle-East observers.

It is believed by most experts on the Middle East that Nasser was trapped into the June, 1967, war, playing the game of Blind Man's Bluff. He knew that he could never remain enthroned as the leader of the United Arab Republic if other aggressive Arab leaders railed against Israel in stronger terms. It is reported that he was caught unprepared when U Thant quickly complied with his order to remove the U.N. observers from the buffer zone which separated the Arabic and Israeli armies. Once this occurred, he had no alternative but to make good his threats.

Israel saw the clear danger of a large-scale Egyptian mobilization in the Sinai peninsula and also the threat of not being able to ship through the Gulf of Aqaba. The Israelites also saw the rapid unification of all Arabic nations into a formidable force surrounding them on three sides. Israeli leaders realized that unless they seized the initiative and attacked, there would be no hope of survival.

What started out to be a bold popularity stunt on Nasser's part, designed to make Israel lose face over the blockade of the Gulf of Aqaba, ended in a fiasco. Rather than be completely humiliated in the eyes of the world, Nasser carried the world to the brink of war.

It is this kind of fierce pride and smoldering hatred against Israel that will keep the Middle East a dangerous trouble spot. No Arab leader could hope to remain in power if he were willing to make concessions in negotiating with Israel.

In July, 1968, the headlines in a news magazine warned, "No Easing of Mideast War Danger." The report said that "The recent visit of Egypt's President Nasser to the Soviet Union—the country that arms him against Israel—turned attention to an area that never seems far from the explosion point."[3]

In December, 1968, the ambassador to the United States from Israel, Yitzhak Rabin, a key strategist in the six-day Arab-Israeli War of 1967, said that he couldn't be optimistic about peace in the near future in the Middle East.[4]

U Thant said of the Egypt-Israeli situation, "Never in the history of the United Nations' experience with peace-keeping has there been such complete and sustained disregard for a cease-fire agreed to by the parties." Mr. Thant went on to say that warfare along the Suez Canal had become so intense he might have to consider withdrawal of U.N. cease-fire observers.[5]

At the time this is being written Nasser is reported to be in poor health. Whether he continues to lead Egypt, or is replaced by some other leader or dead by the time this is published, the clearly predictable course of the Middle East will not be changed. There will be continual crises there and a great involvement of the world's major powers.

The King of the South

Current events in the Middle East have prepared the stage for Egypt's last act in the great drama which will climax with the finale, Christ's personal return to earth.

We are not attempting to read into today's happenings any events to prove some vague thesis. This is not necessary. All we need to do is know the Scriptures in their proper context and then watch with awe while men and countries, movements and nations, fulfill the roles that God's prophets said they would.

Long ago the prophet Daniel spoke of Egypt as "the king of the South." Egypt is identified as this power in chapter 11 where Daniel predicts a long span of history involving warfare between Egypt under the Ptolemaic dynasty and Syria under the Seleucid dynasty.

In Daniel 11:40 Daniel leaps over a long era of time to the events which lead up to the personal, visible appearance of Christ as God's righteous conqueror. The phrase "at the time of the end" speaks unmistakably of the beginning of the last great war of history.

Daniel gives great detail concerning the battles and movement of troops which will take place at the beginning of this war. (The war itself will be developed later in Chapter 12.)

Our interest here is the revelation that Egypt will attack the revived state of Israel, which will then be under the control of a false Messiah. This man will probably be a Jew who works closely with the world dictator who will come to power in Rome. (Meet the "Future Fuehrer" in Chapter 9.)

Notice what Daniel says about this attack on Israel: "And at the time of the end the king of the south shall push at and attack him" (Daniel 11:40 Amplified).

This immediately triggers another invasion of Israel by Russia who is here called "the king of the north."

The movement of Russia and its northern confederacy through "the land bridge of the Middle-East" into Egypt serves an ominous warning to Egypt. Speaking of the Russian invader, Daniel prophesies: "He shall stretch forth his hand also upon the countries: and the land of Egypt shall not escape. But he shall have power over the treasures of gold and of silver, and over all the precious things of Egypt; and the Libyans and the Ethiopians shall be at his steps" (Daniel 11:42, 43 KJV).

As we saw in the last chapter, the Hebrew words "Cush" and "Put," which are translated Ethiopia and Libya, represent the black Africans and African Arabs, respectively. Aside from the obvious evidence of a Russian double-cross of the Egyptians, this passage also indicates that the "black African" and "Arab-African" countries will be involved with Egypt and in line for Russian conquest as well. The statement, ". . . the Libyans and Ethiopians shall be at his (the Russian invader) steps," indicates one of two things: they will be next in line for conquest, or they will submit totally to the Russian will and be assimilated into the northern confederacy.

This invasion of Cush and Put, along with Egypt, and their fall together is mentioned more specifically by the prophet Ezekiel: "And a sword shall come upon Egypt, and anguish shall be in Ethiopia (Cush), when the slain fall in Egypt, and her wealth is carried away, and her foundations are torn down.

Ethiopia, and Put, and Lud, and all Arabia, and Libya, and the people of the land that is in league shall fall with them by the sword" (Ezekiel 30:4,5).

This prophecy, in the first nine verses of Ezekiel 30, refers to the judgment of Egypt and her allies during the Tribulation. The phrases, ". . . the day of the Lord" and ". . . a time of doom of nations" places it in the time just prior to the second coming of Christ. For you students of the Bible, we must add that the latter part of the chapter looks at the time when Nebuchadnezzar destroyed Egypt and her allies, but its greater fulfillment is future.

Are you discovering more pieces of this stirring prophetic puzzle? The Egyptian plan to unite the Arabs and the black Africans into a "third world force" seems to be fulfilling what the prophets have said.

Grace Goes to Egypt

After viewing such a bleak picture of the future for Egypt and its confederacy of nations it may seem as though God has written them off. The truth of the matter is, however, quite the contrary.

Isaiah, reliable prophet that he is, reveals that one of the purposes for the judgment of Egypt is to drive its people from faith in false messiahs and "religion" to faith in the one true Savior.

Isaiah warns of a terrible judgment which would fall on Egypt in the last days. He speaks of Egypt's very life source being judged: "And the waters of the Nile will be dried up, and the river will be parched and dry; and its canals will become foul, and the branches of Egypt's Nile will diminish and dry up" (Isaiah 19:5, 6).

If you think the famous Aswan Dam, which diverts the main channel of the Nile River, will help the Egyptian situation, you're mistaken. Somehow the headwaters of the Nile will be diverted and that important river will be a parched piece of real estate. Imagine the terrifying implications of this to an Egyptian!

Isaiah warns of a powerful dictator who will invade and take them over: ". . . I will give over the Egyptians into the hand of a hard master; and a fierce [merciless] king will rule over them" (Isaiah 19:4 RSV). This refers to the Antichrist of Rome who will possess Egypt after Russia is destroyed.

All of these things will happen to the Egyptians until many cry out to the true Savior, Jesus. Isaiah says, ". . . when they cry to the Lord because of oppressors he will send them a savior, and will defend and deliver them" (Isaiah 19:20).

What a great demonstration of God's loving heart! Often men won't see their need of God until He so shakes up their world that they are helpless to cope with life without Him. It's only then that they turn to trust in God's provision for their shortcomings. Then they discover that Jesus Christ has so paid the penalty for their sins that God can offer a totally free gift of forgiveness and accept them into His eternal family.

A Lesson From Egypt

As you read this book you may have reached the point where you recognize your inability to live in a way that would cause God to accept you. If this is the case, you may speak to God right now and accept the gift of Christ's forgiveness. It's so simple. Ask Christ to come into your life and make your life pleasing to God by His power.

We have found the results to be certain and exciting in our own lives.

Putting It Together

We have seen how current events are fitting together simultaneously into the precise pattern of predicted events. Israel has returned to Palestine and revived the nation. Jerusalem is under Israeli control. Russia has emerged as a great northern power and is the avowed enemy of revived Israel. The Arabs are joining in a concerted effort to liberate Palestine under Egyptian leadership. The black African nations are beginning to move from sympathy toward the Arabs to an open alliance in their "liberation" cause.

It's happening. God is putting it all together. God may have His meaning for the "now generation" which will have a greater effect on mankind than anything since Genesis 1.

Will you be ready if we are to be a part of the prophetic "now generation"?

7 ○ The Yellow Peril

... the great river, the Euphrates ... was dried up, that the way might be prepared for the kings of the east ... And they gathered them together in the place which in Hebrew is called Har-Magedon.

REVELATION 16:12, 16 (NASB)

JOHN THE APOSTLE about A.D. 90

"THE KINGS OF the East" in Biblical prophecy refers to another sphere of power which was to arise in the world at the same time as the great Northern Power (Russia) and the King of the South (Egypt and the Afro-Arabic alliance).

The original Greek words translated "east" (Revelation 16:12) are literally *anatoles heliou*, which mean, "the rising of the sun." This was the ancient designation of the Oriental races and nations. John describes this vast horde of soldiers assembled at the Euphrates River as "the kings of the sun rising" and thus definitely predicts the movement of a vast Oriental army into a war in the Middle East.

The mention of the Euphrates River brings out another important strategic clue about this Eastern confederacy. This great river has figured prominently in military history throughout the ages. It was always recognized as the ancient boundary between east and west. In the late nineteenth century a scholar said of this fact: "From time immemorial the Euphrates, with its tributaries, has been a great and formidable boundary between the peoples east of it and those west of it. It runs a distance of 1800 miles, and is scarcely fordable anywhere or at any time. It is from three to twelve hundred yards wide, and from ten to thirty feet in depth; and most of the time it is still deeper and wider."[1] This clue shows that this power is Oriental, since it comes from east of the Euphrates.

The Euphrates has presented a formidable problem for the corps of engineers of many ancient armies of the past. In this future invasion, however, God Himself will see to it that the river is dried up so that a trap is set for triggering the last great war of mankind.

Another important detail involving this Oriental army is unlocked by the clue involving the Euphrates. The apostle John speaks of the release of four vicious, depraved angelic beings which have been kept bound by God at the Euphrates River (Revelation 9:14-16). Immediately after their release an incredible army emerges from the Euphrates ... it numbers "200 million" (Revelation 9:16). The four demonic spirit-beings somehow incite this great army to invade the Middle East and apparently they are the ones who make the river dry up so that the army can quickly cross this ancient barrier of east and west.

A terrifying prophecy is made about the destiny of this Asian horde. They will wipe out a third of the earth's population (Revelation 9:18). The phenomena by which this destruction of life will take place is given: it will be by fire, smoke (or air pollution), and brimstone (or melted earth). The thought may have occurred to you that this is strikingly similar to the phenomena associated with thermonuclear warfare. In fact, many Bible expositors believe that this is an accurate first-century description of a twentieth-century thermonuclear war.

Another Coincidence?

These predictions, made near the end of the first century, concerned an Asian confederacy which would field the greatest army ever to march to battle. This army would be raised up just prior to Christ's return to the earth.

For centuries Asia has had a tradition of backwardness. Though the peoples of Asia have always been numerous in population, they lagged behind the West in education, science and technology. For hundreds of years Asia chose to remain isolated from the world; then that isolation was broken.

Japan was the first Asian nation to push out into the stream of modern science; it was the first Asian nation in centuries to set out on a course of conquest beyond the Orient. But Japan never truly got outside of the Asian boundaries.

The Japanese navy almost brought a great invasion force into the Middle East during World War II. A convoy set sail for the Red Sea to enter the African and Palestinian campaign and break the Allied resistance there. Nothing could have stopped them. They would have defeated the British who were already extended by Field Marshall Rommel's Afrika Corps.

The British navy had only a handful of ships in the Indian Ocean and they were quickly ordered to flee to Madagascar to avert suicide. Had the Japanese continued as originally planned, World War II could have had a different ending.

It was at this point that a strange thing happened. Admiral Yamamoto, for some unexplainable reason, changed the order, and had the task force turn around in the Indian Ocean and head for the West Coast of the United States. We believe this must have been divine providence.

The intention of this task force was miraculously discovered when some sailors of the U.S. Navy intercepted their radio messages and broke the code. The battle that ensued was really the turning point of the war. With a handful of B-17 bombers and a vastly outnumbered task force, the U.S. Navy turned back the Japanese at the Battle of the Coral Sea.

Japan went on to be defeated and her dreams of world conquest have been put away.

However, the churning of upheaval was taking place in the Orient.

The Dragon Is Awake

With the Communist takeover of China, the real sleeping giant of Asia was awakened. In about 1860 an astute student of prophecy, Dr. Robinson, predicted: "Before another half century shall have rolled away in the providence of God there will be seen revolutions in the Oriental mind of which no one has even a foreboding."[2]

Dr. Cumming in 1864 also foresaw the necessity of the Orient entering the industrial age and later becoming a great scourge to the Western civilization.[3]

In the twenty odd years since the fall of China to the Communists there has been a steady relentless preparation for all-out war with the free world. Though the living conditions of the eight hundred million or more people of Red China are still basically like the nineteenth century, they have made remarkable progress in the production of weapons for war.

Concerning Red China's potential and purpose, Victor Petrov said in 1967, "China does possess all the prerequisites for being or becoming a world power. Communist China's economic growth is evident and has been on the rise. With or without Soviet help, she will be progressing toward her avowed goal of reaching the industrial level of the other major powers of the world . . . a giant, for decades half-asleep, sheepishly watching the rest of the world go by on the path of technological progress. This giant has apparently been awakened."[4]

Red China is definitely on the road to becoming a world power, but her design for the use of this stature is not peace. Within one year after the takeover of China her Communist leaders started the war in Korea. They have since fomented the war in Viet Nam and have traveled to several countries in Africa and the Middle East seeking to aggravate internal subversion and "Communist wars of liberation."

The vaunted Sino-Soviet split is over an interpretation of Communist doctrine. The Chinese insist that the world can be captured only by force of arms and violence: the Russians now believe that the free world can be captured by the relatively limited violence of internal subversion . . . while masquerading under the guise of "peaceful coexistence." It should be marked well, however, that neither have disembarked from their goal of total world conquest for Communism. This is an integral part of the Communist doctrine. Without the total destruction of the capitalist system the basic promise and goal of Communism could not be attained, that is, the changing of man's nature by the complete change of his environment. According to the Communists, as long as capitalism exists in the world it continues to infect man's environment and prevents him from being a creature that loves to work, shares equally his wealth, and loves his fellow man.

The great charge of the Red Chinese against the Russians is the most despicable word in the Communists' vocabulary—"revisionist." They believe that the Russians have "revised" the most fundamental principle of Marxist-Leninism. Lenin succinctly stated this principle. "Marxists have never forgotten that violence will be an inevitable accompaniment of the collapse of capitalism. . . ."[5]

Mao Tse-tung summarized his interpretation of this principle when he said, "Political power comes out of the barrel of a gun . . . the gun must never slip from the grasp of the Communist party."[6]

The basic difference can be described as "external invasion and takeover" versus "internal subversion and takeover."

Because of the Communist Chinese belief that the free world can only be overthrown by all-out war, they have for many years devoted approximately ten per cent of their entire military budget for developing nuclear weapons. In the February, 1969, issue of the *Bulletin of Atomic Scientists*, which was on the theme of "China's Nuclear Options," special note was made of the fantastic technological feat achieved by China's development of the H-Bomb. They went from the testing of a crude atomic bomb to the successful test firing of an H-bomb in two and one half years. This was much faster than the time taken by the other members of the world's Atomic Bomb Club.

In the same issue of the *Bulletin of Atomic Scientists*, Michael Yahuda discussed the various options which the Red Chinese have for a delivery system for H-bombs. He expressed the following opinion: "The third option—an ICBM based strategy—would be the most satisfying psychologically to the present Chinese leadership and to Mao in particular. At one fell stroke, the Chinese would have acquired the most advanced weapon . . . The American mainland would be within range as indeed would the Urals and

European Russia. Current, although incomplete, evidence suggests that the Chinese are striving for an ICBM capability."[7]

Yahuda's speculation is certainly shared by the military planners. This was undoubtedly the prime motivation behind the Nixon administration's push for an anti-ballistic missile system.

Dr. David Inglis wrote in the February, 1965, *Bulletin of Atomic Scientists* regarding this threat, "Our concern should anticipate at least two decades ahead. In such a time the large human and material potential of an upsurging China constitutes a nuclear threat so vast that no effort should be spared to anticipate this threat."[8] This was written before China's successful testing of the H-bomb.

Mao may be dead before this is read, but the course of China's path of destruction will continue. The new leaders of Communist China may be more unstable than Mao.

We believe that China is the beginning of the formation of this great power called "the kings of the east" by the apostle John. We live at a time in history when it is no longer incredible to think of the Orient with an army of 200 million soldiers. In fact, a recent television documentary on Red China, called "The Voice of the Dragon," quoted the boast of the Chinese themselves that they could field a "people's army" of 200 million militiamen. In their own boast they named the same number as the Biblical prediction. Coincidence?

Furthermore, the Chinese leaders claim that even nuclear weapons cannot stop their human wave tactics. They brag about the invincibility of the unbelievable numbers of soldiers they can expend in a given campaign. This "human wave" tactic seems to be behind the strategy of that 200 million man army predicted as invading the Middle East in the battle of Armageddon. Petrov says regarding this, "The abundant population presents an unlimited source of human material for military power, which in our age of machinery and automation has not yet been found obsolete. China's armed forces are formidable in numbers . . . that day apparently is approaching when China will definitely become a member of that small but exclusive group commonly known as the Great World Powers."[9]

The sobering fact that Red China will have ICBM's capable of delivering H-bombs by 1980 at the latest, presents another grisly potential for fulfilling prophecy regarding this Oriental power. Within a decade China alone will have the capacity to destroy one-third of the world's population just as John predicted.

Summing Up

We believe that another sphere of political power is forming its predicted role in the final stages of history. Along with the revival of Israel and the return of the dispersed Jews, the rise of Russia, the formation of the Arab confederacy, China is helping to shape the Orient into its pattern of prophecy.

History seems to be headed for its climactic hour.

8 ○ Rome on the Revival Road

Veni, vidi, vici.   CAESAR, 47 B.C.

WHEN CAESAR SENT his memorable dispatch, "I came, I saw, I conquered," the scribes of his day might have said, "We shall record these historic words immediately. Perhaps Latin students centuries from now will be required to memorize them."

Students who have struggled through Latin declensions and waded with Caesar through campaigns in Gaul know his famous words well. Certainly many other men have expressed themselves more eloquently. But there haven't been many men through the centuries who have had the power of Julius Caesar.

But Rome fell. And Caesar died as any mortal must. And the mighty Roman empire of the ancient world lost its strength.

However, the prophetic Scriptures tell us that the Roman Empire will be revived shortly before the return of Christ to this earth. A new Caesar will head this empire and "Veni, vidi, vici" will leap out of the first-year Latin books and become a reality of the times.

Twenty years ago no one would have dared to believe that Rome as an empire would be put back together. And yet we are seeing significant movements of nations today which are indications that this is what is happening.

As world events develop, prophecy becomes more and more exciting. Also, the understanding of God's prophecies becomes increasingly clear as we look at the Bible and then at the current scene.

We are told in Daniel 12 how prophecy "will not be understood until the end times, when travel and education shall be vastly increased."

We are told that "Surely the Lord God will do nothing without revealing His secret to His Servants the prophets" (Amos 3:7 Amplified).

In other words, when God is going to undertake some significant movement of history as far as His program is concerned, He will reveal it first. This writer doesn't believe that we have prophets today who are getting direct revelations from God, but we do have prophets today who are being given special insight into the prophetic word. God is opening the book of the prophets to many men. This is one reason you will find on Christian bookshelves an increasing number of books on the subject of Bible prophecy.

All Roads Lead To . . .

Where in prophecy do we find a prediction about the revival of Rome? First we shall examine the great prophet, Daniel. Chapter 7 of Daniel was written sometime in the early sixth century B.C., at a time when Babylon was still the ruling empire of the world. In the first part of this chapter the prophet Daniel was shown the successive empires which would come on the stage of history and have authority over the whole earth. A vision of these empires was also described in Daniel 2. The key to these empires is given in Daniel 2:39 where he predicts the successive empires which shall "bear rule" (literally meaning, shall have authority) over all the earth.

First of all, there was Babylon. "You (king of Babylon) are the head of gold."

Then the prophet tells us what kingdoms will rise to power after Babylon.

"And after you shall arise another kingdom [the Media-Persian], inferior to *and* earthward from you, and still a third kingdom of bronze [Greece under Alexander the Great], which shall bear rule over all the earth. And the fourth kingdom [Rome] shall be strong as iron, since iron breaks to pieces and subdues all things; and like iron which crushes, it shall break and crush all these" (Daniel 2:39, 40 Amplified).

These kingdoms would conquer everything that was worth conquering on the known earth of that time.

The Greatest Chapter in the Old Testament

The seventh chapter of Daniel, written before the coming of Jesus of Nazareth, was known by the scribes as the greatest chapter in the Old Testament. Jesus and His apostles referred to it directly or indirectly many times. Many of the predictions from Daniel's dream have been clear in their historic perspective for centuries. However, certain parts have remained obscure until recent times.

Daniel had a dream, and in this dream he saw four great beasts come up out of the sea. The first beast was like a lion, but had eagle's wings. The second beast was like a bear; the third beast was like a leopard, but had four heads. The fourth animal was "dreadful and terrible"—it had iron teeth and ten horns.

If you were an interpreter of dreams, how would you feel if you had a nightmare like Daniel's? Probably you can sympathize with the prophet when he said he was confused and disturbed. But we do not need to be confused by the outward complexity of these descriptions. Daniel had it explained to him by the angels who were the official interpreters of this vision. "These great beasts, which are four, are four kings, which shall arise out of the earth" (Daniel 7:17 KJV).

The first kingdom was Babylon, which became a world empire in 606 B.C. when it conquered Egypt. Nebuchadnezzar took over the Babylonian empire upon his father's death and made it a world kingdom.

The second kingdom, which was like a bear, was the Media-Persian empire (Daniel 8:20). The Babylonian empire was conquered by the Medes and Persians about 530 B.C. when they ingeniously built the dam in the Euphrates River.

For a time the Media-Persian empire was great. The first two kings became believers in the God of Israel. But Daniel predicted long before the Greeks grew in power, when their future leaders were obscure Macedonian hillbillies, that they would become strong and defeat the Media-Persian empire. And so they did. In 331 B.C. Alexander the Great conquered the Persian empire and took it over. The third empire, according to prophecy, became a reality in history.

As predicted in Daniel 8, the Greek empire disintegrated when the first king died prematurely. It was also predicted that four powers from within would divide the empire. And so it happened. Four generals of Alexander the Great took over the empire and divided it into four parts—they lasted until about 68 B.C. when the Romans conquered the last part of the ancient Greek empire. It was then that Rome became the greatest world power to that date.

If you are a careful Bible student you know the common sport in the classroom today, especially in courses called "The Bible as Literature," or something similar. Teachers love to tear the Book of Daniel apart—they especially like to late-date it. Some liberal professors claim that it was written in 165 B.C., in order to discredit the supernatural element of prophecy. However, the authenticity of Daniel and its early date has been carefully defended by such scholars as Dr. Merril F. Unger,[1] Dr. E. J. Young,[2] and Sir Robert Anderson.[3]

Focus on the Fourth Kingdom

The fourth kingdom, Rome, was not given the name of any animal, but it would be a beast unlike any other—more ferocious than all the rest. "Then I would know the truth of the fourth beast, which was diverse from all the others, exceeding dreadful, whose teeth were of iron, and his nails of brass; which devoured, brake in pieces, and stamped the residue with his feet" (Daniel 7:19 KJV).

This verse speaks of the first phase of this fourth kingdom. In phase 1 this kingdom gains world authority (as Rome did), and then disappears to merge again just before Christ returns to establish the Kingdom of God.

Rome: Phase 2

In phase two of the fourth kingdom, Rome, the kingdom will be in the form of a ten-nation confederacy. "And of the ten horns that were in his head, and of the other which came up, and before whom three fell; even of that horn that had eyes, and a mouth that spake very great things, whose look was more stout than his fellows" (Daniel 7:20 KJV).

The meaning of these symbols will become clearer as we continue in Daniel. To the uninitiated these Biblical pictures may seem to resemble the famous Dr. Seuss animals. However, Biblical symbolism is established in historical fact.

Daniel continues with his vision: "I beheld, and the same horn made war with the saints, and prevailed against them; Until the Ancient of days came, and judgment was given to the saints of the most High; and the time came that the saints possessed the kingdom" (Daniel 7:21, 22 KJV).

The "Ancient of Days" who is described here is identified in Daniel 7:13 as "one like the Son of Man" brought on the clouds of heaven—the One who will put down all human authority and establish His kingdom forever.

There is a cohesiveness to the Scriptures that is fascinating. Jesus knew the prophecies of His coming. When He was on trial before the Sanhedrin, which was the Jewish high court, He was put under oath by the high priest to tell who He really was. He was asked directly, "Are you the Son of God?" Jesus answered, "I am." He also said, "Ye shall see the Son of man sitting on the right hand of power, and coming in the clouds of heaven" (Mark 14:62-64 KJV).

Jesus was referring to this verse in Daniel 7:13 and everyone in that court of law knew what He was talking about. The high priests knew the prophets and their writings. They were furious with Jesus and proclaimed Him a blasphemer because He was claiming to be the "Ancient of days" who was coming to set up God's kingdom on earth.

To continue with the second phase of the Roman empire, the Scripture says that the ten horns which were just described are ten kings, or ten nations: "And the ten horns out of this kingdom are ten kings that shall arise: and another shall rise after them; and he shall be diverse from the first, and he shall subdue three kings" (Daniel 7:24 KJV).

When the Scripture says "out of" it means the ten nations (ten kings) which will come out of Rome, since Rome was the fourth kingdom. But who is "another"? This is the beast, the Antichrist.

After these ten nations arise out of the cultural inheritance of the Ancient Roman Empire, another king shall rise "diverse from the first." In other words, he will be different. He will not only be a political leader, but a religious leader. (We shall see this in the next two chapters.) When he comes to power, he will subdue three of these kings or nations. Seven of them, however, will give him authority willingly.

... Couldn't Put Rome Together Again

The Roman influence upon the world is so extensive that it touches Western civilization in every aspect of life. From absorbing epics like *Ben Hur* to the Roman candle we shoot on the Fourth of July, we are saturated with the glory that was Rome. However, Rome disintegrated from within; unfortunately, there is in America the same trend in moral decay that led to the downfall of Rome.

It is interesting to see in history how men have attempted to put together the old Roman Empire. Charlemagne tried to do this in A.D. 800. His "Roman Empire" included what are now the countries of France, Germany, Italy, Holland and Belgium. Charlemagne was crowned by the Pope as Emperor Charles Augustus. But his empire was not the ten-nation confederacy of the Scriptures.

Napoleon tried his strutting best to establish his own Roman Empire. Another Pope, Pius VII, made a tedious trip across the Alps to Notre Dame cathedral in Paris to place an imperial crown on Napoleon, but the new little Caesar snatched the crown from the Pope and put it on himself. His empire was not the revived Roman Empire, either.

And then there was Hitler. Does anyone doubt that he attempted to put Rome together again? He said his Third Reich would last a thousand years. God had other plans and Hitler lost.

In spite of the vain striving of man, of the bold and infamous conquerors throughout the ages who failed in their human attempts, we are beginning to see the Ancient Roman Empire draw together, just as predicted.

If you are racing for your Rand McNally, please spare yourselves the exertion. We are not speaking of a revived Roman Empire in the physical, geographical sense, although some of these countries were part of the Ancient Roman Empire, but we are speaking of those countries which are the depository of the people, the culture, and tradition of Rome.

United We . . . Must

If the formation of the European Common Market were an isolated development in the line of Biblical prophecy, then it would have no significance for our study. However, combined with the other pieces of the prophetic puzzle which we are attempting to develop for you, it takes on immense importance.

We believe that the Common Market and the trend toward unification of Europe may well be the beginning of the ten-nation confederacy predicted by Daniel and the Book of Revelation.

What particular forces are contributing to the evolvement of this federation that the conquerors of history could not command?

First, there is the threat of Communism. One of the great motivating factors in forming this economic community and NATO was the concern over a common enemy. An article about "Mister Europe at Eighty," quotes Jean Monnet, called the father of the Common Market, as saying, "As long as Europe remains divided, it is no match for the Soviet Union. Europe must unite."[4]

The second reason for the formation of the European Common Market was the economic threat of the United States. Europeans realized they could not survive the industrial might of the United States. A charismatic personality on the present-day scene is Jean-Jacques Servan-Schreiber, newspaper editor and author of *The American Challenge,* a book which has received great acclaim throughout Europe. Some have said that the handsome Frenchman is pushing hard for a United States of Europe because he wants to become its first president. Whether this is true or not we would not venture to guess. However, it does seem that he is "furiously trying to push a U.S. of Europe," as one writer expressed it.

Servan-Schreiber is quoted as saying that "a successful response to American technology, organization, and research demands a united European effort."[5]

The third reason this writer feels Europe will form this ten-nation confederacy is that Europeans sense the basic weakness of the United States in its will to resist Communism. They seem to realize that if Europe were really at stake the U.S. would be dragging its feet in reacting against a Russian invasion. As an American it is difficult to write these words, but Europe does not feel that it can count on us in a real showdown.

A fourth factor is that according to the prophetic outlook the United States will cease being the leader of the West and will probably become in some way a part of the new European sphere of power.

Sheath your weapons, please. We realize that the United States is not mentioned in the Bible. However, it is certain that the leadership of the West must shift to Rome, in its revived form, and if the U.S. is still around at that time, it will not be the power it now is.

In spite of many who propose alternatives to a United States of Europe, and the temporary setbacks it appears to have, it seems that the trend is ever onward. An American business magazine said, "Despite its tendency to hang dangerously over cliffs, the Common Market is here to stay."[6]

A fifth factor in the trend toward the ten-nation confederacy is the realization of the great potential of a United Europe. Many men have been preaching this, not just Servan-Schreiber. A few years ago the French foreign minister said that the Common Market will carry with its network of interests and involvements across the world such weight that it will eventually become a world system.

Former Secretary of State Dean Rusk said, "Powerful forces are moving in the European community toward political integration as well. Survival and growth force the nations of Europe to forget their historic antagonisms and unite. Through the pooling of the resources and efforts a mighty new entity is growing out of the chaos left by national rivalries and world wars."[7]

A friend who lives in Germany sent us this translated statement of Dr. Walter Hallstein, who was formerly the president of the European Economic Community. Our correspondent, knowing our interest in Bible prophecy, thought there was significance in Hallstein's words. We'll let you judge.

"Three phases of the European unification are to be noted. First, the customs union, second, the economic union, third, the political union ... what we have created on the way to uniting Europe is a mighty economic-political union of which nothing may be sacrificed for any reason. Its value exists not only in what it is, but more in what it promises to become ... At about 1980 we may fully expect the great fusion of all economic, military, and political communities together into the United States of Europe."

Hallstein cited 1980. The timetable may be accelerating. Developments in Europe have changed so rapidly that an American news magazine had a feature headed "Europe's Dreams of Unity Revive."

One sentence in that story leaped from the page: "Should all go according to the most optimistic schedules, the Common Market could someday expand into a ten-nation economic entity whose industrial might would far surpass that of the Soviet Union."[8]

Imagine that. A "ten-nation economic entity."

Is it any wonder that men who have studied prophecy for many years believe that the basic beginning of the unification of Europe has begun?

What Else Is New?

At the time that this Roman Empire will begin to be revived there will also be a revival of mystery Babylon. If this sounds rather spooky, bring your head out from under the skeptical covers and examine with us in a later chapter the Biblical basis and the current applications.

Heading the revived Roman Empire will be a man of such magnetism, such power, and such influence, that he will for a time be the greatest dictator the world has ever known. He will be the completely godless, diabolically evil "future fuehrer."

9 ○ The Future Fuehrer

The spirit that I have seen may be a devil; and the devil hath power to assume a pleasing shape.   HAMLET

A DICTATOR? WHO is a dictator? What makes a dictator? A dictator is a person with absolute authority, a person who has power over people. Does he appear suddenly on the scene and say, "Stop this outmoded democratic process, I am your leader now"? That isn't the way it happens.

A dictator does not thrust his rule upon people from the top down, without provocation. His tyranny is the end result of chaos in the society that results in his rise to despotic power. The dictionary describes him as a person who seizes the authority over a nation as the result of an emergency.

The chicken and egg principle does not apply here. A troubled society produces the atmosphere for the rise of a dictator, it is not the dictator who initiates the conditions which account for his rise. However, once established as the "Big Cheese," history has shown that the dictator cannot find lasting solutions to the problems.

The power-mad leader of the Third Reich, Adolf Hitler, would not have achieved his terrifying control over the lives of millions if the times had not been ripe for him. In the 1930's the German people were in despair. Economic depression was shaking the foundations of industry. Millions were out of work. Small business enterprises were collapsing. It was a desperate time, with desperate people looking for a way out. Hitler, with his evil genius, knew the mood of the German people. He saw the opportunity to pursue his Putsch in precisely the era that history demanded.

Hitler saw himself as a hero, a savior, a strong man needed by weak underlings—a "great leader" who could guide the Germans to heights of glory, according to his standards. He believed he was above the moral standards of ordinary man. Consequently, he surrounded himself with shady characters of every type. As long as they were useful to him this motley bunch of criminals and sadists were part of the ruling strength of Hitler's inner circle.

When in Rome

Hitler took the name for his empire from the all-powerful First Reich, which was the Holy Roman Empire. It was in Rome that the Caesars introduced universal Caesar worship. Their dictatorial powers, also, were absolute.

A Scottish Bible scholar has written: "The extraordinary fact is that emperor worship was not imposed on the Roman Empire from above; it grew from below."[1]

Shades of Hitler.

However, there were differences between Hitler-allegiance and emperor worship. Hitler's rise to power was rapid in comparison. Emperor worship was a gradual development which grew out of the gratitude of the provincials for what Rome had done for them. When Rome took over a country and unpredictable tyrants were booted out, Roman justice was established. The Roman peace, *Pax Romana*, was unlike anything the world had seen and people were deeply grateful.

It was not enough for the populace to appreciate Rome. This was an impersonal thing. The spirit of Rome needed to be personalized; the emperor of Rome began to be regarded as divine.

Before Christ was born, Caesar was worshiped.

"The first temple to be erected to the godhead of the emperor was built in Pergamum in 29 B.C. Caesar worship had begun."[2]

Can you imagine what happened in Rome? The empire was vast, it had many races and languages. It needed a unifying principle and "religion" can be a very unifying influence. Soon every Roman citizen was compelled to burn a pinch of incense and say, "Caesar is Lord."

Is it any wonder that Caesar worship ran head on into Christianity? When the Christians refused to call Caesar their lord, they were subjected to inhumane persecution. The gigantic movie epics showing the lions in the arena with the Christians and the public killings for the gory amusement of the Roman pagan leaders are not conjured from the imaginations of Hollywood producers.

There are many seeds which are planted in the breeding ground for dictators; anarchy, lawlessness, moral decadence, human desperation, and false hero worship fertilize the fields that produce despots. All the gold carat and two-bit demagogues of history grew out of the soil of the times.

Where Do We Fit In?

Are we living in a peaceful, placid era when people enjoy an environment free of tensions? Ridiculous question to ask, isn't it? But when we slow down our daily lives long enough to take a hard, realistic look at the generation we live in, it's a real shocker.

There are many shoulder-shruggers who say, "Always been crime and wars—always will be—why get all hot and bothered about what's going on today?"

A short time ago we saw a graph in a newsmagazine which indicated the climb in serious crimes in the United States from 1960 to 1968. If you had been an ant on that page you would have had a very steep stairway to climb each one of those eight years. While the number of crimes in America was increasing 122 per cent, the population rose only 11 per cent.[3]

Many people have stopped talking about the "crime rate." They now refer to the "crime epidemic."

Crime is waged on a grand scale by nations. Since World War II the world has been embroiled in conflict that seems to grow increasingly vicious. There has been a rebirth of guerrilla warfare; revolutions and revolutionary movements are becoming a way of life during this latter part of the twentieth century.

War and more war. Has there ever been a time when the potential for self-destruction was as great as it is today?

Another Boom

Some people feel that the concern about the population explosion is exaggerated. They point out that the marvelous technological advances of science will overcome the burgeoning boom in human beings on this earth.

They may be right. However, many experts who have studied and evaluated the population growth have arrived at statistics and conclusions which are rather awesome, to say the least. A 1969 report from the United Nations national policy panel on world population claimed that the population crisis is the world's concern and that it is as important as peace itself. This report projects the world population will reach 7.5 billion by the year 2000. Since the number of human beings on earth in 1968 was 3.4 billion, we see that if the estimate is correct, there will be more than twice as many people in the world thirty years from now.

This same report said "high fertility and high rates of population" contribute to pollution, congestion, urban sprawl, and a host of psychological ailments in developed countries and might mean widespread famine, increased illiteracy, unemployment, squalor, and unrest threatening the foundations of public order in developing countries.[4]

Chairman of the Genetics Department at Ohio State University, J. Bruce Griffing, is quoted as saying that "Unless mankind acts immediately, there will be a worldwide famine in 1985, and the extinction of man within 75 years."[5]

We may not think this will affect us personally, but in 1967 Dr. Stanley F. Yolles, director of the National Institute of Mental Health, said:

"Population movement and the increased pressures of a speeded-up society undoubtedly are causing an increasing amount of emotional disturbance. Between 1960 and 1965 the number of U.S. psychiatrists, psychologists, and other mental health workers rose forty-four per cent. Youngsters are being admitted to mental hospitals in numbers seven times their share of the total population. Many of those left on the outside proclaim loudly their 'alienation from society.'"[6]

If we complain about not being able to find "breathing space," or resent being squeezed into an impersonal computerized society, imagine what it might be like thirty years from now, if we're still around!

Men who are studying population biology, such as Paul Ehrlich, professor at Stanford University and expert in this field, are inclined to be doomsters because of the research they have done. Ehrlich, for instance, says: "Mankind may be facing its final crisis. No action that we can take at this late date can prevent a great deal of future misery from starvation and environmental deterioration."[7]

All Systems Go

It doesn't take a "religious" person to discern the fact that what is happening is setting the world in the proper frame for a dictator. We see anarchy growing in every country. We see established standards of morality thrown aside for a hedonistic brand which is attractively labeled the "New Morality." We see the super-weapons and the threats of atheistic leaders in world powers who would not hesitate to use those weapons if they would further their drive for conquest.

A view seems to be creeping into the consciousness of concerned people that the problems and the tensions of the world need to be controlled by a "strong hand from someplace."

Even Arnold Toynbee, the eminent historian, said on a radio broadcast that "By forcing on mankind more and more lethal weapons, and at the same time making the world more and more interdependent economically, technology has brought mankind to such a degree of distress that we are ripe for the deifying of any new Caesar who might succeed in giving the world unity and peace."

Who Is the "Future Fuehrer"?

The time is ripe and getting riper for the Great Dictator, the one we call the "Future Fuehrer." This is the one who is predicted in the Scriptures very clearly and called the "Antichrist."

The Bible gives a perfect biographical sketch of this future world leader.

If you will follow this Scripture from Revelation, without being bothered by the figures of speech which are used, you will see that the Bible explains the meaning.

"And he stood on the sand of the seashore. And I saw a beast coming up out of the sea, having ten horns and seven heads, and on his horns were ten diadems, and on his heads were blasphemous names.

And the beast which I saw was like a leopard, and his feet were like those of a bear, and his mouth like the mouth of a lion. And the dragon gave him his power and his throne and great authority" (Revelation 13:1, 2 NASB).

You may be saying that this doesn't sound like a human being to you, but just press on and follow carefully how the mystery unfolds.

Revelation continues with this description: "And I saw one of his heads as if it had been slain. . . ." Mark carefully the "as if" in the phrase above. ". . . and his fatal wound was healed. And the whole earth was amazed and followed after the beast; and they worshiped the dragon, because he gave his authority to the beast; and they worshiped the beast, saying, 'Who is like the beast, and who is able to wage war with him?'" (Revelation 13:3, 4 NASB).

This person, the Antichrist, is called the "beast" because from God's viewpoint that is exactly what he is. The passage is obviously talking about a person because the personal pronoun "he" is used. He is also described as a person of great authority.

In the seventeenth chapter of Revelation we are given the meaning of this description of the beast coming out of the sea. Revelation 17:15 says: "And he said to me, 'The waters which you saw where the harlot sits, are peoples and multitudes and nations and tongues'" (NASB).

The "harlot" refers to the religious system which will be tied in with this dictator. This will be described in more detail in the next chapter.

When it says that the beast will emerge out of the sea, it means that he will come out of the chaos of the nations.

In the Old Testament, Isaiah speaks of the chaos of the nations that is to come and says there is no peace for the wicked . . . they are like the "troubled sea," which is a symbolic picture of the Gentile nations (Isaiah 57:20, 21).

Like a Leopard, a Bear, and a Lion

"And the beast which I saw was like a leopard, and his feet were like those of a bear, and his mouth like the mouth of a lion" (Revelation 13:2 NASB).

To understand the meaning of this zoo which is described in Revelation, we go back to the predictive ministry of Daniel. As we studied in the previous chapter, Daniel describes his vision of four great beasts who come up out of the sea in succession. These beasts are the great Gentile empires which would rule the world. Daniel described these kingdoms using figurative expressions of wild animals.

Daniel 8 tells who the first, second, and third empires are; thus we can identify the animal figure by the order of the kingdoms. The first one of these empires which Daniel described was like a lion, which was the Babylonian empire. He said the second great kingdom was like a bear, which was the Media-Persian empire. The third kingdom would be like a leopard, and this was the Greek empire.

Then Daniel said there would arise a fourth kingdom, which would take over what was left of the Greek empire. That was Rome.

In Daniel 7:23, 24, Daniel predicts the fourth kingdom . . . and especially the person who would put it together. He says that the fourth kingdom (Rome) shall "devour the whole earth."

However, we saw in "Rome on the Revival Road" that there is a "phase 2" to the Roman Empire. Daniel says that out of the culture of the first Roman Empire ten kings shall arise, and another king after that who is different from the ten. This king is going to subdue three of the kings.

In other words, when this Roman dictator comes, he is going to take over the ten-nation confederacy. Seven of the kings or leaders will willingly give him their allegiance, but three of them will not. So he will overthrow these three leaders.

Now we are able to see how Scripture fits together. If you return to Revelation 13 and look again at verse one you will understand that the "ten horns" refer to this ten-nation confederacy and the "seven heads" are the seven leaders who form a coalition with the Antichrist.

Der Fuehrer's Personality Traits

Some people have said that they turn to the Book of Revelation to find out how it will all end . . . and then can't understand a thing that is said. Now that we know, however, who the leopard, the bear, and the lion were, we should begin to see what Revelation 13:2 means.

It is said here that the beast (the Roman dictator, the Future Fuehrer, or the Antichrist) will be like a leopard, a bear, and lion. A leopard is quick to seize his prey. The leopard was the Greek Empire. Alexander the Great, the Greek military genius, was known for the speed with which he overcame his enemies. He was fearless and strong, a human counterpart of the great leopard. Alexander was a world conqueror who led his armies to the outermost fringes of the known world of his time.

"A bear" referred to the Media-Persian Empire, which was conquered by Alexander. This kingdom, similar to the animal it exemplifies, was very strong and powerful.

The lion (Babylon) is regal. The way he walks and holds his proud head has class. Babylon was an elegant monarchy. Its palaces were splendid and the famous "hanging gardens of Babylon" were considered one of the seven wonders of the world.

Now we are beginning to see, little by little, the picture emerging of the Future Fuehrer. His conquest will be rapid, he will be very strong and powerful, and there will be an air about him which is self-assured and proud.

It is important to note as we follow in Revelation 13 that "the dragon gave him his power and his throne and great authority" (verse 2b).

Who is the dragon?

If we turn back to Revelation 12:9 we are told who he is.

It says, "And the great dragon was thrown down, the serpent of old who is called the Devil and Satan" (NASB).

We read that the dragon is going to give the Antichrist his power. In other words, Satan himself is going to give him fantastic power. He is going to be able to work all kinds of miracles. This is one reason that Christians should not get too excited when they see a miracle. It may not be a miracle of God. Satan is a miracle-worker and he has been able to work miracles from the beginning.

But there is going to be a time when Satan is allowed to work all kinds of supernatural acts through men. It is said that Satan is going to send this man, his masterpiece, with all sorts of signs and wonders and miracles (II Thessalonians 2:9).

The second thing that will be given this man is a throne. This means world government. This throne was offered to Jesus Christ. In Luke 4 it is told how Satan came to Christ during His temptation in the desert and offered Him all the authority and glory of the world. Satan said He could have all the kingdoms to rule, if He would fall down and worship him. There is only one man who could resist that kind of an offer. Satan offered Him a crown if He would by-pass the cross. But Jesus wouldn't buy it.

Now we are studying a man who will accept this throne wholeheartedly. He will be worshiped as Satan is worshiped, with forms of idolatry that we can only guess in our wildest leaps of imagination.

All around the world today the increase in the mystic, occult, and even devil-worship is so pronounced that people are beginning to question what it's all about. There are churches in some of the major cities of America which actually incorporate into their "religious ceremonies" the worship of the devil. A newspaper report said, "Moving hand-in-hand with astrology in some cities is a rising interest in witchcraft and hypnosis. Courses in the art of the history of witchcraft have popped up at a few recognized colleges and at most 'free universities' (where students design the curricula.)"[8]

A university student told this writer that he knew of several people who had signed up for a college course on witchcraft believing that it was a "how to" course, and after discovering that it was more history than mystery, dropped out of the class.

However, the Satan-worship which will be initiated at the time of the world reign of the Future Fuehrer will make today's antics of the cultists look like nursery school.

A Mortal Head Wound

We are told in Revelation 13:3 that this great world leader will have a fatal head wound which will be miraculously healed. Many people have not known just what to make of this statement. Some have thought that what this means is that one of the empires of the ancient Roman Empire would be miraculously revived and brought back to existence. That is one possible interpretation. However, I do not believe that is the right interpretation. Here is why. . . .

Look for a moment at Revelation 13:14. This is speaking of the False Prophet, who will be an associate of the Great Roman Dictator. The verse says: "And he deceives those who dwell on the earth because of the signs which it was given him to perform in the presence of the beast, telling those who dwell on the earth to make an image to the beast who had the wound of the sword and has come to life" (NASB).

Whoever this person is with this fatal wound will have a statue made of himself, and men are going to worship this idol. You do not make an idol of an empire. You make an idol of a person.

The way in which this dictator is going to step onto the stage of history will be dramatic. Overnight he will become the byword of the world. He is going to be distinguished as supernatural; this will be done by an act which will be a Satanic counterfeit of the resurrection. This writer does not believe it will be an actual resurrection, but it will be a situation in which this person has a mortal wound. Before he has actually lost life, however, he will be brought back from this critical wounded state. This is something which will cause tremendous amazement throughout the world.

We could draw a comparison to the tragic death of John F. Kennedy. Imagine what would have happened if the President of the United States, after being shot and declared dead, had come to life again! The impact of an event like that would shake the world.

It is not difficult to imagine what will happen when this coming world leader makes his miraculous recovery. This man, the Antichrist, will probably not be known as a great leader until the time of his revival from the fatal wound. After that the whole world will follow him.

He will have a magnetic personality, be personally attractive, and a powerful speaker. He will be able to mesmerize an audience with his oratory.

"Who is like the beast, and who is able to wage war with him?" These are the expressions the people who live at the time of the appearance of the Antichrist will be saying. They will accept anyone who offers peace, since this is the great cry of the world.

What does this indicate? We recall that the *Pax Romana*, the Roman peace, was the reason the provincials willingly turned to Rome and eventually initiated Caesar worship. Law and order—peace and security—freedom from war. The same needs, the same desires were expressed in ancient times that the Bible says will be prevalent before the Antichrist begins his rule. He will be swept in at a time when people are so tired of war, so anxious for peace at any price, that they willingly give their allegiance to the world dictator who will promise them peace.

There is another place in the Bible where the words of the people who are alive at the time of the coming of the Antichrist are quoted: "While they are saying, 'Peace and safety!' then destruction will come upon them suddenly like birth pangs upon a woman with child; and they shall not escape" (I Thessalonians 5:3).

This is a direct quote from the people who will live under the false security of this world dictator. It is a cry of relief—a sigh of gratitude. "Peace and safety"—at last!

The mood of the world is being developed toward the acceptance of this person. Remember what Toynbee said: "We are ripe for the deifying of any new Caesar who might succeed in giving the world unity and peace."

I Am God

The Antichrist will deify himself—just like the Caesars did. He will proclaim himself to be God. He will demand that he be worshiped and will establish himself in the Temple of God (II Thessalonians 2:4).

There is only one place where this temple of God can be and that is on Mount Moriah in Jerusalem, on the site where the Dome of the Rock and other Moslem shrines now stand. There are many places in the Bible that pinpoint this location as the one where the Jews will rebuild their Temple.

The Antichrist, who is called by many names in the Bible, but in II Thessalonians is called the "lawless one," will come in on a wave of anarchy. This is why the world will be ready to receive him.

You may be asking, "How can this possibly happen while Christians are in the world?"

It can't. As we understand II Thessalonians 2:6-12, the restraining power of the Spirit of God, within believing Christians, will hold back the rise of this World Dictator. We believe it is not until this "restrainer" is removed that his power and might will be exerted over the entire world.

We shall explain this in detail in the chapter on "The Ultimate Trip."

Authority to Act for Three and One-half Years

"And there was given to him a mouth speaking arrogant words and blasphemies; and authority to act for forty-two months was given to him" (Revelation 13:5 NASB).

Forty-two months is three and one-half years and this is the three and one-half years prior to Christ's personal, visible return to this earth. This period of time will make the regimes of Hitler, Mao, and Stalin look like

Girl Scouts weaving a daisy chain by comparison. The Antichrist is going to be given absolute authority to act with the power of Satan.

"And he opened his mouth in blasphemies against God, to blaspheme His name and His tabernacle, that is, those who dwell in heaven" (Revelation 13:6 NASB).

This is interesting. Why would he "blaspheme" or "badmouth" those who will dwell in heaven? And who are the ones who dwell in heaven; why would he even bother with them? You and I are the ones who are going to dwell in heaven, if we are true believers in Jesus Christ. If we are gone from the earth at this period, which this writer believes the Scriptures prove, how is this fellow going to explain the fact that a few million "religious kooks" are missing? He will, of course, have to discredit the Christian belief, explain it away, or "blaspheme" it and the believers.

"And it was given to him to make war with the saints and to overcome them . . ." (Revelation 13:7a NASB).

It is logical to ask at this point, how is he going to make war with the saints when they are gone from the earth? "The saints" are the people who are going to believe in Christ during this great period of conflict. After the Christians are gone God is going to reveal Himself in a special way to 144,000 physical, literal Jews who are going to believe with a vengeance that Jesus is the Messiah. They are going to be 144,000 Jewish Billy Grahams turned loose on this earth—the earth will never know a period of evangelism like this period. These Jewish people are going to make up for lost time. They are going to have the greatest number of converts in all history. Revelation 7:9-14 says they bring so many to Christ that they can't be numbered.

However, the Antichrist is going to unleash a total persecution of these people.

"And it was given to him . . . authority over every tribe and people and tongue and nation . . ." (Revelation 13:7b NASB).

He will be the absolute dictator of the whole world!

This is the Future Fuehrer.

Who Will Worship Him?

"And all who dwell on the earth will worship him, every one whose name has not been written from the foundation of the world in the book of life of the Lamb who has been slain" (Revelation 13:8 NASB).

The book of life to which this passage refers is for those who put their personal faith in Jesus Christ. Christ is the "Lamb" who was slain.

The Old Testament predicted the coming of Jesus in hundreds of prophecies. Over 300 specific predictions were fulfilled in His life and death. He is conclusively proven as the only One who could be the Messiah.

He has a book. That book contains the names of everyone who simply puts his faith in Jesus for having paid the penalty for his sins. Throughout the history of the Jewish people the Passover Lamb typified a sacrifice. What an incredible thing that so many Jews would not see Jesus as the personification of the Lamb. He was the real Lamb of God.

When John the Baptist, one of the greatest prophets of all time, first saw Jesus coming toward him, he said, "Behold, the Lamb of God that takes away the sin of the world" (John 1:29 NASB). In this statement he summarized the whole significance of the Old Testament. It all pointed to Jesus.

So we see who will worship the Antichrist. Everyone will worship him who has not put his faith in Christ.

Is it possible for a moment to project our thoughts toward that time when the entire world will look upon one human being as the supreme leader? The Antichrist will need a lot of help to carry out his diabolical schemes. His staunchest ally will be

The False Prophet

In Revelation 13:11-18 we are introduced to this infamous character. This person, who is called the second beast, is going to be a Jew. Many believe he will be from the tribe of Dan, which is one of the tribes of the original progenitors of the nation of Israel.

The False Prophet (he is called that in Revelation 19:20 and 20:10) will be a master of satanic magic. This future False Prophet is going to be a devilish John the Baptist. He will aid and glorify this Roman Dictator; he will proclaim him the savior of the world and make people worship him as God.

It is logical to ask how the False Prophet will force this worship of the Roman Dictator. He will be given control over the economics of the world system and cause everyone who will not swear allegiance to the Dictator to be put to death or to be in a situation where they cannot buy or sell or hold a job. Everyone will be given a tattoo or mark on either his forehead or forehand, only if he swears allegiance to the Dictator as being God.

Symbolically, this mark will be 666. Six is said to be the number of man in Scripture and a triad or three is the number for God. Consequently, when you triple "six" it is the symbol of man making himself God.

The cleverness of this economic vise is ghastly to contemplate. But no one could ever accuse Satan of not being clever.

O Come Now. . . .

Do you believe it will be possible for people to be controlled economically? In our computerized society, where we are all "numbered" from birth to death, it seems completely plausible that some day in the near future the numbers racket will consolidate and we will have just one number for all our business, money, and credit transactions. Leading members of the business community are now planning that all money matters will be handled electronically.

Upstage

We believe that the dramatic elements which are occurring in the world today are setting the stage for this magnetic, diabolical Future Fuehrer to make his entrance. However, we must not indulge in speculation about whether any of the current world figures is the Antichrist. He will not be known until his sudden miraculous recovery from a fatal wound.

There would be no earthly advantage in being alive when the Antichrist rules. We believe that Christians will not be around to watch the debacle brought about by the cruelest dictator of all time.

10 ∘ Revival of Mystery Babylon

Beloved, do not believe every spirit, but test the spirits to see whether they are from God; because many false prophets have gone out into the world. I JOHN 4:1 (NASB)

IT IS NOT our purpose to be shocking or offensive. The prophecies of the Bible are a vital part of God's Word, but should not be used for sensationalism. Some of the symbolism in this chapter may seem very strange to modern ears, and some of the indictments of existing beliefs may trigger the defense mechanism in some readers. However, when God's Word is clear, it was never intended that man should dilute what He has to say.

All through the Scriptures we find that Christ dealt strongly with the religious leaders and false prophets who put on their many-colored coats of righteousness and led people astray. Jesus called them hypocrites, fools, and vipers, not exactly soft terms. He tipped over the tables in their places of so-called worship, which was not what men today might consider being broad-minded.

We are told in the Bible that before the seven-year period of tribulation there will be an all-powerful religious system which will aid the Antichrist in subjecting the world to his absolute authority. For a time this religious system will actually have control of the Dictator.

There are several names given to this one-world religion, all of them drawing a perfect analogy in meaning. It is called the Great Harlot, or prostitute; the "harlot" represents a religion which prostitutes the true meaning of being wedded to Christ, and sells out to all the false religions of man.

"Babylon" is another term used for the one-world religion. It is easy to see how a place could also be a system when we consider contemporary examples: Broadway means the theater today, Madison Avenue draws the mental image of the slick advertising world, Wall Street is the hub of finance.

'Tis a Puzzlement

As pieces of the prophecy puzzle appeared to fall into place there was one important part that was lost to me. The Bible outlines very specifically that there would be a one-world religion which would dominate the world in the time before the return of Christ. However, this seemed so remote, with so many different religions competing for the minds and hearts of men, how on earth could people unite in allegiance to just one religion?

Five years ago, for instance, as I surveyed the college campuses where I ministered, it seemed that most of the intellectual community was alienated by any concept of the supernatural. Many of them were not receptive to any form of "religion," which was considered a crutch for the weak, or a rigid set of rules not worth trying to follow.

We should be careful to note at this point that we are using the term "religion," not Christianity. Christianity is not a religion. Religion is the process of man trying to achieve goodness, perfection, and acceptance with God by his own efforts. Christianity, on the other hand, is God taking the initiative and reaching for man. Christianity is God saying that man cannot reach Him except through the one path He has provided—through the acceptance of His Son, Jesus Christ.

But the scene has changed rapidly in the intellectual community in the past few years. Many of those who scoffed at "religion" have become addicted to the fast-moving upsurge in astrology, spiritualism, and even drugs. What does all this mean? Does it have any significance in Biblical prophecy?

We believe that the joining of churches in the present ecumenical movement, combined with this amazing rejuvenation of star-worship, mind-expansion, and witchcraft, are preparing the world in every way for the establishment of a great religious system, one which will influence the Antichrist.

To understand the significance of these movements in relation to this one-world religious system, we should study carefully what the Bible has to say about them. As we begin to examine this in depth, there emerges a pattern which makes the Bible more up-to-date and relevant than any book today.

Origin of Astrology

Many popular American magazines have been commenting recently on astrology and its impact on the contemporary scene; most of these secular writers have done a good job of historical research into the subject. However, few touch upon the best history book of all in doing their reference work.

In Genesis we find that astrology got its beginnings in Babylon, which is verified by secular writers in their historical accounts. There is a remarkable statement in Genesis 11 about the first astrological observatory.

After the great Flood, the Bible tells us, the whole earth had one language. The people who were alive at that time settled in the land of Shinar, which is near the meeting of the Tigris and Euphrates Rivers. This was ancient Babylonia, one of the earliest centers of civilization.

"And they said, Go to, let us build us a city and a tower, whose top may reach unto heaven . . ." (Genesis 11:4 KJV).

Now the city they were speaking about was Babylon, and the tower was the famous Tower of Babel. The interesting thing is that the word "tower" is a word that can mean ziggurat, which was the ancient observatory from which the priests would gaze at the stars.

In many versions of the Bible you will find that in this verse from Genesis 11 the words "may reach" are in italics. This is because they were not in the original Hebrew writings of the Bible. When this passage is studied in Hebrew it becomes obvious that these people had enough intelligence and know-how to realize that they could not build a tower which would actually reach to heaven. It's true that the Babylonian builders were geniuses, but they were not stupid. A tower with its top in heaven meant it would be used to study the stars, chart their courses, and make predictions. Henry H. Halley, who has assembled the comprehensive *Halley's Bible Handbook*, said that the whole purpose of the ziggurats was idolatrous worship.[1]

This origin of astrology was described in what may have been among the first writing known to man, a form of hieroglyphics devised by the ancient race of the Chaldeans who began to give the stars certain meanings. They divided the heavens into the twelve sections of the zodiac and said that the stars control the destiny of men. This religion started to flourish and have its greatest glory of history in the Babylonian Empire, which was primarily made up of the priestly caste of the Chaldean people. These Chaldeans became the aristocracy of the priesthood. We know how esteemed these astrologers and magicians were because every king in Babylon built giant ziggurats for them. The astrologers were considered almost equal in power to the king.

We see God's attitude toward this star-worship when we are told that He destroyed this Babylonian observatory. Nimrod, the first world dictator, was the leader in the Tower of Babel enterprise and through this religious system established at Babylon undoubtedly wished to pursue the ambition of all dictators, and that is to have a one-world government. He did not take God into account, however. God says when you put everyone under one dictator there would be no evil which could be restrained. When the Tower of Babel was destroyed, it was a turning point in history. Where there had been but one language, now God initiated many languages and scattered the people throughout the earth.

This passage shows that God's plan for the world until the Prince of Peace returns is not an international one-world government, but nationalism. This is the one way the world can keep from falling under a dictator who could virtually destroy mankind.

The Scripture says that a Great Dictator is coming and he will be boosted to power, and strengthened in his grasp upon the world with the assistance of the ancient religion called Mystery, Babylon. This is the very religion which started in the Genesis account and made possible the first world dictator.

Some clairvoyants today, without knowledge of Bible prophecy, are saying the same things that the Scriptures tell us. In a publication which specializes in psychic phenomena there was an astounding article which said that "History and many signs of the times point to man's preparation for the coming new world leader." The writer in this magazine dealing with extra-sensory perception, prophecy (not Bible), and spiritual healing, described various events which would precede this new "Leader," among which were. . . . "Conditions shall change and, in the due course of time, people shall be led into a new Age where they have different abilities from those now existing. There shall be clairvoyance and telepathy as there was before the so-called, mis-called, Tower of Babel, in which through the abuse of special powers mankind lost its telepathic abilities *for the time being.*"[2] (Emphasis is ours.)

Mystery, Babylon, Condemned

The great prophet, Isaiah, in chapter 47 of his book, gives an analysis of the Babylonian worship and religion. The description and the judgment to be brought upon this "religion" is so significant for today that we can scarcely contain our continuous excitement over prophetic pictures in the Bible.

Isaiah, speaking predictively in 47:1, says: "Come down, and sit in the dust, O virgin daughter of Babylon, sit on the ground: there is no throne, O daughter of the Chaldeans: for thou shalt no more be called tender and delicate" (KJV).

A glance down to verse 5 will indicate further condemnation of Babylon: "Sit thou silent, and get thee into darkness, O daughter of the Chaldeans: for thou shalt no more be called, The lady of kingdoms" (KJV).

(Literally, the "lady" means the "Queen of kingdoms." When we study Revelation 17 this is going to be a very important figure of speech.)

The prophet goes on to analyze the wickedness of Babylon and the reason why God is going to judge this empire. Isaiah shows how Babylon grew away from the true God and was involved in worldly pleasures. Wisdom and knowledge perverted Babylon, and the prophet says that desolation shall "come upon thee suddenly."

However, the most important thing to see is that Babylon was entangled in "sorceries" and "enchantments," two important words which we shall examine carefully . . . and that this civilization could not be saved by "the astrologers, the stargazers, and the monthly prognosticators" who were the advisers to the Babylonians.

Stay Tuned to the Facts

We are not playing a game of Biblical hopscotch when we turn from one prophet to another. If there was not a strong recurring theme in all the prophets, this book would have no validity. It is the complete agreement of all parts of Biblical prophecy which makes its study so absorbing, so filled with tingling vitality for the twentieth century that it is a wonder that every preacher in every pulpit doesn't shake the ecclesiastical rafters with this subject.

Daniel was a prophet whose themes are far-reaching and who predicted events which are yet to happen in the history of our world, events which we are studying in the context of this book. Daniel was a Hebrew nobleman who was taken captive in Babylon by the king of the empire, Nebuchadnezzar. This king had Daniel and several other Jewish noblemen who showed unusual intelligence put into a special school of the wise men. The "wise men" was a general designation given to the astrologers and magicians of the Babylonian empire and Daniel was trained in all the wisdom of the Babylonians. He became an expert in these fields, but he didn't buy it. It was a tremendous test of Daniel's faith, because he was literally brainwashed by the Babylonian religion, but he kept his belief in God, in spite of all this training.

Nebuchadnezzar had a dream which really bothered him and gave him insomnia. He called the whole gang out to help him with this—all his "magicians and astrologers and sorcerers and Chaldeans" (Daniel 2:2, 10, 27).

The first category or word which is translated "magician" means the special sacred scribes—an order of the wise men who had charge of the sacred writings which were handed down all the way from the time of the Tower of Babel. Some of the earliest-known literature on the face of this earth were these books of magic, astrology, and the black arts.

The next word, "astrologer," means literally to whisper—it came to mean "conjure." These were men who were enchanters who would cast spells through the spirit medium. They had all kinds of chants and low, muttering songs through which they thought they could cast out evil.

The "sorcerers" means the black magic art. The same word is used for the Egyptian magicians who confronted Moses (Exodus 7:11). Through their black art they duplicated several miracles which Moses performed in the court. For instance, they turned water into blood. When Moses cast down his rod and it turned into a serpent these "sorcerers" did the same thing in the court of Pharaoh. It wasn't until God enabled Moses to perform miracles that they couldn't duplicate that these magicians said that this was the finger of God. The Egyptians had all of these arts which the Babylonians exported to them.

The next word, "Chaldeans," was the priest caste of all of them. Wherever you see the word "Chaldean" it can be translated equally well as "astrology." Several great linguists unanimously agree on this point that the Chaldeans studied a person's birthday, asking the very hour a person was born, and then they would cast a horoscope of his destiny. You will find that this thinking has permeated the Aramaic world—the Arabs, the Persians, etc. This is where the idea of Kismet came from; it means it is inevitable, it is fate—what will happen will happen. The ancient astrologers believed that your fate was written in the stars before you were born and you can't alter the course of your destiny.

The Babylonian kings did not make a move without consulting their astrologers, and the Media-Persians who conquered the Babylonians did the same thing. They, too, had their court astrologers and wisemen. When the Greek, Alexander the Great, conquered the Media-Persian empire he also began to follow the astrologers and their wisdom. The practice was transported to Rome where we see the Caesars consulting the augurs, who were experts in astrology, spiritism, and the black arts.

When Nebuchadnezzar called upon his wise men for help and advice, none of them could tell him his dream or the interpretation. Daniel, however, proved he was a true prophet of God when he was able to tell the king what the dream was and then give its interpretation. Daniel really puts the bite on his fellow colleagues and shows them up for the frauds they were.

Nebuchadnezzar's dream, described by Daniel and interpreted by this prophet of God, turns out to be the whole course of world powers that would conquer the world right up to the second coming of Jesus Christ.

Daniel shows that astrologers cannot accurately predict the future. As a matter of fact, God condemns astrology. In Deuteronomy 18 astrologers were commanded in that day under the law of Moses to be put to death.

Astrology is the backbone of the ancient religion of Babylon, but there is no such thing as a man's fate being controlled by the stars.

Man's fate is controlled by God alone.

Whenever a person gets sold out by things like astrology, it will be like the Israelis. Israel was judged and virtually destroyed and taken to Babylon in 606 B.C. because the people became devoted to idolatry, especially astrology. II Kings 23 makes this clear when it says that God wiped out the high places and all of the places where they burned incense to the stars of heaven, or to the constellation (the twelve signs of the Zodiac).

Emergence of the One-world Religion

Now we are coming to some of the most important pieces of the prophetic puzzle which are shown in the Scriptures. In Revelation 17 the apostle John has a vision which shows the future and precisely what is going to happen on earth the last seven years before Christ returns. In Revelation 17 John is given one of the most important prophecies for us to understand because he is exposing a one-world religious system which will bring all false religions together in one unit. Through this system Satan's Antichrist will take over the world—and he is going to do it first with Rome as home base and then from Jerusalem.

Scarlet O'Harlot

Look what John says in Revelation 17:3-5: "And he carried me away in the Spirit into a wilderness; and I saw a woman sitting on a scarlet beast, full of blasphemous names, having seven heads and ten horns. And the woman was clothed in purple and scarlet, and adorned with gold and precious stones and pearls, having in her hand a gold cup full of abominations and of the unclean things of her immorality, and upon her forehead a name was written, a mystery, 'BABYLON THE GREAT, THE MOTHER OF HARLOTS AND OF THE ABOMINATIONS OF THE EARTH'" (NASB).

It is sometimes difficult for the Bible reader to grasp this symbolism. Understanding "the mother of harlots," or the great harlot, is important to the basic understanding of the Christian belief, versus all religions. This church which the prophet describes claims to be united to Jesus Christ in mystical marriage, but is really an adulteress in the spiritual sense. This church professes an allegiance to God, but worships a false religious system.

The main thrust of this passage in Revelation 17 is about Mystery, Babylon, who is typified by this woman. "And I saw the woman drunk with the blood

of the saints, and with the blood of the witnesses of Jesus. And when I saw
her, I wondered greatly. And the angel said to me, 'Why do you wonder?
I shall tell you the mystery of the woman and of the beast that carries her,
which has the seven heads and the ten horns'" (Revelation 17:6, 7 NASB).

We know the meaning of the "beast," for we studied this in the chapter
on "The Future Fuehrer." The ten horns, as we have seen, refers to the revived Roman Empire, or a ten-nation confederacy.

The fact that this woman, who is the Mystery, Babylon, is riding upon
this beast shows that she controls him. Historically this "religion" has
controlled many empires. Notice what John the Apostle, writing in about
A.D. 95, says about these empires which the "woman" has controlled: "Here
is the mind which has wisdom. The seven heads are seven mountains on
which the woman sits, and they are seven kings; five have fallen, one is,
the other has not yet come; and when he comes, he must remain a little
while" (Revelation 17:9, 10 NASB).

We must look at this from the apostle John's perspective. He speaks of
seven kingdoms, five of which have fallen. We must examine what five kingdoms over which this mystery religion of Babylon exerted authority have
fallen. The first great kingdom where the Babylonian religion had great sway
was the Chaldean. The second world power which was virtually controlled
by this religion was Egypt. The great Egyptian pyramids had astrological
significance, as well as being a burial place for the kings, and the sphinx is
the key to where the earth starts in the twelve sections of the Zodiac. The
head of the sphinx is a woman, with the body of a lion. The word "sphinx"
means to "join together" in Greek—it shows that the first part of the circle
of the zodiac is the woman, Virgo, and the last part is the lion, Leo. What
the sphinx does is to put the two together and show the beginning and the
end of the Zodiac.

· The next great world kingdom to be controlled by the mystery religion
was, of course, Babylon itself under the great Babylonian rulers. The fourth
kingdom was the Media-Persian empire, and the fifth was the Greek empire.

John says that "five have fallen, one is." The kingdom which was present
at the time John wrote this was Rome. The mystery religion of Babylon was
in Rome, exerting its great influence over the decisions of the empire. The
other kingdom which "has not yet come" is referring to the revived Roman
Empire.

The Antichrist will come up out of the culture of the ancient Roman
Empire. He will come to the ten-nation confederacy, take it over, and make
it an eighth form of power.

We believe that we are seeing, with all of the other signs, the revival of Mystery, Babylon—not just in astrology, but also in spiritism, a return to the supernatural, and in drugs.

More insight into this last one-world religion is given in Revelation 9:20: "And the rest of mankind, who were not killed by these plagues, did not repent of the works of their hands, so as not to worship demons, and the idols of gold and of silver and of brass and of stone and of wood, which can neither see nor hear nor walk" (NASB).

Some may scoff at the idea that idol worship will become prevalent. Even in America, however, there are growing cults which actually do worship stone and metal idols. At one of California's colleges some young men were seen at dawn, indulging in a primitive sort of sun-god worship on the lawn of a fraternity house. When they were questioned about their rather strange activities they said, "There's a bunch of us up at Big Sur who worship idols and stuff."

And what else will be seen during these times preceding Christ's return? "And they did not repent of their murders nor of their sorceries nor of their immorality nor of their thefts" (Revelation 9:21 NASB).

One of the words here is extremely important—the word "sorceries." It comes from the Greek word *pharmakeia*, which is the word from which we get our English word, pharmacy. It means a kind of occult worship or black magic, associated with the use of drugs. This word is mentioned several times in the Book of Revelation. It is said of the great religious system that "all the nations were deceived by your sorcery" (Revelation 18:23).

If there is anyone today who is not conscious of the spread of drug addiction, particularly among college and high school students, and now reaching down into the junior high and even the grade school level, then they are blind to what is happening. The increase in the use of narcotics and all forms of dangerous drugs has spiralled to such an extent that statistics written today would be out of date by the time this book is published.

A newspaper we saw recently quoted narcotics officials in the juvenile division of a police department saying that they were so alarmed that they thought the situation should be labeled a "Drug Epidemic" and treated by drastic and swift measures before it was more out of hand than it is now. One officer said that whatever they say about the arrests of young people on drug charges is like an iceberg. All they are able to see is what protrudes above the surface. Lurking beneath the known dangers are thousands and thousands of users and pushers that haven't been caught.

I used to wonder how on earth people could see the supernatural things which would occur during the Great Tribulation, the seven-year period before the return of Christ, and still not turn to God. I have seen a graphic example of how minds can be clouded from a person I met in a fraternity house at one of our major universities. He was an outstanding young man and expressed the desire to know more about Christ. I met with him for several weeks and he said, "I believe it, but I just don't want to commit my life to Christ."

When I met him a few months later he looked completely different. He said, "I'm really religious now—I feel sorry for you—I've been taking trips and I've really seen God. Only this God is the King of Darkness—this is the one we worship."

This man had completely blown his mind. He is at this point, apart from a miracle, completely beyond reach. Satan uses these hallucinatory drugs to take man to a deeper level of approach with him. You talk to some people who have been on drugs for a long time and they will tell you, "I know the devil is real—I've seen him."

We believe these drugs reduce a man's thinking and mentality to a point where he is easily demon-possessed. Demons are under the control of Satan and the Bible speaks about them in abundant terms, so we're not talking about spooky things.

There are all sorts of new spirit groups which are worshiping Satan. A newspaper feature article told of "Modern Witches: Old Black Magic but a New Spirit." The story concerned the upsurge in witchcraft in England and told how people take it very seriously. "So ostensibly do the hundreds, perhaps even a few thousand, of witches in Britain who are riding again since the centuries-old Witchcraft Act was repealed in 1951. Covens, assemblies of witches are even said to be thriving in Los Angeles and New York."

As one modern witch describes, "For us it's our religion—we worship a horned god, the prince of darkness, and this makes some people say we're devil-worshipers."[3]

A major television station had a potpourri of news and showed the great interest high school students have in witches. The commentator said, "Nearly every respectable high school these days has its own witch." The program pictured a pretty 16-year-old, eyes staring and voice chanting incantations, conjuring up all sorts of spells. A psychiatrist intoned that he thought the trend toward witchcraft was "healthy" for some because it helps relieve aggressive feelings.

The upsurge of interest in astrology was documented in the first chapter of this book. Man seems to be on this great quest for knowledge and assurance of the future with such intensity that all types of mystic ideas are being accepted today.

Where Is the Church?

We have developed the various forms of religious expressions which we believe constitute a revival of Mystery, Babylon, but have not included the organization which the Bible says will be a definite part of this one-world religion. This is the visible church which is characterized by increasing unbelief and apostasy.

This description of the visible or physical church is given with sadness. We find it difficult not to be disheartened when we see what is happening in the churches which call themselves "Christian." However, if we follow Bible prophecy carefully we see that it is made absolutely clear that in the time preceding the return of Christ there would be a "falling away" from the basic doctrines of Christ by the churches. Some churches are not just falling away, they are plunging recklessly toward destruction with their disbelief and blasphemous programs.

It's not uncommon to hear someone say, usually in a state of anger over some real or imagined injustice, "Why doesn't the church do something about it?"

It is imperative for us to have a clear understanding of who and what "the church" is before we can understand its apostasy. ("Apostasy" means an abandonment or desertion of principles or faith.)

The apostate church is, always has been, and will be, the visible, physical gathering of people who may call themselves Christians. These churches may be of any denomination. They may be magnificent cathedrals or storefront missions, a congregation of thousands or a gathering of a few. However, no matter what sacred or holy name is applied to the visible church, this is no guarantee that it teaches and preaches the truth of God.

The true church, on the other hand, includes all believers in Christ. Many places in the New Testament speak of those who are joined to Christ, the Head of the body. In other words, Christ is the Head of the true church.

"He is also head of the body, the church" (Colossians 1:18 NASB).

"For even as the body is one and yet has many members, and all the members of the body, though they are many, are one body, so also is Christ. For by one Spirit we were all baptized into one body, whether Jews or Greeks, whether slaves or free, and we were all made to drink of one Spirit" (I Corinthians 12:12, 13 NASB).

An organized church may have among its members those who are true believers and those who merely claim to be believers in Christ. We must not make the mistake of saying that everyone who belongs to a church which has strayed far away from the teachings of the Bible is a non-believer. A true believer can be surrounded by apostasy in the church or denomination or the council of churches to which he belongs. Usually, if the believer is aware of what is happening at the policy-making level of his church, he is pretty miserable—or angry—or disgusted.

Some of you may be thinking that every generation has seen this apostasy in the church. This is true, but the Bible says that as the countdown before Christ's return comes closer, the teachings of the false leaders of the church will depart farther and farther from God's Word.

"But false prophets also arose among the people, just as there will also be false teachers among you, who will secretly introduce destructive heresies, even denying the Master who bought them, bringing swift destruction upon themselves" (II Peter 2:1 NASB).

The Harlot

This one-world religious system is not described in delicate terms. A harlot, or a prostitute, is one who is unfaithful. She has prostituted her God-given womanhood. In the same manner, the church which says it belongs to God, but joins in worshiping through a false religious system, is prostituting its purpose.

How can we recognize the apostasy in the church today? What are the characteristics of this harlot?

Peter writes that in the "last days" there would be "mockers" who would say: "Where is the promise of His coming?" (II Peter 3:4 NASB).

John, the apostle of love, spoke strongly about false teachers who deny the fact that Christ will return bodily to earth the second time. He wrote: "For many deceivers have gone out into the world, those who do not acknowledge Jesus Christ as coming in the flesh. This is the deceiver and the antichrist" (II John 7 NASB).

We need to be alert. When we hear church leaders, teachers, or preachers questioning the visible return of Christ, this is a doctrine of apostasy.

The Bible teaches from beginning to end that man is basically sinful. Since this is contrary to so much of the humanistic teachings that surround us today, it is hard for some to swallow. But it does not make it any less true. "If we say that we have no sin, we are deceiving ourselves, and the truth is not in us" (I John 1:8 NASB).

There are many who admire Jesus of Nazareth as a great man, an outstanding teacher, but scoff at His deity. This is another form of apostasy. This is a denial of God, since the doctrine of the trinity is a basic tenet of

Christianity. John says: "Whoever denies the Son does not have the Father . . ." (I John 2:23 NASB).

We have often had people say to us, "Sure, I believe in God, but you certainly don't think Jesus was God, do you?" Of course we do. The Bible also says Jesus was born of a virgin; to deny this is a denial of the miracles of God, what traditional Christianity has said throughout the centuries.

What is happening today in many of our standard brand denominations? One of the first exposés of the beliefs of our future ministers was made by *Redbook* magazine in August of 1961. The publishers hired one of the top pollsters in the nation to survey a full representation of our seminaries which are supposedly preparing men for Christian service in the Protestant churches. Here are some of the results—compare them carefully with what the Bible says about apostasy.

Of the ministers in training, 56 percent rejected the virgin birth of Jesus Christ, 71 percent rejected that there was life after death. 54 percent rejected the bodily resurrection of Jesus Christ. 98 percent rejected that there would be a personal return of Jesus Christ to this earth.

"But false prophets also arose among the people, just as there will also be false teachers among you, who will secretly introduce destructive heresies . . ."(II Peter 2:1 NASB).

We are seeing "destructive heresies" bought in wholesale lots. In the 1968 annual of the *Encyclopedia Brittanica* in a special section on religion the writer wrote that this marks a turn in the history of American theology, for not only are they saying that God is dead, but men who still claim to be Christian theologians are saying that there is no such thing as a personal God at all.

In the February, 1968, issue of *McCall's* a survey of major denominations showed that a considerable number rejected altogether the idea of a personal God. How, may we ask, can a man be a minister today if he does not believe in a personal God?

Although this trend has been accelerated in recent years, this has been going on for a long time. When people move away from Christianity the church will lose its power and influence to a great religious movement, a satanic ecumenical campaign.

The Ecumenical Mania

Years ago when we first heard about the ecumenical movement, we couldn't pronounce it, but we thought it sounded like a great idea. It seemed plausible that all the "good guys" in the churches should join together to fight all the evil on the outside. There are many fallacies in that way of thinking. When all of the various churches begin to amalgamate in one unwieldy body, soon the doctrinal truths of the true church are watered down, altered, or discarded. In their place we see political pronouncements and ecclesiastical shenanigans that astound the believer and repel the nonbeliever. The mass movement of the National Council of Churches and the World Council of Churches toward an umbrella-like structure which would cover all sorts of beliefs and camouflage its motives with "broadmindedness," seems to say: "Come unto me all ye that are weary and heavyladen and I will give you—controversy!"

In May of 1969 the World Council of Churches, for instance, recommended that the churches should support violence if it is the last way to overthrow political and economic tyranny. This group also recommended that churches confess that they are "filled with blatant and insidious institutional racism."[4]

The news media carry stories every day about churches being invaded by pressure groups who "demand" money or recognition. Churches are joining forces with those who oppose everything that is known as traditional Christianity. "Marxist-Christian dialogue" is very popular; not for the purpose of extending the love of God to the atheistic Marxists or Communists, but with the idea of exchanging "truths" and reaching a common ground of understanding.

When Gus Hall, one of the best-known spokesmen for the Communist Party in the United States, says that the current red goals for America are "almost identical" to those espoused by the liberal church, then perhaps it is time (really far past time) that people begin to wake up to what is going on in the apostate church.

"A big and growing trend toward unity is developing in many of America's churches at this time. That trend, some clergymen are saying, could lead to a 'superchurch' of immense religious and political power."[5]

Satan's real intention is not to have a godless political situation, he wants a religious situation. Satan loves religion, which is the reason he invades certain churches on Sunday. Religion is a great blinder of the minds of men.

Where Does Apostasy Lead?

Christ calls His followers, the true Christians, the salt of the earth. If the salt is removed this important preservative will no longer be able to stop the decaying process. When false teachings and doctrines become predominant there will be a decline in the moral climate, for the preservative has been taken away.

Hear what the Bible has to say about the time before Christ's return: ". . . in the last days difficult times will come. For men will be lovers of self, lovers of money, boastful, arrogant, revilers, disobedient to parents, ungrateful, unholy, unloving, irreconcilable, malicious gossips, without self-control, brutal, haters of good, treacherous, reckless, conceited, lovers of pleasure rather than lovers of God . . ." (II Timothy 3:1-4 NASB).

That is a strong indictment of the era in which we live, isn't it? Continuing in that passage, Paul says that learning or intellectualism will increase, but men will not come to the "knowledge of truth."

We have increased in technology so rapidly in the past few years that our grandfather's heads would be spinning at what we take for granted. However, all the educational advances have not brought mankind one step further toward solving the basic needs of love, security, and true happiness; on the contrary, civilization seems more removed from these concepts than ever.

In this letter to Timothy, Paul also cites that there will be a pretense of worship, at the same time denying godliness. When we read of some of the magazines that fall under the category of "religious publications," we can understand what is meant by this pretense. God is not a living, vital reality, personified by Christ, He is hardly more than a "Thing," a "Reality," a "Ground of Being," a "Voice from Somewhere." When there is little to separate the church from a nightclub, a school, a social gathering, a political meeting, even a philanthropic group, then the salt has been taken away, its flavor is no different from any secular organization.

The Power Without the Salt

Although this great religious system of the time of the Tribulation, or the final seven-year period before the return of Christ, will be godless, it will also be powerful.

John says in Revelation 17 that this system would dominate the beast, or the Great Dictator who will be the head of the ten-nation confederacy. As we have said, it would seem that fear of Communism and the need for a common defense against the "King of the North" would drive the one-world political system into the arms of the "harlot" or the one-world religious system. The "harlot" will be "clothed in purple and scarlet, and adorned with gold and precious stones and pearls . . ." (Revelation 17:4 NASB). In other words, this religious system will be splendid on the outside, but corrupt to the core.

This harlot, as described in Revelation, is not only a system, but also a city. There is no question about where the city would be—it was Rome. It says that the woman sits (or rules) on seven mountains. Most elementary students of history or geography know that Rome is the city of seven hills. It is there that the religious system will reign for a time in coalition with the political system.

However, the Bible tells us about the end of this system. The political system and its dictator will hate this religious system after a time, because it controls the Antichrist and he wants to proclaim himself to be God, without any interference. The Great Dictator is not going to be a puppet; if strings are to be pulled, he wants to do the manipulating.

Revelation 18:2 shows that the destruction of the religious system will take place in two phases. "Fallen, fallen is Babylon the great." The first "fallen" refers to the destruction of the religious system by the dictator. This will take place in the middle of the Tribulation, at the end of three and one-half years. The second "fallen" refers to the sudden destruction of the city of Rome.

God-given Compassion

There is a tightrope which is walked by everyone who condemns the actions of churches, their leaders, or any belief which is no more than unbelief. One is accused of being "anti-church," "narrow-minded," or "dogmatic." However, in proclaiming the truths of God, revealed by the Bible and its prophets, we cannot dilute what is said. On the other hand, while loathing the actions and motives of any system which is religious, without knowing Christ, we do at the same time want to introduce persons within these systems to the only way to God, to Jesus Christ Himself. This is a distinction which is difficult for a non-Christian to understand, and sometimes equally difficult for the Christian to follow. It is against human nature to separate the man from the beliefs he appears to follow. We cannot do it alone. Only Christ, working in and through our whole being, can possibly give us compassion and love for what we ourselves have labeled unloving and despicable.

11 ○ The Ultimate Trip

One small step for a man—one giant leap for mankind.

APOLLO 11 COMMANDER NEIL ARMSTRONG

20 JULY 1969

AND THE WORLD caught its breath. Science fiction had prepared man for the incredible feats of the astronauts, but when the reality of the moon landing really hit, it was awesome.

On that historic Sunday in July we watched TV, laughing as Armstrong and Buzz Aldrin loped on the moon's surface. We walked out the front door and looked up at the Old Man and said, "It's really happening—there are a couple of guys walking around up there right now. Amazing."

Astounding as man's trip to the moon is, there is another trip which many men, women, and children will take some day which will leave the rest of the world gasping. Those who remain on earth at that time will use every invention of the human mind to explain the sudden disappearance of millions of people.

Reporters who wrote the historic story of Apollo 11 told how the astronauts collected rocks which may reveal the oldest secrets of the solar system. Those who are alive to tell the story of "Project Disappearance" will try in vain to describe the happening which will verify the oldest secrets of God's words.

What Will They Say?

"There I was, driving down the freeway and all of a sudden the place went crazy. . . . cars going in all directions . . . and not one of them had a driver. I mean it was wild! I think we've got an invasion from outer space!"

"It was the last quarter of the championship game and the other side was ahead. Our boys had the ball. We made a touchdown and tied it up. The crowd went crazy. Only one minute to go and they fumbled—our quarterback recovered—he was about a yard from the goal when—zap—no more quarterback—completely gone, just like that!"

"It was puzzling—very puzzling. I was teaching my course in the Philosophy of Religion when all of a sudden three of my students vanished.

They simply vanished! They were quite argumentative—always trying to prove their point from the Bible. No great loss to the class. However, I do find this disappearance very difficult to explain."

"As an official spokesman for the United Nations I wish to inform all peace-loving people of the world that we are making every human effort to assist those nations whose leaders have disappeared. We have issued a general declaration of condemnation in the General Assembly concerning these heads of state. Their irresponsibility is shocking."

"My dear friends in the congregation. Bless you for coming to church today. I know that many of you have lost loved ones in this unusual disappearance of so many people. However, I believe that God's judgment has come upon them for their continued dissension and quarreling with the great advances of the church in our century. Now that the reactionaries are removed, we can progress toward our great and glorious goal of uniting all mankind into a brotherhood of reconciliation and understanding."

"You really want to know what I think? I think all that talk about the Rapture and going to meet Jesus Christ in the air wasn't crazy after all. I don't know about you, brother, but I'm going to find myself a Bible and read all those verses my wife underlined. I wouldn't listen to her while she was here, and now she's— I don't know where she is."

Rapture—What Rapture?

Christians have a tendency sometimes to toss out words which have no meaning to the non-Christian. Sometimes misunderstood terms provide the red flag an unbeliever needs to turn him from the simple truth of God's Word. "Rapture" may be one of those words. It is not found in the Bible, so there is no need to race for your concordance, if you have one. There are some Christians who do not use the word, but prefer "translation" instead.

The word "rapture" means to snatch away or take out. But whether we call this event "the Rapture" or the "translation" makes no difference—the important thing is that it will happen.

It will happen!

Someday, a day that only God knows, Jesus Christ is coming to take away all those who believe in Him. He is coming to meet all true believers in the air. Without benefit of science, space suits, or interplanetary rockets, there will be those who will be transported into a glorious place more beautiful, more awesome, than we can possibly comprehend. Earth and all its thrills, excitement, and pleasures will be nothing in contrast to this great event.

It will be the living end. The ultimate trip.

If you are shaking your heads over this right now, please remember how many "impossibles" you have said in your lifetime—or how many "impossibles" men throughout the ages have said to many things God has revealed through His spokesmen. And yet they were possible, because nothing is impossible for God.

We have been examining the push of world events which the prophets foretold would lead the way to the seven-year countdown before the return of Jesus Christ to earth. The big question is, will you be here during this seven-year countdown? Will you be here during the time of the Tribulation when the Antichrist and the False Prophet are in charge for a time? Will you be here when the world is plagued by mankind's darkest days?

It may come as a surprise to you, but the decision concerning your presence during this last seven-year period in history is entirely up to you.

God's Word tells us that there will be one generation of believers who will never know death. These believers will be removed from the earth before the Great Tribulation—before that period of the most ghastly pestilence, bloodshed, and starvation the world has ever known.

Examine the prophecies of this mysterious happening—of the "Rapture." Here is the real hope for the Christian, the "blessed hope" for true believers (Titus 2:13-15).

As we see the circumstances which are coming on the world, this hope gets more blessed all the time. This is the reason we are optimistic about the future. This is the reason that in spite of the headlines, in spite of crisis after crisis in America and throughout the world, in spite of the dark days which will strike terror into the hearts of many, every Christian has the right to be optimistic!

You may be thinking now, "Count me out. I like it right here and I have a lot of plans for my future."

Exactly. This is what we are talking about—your plans for the future. In fact, this is what Christ was talking about when He said: "Let not your heart be troubled; believe in God, believe also in Me. In My Father's house are many dwelling places; if it were not so, I would have told you; for I go to prepare a place for you. And if I go and prepare a place for you, I will come again, and receive you to Myself; that where I am, there you may be also" (John 14:1-3 NASB).

According to all the Scriptures we are told that the place He is preparing for us will be utterly fantastic. Eternal life will surpass the greatest pleasures we have known on earth.

I Tell You a Mystery

To avoid confusion, we will refer to the event when the church (those who believe in Jesus Christ as Savior) will meet Christ in the air as the Rapture. If you have grown in a school of Christian thought that uses the "translation," simply substitute this word when you are reading.

In I Corinthians 15:50 important things are revealed about the Rapture. We are told that Christians cannot inherit the Kingdom of God in the type of bodies we now have—that is, in bodies of flesh and blood.

However, according to the gospels and the Old Testament, there will be certain people who will inherit for a time the Kingdom of God in their mortal bodies. This is the Kingdom that Christ will establish after He returns to earth. This does not contradict the previous statement. The Bible is speaking of two separate events.

The distinction between God's dealing with the church and His dealing with another group of believers who are largely gathered around Israel is very important. Revelation 20 and Matthew 25 speak of the time when Jesus will return to the earth and separate the believers from the nonbelievers. For us, as believers, our hope is different from Israel's. This will be clear when we distinguish between the second advent, or the second coming of Christ, and the Rapture.

We are told that we cannot enter the Kingdom of God until we are changed from the type of body we now have into a new model. Then we have this fascinating verse: "Behold, I tell you a mystery; we shall not all sleep, but we shall all be changed" (I Corinthians 15:51 NASB).

The word "mystery" in the original Greek means something which has not been revealed before, but is now being revealed to those who are initiated. It was from this word that the concept of Greek fraternities came—everyone who has been in a fraternity or sorority knows there are certain secrets which are not disclosed until after initiation.

To draw the analogy, every believer in Jesus Christ is initiated into Christ's fraternity. Then, and only then, can he understand some of the secrets of God. These secrets the rest of the world will not accept as those who believe in Christ will accept them and understand them.

What is the secret that had not been revealed anywhere in the Scriptures before Paul wrote this letter to the Corinthians? Here is where the mystery gets exciting.

It says, "We shall not all sleep." Sleep is the word for Christian death. "Sleep" does not mean that your soul, your consciousness sleeps. There are some who believe that when you die your soul, your personality, the real you goes into some strange limbo. However, we are told that the moment a believer breathes his last breath and dies his soul goes immediately to be with Christ—to be face to face with the Lord (II Corinthians 5:1-10; Philippians 1:21-23).

So what does sleep? Your body. The body that disintegrates, Christ will raise into a body which can never see corruption again. "For our citizenship is in heaven, from which also we eagerly wait for a Savior, the Lord Jesus Christ; who will transform the body of our humble state into conformity with the body of His glory, by the exertion of the power that He has even to subject all things to Himself" (Philippians 3:20, 21 NASB).

What about the mystery? The mystery has to do with the believers who will be *alive* when Christ comes for them. "In a moment, in the twinkling of an eye, at the last trumpet; for the trumpet will sound, and the dead will be raised imperishable, and we shall be changed" (I Corinthians 15:52 NASB).

Words are fascinating—and the basis for understanding. The word translated "moment" is the Greek word *atomos*, which is the word from which we get "atom." In the Greek it means that which is indivisible, in other words, it will happen so quickly, in a flash of time which is so short it can't be divided. At that point those who are alive will be brought into the presence of the Lord.

This will take place "at the last trumpet," which refers to something which was the practice of God in the Old Testament. When the Israelites were on their march from Egypt over to the land of Palestine, every morning before they started on their journey they would have seven trumpets blow—to prepare to break camp, fold up their tents, etc. When the seventh trumpet, which was the last trumpet, sounded, this meant—move out!

The idea in this passage is that when God has the last trumpet blow it means He will move out all the Christians—and at that point we shall be changed.

What's in a word? "Changed" means to be changed in essence, but not to be completely changed in appearance. This strengthens the truth which is spoken of in other places that in eternity we are going to recognize people we knew here on earth. If you're not too satisfied with the face or body you now have, you will have a glorious new body. However, you will be recognizable, just as you will recognize others.

We won't have to eat to be sustained, but the Scripture says we can eat if we want to—and enjoy it. For those who have a weight problem, that sounds rather heavenly in itself. Our eternal bodies will not be subject to aging, or pain, or decay.

Just think how excited a woman can get about a new wardrobe. How much more excited we should be about acquiring a new body!

When the Scripture says, "the dead will be raised imperishable" and "for this perishable must put on the imperishable," it refers to the Christians who have died physically. They will be resurrected to meet Christ in the air.

However, when it says, "this mortal must put on immortality," it is referring to those who are alive at the coming of Christ. That's the mystery, the Rapture or translation. That is the hope that Paul offered for the generation which will be alive when Christ returns.

Who Goes First?

The Thessalonians were evidently worried about something that might be concerning you also. They wondered if those who had died and would be resurrected when Christ returned might be in some separate part of God's Kingdom. No Christian would want to miss seeing their loved ones throughout eternity.

However, the apostle Paul assured them that God's plan was perfect: those who had "fallen asleep in Jesus," or the Christians who had died, will join the Lord first. Then the Christians who are alive at that time will be caught up "together with them in the clouds" to meet the Lord in the air (I Thessalonians 4:13-18).

What a great reunion that will be!

The world will not know what has happened, because it occurs in an atom of time.

Debating Another Mystery

Christians sometimes have a theological debate about whether the Rapture occurs at the same time as the second coming of Christ or whether it takes place before the second coming, even before the Tribulation.

It is only fair to sincere Christians who differ about this time element for us to develop the reasons why we believe the Bible distinguishes between the Rapture and the second coming of Christ and why they do not occur simultaneously.

First, there is a great distinction between God's purpose for the nation of Israel and His purpose for the church, which is His main program today. The church is composed of both Gentiles and Jews. We are now living during the church age and the responsibility for evangelizing the world rests upon the church. We should reemphasize here that we are speaking of the true meaning of the church, which is the body of believers in Jesus Christ.

In the Old Testament evangelizing was the task of the Jew. Of course he seldom fulfilled that obligation, which is one of his great failures. But the Scriptures give a vast distinction between God's dealing with the church and that time of Tribulation which seems to be a resumption of God's dealing with Israel. During the Tribulation the spotlight is on the Jew—in the Book of Revelation the Jew is responsible for evangelizing the world again (Revelation 7:1-4).

Another reason why we support the idea that the Rapture and the second coming are separate events is that the second coming is said to be visible to the whole earth (Revelation 1:7). However, in the Rapture, only the Christians see Him—it's a mystery, a secret. When the living believers are taken out, the world is going to be mystified.

Furthermore, we are told when Christ comes at the second coming it is at the height of a global war. Everyone will know that this is the great war predicted by the prophets. There will be no doubt about it. But when Christ comes for the believers, it will not necessarily be at the time of a war.

More proof—when Christ comes to earth for the second time we are told in Matthew 25 that He will divide the believers from the unbelievers. Now if the Rapture were to take place at the same time as the second coming how could the believers and unbelievers be separated on earth? At the Rapture all the living believers will be caught up to join Him in the clouds.

Here is the chief reason why we believe the Rapture occurs before the Tribulation: the prophets have said that God will set up a Kingdom on earth over which the Messiah will rule. There will be mortal people in that kingdom. If the Rapture took place at the same time as the second coming, there would be no mortals left who would be believers; therefore, there would be no one to go into the Kingdom and repopulate the earth.

We need to understand that during the seven-year Tribulation there will be people who will become believers at that time. In spite of persecution as described in the previous chapter, they will survive this terrible period of history and will be taken by Christ to reign with Him for 1000 years. This is the Kingdom which is God's prelude to eternity.

The Church Disappeared

The largest descriptive volume of the Tribulation is found in Revelation 6 through 19. Here is a fascinating revelation about Revelation. In the first five chapters of this book, the church is mentioned thirty times. In fact, in chapters 2 and 3, at the end of each letter to the churches, John says "let him hear what the Spirit saith unto the churches." This is repeated seven times. Then we have the beginning of the description of the Tribulation, and there is not one mention of the churches. The church is conspicuous by its absence. Why? Because the church will be in heaven at that time.

If you are a believer, chapters 4 and 5 of Revelation describe what you will be experiencing in heaven. Talk about mind expansion drugs! We are told we shall expand in understanding and comprehension beyond that of any earthbound genius.

Be Alert

When will the Rapture occur? We don't know. No one knows. But God knows. However, we believe that according to all the signs, we are in the general time of His coming. "But you, brethren, are not in darkness, that the day should overtake you like a thief" (I Thessalonians 5:4 NASB).

In other words, you shouldn't be surprised when Christ returns to take you with Him. Unfortunately, this does not refer to all believers. We may have to go over to some of them and say, "I told you so, friend." It will be a surprise because they don't study the prophetic word. What an exciting time they may have missed on earth! The study and understanding of prophecy is an experience we pray all Christians will have.

"We are not of the night, nor of darkness . . ." (I Thessalonians 5:5 NASB). Darkness refers to the persons who do not have Christ, who cannot understand these things at all.

If you have not accepted Christ in your life this chapter will probably sound like the biggest farce you've ever read.

". . . so then let us not sleep as others do, but let us be alert and sober" (I Thessalonians 5:6 NASB). The idea of sleep is that a person just doesn't know what is going on. He may rationalize along his merry way, not paying any attention to the indications that the world can't go on much longer in the way it is going. He will say, "Something will happen—science will pull something out of the hat." So he puts his faith in science.

If you know what the prophets have said, and if the spirit of God has spoken to you, then you should be alert.

There's nothing that remains to be fulfilled before Christ could catch you up to be with Him.

What's Important?

Have you ever found an electric train, or a bedraggled doll that belonged to you as a child and remembered how terribly important it was to you years ago? When we meet Christ face to face we're going to look back on this life and see that the things we thought were important here were like the discarded toys of our childhood.

What a way to live! With optimism, with anticipation, with excitement. We should be living like persons who don't expect to be around much longer.

12 ○ World War III

There is no defense in science against the weapons which can now destroy civilization. ALBERT EINSTEIN

In the next war, none of us can count on having enough living to bury our dead. J. ROBERT OPPENHEIMER

Mankind must put an end to war—or war will put an end to mankind. JOHN F. KENNEDY, 1961

A war would be an irreversible and fatal occurrence. It would not be the end of difficulties but the end of civilization. POPE PAUL VI

. . . you will be hearing of wars and rumors of wars—then there will be a great tribulation, such as has not occurred since the beginning of the world until now, nor ever shall. And unless those days had been cut short, no life would have been saved. JESUS CHRIST, A.D. 33

FROM THE BEGINNING of man's history he has sought peace, but war has been his chief legacy. Among certain people today the peace sign has become an outward expression of their revulsion against war. This desire is like the people of Jeremiah's day who said, ". . . peace, peace, when there is no peace" (Jeremiah 6:14).

The great men of our day warn us about the insanity of another major war. Many experts, however, feel that it is inescapable. Whether we agree with the conclusions or theories of some of these experts or not, it is important to know what they are saying.

Several years ago a number of Nobel prize-winning scientists from various countries prepared a document and sent it to the leaders of all the world powers. They warned: "Here, then, is the problem which we present to you, stark and dreadful and inescapable: shall we put an end to the human race or shall mankind renounce war? We appeal, as human beings to human beings; remember your humanity, and forget the rest. If you can do so, the way lies open to a new paradise; if you cannot, there lies before you the risk of universal death."[1]

Many of the scientists who were most responsible for the development of the H-bomb signed the document quoted above.

War has greatly increased in frequency and intensity in this century. It has kept pace with the acceleration of technological advances. Some people have undoubtedly become callous to the continuous fighting on our globe, but it is shocking to review the statistics since World War II:

"Since World War II there have been 12 limited wars in the world, 39 political assassinations, 48 personal revolts, 74 rebellions for independence, 162 social revolutions, either political, economic, racial or religious."[2]

Since these statistics were written there have been more major assassinations and several more revolts.

In spite of all the oratory and books that have been aimed at steering man away from another world conflict, all-out war continues to be an ever-impending possibility. Any one of the limited wars such as Viet Nam or the Middle East crisis could at any time strike the spark that ignites World War III.

Why is it that in spite of the terrible lessons learned from history about war and the terrifying predictions of a future war, man keeps playing on the precipice of complete destruction? Jesus predicted that man would not learn from the past nor heed the warnings of the future; man would ultimately plunge the whole world into a war so vast, so utterly destructive, that only the personal return of Jesus Christ Himself to stop it would prevent the total annihilation of all life.

Here is the further solemn prediction of Jesus Christ as He described the world situation that would be present at the moment of His return:

"And unless those days had been cut short [abruptly ended], no life would have been saved . . ." (Matthew 24: 22 NASB).

Why Can't Man Live Without War?

We believe the answer to that question is important to consider before presenting the predicted path that man will take to the last great war which the Bible calls Armageddon.

Man cannot stop war because he will not accept the basic reason and cause for war—nor will he accept the cure for this basic cause. God says: "From whence come wars and fightings among you? come they not hence, even of your lusts that war in your members? Ye lust, and have not: ye kill, and desire to have, and cannot obtain: ye fight and war, yet ye have not . . ." (James 4:1, 2 KJV).

Inside of man there is a selfish, self-centered nature. This is the source of what God calls sin. Sin is basically self-centered seeking and striving—going our own way, with our backs turned on God. It is because of this selfish nature with which we were born that we cannot have consistent peace with ourselves, our family, our neighbor, or, on a broader scale, with other nations.

As one man has said, "What's wrong with the world?" And answered himself truthfully, "I'm wrong with the world."

God didn't intend for man to have this condition. Man was created originally to have fellowship with God. This fellowship is so vital that without it man is like a jet aircraft flying in a dense fog and suddenly losing all its instruments.

God warned man of the consequences when He gave man one simple prohibition. Man understood that to disobey God on this one command was to reject fellowship with God. In spite of all the evidences of God's love and veracity, man went his own independent way and lost fellowship with the only One who can give him the true fulfillment for which he was created.

Man has been turned in upon himself; he has become self-centered and discontented. No matter how much he gets of fame or wealth or power, he is not satisfied. Why? Because he cannot fill the vacuum once filled by God with any other thing. So he fights with himself, with his mate, with his family, and with other nations.

Solution

The only cure for war is to change the hearts of men. Jesus came into the world to bring men back to fellowship with God and consequently make that change in their hearts. The Bible promises, "For Christ also died for sins once for all, the just for the unjust, in order that He might bring us to God . . ." (I Peter 3:18 NASB).

Jesus took the just rap due our sins and died under its penalty so that God might forgive us and receive us back into fellowship. When this occurs God gives us a new heart that desires to follow Him and a love for our neighbor. He gives us a new dimension of life with which we can perceive and know Him. He puts His Spirit within us to live so that He motivates and empowers us to follow God's purpose for our lives.

We begin to experience peace of mind, a new stability, a new sense of purpose, an awareness of Christ's presence, and a healing of our personality that makes us a whole person. We find ourselves concerned about the interests of others. A new kind of love impels us to place others before ourselves. This cannot be done by any system of government, education, psychology, or outer environmental changes. It can be done only by a personal invitation of Christ into the heart and an acceptance of the gift of forgiveness which He gave His life to provide.

Right where you are, as you read this chapter, you can make this decision in the quiet of your heart.

General Douglas MacArthur was eternally right when he said on the deck of the battleship Missouri at the close of World War II: "We have had our last chance. If we will not devise some greater and more equitable system, ARMAGEDDON will be at the door. The problem basically is theological and involves a spiritual recrudescence and improvement of human character that will synchronize with our almost matchless advances in science, art, literature, and all material and cultural developments of the past 2000 years. It must be the spirit if we are to save the flesh."[3]

The sad prediction of the Bible is that mankind will not accept God's diagnosis or His cure. Therefore, they will seek to solve the problem themselves. Fear of war will grow until it prepares man to accept the Antichrist's solution for preventing war. Paul predicts the false hope the world will have in the Antichrist: "While they are saying, 'Peace and safety!' then destruction will come upon them suddenly like birth pangs upon a woman with child; and they shall not escape" (I Thessalonians 5:3 NASB).

Where Are We Going?

In the previous chapters we have shown the predicted powers that would arise shortly before the return of Jesus Christ and how these powers are simultaneously developing in current history. We have outlined how world conditions in this generation are launched into a countdown that will end in the final collapse of man's efforts to run the world without God.

In this chapter we will trace consecutively the predicted events that lead to the Armageddon campaign: the various sequence of battles, the particular powers who fight each other, and how in turn each is destroyed. The crucial prediction of the revived state of Israel's part in triggering Armageddon will also be shown.

The Fuse Was Primed

When the Jews re-established their nation in Palestine they created an unsolvable problem; they displaced Arabs who had dwelt in Palestine for several centuries. All the legal debates and logical dissertations that can be advanced will never change the basic state of hostility that exists between the Israelis and the Arabs.

The Jews will never be convinced that they should leave the land that God gave to their forefathers. They believe that they were robbed of their inalienable right to the land by the Romans. Centuries of persecution have taught them that there is no country in the world where they can be assured of continuing acceptance, much less safety. Remaining as a nation in Palestine is a matter of survival of the race for the Israeli. He feels that it is his only hope in a hostile world.

The Arabs are equally implacable in their unwillingness to accept the Israeli occupation of what they consider to be their land. It has become a matter of racial honor and sacred religious duty to drive out the Israelis.

Israel's Treaty With Hell

According to the Bible, the Middle East crisis will continue to escalate until it threatens the peace of the whole world. The focus of all nations will be upon this unsolvable and complex problem which keeps bringing the world to the precipice of a thermonuclear holocaust. This is apparently the first major problem that the incredible Roman leader will solve after taking over the ten-nation confederacy of European nations.

Some 2500 years ago the prophet Daniel said that a prince would come to power from the people who would destroy the city of Jerusalem and the second Temple (Daniel 9:27). The Romans under Titus did the destroying, so the coming prince would have to be someone out of the Roman culture. This Roman prince, as we described in "The Future Fuehrer," will come to power just before the return of Christ. He will make "a strong covenant" with the Israelis, guaranteeing their safety and protection. The word translated "strong covenant" has the idea of a treaty or mutual protection pact. The Israelis will then be permitted to reinstitute the sacrifice and offering aspect of the law of Moses. This demands that the Temple be rebuilt, because according to the law of Moses, sacrifices can be offered only in the Temple at Jerusalem. Apparently all this will be done under the protection of the Antichrist of Rome.

(P.S. The Arabs are not going to like this idea of rebuilding the Temple one bit.)

According to Daniel's prophetic chronology, the minute the Israeli leader and the Roman leader sign this pact, God starts His great timepiece which has seven allotted years left on it. This event marks the beginning of the period of Biblical history previously noted as the Tribulation.

Isaiah prophetically expressed warning to the Jews concerning this covenant when he declared: "Because you have said, 'We have made a covenant with death, and with Sheol we have an agreement; when the overwhelming scourge passes through it will not come to us; for we have made lies our refuge, and in falsehood we have taken shelter'; Then your covenant with death will be annulled, and your agreement with Sheol will not stand; when the overwhelming scourge passes through you will be beaten down by it" (Isaiah 28:15, 18).

It is through an ingenuous settlement of the Middle East problem that the Antichrist will make good his promise to bring peace to a world terrified of war. After this he will rapidly bring all nations under his control. The world will experience great hope and put its full trust in the genius of Rome. He will begin to bring in fantastic plans of economic prosperity, even to the underdeveloped countries. War will seem to be a curious game that men used to play. The world will be universally acclaiming the Dictator.

"Who is like the Dictator, and who is able to make war with him?"

After three and a half years of remarkable progress, the Antichrist will become worshiped for his brilliant statesmanship and the wonderful progress in the world. The believers in Christ will oppose his rule and be ruthlessly exposed. Publicly, they will not be able to buy, sell, or hold a job. They will be executed en masse as examples to those who would hinder the "brotherhood of man," because they will insist that Christ is the only lasting hope for man.

Riding upon the crest of public worship the Roman Dictator will go to Jerusalem and in the Temple proclaim himself to be God incarnate (II Thessalonians 2:4; Matthew 24:15). As mentioned, this will be the great warning sign to the believers of that day that Armageddon is about to begin. The residents of Israel who believe in Jesus will flee to the mountains and canyons of Petra for divine protection, as promised (Matthew 24:16; Revelation 12:6, 14).

The Red Horse Unleashed

"And another, a red horse, went out; and to him who sat on it, it was granted to take peace from the earth, and that men should slay one another; and a great sword was given to him" (Revelation 6:4 NASB).

Almost immediately after the Antichrist declares himself to be God, God releases the dreaded second of the four horsemen of the Apocalypse. This is a figure of the unleashing of war upon the earth.

That beautiful balance of power established by the Antichrist is suddenly ruptured. God begins to show man that the Antichrist's promises cannot stand. The thing which man feared most, an all-out war, now rushes upon him.

The Beginning of the End

"At the time of the end the king of the south shall attack him (Israeli leader)" (Daniel 11:40a).

We have identified the characters of this passage. The Arab-African confederacy headed by Egypt (King of the South) launches an invasion of Israel. This fatal mistake spells their doom and begins the Armageddon campaign. ". . . but the king of the north shall rush upon him (the Israeli leader) like a whirlwind, with chariots (mechanized army) and horsemen (cavalry), and with many ships" (Daniel 11:40b).

Chart one shows the movement of troops.

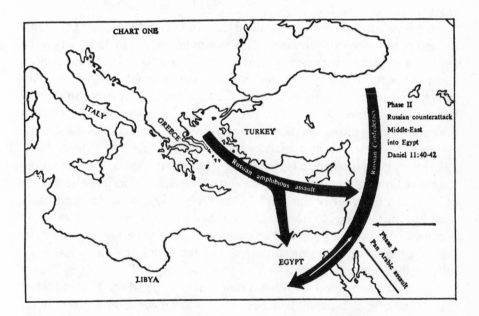

Russia and her allies use this occasion to launch an invasion of the Middle East, which Russia has longed to do since the Napoleonic wars. Ezekiel 38 describes the development of this great Russian force, and its plan to attack Israel.

Twenty-six centuries ago Ezekiel described the plot of the Russian leaders against revived Israel: "Thus says the Lord GOD; On that day thoughts will come into your mind, and you will devise an evil scheme and say, 'I will go up against the land of unwalled villages; I will fall upon the quiet people who dwell securely, all of them dwelling without walls (i.e. fortifications), and having no bars or gates'; to seize spoil and carry off plunder; to assail the waste places which are now inhabited, and the people who were gathered from the nations, who have gotten cattle and goods, who dwell at the center of the earth" (Ezekiel 38:10-12).

The Russians will make a great tactical blunder by invading Israel. They will construe the defenseless posture of Israel, who will be trusting in the Antichrist's protection, as an opportunity to finally conquer the great land bridge of the Middle East. They will be motivated by the great material wealth of the restored nation of Israel. Their purpose is thus revealed by Ezekiel ". . . to seize spoil and carry off plunder. . . ."

The wealth of Israel is also predicted: ". . . the people who were gathered from the nations, who have gotten cattle and goods."

True Bible scholars have recognized that some day there would be a vast concentration of wealth in Israel. Harry Rimmer wrote in 1940, when the land was scrub brush in comparison to what it is today: ". . . The development of the resources of that land has only commenced. Ten years of uninterrupted industry there will make Palestine the richest concentration of treasure this world has so far witnessed. Even five years of unbroken application to the cultivation of her natural resources would make Palestine the envy of the world, and a land very well worth robbing, indeed."[4]

The prophetic indication is that Israel will become one of the most prosperous nations on earth during the reign of the Antichrist. It is also said to be, ". . . at the center of the earth." Geographically, this is approximately true, but more seems to be meant here than physical location. Israel will become a cultural, religious, and economic world center, especially at Jerusalem. The value of the mineral deposits in the Dead Sea alone has been estimated at one trillion, two hundred and seventy billion dollars. This is more than the combined wealth of France, England, and the United States!

I was talking to a prominent Los Angeles engineer after a message on this subject and we discussed the need for a cheap source of energy by which these Dead Sea minerals could be refined. He said that he is certain that there is enough steam trapped under the numerous faults in the earth around Israel to provide power to run turbines to produce electricity very economically. He called this new process geo-thermal energy. In the near future Israel will discover a way to produce cheap energy to develop this gold mine of riches.

One of the chief minerals in the Dead Sea is potash, which is a potent fertilizer. When the population explosion begins to bring famine, potash will become extremely valuable for food production.

It is strategic wealth of this sort that will cause the Russian bloc to look for an opportunity to invade and conquer Israel, according to Ezekiel.

The strategic military importance of "the land bridge of the Middle East" which begins in the north with the Bosphorus (the narrow channel which divides Turkey connecting the Black Sea with the Mediterranean), and extends southward to Egypt, has been established by centuries of military conflicts. The one who would control Europe, Asia, and Africa must control this area, which literally connects the three continents. This must figure into the Russian motivation for future conquest. Since Israel lies in the center of this land bridge, it has been made a battleground innumerable times.

This writer is indebted to Col. R. B. Thieme, Jr., a man who is uniquely qualified to explain this passage, since he is both a scholar in military history and in the original languages of the Bible, for pointing out the military aspects of this war.

The Classic Double-cross

When the Russians invade the Middle East with amphibious and mechanized land forces, they will make a "blitzkrieg" type of offensive through the area. As Daniel saw it centuries ago: ". . . and he [Russians] shall come into countries [of the Middle-East] and shall overflow and pass through. He will come into the glorious land [Israel]. And tens of thousands shall fall" (Daniel 11:40b, 41a).

Ezekiel describes the same invasion as follows: "Therefore, son of man, prophesy, and say to Gog [the Russian leader], Thus says the Lord GOD: On that day when my people Israel are dwelling securely, you will bestir yourself and come from your place out of the uttermost parts of the north [Daniel's king of the North], you and many peoples with you [i.e., the European iron curtain countries], all of them riding on horses, a great host, a mighty army; you will come up against my people Israel, like a cloud covering the land. In the latter days, I will bring you against my land . . ." (Ezekiel 38:14-16).

As previously quoted the Russians will make both an amphibious and land invasion of Israel. The current build-up of Russian ships in the Mediterranean serves as another significant sign of the possible nearness of Armageddon. They now have more ships in the Mediterranean than the United States, according to several recent news releases. The amphibious landings will facilitate a rapid encirclement of the middle section of "the land bridge."

The might of the Red Army is predicted. It will sweep over the Arab countries as well as Israel in a rapid assault over to Egypt to secure the entire land bridge. It is at this point that Russia double-crosses the United Arab Republic leader, Egypt. After sweeping over tens of thousands of people Daniel says of the Red army: "He shall stretch out his hand against the countries [i.e. Arab countries of the Middle East], and the land of Egypt shall not escape. He [Russian leader] shall become ruler of the treasures of gold and of silver, and all the precious things of Egypt; and the Libyans [African Arabs] and the Ethiopians [African blacks] shall follow in his train" (Daniel 11:42, 43).

As we saw in Chapters 5 and 6, this prediction indicates that the Russian bloc will double-cross the Arabs, Egyptians, and Africans, and for a short while conquer the Middle East. At this time, with the main Russian force in Egypt, the commander will hear alarming news: "But rumors from the east [the Orient mobilizing] and from the north [the Western Europeans mobilizing] shall alarm and hasten him. And he shall go forth with great fury to destroy and utterly to sweep away many" (Daniel 11:44 Amplified).

As shown in Chart two, the Russian force will retrace its steps from Egypt to consolidate for a counter-attack in Israel. The Russians will be alarmed at the news of the Roman Dictator mobilizing forces around the world to put down this breach of peace. Apparently it will surprise the Russian leader who underestimated the revived Roman Empire's will to fight.

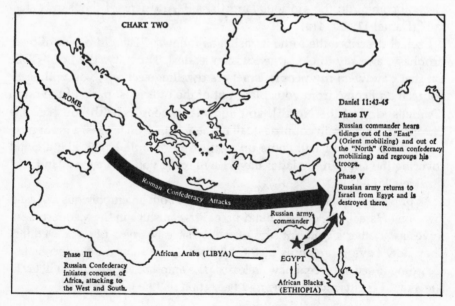

CHART TWO

ROME

Daniel 11:43-45

Phase IV

Russian commander hears tidings out of the "East" (Orient mobilizing) and out of the "North" (Roman confederacy mobilizing) and regroups his troops.

Phase V

Russian army returns to Israel from Egypt and is destroyed there.

Roman Confederacy Attacks

Russian army commander

Phase III

Russian Confederacy initiates conquest of Africa, attacking to the West and South.

African Arabs (LIBYA)

EGYPT

African Blacks (ETHIOPIA)

It is conjecture on this writer's part, but it appears that the Oriental powers, headed by Red China, will be permitted to mobilize its vast army by the Roman Dictator, thinking that they would be loyal to him against Russia. However, the Orientals will eventually double-cross him, and move a 200 million man army against the Antichrist, as we have seen in Chapter 7.

This Russian double-cross of the Arabs is predictable by any astute observer of the Middle East situation today. It is obvious that the Russians are playing games with the Arabs in order to accomplish the old Russian dream of year-round seaports and oil supplies. The Arab leaders think that they can accept Russian loans and supplies without strings, but there are steel cables of conditions behind every Russian ruble given in aid and they are used eventually to pull a country behind the iron curtain.

The Russian force will establish command headquarters on Mount Moriah or the Temple area in Jerusalem. Daniel pointed this out when he said: "And he shall pitch his palatial tents between the seas [Dead Sea and Mediterranean Sea] and the glorious holy mount Zion; yet he shall come to his end with none to help him" (Daniel 11:45 Amplified).

As the Russian commander confidently prepares to meet the forces of the revived Roman Empire in Palestine, he seeks to utterly destroy the Jewish people. This is the apparent meaning of verses 44 and 45. Perhaps no other great army of history has ever been so totally destroyed as this one will be.

The Russian Waterloo

Ezekiel sounded the fatal collapse of the Red Army centuries ago when inspired by the Spirit of the living God he said: "But on that day, when Gog shall come against the land of Israel, says the Lord GOD, my wrath will be roused. For in my jealousy and in my blazing wrath I declare, On that day there shall be a great shaking in the land of Israel; the fish of the sea, and the birds of the air, and the beasts of the field, and all creeping things that creep on the ground, and all the men that are upon the face of the earth, shall quake at my presence, and the mountains shall be thrown down, and the cliffs shall fall, and every wall shall tumble to the ground. I will summon every kind of terror against Gog, says the Lord GOD; every man's sword will be against his brother. With pestilence and bloodshed I will enter into judgment with him; and I will rain upon him and his hordes and the many peoples that are with him, torrential rains and hailstones, fire and brimstone" (Ezekiel 38:18-22).

". . . then I will strike your bow from your left hand, and will make your arrows drop out of your right hand. You shall fall upon the mountains of Israel, you and all your hordes and the people that are with you; I will give you to birds of prey of every sort and to the wild beasts to be devoured. You shall fall in the open field; for I have spoken, says the Lord GOD" (Ezekiel 39:3-5).

The description of torrents of fire and brimstone raining down upon the Red Army, coupled with an unprecedented shaking of the land of Israel could well be describing the use of tactical nuclear weapons against them by the Romans. It explicitly says that this force would fall "in the open field," so apparently this position enables the use of nuclear weapons.

God consigns this whole barbarous army, which will seek to annihilate the Jewish race, to an utter and complete decimation. Ezekiel speaks of the Russians and ". . . all your hosts and the peoples who are with you . . ." being destroyed in Israel.

Nuclear Exchange Begins

A fearful thing is predicted as occurring at the time of the Red Army's destruction. God says, "I will send fire on Magog [Russia] and upon those who dwell securely [false hope] in the coastlands [various continents] . . ." (Ezekiel 39:6 Amplified). According to this, Russia, as well as many countries who thought they were secure under the Antichrist's protection, will have fire fall upon them. Once again, this could be a direct judgment from God, or God could allow the various countries to launch a nuclear exchange of ballistic missiles upon each other.

What About the United States?

The United States may be aligned with the Western forces headed by the ten-nation Revived Roman Empire of Europe. It is clear that the U.S. cannot be the leader of the West in the future. It is quite possible that Ezekiel was referring to the U.S. in part when he said: "I will send fire—upon those who dwell securely in the coastlands. . . ."

The word translated "coastlands" or "isle" in the Hebrew is *ai*. It was used by the ancients in the sense of "continents" today. It designated the great Gentile civilizations across the seas which were usually settled most densely along the coastlands. The idea here is that the Gentile nations on distant continents would all experience the impact of sudden torrents of fire raining down upon them. This can include prophetically the populated continents and islands of the Western hemisphere as well as the Far East. It pictures cataclysmic events which affect the whole inhabited earth.

The Greatest Battle of All Time

With the United Arab and African armies neutralized by the Russian invasion, and the consequent complete annihilation of the Russian forces and their homeland, we have only two great spheres of power left to fight the final climactic battle of Armageddon; the combined forces of the Western civilization united under the leadership of the Roman Dictator and the vast hordes of the Orient probably united under the Red Chinese war machine.

The Mobilization

There may be a short lapse of hostility in the world after the destruction of Russia and allies while the armies mobilize. The apostle John predicts the mobilization of the oriental power as mentioned in Chapter 7. "And the sixth angel poured out his bowl upon the great river, the Euphrates; and its water was dried up, that the way might be prepared for the kings from the east" (Revelation 16:12 NASB).

The Chinese, as previously discussed, will be the most logical leader of this great army. They will use the chaos caused by this conflict in the Middle East to march against the Roman Dictator in a challenge for world control.

As this incredible Oriental army of 200 million soldiers marches to the eastern banks of the Euphrates, the Roman Dictator will begin to prepare his armies to meet them for the showdown in the Middle East. The apostle John predicts the supernatural power that the Antichrist and the False Prophet will use to gather all remaining nations together to confront the Oriental armies: "And I saw coming out of the mouth of the dragon [Satan] and out of the mouth of the beast [Roman Dictator] and out of the mouth of the false prophet, three unclean spirits like frogs; for they are spirits of demons, performing signs, which go out to the kings of the whole world, to gather them together for war of the great day of God, the Almighty. And they gathered them together to the place which in Hebrew is called Armageddon" (Revelation 16:13, 14, 16 NASB).

Several things must be noted from this passage. First, this whole sequence of events constitutes the final judgments of God against the Christ-rejecting world. They are called in the Book of Revelation the seven bowl or vial judgments and they occur just before and during the visible return of Jesus Christ to the earth. Secondly, the passage shows that the Roman Dictator and his sensational religious cohort, the False Prophet, will speak a satanically originated message to the non-oriental world—a message energized with great demonic power. They will persuade the nations of the whole world (i.e. not aligned with China) that they should send armies to the land of Palestine to destroy the last great warlike force on earth. They will probably promise an age of everlasting peace after the troublesome communist forces of the Orient are destroyed. Thirdly, the passage indicates that "leaders of the whole world" will send armies to the Middle East to fight under the Antichrist's command against "the kings of the east." Such countries as Western Europe, the United States, Canada, South America, and Australia undoubtedly will be represented.

Fourthly, these armies will be assembled and deployed for battle in the place called "Armageddon" or "Harmageddon."

What and Where Is Armageddon?

Armageddon is a byword used through the centuries to depict the horrors of war. Dr. Seiss sums up its true significance as follows: "Harmageddon (Armageddon) means the Mount of Megiddo, which has also given its name to the great plain of Jezreel which belts across the middle of the Holy Land, from the Mediterranean to the Jordan. The name is from a Hebrew root which means to cut off, to slay; and a place of slaughter has Megiddo ever been."[5]

In Biblical history countless bloody battles were fought in this area. Napoleon is reported to have stood upon the hill of Megiddo and recalled this prophecy as he looked over the valley and said, ". . . all the armies of the world could maneuver for battle here." In the Old Testament book of Joel this valley was called the "valley of Jehoshaphat."

Today this valley's entrance has the port of Haifa at its Western end. This is one of the most accessible areas in Palestine for amphibious landing of troops. It also affords a great area for troop assembly, equipment, and organization. Some troops will doubtlessly be airlifted in as well, and this large valley is suited for that, too.

The Valley of Decision

Some twenty-seven centuries ago the prophet Joel focused upon this same scene and said: "Proclaim this among the nations: Prepare war, stir up the mighty men. Let all the men of war draw near, let them come up. Beat your plowshares into swords, and your pruning hooks into spears; let the weak say, 'I am a warrior.' Hasten and come, all you nations round about, gather yourselves there. Bring down thy warriors, O LORD. Let the nations bestir themselves, and come up to the valley of Jehoshaphat; for there I will sit to judge all the nations round about. Put in the sickle, for the harvest is ripe. Go in, tread, for the wine press is full. The vats overflow, for their wickedness is great. Multitudes, multitudes, in the valley of decision! For the day of the LORD is near in the valley of decision" (Joel 3:9-14).

Joel reveals that it is in this very place that the Messiah will destroy the armies of the world and establish his kingdom of true peace and everlasting happiness. He also confirms the world-wide assemblage of armies there.

It is extremely important to note the accuracy of Bible prophecy in relation to this last conflict. In this day of H-bombs and super weapons, it seems incredible that there could ever be another great land war fought by basically conventional means, yet the Chinese believe that with a vastly superior numerical force, they can absorb devastating losses and still win a war. They also believe that all war is still determined on the ground by land forces.

Another interesting fact is that a force of 200 million soldiers could not be transported by China and its foreseeable allies by air or sea. They do not possess the industry to produce a transportation system for such an army. This necessitates the movement of troops across the land as is indicated in Revelation 16:12.

India has revealed recently an important development. It is reported that 12,000 Chinese soldiers are at work inside Pakistan-held Kashmir on the road which would give Chinese troops in Tibet a shortcut to the subcontinent. India calls the Chinese road-building activities a "threat to peace in Asia." It was said that "a flurry of road-building throughout the Himalayas is taking on increasing strategic importance."[6]

When this road is completed, it will make possible the rapid movement of millions of Chinese troops into the Middle East. It will literally pave the way for John's prophecy to be fulfilled: ". . . unless those days had been cut short, no life would have been saved . . ." (Matthew 24:22 NASB).

So here it is—the last great conflict. After the Antichrist assembles the forces of the rest of the whole world together, they meet the onrushing charge of the kings of the East in a battle line which will extend throughout Israel with the vortex centered at the Valley of Megiddo.

According to Zechariah, terrible fighting will center around the city of Jerusalem (Zechariah 12:2, 3; 14:1, 2).

Isaiah speaks of a frightful carnage taking place south of the Dead Sea in ancient Edom (Isaiah 63:1-4).

The apostle John predicts that so many people will be slaughtered in the conflict that blood will stand to the horses' bridles for a total distance of 200 miles northward and southward of Jerusalem (Revelation 14:20).

It seems incredible! The human mind cannot conceive of such inhumanity of man to man, yet God will allow man's nature to fully display itself in that day. No wonder Jesus said: ". . for then there will be a great tribulation, such as has not occurred since the beginning of the world until now, nor ever shall" (Matthew 24:21 NASB).

World-wide Destruction

The conflict will not be limited to the Middle East. The apostle John warns that when these two great forces meet in battle the greatest shock wave ever to hit the earth will occur. Whether by natural force of an earthquake or by some super weapon isn't clear. John says that all the cities of the nations will be destroyed (Revelation 16:19).

Imagine, cities like London, Paris, Tokyo, New York, Los Angeles, Chicago—obliterated! John says that the Eastern force alone will wipe out a third of the earth's population (Revelation 9:15-18).

He also predicts that entire islands and mountains would be blown off the map. It seems to indicate an all-out attack of ballistic missiles upon the great metropolitan areas of the world.

Prophecy indicates that U.S. Representative John Rhodes was right when he said concerning the danger of Red China and nuclear weapons, ". . . anyone who expects restraint from Red China ignores history and imperils future generations of Americans."[7]

Isaiah predicts in Chapter 24 concerning this time: "Behold, the Lord will lay waste the earth and make it desolate, and he will twist its surface and scatter its inhabitants."

"The earth lies polluted under its inhabitants." (Perhaps this refers in part to water and air pollution.)

"Therefore, a curse devours the earth, and its inhabitants suffer for their guilt; therefore the inhabitants of the earth are scorched [burned], and few men are left" (verses 1, 5, 6).

In the same chapter Isaiah says: "The earth is utterly broken, the earth is rent asunder, the earth is violently shaken. The earth staggers like a drunken man, it sways like a hut . . ." (verses 19, 20).

All of these verses seem to indicate the unleashing of incredible weapons the world over.

A Bright Spot in the Gloom

As Armageddon begins with the invasion of Israel by the Arabs and the Russian confederacy, and their consequent swift destruction, the greatest period of Jewish conversion to their true Messiah will begin. Ezekiel predicts that the destruction of the great Russian invading force will have a supernatural element to it which will cause great numbers of Jews to see the hand of the Lord in it. Through the miraculous sign of the destruction of this enemy who sought to destroy all Jews they come to see the name of their true God and Messiah, Jesus Christ.

Ezekiel quotes God as saying: "I will send fire on Magog [Russia] and on those who dwell securely in the coastlands; and they shall know that I am the LORD. And my holy name I will make known in the midst of my people Israel; and I will not let my holy name be profaned any more; and the nations shall know that I am the LORD, the Holy One in Israel. Behold, it is coming and it will be brought about, says the Lord GOD. That is the day of which I have spoken" [i.e., in the prophecies] (Ezekiel 39:6-8).

Zechariah predicts that one-third of the Jews alive during this period will be converted to Christ and miraculously preserved.

"In the whole land, says the LORD, two thirds shall be cut off and perish, and one third shall be left alive. And I will put this third into the fire, and refine them as one refines silver, and test them as gold is tested. They will call on my name, and I will answer them. I will say, 'They are my people'; and they will say, 'The LORD is my God'" (Zechariah 13:8, 9).

The Greatest Moment

As the battle of Armageddon reaches its awful climax and it appears that all life will be destroyed on earth—in this very moment Jesus Christ will return and save man from self-extinction.

As history races toward this moment, are you afraid or looking with hope for deliverance? The answer should reveal to you your spiritual condition.

One way or another history continues in a certain acceleration toward the return of Christ. Are you ready?

13 ○ The Main Event

The purposes of the United Nations are: to maintain international peace and security, and to that end: to take effective collective measures for the prevention and removal of threats to the peace. U. N. CHARTER, 1945

These things I have spoken to you, that in Me you may have peace. In the world you have tribulation, but take courage; I have overcome the world. JESUS CHRIST

WRITTEN UPON THE cornerstone of the United Nations building is a quotation of part of a prophecy. It reads: ". . . they shall beat their swords into plowshares, and their spears into pruning hooks; nation shall not lift up sword against nation, neither shall they learn war any more" (Isaiah 2:4).

This is a noble thought and has been quoted often by men who seek peace for this troubled world. There is a problem in the phrase, however, and we believe this is why the United Nations will never bring a lasting peace to the world. This quotation has been taken out of context. The meaning of the passage speaks of the time when the Messiah would reign over the earth out of Jerusalem and judge between the nations in a visible, actual, and historic Kingdom of God on earth. The people of the earth will come to the Lord in that day and ask Him to teach them His ways. Knowledge of God will be universal (Isaiah 2:3). This is the era for which Jesus taught us to pray in the Lord's Prayer, ". . . Thy kingdom come, thy will be done on earth as it is in heaven" (Matthew 6:10).

Men today vainly seek after peace while they reject and shut out of their lives the Prince of Peace, Jesus Christ. The name of Christ is not mentioned at the close of prayer in the United Nations. In fact, Jesus has been excluded from the premises. Man has shut out the only hope of peace, according to the Bible. The spirit of "antichrist" reigns in the governments of the world, for Christ is said not to be relevant to the problems we face.

Peace is available to the individual today as he invites Christ into his heart and allows Him to reign upon the throne of his life. But the Bible teaches that lasting peace will come to the world only after Christ returns and sits upon the throne of David in Jerusalem and establishes His historic kingdom on earth for a thousand years (Revelation 20:4-6).

The rulers of the world are told by many prophecies that God would send His king to rule over the earth and establish a reign of peace, righteousness, and justice in place of their godless, selfish, and violent rule. Jesus will return at a time of world-wide catastrophe, when man is on the brink of self-destruction. Men, for the most part, will have utterly rejected the true God and His Son, Jesus the Messiah, as predicted long ago by the psalmist: "The kings of the earth set themselves, and rulers take counsel together, against the LORD and his anointed [Christ], saying, 'Let us burst their bonds asunder, and cast their cords from us'" (Psalm 2:2, 3).

In spite of all that man will try to do to establish his rule and push God out of the world, God will establish His king, the Messiah Jesus, as the psalmist goes on to predict: "Yet have I set my king upon my holy hill of Zion" (Psalm 2:6 KJV).

Many so-called Christian leaders today do not believe that Jesus Christ will literally and physically make a personal return to the earth. Some teach that Christ returns spiritually when people accept Him and say that this is all that is meant by the various predictions of His return. Others teach that Jesus may return some day, but that it is irrelevant to study or to talk about it. The latter are worse than the former, for one out of every twenty-five verses in the New Testament is related to the second coming of Christ, and the survival of mankind as well as the fulfillment of hundreds of unconditional promises especially made to the believing remnant of the Jewish race are dependent on the second coming of Christ to this earth. As a matter of fact, in the Old Testament there were more than 300 prophecies regarding Christ's first coming (all of which were literally fulfilled), but more than 500 relating to His second coming. Many of these two different themes of prophecy were disclosed in the same sentence.

We have read that the apostle Peter clearly warned that in the days just prior to Christ's return false teachers would arise in the church and say: "Where is the promise of His (Jesus') coming? For ever since the fathers [apostles] fell asleep, all continues just as it was from the beginning of creation" (II Peter 3:4 NASB).

Characteristics of Christ's Return

Immediately after Jesus physically departed from the Mount of Olives and while His disciples were staring after Him with awe and amazement, the following promise was given: "And as they were gazing intently into the sky while He [Jesus] was departing, behold, two men in white clothing stood beside them; and they also said, 'Men of Galilee, why do you stand looking into the sky? This Jesus, who has been taken from you into heaven, will come in just the same way you have watched Him go into heaven'" (Acts 1-10, 11 NASB).

The word in the original translated "in just the same way" means "in exactly the same manner." Just as Jesus departed physically, visibly and personally from the earth, so He will return. Just as Jesus departed with clouds, so He will return.

His Return Will Be Visible, Personal, and Physical

The apostle John said: "Behold, He [Jesus] is coming with the clouds, and every eye will see Him, even those who pierced Him; and all the tribes of the earth will mourn over Him" (Revelation 1:7 NASB).

Zechariah predicted the same picture 500 years before Christ was born: ". . . and they [believing Israelites] shall look upon me [Jesus] whom they have pierced, and they shall mourn for him, as one mourneth for his only son . . ." (Zechariah 12:10 KJV).

To mourn over the one who was pierced necessitates that man recognizes Jesus who was crucified and rejected. This demands a dramatic personal and physical appearance.

Jesus promised under oath before the high priest at His trial: ". . . nevertheless I tell you, hereafter you shall see the Son of Man sitting at the right hand of Power [God], and coming on the clouds of heaven" (Matthew 26:64 NASB).

This statement was the official ground of His condemnation for blasphemy and the death sentence. Jesus dared to be the One who would fulfill two of the best-known prophecies concerning the Messiah's coming in glory to rule the earth. The first is from the Psalms, predicted before 1000 B.C.: "The LORD [God, the father] said unto my Lord [God, the Son], Sit thou at my right hand, until I make thine enemies thy footstool" (Psalm 110:1).

The second is from Daniel, predicted about 550 B.C.: "I saw in the night visions, and behold, one like the Son of man came with the clouds of heaven, and came to the Ancient of days, and they brought him near before him. And there was given him dominion, and glory, and a kingdom, that all people, nations, and languages should serve him: his dominion is an everlasting dominion, which shall not pass away, and his kingdom that which shall not be destroyed" (Daniel 7:13, 14 KJV).

No wonder the Jewish supreme court (the Sanhedrin) went into orbit. When Jesus made such a fantastic claim as that in one terse sentence, they either had to fall down and worship Him or kill Him. They chose the latter.

His Coming Will Be Sudden and Startling

Jesus predicted the suddenness of His return as follows: "For just as lightning comes from the east, and flashes even to the west, so shall the coming of the Son of Man be" (Matthew 24:27 NASB).

And again He said: ". . . and then the sign of the Son of Man will appear in the sky, and then all the tribes of the earth shall mourn, and they will see the Son of Man coming on the clouds of heaven with power and great glory" (Matthew 24:30 NASB).

Perhaps the "sign of the Son of Man" will be a gigantic celestial image of Jesus flashed upon the heavens for all to see. This would explain how all men suddenly recognize who He is and see the scars from His piercing at the cross.

His Coming Will Be With the Saints

It is significant to note that many references to Christ's return speak of His return accompanied with "the clouds of heaven." We believe that the clouds refer to the myriads of believers who return in white robes with Jesus. Believers are referred to as "a cloud of witnesses" in Hebrews 12:1. The clouds then would be all of the church age believers, you and I, returning in immortal glorified bodies, having been previously caught up to meet Christ in the air in "the ultimate trip," prior to the seven years of Tribulation on earth, and the resurrected saints of the Old Testament (Revelation 19:14).

The word "saint" means someone who is set apart as God's possession. It is used to designate all who have believed in Christ as Savior. This word is used many times to refer to those who will accompany Christ at His return.

As Zechariah referred to the Messiah's second coming he said: ". . . and the LORD my God, shall come, and all the saints with thee" (14:5 KJV).

The apostle John speaks of the apparel of the saints as they return with Christ: "And the armies which are in heaven, clothed in fine linen, white and clean, were following Him on white horses" (Revelation 19:14 NASB).

John explains the white linen robes: "And it was given to her [the church made up of all believers who have been caught up in the Rapture] to clothe herself in fine linen, bright and clean; for the fine linen is the righteous acts of the saints" (Revelation 19:8 NASB).

His Coming Will Be With Violent Judgment

When Jesus came the first time it was not to judge the world, but to save it. He came as the Lamb of God who gave His life to take away the sin of the world. The one thing that God has established for man to do is to believe in His Son as Savior. When Jesus returns the second time it will be as a lion to judge those who rejected the free gift of salvation from sin. Man will have completely demonstrated his worthiness of judgment.

According to Zechariah, "all nations will be gathered against Jerusalem to battle." The Jews who live in the area will be on the verge of annihilation when God gives them supernatural strength to fight. Then the Lord will go forth to fight for them and save them.

Jesus' feet will first touch the earth where they left the earth, on the Mount of Olives. The mountain will split in two with a great earthquake the instant that Jesus' foot touches it. The giant crevice which results will run east and west through the center of the mountain. It will go east to the north tip of the Dead Sea and west to the Mediterranean Sea (Zechariah 14).

It was reported to me that an oil company doing seismic studies of this area in quest of oil discovered a gigantic fault running east and west precisely through the center of the Mount of Olives. The fault is so severe that it could split at any time. It is awaiting "the foot."

Zechariah predicts a strange thing with regard to the ensuing split in the earth. The believing Jewish remnant in Jerusalem will rush into the crack instead of doing the natural thing of running from it. They will know this prophecy and realize that this great cavern has opened up for the Lord to protect them from the terrible devastation that He is about to pour out upon the godless armies all around. It will be used as a type of bomb shelter.

The nature of the forces which the Lord will unleash on that day against the armies gathered in the Middle East is described in Zechariah 14:12: "And this shall be the plague wherewith the LORD will smite all the people that have fought against Jerusalem; Their flesh shall consume away while they stand upon their feet, and their eyes shall consume away in their holes, and their tongue shall consume away in their mouth" (KJV).

A frightening picture, isn't it? Has it occurred to you that this is exactly what happens to those who are in a thermonuclear blast? It appears that this will be the case at the return of Christ.

His Return Will Be to Set Up God's Kingdom on Earth

After Christ destroys all ungodly kingdoms, Zechariah says, "The Lord shall be king over all the earth; in that day shall there be one Lord, and His name one."

Most ministers and religious leaders today reject even the possibility that Christ will establish an actual physical kingdom of God upon the earth.

Many who believe in a personal return of Christ reject that He will establish a thousand year kingdom of God and rule mortals from the throne of David out of Jerusalem after His return.

The Latin word for "1000" is "millennium" and down through history the teaching concerning this earthly kingdom came to be known as the "millennial kingdom." Those who reject that Christ will establish a 1000 year kingdom after His return are known theologically as "amillennialists," meaning "no millennium." Those who believe that Christ will return and set up a 1000 year kingdom are called "premillennialists," meaning Christ returns first, then establishes the kingdom on earth.

There used to be a group called "postmillennialists." They believed that the Christians would root out the evil in the world, abolish godless rulers, and convert the world through ever increasing evangelism until they brought about the Kingdom of God on earth through their own efforts. Then after 1000 years of the institutional church reigning on earth with peace, equality, and righteousness, Christ would return and time would end. These people rejected much of the Scripture as being literal and believed in the inherent goodness of man. World War I greatly disheartened this group and World War II virtually wiped out this viewpoint. No self-respecting scholar who looks at the world conditions and the accelerating decline of Christian influence today is a "postmillennialist."

We are "premillennialists" in viewpoint. The real issue between the amillennial and the premillennial viewpoints is whether prophecy should be interpreted literally or allegorically. As it has been demonstrated many times in this book, all prophecy about past events has been fulfilled literally, particularly the predictions regarding the first coming of Christ. The words of prophecy were demonstrated as being literal, that is, having the normal meaning understood by the people of the time in which it was written. The words were not intended to be explained away by men who cannot believe what is clearly predicted.

The opponents of the premillennial view all agree grudgingly that if you interpret prophecy literally it does teach that Christ will set up a literal kingdom in time which will last in history a thousand years and then go into an eternal form which will never be destroyed.

To us the biggest issue is over the question, "Does God keep His promises?" For God unconditionally promised Abraham's descendants a literal world-wide kingdom over which they would rule through their Messiah who would reign upon King David's throne. The Jews who believe in the

Messiah will also possess the land which is bordered on the east by the Euphrates River, and on the west by the Nile (Genesis 15:18-21).

It is promised that Jerusalem will be the spiritual center of the entire world and that all people of the earth will come annually to worship Jesus who will rule there (Zechariah 14:16-21; Isaiah 2:3; Micah 4:1-3). The Jewish believing remnant will be the spiritual leaders of the world and teach all nations the ways of the Lord (Zechariah 8:20-23; Isaiah 66:23).

Paradise Restored

God's kingdom will be characterized by peace and equity, and by universal spirituality and knowledge of the Lord. Even the animals and reptiles will lose their ferocity and no longer be carnivorous. All men will have plenty and be secure. There will be a chicken in every pot and no one will steal it! The Great Society which human rulers throughout the centuries have promised, but never produced, will at last be realized under Christ's rule. The meek and not the arrogant will inherit the earth (Isaiah 11).

Prelude to Eternity

As it was mentioned in Chapters eight and nine, Daniel predicted the four great world ruling kingdoms that man would set up during the time from the sixth century B.C. until the coming of the Messiah. We noted these four human empires as Babylon, Media-Persia, Greece, and Rome, with its revived form in the last days. The fifth world kingdom, which according to Daniel will conquer the revived form of the Roman Empire, is the Messianic kingdom (Daniel 7:13-27).

This kingdom will begin in time with mortal subjects (Revelation 20:4-6), last 1000 years, and at the end of that time some of the children of the believers who started in the kingdom will apparently prove to be unbelievers and start a rebellion against Christ and His rule. Christ will bring swift judgment upon them before the rebellion reaches the actual fighting stage (Revelation 20:7-10).

After this event there will be no more human history with mortal men. All unbelievers, it seems, will be judged in the crushing of the last rebellion which is led by God's old adversary, Satan. Satan will have been bound for a thousand years, but is released momentarily so that he could reveal the rebellion in the unbelieving hearts of those who rejected Christ as Savior

(Revelation 20:7, 8). All who remain as mortals will be changed into immortality at this point, and the Kingdom of God will not cease, but simply change form and be reestablished in a new heaven and a new earth (Revelation 21).

The sequence is clear in the last chapters of Revelation. First there is the return of Christ at the climax of the greatest war of all time. Second, Christ separates the surviving believers from the surviving unbelievers; the unbelievers will be judged and cast off the earth (Revelation 20:1-6; cf. Matthew 25:41-46). Third, Christ establishes the millennial kingdom and the surviving believers go into it as mortals and repopulate the earth (Revelation 20:11-15; cf. Matthew 25:31-40). Fourth, at the end of a thousand years the unbelieving children rebel, Christ judges them, then He completely changes the old heaven and earth and creates a new one (Revelation 21; Isaiah 65:17; II Peter 3:8-13). This is the ultimate destiny of all persons who are redeemed by Christ.

How many times have we wondered what heaven will be like? According to such passages as Revelation 21 and 22, heaven is a real and breathtaking place. We will not wander about as disembodied spirits, playing harps throughout an ethereal expanse. We shall live forever in the presence of God, fellow heirs with Christ, as kings and priests forever, with no more sorrows or tears. We shall know an ecstatic, endless joy surrounded by an earth and heaven of indescribable beauty. If you can think of the most beautiful place you have ever been, then amplify its beauty beyond your comprehension and imagine what it would be like without death, disease, or any curse upon it, you may have an inkling of heaven.

The word translated "new" in Revelation 21:1 means "new in kind or order" as distinguished from merely new in point of time. Peter describes the process the Lord will use in renovating the heaven and earth that now exist: "But the day of the Lord will come like a thief, in which the heavens will pass away with a roar and the elements will be destroyed with intense heat, and the earth and its works will be burned up. Since all these things are to be destroyed in this way, what sort of people ought you to be in holy conduct and godliness, looking for and hastening the coming of the day of God, on account of which the heavens will be destroyed by burning, and the elements will melt with intense heat. But according to His promise we are looking for new heavens and a new earth, in which righteousness [only] dwells" (II Peter 3:10-13 NASB).

The word translated "elements" is *stoicheiov*, which means the most basic element of nature. Today we know the atom is the smallest building block of nature. Now Peter says that these elements will be "destroyed." The literal meaning of the word "destroyed" is "to loose something." It was frequently used for untying a rope, or a bandage as in John 11:44. In other words, Christ is going "to loose" the atoms of the galaxy in which we live. No wonder there will be a great roar and intense heat and fire. Then Christ will put the atoms back together to form a new heaven and earth, in which only glorified persons without their sinful natures will live. There will be no more rebellion of man's will against God; only righteousness, peace, security, harmony, and joy.

That's where we want to be!

14 ∘ Polishing the Crystal Ball

Go your way, Daniel, for the meaning of the words of prophecy is shut up and sealed until the time of the end. Many shall travel about and knowledge shall increase. None of the wicked shall understand these words, but those who are wise shall in the last days understand.   GOD TO DANIEL ABOUT 520 B.C. (LITERAL TRANSLATION)

No OTHER PROPHET has ever had more numerous, far-reaching prophecies revealed to him than Daniel; and yet a great deal of what he received in God-given visions and revelations he didn't understand. Many of his predictions had to do with "the end times" or the events immediately preceding the coming of the Messiah-Jesus to set up God's kingdom.

At the close of Daniel's written account of his prophecies, he reveals his bewilderment about when and how all the things he had predicted would occur: "How long shall it be to the end of these wonders?" (Daniel 12:6 Amplified).

A special angelic messenger replied to Daniel and said, ". . . when the shattering of the power of the holy people [Israel] comes to an end all these things would be accomplished" (Daniel 12:7).

Daniel replied, "I heard, but I did not understand." Then he said, "O my lord, what shall be the issue and final end of these things?" (Daniel 12:8 Amplified).

The messenger replied, "Go your way, Daniel; for the words [of prophecy] are shut up and sealed till the time of the end" (Daniel 12:9 Amplified).

In other words, God revealed to Daniel that his prophecies would not be clearly understood *until* the end times, i.e., the times when the events predicted would begin to take shape. The key that would unlock the prophetic book would be the current events that would begin to fit into the predicted pattern.

Christians after the early second century spent little time really defining prophetic truth until the middle of the nineteenth century. Then there seems to have been a great revival of interest in the prophetic themes of the Bible. Today, Christians who have diligently studied prophecy, trusting the Spirit of God for illumination, have a greater insight into its meaning than ever before. The prophetic word definitely has been "unsealed" in our generation as God predicted it would be.

Now I am about to walk into the lion's den. Perhaps it would be wise to follow Churchill's tactic when he said, "You know I always avoid prophesying beforehand, it is much better policy to prophesy after the event has already taken place." However, in this chapter I will make a number of forecasts about the future which are based on a careful study of the prophetic truth and the writings of many scholars on the subject. I believe that these forecasts are based upon sound deductions; however, please don't get the idea that I think that I am infallibly right in the same way that a Biblical prophet speaking under the direct inspiration of God's Spirit was. I believe that God today gives us illumination to what has been written, but that He doesn't give us infallible revelation as He gave the authors of the Bible. Here, then, are the things that I believe will happen and develop in the near future.

The Religious Scene

In the institutional church, composed of professing Christians who are in many cases not Christian, look for many things to happen:

With increasing frequency the leadership of the denominations will be captured by those who completely reject the historic truths of the Bible and deny doctrines which according to Christ Himself are crucial to believe in order to be a Christian. In some of the largest Protestant denominations this has already taken place. The few remaining institutions which are not yet dominated by the disbelievers will go downhill in the same manner.

There will be unprecedented mergers of denominations into "religious conglomerates." This will occur for two reasons: first, most denominations were formed because of deep convictions about certain spiritual truths. As more of these truths are discarded as irrelevant because of unbelief in Biblical authority, there will be no reason to be divided. Unity is certainly important to have, but never, according to the teachings of Christ, at the expense of the crucial truths of Christianity.

Secondly, as ministers depart from the truths of the Bible they lose the authority and power that it has to meet real human needs, and as many ministers are not truly born spiritually themselves and are consequently without the illumination of God's Spirit, they no longer will be able to hold their present congregations, much less attract others. So they resort to "social action gimmicks," super-organization, and elaborate programs as a substitute.

As Paul predicted concerning these ministers in the last days: "holding to a form of godliness [literally religion], although they have denied its power...." And again he says, "... they are always learning and never able to come to the knowledge of the truth" (II Timothy 3:5, 7 NASB).

Young people will continue to accelerate their exodus from the institutional churches. Several surveys taken by church leaders indicate this. Youth today reject impersonal, highly structured organizations with their emphasis upon buildings and material affluence. In talking with many young people from various backgrounds I have found that the institutional churches are viewed by them as a reflection of all they despise in what they consider materialistic, hypocritical, and prejudiced elements within our American culture.

Above all, young people want a simple, personal, and relevant answer to life that isn't based upon self-centered materialism, but upon real life, selfless love. When they are shown that this idealistic view of life cannot be achieved by various shades of welfarism, socialism, or drugs, but only through a personal relationship with Christ that is not tied to joining an institutional church (or religious country club as they call it), then many respond and receive Jesus Christ.

Some traditional churches have learned to provide the personal ministry of God's truth to the youth and you will find their youth departments are flourishing. But they are the exception, unfortunately. Most churches seem to be on the wrong wave length altogether. Some have the truth, but can't communicate it to today's youth; others simply don't teach the truth, and though they try "underground church" approaches, they can't compete with the radical political organizations.

Many youth are going to be on the front edge of a movement toward first century-type Christianity, with an emphasis upon people and their needs rather than buildings and unwieldy programs.

There will be an ever-widening gap between the true believers in Christ and those who masquerade as "ministers of righteousness." I believe that open persecution will soon break out upon the "real Christians," and it will come from the powerful hierarchy of unbelieving leaders within the denominations. Christians who believe in the final authority of the Bible, salvation through the substitutionary atonement of Christ alone, the deity of Jesus Christ, etc., will be branded as prime hindrances to "the brotherhood" of all men and the "universal Fatherhood of God" teaching, which is so basic to the "ecumaniacs" who don't believe in the very heart of Jesus' teachings. Jesus taught that God is the Creator of all, but the Father of only those who believe in Him (John 8:44; Galatians 3:26).

Because of the persecution of believers, there will grow a true underground church of a believing remnant of people.

Look for vast and far-reaching movements toward a oneworld religious organization, spearheaded mostly by the unbelieving leaders of the institutional churches; also look for this movement to become more politically oriented than it is now.

Look for movements within Israel to make Jerusalem the religious center of the world and to rebuild their ancient Temple on its old site.

The Political Scene

Keep your eyes on the Middle East. If this is the time that we believe it is, this area will become a constant source of tension for all the world. The fear of another World War will be almost completely centered in the troubles of this area. It will become so severe that only Christ or the Antichrist can solve it. Of course the world will choose the Antichrist.

Israel will become fantastically wealthy and influential in the future. Keep your eyes upon the development of riches in the Dead Sea.

The United States will not hold its present position of leadership in the western world; financially, the future leader will be Western Europe. Internal political chaos caused by student rebellions and Communist subversion will begin to erode the economy of our nation. Lack of moral principle by citizens and leaders will so weaken law and order that a state of anarchy will finally result. The military capability of the United States, though it is at present the most powerful in the world, has already been neutralized because no one has the courage to use it decisively. When the economy collapses so will the military.

The only chance of slowing up this decline in America is a widespread spiritual awakening.

As the United States loses power, Western Europe will be forced to unite and become the standard-bearer of the western world. Look for the emergence of a "United States of Europe" composed of ten inner member nations. The Common Market is laying the groundwork for this political confederacy which will become the mightiest coalition on earth. It will stop the Communist take-over of the world and will for a short while control both Russia and Red China through the personal genius of the Antichrist who will become ruler of the European confederacy.

Look for the papacy to become even more involved in world politics, especially in proposals for bringing world peace and world-wide economic prosperity.

Look for a growing desire around the world for a man who can govern the entire world.

Look for some limited use of modern nuclear weapons somewhere in the world that will so terrify people of the horrors of war that when the Antichrist comes they will immediately respond to his ingenious proposal for bringing world peace and security from war. This limited use could occur between Russia and China, or upon the continental United States.

On the Sociological Scene

Look for the present sociological problems such as crime, riots, lack of employment, poverty, illiteracy, mental illness, illegitimacy, etc., to increase as the population explosion begins to multiply geometrically in the late '70's.

Look for the beginning of the widest spread famines in the history of the world.

Look for drug addiction to further permeate the U.S. and other free-world countries. Drug addicts will run for high political offices and win through support of the young adults.

Look for drugs and forms of religion to be merged together. There will be a great general increase of belief in extrasensory phenomena, which will not be related to the true God, but to Satan.

Astrology, witchcraft, and oriental religions will become predominant in the western world.

Where Do We Go From Here?

We believe that in spite of all these things God is going to raise up a believing remnant of true Christians and give one last great offer of the free gift of forgiveness and acceptance in Jesus Christ before snatching them out of the world as it plunges toward judgment.

After considering the incredible things in this book, what should our attitude and purpose be?

First, if you are not sure that you have personally accepted the gift of God's forgiveness which Jesus Christ purchased by bearing the judgment of a holy God that was due your sins, then you should do so right now wherever you are. It may be that you are bothered because you can't understand it all, or you feel that you don't have enough faith. Don't let either of these things stop you. The only thing you need to understand is that God offers you in Jesus Christ a full pardon and new spiritual life. If you truly desire to receive Jesus Christ into your life, then you have enough faith to enter God's family and change your eternal destiny.

Jesus put the whole thing in a very picturesque way when He said: "Behold, I stand at the door [of your heart] and knock; if any one hears My voice and opens the door, I will come in to him, and will dine [have fellowship] with him, and he with Me" (Revelation 3:20 NASB).

Right at this moment, in your own way, thank Jesus for dying for your sins and invite Him to come into your heart. The door of the above illustration is your desire and will. You open the door by inviting Jesus Christ into your life.

Did you do it? If you did, then where is Jesus Christ right now? According to His promise (and He can't lie), He is in your heart.

Jesus further promised, "I will never desert you, nor will I ever forsake you" (Hebrews 13:5 NASB).

He has come into your heart to stay and to bring new purpose, peace of mind, stability, in spite of circumstances, and true fulfillment to your personality as well as eternal life.

Secondly, if you have received Jesus Christ as Savior, then He wants to change your desires about life to God's desires, and empower you to live for God. God doesn't want us to try to clean up our own lives, but rather to be available to His Spirit who now lives personally within us.

As we trust Christ to deal with our temptations and to work in us His will, then He produces a real life righteousness in us which is characterized by an unselfish love for God and for others. The more we learn of God's love and unconditional acceptance of us, the more we want to please Him and the more we are able to trust Him to work in us. We also will desire to learn His Word which renews our minds to His viewpoint.

Ask Christ to teach you God's Word as you study it and He will.

Third, far from being pessimistic and dropping out of life, we should be rejoicing in the knowledge that Christ may return any moment for us. This should spur us on to share the good news of salvation in Christ with as many as possible. The Holy Spirit is working upon men in a dramatic way and He will lead you to people who are ready or who will be shortly if you trust Him.

Fourth, we should make it our aim to trust Christ to work in us a life of true righteousness. We all grow in this, so don't get discouraged or forget that God accepts us as we are. He wants our hearts to be constantly set toward pleasing Him and have faith to trust Him to help us. John said it this way: "See how great a love the Father has bestowed upon us, that we should be called children of God; and such we are. For this reason the world does not know us because it did not know Him. Beloved, now we are children of God, and it has not appeared as yet what we shall be. We know that, if He should appear, we shall be like Him, because we shall see Him just as He is. And every one who has this hope fixed on Him purifies himself, just as He is pure" (I John 3:1-3 NASB).

Fifth, we should plan our lives as though we will be here our full life expectancy, but live as though Christ may come today. We shouldn't drop out of school or worthwhile community activities, or stop working, or rush marriage, or any such thing unless Christ clearly leads us to do so. However, we should make the most of our time that is not taken up with the essentials.

Right after one of the major passages of the apostle Paul concerning the Rapture, he gave this promise: "Therefore, my beloved brethren, be steadfast, immovable, always abounding in the work of the Lord, knowing that your toil is not in vain in the Lord" (I Corinthians 15:58 NASB).

As we see the world becoming more chaotic, we can be "steadfast" and "immovable," because we know where it's going and where we are going. We know that Christ will protect us until His purpose is finished and then He will take us to be with Himself. We can "abound in His work" as we trust Him to work in us and know that it is not in vain because He will give us rewards to enjoy forever for every work of faith.

So let us seek to reach our family, our friends, and our acquaintances with the Gospel with all the strength that He gives us. The time is short.

In the early centuries, the Christians had a word for greeting and departing; it was the word, "maranatha," which means "the Lord is coming soon." We can think of no better way with which to say good-by—

MARANATHA!

NOTES

CHAPTER 1

1. *Time*, March 21, 1969.
2. *Family Weekly*, July 14, 1968.
3. *Los Angeles Times*, November 19, 1968.
4. *Time*, January 15, 1965.

CHAPTER 3

1. Douglas MacArthur, *Reminiscences* (McGraw-Hill: New York, 1964).

CHAPTER 4

1. *U.S. News and World Report*, Oct. 30, 1967.
2. William F. Albright, *From the Stone Age to Christianity* (Doubleday & Co.: Garden City, New York, 1946).
3. John Cumming D.D., *The Destiny of Nations* (Hurst & Blackette: London, 1864).
4. James Grant, *The End of Things* (Darton & Co.: London, 1866).
5. David L. Cooper, *When Gog's Armies Meet the Almighty in the Land of Israel* (Biblical Research Society: Los Angeles, 1940).
6. Arthur W. Kac, M.D., *The Rebirth of the State of Israel* (Marshall, Morgan and Scott: London, 1958).

CHAPTER 5

1. Walter Chamberlain, *The National Resources and Conversion of Israel*, (London, 1854).
2. John Cumming, M.D., *The Destiny of Nations* (Hurst & Blackette: London, 1864).
3. Chamberlain, op. cit.
4. Louis Bauman, *Russian Events in the Light of Bible Prophecy*, (The Balkiston Co.: Philadelphia, 1952).
5. Cumming, op. cit.
6. Wilhelm Gesenius, D.D., *Hebrew and English Lexicon*.

7. C. F. Keil, D.D. and F. Delitzsch, D.D., *Biblical Commentary on the Old Testament* (Eerdmans Publishing Co.: Grand Rapids, Michigan).

8. Gesenius, op. cit.

9. Cumming, op. cit.

10. Gesenius, op. cit.

11. Gesenius, op. cit.

12. W. S. McBirnie, *The Coming Decline and Fall of the Soviet Union* (Center for American Research and Education: Glendale, California).

13. Robert Young, LL.D., *Young's Analytical Concordance* (Eerdmans Publishing House: Grand Rapids, Michigan).

14. Gesenius, op. cit.

CHAPTER 6

1. *Current History*, "Nasser's Egypt," Gordon H. Torrey, May, 1965.

2. Ibid.

3. *U.S. News and World Report*, July 22, 1968.

4. *Santa Monica Evening Outlook*, December 3, 1968.

5. *Los Angeles Times*, July 9, 1969.

CHAPTER 7

1. J. A. Seiss, *The Apocalypse* (Zondervan Publishing House: Grand Rapids, Mich., 1962).

2. Cumming, op. cit.

3. Ibid.

4. Victor Petrov, *China: Emerging World Power*, (D. Van Nostrand Co., Inc.: Princeton, N.J., 1967).

5. W. Cleon Skousen, *The Naked Communist*, (The Ensign Publishing Co.: Salt Lake City, 1961).

6. *Quotations from Chairman Mao Tse-Tung*, "Problems of War and Strategy" (November 6, 1938), Selected Works, Vol. 11, P. 224. Quoted from a research pamphlet of the Center for American Research and Education, Glendale, Calif.

7. *Bulletin of Atomic Scientists*, "China's Nuclear Options," Michael Yahuda, February, 1969.

8. David Inglis, February, 1965.

9. Petrov, op. cit.

CHAPTER 8

1. Merrill F. Unger, *Introductory Guide to the Old Testament* (Zondervan Publishing House: Grand Rapids, Michigan, 1965).

2. Dr. E. J. Young, *The Prophecy of Daniel* (Eerdmans Publishing Co.: Grand Rapids, 1949).

3. Sir Robert Anderson, *Daniel in the Critic's Den* (New York, n.d.) .

4. *Look*, November 26, 1968.

5. *New York Times Magazine*, May 19, 1968.

6. *Nation's Business*, November, 1966.

7. "Trade and Atlantic Partnership," Dept. of State Publication 7386, Secretary of State Dean Rusk at the Conference on Trade Policy, Washington, D.C., 1962.

8. *Time*, July 4, 1969.

CHAPTER 9

1. William Barclay, *The Revelation of John* (Westminster Press: Philadelphia, 1960).

2. Ibid.

3. *U.S. News and World Report*, August 25, 1969 (source: F.B.I.).

4. *Los Angeles Times*, May 25, 1969.

5. *Columbus Dispatch*, August 21, 1969.

6. *U.S. News and World Report*, November 6, 1967.

7. *Natural History*, May, 1968.

8. *Los Angeles Times*, May 28, 1969.

CHAPTER 10

1. Henry H. Halley, *Halley's Bible Handbook* (Zondervan Publishing House: Grand Rapids, Michigan).

2. *Chimes*, October, 1968.

3. *Los Angeles Times*, May 18, 1969.

4. *Los Angeles Times*, May 25, 1969.

5. *U.S. News and World Report*, July 25, 1966.

CHAPTER 12

1. Bertrand Russell, *Has Man a Future?* (Simon & Schuster: New York, 1962).

2. *U.S. News and World Report*, December 25, 1967.

3. Douglas MacArthur, *Reminiscences* (McGraw-Hill: New York, 1964).

4. Harry Rimmer, *The Coming War and the Rise of Russia* (Eerdmans Publishing Co.: Grand Rapids, Michigan, 1940).

5. J. A. Seiss, *The Apocalypse* (Zondervan Publishing House: Grand Rapids, Michigan, 1962).

6. *Los Angeles Times*, August 20, 1969.

7. *Human Events*, August 26, 1967.

SATAN IS

ALIVE & WELL

ON

PLANET EARTH

O O O o o . o o O O O

In memory of Kent Carlson, the son of my dear friends, Carole and Ward Carlson. Kent, eighteen, was killed in a plane crash on the day this book was being completed. His life was a tribute to a godly home where he was taught the love of Christ, his fellow-man, and his country. Earth is poorer, but heaven is richer because of the entrance of this wonderful young man.

CONTENTS

INTRODUCTION

A FEW YEARS ago I came face to face with a complete reversal in the academic community. An unusual change came over many who had denied any belief in the power of a supernatural God. The indifferent, the scoffers, the proud agnostics in the Age of Rationalism, began to turn to another form of the supernatural. They became involved with psychic research, parapsychology, ESP, mystic philosophies, and Eastern religions. Recently there has been an upsurge in all forms of the occult!

Witchcraft and Satan worship spread throughout campuses and cities. In America, a so-called civilized country, people are involved in weird rites and rituals.

This book is an attempt to define a personal enemy who rules our world system. Whether we know it or not, he also influences every life to some degree. Until recent years his very existence has been doubted. Our churches have denied or underestimated him. But he is here—alive and well!

My wife Jan and I were having dinner with Carole and Ward Carlson, my co-author and her husband, when we first discussed *Satan Is Alive and Well*. A restaurant overlooking the Pacific didn't seem to be the right scene for the subject; the world and its problems were too remote. However, I felt compelled to warn them that anyone involved in this project would be a target for the central character.

We all discovered the reality of our adversary.

At times I thought I'd shelve the whole idea, but every time the progress on the manuscript was slowed down, I was shown another reason for the urgency of this message. I have never before come under such personal attack. It was not my imagination.

We are all part of an unseen conflict in the world and within ourselves. Yet we don't have to lead defeated lives, no matter what is thrown at us.

Consider what is said about this clever character, Satan. Anyone who has dominated history as he has cannot be ignored, especially in these days. To do so may be at the peril of your very life.

1 ∘ What's Happening?

"Millions of spiritual creatures walk the earth unseen, both when we wake, and when we sleep."
                                                        JOHN MILTON, *Paradise Lost*, A.D.1667

WHAT A CHANGE! I had shelved my usual life style of teaching among the youth culture of California for a few quiet days with my wife, Jan, and a group of professional people at a conference in Indiana. No pressures, an easy pace, a chance to recharge the batteries.

If I had known what was going to happen in that reserved atmosphere, I probably would have belted back to the refuge of the mad West.

We had two days of lectures which were calm enough. No past midnight rap sessions, no crisis calls at 2:00 A.M., no emergencies that couldn't wait while we ate dinner. We had unwound and were feeling great.

The last day we decided to have breakfast with some women who had come to the conference together. One of them had attracted our attention because every day she wore an unusual plaid skirt. All of the women were high fashion, but this one was a striking individualist.

The comments at the breakfast table drifted to prophecy, and the Scottish kilt gal dropped a bomb in the conversation when she said, "I've always been able to look into the future and foresee what is going to happen."

I gulped my coffee and snapped to attention. I began to question her.

"This isn't something new. . . . I've had a gift of psychic power all my life—inherited it from my mother and grandmother, I guess."

To this day I have a difficult time describing the change in the atmosphere. I looked at her more closely and realized that she was a woman with deep problems.

After we had discussed some of the results of this psychic ability, one of her friends said, "I know she has something unusual. She's told me things about my life she couldn't possibly have known by natural means."

The psychic woman added, without any attempt to boast, "I've always believed this power is from God."

Before I had really thought about it, I blurted out, "This is not of God. And if you don't reject this power, it will destroy you."

Everyone at the table was startled. I almost choked, but as soon as I had said it, I knew it was right. There had been a growing sense of uneasiness (that's an understatement—it was a sensation of the presence of evil) from the time the woman had mentioned her psychic ability.

Then I noticed she was wearing an unusual ring. I recognized the head of the ram with a woman's breasts, the symbol usually worn by Satan worshipers.

The group broke up quickly—whether out of embarrassment at my rudeness or as an excuse to go to the morning seminars, I don't know.

Our friend in the plaid skirt remained, however, obviously willing to hear me out. As a conversation opener, I asked her about the ring, and she said that she had been attracted to artifacts like this since childhood and possessed hundreds of dollars' worth of these things. She didn't seem to be aware of their Satanic significance.

It was a bright morning, yet I could feel an uncanny oppression around us. We talked about her life, and she began to confide that she was having some real personal heartaches. She told me her husband had left her recently; when I asked her if she knew why, she began to reveal some eerie things.

In recent years, she said, she had times of depression when she would like to sit alone in her darkened house. She said that "a spirit" began to come to her at night, trying to totally possess her being. A couple of times she went into convulsions. She began to drink heavily. Her life became restless and disoriented, and in the midst of all this her husband walked out.

As I talked with her, a sense of unexplainable fear kept gnawing at me. I wanted to run and forget this whole thing. It wasn't that the woman herself was evil; it was extrasensory, some sort of unnerving spiritual presence.

I knew, as I had from the beginning but didn't want to admit to myself, I was dealing with something that until this time had been only a doctrine from my seminary training. I knew what the Bible had to say about such manifestations, but I had never been called upon to deal with someone who was under the influence of an evil spirit.

What happened during the following hours was an amazing experience, and I'll tell you more about it later in the book. At this point, it is sufficient to say I witnessed a miracle! This woman was freed from an evil spirit. Not in Africa, not in the remote regions of the Amazon, but in the sunshine of an American college campus.

This incident awakened me to the widespread phenomenon of the occult. It alarmed me that the increase in astrology, extrasensory perception, witchcraft, black magic, fortunetelling and Satan worship, which you might expect among the youth of the West Coast, was evident in other places. The occult influence went deeper into American life than I had imagined.

American Jungles

The drug epidemic was the alarm sounded in the middle and late 1960s by law enforcement officials. Statistics mounted to fever level and realistic, compassionate men like Commander Bob Vernon of the Los Angeles police force watched the sickening results on young lives. The disease started largely in the West and quickly spread from coast to coast.

An interview with Commander Vernon in the early 1970s revealed a shifting scene, a new upsurge. This time the infection was bizarre. Some of the events he related were happening right at our doorstep.

As we sat in Commander Vernon's office, listening to the incredible stories he told us, we found our shockproof constitutions were beginning to shatter.

By the time this book is published these stories may have become so commonplace that most of us will have developed attitudes which are beyond the realm of being surprised by anything.

I would like to repeat parts of the interview verbatim, without comment. Add your own exclamation points.

"Do you see indications of witchcraft or Satanic cults in the Los Angeles area?"

"Yes, and they're increasing all the time. We've found evidence of animals, mostly dogs, who have been skinned and all the blood drained from them. We discovered through talking with some of the cult members that the blood is put into caldrons, mixed with LSD, and then used as a drink during their rites or ceremonies."

"What are some of the actual cases of Satan worship and these blood sacrifices?"

"Not too long ago a woman called us and said that she had seen a van pull up to the beach and some of the occupants take out a box and bury it in the sand. She thought they were trying to dispose of a baby. We arrived on the scene and found that the box contained the remains of an animal that had obviously been skinned.

"We have also encountered a case where a part of the ceremony required skinning a dog without killing it. It was a careful job and one of the most pitiful sights I've ever seen."

"Where are some of these cults located?"

"Many live in communes. Our Metro squad made a raid into a canyon near here where they had to let down ropes to get into the area and haul up the occupants. They were living in the most primitive way you can imagine—just a short distance from one of the most affluent neighborhoods in the country—indulging in acts of sexual deviation, pagan ceremonies, and rites which defy imagination."

"Is Satan worship tied into the drug scene?"

"It's a part of it. However, some of these procedures have little or no relationship to drug usage. Not too long ago there was a 'Kiss-In' on a Santa Monica beach. I walked into the area and was struck by the similarity between what I saw and what I knew of the rites of African savages. There were about four hundred people, so tightly packed together that they were just one big mass swaying to the throb of drums and weird music. Although it was early in the afternoon and we found little drug evidence, they soon became glassyeyed—transported, so to speak, into another world. Some of them began to peel off their clothes. Some began to indulge in open sex, oblivious to any around them. We noticed that most of them wore charms around their necks. They believe in the spirit world and will readily tell you that the Devil is very real to them."

"Are there leaders in these groups of Satanists or Devil-worshipers?"

"Usually. We had a strange one in the station not too long ago. He said his name was 'Om' and that he was God. He had a following who believed that the only way to worship was through sexual deviations, and they practiced all of them. 'Om' has a group of followers who are so perverted it's impossible to describe. We asked him how old he was and he replied, 'Before the world was, I am.' We pressed him for his age and he replied, 'Through the illusion of time the way you mortals view it, I am thirty-two.'"

"You've talked about animal blood sacrifices. Have you ever found evidences of human sacrifices?"

"A highway patrolman apprehended a man who was said to have killed another man and eaten his heart. When the officer searched him, he found knuckles of a human in the suspect's pocket. He was part of a Satanic cult,"

"Do you have an explanation for the trend toward witchcraft, Satanism, and some of these other bizarre cults?"

"For one thing, I know there is a spiritual hunger among people today. Many of them have gone to a church and haven't found the answer to that hunger. Someone comes along and offers them a feeling of belonging, a sense of being loved by a group, and they fall for it. There are other reasons, of course, but longing for acceptance and a place in the world is what I see as being a very important part of the insane direction many are taking into the supernatural."

Commander Vernon is a no-nonsense man. He reports it as he sees it.

The Satanic Age

Are we in a new age of Satan? Many people would be revolted by the so-called churches which openly worship Satan. The most widely publicized establishment of this kind is the First Church of Satan in San Francisco, headed by Anton LaVey, the High Priest.

The bald, narrow-eyed LaVey was quoted as saying, "The Satanic Age started in 1966. That's when God was proclaimed dead, the Sexual Freedom League came into prominence, and the hippies developed as a free sex culture."[1]

Satanic cults are expanding in every major city in the United States. "We have received reports from other California cities which show the existence of three Satanist groups in Berkeley, two of them communes, one in Big Sur, one in Venice, five in San Francisco, and one in San Diego. The number of Satanist circles gathering in Los Angeles County is indeterminate."[2]

Some of the churches of Satan are brazenly open, such as LaVey's establishment, an impressive three-story Victorian home, while others are camouflaged by storefronts or meeting halls.

In Europe Satanic masses are held in ruined churches and monasteries, but we should not be deceived by creaking castles or shadowy figures in musty rooms. Satanism is not just an old-world phenomenon.

Arthur Lyons says, "Satanism is not only present in Europe, but in the United States as well. In fact, the United States probably harbors the fastest-growing and most highly organized body of Satanists in the world."[3]

In the "churches" entangled in Satan worship the rites are opposite from those of a Christian church. Every desecration of Christianity is emphasized, from the upside-down cross to the flagrant use of sex and sexual stimuli. In Hollywood the altar was a glass tank filled with formaldehyde, containing the body of a dead baby. Lyons reported that the "high priest" had a hypnotic effect upon a teen-age girl. The ritual in which she became involved was so debasing he couldn't describe it.

We are reminded of the sordid spectacle of the girls who were mesmerized by Charles Manson. In a personal interview with a former Manson family member, I found they indulged in all types of Satanism and witchcraft. Manson was said to have had visions and magic powers. There were stories of his being physically transported from one end of the Spahn ranch to the other. Group sexual experience, an indulgence of some witch covens, was commonly practiced by the Manson cult. The twisted reversal of Christianity was evident. Manson was called "God," "Jesus," and "Satan" by his followers.

After Manson's conviction for the seven Tate-LaBianca murders, five members of his "family," girls with their heads shaved to prove their loyalty to their leader, led a trek through Hollywood on their knees "in witness to the second coming of Manson."[4]

Bubble, Boil, and Trouble

The steps which separate witchcraft and Satanism are almost invisible. Their histories, rites, and followers are intermingled. Statistics of witch covens given today would be out of date in a month. *Life* magazine reported in 1964, "It is difficult to estimate numbers as not all covens are known to one another, but the interest appears to be growing."[5]

Seven years later a Ph.D. from Harvard wrote, "It is undeniable that the rising addiction to mysticism has swelled to a veritable epidemic."[6]

In Switzerland an ex-priest and his mistress were charged with the murder of one of their followers. They said she had been sexually and physically possessed by the devil.[7]

In France 60,000 sorcerers are taking in $200,000,000 a year.

In Frankfurt, Germany, there are reportedly tens of thousands who believe in witches.[8]

The bishop of Exeter said that more Britons are turning toward black magic as their interest in traditional religion declines.[9]

The chairman of the psychology department at the University of the Pacific in Stockton, California, advertised for a woman who felt she was a witch or had unusual psychic powers to assist in a course on extrasensory perception.[10]

"The Golden State is the new holy land of Satanism, and its occult flood has divided itself into two main streams, two types of witches—the drugged and the drugless."[11]

One estimate says there are five hundred witches in Manhattan.[12]

Why Witch?

Louise Huebner, who claims to be Los Angeles County's official witch, describes the recent revival of the "Old Religion," as witchcraft is often called, and its attraction to young people in this way:

"You see, witchcraft is a participatory religion. This isn't a religion where you go somewhere and sit to listen to a sermon. We all get involved.

"This attracts the young person, because he or she is sick of the organized and recognized religions. They want to be active—to take part. Witchcraft offers them just such an opportunity.

"Witchcraft is actually a return to nature, a worship of the natural gods as opposed to the chrome and glass gods you find in society. We're more interested in finding powers within ourselves, in broadening our own minds."[13]

In Orange County, California, an area known for its family living, Knott's Berry Farm and Disneyland, an attractive witch housewife, Cassandra Salem (an assumed name), made another observation on witchcraft.

"Our whole religion is based on the lunar cycle, moon worship, and we really were the first ones interested in ecology, which you are hearing so much about right now.

"We're the ones who are pushing for a return to nature, and we may be on the right track. At least witchcraft seems to be growing faster right now than any other religion."[14]

Unhook My Nose

Many witches are seriously concerned about their image. They make it clear that there are, according to their views, good witches. Dr. Robert Ellwood, assistant professor of religion at the University of Southern California, recently offered a course on "New Religious and Philosophical Movements in Southern California." He said that a meeting he attended of eight or nine witches, magicians, and Satanists "took on aspects of a Protestant church meeting." In describing the witches he commented:

"They rejoice in being witches and being pointed out, but at the same time they expressed concern to one another about their bad 'image' because of publicity about the Manson family, a recent article in *Esquire* magazine, and the motion picture *Rosemary's Baby*."[15]

Merry England

The image concern among the witches extends to England, where spooky castles and eerie happenings have long been a rather romantic part of legend and life. Tourists are delighted if they can stay in a haunted house.

Modern English witches are different. For one thing, they insist that they have a vital and growing religion. According to one report, there are as many as 6,000 witches meeting regularly in small groups throughout England.[16]

The witches of England work at their religion seriously. They meet regularly and perform their rituals in a manner of worship, not of magic-making as many in America are doing. The witches' deities are a sun god and a moon goddess, and according to one "high priestess," who is a housewife and a manager of a home for the aged, "We witches are simple people with simple beliefs." She describes candidly the type of people in their covens.

"We are just ordinary people going about our own particular jobs. We are reasonably intelligent. We have doctors, teachers, businessmen, farmers, nurses, theatrical people, office workers, and housewives among us. Most of us have studied comparative religion. We do not try to convert others, but we do encourage people who have a leaning towards our craft. We do not take everybody who wants to come in."[17]

This would imply that witchcraft is a rather exclusive club of believers.

Brooms Are Out

When witchcraft is mentioned today in many circles, some people become defensive and say, "You really don't believe in witches, do you? That went out with the Salem trials."

It is true that any study of witchcraft revives scenes of a medieval inquisition where many innocent victims were self-righteously judged in the name of "Christianity" or "The Church." However, this is not the impression the witchcraft devotees want to give us. It must appear to be exciting, sophisticated, inviting, or perhaps just a little amusing.

No one is attracted by fangs and raspy cackles.

Trust Hollywood

I was introduced to a clever place in Hollywood by a calling card announcing the "Sorcerer's Shop." The shop was appealing in every way with an atmosphere of quality. A raven with the predictable name of "Lucifer" greeted me, while a large owl with the equally appropriate name of "Solomon" ogled me from his perch near the door.

The shopkeeper was about twenty-two years old; he told me he was a college graduate with a degree in political science. He was dignified, gracious, and serious.

Some of the usual accouterments of witchcraft were visible: the cauldron, the jars containing special herbs for spells, the various types of incense and candles. There were dozens of instruction books on witchcraft, potions, spells, astrology, tarot, and the occult. The host told me that some spirits had been there a few nights previously and that a sword had flown off the wall. He said that this was probably the work of a poltergeist (a spirit that causes solid objects to move from one place to another).

Covens on the Campus

Witchcraft has become so widespread that most high schools and colleges have their own special witches. They live in dorms, go to class, and on the side meet in their covens. A coven is a circle of witches and warlocks (male wizards or witches) numbering thirteen. The rites, rituals, and literature of witchcraft are ancient and established.

In the Bible Belt of the Midwest at a girls' college, conservative in outlook and rated high academically, the school newspaper which was issued at the beginning of the fall semester contained an editorial that told of a strange occurrence. Thievery was evidently a severe problem at the school library, because almost 2,000 books were missing after the inventory was taken at the end of the summer. The part of the editorial which caught my attention was the information that all of the books on witchcraft had been taken—completely removed from the shelves.

On the same campus I watched a televised talk show on the college station featuring a coed who said she was a witch. It was an impish interview, leaving the audience with the impression that this was not something we should take seriously.

The pretty coed said, "To be a witch I had to say the Lord's Prayer backwards three times while staring at a candle."

When asked about Christian beliefs, she became quite animated, but also defensive.

"I have nothing against Christianity," she said. "You're wrong if you think witchcraft is against Christianity. It isn't."

She continued to say that there was a "pyramid" that must be ascended in graduating steps before you could become a witch. That witch's pyramid involved faith, will, and imagination. However, she could not divulge how to become a witch.

The *New York Times*, in commenting on the campus scene, described a certain Catholic university where a coven of warlocks was discovered. The dean of the institution said, "We've really become progressive around here. A couple of hundred years ago we would have burned them at the stake. Twenty-five years ago I would have expelled them. Now we simply send them all to psychiatrists."[18]

Witchcraft and Sorcery Convention

I could have registered at the Witchcraft and Sorcery Convention and no one would have thought it was strange. It was held in the plush suites of one of the major Los Angeles hotels. The registrants were a cross section of respectable America with the intent smiles and programmed schedules of any convention. Most of them were promoting supernatural comic books or occult artifacts. The majority of speakers were members of the publishing industry specializing in weird tales. However, beneath the businesslike surface was an undercurrent which emerged after a few meetings. Then the big announcement was made: Nick Nocerino (not his real name) was going to speak; as a parapsychologist teaching in the occult, he was considered an expert in the field. He announced that he was a wizard ("Not a warlock, please. That is a perversion of my craft.") and proceeded to describe in a series of lectures some fascinating trade talk.

Nocerino differentiated between what he called "witchcraft" (of which he is a part) and "wickedcraft," which is what he termed a perversion of his art. He called witchcraft a religion and said that ten years ago he could not find five good books on the subject, but that today he knows of at least five hundred books on the market. He said witches are everywhere. There are ten million in the United States, and about two thousand in Los Angeles. However, he added secretively, "What is known publicly about the number of witches is just what has to be known."

He said that in the past few years he had seen an outpouring of "wickedcraft" in the national magazines, such as *Esquire* and *McCall's*, and "it scared me . . . and I've been around for a long time." He thought it was a crime that his craft was being perverted by bad publicity. He indicated there are witches in every part of the world, but they are more open in France, Germany, and England. In Italy, he said, witchcraft is practiced in conjunction with the church, but the church will not admit it.

"There is a move today," explained the famous wizard, "to bring witchcraft into the open as a religion."

"Many witches are very active in their churches," said Nocerino, "but no witch says, 'I'm a witch.' The stigma is too great."

Nocerino does not associate true witchcraft, as he called it, with Satanic cults. He explained that people are selected very carefully for a coven of witches and not just anyone who would like to be a witch or a wizard is accepted.

You Can't Be Serious

Many regard witchcraft with the same degree of amused tolerance they granted to goldfish swallowing, telephone booth cramming, and other fads. The news media is giving it an aura of gentle fun. If a self-proclaimed witch is blonde and shapely, this is good copy. A recent wire story in one of the West Coast's leading newspapers told about a beautiful witch who was raising funds to combat the effects of movies that portray witches in a bad light.

"We get such bad publicity from crummy movies. Black witches are the bad witches who practice voodoo, for one thing. White witches are your goodie two-shoes who read your palm for $2."

This lovely lady is a gray witch, she says, which is neither good nor bad.[19]

To get the message to the public there are record albums of "how to's" concerning witchcraft. One of them has a seductive advertisement featuring "The Gray Witch," who will tell you what you can gain today from practicing witchcraft.

"She introduces you to witches and warlocks who'll describe everything from the appearance of a demon to the everyday problems of witchcraft in a modern society. Barbara will tell you how to develop and practice your witchcraft ability even if you're only a mortal."

The Teen-Age Witch

Cheryl may have answered an ad on how to be a witch. Who knows? She didn't tell me that, but as we sat on the floor of the coffee house rapping about her experiences, she told me she was sixteen—well, almost sixteen. She was pretty, spoke softly, and had a sharp mind.

Cheryl had traveled the drug route since she was twelve or thirteen. She had uppers and downers, bad trips and good ones. Most of her associates were older, and as she watched them in the moments when her mind was clear, she decided that unless she split she'd fall apart. So Cheryl took another route. She became a witch.

At first she pretended it was just a prank. Someone bought her a crystal ball, and she spent hours staring into it and interpreting the visions she saw.

One day she told one of her friends in school that her friend's father was going to die. When he met with an accidental death two days later, Cheryl felt little sadness; she was high with power!

"It shook me at first," she said, "but I was fascinated by it. I had something no one else had! I had been doing a lot of reading about potions and chants, and I knew that I had this power over people. I could burn a hole right through someone by just looking at them."

A few years ago I might have listened to Cheryl and thought that she was a cute teen-ager with a lively imagination.

Not any more.

"Recent history has shown terrifyingly enough that the demonic lies barely beneath the surface, ready to catch men unawares with new and more horrible manifestations."[20]

Witches and Satanists, spirits and demons have surfaced in our generation. But underneath is the cauldron of cults, claiming for its victims the gullible and the young.

Who will be the victims? And the victorious?

2 ○ Perilous Tide From the Other Side

"There is a way which seems right to a man, but its end is the way of death."

Proverbs 14:12

A WASHINGTON NEWSPAPER reporter and a dead man have written a best seller about the "first inside, eyewitness account of the Hereafter."

Ruth Montgomery, one-time friend and confidant of Jeane Dixon, and Arthur Ford, deceased spiritualist and the medium the late Bishop Pike used to contact "the other side," are the co-authors of a book which is supposed to answer every major metaphysical and theological question that has plagued mankind since the beginning of time.

Ruth Montgomery sat at her typewriter in a trance and Ford transmitted through her fingertips the information about what is going on in the beyond. Evidently the world-famous personalities who have passed on are involved in the same interests they had on earth. Robert Kennedy is occupied with civil rights. J.F.K. is peacemaking in the Middle East. Churchill is arguing world politics with Franklin Roosevelt.

Arthur Ford says (through Montgomery's automatic writing) that in the spiritual realm everything is basically the same as on earth, except thought patterns replace physical form.

Ruth Montgomery explains why she believes she was chosen to write about the hereafter: "I guess Arthur and the others decided that because of my journalistic background, I'd be good to write it . . . and it's the Age of Aquarius, so the time was right for revelations about the unknown."[1]

Travels Back With A. Ford and J. Pike

In 1967 Arthur Ford, probably the best known medium of modern times, went into a public, televised trance on a program with Bishop James Pike. The Bishop's direct involvement with spiritualism was revealed to people across the country. Interest in the occult was given a new boost by Pike's testimony that he had communicated with his deceased son, Jim. Ford gave credence to Pike's revelations.

The publication of Pike's book, *The Other Side*, popularized spiritualism. Through seances, mediums, and other spiritualistic phenomena Pike claimed to have had many dealings with the spirit world. He believed that communication with the dead was possible and during his lifetime wrote and lectured extensively on this subject.

Now Pike is dead, too. His body was found in September of 1969 in the desert area surrounding the Dead Sea. I have no way of knowing what drew him into that bleak area where he met his death. A friend of mine who was in that vicinity a month after the mishap questioned some of the inhabitants, and they said no one in his right mind would have gone into that remote region without skilled and knowledgeable guides.

Ford is supposed to have seen Pike struggling for his life in the wilderness. He probably did, because Ford was not a fraud! If that statement surprises you, hold your fire until we have investigated the amazing evidence together.

Dr. Merrill Unger, a renowned archaeologist and theologian, writes, "This human spirit does possess mysterious powers, but the *greater* power of demonic spirits to delude humanity is the unrecognized peril surrounding parapsychologists and spiritualists."[2]

On the other hand, Hans Holzer, assistant professor of parapsychology at the New York Institute of Technology and the author of twenty-six books on psychic phenomena, says, "Psychic phenomena don't hurt anyone. In fact, they're good for you. They expand the mind, expand your sense of man's purpose."[3]

Chris Pike, the son of the late Bishop Pike, would not agree with Holzer. Pike, who speaks cautiously of his famous father, told me in a personal interview that while practicing yoga and meditation he became possessed by spirit beings who nearly destroyed his life. He has denounced that way of life and today is a witness to the transforming power of Jesus Christ. His own life has been completely changed, and I believe the world will soon hear from this brilliant young man.

Look Inward, Angel

Meditation is very big. The president of the National Center for the Exploration of Human Potential said, "Many young people today are engaged in an extensive search for the meanings and values of life. They are endeavoring to make peace, love, and tranquillity part of their daily lives.

They are rediscovering the spiritual dimensions of their being. There is a widespread interest in meditation, and the Transcendental Meditation Movement currently has 30,000 members on U.S. campuses."[4]

A study made over a period of three years of twenty-two communes in the United States shows that "widespread reports of psychic phenomena can be attributed to the altered states of consciousness induced by drugs in some cases and by yoga-type meditation in others."

These mental states, according to Dr. Stanley Krippner, tend to make a person become skeptical of God, doubt any concept of life after death, and discard many beliefs he may have had before he delved into meditation and psychic phenomena.[5]

It's in the Tarot Cards

The ancient art of reading tarot cards has been revived in our time. One expert on the subject says that tarot is derived from the pages of the oldest book in the world, originating in Egypt at a period when magic, astrology, and other mystic sciences flourished.

The object is to be able to read the cards as they fall in relation to one another, to solve a person's problems or read his future. An expert who has made a great study of this subject and has written several popular books on the art of reading tarot cards advises her readers to "Go deep within in meditation; find your own divine center, and you will understand by direct intuition that which the Tarot only hints at. . . . Prepare to pass through the beautiful gate of symbolism into the starry world beyond."[6]

The Tarot is supposed to have its own "divinatory powers and its own spiritual content." The reader, who interprets the cards, is particularly interested in your character analysis, your future, and solutions to immediate problems, much as the palmist or the fortuneteller. It is emphasized that "there are also those who will value the Tarot's help in meditation."[7]

Nichiren Shoshu

This Buddhist sect began a few years ago with most of the membership being in their teens and twenties. In the past few years older persons have been drawn into membership. A typical meeting is a cross section of Americans, all seated lotus-fashion, chanting the same words over and over again. One report said that in the United States there were 25,000 followers in 1965 and 200,000 in 1971.[8]

Willie Davis, an outfielder for the Los Angeles Dodgers, is involved in Nichiren Shoshu. He chants all the time. Davis said he does most of his chanting to a scroll at home with his family, but that he "might be chanting at all times during the day."

"It scares people when you say Buddhism," he said, "because right away they think it's some kind of witchcraft. It's a philosophy, a true philosophy."[9]

An owner of a grocery store in Manhattan chants at a Nichiren meeting because "Going makes me feel good, it's soothing, it calms me down. . . . Nichiren Shoshu is nice because you participate. Let's face it, the church has lost it. They lost most of my generation and I would say all of the next generation."[10]

Eastern religions, their chants and meditations, are flourishing in Western soil.

How Does a Guru Grow?

On a speaking tour in Texas I was invited to appear on a television show with Peter Max, the well-known pop artist. Max, whose psychedelia in the art media has influenced many of the art forms of the youth culture, told me how he was one of the first persons to bring gurus from the East to teach meditation, reincarnation, and transcendentalism.

Entertainers have been leaders in this movement, seeking the advice of "holy men" and even making pilgrimages to India to consult with their own special guru of the moment.

Along the sun-drenched shopping malls of our California cities is another sect from the Eastern religions called Hare Krishna. Mingled with the longhairs of their own generation, the shaved heads and long yellow robes of this group present sharp contrasts. The Krishna devotees approach anyone who hesitates in his walk and try to sell their magazine. They sing, dance, and chant, seemingly immune to any criticism or ridicule.

Los Angeles is fair game for touring gurus. A thirteen-year-old guru visiting from India sent out publicity releases stamped "Top Sacred," which described the youth as "empowered to impart the imperishable word of God to all sincere aspirants who seek for perfect tranquillity of mind through spiritual insight."[11]

It was reported that millions believe the "world's youngest guru" is the new son of God. He travels by jet as the "Lord from Heaven," bringing what he says are messages of hope and wisdom to troubled souls. Some of his devotees who come to worship him say they are saved in his presence.

McCandlish Phillips, of the *New York Times*, writes, "Demons of the East are coming into the United States now, bringing with them the religious teachings and the occult arts with which they have long deceived the people there."[12]

Religions of the East may seem alien to the life style of many Americans, but other cults are acceptable in the urge for self-improvement and fulfillment.

Scientology

Most cults have a strong founder-image. L. Ron Hubbard, the man who dreamed up Scientology, is practically worshiped as being an indestructible force. He is an authoritarian leader with a missionary zeal to spread the word of his discoveries. The literature of the cult declares that "In 1950 one man, one book touched off the spark that has become a star for all of Mankind."[13]

Not to be outdone in modesty, another Scientology publication states that Hubbard is author of the book *Dianetics, The Modern Science of Mental Health* which has done more than any other book to change the fate of Mankind.[14]

Scientology claims to be both a religion and a science. It has coined its own vocabulary, which is weird to the uninitiated. They have "dianetics" courses, "power processing," and steps to follow to achieve their goal to "Go Clear."

Scientology claims, "We are evolving Man to a higher state."[15]

Its membership and new centers are growing at an astonishing rate. The eager young man I spoke with at one of the centers said that Scientology has doubled every six months since 1966. When asked how he accounted for this amazing growth, he said simply, "It works."

A *Life* magazine writer traveled some of the steps recommended by the cult and arrived at some personal conclusions. He wrote, "Scientology is scary—because of its size and growth, and because of the potentially disastrous techniques it so casually makes use of."[16]

The young writer said, "I have Hubbard to thank for a true-life nightmare that gnawed at my family relationships and saddled me with a burden of guilt I've not yet been able to shed."[17]

Christian ? Spiritualism

Spiritualism has found a home in many churches. One spiritualism denomination called the Universal Church of the Master began in 1966 and now has 125 active churches. In the Los Angeles phone book there are eight congregations listed.[18]

Raphael Gasson, a former member of a spiritualism church and a medium, writes, "Many people are unaware of the challenge which spiritualism presents to the true Church of God, and they should be warned not to treat too lightly what is one of the diabolical delusions that Satan is using. Many have suffered greatly because they started investigating into this thing and have eventually been brought to distraction when they have attempted to free themselves from it."[19]

A friend of mine, a successful young banker, became involved in a spiritualist church which is well advertised—Rosicrucians. He recognized evil in the movement, but thought there was enough good in it to offset some of its more unsavory aspects.

This particular thought-line is called "Christian Metaphysics." As we sat in a brightly lit restaurant having an informal lunch, the young executive told me of some of the strange happenings in this movement. He spoke of auras surrounding the bodies of participants, of spirit-controlled men and women. For anyone who has once been deep into the occult, it's difficult, if not dangerous, for him to tell of his experiences. To relive the past involves unnecessary discomfort, and for this reason I stopped him from relating some of his experiences when he became definitely uneasy.

Passport for a Psychic Tour

On a recent trip to the Middle East I noticed an interesting sign of our times in a Pan American Airlines magazine. Pan Am is pushing a tour to explore the occult revival in Great Britain. The psychic scene is a fourteen-day package including a banquet given by the Spiritualist Association of Great Britain.

I'm sure it is not a coincidence that one of the highlights of the tour will be lectures by Ena Twigg, who was the go-between when Bishop Pike wished to talk with his departed son. Twigg is also said to have established contact between Mrs. Pike and the Bishop after he died in the desert.

The tour company promises personal astrological/numerological charts prepared for the participants.

Psyched Out in Russia

Some remarkable research has been done on the extensive use of psychic phenomena in Russia. These studies do not involve the ghoulishness or foolishness of witchcraft, but are careful works done by men of science. Some of these findings bear ominous warnings to the free world of the type of mind and thought manipulations which are being employed today in an anti-God society. It's interesting that the occult realm has been made scientifically respectable under the academic guise of "parapsychology."

In forces which are more scientific or refined than Satan worship or witch covens we find effects which could be more insidious. In a recent book, *Psychic Discoveries Behind the Iron Curtain*, the writer-researchers say: "In the early sixties, the Stalinist taboo against all things psychic vanished with a bang. Top-level physiologists, geologists, engineers, physicists, and biologists abruptly plunged into work on ESP. A freewheeling, little known psychic renaissance hit Russia. Bankrolled by their governments, not just Russians, but Bulgarians, Czechs, and Poles are pursuing clues to telepathy, prophecy, and psychokinesis, the ability to move matter with mind alone."[20]

This is the same Russia of sputnik—the Russia of the scientific man, where leaders since the Communist revolution have been wary of anything that could not be seen in the materialistic manner.

Russia's extensive interest in researching "inner space," just as the scientific community has sought to conquer outer space, has ominous undertones. For instance, the authors say: "Highly placed Soviet scientists take parapsychology seriously, not snickeringly.... It was hoped that suggestion at a distance could induce individuals, without their being aware of it, to adopt the officially desired political and social attitudes."[21]

Does that sound like brainwashing through telepathy? It was further described in this book that confidential reports have been seen that indicate the Soviets are attempting to train clairvoyants for spy purposes.

Is It All a Bad Joke?

Witchcraft, Satan worship, cults, occult, spiritualism, psychic phenomena—should we take any of these movements seriously? Is it just a passing trend? Will they ever touch our lives or influence our future?

I believe that man's search for truth and reality may take him into realms of mind expansion where serious harm may be done to his mental health and his ability to cope with real life situations. The *Journal of the American Medical Association* said, "The new occult craze—and that is just what it is— has given rise to all manner of flimflam and hocus-pocus with people's health. In this Age of Aquarius, quackery is thriving as a surprising number of people, young and old, are fleeing into superstition and unreality."[22]

All of these cults, ventures into spiritualism, fortunetelling, and psychic avenues, have a common danger: they open the mind to associate with the spiritual realm and to seek contact with the world beyond. The will is made available to any experience which is beyond the senses. Whether it is realized or not, the person exposed in this manner can be brought under the direct influence of powerful spiritual personalities who are dedicated to enslaving his life.

There are phenomena beyond the realm of the senses. They are beginning to be accepted in scientific circles, and we may scoff or laugh at our own peril. They are not related to the true God, but to the one whom Jesus Christ called "the god of this world."

I believe that people are being given superhuman powers from Satan in order that they may promote his work on earth. *We are only at the beginning of this explosion.* There will be inventions which will come from the spirit world and fantastic displays of miracles and wonders that the ancient Scriptures predicted would occur in the days just before this present civilization would end.

We should not be fooled by miracles worked through the extrasensory powers of Satan. This is a time when people need to know what is behind the eruptions that are disfiguring our world. More important, we need to know *who* is behind it all.

In the following pages I will take you back into the dawn of history to an account which is stranger than fiction; but without a knowledge of it you could never understand the mess in which the world finds itself.

Some of the propositions in the next few chapters may seem fairly heavy to you. On the other hand, the food for thought may taste unusual. Whatever your background, if you approach this subject boldly and openly, I believe you will find that the conclusions are justified.

3 ○ Birth of
the Black Prince

"How you have fallen from heaven, O star of the morning, son of the dawn!"
ISAIAH 14:12

"You were blameless in your ways from the day you were created, until unright-eousness was found in you."
EZEKIEL 28:15

IN 1966 A friend of mine submitted a manuscript to a well-known publisher. It was rejected with the explanation that the subject was a dead issue and no one believed in that sort of thing any more. The book was entitled *The Dark Prince,* and it presented a very real spiritual being who is sometimes called Satan.

Would anyone dare to say this is a dead issue today?

Recently a brilliant young Englishman named Os Guinness began searching through the vast libraries of London for literature on witchcraft, magic, and the occult. He found that most major works on history listed these subjects as phenomena which were almost extinct and had been dealt a deathblow by the Renaissance and modern science. However, beginning about 1967 he discovered a veritable explosion of literature and documentation on the subject.

I am convinced that the vast majority of people today, even those directly involved in ESP, astrology, the occult, and various forms of Eastern religions, do not realize with whom they are dealing.

How many believe they are making contact with a powerful, incredibly intelligent spiritual being who heads a vast, highly organized army of spiritual beings like himself? This host is dedicated to blinding men's minds to the gift of forgiveness and love which God offered through Jesus Christ and to destroying or neutralizing those who have already believed in Him.

Just how clever this spiritual being is (he is often called Satan) may be comprehended by the strategy he has used in modern history. Beginning in the Renaissance period and extending to the first two-thirds of the twentieth century, men progressively rejected phenomena which were beyond their senses. Many medieval superstitions related to demons and devils were exposed as foolish by scientific discoveries and education, as they should have been. However, from the seminaries of Germany in the 1800s came a group which called itself the "Higher Critical School." These liberal biblical scholars began to question the historicity of the Bible. Using subjective literary methods of analysis (not based on hard facts of history or archaeology), they dissected the books of Moses and attributed them to a host of different writers. Many of these critiques were made on the basis of different names for God being used in various sections of Moses' writings. On this tenuous basis, these men rejected all of the witness of history which attributed the first five books of the Bible to Moses and ignored the fact that all through the books themselves it is repeatedly stated that they are the writings of Moses.[1]

From Moses to Myth

From the books of Moses, the "Higher Critical School" went on to attack other crucial books of the Old and New Testaments. The effect was to render the entire Bible a mass of unhistorical myths and folklore of the Jewish people. Each of these biblical mythologists more or less denied the possibility of the supernatural. Some were less subtle and blatantly denied all supernatural manifestations.

This type of teaching began to spread, and young theologians from the rest of Europe and the United States who studied under the influence of these intellectuals returned to their seminaries and churches and began to introduce these new doctrines. By 1925, many of the major seminaries of America had taken this point of view. In the colleges and universities of the United States it became the vogue to cast out the Bible as unhistorical and unfit for honest academic consideration.

In universities today, Bible courses are often taught by men who are biased against a normal, historical approach and who usually show hostility toward acceptance of the miraculous. In some of the "Bible as Literature" courses that I have observed, the teachers were agnostics.

Over the past fourteen years hundreds of students have reported to me that they felt their faith was deliberately and relentlessly attacked or discredited in university religion and philosophy courses. Some actually received poor grades on papers which were well done simply because they expressed a Christian point of view which centered on believing the Bible as literally true.

What began in the "Higher Critical Schools" of Germany has brought about an almost universal rejection of the Bible as a historically reliable document in the colleges and universities of the world today.

The irony is this: the Bible was discredited and discarded because of a general rejection of the supernatural. However, beginning with the late 1960s a new trend began to grow with the acceptance of ESP and other forms of the supernatural. Unfortunately, the Bible has been left out of this acceptance.

Now we have some members of the academic community as well as our youth experimenting with ESP and the occult without any reliable criteria to understand the origin of the phenomena they may experience.

A professor at the prestigious Massachusetts Institute of Technology describes an experience he had in a seminar with some of the best students of that institution. He said the progression of topics ran from Asian philosophy to meditation, yoga, Zen, then to *I Ching* (a book presenting an ancient Chinese divination device which supposedly enables one to make decisions), the yang-yin macrobiotic diet, Maher Baba, astrology, astral bodies, auras, U.F.O.'s, tarot cards, parapsychology, witchcraft, and magic. He added that the students were not dallying with these subjects, but were involved in them.

"And they weren't plebeians," the professor said. "Intellectually they were aristocrats with the highest average math scores in the land, Ivy League verbal scores, and two to three years of saturation in M.I.T. science."[2]

I do not believe this trend of history has happened by chance. Satan does not want a world that rejects the supernatural; he wants a world that is "religious" and accepts supernaturalism because it sets the stage for him to be worshiped in the person of a coming world leader known as the Antichrist.[3] The first step was to discredit the Bible so that Satan's true nature and plan would not be discovered. Satan wants a religious world, but one which rejects God's offer of a personal relationship with Him through Jesus Christ.

If you are having trouble accepting some of these assertions, if you are saying, "How can any educated person really believe in a personal Devil?" I dare you to read on with an open mind and ask God to reveal what is true. There is historical evidence of the reality of this being, and the evidence is increasing.

I realize that in man's long attempt to explain the continual existence of evil in the world, many myths and superstitions have sprung up. But the account that we are investigating here is found in the record of the ancient Hebrew Scriptures. I believe that this account has proved to be the most consistent explanation of the rebellious nature of man and society.

To understand what is happening today and in the near future, we must reach back into these ancient documents and look into events that occurred before man came into existence. The account of how an exalted supernatu-

ral being of incredible beauty, power, and intelligence named Lucifer came
to be Satan is stranger than fiction. The Bible chronicles the origin of Satan
with the same factual precision as any other historical event it covers. The
key to understanding man's purpose and destiny is related to the pre-history
conflict that began with Lucifer's revolt against God.

Curtain up on Pre-history

Ancient history can be pretty dull. I'm sure some of you may have dozed
through classroom lectures on the subject. However, God's ancient history
is something else. It's exciting because it has meaning to every one of us; it
hits us where we are today.

Let's examine the Book of Job, for instance, which was written about four
thousand years ago. Job was a fellow who had a few problems. As things
started to pile up, he began to do what a lot of us do—he began to question
God's judgment.

God asked Job some pointed questions designed to show him that he
didn't have enough wisdom to sit in judgment upon God. Consequently,
God revealed some fantastic information about the creation of this planet
and all its surrounding galaxy.

"Where were you when I laid the foundation of the earth!
Tell Me, if you have understanding,
Who set its measurements, since you know?
Or who stretched the line on it?
On what were its bases sunk,
Or who laid its cornerstone,
When the morning stars sang together,
And all the sons of God shouted for joy?" (Job 38:4-7)

Here we are introduced to some interesting descriptions: "morning stars"
and "sons of God." A careful study of these titles reveals that in the Old
Testament they are used only in regard to angels. Angels are higher than
man; they have greater intelligence and more power than man. They have
a personal audience with God.

Now when God created the universe, these spirit beings, these spirit personalities "shouted for joy" at the demonstration of God's tremendous
power. What a great picture!

They weren't fighting or arguing about their positions in God's kingdom.
This passage says clearly that they *all* shouted for joy, indicating complete
harmony among the angels. Obviously no rebellion had taken place at this time.

Lucifer the Perfect

The highest and most exalted position of this spirit realm was held by Lucifer, a creature who was perfect in all of his ways from the day he was created. The way we are introduced to him is important in itself.

In Ezekiel 28:1-2 a ruler is introduced as the *prince* of Tyre. He is described as a man who became so vain about all of his riches and intelligence that he claimed to be God. In Ezekiel 28:12 we are introduced to someone who, according to the description, is a different person. He is called the *king* of Tyre. The king of Tyre is the real power behind the prince of Tyre.

Again the word of the Lord came to me saying, "Son of man, take up a lamentation over the king of Tyre, and say to him, 'Thus says the Lord God, "You had the seal of perfection, full of wisdom and perfect in beauty. You were in Eden, the garden of God; every precious stone was your covering: The ruby, the topaz, and the diamond; the beryl, the onyx, and the jasper; the lapis lazuli, the turquoise, and the emerald; and the gold, the workmanship of your settings and sockets, was in you. On the day that you were created they were prepared. You were the anointed cherub who covers; and I placed you there. You were on the holy mountain of God; you walked in the midst of the stones of fire. You were blameless in your ways from the day you were created, until unrighteousness was found in you"'" (Ezekiel 28:11-15).

God truly mourned over this person; he is described as "having had the seal of perfection," which in the original Hebrew means a pattern of perfection. He is even described as having been "full of wisdom and perfect in beauty," the most beautiful and wise of all God's creation!

We will be able to understand how perfect is perfect (which is in no way a relative term when God is describing Lucifer) by some of the descriptions applied to him. He is called "the anointed cherub who covers." A cherub is an angelic being of high rank, associated with God's holy presence and His glory. Cherubs are celestial beings who proclaim the righteousness of God.

He is called "the anointed" one, which indicates supreme favor from God. "Anointed" is the same word that is used of the Messiah, God's anointed king. This person was the ruler and leader of the angelic beings and apparently led them in their praise of God and shouts of joy. The Hebrew word translated "who covers" in Ezekiel 28:14 and 16 literally means "who leads."

All the fabulous jewels were given to him, further indicating his exalted rank. He had been in "Eden, the garden of God" and "on the holy mountain of God." He had walked "in the midst of the stones of fire," which is a symbol often used of God's holy presence. Such a description could not be applied to a mere human.

This passage is speaking of the greatest being God ever created, one who had unequaled strength, wisdom, beauty, privilege, and authority. This is the one who according to Isaiah was named "Lucifer" and "the Son of the Morning." His name literally means "the shining one" and is a word for great beauty.

The crisis point of the universe is described in Ezekiel 28:15 where it says, "You were *blameless* (literally perfect) in your ways from the day you were created. . . ."

Could this have been an ordinary man? No. First of all, man is not created; (since Adam) he is born. Second, no man is born perfect. The blameless, perfect Lucifer was created without any form of evil, which is something which could not have applied to any *man* after Adam.

What happened to Lucifer?

The Big "Until"

Lucifer was perfect in his ways *until* "unrighteousness was found in him." This marked the fall of Lucifer and the birth of Satan. What this unrighteousness or evil was is described more fully in Isaiah 14:12-14.

It is important to note that God addresses Satan through the person of the prince of Tyre. Satan is the unseen source of this prince's arrogance and self-deification. Scofield describes other instances of indirectly addressing Satan through a man or another creature: when God addressed the serpent in the garden in Genesis 3:14; when Jesus spoke to Satan through Peter in Matthew 16:23. "The vision is not of Satan in his own person, but of Satan fulfilling himself in and through an earthly king who arrogates to himself divine honors" (*Scofield Reference Bible*, page 871).

Five "I Wills"

In Ezekiel we have the key to the origin of evil. In Isaiah 14:12-14 there is a description of the same supernatural being who introduced all the suffering into the universe. When this passage was written in the original Hebrew, it was a song of sorrow. God was mourning over this creature whom He had created and loved.

How art thou fallen from heaven, O Lucifer, son of the morning! how art thou cut down to the ground, which didst weaken the nations! For thou hast said in thine heart, I will ascend into heaven, I will exalt my throne above the stars of God: I will sit also upon the mount of the congregation, in the sides of the north: I will ascend above the heights of the clouds; I will be like the Most High (Isaiah 14:12-14, KJV).

He was described first as Lucifer, the "shining one." He was so beautiful he literally shone, and he was no stranger to holiness because apparently he was created with the very glory of God. However, when the verse in Isaiah begins "For thou hast said in thine heart," this is the real description of evil. This is where sin originates—in the heart. Five times he said in his heart, "I will!"

Lucifer filled his heart with the violence of rebellion; he wanted to act independently of God. He was saying to God, "After all, since *I* am so magnificent, so beautiful, so filled with power, why shouldn't *I* have some of the worship of the universe for myself?"

He said, "I will ascend to heaven." In other words, "Move over, God, I'm going to be in charge here." He said, "I will make myself like the Most High." He wanted to be God!

God Doesn't Manufacture Robots

When God created the angelic realm (and apparently Lucifer was the leader of all the angels), He took a calculated risk. He created Lucifer with the greatest intelligence of any created being, endowing him and the other angelic beings with self-determination. God did not want robots. He wanted creatures who could respond to His love and have spontaneous fellowship with Him.

God believed it was worth the risk to create these beings with the ability to act independently of His will and have the choice of rejecting or obeying Him. Lucifer, realizing how beautiful he was, inflated with power and pride, rebelled against God. He broke his relationship with God when he said, "I will be like the Most High."

Apparently a great rebellion erupted throughout the universe at that time. Lucifer led a revolution among the angels. We are told in Revelation 12 that one-third of the angelic realm followed Lucifer in this revolt. After Lucifer rebelled and became the first sinful creature, he lost none of his great intellect, beauty, or power. He used this to entice many angels to join his ranks. However, he lost the one trait which would make him function correctly, and that was a personal relationship with God.

When the perfect Lucifer, the one who had authority over all of God's creation and walked in unity with God, became inflated with pride and fell from his high position, God's perfect universe became impure. Pollution entered in such a rush that God brought the greatest polluter of all time to trial and pronounced judgment upon him and all those angels who had revolted with him.

Satan Was Born!

Evidently when God judged the crimes of Lucifer, He changed his name to Satan, the Devil, the Evil One. "Satan" means "the resister or adversary"; the name "Devil" means "the accuser and slanderer."

Satan was sentenced to eternal banishment. In Matthew 25:41 Jesus says that hell was created for the Devil and his angels.

After God pronounced Satan's judgment, His first act was to clear off one of the planets of the universe, beautify it, and call it "earth." This little planet was to become the arena of the mightiest contest of all time: a contest where God Himself would be wounded in a life-and-death struggle with the powers of darkness. God had a plan, a method to resolve this pre-history rebellion led by Satan, which involved the creation of another creature with whom all of you are familiar.

I realize that this account may appear to some as wild conjecture based on only a few verses, but I have projected the light shed by the rest of the Bible into an area where little is actually disclosed. However, as you read on you will see that it is consistent with all that is revealed of God's working in human history.

4 ○ "D" Day Earth

*"In the beginning God created the heavens and the earth. And the earth was formless
and void, and darkness was over the surface of the deep; and the Spirit of God was
moving over the surface of the waters. . . . And God created man in His own image,
in the image of God He created him; male and female He created them."*

GENESIS 1:1-2, 27

WHEN GOD MADE Planet Earth, He established a giant, complex
research and development center where a strange creature called "man" was
going to be tested. However, before man was created, God restored the earth
from the chaotic mess caused by Satan's rebellion and brought forth life in
the form of animals, fish, and fowl to inhabit that earth.

God could have left the earth as a gigantic perpetual zoo, but instead He
did something about which many have mixed emotions—He gave us our first
parents.

Why would God do a thing like that? Why did God create man? These
are the most basic questions of all time: Why is man? Why does he exist? Why
are we here?

Footnote in the Sands of Time

I don't want to inject heavy theology here, but instead will attempt to
answer some speculations concerning the universe of eternity past.

Some believe that God created the world in six stages, at six intervals
separated by long expanses of time. This is called the age-day theory. Others
believe that God spaced different stages of evolution which developed into
the world of today.

Another belief centers upon the concept that Genesis 1 and 2 describe an
original and recent (in relationship to eternity) creation of the world.

I believe that chapters 1 and 2 do not explain the original creation of Planet
Earth and the universe, but assume their prior existence. If we consider this
view, then these two chapters describe a *reconstruction* of the earth and its
galaxy by God in six literal solar days.

The chronology of Job 38:4-7 indicates that God created the material universe before the angelic revolt and consequently before man's appearance
on the planet. In Job 38:4 the context begins, "Where were you when I laid
the foundation of the earth?" and continues to speak of the great acts of cre-

ation. Then in verse 7 God says, "When the morning stars sang together, and all the sons of God shouted for joy?" As mentioned in chapter 3, this refers to angels. The passage also indicates that *all* the angelic beings were in harmony as they shouted for joy at this demonstration of God's great power. Two vital things are involved here: the earth was created *after* the angels were and yet *before* the angelic rebellion. I believe, after carefully piecing together the few rays of light from the Scripture about things prior to Genesis 1, that the earth was somehow devastated when God rounded up Satan and his cohorts and brought them to judgment.

The only original acts of creation in Genesis 1 and 2 are described by the Hebrew word "bara," which is used in the sense of bringing something into existence out of nothing. It is used in Genesis 1:1, where it refers to the original act of creation in the undisclosed past; again in Genesis 1:21, where the creation of all subhuman creatures is described; and in Genesis 1:27, where the creation of the life and personality of man is described.

Other words which are used in connection with creation do not necessarily imply any original acts, but rather *restoration* of a galaxy which is described in Genesis 1:2 as being in a state of chaos. This chaotic condition is the literal meaning of the Hebrew words "tohu-wa-bohu," translated "without form and void." This expression doesn't just mean "undeveloped," but rather something that is the result of a catastrophe.

This is sometimes called the "gap" theory, so named because of the expanse of time which elapsed between Genesis 1:1 and Genesis 1:2.

Barnhouse describes the time between the original creation of the earth and its restoration from chaos as "The Great Interval." One of the most cogent statements he makes to substantiate this view is, "If a perfect God should create a very imperfect world, chaotic, waste and desolate, a wreck and a ruin, it would be a violation of one of the great spiritual principles stated by the Holy Spirit Himself: 'A fountain cannot send forth sweet water and bitter (James 3:11)'"[1]

After the subsequent formation or reconstruction of the same earth which had been turned into chaos, God *created* man, and he has the center stage now.

Footprints in the Sands

In eternity past there was only one will, the will of God. There was no evil whatsoever, only harmony, holiness, and righteousness. When the second will entered the universe, generated by the heart of Lucifer, rebellion broke out. Time, as we know it, began with two wills in existence.

One great Bible scholar says that the shortest definition of sin is simply, "I will."[2]

When Satan was born and stated his proud "I will's," God didn't hesitate; God ousted Satan from his position of authority in His government.

The declaration of war had been made, but God was not taken by surprise. He had His plan ready to be launched with Operation Man.

Doubtless God had many reasons for creating man which we cannot fathom, but I believe the following are primary. God wanted to prove His perfect love and to show the angelic beings who chose to stay with Him that He had been neither unjust nor unloving to Satan and his followers by sentencing them to eternal banishment. God demonstrated this love to the fullest at Golgotha.

Perhaps another reason was to show the complete folly of choosing to reject God's will. And finally, God wanted to elevate man above the angelic realm and to fellowship with Him.

In the Book of Hebrews God shows that man will rule the world to come; angels will actually be under man's rule: "For He did not subject to angels the world to come, concerning which we are speaking. But one has testified somewhere, saying, 'What is man that Thou rememberest him? Or the son of man, that Thou art concerned about him? Thou hast made him for a little while lower than the angels; Thou hast crowned him with glory and honor, and hast appointed him over the works of Thy hands; Thou hast put all things in subjection under his feet' " (Hebrews 2:5-8).

The Apostle Paul says the same thing in 1 Corinthians 6:3: "Do you not know that we shall judge angels? How much more, matters of this life?"

But man is not just a pawn for a divine demonstration. He has destiny himself. God has great love and concern for each person and total forgiveness for the man who places his faith in the reconciliation God offers.

God's Crown of Creation

Out of the millions of galaxies of the universe God chose one galaxy for His great creative efforts. He set apart one of the planets to be the stage of testing, a complex experimentation center, more comprehensive than any progressive corporation board of directors could imagine.

God chose to construct the world in six days. (Although I believe He could have created it in a split second if He had chosen.) On the sixth day we read of God's greatest creation—man.

"Then God said, 'Let us make man in our image, according to our likeness; and let them rule over the fish of the sea and over the birds of the sky, and over the cattle and over all the earth, and over every creeping thing that creeps on the earth.' So God created man in His own image, in the image of God He created him; male and female He created them" (Genesis 1:26-27).

The important part is that man's immaterial being was created in the very image of God. God doesn't have arms or legs or a body in His essential being; the image of God in man is the possession of will, intellect, emotion, moral reason, and everlasting existence. All of this is part of what the Bible calls the soul of man.

Angels also possess these qualities, with a few superior additives which set them apart from humans: angels have greater mobility and intelligence than man. However, men and angels have a vitally important quality in common—they both possess freedom of choice and the intellect to make choices.

No Place to Hide

Once man had been created, he was watched by both the angels of God and the fallen angels. Fantastic thought, isn't it? We believe that we can take ourselves to a remote Pacific Island or an isolated mountain retreat and get away from everybody and everything. However, we still are being watched by angels. We know this from many passages in the Bible.

In Luke 2:8-14 the angels visited the shepherds and told them of the birth of the Savior. In Ephesians 3 it says that God is teaching "rulers and the authorities in the heavenly places" (terms used only about angels, describing their rank and order) many things about Himself through man.

If man is the object of a great deal of study on the part of angels, we must ask "why?" What are they observing? What are they learning? I believe that God is demonstrating to angels that He was perfectly just in His eternal judgment of them and that His love is so great it cannot be fathomed by any created being.

Paradise Found

Man's immaterial being will always exist; it will always live. In that sense, man is also in the image of God. At the time of his creation man was given legal authority to rule himself and all of the earth. The responsibility is spelled out clearly in Genesis 1:28: "And God blessed them; and God said to them, 'Be fruitful and multiply, and fill the earth, and subdue it; and rule over the fish of the sea and over the birds of the sky, and over every living thing that moves on the earth.'"

That is an important fact to remember: when God gave man that legal right, he was put into a garden where he was provided with every conceivable need that he might have. We may allow our human imaginations to take over here, visualizing what a perfect environment would have been. There would have been no need for Earth Day advocates, Federal Water Quality boards, or Air Pollution Control departments in the Garden of Eden.

When God created man, He saw that he was going to need a companion with whom to share Paradise, so He created the loveliest creature in the form of a woman. Eve must have been the most gorgeous female ever to exist. Too often today we think of ancient man looking quite inferior to modern man. However, the very reverse was true. Adam and Eve were the most beautiful specimens of Homo sapiens ever to walk this planet, according to the Bible. They were the direct creation of God. The idea is often embraced by man that if he had the most beautiful woman as a mate, all problems would fade away; the woman thinks if she had the perfect, handsome man her problems would be solved. Others think, *If only we had a secure society with a perfect ecological balance of nature and all material needs provided, we would have no problems.* Adam and Eve had all this plus personal fellowship with God, but they threw it away.

Rebel With a Cause

What a drama in Genesis 3! No clever playwright with all the skills of manipulating characters and providing psychological tricks of suspense could dream up a better plot than the one that happened in the Garden of Eden.

On stage we see Adam and Eve, living in fellowship with God, seeing the evidence of God's love on every side. However, there was one prohibition: man was not to eat the fruit of a certain tree in that garden. The tree was called "the tree of the knowledge of good and evil." (The Hebrew word for knowledge means "experiential knowledge.") We do not know the kind of fruit the tree had on it, but it was to provide the test which would determine whether man wanted to stay in perfect fellowship with God or not. The test would set the stage for God to demonstrate His justice and His love to the angelic realm.

Man was told that if he ate from this tree, he would die. The evil was not in the tree—it was not sprayed with some lethal insecticide which would poison the fruit. The evil was in rejecting God's revealed will and consequently rejecting fellowship with God.

The stage was set, and Satan was allowed to enter the scene. He was off-stage in the wings all the time, waiting for his entrance cue, plotting how he could make man rebel against God just as he had done. He apparently thought that the whole onstage contest revolved around this act, the act of making man fall.

Satan may be extremely wise, but he is battling against a far wiser being. For when Satan made man fall, he played right into the hand of God. Far from defeating God, he set a trap for himself. He set up a situation through which God could demonstrate His justice and His love to the infinite degree.

God did not want man to fall, but He wasn't surprised when he did. And He had a plan—a plan to save man from his own rebellious state.

How Did Satan Make Man Fall?

Genesis 3 is probably one of the most important chapters in the Bible. We must understand it to grasp anything of history. In Genesis 3:1 it says: "Now the serpent was more subtle than any beast of the field which the LORD God had made." (KJV)

This does not mean "subtle" in the sense of being clever, although we know he is that. In this case subtle means graceful and lovely. We tend to think of a serpent as a slimy thing which wiggles around on its belly, but that wasn't what the serpent looked like then. The word "serpent" in the original Hebrew means something shining and beautiful. It is similar in meaning to "Lucifer."

Apparently at that time the serpent walked around on legs, as indicated by the description "beast of the field." It was shrewd, an extremely wise and cunning member of the animal kingdom. As Satan began to work his wiles, it was obvious he had done his homework thoroughly. He studied man and woman to see how he could make them rebel against God; he analyzed the situation and saw that the more susceptible of the two might be the woman. Satan also saw that if he could get Eve to rebel, Adam would probably follow after her rather than follow God.

Satan was a master of timing in this first encounter in the garden. He waited until the perfect moment to fire his temptation at Eve. He knew that if the temptation didn't work, it would be twice as hard to fool her the second time. Also, he didn't come directly to tempt Eve, but he used a beautiful creature.

Where was Eve when all of this took place? It is obvious from the context of the chapter that she was by the tree of the knowledge of good and evil. She was already curious about it, a trait which has meant trouble for many!

Poor Eve didn't sense that powerful and evil dignitaries were breathlessly watching as she eyed the forbidden tree. She was just standing there, probably thinking, *I wonder why God doesn't want us to eat from this tree.*

Satan had already put into her mind the suggestion to look at the tree. This is how he works upon man—planting an idea here, an innuendo there.

Satan, the super-intelligent being, invented one of the cleverest attacks of all time. He invented the power of suggestion, the ability to put thoughts into our minds about things we already desire. He knows our natural weaknesses; he knows the areas where desire is strongest in us. He knew Eve and her basic curiosity, and he hit her at just the right time. We see how adroit and fiendishly clever this foe is when we understand that the original Hebrew in which Genesis 3:1 was written gives just the right inflection to the serpent's words. Try asking this question out loud and see how it sounds:

"Indeed, has God *really* said, 'You shall not eat from *every* tree of the garden?'" (Literal translation.) Wow! Satan can really get it together when he wants to tempt! He doesn't come to a person with a dogmatic statement, "God's word isn't true." Rather, he will ask a question carefully designed to start the doubt gnawing at our minds. Notice how he said to Eve, "You shall not eat from *every* tree of the garden." How many trees could she use to satisfy her hunger, her desire, and her needs? Every tree but one, we are told. So what was Satan focusing upon? The one limitation, of course. This question was planned to take Eve's eyes off all that God had given her and make her center upon the one thing He had forbidden. Satan is a master at this.

The Poison Planter

Satan is a master at planting seeds of doubt. He fogs us in and we become confused. This is exactly what he did with Eve.

When Eve answered the serpent's question about eating from the tree, we see that Satan's poison had begun to work. She said, "From the fruit of the trees of the garden we may eat; but from the fruit of the tree which is in the middle of the garden, God has said, 'You shall not eat from it or touch it, lest you die'" (Genesis 3:2-3).

Wait a minute! There's only one problem. Eve added her own embellishment to the original command in Genesis 2:17. She said, "or touch it." She showed that she didn't know what the real issue was; she thought there was something in the material of the tree that was evil. God didn't say, "Don't touch." She was making sin something material or tangible, rather than a choice of the mind. She was psyched out! Already she had the wrong issue.

Satan saw that he had her where he wanted her and zeroed in with an outright denial of the word of God. It is his special technique: first he makes suggestions in an area where we are uncertain or doubtful; then he will come along with a direct repudiation of what God said. In Genesis 3:4 he said, "You surely shall not die!"

Eve was probably gazing at the tree, listening to Satan's smooth talk, and the next thing she thought was, "What is God's *motive* for not wanting me to eat from this tree?" Satan was right on the spot with the reason. He said: "For God knows that in the day you eat from it your eyes will be opened, and you will be like God, knowing good and evil" (Genesis 3:5).

What Satan was saying to Eve was that God's motive was jealousy. Satan implied, "Look, Eve, He's holding out on you because if you eat from this tree you'll have the experiential knowledge of good and evil and you'll be like God."

This is another of Satan's methods: he takes clear truth and drops just enough poison in it to kill us. It was true that if Adam and Eve ate from the tree they would get the experiential knowledge of good and evil, but it was not true that they would be like God. See how clever Satan is? He got this woman, who was already confused and missing the point, to reject God's Word outright and to accept the idea that God had impure motives and was holding out because He didn't love mankind. Once that insidious thought was planted, Satan had his ally—the lust of the eye.

Arsenic in the Race

Eve ate from that tree and immediately things began to happen. For one thing, I believe there was a visible change in Eve. Before this she was covered with light, a beautiful glow from God, but after she ate she lost this ethereal shine. What is more amazing, she "also gave some to her husband, and he ate."

We can say that the woman was confused, that she was deceived and therefore wasn't legally responsible for sin. However, there was no excuse for the man at all. "And it was not Adam who was deceived, but the woman being quite deceived, fell into transgression" (1 Timothy 2:14).

Adam gave in without a fight! There was not one word given directly to the man, not one temptation. He walked into transgression with his eyes wide open. It seems that he simply chose to stay with Eve rather than continue with God. He made a cool and calculated decision to reject God. Adam had the legal power of attorney over himself and the world, but he betrayed the trust God had given him and forfeited his authority to Satan.

Satan, this fantastically superhuman being, achieved what he thought was a great victory—leading man to go against the will of God. Things really happened when Adam and Eve rejected God and obeyed Satan; in a flash of time mankind had some drastic results.

Man: Down for the Count

One, man died instantly, just as God had said, "... *in* the day that you eat from it you shall surely die" (Genesis 2:17). He lost spiritual life, the most important sphere of life we have. Man is made up of body, his material being; soul, his immaterial life; spirit, his spiritual life with which he is able to communicate with God. The instant man disobeyed God, he lost this spiritual life and severed that direct line of communication with his Maker. As it is written, "... you were dead in your trespasses and sins" (Ephesians 2:1), "being darkened in their understanding, excluded from the life of God" (Ephesians 4:18).

Two, man received a nature of self-centeredness and rebellion against God. We see this result throughout the history of mankind. God describes it this way: "The heart is more deceitful than all else and is desperately sick; who can understand it?" (Jeremiah 17:9). This rebellious nature is the root of what the Bible calls sin.

Three, Satan became man's absolute master; man became the slave. It's really a heavy scene, but according to the Bible Satan is ruling all those who have rejected God. Jesus Christ brought this out clearly when He commissioned Paul: "... I am sending you, to open their eyes so that they may turn from darkness to light and from the dominion of Satan to God..." (Acts 26:17-18).

Four, when man rebelled, the world was legally handed over to Satan. Adam actually became the Benedict Arnold of the universe. When he obeyed Satan, he turned the title deed of himself, all his dominion, and all his descendants over to Satan. This is why Jesus called Satan the "ruler of this world" (John 12:31).

God: Into the Arena

Satan won the first round in the garden. He thought the fight was all over, but it was just beginning. We are a part of this massive conflict which is settling an ancient battle between these extraterrestrial beings and God, because after man fell God gave the promise that the seed of woman would ultimately triumph over Satan (Genesis 3:15). Those today who plant doubt about the virgin birth of Jesus Christ should mark well that it was the seed of woman, not the seed of man, that God promised would eventually conquer Satan. Jesus Christ, the Promised One, would be greatly wounded in this battle with His adversary, but would later give Satan a mortal wound.

When man fell into Satan's hands, God immediately launched His plan to redeem man from this helpless situation. What Satan didn't count on was that God would be so just that He wouldn't forgive man unless divine justice was satisfied. And something much more incredible—that God would be so loving that He would be willing to step down from heaven and temporarily lay aside all of His divine rights and become a man. Satan didn't anticipate that God, as a man, would later go to a cross and bear His own righteous judgment against the sin of the whole universe.

Just Thinking . . .

Perhaps Satan figured if he could get God's new creation to sin, rather than condemn man, God would bend His justice and let Satan go free as well.

Satan may have reasoned: *If I can get enough of mankind to reject God, then God will not be able to bring Himself to judge them all, and ultimately He will let them go free. Once God compromises His justice with man, He will have to do the same with me and my angels.*

Have you ever heard someone say, "I *can't* believe that God would condemn *all those people*"? Now where do you think they get that line of reasoning?

God, taking the form of man, poured out upon Himself all of the just wrath that was due the whole human race, so that anyone who gets beneath the cross with Jesus will be shielded from that wrath. To be brought into God's family, all we need to do is accept the fact that Jesus Christ died in our place with our sins and simply receive this gift of forgiveness which our Substitute provided for us. The Spirit of God describes it beautifully: "When we were utterly helpless with no way of escape, Christ came at just the right time and died for us sinners who had no use for him. Even if we were good, we really wouldn't expect anyone to die for us, though, of course, that might be barely possible. But God showed his great love for us by sending Christ to die for us while we were still sinners. And since by his blood he did all this for us as sinners, how much more will he do for us now that he has declared us not guilty? Now he will save us from all of God's wrath to come. And since, when we were his enemies, we were brought back to God by the death of his Son, what blessings he must have for us now that we are his friends, and he is living within us!" (Romans 5:6-10, *Living Bible*).

When God accomplished this on the cross, it showed conclusively that He is perfectly just because He didn't bend His justice to salvage man out of this whole conflict; He showed how great His love is because He was willing to become a man and bear His own judgment to set man free.

"God showed how much he loved us by sending his only Son into this wicked world to bring to us eternal life through his death. In this act we see what real love is: it is not our love for God, but his love for us when he sent his Son to satisfy God's anger against our sins" (John 4:9-10, *Living Bible*).

This is the ultimate demonstration of both the justice and the love of God! All this was done that God might be both "just and the justifier of the one who has faith in Jesus" (Romans 3:26).

Satan thought if he could destroy the Man who was the Son of God, if he could destroy the humanity of Jesus Christ, he would win. He thought that Man would never be able to be raised from the tomb. Once dead, He would stay buried!

The resurrection of Jesus sealed Satan's defeat. It was God's proof that Jesus had completely paid for every sin that would ever be committed. Even one sin not paid for would have held Christ in the grave. The fact that Jesus is alive proves that all who believe in Him are declared righteous before a Holy God (Romans 4:25).

Now Satan has no legal authority over the believer.

Satan's Blindfolds

Satan may have won a battle in the garden, but he has not won the war. He has already been defeated, and he knows it! However, he is going to use every tactic in his bag of deceptions to keep as many individuals as possible from knowing it, especially those who are believers in Jesus. He already has the unbelievers in his grasp by blinding them to the good news of the pardon that God freely offers through Jesus Christ.

"If the Good News we preach is hidden to anyone, it is hidden from the one who is on the road to eternal death. Satan, who is the god of this evil world, has made him blind, unable to see the glorious light of the Gospel that is shining upon him, or to understand the amazing message we preach about the glory of Christ, who is God" (2 Corinthians 4:3-4, *Living Bible*).

Right . . . Right Now

Where do you stand in this conflict? Perhaps you're having trouble accepting these things. If you are, guess who is helping you think that way?

The most important thing to realize is that you don't have to believe everything to become a member of God's forever family. All you need is faith enough to call out to God in your heart and thank Him that Jesus Christ died for *your* inability to measure up to His perfect standards. Receive the forgiveness of your sins and thank Him for it. Tell Jesus Christ that you want Him to come into your life right now and begin to make it pleasing to God.

If you did this, on the authority of God's Word, I assure you that you have eternal life right now.

5 ○ Three Dimensional Warfare

"For thou didst gird me with strength for the battle...."   KING DAVID, PSALM 18:39

Dr. FRANCIS SCHAEFFER, the Christian scholar of L'Abri Fellowship, Switzerland, recently told me, "This is not an age to be a soft Christian."

He shared with me his concern for something which has stirred me also. He feels there is a tremendous need to reach out to the tens of thousands of young men and women who are turning to Christ in the Jesus Revolution and give them in-depth training in their new faith.

I believe that Dr. Schaeffer is right on! It has greatly thrilled me to observe firsthand the amazing work the Spirit of God is doing among the youth of America and other parts of the world, especially in what was once known as the hippie and drug culture. I have seen youth delivered from hopeless addiction to acid and heroin through faith in Jesus Christ. Radicals for Mao Tse-tung's principles have become radicals for spreading the love of Jesus. Weathermen and Hell's Angels are now true disciples of Jesus Christ. No man or group can take credit for what is happening. It's a work of God.

But great as this is, I fear that unless mature and trained teachers who can communicate with the "Jesus People" begin to influence and instruct them, they will be swept into terrible error and excesses. Few Christians today realize that we are engaged in a three-dimensional warfare. At stake is whether we will enjoy the tremendous sense of inner peace, purpose for life, and new source of strength that is the heritage of every believer.

Either your life will count for God or it will be sidetracked and neutralized through the opposition of little-understood enemies.

Battlefield Strategy

If we have come to a point in our lives where we believe in Jesus Christ and accept Him as the One who is our Savior, one of the first desires that comes to us is that we want to live a life which is pleasing to Him. This comes from a new nature He puts within us. At this point we all find there are many handicaps which hinder us from being the type of person we want to be.

We are, whether we know how to express it or not, fighting a warfare on three fronts. These have been called the world, the flesh, and the Devil.

Throughout history leaders have never approached an enemy in warfare like a child brandishing a stick, flailing in all directions. They have used careful strategy and have studied the way in which the enemy maneuvers. General Albert Wedemeyer, a top military strategist of World War II, told of attending the German War College in the late 1930s and learning from the very men who would later become his opponents in war. He said, "The Germans stressed the campaigns of Frederick the Great, Napoleon, Caesar, Alexander and Philip of Macedon.

"When we studied a campaign of Frederick the Great or Napoleon, we generally went to the area where the battle had been fought," General Wedemeyer wrote. "The military history instructor reviewed the situation, analyzed dispositions and tactical decisions, and injected interesting anecdotes."[1]

If we are to understand and study the warfare we are in, we must know the area where the battles are being fought. The "flesh" is one battlefield where our enemy Satan constantly hinders us from doing what God wants.

The Flesh Trap

The term "flesh" ("sarx" in the original Greek) is used in many ways in the New Testament. Sometimes it is used to mean simply the stuff that covers our bones, as in Luke 24:39. "See My hands and My feet, that it is I Myself; touch Me and see; for a spirit does not have flesh and bones as you see that I have."

Sometimes flesh is used to represent the whole body, as in Acts 2:26. "Therefore my heart was glad and my tongue exulted; moreover my flesh also will abide in hope."

And sometimes flesh is used in the sense of our physical, earthly limitations, as in Second Corinthians 10:3-4. "For though we walk in the flesh, we do not war according to the flesh, for the weapons of our warfare are not of the flesh, but divinely powerful for the destruction of fortresses."

But the sense in which it is used as an area of warfare is most fully developed by the Apostle Paul. Drs. Arndt and Gingrich comment as follows: "In Paul's thought especially, the flesh is the willing instrument of sin and is subject to sin to such a degree that whatever flesh is, all forms of sin are likewise present, and no good thing can live in the flesh itself."[2]

A careful study of the many passages on the "flesh" when it is used in this sense reveals the following facts:

1. It is a basic nature or principle which operates within us from the time we are born physically. This nature is in rebellion against God; it is self-centered and wants its own way (Romans 7:14-24; 8:5-9).

2. It is an inseparable part of our material body and cannot be eradicated until we receive our transformed resurrection bodies (Romans 7:25; 1 John 1:8, 10).

3. Though it cannot be eradicated, its power to *operate* in the life of the Christian has been neutralized by our being united with Christ in His death to sin. The flesh has no right to reign in the Christian's life any longer, and its power is broken in our lives when we count this as being true (Romans 6:1-14).

The attitude of believing that God has already broken sin's and/or the flesh's power over us sets the Spirit of God free to make victory a reality in our experience (Romans 8:1-4).

Here is just a partial list of what the flesh does in our lives when we don't consider its power broken and depend upon God's Spirit: "Now the deeds of the flesh are evident, which are: immorality, impurity, sensuality, idolatry, sorcery, enmities, strife, jealousy, outbursts of anger, disputes, dissensions, factions, envyings, drunkenness, carousings, and things like these, of which I forewarn you just as I have forewarned you that those who practice such things shall not inherit the kingdom of God" (Galatians 5:19-21).

Most of these words which are used for the deeds of the flesh need amplification. Briefly, here are some of the specifics:

Immorality: from the word "porneia," it means all sexual intercourse outside of marriage.

Impurity: impure thoughts and actions, especially in the area of sex.

Sensuality: living primarily to please the senses (out-of-control appetite for foods, music, sex, creature comforts, etc.).

Idolatry: anything that we place ahead of Christ as an object of our attention and devotion; this could be a girl friend or a boyfriend, our children, a job, an education, a beautiful home, clothes, a sleek body, or a fast car.

Sorcery: from the word "pharmakia"; the practice of witchcraft and occultism in association with drugs.

Enmities: to be at odds with people; carrying grudges.

Disputes: modern man calls these "personality conflicts," but "selfishness" is more accurate.

Dissensions: literally division; causing conflicts and taking of sides between people.

Factions: literally heresies; leading astray with false doctrine and forming sects.

Envyings: attitudes of dissatisfaction which cause you to desire what others have.

Drunkenness: any loss of normal judgment and awareness through the use of alcohol or drugs. The idea of better living through chemicals instead of the Spirit of God.

Carousings: seeking to escape reality through excessive pursuit of entertainment.

These are only some of the deeds of the flesh, not all of them! When the apostle says that those who practice such things "shall not inherit the kingdom of God," he means that those who *habitually* indulge in them are evidencing the fact that they have never received the new nature which hates sin.

It is impossible for a Christian to regularly practice the deeds of the flesh without a change of heart before God. Because of the fact that the Holy Spirit dwells inside of us, we can't be continually happy in sin. Sooner or later the Christian will acknowledge his sin and turn back to trusting Christ to deliver him from its power; and from the standpoint of his happiness, the sooner the better.

Continuous, unbroken toleration of the deeds of the flesh should cause a person to question whether he has really been born spiritually. A true Christian can and does experience these deeds of the flesh, but he will have a desire to be delivered from them for Christ's sake. A non-Christian just wants to be delivered from the consequences.

Deeds of the Flesh and Demons

Some well-meaning Christians today have a tendency to go overboard about demons. I want to be sure no one falls into the trap of attributing to demons what is actually the work of the flesh.

You may have heard people speak about the "lying demon," the "lust demon," the "envy demon," and others. I do not believe that there are specific demons such as these who can only do one thing.

Consider a fellow who is constantly thinking about sex. He is consumed by lascivious thoughts every day. If he has heard of such things, he may begin to think, "Maybe I have a lust demon."

He shares his thoughts with some of his Christian friends, and they have a little prayer meeting and "cast the demon out." Sanctimoniously they may say, "We've cast out the lust demon. Praise the Lord."

Our Christian friend, thus assured by his own feelings and the pronouncements of his friends, takes his wife to a restaurant, smug in his victory over himself. A curvaceous waitress in a mini-skirt comes to the table, and in a flash the old demon is back.

The danger in this concept is that a deed which is actually a part of the flesh or the old sin nature is attributed to a demon. It is vital that we assign things to their proper cause. There is no "lust demon" per se. Lust is a sin which comes from the flesh. But there are demons who will use the lust of the flesh to guide us into moral disaster. Satan can take a natural drive and use it, but he is not the originator of it. He capitalizes on something which is already going on in our hearts

Along with many other doctrines which become distorted in popular usage, the theme of Satan probably has more false clichés attached to it than any other.

"The Devil made me do it" is a cop-out.

When Satan takes the desire which you have and uses it for his purposes, he doesn't force you. If you really express the truth when overtaken by a sin of the flesh, you would say, "I did it because I chose to follow the desires of my old nature." Now that is not as easy to say as "The Devil made me do it," but it is more honest.

Puzzled Apostles

Mark 7 gives a good description of the flesh. Jesus had told the disciples a parable, and they questioned Him about it. We can almost see Him shaking His head when He said, "Are you so uncomprehending?" Then He explained: "That which proceeds out of the man, that is what defiles the man. For from within, out of the heart of men, proceed the evil thoughts and fornications, thefts, murders, adulteries, deeds of coveting and wickedness, as well as deceit, sensuality, envy, slander, pride and foolishness. All these evil things proceed from within and defile the man" (Mark 7:20-23).

Jesus is talking about the flesh, the source of this sinful nature. He shows that our major problem is not our environment but our inner nature of the flesh.

It's not a sin to have an evil thought flash into the mind; it is only a sin when we fail to say "no" to it and do not rely upon Christ to put it down. Temptation and sin are different. The old saying applies, "You can't stop a bird from landing on your head, but you can stop it from building a nest in your hair."

When the Bible speaks of the temptations of the flesh, it is always in terms of a continued need to overcome them. It is a matter of moment-by-moment reliance upon the Holy Spirit by deliberate choice to overcome the lusts of the flesh. Victory is never achieved by freedom *from* temptation, but by overcoming temptation through the power of the indwelling Holy Spirit.

Galatians 5:16 says: "But I say, walk by the Spirit, and you will not carry out the desire of the flesh."

To walk in the Spirit means to have a continuing attitude of reliance upon the Holy Spirit and not on your own human resources. Note: it does not say that if you walk in the Spirit you will not *have* temptations; it does say that you will not fulfill them. The Spirit-controlled believer will be tempted, but it is not sin until you stop trusting the Spirit to fight it.

The Bible talks about overcoming the flesh, or going to battle with it in dependence upon the Holy Spirit who lives in every believer. However, as the Bible speaks of "the world," it talks of claiming victory which has already been won.

Christ has won a victory over the world and Christians are to claim that victory. This will be amplified later in the chapter "Weapons of Warfare."

The World

In most cases the term "world" as used in the Bible comes from the word "kosmos." Basically it has three ideas in its verbal form: to put things into order, to systematize, and to adorn or decorate. In the latter form the word became used as "cosmetics," which is the concept of adorning the outer appearance.

First idea: in the New Testament, "world" is used in the sense of the planet Earth, the material planet. This is the way it is used in Acts 17:24 and John 1:10.

Second idea: "world" is used to mean the inhabitants of the Earth. First, referring to people in general, not viewing them as good or evil, as in John 3:16—"God so loved the world"; and second, referring to all unbelievers, alien toward God, as in John 14:17 and John 15-18.

Third idea: vital to our study, it is used to describe the world *system*, beautifully organized and arranged to function without God, opposed to all that is true in Jesus Christ. The world system is adorned with the beautiful concepts of culture, music, art, philosophy, knowledge, social concerns, programs of welfare, science, politics, religion, and pleasure. It embraces all these things in an orderly system. These are not evil in themselves, but Satan weaves them into a world order so that he can take man's heart away from a true relationship with God and center him on those things which are both temporal and material.

Beginning of the World System

In the Garden man gave the title deed of the world to Satan, and since then the world has been under his control. Before man's rejection of God, there was no "cosmos" in the sense of an ordered world system alien to God. There was only the planet Earth and God's appointed regent, man. When man chose to reject fellowship with God and follow the lie of Satan, he not only handed over to Satan the title deed to man's life, but to that of the Earth itself. It was then that the world system began to develop.

Adam had been given authority over Planet Earth, including its creatures and elements. "And God blessed them; and God said to them, 'Be fruitful and multiply, and fill the earth and subdue it; and rule over the fish of the sea and over the birds of the sky, and over every living thing that moves on the earth'" (Genesis 1:28). Adam had complete power of attorney; when he chose to reject God and follow Satan, legal ownership of mankind, animals, and the Earth was transferred to Satan.

God, being just, had to honor this legal right, even to Satan. Man and the world could not be taken back until sin, which caused the forfeiture of ownership to Satan, was paid for.

Jesus certainly knew Satan had won legal right to the world. When Satan personally tempted Jesus, displaying at that time his ability to deceive, the Scriptures say, "And the devil said to Him, 'I will give You all this domain and its glory; for *it has been handed over to me*, and I give it to whomever I wish'" (Luke 4:6).

Our earthbound minds can't comprehend the mysterious power it took to show Jesus all the kingdoms of the world in a moment. Satan probably made it look like the most dazzling movie production, combining a panorama of nature's beauty and the pomp and glory of kingdoms. Satan can make the things of the world appear so good that men would give their lives for them—and some do. (See 2 Timothy 4:10 for the tragedy of a promising young minister, Demos.)

Jesus didn't dispute Satan's claim to the world; He knew that Adam had handed over the legal ownership to the whole planet and all on it.

The Arch Architect

Satan lost no time in beginning to set up a whole scene that would carry man's mind away from God. Genesis 4 records the beginning of the system.

One of the most basic parts of the world system is religion. Religion is based on man's pride. It assumes that man can do something to earn God's acceptance. True faith says you can only be accepted with God through receiving forgiveness as a gift on the basis of a God-provided substitute bearing the penalty for sin. Abel approached God the true way. He brought the appointed animal sacrifice as a substitute to die for his sins. Cain, on the other hand, came the way of the world system. He brought the fruit of his own works. Abel was accepted—Cain wasn't.

God even reasoned with Cain and sought to get him to come the true way. "Then the Lord said to Cain, 'Why are you angry? And why has your countenance fallen? If you do well, will not your countenance be lifted up? And if you do not do well, sin is crouching at the door; and its desire is for you, but you must master it'" (Genesis 4:6-7).

Cain's pride was inflamed. Rather than come by faith in God's provision, he did what religion has been doing for centuries; he murdered the one who represented God's truth. Religion can't stand the truth because it is a rebuke to man's self-centeredness and pride. This is why some of the greatest crimes in history have been done in the name of false Christianity and religion. The false cannot stand the true.

The world system began with the underlying principles of pride, rejection of God's truth, and force.

What Cain Raised

We see the world system further developed as Cain "... went out from the presence of the Lord" (Genesis 4:16). Cain established a highly developed society and culture which left God out; he built the first city mentioned in the Bible, called Enoch.

In the generations that immediately followed, many advancements were made. "Jabal ... was the father of those who dwell in tents and have livestock" (Genesis 4:20). Agriculture began to develop and flourish.

"Jubal ... was the father of all those who play the lyre and pipe" (Genesis 4:21). Music, art, and culture were introduced to take their places in the world system.

"Tubal-cain (was) the forger of all implements of bronze and iron ..." (Genesis 4:22). And now we see the development of industry becoming involved in the early world system.

These things were not evil in themselves, but there was one glaring problem—they left out God. Man's achievements became a snare to take his heart further away from God. Here was an entire civilization organized and developed around the material and temporal. Man's proud self-sufficiency, rejection of God's truth, and violence permeated the whole system.

It wasn't until Adam's son Seth had a son named Enosh that it says, "*Then* men began to call upon the name of the Lord" (Genesis 4:26).

The first world system became so permeated with every kind of evil that God had to destroy it (Genesis 6-7).

Alienation of Affections

The real battle with the world has to do with something as basic as our affections. When Satan can't reach a person through temptations to do the more obvious gross sins of the flesh, he will switch to such innocent and worthwhile avenues as education, careers, nature, money, fame, or a myriad of other pursuits. If he can shift anything from the world system into being first in our affections, taking Christ's place of priority, he has effectively sidetracked us into the web of worldliness. This is why John warns, "Do not love the world (cosmos), nor the things in the world. If any one loves the world, the love of the Father is not in him. For all that is in the world (system), the lust of the flesh and the lust of the eyes and the boastful pride of life, is not from the Father, but is from the world (system)" (1 John 2:15-16).

Friendship with the world is hostility toward God because the philosophy of the world, its whole life view, is in contradiction to God's viewpoint of life. Embracing the world and its ways will inevitably drive our affections away from God. There is no neutral ground. This is why John warned, "... if any one loves the world, the love of the Father is not in him."

Behind all that is tangible in the world system there is the intangible genius of Satan, the master deceiver. Behind "the things of the world system" is the mastermind who uses them to shift our focus from devotion to Christ to devotion to things. Once this is done, the inevitable ever-increasing force of greed sets in. Because things can never take the place of fellowship with God, we are never satisfied. The more we get, the more we want. James zeroed in on this when he said, "You lust and do not have; so you commit murder. And you are envious and cannot obtain; so you fight and quarrel. You do not have because you do not ask. You ask and do not receive, because you ask with wrong motives, so that you may spend it on your pleasures. You adulteresses, do you not know that friendship with the world is hostility toward God? Therefore whoever wishes to be a friend of the world makes himself an enemy of God" (James 4:2-4).

Satan: Ruler of This World

The diabolical mastermind backing up the world system deceives and ensnares the minds of people. He does a good job with those who do not believe in Christ and a fair job with those who do.

Three titles describe Satan's work: first, he is "the ruler of this world," which means he is constantly at work in human government and its political systems.

Before you accuse me of being an anarchist, I don't mean that every government is totally evil or immoral, but that Satan is capable of manipulating all forms of government for his purposes.

Jesus gave us many details about this person who pulls the political strings of the world system. Even those who see Jesus as only a historical figure or a great teacher must admit He wouldn't have taught anything which He couldn't prove by experience. Here are a few passages where Jesus speaks of "the ruler of this world":

"Now judgment is upon this world; now the ruler of this world shall be cast out" (John 12:31).

"I will not speak much more with you, for the ruler of the world is coming, and he has nothing in Me" (John 14:30).

"And concerning judgment, because the ruler of this world has been judged" (John 16:11).

The Greek word for ruler in the previous passages is "archon." The Greeks were specific in their meanings, and when "archon" is used it stresses the vise that Satan has upon the world. It literally means a political ruler. It emphasizes Satan's control over the political systems of this earth.

Let's look at an example of this from the Book of Daniel. Daniel was one of God's great prophets. At one time he was given a prophetic vision which he couldn't interpret. He prayed that God would reveal its meaning to him.

Daniel spent twenty-one days in prayer. Then an angel appeared to Daniel and told him that he had come to reveal the meaning of the vision. The angel explained to Daniel that he had been detoured in an unusual manner. "The prince of the kingdom of Persia was withstanding me for twenty-one days" (Daniel 10:13).

At that time Persia was ruling the world. It was no mere human who held up one of God's angels, but a demon (or fallen angel), one of Satan's generals, who was controlling the prince of Persia. This mighty spiritual power behind the Persian prince actually withstood the angel for three weeks, until God sent Michael, one of His chief angels, to overcome the demon and send the messenger on his way to Daniel.

This is not just ancient history, something we delegate to Daniel's time. According to the Bible, an unseen warfare is being waged behind world events all the time. The Bible describes this "invisible warfare" from Genesis to Revelation. The vast, highly organized army of demons behind the world system is clearly revealed in Ephesians 6:12: "For our struggle is not against flesh and blood, but against the rulers, against the powers, against the world-forces of this darkness, against the spiritual forces of wickedness in the heavenly places."

Prince of the Power of the Air

Satan's second title is "prince of the power of the air." Before a person becomes a Christian, he is spiritually dead and ruled by this prince. "And you were dead in your trespasses and sins, in which you formerly walked according to the course of this world, according to the prince of the power of the air, of the spirit that is now working in the sons of disobedience" (Ephesians 2:1-2).

The word translated "air" literally means the air we breathe. However, in this context it is obviously not used in a literal sense. The clause prior to it, ". . . the course of this world," looks at the world in the sense of the thought forms and environment of the world view of this godless world system.

The clause following it, "the spirit that is now working in the sons of disobedience," looks at the energizing spirit of evil within the unbelieving world. Both clauses speak of the dynamics that motivate and shape the way men think and act. Therefore, in context the word "air" must be speaking of the "mood" or "atmosphere of thought." We often use the term "atmosphere" in this sense. For instance, "Paris has a romantic atmosphere" or "The atmosphere in the room was oppressive."

Satan is said to be the prince and power behind the atmosphere of the thoughts of this world system that are hostile to God. Before we believe in Jesus Christ and are born spiritually, we are unwittingly dominated by this atmosphere of thought.

As "prince of the air," Satan rules over the thoughts of the world system. He originated the concept of brainwashing long before human rulers used it to manipulate prisoners of war.

In this role Satan injects his treachery into the educational system, the philosophy, the mass media, the arts, the style, and the culture. He will use a lake of truth to disguise a pint of poison. His deceptions about life and its purpose are lethal. Any flirting with the ways of the world can lead to spiritual adultery (James 4:4).

When we think that he is the ruler over all of these thought forms and realize the ways in which we are bombarded every day by these sources, we begin to see how deadly the world system can be. At the same time, we begin to understand the importance of the promise of 1 John 5:4: "For whatever is born of God overcomes the world; and this is the victory that has overcome the world—our faith. And who is the one who overcomes the world, but he who believes that Jesus is the Son of God?"

With our hearts focused on Jesus, we are constantly having our minds renewed with God's view of life, which is alien to the human viewpoint of the world system.

The human viewpoint of life looks at the daily problems as well as all the complications of living in this world from the standpoint of the human ability to cope with them. The divine viewpoint looks at life from God's ability to handle it through a yielded you. It is His job to deal with your temptations and needs. There is peace of mind, stability, and power for the one who has the divine viewpoint.

This is why Romans 12:2 says: "Don't let the world around you squeeze you into its own mold, but let God remold your minds from within" (Phillips' translation).

God of This Age

Satan's third title is "the god of this *age*," which is from the Greek word "aion." This often means the prevailing thought of a particular era. Satan is constantly changing the "in thing" so that when you get "where it's at" you find you're where it was. The pace is accelerating; the world system is changing so fast that even the world can't keep up with it.

In the future, old institutions are going to change so rapidly that people will reach a tremendous state of instability and emotional disturbance resulting in psychological problems. Nothing will be dependable, stable, or certain.

"The god of this age" also refers to Satan's activity in relation to religion. He loves religion. It's his ace trump for blinding our minds to the truth. He is *the god* of all those who do not follow Jesus Christ. Those who worship in any religious form apart from Christ are ultimately being deceived by Satan.

It is comforting to know, however, that Satan can't permanently blind the minds of those who are truly seeking to know God. Wherever a person may be, whether in Lapland or Africa, Dubuque or Denver, the Scripture says that he can come to a God-consciousness. "But God shows his anger from heaven against all sinful, evil men who push away the truth from them. For the truth about God is known to them instinctively; God has put this knowledge in their hearts. Since earliest times men have seen the earth and sky and all God made, and have known of his existence and great eternal power. So they will have no excuse" (Romans 1:18-20, *Living Bible*).

If a man sincerely wants to know God, then God will move heaven and earth to get enough light to him so that he will have the knowledge to throw himself upon the mercy of God. "And you will seek Me and find Me, when you search for Me with all your heart" (Jeremiah 29:13).

Although Satan can't blind the mind of the person who is sincerely seeking God, he does blind those who reject the light that they have. This is a hard fact which each person, no matter how good he is in his own opinion, no matter what good principles he obeys, no matter how many good works he performs, should confront. If he is not following Christ, he is unwittingly following Satan, "the god of this age."

"If the Good News we preach is hidden to anyone, it is hidden from the one who is on the road to eternal death. Satan, who is the god of this evil world, has made him blind, unable to see the glorious light of the Gospel that is shining upon him, or to understand the amazing message we preach about the glory of Christ, who is God" (2 Corinthians 4:3-4, *Living Bible*).

Traveling Incognito

"The Devil's cleverest ruse is to make believe that he does not exist."[3]

This is the reason we see the ridiculous pictures of Satan with his horns and red suit, sporting a tail and an evil grin. If he is a comic figure or a mythical villain, there is little harm he can do except give us an occasional nightmare.

Satan's incognitos are cleverer than movie star disguises. He hides behind religion, intellectualism, poetry, art, music, psychology, human understanding, and even our human "self." The Bible says, "The whole world lies in the power of the evil one" (1 John 5:19).

All men are under Satan's rule until they are brought to Jesus Christ.

That's heavy! When we are faced with an "either-or" situation or a black and white choice, most of us would like to wiggle in the center with a "maybe" or charge through the middle wearing a gray hat. Modern thought rejects the antiquated idea that Satan is the origin of evil and has the world in his control. Man has so many explanations for evil: poverty, pollution, politicians, police, parents, employers, unions, racial minorities, racial majorities . . . choose your cause! Put the rap on someone, man says, but don't tell me about Satan. That's negative—unpleasant.

Christians are not exempt from this inability to understand where and how Satan is working. In fact, because his doctrine has been neglected for so long, they are sometimes the least discerning of all in understanding the world system. Young Christians are particularly vulnerable. As Francis Schaeffer has said, "We have left the next generation naked in the face of 20th century thought by which they are surrounded."[4]

Satan is not the man below, heaping coals into an eternal furnace. He's the original "jet-setter"; he's "right on" with the latest cause. When God asked Satan a direct question, his answer showed outrageous arrogance: "And the Lord said to Satan, From where do you come? And Satan—the adversary and the accuser—answered the Lord, From going to and fro on the earth, and from walking up and down on it" (Job 2:2, *Amplified Bible*.)

What a picture! Satan trucking all over the earth, constantly doing his thing in every spot he can! He's working in our world system through governments, education, business, and culture. You name it—he'll tame it.

This modern "promoter" has had some help from his advance men who began planning his twentieth century campaign a few hundred years ago. Stand by for the shock waves from the nineteenth century thought-bombs that are threatening to bring the whole civilization into Armageddon.

6 ∘ Thought Bombs

"For the wisdom of this world is foolishness before God."

APOSTLE PAUL TO THE CORINTHIANS

"Our dialectical philosophy abolishes all the notions of absolute and definitive truth."

FREDERICK ENGELS IN A EULOGY TO KARL MARX

DATELINE WASHINGTON, NOVEMBER, 1971.

"The 5-megaton atomic explosion set off by the United States beneath Amchitka Island Saturday caused the largest earth tremor produced by man but resulted in no apparent damage outside the immediate vicinity of Amchitka."[1]

Who remembers Amchitka? The explosion on that remote island made Hiroshima look like a firecracker. And yet the blast from Amchitka was minor compared to the thought bombs set off by a few eighteenth and nineteenth century men who dreamed up ideas which have sent shock waves to rock our thinking today.

The contamination of these explosive ideas has been so devastating that it has completely permeated twentieth century thinking. The men who devised these thought bombs are the subject of this chapter. Satan took their concepts and wired the underlying frame of reference for our present historical, educational, philosophical, sociological, psychological, religious, economic, and political outlook. You and I and our children have been ingeniously conditioned to think in terms that are contrary to biblical principles and truths in all of these areas—and without our even realizing it.

There is only one person who had anything to gain by so radically conditioning the thinking of mankind, and that person is Satan. He was the real genius and impetus behind each of these men and their ideas which we are going to discuss.

I realize it is a serious charge to imply that these brilliant men, who in many ways made significant contributions to our world, were instruments of Satan to lead men's thinking away from eternal truths, but as the case against them unfolds I believe the conclusions will be justified.

You may find some of this pretty heavy reading, but it is absolutely essential that we understand how we have come to this present hostility toward God's viewpoint of life. The analysis of each man and his philosophy will be brief and confined to the specific areas where his thinking came into conflict with the Bible.

Bomb One: Kant

Immanuel Kant was a German philosopher. He never traveled more than sixty-nine miles from his home in Prussia, where he lived from 1724 to 1804, and yet his original thinking formulated principles which still sway the civilized world.

Until Kantian philosophy began to influence the intellectuals of the age, classical philosophy was based upon the process of antithesis, which means that man thought in terms of cause and effect. This means if A is true then non-A cannot also be true. According to classical philosophy, values were absolute.

The world at large accepted these possibilities of absolutes in both knowledge and morals. Before Kant you could reason with a person on the basis of cause and effect. However, this one man and his critiques began to question whether people could actually accept things which were beyond their five senses.

A modern French philosopher describes the Kantian thinking this way: "Kant was able to go definitively beyond scepticism and realism by recognizing the descriptive and irreducible characteristics of external and internal experience as the sufficient foundation of the world."[2]

In Kant's analysis of the process of thought he proposed that no one can know anything except by experience. He believed that individual freedom lies in obedience to the "moral law that speaks within us."[3]

Kant, therefore, finding no personal basis for accepting absolutes, triggered the ideas which would result in the philosophy introduced by another German.

Bomb Two: Hegel

Hegel took the ideas of Kant and began to press them forward. He lived from 1770 to 1831 and left a heritage of brutal and violent fallout which has invaded our century.

He was called the philosophical dictator of Germany. He believed that one fact or idea (thesis) working against another fact (antithesis) would produce a new fact (synthesis). This philosophy was the basis of the communistic political and economic ideas of Karl Marx and the National Socialism of Adolf Hitler.

Hegel glorified the state. He taught that the state did not have to obey moral laws, nor did governments have to keep agreements. Hitler followed this philosophy to perfection.

According to the Hegelian thought, everything was relative. This gave man an approach to truth, an approach to life, in which there were no absolutes, only terms of relativity.

When Hegel introduced the philosophical basis for relative thinking and rejected absolutes, he literally altered the future course of the world. Absolutes are unchangeable truths from which you can reason from cause to effect. In relative thinking you are dealing with subjective thought in which cause and effect have no part. Relativity is based upon changeableness. When you think in this manner, you say, "Well, how do you feel about it now?"

As Hegel did away with cause-and-effect logic, there was no need for ultimate truth. With the elimination of an ultimate cause or truth, man could plunge headlong away from any necessity of believing in a Creator-God.

This philosophy of relative thinking soon permeated the higher educational systems of Europe and America. The sad progress (?) afterward was simple: the more educated people became, the more they rejected absolutes of God, truth, and morals. Even those who had a true faith in Jesus Christ found their faith weakened in college, but it was hard to discover why.

Dr. Francis Schaeffer in his great book, *The God Who Is There*, shows that it wasn't so much that truth was being attacked as it was the very presuppositional basis for truth. This was much more subtle.

Today the average college student who hasn't been born spiritually through personal faith in Jesus Christ doesn't believe in the possibility of absolute truth. Relative thinking has now been brought down to the earliest levels of elementary education. It is a Trojan Horse which few Christian parents understand, much less actively fight.

Bomb Three: Kierkegaard

Out of Denmark in the nineteenth century came a philosophical theologian, Soren Kierkegaard. Although he came from a Christian environment, he rejected the generally accepted beliefs of the Lutheran Church, the established church of Denmark.

Kierkegaard was a great influence in the theology of his time and is considered the father of contemporary existentialism. His writings are a denial of the basic tenets of the Christian faith and show a disdain for those who do not agree with his intellectual pursuits. He was the first man to launch a system of thought in which despair was the underlying current. In two books which Kierkegaard himself called "the most perfect books I have written," *Fear and Trembling* and *The Sickness Unto Death,* the very titles reflect that mood of despondency.

Kierkegaard believed that a man comes to a point in his life when he concludes that he cannot find any definite reasons for truth or for life. To find purpose he has to take a leap of faith which has no rationality behind it at all.

In the writings of Kierkegaard there is contempt for those who do not think on his intellectual plane. It is understandable that his philosophy would not accept biblical truths. For instance, in his volume *Fear and Trembling* he wrote scornfully, "One not infrequently hears it said by men who for lack of losing themselves in studies are absorbed in phrases that a light shines upon the Christian world whereas a darkness broods over paganism. This utterance has always seemed strange to me, inasmuch as every profound thinker and every serious artist is even in our day rejuvenated by the eternal youth of the Greek race."[4]

Kierkegaard was one of the foremost proponents of the philosophy which has swept the intellectual world right down to our time. He introduced the tenets of Kant and Hegel into the theology of the Christian faith. The idea that there is no rational basis for things beyond the five senses, but that we must take an irrational leap of blind faith to find purpose in life came out of Kant's teaching. The idea that there is no absolute truth and we must therefore find relative reasons upon which to base our life resulted from Hegel's teaching. This was the beginning of "existential thought."

I believe this gave a philosophical framework for "the doctrines of demons" which Paul said would sweep the world in the latter times before the return of Christ. When Karl Barth came along in the early twentieth century and developed a "new" system of theology called "Neo-Orthodoxy" (which was neither new nor orthodox), this existential, relative thinking became thoroughly spread throughout the Christian church.

Bomb Four: Marx

Karl Marx, one of the most influential men to explode his ideas onto the world scene, was a German who was born in 1818 and came from a long line of outstanding scholars and rabbis. His father broke his religious family tradition and became a Protestant when Karl was a child.

Karl was a brilliant student and, from what we learn from his biographers, a man who did not make or keep friends. Hot-tempered, brooding, and intense, he allowed his wife and half-starved children to live in cruel poverty while he devoted himself to his intellectual studies.

Marx and the only close friend he ever had, Friedrich Engels, were co-workers for many years in the movement which has changed the course of modern history.

As we see the vast chain of influence established by the philosophers and writers in the nineteenth century, it shouldn't be surprising that Marx became involved at the University of Berlin with a left-wing group which followed the philosophy of Hegel. Their main thrust at that time was to throw out Christianity. Marx was inspired in his intellectual quest to start a movement to remake the world. (At least that desire was partially fulfilled generations after his death.)

When Marx and Engels got together to formulate the great blueprint which would make this warring planet a utopia, they had already decided that the main way it could be achieved was through a classless society. They saw the proletariat (the class of wage labor) in a state of war, or conflict, with the bourgeoisie (the class of property ownership). According to Marxist thinking, the property owners were the exploiters, and the workers were the exploited.

Marxism applies the principle of dialectics, or the art of reasoning, to this inevitable class struggle in a manner in which we may readily see the influence of Hegel. Three elements are at work: the thesis (a positive force) and the antithesis (the opposing force) resulting in a clash which would produce a new idea of force (a synthesis). This clash would provide the dynamics which would catapult society into some new development.

Marx and Engels believed that this great and glorious class struggle would eliminate the cause of all past conflicts in society. They thought that the cause of all the human struggles and war could be traced to that terrible evil— private property. If the great class uprising overthrew private property, then there would be nothing to fight over and everyone could live happily ever after.

To remake the world along the lines of this classless society, Marxism employs every weapon: not just bombs, guns, and tanks, but also the weapons of education, religion, trade, economics, and culture. The material improvement of society will be brought about by whatever methods are useful to the cause. The end justifies the means.

Goals established by Marx were: abolish private property; centralize all power in the hands of the state; control the world. Collectivize, centralize, control.

Marx believed the property class used religion as a device to suppress the "exploited class." This extended into the philosophy of modern Communism which has a few basics: everything can be explained by matter (the

Russian cosmonaut who saw no signs of God in the stratosphere); materialism is the beginning and end of reality.

"The communist intellectual believes that everything in existence came about as a result of ceaseless motion among the forces of nature. Everything is a product of accumulated accident. There is no design. There is no law. There is no God. There is only matter and force in nature."[5]

Marx justified violence to achieve the new classless society, although he expounded the social and economic ideals of utopian Communism. His ideas and his aims have permeated every aspect of twentieth century thought and life.

The late J. Edgar Hoover said, "Communism is many things: an economic system, a philosophy, a political creed, a psychological conditioning, an educational indoctrination, a directed way of life."[6]

It is time for the world to realize that Communism is not just another political philosophy, but a religion--a religion which promises utopia to its devotees. The state is worshiped in place of God. Communism deals with such basic issues as: What is man? What is man's most basic problem? How can man be delivered from his problem? What is man's destiny? In all these points Communism gives answers which are diametrically opposed to God's truth.

Bomb Five: Darwin

When Charles Darwin, an Englishman of the nineteenth century, came on the scene, he caused a real sensation in the scientific and nonscientific world. Darwin amassed a vast amount of scientific facts and presented a theory dealing with the development of plants and animals. This theory, in simple form, said that living things increase more rapidly than people realize. Earth cannot provide room and food for all the offspring of these living things; members of each species then compete for a chance to live. This competition brings about a process called natural selection, or the preservation of those life forms best adapted to survive in the struggle for existence. In essence, this is the belief that lower forms advance to higher forms in this struggle for existence.

When Darwin took his theories out of the plant and animal kingdoms and transferred them to man, the sparks flew that ignited educational fires right into our time. On one hand was Darwin's widely held theory that all life, including man, evolved from lower forms, and on the other was the

Bible which in the Genesis account states that God created man, animals, and plants "after their kind"; they did not evolve from lower forms.

Conflict! Hegel and Marx would be happy—a scientist using their theories of thesis, antithesis, and synthesis.

Today, although we hear a great deal about the *theory* of evolution, even some reference books place it in the category of fact. A new reference series says, "The popular conception that Darwinism is simply the theory of evolution applied to the origin of man is far from correct. Its novelty lies not in the conception of evolution, but in an explosion of a probable cause of evolution so clear and cogent as to remove the theory from the sphere of philosophical speculation to that of practical life."[7]

In *The Naked Ape*, a book which has been widely recommended by high school and college teachers to their psychology students, the author states, "If we accept the history of our evolution, then one fact stands out clearly: namely that we have arisen essentially as primate predators."[8] This nurtures the idea that since man is no more than an animal, he should act like one.

Hegel introduced the philosophical basis for man to see no necessity for a Creator-God. Darwin introduced what seemed to be a scientific basis for not believing in a Creator-God to whom man was responsible. The impact of this thought bomb is that since man had no special beginning, he has no special purpose or destiny. This thinking leads many to sink into amoral behavior, disorientation, and despair.

Bomb Six: Freud

Sigmund Freud, born in the middle of the nineteenth century in Austria, was "very attracted to Darwin's theories because they offered the prospect of an extraordinary advance of human knowledge."[9]

Freud, the founder of psychoanalysis, was an atheist. His ideas, his teachings, his concept of the unconscious have become so fundamental to the mental attitude of the twentieth century that "without them much of modern life is unintelligible."[10]

Freud defines psychoanalysis as a "method of treatment for those suffering from nervous disorders."[11] The doctrine which promoted this type of treatment is based upon Freud's fundamental views of human nature—views which have formed the basis for the permissive society in which we live today.

Whether a person today knows anything about Freud or not, whether he only thinks Freud is someone who invented those "slips" we hear mentioned so frequently, or whether he is a student who has studied his works for years, all are products of the Freudian ethic.

What did Freud believe? The human race is motivated chiefly by pleasure; everything starts and ends with sex. Man is repressed by society in the fulfillment of his unconscious drive for gratification of his erotic desires; this repression makes him unhappy. The consequence of the conflict between our pleasure-seeking instincts and the repression exerted by our society is neurosis.

"Freud's doctrines, and particularly his ethics, are the product of his concept of the human race. There is no purpose in man's existence. There is no goal in mankind's presence on earth. There is no God . . . and if this is so, all is permitted."[12]

Freud firmly laid the groundwork for extreme permissiveness. He simply set forth the logical conclusions of behavior for man as the highest form of the evolutionary chain.

A prominent doctor has written, ". . . the intellectuals and the wealthy promote and defend an extreme permissiveness without even realizing that they are contaminated by the Freudian ethic, the ethic which declares that all is permitted, that the permissiveness syndrome is the natural drive of a human being to be free from society and that it should not be repressed or even controlled."[13]

The interest in sex, which was just getting a fleshhold in the beginning of American Freudianism, has exploded in our time. It is ironic, however, that the influence of the Freudian ethic is growing fast while his brainchild, psychoanalysis, seems to be dying.

Freud's Fruits

We are reaping the fruits of permissiveness. There is a criminal homicide every thirty-three minutes in the United States. America is "maintaining its long held, unhappy distinction of leading advanced Western nations in the rate at which its citizens destroy one another. . . . It has led many behavioral scientists to begin talking about a national 'crisis of violence'."[14]

The pattern we see is from permissiveness to disintegration. The state of disarray in the American family, fostered in our permissive society, has contributed to the runaway phenomenon. Each week more than 10,000 American children run away from homes, schools, and institutions. Why? The shock waves from these thought bombs are beginning to rip our society apart.

One young runaway said, "I was really spoiled by my mother. She should have said 'No' to me when I was small. Now she's trying to correct the mistake and says 'No' to everything, but it's too late."[15]

A police officer in an upper-class Chicago suburb said, "It becomes a form of blackmail that the kids use on the parent. Maybe the parent won't let the kid stay out as late as he wants, so he runs away. Some of these parents have taken threats from their kids from the time they were small. They ought to call the kids' bluff and not give in."[16]

Many of our modern mind manipulators, the educational theorists of twentieth century America, don't know the difference between a free society and a permissive society. One syndicated columnist wrote: "Under their mushy tutelage, we have raised two generations of children to suppose that discipline is cruel, that obedience is a sometime thing."[17]

The advocates of the permissive school are watching with horror the grades which are being handed out in the form of violence, alienation of their children, and tragic disintegration of families.

Evolution to Revolution: Lenin

The thought bombs are coming closer to our age. Lenin died some fifty years ago, leaving a heritage of brutality and violence to following generations. Probably more than any other man, Lenin is the builder of modern Communism. He took a philosophy and added the activism.

Lenin was not a simpleton. He had an outstanding record as a law student and became a staunch Marxist. He had one very basic belief: atheism. He referred to religion as the "opiate of the people."

Lenin used terror, murder, and secret police to crush all opposition to his counter-revolutionary ideas and emerged the dictator of Soviet Russia. He believed that to be successful revolution must be masterminded by a small, utterly loyal group of trained revolutionaries, and with this intensity of belief he succeeded in creating a force which would cross national boundaries and unite socialists in a universal class. This group would settle for nothing less than a world-wide Communist victory.

In 1917 Lenin declared, "We will destroy everything and on the ruins we will build our temple! It will be a temple for the happiness of all. But we will destroy the entire bourgeoisie, grind it to a powder. . . . I will be merciless with all counter-revolutionaries."

Since 1917 history has witnessed the impact of what Lenin meant: Hungary, Czechoslovakia, East Germany, The Balkans, Cuba, China.

In the Communist philosophy, man is treated with the cold logic of "survival of the fittest." Since there is no God, and since man has no special destiny or purpose, but is simply matter in motion, he can be disposed of without conscience. Individual life is unimportant. The State is all.

Demons on the Front Line

At times Satan works openly in the world system through the governments and leaders of countries. It has frequently been said, even by those people who have little knowledge or belief in supernatural beings, that Adolf Hitler was demon-possessed. However, the extent of influence upon the course of Germany's history by another strange and little-known man, who by his own admission was demon-possessed, is an astonishing fact shared by William L. Shirer. "It is probably no exaggeration to say, as I have heard more than one follower of Hitler say, that Chamberlain (Houston Steward Chamberlain, one of the strangest Englishmen who ever lived) was the spiritual founder of the Third Reich."[18]

Here is Shirer's description of Chamberlain, the man who inspired Hitler and his insane reign of terror and power: "Hypersensitive and neurotic and subject to frequent nervous breakdowns, Chamberlain was given to seeing demons who, by his own account, drove him on relentlessly to seek new fields of study and to get on with his prodigious writings. One vision after another forced him to change from biology to botany, to the fine arts, to music, to philosophy, to biography, to history. Once, in 1898, when he was returning from Italy, the presence of a demon became so forceful that he got off the train at Gardone, shut himself up in a hotel room for eight days and, abandoning some work on music that he had contemplated, wrote feverishly on a biological thesis until he had the germ of the theme that would dominate all of his later works: race and history.

"Since he felt himself goaded on by demons, his books (on Wagner, Goethe, Kant, Christianity, and race) were written in the grip of a terrible fever, a veritable trance, a state of self-induced intoxication, so that, as he says in his autobiography, *Lebenswege*, he was often unable to recognize them as his own work.

"But it was on the Third Reich, which did not arrive until six years after his death but whose coming he foresaw, that this Englishman's influence was the greatest. His racial theories and his burning sense of the destiny of the Germans and Germany were taken over by the Nazis, who acclaimed him as one of their prophets. During the Hitler regime books, pamphlets and articles poured from the presses extolling the 'spiritual founder' of National Socialist Germany.''

The Deep Things of Satan

As I examined the philosophies of the men and movements which have influenced the past two centuries, I began to understand what Revelation 2 means when it speaks of the deep things of Satan (Revelation 2:24). There are very deep things behind the thought patterns of our time, introduced by many of the philosophical munitions-makers from the past. These are the men who led the way for man's approach to truth today.

Most secular education (apart from that which is related to the Christian form of truth which is in the Bible) is based upon these concepts. When we think about morality in the world, there is no way of establishing what is right and what is wrong because there is no way of relating it to God. Morality becomes a system based on the Gallup Poll. That's where we're at. That is the kind of thinking that has spread throughout the educated world.

The world system has established this atmosphere of thought that subtly seeks to gain footholds in the believer's thinking. Once this is done, a steady pressure is exerted to pull him away from the divine viewpoint of life.

Thank God that ". . . the weapons of our warfare are not of the flesh (i.e. human resources), but divinely powerful for the destruction of fortresses. We are destroying speculations and every lofty thing raised up against the *knowledge of God*, and we are taking every *thought* captive to the obedience of Christ" (2 Corinthians 10:4-5).

As we simply keep our eye of faith focused upon Jesus' ability to work within us and keep trusting Him to teach us God's Word, we find that "greater is He who is in you than he who is in the world (system)" (1 John 4:4).

7 ○ Mind Manipulators

"Never in American history has there been a time when people more need to know what is behind the eruptions and disruptions that are beginning to rend society and disfigure history." MCCANDLISH PHILLIPS, *NEW YORK TIMES* NEWSMAN

THOUGHT CONTROL REVOLTS me. Free men should be able to think for themselves.

I remember a science fiction movie which impressed me with its far-reaching implications. It was probably grade B, rated G—scarcely a contestant for an Academy Award—but I'll never forget it.

Creatures from outer space invaded this planet, captured human beings, and took them to their space ship. When they had the earth people bound and anesthetized, they planted little electrical receivers in the back of their heads. The invaders held the controlling transmitters and returned the earthlings to their jobs and society. Some of the people on remote control killed their own husbands and wives, committed despicable crimes, and changed their life styles into parodies of their former selves because their thoughts and actions were being controlled by these extraterrestrial invaders.

That describes Satan exactly. He is an extraterrestrial invader who has planted his receiver deep in every human heart. This receiver is called "the flesh" or the sin nature. He also flashes his messages into our minds through the vast, highly organized world system he controls. This is why God tells us, "For the weapons of our warfare are not of the flesh, but divinely powerful for destruction of fortresses. For our struggle is not against flesh and blood, but against the rulers, against the powers, against the world-forces of this darkness . . ." (2 Corinthians 10:4; Ephesians 6:12).

Extremes of criminal behavior are not the only ways in which Satan works. His control of the atmosphere of thought in the world system is more deadly than the cold steel of a gun in your back. His *modus operandi* has been so successful that even Christians are constantly being lured from the divine viewpoint of life into Satan's web of deceit. Bombarded from every direction, undermined by the philosophy, education, art forms, music, mass media, styles, and fashions of the day, the world system will whirl us into its cesspool if we do not understand how we are being pushed and where we can slip.

Satan has always created confusion in the world. Nineteen centuries ago the Apostle Paul emphatically warned Christians: "See to it that no one takes you captive through philosophy and empty deception, according to the tradition of men, according to the elementary principles of the world, rather than according to Christ" (Colossians 2:8-9).

This is the warning: we are not to be taken captive by Satan through philosophy, which he has always used as a subtle, logical means of leading the minds of men away from the Truth. Today these philosophical deviations are more powerfully used than at any other time.

Twentieth century mind manipulation takes many forms. In the fields of psychology and sociology one of the modern social planners to hit the scene in a big way is B. F. Skinner.

Skinner Dipping

In 1971 *Time* magazine had a cover story about the man who says "we can no longer afford freedom, and so it must be replaced with control over man, his conduct and his culture."[1] This thesis, proposed not by a fiction writer, but by a man of science, raises the specter of a 1984 Orwellian society that may become reality.

B. F. Skinner, called by *Time* the "most influential of living American psychologists," reasons that free will is an illusion; he claims that since man is already controlled by external influences, he should plan his environment so that desired behavior will be guaranteed. In the Skinnerian world, utopia would be achieved by conditioning man to serve group interests.

How could this be done? Skinner believes that "human behavior can be predicted and shaped exactly as if it were a chemical reaction." The way to do it, he thinks, is through "behavioral technology," a developing science of control that aims to change the environment rather than people, that seeks to alter actions rather than feelings, and that shifts the customary psychological emphasis from the world inside men to the world outside them.

Skinner is said to believe that an "inner man is a superstition that originated, like belief in God, in man's inability to understand his world."[2] This leading exponent of behaviorism would deny the very existence of a soul-life, much less the possibility of needing a spiritual birth.

This is an extreme view of manipulating man, and many reputable psychologists reject Skinner's methods. However, the frightening thing about Skinner's book, *Beyond Freedom and Dignity*, is that some young intellectuals are beginning to take it seriously. Who would have dreamed that the writings of Karl Marx would find such dedicated adherents—or that Chamberlain's mad thesis of a master race would inspire fanatic zeal for its principles within one generation?

All that radical new panaceas for world problems need in order to flourish are crisis times and satanically inspired leaders like Lenin and Hitler. Could it be that the long-dreaded figure of Bible prophecy, the Antichrist, will rise up to implement Dr. Skinner's basic tenets into reality? According to the latest projections of scientists, scholars, and statesmen, the times just ahead will be right for such a phenomenon. The greatest crises in the history of man are a mathematical certainty according to the computerized projects of "Project Predicament of Man," sponsored by the prestigious international group called the Club of Rome.[3]

But before the young intellectuals of high school and college age are confronted with some of the more advanced techniques of a Skinner, they have been made pliable by the mind-bending in their pre-school and public school years.

Never Bend Over

Perhaps nowhere does the modern world viewpoint become more obviously opposed to God's viewpoint than in the area of the parent-child relationship. Basic concepts of discipline, respect for authority, absolutes, and morality have been radically changed in the concepts of child-rearing and the public educational system.

The permissive syndrome is not something new, but recent generations have been nurtured on it from the seeds planted by such men as Freud, Dewey, and Spock. These men led the way in applying relative thinking and life patterns without rules at the child level.

Freud's philosophy is complex, but is best described by his theory of "repression." Again and again in his writings, Freud returns to the question of man's repression by the society in which he lives. "Repression is the basic factor in man's unhappiness, in his inner conflicts, for society represses the individual, and thus the individual is forced to repress himself."[4]

Freudian thinking is that problems from childhood to adulthood are the result of being repressed, but the Bible says: "Correct your son, and he will give you comfort; He will also delight your soul" (Proverbs 29:17).

John Dewey, a man who threw out the traditional concepts of a few generations ago (that there are fixed moral laws and eternal truths), was a man who rejected God and the idea that man has a soul. His educational theories scorned individualism and promoted the idea that man should lose his individuality by finding acceptance and absorption in the great mass. Dewey's educational philosophy was built upon permissive principles, although the ideas were termed "progressive education," not permissive education. The Progressive Education Association, inspired by Dewey's views, put some of his doctrines into their code by expressions such as these: "The conduct of the pupils shall be governed by themselves, according to the social needs of the community," and "Interest shall be the motive for all work."[5]

What does all this mean? Erich Fromm, well-known psychologist, wrote: "The basic principle of such self-determination was the replacement of authority by freedom, to teach the child without the use of force by appealing to his curiosity . . . this attitude marked the beginning of progressive education and was an important step in human development."[6] Certainly a teacher should strive to be interesting and to capture the child's natural curiosity. But what these men proposed was education without specific requirements or structure.

Diametrically opposed to this way of thinking stands God's instructions, "Foolishness is bound up in the heart of a child; the rod of discipline will remove it far from him" (Proverbs 22:15).

Dr. Benjamin Spock, the pediatrician turned politician, in his famous handbook for parents, *Baby and Child Care*, advised the parents of the present generation not to restrict the permissiveness complex of children. Spock's advice was followed by thousands of inexperienced parents who raised their children with his book under one arm and the baby in the other. Parents were told not to spank, but to reason. According to the Dewey-Spock school of thought, the old-fashioned strap and woodshed principles were not a demonstration of love.

God wants us to discipline our children, but He certainly doesn't condone brutality. Some of the cruel beatings and punishments which are practiced by those who vent their own frustrations and hatreds upon children are despicable.

Children will test their parents to the limit. They will irritate, misbehave, and disobey until parental authority is backed up with action, not occasionally, but consistently.

God is not cruel; He is just—which is why He disciplines His children with love. And this is how He commands us to discipline our children—in love, not anger.

The Bible says, "He who spares his rod hates his son, but he who loves him disciplines him diligently" (Proverbs 13:24).

To discipline diligently means steadily, constantly, tirelessly, and patiently. It is not a sometime thing.

Radical Result in Education

Although the permissive philosophy of the Dewey followers has seeped through our educational system in various ways, there are few who would admit that the extreme theories of a comparative unknown by the name of A. S. Neill are acceptable in our public school systems. However, if you ask most college students in teacher-education courses if they have heard of "Summerhill," they would say "yes."

A. S. Neill started his radical approach to child rearing at his school, "Summerhill," in England. The Summerhill method has spread to the United States and is being used in many private schools and experimental public schools. If Neill's ideas were not required reading in so many college courses and were not so widely accepted in intellectual circles, they might not be important in this section about education. But what B. F. Skinner is to the extreme in psychological thought, Neill is to the extreme in educational circles.

At Summerhill, and the other schools patterned after it, there are no rules, no established courses of study. Freedom is the ultimate; happiness is the aim. "There is no need whatsoever to teach children how to behave. A child will learn what is right and what is wrong in good time . . . provided he is not pressured."[7]

Neill believes that all children are born good; therefore, there is no need for redemption. He believes that moral instruction makes a child bad, that "there is no case whatever for the moral instruction of children."[8]

The man who has spawned this radical approach to education writes: ". . . I repeat that parents are spoiling their children's lives by forcing on them outdated beliefs, outdated manners, outdated morals."[9]

The Bible says, "Train up a child in the way he should go, even when he is old he will not depart from it" (Proverbs 22:6).

Train . . . in the Way He Should Go

A cartoon in the Los Angeles Times showed a bound and gagged Statue of Liberty with a professor leaning over her saying, "Look, all I want is the truth, the whole truth, and nothing but the truth . . . as I see it."

Much of the formal education we have today is a product of "the truth . . . as I see it." As the permissive school of education has been built, the social engineers have been the builders—striving for a new world, a better society through guiding man and his behavior.

Bertrand Russell said: "Man now needs for his salvation only one thing: to open his heart to joy. He must lift up his eyes and say: 'No, I am not a miserable sinner.'"[10]

The Bible says, "It is a trustworthy statement, deserving full acceptance, that Christ Jesus came into the world to save sinners . . . for all have sinned and fall short of the glory of God" (1 Timothy 1:15; Romans 3:23).

H. G. Wells said: "It is the triangle of Socialism, Law and Knowledge which frames the Revolution that may yet save the world."[11]

The Bible says of Jesus, "And there is salvation in no one else; for there is no other name under heaven that has been given among men, by which we must be saved" (Acts 4:12).

These men will never come up with an adequate cure for man's basic problems because they have started with a wrong diagnosis.

And so the social planners and educational engineers continue, believing man is basically good and that he can somehow elevate society and create a better world by his own efforts. Meanwhile, the school system abolishes absolutes and rips moral values as it is caught in the grip of the world system.

Students and parents must wake up! We need to carefully evaluate what the educational system is advancing in the methods of the mind manipulators. As further effort is made to centralize and control education, there is more urgency than ever to learn and understand what God's truth is.

Mind Manipulators . . . in Art

It's "in" to be arty. There is no doubt that art has a real impact on the times. Or perhaps we should say that the times have an impact upon art.

A professor of fine art at the University of Edinburgh said, "Art is a mirror of its age . . . each age gets the art it deserves."[12]

A man's world view will permeate everything he creates. If the artist accepts a philosophy of life where there are no absolutes, no way of knowing definite purpose, his art will reflect this. This is one reason why a psychoanalyst will ask a patient to draw a picture. The way the patient sketches his surroundings and life can be very self-revealing.

Much art today ranges from the lewd to the absurd. You don't have to be a connoisseur to be hit in your subconscious by the obscenities which are expressed by some modern artists. Art is one of the most powerful mediums which affect the way a person thinks about life.

In analyzing some of the leading exponents of the new art, an art critic wrote: "There is some evidence that the climate of New York may now have become almost too favorable for heresies and radical experiments of all kinds. The appearance of a large and militantly avant-garde audience, a shockproof public that greedily accepts whatever is offered in the name of art so long as it is certifiably new and it has impressed Duchamp, among others, is proof that the long decline of Western art has now reached its nadir."[13]

H. R. Rookmaaker, an art history professor in Amsterdam, in documenting the main art trends from the Renaissance to the twentieth century, says, "Modern art in its more consistent forms puts a question mark against all values and principles."

Modern art, according to Rookmaaker, has won the battle and become the official art of today. "If in the wake of this avalanche of modern work of all kinds there is a strong anarchistic trend among the younger generation we must not be surprised." He believes that the modern movement of revolution in art has won because Christians were not alert. He says that his fellow Christians have not understood that art and literature, philosophy and even popular music are the agents of the "new spirit of the age" and have "left these alone or optimistically assumed they were too remote to be of influence."

Music . . . for the Masses

Satan works subliminally in the area of music. We are being bombarded, and we don't know what is hitting us. I was astounded as I began to study this subject. Basically I'm ignorant about music, and yet I realize that it is a powerful means of provoking emotions. Henry Thoreau, the new-old hero of many youth, prophesied in *Walden*: "Even music may be intoxicating. Such apparently slight causes destroyed Greece and Rome, and will destroy England and America."

I heard a professor of sociology speak on trends in music, and about rock in particular. This man was not an ivory-tower member of the academy speaking without experience. He was a member of the musician's union and had been a professional trumpet player for fifteen years. He explained that harmonic and rhythmic fabrics of rock music are critically important. And it's not necessary to comprehend the intricacies of music to understand what's being done with it.

This former jazz man described how changes in rhythm and other musical techniques can be used to sell attitudes and concepts. Many of Pavlov's experiments were conducted with a metronome to research the effects of rhythms as a conditioning agent.

By changing the rhythm within a musical piece, you may have a strong impact on the listener. The subconscious effect is to push the message more strongly.

The ability of music to excite and incite is nothing new. In primitive societies music's chief function is arousing emotion and action. However, in civilized countries music is more a means of communicating pleasurable emotions, not creating havoc.

Today, in some of our popular music at least, we seem to be reverting to savagery. The most dramatic indication of this is the number of times that rock concerts have erupted into riots.

I'm not trying to blast all modern music, but I think we should be aware of the fact that Satan can use it as his tool to pull us away from God and into chaotic thinking.

Poison in the Popcorn

When movie critics open their reviews with a social analysis of cinema artlessness, it is a sign that the concern for the evil impact of the media is widespread. A reviewer on one of America's largest dailies wrote: "As has often been observed, the loss of faith in technology in these perilous times is reflected in the resurgence of interest in astrology, psychic phenomena and even Satanism.

"The new preoccupation with the occult is also reflected in movies. The overwhelming success of Rosemary's Baby showed that film makers no longer needed to come up with rational last-reel explanations for seemingly supernatural goings-on. . . . In short, what several years ago most people would have dismissed as superstition in its ugliest form is in some quarters being taken seriously, regarded as 'purifying' or 'enlightening'."[15]

It's not difficult to see how Satan is using the world of entertainment to advance his kingdom. When movies are not presenting sex, violence, or Satanic themes, we see blatant mocking of the Christian faith. One movie rated GP (which means parents send their children in blind confidence) was The Reincarnate. The advertisement blared "No Heaven . . . No Hell . . . No Guilt! Eternal life is the only reality!" The subtitle to the film announced it was "A fascinating tale of the occult."

We've come a long way since the old Clark Gable era when the most daring escapade in the movies was a scene in "It Happened One Night" where Gable and Claudette Colbert made a curtain out of a blanket and put it between their beds when they were forced to spend the night in a cabin. They called the blanket the "Walls of Jericho," but today the movie makers have torn down the walls and turned them into crumpled bed sheets.

Reel life is supposed to depict real life, but the themes of some of the films are unreal. Counterfeit Christianity is one favorite. One issue of *Time* magazine carried two reviews, one of a film called *Black Jesus*, the other *Sweet Savior*. The first described a scene in which an African leader, a world-famous apostle of nonviolence, was brought before the local Pontius Pilate, cast into jail with a thief, and tortured with nails driven into his hands. The *Sweet Savior* description said: "The movie gloats over its scenes of degenerate sex and reaches a climax in human butchery . . . a symptom of a social disease."[16]

To their credit, many movie makers are trying to cure this social disease, but the virus has a head start.

The Eye in Our Living Room

Nowhere is the theme of permissiveness more subtly presented than through television. One popular comedy program shows "love" as the inevitable chase in and out of the bedroom, enjoyed in unmarried bliss. Many programs glamorize the social drink and burlesque the social drunk. The media is sanctimonious about eliminating cigarette advertising but liberal with suggestive jokes.

Talk shows have a way of reflecting the bias of the interviewer and the opinions of the audience. On one interview show a much-married celebrity was telling about a wedding ceremony he had recently attended where the vows exchanged between the bride and groom ended ". . . as long as we both shall love." The comments from Mr. Celeb were: "Isn't that a groovy idea. None of this Victorian idea of repeating 'as long as we both shall live.' " The audience reacted with applause, and the master of ceremonies agreed.

From cartoons to comedy, the mind benders use the television controls to channel us in the mold of the world system.

One World Economic System

Satan . . . the unifier. System and control are essential ingredients in his world system. In the vast area of economics and business, a trend toward a world economy with a centralized money exchange would be one tool which could be used to manage the purse strings of the world.

Is a world economic system possible?

A UPI report in 1968 said: "Rune Hoglund, president of Sweden's largest bank, said the long-term solution of international gold and monetary problems is establishment of an international paper currency issued by the International Monetary Fund."[17]

Most of us have little knowledge of the machinations of international banking or what effects it has upon our personal lives. However, one trend toward a moneyless society should be obvious to all of us with our bulging billfolds. Credit card living is a future probability. "Bankers in one city after another refer to it as 'the credit card revolution'."[18]

According to a 1967 report, in a two-year span of time the number of banks offering credit card services jumped from one hundred to fifteen hundred. Two years later *U.S. News* reported "an upheaval now going on in banks across the country."[19] This involved setting up holding companies which own a bank in addition to other businesses. The chairman of the Federal Reserve Board feared that holding companies might lead to undue concentration of economic power in the hands of the banks.

Many other economic manipulations can be used to centralize control in the hands of a few: industry taken from the free market economy and placed under state control; destruction of individual initiative through excessive taxation; regulatory laws which strangle private enterprise; government intervention into every aspect of private affairs.

A future world ruler will have his stage set if a one-world economic system is within his grasp.

Short Change

This whole system of thought has one fatal presupposition. "You can cure all of man's ills by changing or manipulating his environment."

The center of Jesus Christ's teaching was that man's problem is in his very heart and nature, and that you can only heal man by giving him an inner transformation, a new nature. Such a thing is possible only by a miraculous working of God's power called "the new birth." Jesus explained that man must be born spiritually because he is born into this world with a vacuum at the center of his being. He has physical life by which he can relate to the phenomena of this world, but he is without a spiritual dimension through which he can know God personally.

Jesus said, "Men can only reproduce human life, but the Holy Spirit gives new life from heaven; so don't be surprised at my statement that you must be born again!" (John 3:6-7, *Living Bible*).

Stop the World, I Want to Get Off

Any normal, sane person must be saying by now, "Stop the world, I want to get off!" But we can't stop the world or the world system. What can we do then? Mainly, we must be aware of how Satan is using art, music, philosophy, education, economics, and the mass media to entice us away from God's view of life. I think it's about time that we realize what is meant in James 4:4: "You adulteresses, do you not know that friendship with the world is hostility toward God? Therefore whoever wishes to be a friend of the world makes himself an enemy of God."

Why does James use the word "adulteresses"? If you have personally believed in Jesus Christ and accepted forgiveness from Him, you are married to Christ in a spiritual sense. When you go back to the world's way, figuratively you are committing adultery.

"Do you not know that friendship with the world is hostility toward God?" means that anyone who makes a friend of the world system is an enemy of God.

The world is a real battlefield in the area of our minds and our affections. We need the Spirit of God to give us careful discernment about what we allow to bombard our minds. This is why the Scripture says: "Do not love the world, nor the things in the world. If any one loves the world, the love of the Father is not in him" (1 John 2:15).

What Wavelength Are You On?

If we think we can get into these deceptive things of the world and still remain on intimate terms with God, we are deluding ourselves. We won't lose our relationship with God, but we will get so disoriented spiritually that we cannot think God's thoughts. We can't be intimate with God when our affections are dominated by the world. We are on a different wavelength.

When Jesus told us we are to be "*in* the world but not *of* it," He meant that we are not to cop out or drop out but to reject the world's hold on our affections and mental attitudes. Then we can be part of the solution for the world instead of part of the problem.

We need more Christian writers, artists, business people, and educators who will produce works that express God's viewpoint. This is not a time for withdrawal; this is a time for involvement!

Needed: A New World

H. G. Wells said, "Either Mankind collapses or our species struggles up by the hard, fairly obvious routes I have collated in this book to reach a new level of social organization."[20]

The philosophers of the day try to find unity and reason in this mixed-up world. However, they shut themselves off from the only hope—Jesus Christ.

More and more I see what Jesus meant when He said, "You shall know the truth, and the truth shall make you free" (John 8:32).

Jesus Christ is not a concept of truth; He is Truth. That is why He is the only one who can set us free from the established world order. He is the only one who can give us the freedom to find the full potential that God intended us to have. He is the only one who can give meaning and definition and purpose to life.

I am not speaking theoretically. I am speaking out of experience.

By the time I was twenty-six years old, I had tried everything and was saying, "Okay, now what do I do for an encore?" I'd run out. I began thinking about committing suicide. It was only then that I reached out, with no faith at all, to read the third chapter of John. To my amazement, Someone took my hand; He turned on the lights, and I found that Someone was Jesus Christ.

In this world where men have cut their moorings from God and values, there is only one real hope: to be born spiritually by faith in Jesus Christ. For those who are, it is the most exciting time to be alive. Things are happening so quickly today that I can hardly keep them catalogued—no one can.

Revolutionaries, social planners, humanistic philosophers . . . attention, please! A New World order will be established someday. When Jesus Christ returns, He is going to throw out the garbage of the world system and then —and only then—we will see perfect equality and peace.

That time is coming when believers in Jesus Christ are going to walk upon this earth and see it in perfect condition. Pollution will be passé.

Jesus Christ is going to recycle the late great Planet Earth.

8 ○ Angels of Light

"...for even Satan disguises himself as an angel of light. Therefore it is not surprising if his servants also disguise themselves as servants of righteousness...."

2 CORINTHIANS 11:14-15

As THE MASS media bombards us with instant news, it also programs us with future forecasts. Modern-day prophets manipulate minds by anticipating things to come.

Newspaper columns, best seller lists, and television talk shows are spouting prophecies, and the current prophets are prolific in their outpourings. The late Edgar Cayce, known as "the sleeping prophet" because his "readings" came to him during periods of trancelike slumber, left so many prophecies in stenographic records that there is a special library devoted to them.

How should the public evaluate these people and their pronouncements? Each individual has the freedom to discredit or believe them, but the Christian must judge these prophecies on the basis of God's standards.

What About Jeane Dixon?

If that question has been asked me once—well, you know the rest. Mrs. Dixon is perhaps the best known psychic of modern times with an impressive list of amazing predictions, some of which have come true and were fairly detailed.

In her book, *The Call to Glory*, which deals with her views of Jesus Christ, among other things, Mrs. Dixon claims that: "It is my belief God has given me a gift of prophecy for His own reasons, and I do not question them."[1]

How does she receive these prophetic powers?

"I empty my mind in order that I may be filled with the Spirit of God. Finally, during my meditations, when my spirit is calm and He is ready, God talks to me. I know then, beyond all doubt, that the channel is coming directly to me from the Divine, the Lord our God, because *I feel it* and sense it. I know it is not the channel of Satan, because his channel I have felt and sensed too; and I definitely know the difference. So according to my wisdom I follow the Lord's channel...."[2]

She claims, "The future has been shown to me to 2037 A.D."[3]

She predicts such things as the rise of the Antichrist, major world conditions leading up to and following this, the Second Coming of Christ and a time of unprecedented blessing to follow.

Many of her new predictions are very close to biblical prophecies of these events, but the whole timetable for their occurrence does not fit with the biblical pattern. According to my understanding of the biblical prophets, all of the events which are associated with the Second Coming of Christ will occur within a time period of seven years immediately preceding His visible and personal return to the earth (Daniel 9-11).

She also speaks authoritatively about how to know Jesus Christ and enter God's kingdom.

When a person makes the sort of claims for herself that Jeane Dixon has made, either she is a remarkable modern-day prophet of God and we should analyze her prophetic utterances as new revelations from God on the level with Scripture, or she is a counterfeit prophet who, though appearing as an angel of light, is setting up the unwary for great deception.

Appointment Arranged

To be as fair and discerning as possible with Mrs. Dixon, I prayed that God would somehow get me an interview with her. This was next to impossible, but through an incredible set of circumstances, not long after my prayer I found myself in a face to face encounter with her, an interview which lasted for some time.

Mrs. Dixon is a charming and sincere person who is genuinely interested in people and speaks of God in a natural and easy manner. I liked her immediately and enjoyed several hours of fascinating conversation with her.

As I had anticipated our meeting I had searched the Scriptures to find what is most important in discerning whether a modern-day prophet is really a true prophet of God or not. I found that the most important issues are what one believes about Jesus Christ and what one thinks the requirement is to become a true Christian. Therefore, I was concerned about Mrs. Dixon's view of what a person must believe to be forgiven of sin and accepted into God's kingdom. This is a most crucial issue, and I could not find a clear statement on this subject in any of her books. In her many illustrations of prominent people whom she had helped get right with God, she told of emphasizing to them that they could find God by finding their talent in life and using it in the service of humanity.

Mrs. D. and Salvation

In *The Call to Glory* Mrs. Dixon makes the nearest thing to a definitive statement about her view of how to become a Christian. In the chapter on "Getting to Know Him," she says, "The present Jesus Christ becomes known by bringing the knowledge of His historical life and teaching into our lives; this is the way we bring Jesus Christ into our lives, for was it not He who said, 'I am the way, the truth and the life.'"[4]

In another section of the same chapter she says, "His (Jesus') major message was if we follow His teachings and strive for the kingdom of God while on earth, then we will have a much better life on earth, and the assurance of eternal life in heaven."[5]

Mrs. Dixon confirmed this thinking in our conversation. But the above statements are not the Gospel that Jesus Christ has given us to share with man so that he may enter God's kingdom. They set forth a salvation by works plus faith and exactly what we are to believe is not made clear.

The Bible declares, "For by grace you have been saved through faith; and not of yourselves, it is the gift of God; not as a result of works, that no one should boast" (Ephesians 2:8-9).

This verse shows that if we *strive* to gain God's acceptance by our own works, we won't make it.

When some sincere religious seekers asked Jesus what works they could do to inherit eternal life, Jesus said, "This is the work of God, that you *believe* in Him whom He has sent" (John 6:29).

The only way to come to God is to accept the work which Jesus did for us at the cross and believe in Him as our personal Savior from sin and its consequence, which is eternal separation from God.

We are saved by grace, not by works or human merit. "But if it is by grace, it is no longer on the basis of works, otherwise grace is no longer grace" (Romans 11:6).

The only possible way of receiving grace is through the agency of faith. Faith is the one thing that man can do and still not accomplish anything meritorious. Biblical faith is receiving the work of another on my behalf based on the realization that I can't help myself.

Even my works for God as a Christian must be done in my life through faith. For the Bible says, "And without faith it is impossible to please Him . . ." (Hebrews 11:6).

As I depend upon Christ for strength and direction, the following becomes true: "For it is God who is at work in you, both to will and to work for His good pleasure" (Philippians 2:13).

Mrs. D. and Faith

Not once does Mrs. Dixon make clear the object of saving faith, which is the significance of Christ's substitutionary death, bearing our judgment for not being able to measure up to God's perfect law.

The Bible says, "He made Him who knew no sin to be sin on our behalf, that we might become the righteousness of God in Him" (2 Corinthians 5:21). "Even the righteousness of God through faith in Jesus Christ for all those who believe; for there is no distinction; for all have sinned and fall short of the glory of God, being justified as a gift by His grace through the redemption which is in Christ Jesus" (Romans 3:22-24).

To be justified means to be declared righteous and blameless in God's sight.

In talking with Mrs. Dixon, I asked her why she hadn't made salvation and faith clear in her books, and she said, "Because the world is not ready for that yet."

Is the world not ready to hear a message which God commanded to be preached to every creature?

In all fairness, I must state that when I went through the facts of the true Gospel of Christ with Mrs. Dixon she said that she had always known and believed those things. Assuming that she actually does believe them, it is difficult for me to understand why she doesn't make them clear, but rather stresses a message of works.

A prophet's chief goal should be to lead people to a saving faith in Jesus Christ. "For the testimony of Jesus is the spirit of prophecy" (Revelation 19:10).

Is She a Prophet of God?

Rene Noorbergen, the writer of Mrs. Dixon's book, *My Life and Prophecies*, raises twenty issues in the prologue which are designed to lead the reader to the conclusion that Jeane Dixon has a God given gift of prophecy which is in accord with the Scriptures.

At the close of this list, Noorbergen writes, "Jeane Dixon's record of accuracy is unequaled."[6]

I would like to raise the question, "Unequaled in comparison to whom?"

If Noorbergen is comparing Jeane Dixon's record to the records of modern-day prophets such as Edgar Cayce, Maurice Woodruff, and others, Mrs. Dixon *is* the most accurate. If Noorbergen means to compare her with the biblical prophets, there is no contest. A biblical prophet was a person called of God and given a unique gift and commission which always fit into God's ultimate goal of bringing men to a change of heart and faith in His provision for salvation from sin.

One of the chief credentials of a true prophet of God was that he had to be 100 percent accurate on all predictions. Noorbergen and Jeane Dixon left this credential out of the list of twenty given in *My Life and Prophecies*.

While talking with Mrs. Dixon, I brought up the passage in Deuteronomy 18:9-22 which gives the description of a true prophet of God. She said that she knew the passage well; however, I observe that it was strangely absent in all of her books.

In this portion of Scripture Moses warned the Israelites about seeking to obtain secret information and guidance through the occultic practices common to the people whom they were expelling from the land of Canaan. Instead of looking to these forbidden pursuits, they were to obtain all their guidance and understanding through prophets who would be sent from God, as Moses was.

Moses put it this way: "When you enter the land which the Lord your God gives you, you shall not learn to imitate the detestable things of those nations. There shall not be found among you anyone who makes his son or his daughter pass through fire, one who uses divination, one who practices witchcraft, or one who interprets omens, or a sorcerer, or one who casts a spell, or a medium, or a spiritist, or one who calls up the dead. For whoever does these things is detestable to the Lord; and because of these detestable things the Lord your God will drive them out before you" (Deuteronomy 18:9-12).

Divination

This is a term from the previous passage which needs careful definition. There are many means of divination, but all forms seek to obtain secret knowledge of past, present, and especially future events by supernatural means. The most amazing display of divination is called "inspirational divination" in which the medium is given direct communication from demons of events that could not have been known by normal means. In this form of divination, the medium is conscious of contact with real spirit beings, though erroneously thinking that it is the Spirit of God.

The pagan world was filled with diviners, which were a counterpart of God's prophets. Every king of the ancient world had his cabinet of diviners, soothsayers, magicians, and astrologers. Daniel mentions this practice throughout his book. (See also Leviticus 19:26, 31; 20:6; Joshua 13:22; Jeremiah 27:9.)

If a person receives accurate secret knowledge which cannot be attributed to fakery, then there are only two possible sources. The person is either a prophet of God and receiving revelation from the Holy Spirit, or he is a divining medium receiving revelation from a demon, called in Acts 16:16 "a spirit of divination." The Bible leaves us no other option.

Whispering Wizards

Isaiah lashed out against the nation of Israel because they had departed so much from their true faith that they were turning from the true prophets to the occult diviners. Listen to his inspired warning: "And when they say to you, 'Consult the mediums and the wizards who whisper and mutter,' should not a people consult their God? Should they consult the dead on behalf of the living? To the law and to the testimony! If they do not speak according to this word, it is because they have no dawn" (Isaiah 8:19-20).

The challenge of Isaiah is appropriate for our day. As the nation Israel had been drawn away from the true faith, so America is rushing headlong into apostasy today. For discernment as to what is true and false we must evaluate all things by "the law" and "the testimony," which means the Bible. If any phenomenon, no matter how seemingly moral, religious, and supernatural, doesn't jibe with God's Word, it is because these false prophets have "no dawn," or literally "have no light" (i.e., they don't have light from God's Spirit).

As Moses condemned all forms of occult practice and predicted that other prophets like himself would be sent to give God's Word to Israel, he perceived a question that was already in everyone's mind: "How shall we know the word which the Lord has not spoken?" (Deuteronomy 18:21). In other words, how are we to tell who is a "diviner" and who is a "prophet sent by God"?

Test of a True Prophet

Moses gave the acid test: "When a prophet speaks in the name of the Lord, if the thing does not come about or come true, that is the thing which the Lord has not spoken . . ." (Deuteronomy 18:22).

Two important things are to be observed here. First, nowhere is there any authorization for obtaining secret knowledge of past, present, or future things except by the sovereign will and inspiration of the Spirit of God. "For no prophecy was ever made by an act of human will, but men moved by the Holy Spirit spoke from God" (2 Peter 1:21).

God says again on this matter, "The secret things belong to the Lord our God, but the things revealed belong to us and to our sons forever, that we may observe all the words of this law" (Deuteronomy 29:29).

Only God's prophets are authorized to reveal secret things and only with a purpose of bringing men into obedience to His Word.

Whatever God's Spirit reveals to a prophet is always spoken in the Lord's name. This is why the statement, "Thus says the Lord," appears hundreds of times throughout the Bible.

A New Testament prophet named Agabus said, "This is what the Holy Spirit says. . ." (Acts 21:11).

Everything spoken in the name of the Lord, or the Spirit of God, must come true exactly as predicted. In Israel, before her apostasy, a prophet was either 100 percent accurate or he was stoned (with rocks, that is)!

No prophet called of God was given authorization to hedge his predictions! Nowhere does a Bible prophet claim that some predictions are the thoughts of men and thus, because men can change their minds, may be excused for inaccuracy. God, who has perfect foreknowledge of all things, is never fooled by men changing their minds. He even knows when this will occur, and His prophecies take it into account.

Mrs. D. and the Bible

Let's examine Jeane Dixon's claims in the light of the biblical standards of accuracy and purpose.

Her prophecies do not all come true. Though the accurate predictions are greatly publicized, the inaccurate ones are usually ignored. Just a few of her failures are listed here:

World War III would begin in 1958.

Red China would be admitted to the United Nations in 1958.

The Vietnam War would end in ninety days (i.e., from 7 May 1966) on terms not satisfactory to the U.S.

On 19 October 1968 she said that Jacqueline Kennedy was not thinking of marriage. The next day she married Onassis.

How does she explain her failures? Mrs. Dixon gives a curious answer. She has several categories of prophecies which she makes. First, she claims that divine revelations are always accurate. The other categories are based on "tuning in" on the thoughts of men via mental telepathy through a number of methods, such as touching their fingertips, getting them to look into a crystal ball while she reads their thoughts, putting her hand on a deck of cards she received from a gypsy fortuneteller, or dreams and visions.

Mrs. Dixon claims that at the time she reads the person's thoughts, she accurately predicts what he intends to do. But since these are only the plans of men, intentions can change and then the prediction does not come true.

As fascinating as this explanation may be, it does not square with the Word of God. She may receive secret information, but if she does it is not from the Spirit of God. If it were from God, it would be accurate in spite of any change of mind on the part of men.

The Bible does not authorize hedging a prophetic bet with qualifications. Any prediction of the future must come true or it is not from God.

Her prophecies are not given in the name of the Lord. God-given revelations of the future must be given in the name of the Lord; no other kinds of predictions are authorized. All other prophets are branded false prophets and divining mediums. Even pagan prophets used to predict some things accurately, but not in the Lord's name (see Deuteronomy 13:1-5).

She obtains secret information supernaturally, but not through the Spirit of God. This is an intrusion into an area expressly forbidden by God. "The secret things belong to the Lord."

Mrs. Dixon's prophetic insight into the lives of people both for present and future events is clearly occultic.

Her prophecies do not line up with the biblical purpose for prophecy. True prophecy has two purposes: first, it should bring people to obedience to God's Word (Deuteronomy 29:29); second, it should bring people the testimony about Jesus Christ (Revelation 19:10).

Mrs. Dixon makes predictions about such things as fashion changes, horse races, and prominent celebrities. When she tells the future of well-known personalities, no attempt is made to bring them to a personal faith in Jesus Christ or to challenge some of their moral and spiritual problems.

She gives a lot of political advice but doesn't consistently exhort people for failing to believe in Jesus Christ as personal Lord and Savior. Some leaders from the East come to her, and no issue is made concerning personal faith in Jesus Christ instead of their false religions. Yet the Bible declares, "And there is salvation in no one else; for there is no other name under heaven that has been given among men, by which we must be saved" (Acts 4:12).

Jesus Christ is the theme of all true prophecy (Revelation 19:10). All prophecy must either bear direct witness or authenticate a witness as to how men can be forgiven of their sins and be born again spiritually.

Mrs. Dixon's predictions are about everything from the mundane to international political affairs, with no true witness to the Gospel of the grace of God attached to them.

She uses artifacts of the occult to receive her prophecies. I questioned Mrs. Dixon at length about why she uses a crystal ball, a deck of cards from a gypsy fortuneteller, palmistry, astrology, numerology, etc, and she had an explanation for each of these things.

About the crystal ball: she said that she doesn't ever receive visions in the ball itself, but rather uses it as a means of helping the person whom she is "reading" to clear his mind and concentrate. Then she reads his mind by "vibrations" or "telepathy." Both are contrary to the teaching of Scripture.

Both cases are an example of intruding by human will into the area of "secret things" which the Lord has forbidden. God says, "But know this first of all, no prophecy of Scripture is a matter of one's own interpretation" (2 Peter 1:20). This means that God's prophets didn't initiate or give their own interpretation of life and history. It continues, "For no prophecy was ever made by an act of human will, but men moved by the Holy Spirit spoke from God" (2 Peter 1:21).

Furthermore, no prophet of God made a practice of using artifacts to receive a vision or a prophecy, especially things that have been historically associated with the occult such as Mrs. Dixon uses.

Contradictions in the Crystal Ball

Mrs. Dixon seems to contradict her own claim of "not seeing things in the crystal ball."

As she described her meeting with the gypsy at age eight when she first received the crystal ball, she said, "I looked into it and what I saw was so beautiful it almost made me cry. I saw a wild, rocky coast in a far-off land and a turbulent sea crashing into the jagged edges of the crumbling rocks."[7]

The fortuneteller was deeply moved and said that Jeane had just described her homeland. On this basis she gave Jeane the crystal ball. If words mean anything, Jeane Dixon said she "looked into the crystal ball and saw" that vision.

Mrs. Dixon describes another incident which happened in 1948: ". . . suddenly the crystal ball was filled with tumult. I saw helmeted police and heavily armed soldiers leading and dragging sullen and belligerent men through angry crowds, etc."[8]

Note that she said, "the crystal ball was filled with tumult . . . etc."

My question is this: if Mrs. Dixon doesn't see her visions in the crystal ball, why does she need it at all? Aren't there other means of helping a person to relax and concentrate? Why use something that is contrary to any biblical pattern of prophecy and which has always been associated with the occult?

The partial deck of "blessed cards" was given to Jeane when she was a young girl by the gypsy fortuneteller, who was clearly a medium, possibly demon-possessed. "Cartomancy," described by Kurt Koch, is the technique of fortunetelling by means of cards. Koch cites many examples (he has examined over 20,000 case histories) of a pattern of occult involvement being established by experiences with mediums.[9]

The fortuneteller's cards are examples of the types of artifacts clearly condemned in the Scriptures. In witchcraft, for instance, certain artifacts carry a strong presence of demon influence. This is why it is reported in Acts 19:18-19: "Many also of those who had believed kept coming, confessing and disclosing their practices. And many of those who practiced magic brought their books together and began burning them in the sight of all; and they counted up the price of them and found it fifty thousand pieces of silver."

To be delivered from demonism these people confessed their practice of black magic and burned their artifacts. Whenever I lead a person to Christ who has been involved in the occult, I immediately urge him to confess his complicity with demons to God and get rid of all artifacts associated with the occult such as crystal balls, tarot cards, books on the occult, jewelry of the occult, ouija boards, astrology paraphernalia or fortunetelling bric-a-brac.

The use of astrology plays a role in Mrs. Dixon's analysis of a person. One of the first things she asked me was, "What is the date of your birth?"

She has a regular syndicated astrological column in over three hundred newspapers in the United States.[10] Mrs. Dixon said that she began the horoscope column because this was a way of giving helpful advice about life to many people who were requesting her help.

God condemns the practice of astrology, which began in ancient Babylon along with all kinds of witchcraft and black magic. It grew out of the pagan belief that each star was a god who exercised control over men's lives. It was a pseudo-science as well, which has been proven absurd in the light of modern science.

The prophet Daniel clearly declared that the things of God could not be understood or predicted by the occult representatives of his day: "Daniel answered before the king and said, 'As for the mystery about which the king has inquired, neither wise men, conjurers, magicians, nor diviners are able to declare it to the king. However, there is a God in heaven who reveals mysteries, and He has made known to King Nebuchadnezzar what will take place in the latter days" (Daniel 2:27-28).

Astrology was the chief means of divining in the kingdom of Babylon. The king financed the building of elaborate towers for the astrologers to use in their study of the stars. The ruins of these "observatories" are still visible today in Iraq.

Isaiah condemned the astrologers and sorcerers in Babylon and predicted their destruction. "Stand fast now in your spells and in your many sorceries with which you have labored from your youth; perhaps you will be able to profit, perhaps you may cause trembling. You are wearied with your many counsels, let now the astrologers, those who prophesy by the stars, those who predict by the new moons, stand up and save you from what will come upon you. Behold, they have become like stubble, fire burns them; they cannot deliver themselves from the power of the flame; there will be no coal to warm by, nor a fire to sit before!" (Isaiah 47:12-14).

No child of God has any business toying with astrology, much less practicing it as Mrs. Dixon does.

So As to Mislead

In conclusion, I believe many lessons should be learned from the case of Jeane Dixon. This is why I have gone into so much detail about her. I believe many prophets like her will appear in the near future. Jesus said, ". . . false prophets will arise and will show great signs and wonders, so as to mislead, if possible, even the elect. *Behold, I have told you in advance*" (Matthew 24:24-25).

With real regret I told Mrs. Dixon that I believed her prophetic ability was *not* from God. I told her I sincerely believed that if she didn't reject this psychic power, it would lead to her destruction.

She said she was certain her gift was from God and that she knew beyond doubt the "feeling" of God's presence.

When I left her, I quoted Proverbs 14:12; "There is a way which seems right to a man, but its end is the way of death."

When our "feelings," no matter how right they may seem, contradict Scripture, we must conclude that our feelings are wrong.

May God graciously touch Jeane Dixon and bring her fully to the truth.

In the meantime, reader, be discerning.

9 ○ Signs and Wonders

"Bread obtained by falsehood is sweet to a man, but afterward his mouth will be filled with gravel."
PROVERBS 20:17

We ARE LIVING in a time when history is racing toward a climax. The pattern of events which the prophets said would occur before the Second Coming of Christ are coming together rapidly.

After hundreds of years of being scattered throughout the world, the Jews have returned to their homeland to establish a nation again. They have recaptured Old Jerusalem and have sustained sovereign possession of it for the first time in 2600 years.

The Arabs have united with the mutual desire of attacking Israel to regain their land.

To the north of Israel a great military power has formed in Russia.

In the Orient there is a great power that can field an army of 200,000,000 men—Red China.

There are rumblings of the revival of the ancient Roman culture in Europe uniting to form a ten-nation confederacy in the Common Market.

Scientists, confronted with the reality of the world situation, are predicting famines on a scale never seen by man—in the next ten to fifteen years.

Earthquakes are increasing mysteriously; pollution promises to be a greater and greater problem.

All of these things are predicted in the Bible, and they are fitting together simultaneously. We are in an unparalleled time in human history in which the most wonderful event of all, Jesus Christ coming secretly to snatch out all of those who truly believe in Him, could happen at any moment.*

Prophecy of Deceptions

Along with these events, there is another great prophetic sign of the imminent return of Christ: the emergence of Satanic deceptions through the activity of counterfeit miracles and false prophets.

---

* For a more detailed account read *The Late Great Planet Earth.*

The Bible gives a series of sober warnings both to those who know Jesus Christ personally and to those who don't know Him or may be putting off this decision.

The first warning was given by Christ Himself in one of His last great public messages. As Jesus was about to be arrested and taken to the cross, He said that we should watch because there would be great deceptions during the last times; there would be false messiahs, people who would come in with a plan for saving the world, for bringing about a utopian society (Matthew 24:4-5). He warned that there would be false prophets who would mislead many (Matthew 24:11).

These warnings are not just to the world, but to the believers—to those who know Jesus Christ. He said, "For false Christs and false prophets will arise and will show great signs and wonders, so as to mislead, if possible, even the elect" (Matthew 24:24).

The Apostle Paul prophesied that these counterfeits would be a part of the activities which would prepare the way for the great world dictator known as the Antichrist. "That is, the one whose coming is in accord with the activity of Satan, with all power and signs and false wonders, and with all the deception of wickedness for those who perish, because they did not receive the love of the truth so as to be saved" (2 Thessalonians 2:9-10).

The prelude to this dictator will be a build-up of supernatural phenomena through Satanic power. The same words used to describe the miracles of Christ in the gospels are used here, which clearly indicates that in the last days Satan will be permitted a greater freedom to counterfeit the miracles and gifts of the Holy Spirit.

What/Who Is a False Prophet?

A false prophet claims to have a revelation from God, but doesn't; he appears to be someone sent from God, but isn't. He doesn't simply step out on the center stage of humanity and say, "Behold, I am a false prophet, so don't listen to what I have to say." He comes in sheep's clothing, but inside he's a ravening wolf. He makes proclamations and predictions mixed with just enough truth to make them plausible.

The Scriptures clearly tell us that false teachers and prophets have the ability to mix truth with deception.

As the days draw near for the return of Christ, the Bible says that God will allow these false prophets to work miracles in the power of His archenemy—Satan himself. They will work great signs, so that even those who know Jesus Christ will be deceived—but not utterly deceived, for that's not possible.

In the Power of Satan

What kinds of miracles can we expect to see in the last days? In Acts 8 we find one example of the power of Satan. "Now there was a certain man named Simon, who formerly was practicing magic in the city, and astonishing the people of Samaria, claiming to be someone great; and they all, from smallest to greatest, were giving attention to him, saying, 'This man is what is called the Great Power of God'" (Acts 8:9-10).

Here was a man who through black magic had performed such things before people that they thought it was the power of God, but he did it by the power of Satan!

We have examples from the days of Moses when God sent him into the court of Pharaoh and he worked some real wonders before the Egyptian people. We are told that the magicians who practiced black magic duplicated the first several signs that Moses worked; they were able to counterfeit the miracles of God.

Many people do not realize that Satan has this power. He has the power to come as an angel of light; he has his own ministers. He may work through someone who appears to be righteous. He may perform feats of the supernatural which appear to be direct acts of God.

I do believe that God is working miracles today and that we haven't seen anything yet! We are in the day of a special outpouring of the Spirit of God that will parallel the early days of the Church. God is beginning to show the miraculous in reauthentication of His Word and His message. However, Satan is also going to be allowed to counterfeit these miracles.

And, this is why we must . . .

Be Discerning

Christian, be warned! You may see and be involved in acts which appear to be supernatural. You may be inclined to think, "Wow, this must be of God; it's miraculous!"

Watch out.

One of the ways in which great deceptions are going to capture individuals is through the popularity of the occult.

At the check-out counter in a supermarket you can buy a 25¢ booklet on *Everyday Witchcraft*. The cover shows a white cat, a black candle, and the enticing words, "Love magic, charms and spells, fortunetelling; everything you need to know to enjoy occult power!"[1]

What a come-on. So innocent. So appealing.

Women, especially, are going in for palmistry and fortunetelling in a big way. Political, charitable, and philanthropic organizations, searching for the newest in modern motifs for their luncheons or fund-raising events, are turning to the occult theme.

If you have read this far and still do not believe in the danger of these things, the following is a true story about a man who was equally hard to convince.

A Little Dabble Do Ya

A young minister wanted to expose the folly of astrology to his congregation. Rather than showing them the demonic spirit behind astrology, he figured the best way was through involving himself, so he had his horoscope cast. *Why not*, he thought. *This is all ridiculous, and I'm going to show my people how absurd it is.*

He told his church what he had done and even told them what had been predicted about his life. To his amazement, those things started coming true. He began to have periods of terrible fear; he lost his discernment. He read the Bible but didn't have the understanding he had had previously. As the conflict in the spiritual realm became almost unbearable, he finally went to God on his knees and confessed that he had sinned by dabbling in this art, realizing that it wasn't just a bunch of fakery.

When he went to God and confessed, he was delivered from his spiritual oppression and immediately the remainder of that horoscope began to be wrong.

There are many case histories of this type in Dr. Kurt Koch's book *Between Christ and Satan*.[2]

Any time you submit yourself unreservedly to the spiritual realm, turn off your mind and cease to be discerning, you are opening yourself up to possible demon deception. As you study the Scriptures on this, you will find that even though you may be sincere, earnestly seeking God, not immoral or involved in some gross sin, this will not keep you from being deceived.

Jesse Penn Lewis tells how a great revival in Wales was completely neutralized by an invasion of demonic power.[3] The demons began to get into this movement through people who sincerely wanted to know God in a deeper way and began to open themselves up for all kinds of spiritual contact and leading. You may say, "Well, if that's true, should I ever open myself up to God?" Of course you should. We are commanded to submit ourselves to Him. However, since there's more than one spirit which will try to contact us in the spiritual realm, we are warned to "try the spirits" to see whether they are of God or not. As we depend on the Holy Spirit and have the Word of God in our hearts, the Holy Spirit will never lead us contrary to His written word.

Sometimes this discernment will take time; we may not understand what the Holy Spirit is seeking to reveal to us. Our hearts may cry out, "I want to have something dramatic happen—something which will show me God's power in a fantastic way. I want to know it all—right now!"

Instant Maturity

A deceiving spirit can get into a person's life when he begins to believe there is some experience which is going to give him instant maturity.

The Scripture tells us that when we become believers in Jesus Christ we have the Holy Spirit indwelling us. As believers we must come to understand that we can walk in dependence upon the power of the Spirit of God Himself. We can have His power to live for Christ, to understand God's Word, to minister for Christ according to our spiritual gifts, and to overcome temptation. Any believer can have this. A babe in Christ who submits himself to God and walks by faith and dependence upon Christ can be empowered by the Spirit.

However, there is no such thing as instant perfection or instant maturity!

When, as a young believer in Christ, I first learned I could have the power of the Holy Spirit in my life, I claimed this by faith and God began to overcome hangups in my life. He began to do things through me that I had never seen before in my whole life. As I look back with the mature perspective I have now, I know God was blessing my faith and my understanding as far as it went, but there were big areas that I didn't understand, and God just didn't hold me accountable for those areas.

The Christian life is a maturing process. We are to keep growing in grace and knowledge of Christ. There are many Christians, especially young Christians today, who want everything now. Some seek an experience by which they instantly have total victory over the flesh—no more temptations. They want to have great power and wisdom so that they suddenly know more than the Bible teachers, more than their pastors.

God may graciously grant us an experience that will give our faith such a jolt that we start believing in Him. We may suddenly come to realize for the first time that the Holy Spirit is dwelling in us and that we can count on Him for power. For many people this may come as such a welcome revelation that they would describe it as a "second blessing." Some even conclude that they must have received the Holy Spirit for the first time because His indwelling Presence has become so real to them. This, of course, is unscriptural. Every believer has the Holy Spirit indwelling him, but not necessarily filling or empowering him.

When we initially become aware of His personal power and Presence within us and yield to His control, we may experience anything from a quiet sense of assurance to an emotional sense of release. The point is, however, that we still have to grow in knowledge; we have to know how to apply the truth of the Scripture to our life day by day; we have to grow in our ability to depend upon God in our daily circumstances and to live by faith, claiming His promises. If we try to jump over this process of growth, we can get into a situation where we can be badly deceived.

One of the most controversial subjects in the Christian world today, and one which I write about only after years of study and much prayer, is this matter of the supernatural gifts of the Spirit, particularly tongues. Now and then I run into people who have never heard about this phenomenon. Many others are confused by the profusion of books on the subject—both pro and con—and are genuinely seeking a calm, reasonable, and biblical approach to this issue. For this reason I feel that it is necessary to deal with the subject in a book such as this. Mine is by no means an exhaustive study; a whole book would be necessary for that. But I do want to set forth some of the prevalent thinking about this matter and my own conclusions.

There are different views among those who speak in tongues regarding the purpose of tongues, kinds of tongues, what tongues indicate, and who must speak in tongues. The old-line Pentecostals and a new breed of articulate writers and speakers who have sought to be the spokesmen for the new tongues phenomenon, usually referred to as the charismatic movement, do not agree on all points.

Similarly, many evangelicals have spoken out strongly against this modern-day manifestation, and their denunciation ranges from accusations that "all tongues are of the Devil" to "God may be giving the gift today, but you're better off staying away from it."

As the present charismatic phenomenon began to grow to epidemic proportions in many areas of the world, I felt I needed to take a second look to see if any of it was of God and for the church today. I had previously believed that all of the sign gifts such as healing, miracles, tongues, and prophecies ceased as bona fide gifts of the Spirit about the end of the first century, just after the New Testament was completed.

The Scripture usually cited to prove this thesis is First Corinthians 13:8-12: "Love never fails; but if there are gifts of prophecy, they will be done away; if there are tongues, they will cease; if there is knowledge, it will be done away. For we know in part, and we prophesy in part; but when the *perfect* comes, the partial will be done away. When I was a child, I used to speak as a child, think as a child, reason as a child; when I became a man, I did away with childish things. For now we see in a mirror dimly, but then face to face; now I know in part, but then I shall know fully, just as I also have been fully known."

There are many biblical scholars who believe that the "perfect" in this passage refers to the completed New Testament canon of Scriptures. This school of thought contends that after the New Testament was written there was no longer any reason for God's message to be authenticated by special supernatural signs, so the gifts were taken away. For this reason, they look sceptically upon any present-day manifestation of these sign gifts.

This is admittedly a difficult passage of Scripture, but I have come to believe that the "perfect" refers to a condition which will be true of us when Christ returns for the Church and gives us glorified bodies like His own. Then we will see Him face to face and know as we have been known. Therefore it is my opinion that this passage alone is not enough to warrant the forbiddance of tongues today.

What Is "Tongues" Anyway?

From passages in both Acts and First Corinthians, "tongues" appears to have been an actual language which had never been learned by the speaker. In First Corinthians 14 the believers were both speaking and praying in an unknown tongue. I don't believe it was gibberish. I believe it was the same phenomenon as on the day of Pentecost—an actual language. If used in public worship, it needed an interpreter; but not if used in private prayer.

There are some who believe that there are two different kinds of tongues: the first a heavenly language (sometimes called a prayer language), which is unintelligible to anyone on earth, and the second the gift of tongues, which is a language unknown to the speaker but intelligible to someone, somewhere in the world.

However, the same words are used in the original language throughout the New Testament to describe the manifestation of tongues, thus showing its unity of meaning. I am not convinced that there is solid biblical ground for asserting that there is a genuine phenomenon of tongues that is other than the gift of tongues which is an actual language.

Speaking in tongues is first recorded in the New Testament in the Book of Acts. Following Christ's resurrection, He told His followers (about 120 of them) to wait in Jerusalem until they were given the Holy Spirit. When the Holy Spirit came, He would give them power to become bold witnesses to the whole world.

In Acts 2 we read of the fulfillment of this promise. The Holy Spirit filled all of the believers in the upper room, and they all began to speak in different languages, languages which they had never learned. They went out into the streets and began telling the wonderful works of God and praising Him, and everyone heard the message in his own language. In this instance the major purpose of tongues was to enable the disciples to preach the message of Christ to the mass of foreigners in the city during that religious festival. There were dozens of dialects represented in the crowds, and many hardened heathen were astonished at hearing the message of a Jewish Savior in their own language.

The Real Miracle

But the real miracle on the day of Pentecost was that after weeks of discouragement and cowardice, these believers were now filled with an overwhelming boldness to witness, and it was this boldness which confirmed to them that they had received the Holy Spirit—*NOT* just the fact that they had spoken in tongues or that tongues of fire and rushing winds had also been present.

I remember a story Dr. J. Edwin Orr used to tell student groups. He told of speaking with a college boy about his drinking habits. The boy would get drunk on Monday night on gin and soda. On Tuesday night he got high on whiskey and soda. Wednesday night his inebriation was brought on by vodka and soda. On Thursday it was vermouth and soda. Then Dr. Orr would ask the question, "What do you suppose it was that got the boy drunk? Obviously it was the soda."

In the same way, people often draw the conclusion that since tongues were associated in *some* cases with the filling of the Spirit in the Book of Acts, that obviously tongues are the evidence of having received the fullness of the Spirit. But if we are going to believe the witness of the Book of Acts, *power* and *praise* are the chief evidence of having been filled with the Spirit since they are the *common* factors mentioned each time a believer was filled. The same thing can be said of the epistles' witness on this matter.

Original Purpose of Gifts

I believe that the primary reason God originally gave the gifts of the Spirit to believers is what Paul painstakingly tries to point out in First Corinthians 12-14. Paul paints a beautiful word picture of what the Church is really like. He says that we're like a body: Christ is the head, and each of us has been placed, ever so lovingly and conscientiously, into our proper place in the body by the Holy Spirit. He picks out the role that each of us is to play in the body. Everyone can't be an eye and everyone can't be an ear. I'm sure that there are certain parts of any body which are more glamorous than others, and no one is really excited about being a big toe. But Paul says that the Spirit has placed us in the body, *as He wills*, on the basis of the gift. He has given us. In other words, your place in the body is determined by your gift, and we won't all have the same place because we don't all have the same gift.

The very thing Paul was dealing with in this letter to these carnal Corinthian believers was that they were "big-timing" one another with their gifts and especially the gift of tongues. In effect he was saying, "Look, the Spirit doesn't make any mistakes. He knows what gift you need to function properly in the body. It isn't necessary to beg Him for this gift or that, or to flaunt it in people's faces once you've discovered it. Just stay a healthy member of the body and God will use your gift to edify you and the rest of the body and to bring more members into it."

The Sign Gifts—What and Why?

In the list of spiritual gifts which Paul enumerates in Romans 12 and First Corinthians 12 there are about ten that would be considered fairly normal abilities, although any spiritual gift is attended with divine power when exercised in the Spirit. However, there are several gifts mentioned that are definitely supernatural in their manifestation: the gifts of healing, miracles, tongues, prophecies, and interpretations.

In Hebrews 2 the writer spells out clearly why the supernatural gifts were given. "For this reason we must pay much closer attention to what we have heard, lest we drift away from it. For if the word spoken through angels proved unalterable, and every transgression and disobedience received a just recompense, how shall we escape if we neglect so great a salvation? After it was at the first spoken through the Lord, it was confirmed to us by those who heard, God also bearing witness with them, *both by signs and wonders and by various miracles and by gifts of the Holy Spirit* according to His own will" (Hebrews 2:1-4).

The Gospel of redemption in Christ had to have strong authentication for the Jew to accept it as a message which superseded what he had always been taught. The pagan world also had to be convinced that the disciples were not just bringing a story about another god among many, but that their message was from the one true God.

It is an undeniable fact that these gifts ceased to be widely known from around the middle of the second century until modern times. This can't be explained away by saying that all the believers down through those centuries just wouldn't believe God for those gifts. More likely, the truth is that there was simply not the same need for authenticating the gospel message as there had been prior to the completion of the New Testament. This is why there is little if any record of public use of the gift of tongues during those centuries. Perhaps there was private use of the gift as a secondary purpose, since the primary need no longer existed.

Resurgence of Tongues

Our present day seems to be another era when strong authentication for God's Word is needed. The "sign" gifts have made a remarkable inroad into the Jesus Movement. There are many reasons for this, and not all are good. Many young people who have been turned on to drugs have had supernatural experiences with demons and Satan, and they might not have much use for a God who couldn't pull off some miracles bigger than those they've already experienced.

Another place where a renewed validation for the Scriptures is needed is in many church denominations which have swallowed the liberal theologian's destructive views of the validity and historicity of the Bible. Neo-orthodoxy seeks to find spiritual values in the Bible while siding with the liberals against its historical accuracy. The results have been a bewildered group of sincere seekers after God who can't find Him in the institutional churches.

In some of the major old-line denominations where these conditions have existed to the greatest degree, a strange phenomenon sprang up. People began to receive the gift of speaking in tongues. Even ministers who had been in the ministry for years began experiencing this gift of the Spirit as they came alive in Christ, many for the first time. A true revival has resulted in many areas. Thousands have come to experience new life in Jesus Christ and are excited about living and witnessing for Him. This has also split churches and divided friendships of long standing, but there is no denying that many impotent, defeated Christians have come gloriously alive in Christ.

Remember Dr. Orr's little story about the "whiskey and soda"? What got the boy drunk, the whiskey or the soda? What has transformed these earnest believers? Is it tongues or is it the Holy Spirit? It is the Holy Spirit! With or without tongues, when you begin to walk in utter dependence upon the Spirit's power in you; when you make yourself available to all that God has made available to you; when you step out of the picture, admitting your weakness, and let Him take control; then you too will know the experience of a transformed life.

But Mr. Deception himself has sneaked in along with this new charismatic revival. We can count upon the Devil to be consistent. Wherever there is a victory, he will bring about a counterattack. And perhaps no spiritual gift is more susceptible to Satanic counterfeit and confusion than the gift of tongues. This statement is not made with any attempt to belittle or downgrade the genuine gift, but rather to caution those who have gone overboard with their experience and are not carefully relating it to the Scriptures.

Slips of the Tongues

The first confusion that has slipped in upon the excited but unwary "tongues" enthusiast is that everyone can and should have the experience of speaking in tongues. This is a logical conclusion based on his own experience. Many were either not really born again or may have been Christians who were never taught that the Holy Spirit dwelt in them from the time of their conversion and was there to empower their lives.

Most of them have been taught that if they could get this gift of tongues, then they could have all of the Spirit's fullness and power; this is referred to by them as "the baptism of the Spirit." Naturally, once they got this gift, it turned their focus onto the Holy Spirit and they believed He was filling them—and all that is needed for the Holy Spirit to fill us is for us to believe that He is. If I tell you repeatedly that you can have the Spirit's fullness and power as soon as you can induce goose pimples on your right arm, then the day you get those goose pimples you will begin to believe that the Spirit is filling you. When you believe that, He does fill you. But don't go around trying to get everyone to have goose pimples! Introduce people to the fact that the Holy Spirit lives in them and that His desire is to fill them with the life of Jesus; they will have plenty of goose pimples if that is God's plan for them. If they never get your particular gift, they can still have the Spirit and His power; otherwise, all of the epistles are a mockery on this subject.

In the books of the New Testament called the epistles, Paul, Peter, and John explain the meaning of the historical events chronicled in the gospels and the Book of Acts. To teach that everyone must experience speaking in tongues to gain the full power of the Spirit for living the Christian life is a contradiction of the epistles. In the Book of Romans, for instance, where Paul gives his fullest and most definitive statement about salvation and the central truths of Christianity, tongues are not mentioned once, and yet every other doctrine vital to living in this world as a believer is carefully expounded. Faith in God's promises alone is stressed. Would Paul have left out of this important treatise a truth that was the *key* to receiving power for serving and living for God?

God Does the Choosing

Paul has plenty to say about the gift of tongues, but not what is generally being taught in the charismatic movement today. In First Corinthians 12:28-30 Paul climaxes his argument with three key points: the Holy Spirit decides who gets what spiritual gift; we cannot all have the same gift; and no one is inferior for not having certain gifts that are more spectacular. He says, "And God has appointed in the church, first apostles, second prophets, third teachers, then miracles, then gifts of healings, helps, administrations, various kinds of tongues. All are not teachers, are they? All are not workers of miracles, are they? All do not have gifts of healings, do they? All do not speak with tongues, do they. All do not interpret, do they?"

Each question demands a negative answer. So, when Paul asks the question, "All do not speak with tongues, do they?"—the answer is "no!" All cannot speak with tongues any more than all could be apostles, prophets, evangelists, or teachers.

It should be carefully noted that Paul doesn't say all do not have the "gift" of tongues. Some have taught that there is a gift of tongues and then there is a sign of tongues, which is different from the gift and is given as an evidence of what they call the "baptism in the Holy Spirit." In this teaching, although one may speak in tongues as a sign of having received the Spirit's fullness, one may not have the gift. This is grasping at straws to try to make all of the Scripture's teaching fit experience, and it simply cannot be supported by a careful study of the Word. Even if it could, Paul denied that either kind of tongues must be true of everyone when he said, "All do not *speak* with tongues, do they?"

If the full power of the Holy Spirit is only available to those who experience the "baptism of the Holy Spirit," as it is called, and its sign, tongues, then Paul is saying that there are some who could never have the full power of God for living. For, again, Paul says, "All do not speak with tongues, do they?"

Further Confusion

A second confusion in the tongues movement grows out of the first. It is generally taught by those who emphasize tongues that since you can't really have all of the Spirit's power until you speak in tongues, then naturally all should seek the experience.

I can see the genuine concern for others that would bring them to this conclusion, but I must confess that this particular practice has distressed me greatly. I've seen many seeking the "baptism" with agonizing earnestness, and they have not received it. Their Christian life is in low gear and they feel God simply cannot use them or empower them because they can't speak in tongues. They will not believe the unconditional promises of the Bible about their spiritual assets because they've been taught that those can only be theirs once they've received their "baptism."

Many people go from one "tarrying" meeting to another, somehow hoping that they can get this mysterious "it" they've been seeking.

My spiritual gift happens to be the gift of teaching. I didn't seek it, tarry for it, or even unnecessarily concern myself about what it was. When the Father felt I was ready to handle the gift He had for me, He began to use me and gave great blessing to my first feeble attempts. As I grew in my knowledge of the Word and He continued to bless in a greater way, I realized that He had given me the gift of teaching.

Now, naturally, I'm enthused about the gift which the Lord has chosen for me. I am personally blessed and ministered to as the Spirit of God works through this gift. But what a sorry spectacle it would be—and how completely frustrating for all—if I began to have "after" meetings each time I spoke in which I encouraged people to come forward to tarry for my gift of teaching. It would be frustrating because, let's face it, God just didn't plan that everyone in the Body of Christ should be a teacher. "All are not teachers, are they?"

I have never spoken in tongues, nor do I honestly see any scriptural evidence that I should seek it. I've enjoyed a Spirit-filled walk for many years and have discovered progressively that all God has is available to me when I am available to Him. I don't need to try to get more from God, but to simply claim by faith and enjoy what He has already given me.

Paul wrote to the church at Corinth that "Things which eye has not seen, and ear has not heard, and which have not entered into the heart of man, all that God has prepared for those who love Him. For to us God revealed them through the Spirit . . ." (1 Corinthians 2:9-10). And I have that wonderful Holy Spirit in me doing just that.

In the Scriptures, the order for growth as a believer is *fact, faith, feeling.* The "feelings" should never run the life. Satan can give the most electrifying feelings to an unwary believer who has turned off his understanding of the Scriptures and opened himself up for any experience that will solve his spiritual "blahs." If the end result is to get a believer off into false doctrine and a wrong emphasis, Satan will even help him have some seemingly great personal experiences. He is a master at pulling texts out of context and piecing them together into a patchwork of false doctrine. It is diabolical that most false doctrine has just enough truth in it to make it lethal.

Why Speak in Tongues Today?

Why do people want to speak in tongues today? I think you can see from all I have said that they are sincerely convinced it will give their Christian life a tremendous shot in the arm and cure most of their spiritual problems. Who wouldn't want an easy antidote for the ills of the soul?

The problem is, though, that many dear believers, having had their "baptism in the Spirit," find to their great dismay that all of their problems are not miraculously solved. Day by day they find they still have to cope with the world, the flesh, and the Devil; and for some, great disillusionment sets in. Others live from experience to experience and in this subtle way keep focusing on the gift rather than the Giver, and that is tantamount to walking by sight rather than walking by faith.

Why have I made so much of this point? Because the Scripture says that we are to *walk in the Spirit* and we will not fulfill the lusts of the flesh (Galatians 5:16). Paul pleads with us to allow ourselves to be *continually filled* with and controlled by the Holy Spirit (Ephesians 5:18). Walking in, and being continually filled with, the Holy Spirit are not one shot deals. It's a whole pattern of life God is talking about.

Summing It All Up

I believe there is a genuine gift of tongues which God is giving today. It often quickens a person to believe God for the power of the Spirit to live a godly life. Many people have received this gift without even seeking it, and others who have sought it have been graciously granted it because it was obviously one of the gifts God had already planned for them. The exercise of this gift, both in private and public, has been a personal blessing to them. Some feel that when they pray in tongues they are able to express the inexpressible to God. Others sing in tongues, letting the Spirit compose the music and words as they yield their vocal cords to Him.

I would not in any way want to rob these people of their new love for Christ. It isn't necessary. The exercise of any spiritual gift can greatly bless the life of the one using it, and no one has a right to deny anyone the blessing God has intended for him. As a person walks in the Spirit and exercises his spiritual gift, it can't help but give him a deeper love for Christ and for the lost world.

Here are my only words of caution. It is so easy to become unbalanced in our Christian walk if we are not rightly dividing the Word and walking only in the light of it. The charismatic movement has placed an unbalanced emphasis on the importance of tongues. They have drawn unscriptural conclusions about a genuine and bona fide spiritual gift. The more the Christian world has criticized their movement, the greater the claims they have made for tongues. The more they have sought to validate their emphasis with biblically unsupportable claims, the more conservative biblical scholars and Christians have resisted them.

With a polarization like this, who do you think is the winner? You guessed it! Satan. He goads both sides on in their causes and then stands back and laughs while they battle each other instead of him.

Investigation of Manifestations

If there are certain areas of God's Word where we're a bit shaky, it's important to take them out and examine them occasionally.

In the first century when someone stood up and gave a revelation, or spoke in a tongue, they were to: "Let two or three prophets speak, and let the others pass judgment" (1 Corinthians 14:29).

The words "pass judgment" in Greek mean to "thoroughly discern"—to thoroughly investigate. Deceiving spirits can easily work through people who say they have a prophecy. Someone stands up and says something which has beautiful truth in it while underneath it is deceptive, and he leads others astray by false guidance.

We must depend upon the Holy Spirit and give our renewed mind to the Word of God—to learn and constantly be discerning. I believe Christians could, to some degree, "coast" in times past, but we can't coast now!

We are in a time of the greatest opportunity for service and the greatest possibility of peril. We need to snatch the opportunity and not get caught up in deception. We need to depend upon the Lord and to check out the Word. Only God's truth drives away error.

Paul said that perilous times would come and that "Evil men and impostors will proceed from bad to worse, deceiving and being deceived" (2 Timothy 3:13).

Then he exhorted Timothy, "You, however, continue in the things you have learned and become convinced of, knowing from whom you have learned them" (2 Timothy 3:14).

"All Scripture is inspired by God and profitable for teaching, for reproof, for correction, for training in righteousness" (2 Timothy 3:16).

The antidote for Satan's error is God's truth.

10 ○ Diagnosing Demon Possession

"Behold, I have given you authority to tread upon serpents and scorpions, and over all the power of the enemy, and nothing shall injure you." LUKE 10:19

THE STREETS OF Old Jerusalem are narrow and winding. When two or more are gathered together, it's a crowd. We were pushing our way through the stalls filled with pungent odors, jostling cameras with our American friends on a Holy Land pilgrimage, when we were halted by a traffic jam of eight or ten people listening to a disheveled man making a violent speech.

Jan and I were rather uneasy about the man because he seemed to be looking at us; each time we moved on up the street to get away from him, he followed us. He kept repeating the same short speech in an almost insane frenzy. The only two words we recognized were "Americans" and "Mohammed." He was carrying a large picture of Mohammed.

As a larger crowd began gathering, I quickly snapped a picture of the man and then turned to Jan and said, "Let's get out of here." We headed for the Damascus Gate at a fast pace, and the man, still shouting, followed us right through the gate. Needless to say, we were mighty glad to be out of that potentially explosive situation.

The first time I showed the pictures of our trip after we came home, I was startled as I came across the photograph of that wild character. I remembered what I had been thinking as we watched him in Israel and knew that my original evaluation was correct. His entire facial expression, particularly his eyes, verified to me that he was demon-possessed.

I don't approach this subject flippantly. When you begin to investigate, the tendency is to see everyone as demon-possessed. This is to be avoided as much as pure ignorance.

When we seek to diagnose whether a person is demon-possessed or not, we need discipline and prayer to be able to observe a combination of traits. I don't think any one of the following characteristics applied by itself to someone provides an iron-clad certainty that a person is demon-possessed.

Psychic or Occult Powers

Be wary of those who have psychic powers. This would be the ability to sense things about people, the ability to foretell the future, to have insight into people without having any knowledge of them. It can be a gift of discernment from God, but it can also be a counterfeit from Satan and a symptom of demon possession.

Paul and Silas had an encounter with a girl who had these powers: "And it happened that as we were going to the place of prayer, a certain slave-girl having a spirit of divination met us, who was bringing her masters much profit by fortune-telling" (Acts 16:16).

Divination, as we saw in Chapter Eight, is the ability to foretell future events or discover hidden information. A Bible scholar says that divination is the "Satanic counterfeit of Biblical prophecy."[1]

The fortunetelling slave was a pest. "Following after Paul and us, she kept crying out, saying, 'These men are bond-servants of the Most High God, who are proclaiming to you the way of salvation'" (Acts 16:17).

Two things of importance are noted in this incident. First, the fortuneteller was accurately describing Paul's and Silas's mission. They were "servants of the Most High God." Secondly, she mixed error subtly with the truth. In the original Greek of this passage she literally said, "who are proclaiming to you *a* way of salvation."

The implication was that Jesus Christ was "a way" of salvation, but that there were other ways. The Scripture, however, is explicit on this: "And there is salvation in no one else; for there is no other name under heaven that has been given among men, by which we must be saved" (Acts 4:12).

Notice how demons do things. The slave girl was speaking in the power of a demon, and without knowing Paul and Silas, she was telling the truth about them. Then, as fortunetellers go, error was camouflaged by fact.

Such persistence! "She continued doing this for many days. But Paul was greatly annoyed. . ." (Acts 16:18).

Why was Paul so agitated by this fortuneteller's witnessing as to his mission? He recognized it as Satan's old "if you can't beat 'em join 'em" tactic. To have accepted the witness of a demon-possessed fortuneteller would have done several things. First, in the eyes of the people, it would have been an act of approval of her abilities. This would have exposed many to deceptions, because Satan will inspire much truth only to slip in later with clever lies. Secondly, it would have exposed Paul to demonic attack.

Paul obviously had the gift of discerning spirits, for he settled the problem when he "turned and said to the spirit, 'I command you in the name of Jesus Christ to come out of her!' And it came out at that very moment" (Acts 16:18).

Any complicity with demon activity, whether it be ouija boards, tarot cards, horoscopes, crystal balls, palm readings, or fortunetelling, makes one vulnerable to demonic influences. I have encountered cases where heavy demon influence began in this way.

We are commanded: "resist the devil and he will flee from you" (James 4:7). If we don't resist, we will make an opening in our lives that Satan will be quick to enter.

Playing with any form of the occult is definitely not resisting but assisting the Devil.

As in the case of the demon-controlled slave girl, a fortuneteller may be able to tell you about your past and present and be absolutely accurate. This might give you confidence that this person really has supernatural power and you would accept the possibility of her predictions coming true. Consequently, you could be directed into a self-fulfilling prophecy. We saw how this could happen with the young minister in the last chapter.

When a fortuneteller's prophecy comes true, a person can come under demonic enslavement. A young man in one of my classes told about a fortuneteller who came to the door of his mother's house when she was pregnant with her first child. The fortuneteller told her that she would not have children until she was much older and that she was going to have a tragedy in her family very soon. Since the woman was already pregnant, but not noticeably, she laughed off the fortuneteller as being a fraud.

However, the baby she was carrying did die and her next child also. She became depressed to the extent that she was caught in the demonic snare of the fortuneteller's power.

Don't play with fortunetelling—no matter how innocent it may appear to be!

Magic

Involvement in magic should be suspect when we understand how open a person can be to demon possession. We're not talking about those who do sleight of hand tricks or entertain us with clever showmanship. That's fun and a legitimate form of entertainment. But there is another form of magic which involves mesmerism, black magic, and supernatural powers.

The type of magic we refer to as a sign characteristic of demon possession is a "divinely forbidden art of bringing about results beyond human power by recourse to superhuman spirit agencies."[2]

Sceptics of our time tend to deny the reality of both divine and demonic power, according to Dr. Unger, one of the finest Bible scholars in the world. Combined with this scepticism is a confusion over the nature of magic. For our study, the important point is to understand that many of the phenomena which involve the spirit realm and result in spirit-rapping, moving furniture, apparitions, and other weird occurrences are a part of diabolic deceptions.

Some persons may claim to have magic powers which are from God. The Scriptures tell us of one magician who made such false claims: "Now there was a certain man named Simon, who formerly was practicing magic in the city, and astonishing the people of Samaria, claiming to be someone great; and they all, from smallest to greatest, were giving attention to him, saying, 'This man is what is called the Great Power of God.' And they were giving him attention because he had for a long time astonished them with his magic arts" (Acts 8:9-11).

The man named Simon was so involved in magic that even though he made a profession of belief, his belief was not genuine. Peter pulled him up by the scruff of his deceiving neck and said: "May your silver perish with you, because you thought you could obtain the gift of God with money! You have no part or portion in this matter, for your heart is not right before God. Therefore repent of this wickedness of yours, and pray the Lord that if possible, the intention of your heart may be forgiven you" (Acts 8:20-22).

The history of magic with devilish works and any involvement with black magic, should be shunned.*

Necromancy

Necromancy means calling up the dead or foretelling the future by communicating with the dead. Usually when a medium calls up someone from the dead, it is a demonic deception: that is, a demon impersonating someone who is dead will begin to speak through the medium. Necromancy has been practiced from the beginning of recorded history. The Bible gives a vivid example in the Old Testament.

---

* For a study on this subject, to be read with Christian discernment, see *The History and Practice of Magic* by Paul Christian, The Citadel Press, Inc., New York, 1963.

Saul, the first king of Israel, through repeated disobedience had lost communication with God. God ceased sending him instructions through priests or prophets. Furthermore, the most respected and trusted prophet, Samuel, who had been Saul's friend, was dead.

When the enemies of Israel gathered a great army and threatened to invade, Saul committed his worst sin of all. In an hour of desperation he sent for a medium to call up Samuel from the dead. In other words, he wanted a seance. Saul knew this was forbidden, for he had previously run all the spiritists and mediums out of the land (Deuteronomy 18:10-12; 1 Samuel 28:3).

Saul's men located a medium at a place called Endor. Disguising himself, Saul persuaded the medium to conduct a seance and to call up Samuel.

When Samuel appeared, he rebuked Saul directly for his sin and predicted that Israel would be defeated by the Philistine army and that Saul and his sons would die in battle.

The sin of necromancy was considered by God to be the final straw for Saul. He and his sons did die in battle the next day and Israel was routed.

My young twin daughters have told me of classmates attempting to conduct seances with older students. Seances are considered popular pastimes these days on many junior high, high school, and college campuses, and it should be understood by all that God considers this an extremely serious matter.

Listen again to the warning of God through Moses: "There shall not be found among you anyone . . . who casts a spell, or a medium, or a spiritist, or one who calls up the dead. For whoever does these things is detestable to the Lord" (Deuteronomy 18:10-12).

Any playing with seances may open the door for strong demonic influence in your life, whether you are a Christian or a non-Christian. It may even lead to an early death.

Bishop Pike was deeply involved with mediums and necromancy before he was led to his death.*

Marked Change in Intelligence

When a demon is heavily influencing a life, there may be a sudden or sporadic increase in the person's intelligence. The greatest example of this was Adolf Hitler. This man had incredible intelligence, yet had no formal

* See Dr. Merrill Unger's *The Haunting of Bishop Pike* for a detailed account.

education. After he became involved with the Nazi party, he began to show unusual mental ability and oratorical power. His skill in speaking was obviously demonic.

Hitler mesmerized the German people, and they followed him willingly. His great oratorical ability was the deadly Pied Piper for millions.

The operation of demonic power is strong in an area where people are willing to follow a demonic leader. If ruthless ambition and the desire for prominence take over a man's life, Satan can gain a foothold.

Satan, Give Me Strength

Demons are able to energize people with incredible strength. In the case of the demoniac of Gerasene in Mark 5, it was said that he was bound with heavy chains and he broke them. No one could subdue him.

Since studying about demon possession and encountering its reality, I recall a neighbor who was thought by everyone to be mentally ill. From the characteristics he showed, I believe that he was demon possessed. One night he almost killed his wife with a hammer. The police came to get him and handcuffed him. He was only about 5'6" tall and weighed around 130 pounds, but he was able to break those handcuffs. It took several policemen to drag him down and lock him in a squad car.

I know now that this was something more than human strength.

I saw a demon-possessed man at Berkeley with such superhuman power it took six men to hold him down to keep him from doing physical harm to himself or others.

Depression, Despondency, and Suicidal Tendencies

Another word of caution: we must be careful to weigh any of these symptoms, because they may have been brought about by other causes. However, in combination with other symptoms they could be a strong indication of demon possession or influence.

Some examples from Scripture: after Satan had used Judas for his purpose, he then used the power of guilt to drive Judas to self-destruction (Matthew 27:5-10).

The demon-possessed boy in Matthew 17:14-15 had a strong tendency toward self-destruction. He threw himself into fire and then into water. This was the result of the demon attempting to inflict harm and self-destruction upon the child.

The demoniac of Gerasene continually gashed himself with stones, indicating how demons arouse a tendency toward self-destruction.

Although we probably have no way of telling after the act has been committed, we certainly should admit there is a strong possibility that persons who douse themselves with gasoline and light a match are driven by demons.

In combination with other symptoms, it is possible to observe a person's face and see evidences of demon possession. You recall the story of the Jerusalem orator at the beginning of this chapter. His eyes were wide open and wild, his face a chilling contortion of evil. I have seen the expressions of those who have been demon possessed and the vivid way in which Christ is able to work a miraculous change.

Filthy, Uncontrolled Swearing

A person's almost spontaneous reaction of swearing and cursing when the name of Jesus Christ or God is mentioned can be a symptom of an unclean spirit or demon. Jesus often confronted this.

A continual compulsion to blaspheme the name of God and Christ can, in connection with other symptoms, be a sign of demon possession or influence.

Radical Change in Personality

This characteristic of demon possession was vividly dramatized in one of the letters received from a reader of *The Late Great Planet Earth*.

A woman in the Northwest told how her husband, who was normally a pleasant family man, became fascinated with a ouija board at a party. When the ouija board began to spell out accurate answers to questions about himself and others, he became furious. He determined to prove that it was all a hoax. The next evening he came home from work with a ouija board and urged his wife to participate. Once again the board began to predict that he was to become a great leader and help bring peace to many. To do this, he was told, he would have to abandon his family.

These prophecies continued. His personality began to change radically. He stayed away from home and drank heavily. He moved out, coming home just for short visits.

Whenever he was home, he continued to pressure his wife into sessions with the ouija board. The poor woman became increasingly alarmed about the whole thing and sought help from friends who were believers in Christ, a subject her husband could not stand.

Finally, one evening while they were asking the ouija board questions, it spelled out that they would no longer have to use the board; the spirit would give guidance directly through the husband.

The wife was amazed as her husband immediately fell into a trance and a voice—not her husband's—spoke out of him. The spirit, which was a demon, reiterated all the things previously spelled on the board and told her that it was time for her husband to leave on his mission of destiny.

Shortly afterward a friend told the woman that I was to be in town speaking on the rise of the occult. She persuaded her husband to come with her to the meeting, and they were shocked to find that they were involved with demons through initial contact with the ouija board.

They obtained a copy of *The Late Great Planet Earth;* the wife read it and finally persuaded her husband to read it. As a result he renounced his involvement with demons, asked for forgiveness, and received Jesus Christ as his Savior.

His personality changed immediately for the better. He moved back home, and he and his wife became real witnesses to the saving power of Jesus Christ.

Can a Believer Be Demon Possessed?

Semantics separating demon possession and demon influence seem important to some people. A person who is demon influenced is under the power of evil spirits which may result in anything from mental torment to extreme abnormal behavior. Both believers and non-believers can be subjected to demon influence.

Most Bible scholars and missionaries who have studied or dealt with the problem understand demon possession as the indwelling of one or more evil spirits in a person's body, resulting in the personality of the demon taking dominant control. In a demonized condition the personality of the victim is enslaved and the demon virtually exercises complete control.

Dr. Unger has an excellent study on whether a Christian can be demon possessed.[3] He states that a non-Christian can be totally controlled and manipulated by demonic power, but a Christian rarely has the same degree of complete subjugation. This is my position, also. However, I've talked to many missionaries who have had to deal with these things personally, and I must say that it seems to be possible for a Christian to have a certain degree of demon possession.

An example of a demon-possessed Christian was given me by Dick Hillis of Overseas Crusades. Dick is a man who knows the Scriptures, not just as a theologian, but as a warrior of the faith. A man of careful discernment, not given to sensationalism, he has spent most of his life on the mission field. Hillis told me of one incident which happened while he was in China, before the Communist takeover, when one of the elders of his church, who was unquestionably a believer, became so demon possessed that his personality changed. He became vile and profane in his language and extraordinarily strong. Some of the members of the church locked him up in a room and sent for Hillis.

When Dick walked in the door, this man became violent and a strange voice shouted, "I know who you are."

Hillis said, "And I know who you are," and began to speak to the demon.

This was a case when a believer was actually possessed by a demon who spoke in another voice.

In countries where there is open worship of idols, such as China, a person is much more susceptible to demon influence and possession. As Unger says, "In lands where demon-energized idolatry has flourished unchecked by the Gospel for ages, new believers who were delivered from demon possession have been known to become repossessed when they return to their old idols."[4]

The main argument advanced against a Christian being demon possessed stems from the fact that the Holy Spirit dwells in the Christian. Therefore, a demon cannot dwell in the same place where the Holy Spirit dwells.

However, in Acts 5 two believers named Ananias and Sapphira certainly were controlled by Satan. Peter said, "Ananias, why has Satan *filled* your heart to lie to the Holy Spirit?" (Acts 5:3).

The word translated "filled" is the same one used in Ephesians 5:18 to describe the Holy Spirit's controlling and empowering ministry to the believer. It means the same here, only it is Satan doing the controlling.

For one person to *fill* another person literally means for one to control the other by his consent. Therefore, the one being controlled is responsible because he received the control. This responsibility is brought out clearly when Peter says to Ananias again, "Why is it that *you* have conceived this deed in your heart? *You* have not lied to men, but to God" (Acts 5:4).

The main point is that Ananias was a believer whose heart became controlled by Satan. I believe a serious warning is given us here. Whenever we deliberately turn from depending on the Holy Spirit to resist temptation, and then knowingly plot to commit sin, we open ourselves up for the possibility of Satanic attack and even control.

When Jesus announced to His disciples that He was going to be arrested and put to death, and Peter rebuked Him and said this would never happen, another important statement was made. Jesus said to Peter, "Get behind Me, *Satan!* You are a stumbling-block to Me; for you are not setting your mind on God's interest, but man's" (Matthew 16:23). Jesus addressed Peter as Satan because obviously Satan was influencing him and misleading him at this point. It was Satan who was taking Peter's eyes off God's purpose and turning them to the human viewpoint.

l believe that these and other incidents show how a believer can be possessed to a certain degree, though only temporarily and never as completely as a non-believer. It is certainly an incentive to us to walk in continual dependence upon the Holy Spirit and not try to live by human power.

It should be understood clearly that Satan cannot get control of a believer who is walking by faith and available to the Holy Spirit. Much more will be said about this in Chapter Thirteen.

Exorcists

The ancient subject of exorcism or casting out evil spirits has reentered our streamlined society. *The Exorcist* has become a national best seller. For those in our modern culture who may think all of this is some weird new venture into unreality, we should recall exorcism's pagan origins.

Magic formulas and rituals to expel evil spirits have been practiced for centuries. Many of the methods were painful to the one possessed and involved beating, pinching, burning, and other types of physical abuse. Unger tells us of a shrine in India which is well-known among Hindus and Muslims as a place where demons are exorcised. Violence and the infliction of pain are common, but when the demon that is to be driven out is particularly obstinate, cotton wicks soaked in oil are lighted and stuffed up the nostrils of the possessed. The cruelty of professional exorcists is beyond human understanding.

When we read and hear of the methods of casting out demons used by unbelievers, we understand that it is even possible under the power of Satan to cast out demons, if it furthers his teachings and purpose.

Contrast With Christ

The method which Jesus used to cast out demons was in sharp contrast to the Jewish and pagan exorcists. Matthew 8:16 tells us that when the disciples brought to Him many who were demon possessed, He cast out the spirits with a word. He did not resort to rituals.

His disciples cast out demons "in the name of Jesus Christ." Christ gave them this authority when He spoke to them following His resurrection. He said: "And these signs will accompany those who have believed: in My name they will cast out demons" (Mark 16:17).

The name of Jesus stands for the infinite and omnipotent God behind the name and has no magical power in itself. There is no hocus-pocus about saying, "In the name of Jesus." The warning to the young or immature believer must be emphatic at this point. We need to know what our authority is as believers and learn the truth from God's Word before attempting to "cast out demons" from someone whom we may believe is possessed.

Christ said, "Behold, I have given you authority to tread upon serpents and scorpions, and over all the power of the enemy, and nothing shall injure you. *Nevertheless* do not rejoice in this, that the spirits are subject to you, but rejoice that your names are recorded in heaven" (Luke 10:19-20).

This is a promise given by the Lord which everyone involved in this study needs to grasp. As believers we are given authority over demons, and the only way that demons can get a stranglehold on us is when we deliberately, knowingly, and persistently walk in some sin.

As we walk with Christ, we may be in fearful situations, but nothing can injure us if we claim our authority over the enemy. If we get into this area of the Satanic and do not know our authority, we are going to get into trouble.

Satan will bluff us as far as he can; he will take all the ground we will give him. But if we stand on the promises of God and use our authority from the Scriptures, he will respect that authority and flee. We are not talking about human bravado or the whistle-in-the-dark front; we are talking about the victory of the cross. We must stand behind that victory and have a healthy respect for Satan's power.

One of the dangers of immaturity in the Christian faith is at the point when God begins to show works of power and answers this newly acquired faith. It is easy to become enamored with the power and captured by the gifts instead of the Giver. The great danger in spiritual adolescence is to have a little knowledge and not know it is *a little knowledge*.

Recently I was given an old and priceless book which has some deep perceptions into this subject. The writers were scholars and Christians of great understanding and depth. They said: "For the deliverance of souls under the bondage of evil spirits in possession, much knowledge of God and of spiritual things is needed."[5]

If a believer encounters what he thinks is a true manifestation of demon possession, I believe he should, in most cases, call upon a trusted, mature believer and the two should pray for guidance together as to how to deal with the situation.

What Happened to the Socialite at the Conference?

Before this book was begun, I had never cast a demon out of anyone. It's not something I would seek to do or a ministry I would find particularly enjoyable. But I believe the Lord gave me the experience I described briefly in Chapter One so I would have a better understanding of this entire realm.

When the socialite from the Midwest (see Chapter One) showed me the ring on her finger, the sign of a Satan worshiper, and described the evil spirit which hurled her into periods of great depression and despondency, she also told me that her mother and her grandmother had been fortunetellers. Apparently she had inherited her psychic ability from them.

It wasn't easy telling this woman what her real problem was. With genuine compassion, I told her she was possessed by a spirit of divination, a demon that specializes in fortunetelling. She listened intently while I explained that according to many case histories I had read, this usually occurred in families with a history of occult powers.

I insisted she renounce this psychic power and turn to Jesus Christ, who alone could liberate her, or this demon would destroy her life.

"Would you like to be delivered from this spirit and receive Jesus Christ into your life?"

She didn't hesitate. "If it means finding peace of mind, I sure do."

I then prayed according to the pattern of the Apostle Paul in Acts 16:18. "You evil spirit, I command you in the name of Jesus Christ to come out of this woman and leave her alone."

Never have I experienced such a sense of authority in the name of Jesus Christ as I did at that moment.

The woman shook slightly and began to sob.

"Pray this prayer out loud," I continued. "I believe that Jesus Christ is the Son of God who died for my sins. Jesus, come into my life and make it pleasing to You."

The woman fought to speak for about three minutes. Her throat seemed to be constricted by an unseen hand.

I prayed silently for Jesus to bind the influence of Satan. Finally she prayed the prayer aloud.

As soon as she had finished, her whole countenance changed before my eyes. She became radiant. She exclaimed, "I'm free!" It had a different meaning for her than it does for most people.

She left me abruptly and started toward the final meeting of the conference. The first person she encountered was Jan. She blurted out, "Do you know what your husband just did? He cast a demon out of me."

My wife, who is not easily surprised, immediately saw the startling change in the woman. Sensing her immediate spiritual need, Jan said quietly, "Did Jesus Christ come in?"

"You bet He did," she said jubilantly.

She then found the friends who had brought her and amazed them with the good news.

As the former psychic was about to leave, I instructed her to get rid of all her artifacts of the occult because this is a way demons can keep a foothold in a life. She agreed to do this.

Then I got a real jolt. She pointed to the Scottish kilt she had worn all weekend.

"Do you recognize this plaid?"

I studied it for a moment and said, "I believe it's the Lindsey plaid."

"Right," she answered. "A few weeks ago I was in Scotland. While I was there, I had a premonition that I was going to meet someone named Lindsey and that he would have a profound effect upon my life. That's the reason I bought the plaid kilt."

I was speechless. Later, in reflecting upon the incident, a thrill went through me. The power of Jesus Christ was so real to me!

11 ○ Doctrines
of Demons

"The Devil can cite Scripture for his purpose."

SHAKESPEARE, *The Merchant of Venice*, 1597

"But the Spirit explicitly says that in later times some will fall away from the faith, paying attention to deceitful spirits and doctrines of demons."

I TIMOTHY 4:1

SATAN, IN HIS role as "the god of this age," has conducted a relentless, well-planned strategy to blind men's minds to the truth about God and how to know Him. If you were Satan, out to control men, where would you launch your heaviest attacks?

Against the Bible and those who preach and teach it and against the church, of course!

With the Bible generally accepted as a revelation from God, mankind could not easily be blinded. As long as there were ministers who preached and taught the Bible, the Christian would keep growing in his faith, vitally witnessing to the world, and not easily deceived. While churches were organized and functioning according to the New Testament pattern, they could not be swept away from their real purpose of building disciples and reaching out to the world with the "good news about Christ."

When the apostles realized they were nearing the end of their lives, they warned about the coming attacks upon the truth and the church that would be accelerated in the days just before Christ would return to earth in His Second Coming.

In Paul's last session with the elders of the church at Ephesus, he gave the following exhortation: "Be on guard for yourselves and for all the flock, among which the Holy Spirit has made you overseers, to shepherd the church of God which He purchased with His own blood. I know that after my departure savage wolves will come in among you, not sparing the flock; and from among your own selves men will arise, speaking perverse things, to draw away the disciples after them. Therefore be on the alert, remembering that night and day for a period of three years I did not cease to admonish each one with tears" (Acts 10:28-31).

Paul predicted that there would be ministers from within the church who would teach perverted things while posing as teachers of truth. The antidote to this coming apostasy is given in verse 32. "And now I commend you to God and to *the word of His grace,* which is able to build you up and to give you the inheritance among all those who are sanctified."

Paul exhorted the church leadership to place heavy reliance upon "God and the *Word of His grace.*"

When a minister ceases to teach and emphasize a personal faith-walk with God upon the principle of grace instead of law, he has taken the first step down the road to apostasy.

Why Revivals Fizzle

History is strewn with evidence of movements born in the fires of revivals that after a few generations have departed into error and eventual apostasy. Many of the great denominations of today bear little resemblance to the faith and fervor of their original founders.

Christians have been bewildered at this continual trend away from God and have asked "why?" In most instances the trend began in a departure from the grace of God into "legalism."

Legalism—seeking to live for God by the principle of the law—is the first and the worst doctrine of demons. It is the dent in your armor at which Satan will chip away until he has a hole big enough to drive a truck through. I don't know another doctrinal distortion that has been more devastating to believers. The awful thing is that it can sidetrack a mature believer as well as a young one. In fact, this demonic doctrine seems to find especially fertile soil in the life of a growing believer who is intent upon pleasing God in his life.

It was concerning teachers of legalism that Paul wrote, "But I am afraid, lest as the serpent deceived Eve by his craftiness, your minds should be led astray from the simplicity and purity of devotion to Christ. . . . For such men are false apostles, deceitful workers, disguising themselves as apostles of Christ. And no wonder, for even Satan disguises himself as an angel of light. Therefore it is not surprising if his servants (literally ministers) also disguise themselves as servants (ministers) of righteousness, whose end shall be according to their deeds" (2 Corinthians 11:3, 13-15).

According to this warning, Satan has his own corps of dedicated ministers who masquerade as "ministers of righteousness." What could be more effective than a minister, sincere and moral, quoting the Bible, yet missing the emphasis of grace?

Some ministers who truly belong to God's family become tools of Satan by putting their flock "under the law."

If we do not understand the difference between the principle of law and the principle of grace when it comes to relating to God, we will not understand why we sin.

Why Do We Sin?

Sometimes when we sin we like to say, "The Devil made me do it." It helps get us off the hook in our own minds, but we can't blame Satan for all our sinning.

There are two ingredients necessary for a person to sin. In Romans 7:5 Paul says, "For while we were in the flesh (that is, before we became believers), the *sinful passions*, which were *aroused by the Law*, were at work in the members of our body to bear fruit for death."

Paul indicates that there are two things at work within a non-believer to make him sin: his sinful passions or sin nature as it is sometimes called, and the law. When the law stirs up the sinful passions, rebellion against the law occurs and that is what the Bible calls "sin."

Later on in Romans 7:7-8 Paul says that the law works exactly the same way in the life of a believer. ". . . I would not have come to know sin except through the Law; for I would not have known about coveting if the Law had not said, 'You shall not covet.' But sin, taking opportunity through the commandment, produced in me coveting of every kind; for apart from the Law sin is dead."

Paul might just as easily have said, "My sin nature, which used to be aroused by all the laws before I became a Christian, is still getting stirred up by the law even though I'm now God's child. If I could get away from all those laws, then I wouldn't have to be worrying about all this sinning."

Reverse Psychology

Psychology has noticed this same tendency in man to do just the opposite of what he is commanded to do. We call it the "law of reverse psychology." If you want someone to do something, tell him to do just the opposite. Most parents have figured this out before their children get very old.

A classic example of this is a story that appeared in a national publication a few years ago. A new luxury hotel was built out on a pier in Galveston, Texas. As they were about to have their gala opening and the manager was inspecting a room with a Gulf view, it suddenly occurred to him that people were going to be tempted to fish off the balconies. If they did, when they cast out their lines with heavy sinkers on them, the wind might blow them back into the windows below and cause a lot of breakage.

There was a little panic for a while as the management tried to decide what to do. They finally put cards under the glass on each room desk saying that fishing off the balconies was absolutely forbidden!

Opening week came. You guessed it! A number of windows were broken. The management was shaken. Finally one hotel clerk suggested, "Why not throw away the cards and see what happens?"

Immediately the damage stopped. There was no more "law" to stir up the "sinful passions" of all those hotel patrons!

The Law Is Not the Culprit

I know that all of this tends to make the law, whether God's law or man's law, look bad. But the law isn't the real problem. Those sinful passions or sin natures that get stirred up by the law are the problem.

You might wonder why God would give the law if He knew that it would work against us rather than for us. There are four basic reasons why God gave His law.

The first reason is to show man what sin is. The law is a principle which guides our behavior by setting up standards of conduct and threatening certain consequences if the standards are not met.

There are several kinds of law set forth in the Bible. The first *is the law of conscience*. When Adam and Eve ate of the tree of the knowledge of good and evil, they developed a conscious knowledge of what they should and should not do.

The Apostle Paul referred to this law of conscience in Romans 2:14-15. "For when Gentiles who do not have the Law (the Law of Moses) do instinctively the things of the Law, these, not having the Law, are a law to themselves, in that they show the work of the Law written in their hearts, their conscience bearing witness, and their thoughts alternately accusing or else defending themselves."

The only problem with the conscience as a reliable standard of conduct is that it can easily be seared. Within the few hundred years it took to go from Adam to Noah, man had so deadened his conscience that God was sorry He had even made man.

In modern times you can see how effective the searing of the human conscience has been. Jane Russell's seductive film, *The Outlaw*, made in the

1950s, is so tame by present-day standards that it could be shown at a Sunday school picnic.

God rejected the law of conscience as a means for man to know Him. About the time that Moses came along, the people had so little consciousness of what sin was that God saw their need for an objective standard that would forever nail down what He considered to be sin.

The "Big Ten"

When God gave the Ten Commandments and the various other laws to the nation of Israel, for the first time the people knew just how far they could go and still not sin. Before the law was given, if a man had a weakness for sleeping with other men's wives and his conscience didn't bother him, then it wasn't sin. The other husbands may not have liked it, but there was no law to which they could appeal to convict the other man of wrongdoing. There may have been certain tribal laws, but there was no larger moral law which could be invoked against the man.

During the hundreds of years that passed until Jesus came on the scene, the Jews had so stringently interpreted their laws that they had evolved into a mere keeping of outer form and ritual. Jesus' indictment of them was that outside they were like whitewashed tombs, but on the inside they were full of dead men's bones (Matthew 23:27).

Sermon on the Mount

The Sermon on the Mount was the greatest "hellfire and damnation" sermon ever preached. In no uncertain terms, Jesus said that it wasn't just what you did on the outside that was a sin, but even what you were thinking on the inside.

Nothing could have pricked the self-righteous hearts of those religious people more than to hear that "good works" weren't enough to get them to heaven. Over and over again Jesus pulled the rug out from under them by saying, "You have heard it taught," and then quoting one of the Ten Commandments. "But I say to you, it isn't just what you *do* wrong that will convict you, but even your wrong thoughts that will bring you condemnation." Jesus sought to show them what the basic intent of the law of Moses had always been.

So we can see that the teachings of Jesus about man's conduct were a further amplification in the definition to mankind of what sin really was.

New Testament Injunctions

All of the New Testament epistles are filled with words of warning, words of admonition, and words of definition regarding what a Christian should and should not do. This "law of the New Testament" is the most definitive and exacting law given to man. You can see the progression from the easygoing "law of conscience" to the demanding "injunctions of the New Testament."

What if the law hadn't been given?

Suppose Jesus had come and announced to the world, "I'm here. I'm going to die for your sins. I'm the solution to your problem."

If the law hadn't been given, what would they have said? "What problem? We don't have any problem. My conscience doesn't bother me. What problem are you talking about?"

That's the first reason the law was given: to show us what sin is in order to give us a standard against which to compare our lives. When we see that we don't measure up, we're forced to admit we have a problem. Now when Jesus comes and says He is the solution to our problem, we look at the law and we look at our lives and we say, "Man, I need a solution!"

The law is much like pain. If it weren't for pain, we'd be in trouble physically. The most insignificant injury could end up being fatal if we didn't have pain to signal its severity to us.

Man is born into this world with a tremendous injury in his soul, and if it weren't for the "pain" of the law jabbing into his sinful passions and arousing them, he'd go merrily on his way to hell saying, "Problem, what problem?"

That Sin Might Increase

I know it's going to be hard to accept the second reason God gave the law, but it's true. The law was given to provoke man's sin nature to sin more. Paul said in Romans 5:20, "And the Law came in that the transgression might increase. . . ." God wants the unbeliever to get so loaded with sin that there's no way he can fail to see how utterly sinful he is and how much he needs a Savior.

In First Corinthians 15:56, Paul said, ". . . the power of sin is the law." According to this verse, even the sin nature of believers gets a stranglehold on them from the prodding of the law. It seems that God is working against Himself to get us to sin more, but this is God's way of bringing us to total despair of self-effort in living for Him.

And that's the third reason God gave the law: to drive us to despair of self-effort. When we have despaired of self-effort, we're ready for the fourth reason God gave the law: to bring the unbeliever to Christ for salvation and the believer to the Holy Spirit for His empowering.

The Law Is Our Schoolmaster

When Paul wrote his letter to the Galatian believers, he used a terrific illustration of how the law works on unbelievers. In Galatians 3:24-25 he says, "The Law has become our tutor to lead us to Christ, that we may be justified by faith. But now that faith has come, we are no longer under a tutor."

A tutor was a specially chosen slave whose job it was to take a Roman child by the hand every morning and lead him to the school. He would wait there until the lessons were done and then lead the child home again. Once the child's school days were over, he no longer needed his "tutor."

The law takes the unbeliever by the hand and gently leads him to Christ for salvation. Once he has come to Christ, he no longer needs his "tutor," the law.

The law also is designed to do the same thing to a believer.

In Romans 7:14-24, we see a picture of a man who was at the end of himself, and the law had brought him there: ". . . but I am of flesh, sold into bondage to sin. For that which I am doing, I do not understand; for I am not practicing what I would like to do, but I am doing the very thing I hate. . . . For I know that nothing good dwells in me, that is, in my flesh; for the wishing is present in me, but the doing of the good is not. For the good that I wish, I do not do; but I practice the very evil that I do not wish. . . . Wretched man that I am! Who will set me free from the body of this death?"

Do you know who uttered those heartrending words? The Apostle Paul! There he was—right where the law was designed to bring him—at the end of himself. At that point the law tenderly took him by the hand and led him to the Lord Jesus Christ, who set him free as he began to walk in the Spirit.

In Romans 8:3-5 Paul said that what the law couldn't do for him, God had done. God produced in Paul the righteous life which the law demanded of him, and this happened as Paul just walked in the Spirit.

The Law Has Done Its Job

The law has shown us what sin is, and it has actually made us sin more. It has driven us to despair of human effort and it has finally brought us to Christ for salvation and for the moment-by-moment power to live for Him. When this progression is finished, then the law is finally done with the believer.

Because it is so difficult for us to understand and accept this, it is a constant nemesis to the Christian.

The law is through with us, but we won't let go of it. Let's look at what we've done with the law in our Christian lives today. Many say, "Sure, we're free from the law of Moses, but we're under the higher 'Law of Christ,' which means that we have to keep the Sermon on the Mount and all of the laws of the New Testament."

If the law of Moses was impossible to keep, and it was, how on earth do we suppose that we can keep the laws of the New Testament which are a thousand times tougher? The Old Testament laws were external, but most of the New Testament laws are internal, dealing with our emotions and our thought life.

The problem with Judaism was that the Jews thought if they could just be obedient to their laws, then they could obtain righteousness. Paul said that they didn't obtain righteousness because they tried to get it by obedience, rather than by faith (Romans 9:30-32).

One thing you can say for them: they had a zeal for God. But unfortunately, it wasn't in accordance with God's plan (Romans 10:1-3).

We're Guilty Too!

We've done just what the Jews did, with our own refinements, of course. We've had a lot of zeal for God, but much of it has not been according to knowledge. We've made rules about how to be a "good Christian" and we've said, "Okay, here are the things we can do, and here are the things we can't do."

The Jews tried to become righteous by obeying the Ten Commandments, and it didn't work. We've tried to bring righteousness into our lives by obedience to the Sermon on the Mount and all the teachings of Paul plus a few man-made taboos, and that hasn't worked either.

The Solution

What is the answer to a righteous and obedient life?

"Christ is the end of the law *for righteousness* to everyone who believes" (Romans 10:4).

". . . if a law had been given which was able to impart life, then righteousness would indeed have been based on law" (Galatians 3:21).

"Now that no one is justified by the Law before God is evident; for 'The righteous man shall live by faith.' However, the Law is not of faith . . ." (Galatians 3:11-12).

"I do not nullify the grace of God; for if righteousness comes through the Law, then Christ died needlessly" (Galatians 2:21).

"For the law was given through Moses; grace and truth were realized through Jesus Christ" (John 1:17).

The answer to a righteous and obedient life is to walk in the Spirit and walk by faith in His ability to produce God's righteousness and obedience to His laws within you. "In order that the requirement of the Law might be fulfilled in us, who do not walk according to the flesh, but according to the Spirit" (Romans 8:4).

Don't Get the Cart Before the Horse

In the Christian life there is only one *source* of power—the indwelling Holy Spirit. There is only one *means* of releasing that source, and that is faith. There are hundreds of *results* in the life of the Christian who releases the Spirit in him by faith: witnessing, holiness, obedience, good works, power, boldness, praise, faith, etc.

Some of you may still be concerned about how you're going to keep all the commands in the Bible. These commands are simply *"results"* of the Spirit-produced life. We are only to concern ourselves with walking in the Spirit, and He will concern Himself with making all these biblical admonitions a reality in our life. This turns the commands in the Word into promises of what He can be trusted to do in us.

If *we* try to produce the holy life we see expected of us in the Bible, then we are focusing on the *"results"* of the Christian life rather than on its source, Jesus. We are doomed to end up in utter frustration.

We don't get up in the morning and say, "Now I must be obedient today. I must check over all my lists of things that Christians do and don't do. I must do my best to live for God today."

Do you know what happens when you do that? It's like throwing a truckload of fresh meat into a cage of half-starved lions. All your resolve, determination, and good intentions will be torn to shreds before the day is half over. All your sin nature has been waiting for, to turn it into a raging beast, is a "truckload" of law.

If you seek to be made righteous as a believer by obedience to the law, any kind of law, you have cut off the power of Christ in your life. That's what Paul says in Galatians 5:1-5.

Obedience is a *result* of a Spirit-filled relationship with Christ, not the means of producing it.

How Has God Made Us Holy?

We've looked at the law; we've seen what it is. We've examined what its purpose is in both the unbeliever and the believer. We've seen what it has done to us and how we've misused it.

Now then, what has God done about the law and the believer's relationship to it?

He has taken us out from under the jurisdiction of the law and placed us under His grace. The law is still there, but we're not under it.

"But now we have been released from the Law, having died to that by which we were bound, so that we serve in newness of the Spirit and not in oldness of the letter" (Romans 7:6).

The law just doesn't speak to us anymore as a basis of operation in the Christian life. When Christ died, was buried, rose, and ascended, we died with Him to the law and its power over us.

A friend of mine tells a story to illustrate this. You're in a car going twenty in a twenty-five-mile zone. A cop is following you, and you're really watching yourself. Overhead, there's a bird doing forty. You glance at the policeman, but he doesn't move. Why? Because the law of twenty-five-miles-an-hour just doesn't have jurisdiction over that bird.

Law and Grace Are Mutually Exclusive

It is imperative that we realize that law and grace are complete systems in themselves. They are mutually exclusive. To mix these principles robs the law of its bona fide terror and grace of its creative freeness.

What does this mean to us in a practical way?

First of all, it means that there is nothing we have to do to earn favor with God. Under grace, our acceptance with God is based on the fact that we are *in* Christ and God accepts Him completely. Therefore He accepts us the same way. Our acceptance is based on Christ's performance for us.

If we insist on relating to God by the principle of law, then our acceptance with Him is based on our own performance. I don't know a more heartbreaking sight than earnest, well-meaning, but dead-wrong believers plugging away, trying to improve their status with God by all their righteous deeds. If they could only know that all of that is futile. Their acceptance is already a settled fact and *in no way* can it be improved upon.

Grace emphasizes love as a motivation for obedience and service, but law uses a fear-threat motive. Satan subtly makes you think, "Something awful will happen to me if I don't shape up in my Christian life. God will take one of my children or let me be in a crippling accident."

There is no way to feel loved by God or loving toward Him under a law-based relationship. Everything depends on your own ingenuity to keep God happy with you, and that's just too heavy a burden of responsibility to bear.

Grace That Is Greater Than All My Sin

Do you know what grace really means and what God's grace has made available to His dearly loved children?

It means that there is not now, nor can there ever be again, for any reason, any condemnation of us by anyone, including ourselves and God. It means that we are totally accepted by God in our present, unfinished condition. It means that He has set Himself so free to minister in us and to us that He will do it without our even asking Him (Romans 8:1).

Now that's a lot to digest, but it's just a glimpse of what His grace is. It will take all eternity to fathom it.

What Results?

When we come to know and truly believe that we are no longer under law, but under grace, it sets the Holy Spirit free to produce holiness in us. Love, praise, obedience, and performance will all result from the Holy Spirit making this a reality in our lives.

We feel like responding in love to someone who has done so much for us. "We love, because He *first* loved us" (1 John 4:19).

Doctrine of Demons

Perhaps you've wondered why I've taken so much time to show the devastating effects of "legalism" on the church. It's because this doctrine is tolerated in churches today that make an absolute fetish of being doctrinally pure in every area. Satan has completely blinded them to the fact that what they are doing to their people by keeping them under law is guaranteed to wipe out their Christian life.

I know of Christians today who talk about grace, who believe in grace, and who at the same time have almost put grace under the law.

God grant that their eyes will be opened to see the liberty there is in Christ. A true understanding of grace will never produce license, but I have seen plenty of license produced by legalism. Satan is in there pitching all the time.

The Trial of the Truth

Legalism is joined by another "doctrine of demons." This took on steam in Germany in the 1880s when the so-called "Higher Critical" movement (mentioned briefly in Chapter Three) launched its attack against the historicity and authenticity of the Bible.

This biased group brought such convincing arguments to bear upon the Bible that young seminarians became crusaders to spread "the honest truth" about the Bible to other seminaries and from there into the various churches.

These religious liberals, who started with the basic assumption that there can be no real supernatural occurrences, vigorously attacked the accounts of Christ's life in the four gospels. It was dogmatically asserted, with no hard evidence from history or archaeology, that the followers of Jesus had embellished and rewritten the accounts of His life and had inserted the miracles as fanciful myths.

These men, primarily on the basis of speculation, dated the writing of the gospels and other New Testament books, for the most part, in the second century. This permitted them to argue that the writers were so far removed from the actual facts that the original readers had no way to check the accuracy of the books.

Recent archaeological discoveries may explode this "liberal mythology." Perhaps one of the most exciting archaeological finds of this century relating to the New Testament was reported, with little prominence, in the news media. The article by Louis Cassels of United Press was headlined "Bible Accounts Strengthened by Scholar's Finds." These archaeological discoveries concerned the identification of certain pieces of papyrus which were found among the Dead Sea Scrolls in 1947 as possibly being parts of Mark's gospel, written around A.D. 50.

The newspaper account continues: "The date is what matters. Biblical scholars have long assumed that Mark's gospel, based on the recollections of the Apostle Peter, was set down in writing shortly before Peter's death in Rome, which would date it around A.D. 68.

"Since Jesus was crucified about A.D. 33, the previous dating of Mark's gospel—generally regarded to have been the first one written—left a hiatus of 35 years in which the historical details of the life of Jesus either were transmitted by word of mouth or by now lost records. . . .

"German biblical scholarship, sometimes called 'form criticism' has been predicated since the 19th Century on the assumption that during this lapse of 35 years the actual facts of Jesus' life became heavily intermixed with myth and legend."[1]

The papyrus fragments identified by Professor Jose O'Callaghan, a scholar at the Pontifical Biblical Institute in Rome, have been dated by scientific methods as possibly having been in existence from about A.D. 50, which indicates that Mark's gospel might have been in circulation within a dozen years of the time of Jesus' death.

As Louis Cassels points out, if this early date for the gospel is correct, it "means Mark's record had to survive the test of any journalistic or historical writing—being published at a time when it could be read, criticized, and, if inauthentic, denounced by thousands of Jews, Christians, Romans, and Greeks who were living in Palestine at the time of Jesus' ministry.

"That the early church chose Mark as one of only four gospels out of dozens once in circulation to be preserved for posterity in the New Testament also indicates the people closest to the events—Jesus' original followers—found Mark's report accurate and trustworthy, not myth but true history."[2]

Scholars may be working to prove or disprove this and other finds for years to come, but as each day we live becomes history, we will see more evidence of the authenticity of the Bible unfold before the unbelieving world.

For centuries Satan has delighted in making biblical Christianity appear non-intellectual in the eyes of the world. But how great it is to know that we do not have to put our intellect on the shelf to believe the message of God's transforming power through Christ.

12 ○ The Guilt Trip

"I, even I, am the one who wipes out your transgressions for My own sake; And I will not remember your sins."   THE LORD, ISAIAH 43:25

IF YOU WERE the captain of an invading army, you would find the weakest spot in your opponent's defenses and go in for the kill.

Satan, the archenemy of the saints, has a way of wiping Christians out—over and over again. He moves in on our blind side and steers us in the direction he wants.

When a person becomes a true believer in Christ, he is born into the family of God and out of the family of Satan. Satan does everything he can to keep us blinded to the offer of forgiveness in Christ, but millions have thrown off his shackles and gone from death to life. This has absolutely infuriated Satan, and each time someone responds to the Gospel, it's a slap in his face.

C. S. Lewis, in his amusing book *The Screwtape Letters*, satirizes the daily routine in hell and the foibles and headaches of hardworking demons who just try to put in an honest day's work fouling up Christians.

One of the most successful tactics the demons used in neutralizing their enemies (the Christians) was to get them to dwell on all of their failures. Once they began feeling guilty about their performance in the Christian life, they were no longer any threat to Satan's program.

Things haven't changed much in Satan's tactics. Why should they? He's got a winner.

There's nothing Satan likes better than to get a believer started on the guilt trip.

As I look back over my own life, I realize that guilt is a handle that the Devil constantly tries to grab to steer me. One classic illustration that comes to mind happened to me my third year in seminary. One fellow was a real close buddy of mine. We had had three years of great times together. Then I borrowed some money from him. I told him I would be able to pay him back in about two weeks.

After a week went by, I began to be concerned a little about where the money was going to come from to pay him. But I had another week to work on it, so I wasn't too worried.

The second week went by, and I just couldn't raise the money anywhere. I felt kind of strained around my friend, but I didn't bring the subject up because I'd hoped he'd forgotten what the date was.

As the days went by, it seemed to me as though he was looking at me with an accusing expression every time I saw him, and I did the best I could to stay out of his way. After the deadline had passed by two weeks, I began planning my day so I wouldn't run into him. It was awful. I felt terrible to have lost such a good friend, but on the other hand, I couldn't see why he wasn't more understanding of my problem. Mind you, not a word had passed between us regarding the money, but I felt so guilty that I was sure he had written me off as a friend.

Finally one day, to my horror, I saw him coming toward me in the hall. There was no place to hide! He cornered me and said, "Okay, Hal, what's the matter with you?"

"Well, it's about that money I owe you," I answered defensively.

He laughed and put his big hand on my shoulder and said, "Brother, I thought that was it. Look, Hal, I haven't changed. I don't feel any different toward you than I did a few weeks ago. If you had the money, I know you'd pay me. But money doesn't mean that much to me. Your friendship means a lot more, and I'm still your buddy."

For three weeks I had been going around thinking he was condemning me. But that wasn't true at all—he was still my best friend.

That taught me an unforgettable lesson. If we think someone is holding something against us, we become alienated and hostile toward them. It's simply an inevitable reaction, a defense mechanism.

I believe this is the number one reason why Christians fail in their relationship with God. Because we're always aware that in many ways we fall short of what we should be as Christians, it's only natural to assume that God must be displeased with our performance. The more we let God down, the more we assume His anger, until such alienation sets into our minds that it is virtually impossible for us to enjoy a vital fellowship with God.

And the pitiful tragedy is that all this is just in our minds. God isn't mad at us!

I know what some of you are thinking. You can hardly believe that what I'm saying is true. On the human level if we let people down or offend them, it does produce alienation on their part. And besides, if you've been riddled with guilt, then you have a gnawing suspicion that you really deserve God's hostility.

I want to say something loud and clear, in no uncertain terms: "He has now reconciled you in His fleshly body, through death, in order to present you before Him holy and blameless and beyond reproach—" (Colossians 1:22).

When do you become "holy and blameless and beyond reproach"? The minute He reconciles you to the Father, and that happens the moment you believe in Christ's substitutionary death on your behalf.

Let's substantiate this from the Scripture.

There are several words in the original Greek New Testament for reconciliation. One is found in Matthew 5:24: "*diallasso*," which means that two parties are at enmity with each other and need to be reconciled by removing the cause of the enmity. This word is used strictly of human relationships in the Bible.

There is another word, however, which is always used in connection with God and man: "*apokatallasso*," meaning that only one party has enmity in his heart and needs to have the barriers separating fellowship removed, while the other party has no enmity. You see, God has no hostility toward us. He has always loved man. This is why He became a man, so that as our substitute He could bear the judgment due us and in so doing remove every barrier that our sin had erected between Himself and us. God never needed to be reconciled; man is the one who needs it.

As the Scripture puts it, ". . . God was in Christ reconciling the world to Himself, not counting their trespasses against them . . . ," for "He made Him who knew no sin to be sin on our behalf, that we might become the righteousness of God in Him" (2 Corinthians 5:19, 21).

It doesn't seem like an even exchange; He gets our sin and we get His righteousness. But there you have it. It was God's incomparable plan to reconcile man back into fellowship with Him.

This is why God can say in effect to all who receive Christ, "You are *now* holy and blameless *in my sight*" (Colossians 1:22; Ephesians 1:4).

Can you think of another human being, including yourself, who views you as totally holy and blameless? I can't! Yet, in God's eyes we are already perfect; not will be, but *are*!

This is not a status which is given on a temporary basis while we try to become worthy of it as Christians. Once God puts us into union with His Son, we become clothed with His righteousness and God sees us as holy and blameless because that's the way He views Jesus. Experientially we may be quite imperfect, but our acceptance in God's eyes is never based on how we perform, but rather on the fact that we are *in* Christ and God accepts Him perfectly.

Knowing these liberating facts and counting them true on a moment-by-moment basis is the most important factor in living a life pleasing to God.

You can't help but respond with love and obedience to someone who loves and accepts you.

Now Satan is dedicated to keeping Christians from finding out what I've just told you, and he's done a pretty good job in the Christian world today. He lets them have a little taste of victorious living and then he moves in on them with his heavy artillery. He'll get them to fail God and get their eyes on themselves. After a series of failures, Satan gets them into a pattern that I have called "the sin syndrome."

The Sin Syndrome

First, we knowingly *sin*. The inevitable result, if we don't relate the sin to the Cross, is that we develop *guilt*. And guilt always leads to *estrangement*. There's the syndrome: *sin, guilt, estrangement*.

Now man can't live with guilt. So he tries to deal with guilt in one of two ways—both of them wrong.

If he is the type who doesn't have a particularly sensitive conscience, he tries to *justify* himself. He makes excuses and offers valid reasons why he did something:

"It was only a little lie, and it was easier on everyone involved."

"After all, the government spends my tax money on things I don't agree with anyway."

"But we really love each other, and everyone is doing it."

When we justify our actions, the result will be a feeling of loss of fellowship with God, because deep down inside we know that we haven't been honest with ourselves or God. We sense we've offended God by our deviousness. And when we feel that God has been offended, then we will also feel estranged from God. Remember, God isn't mad, but we think He is.

Another way man deals with guilt, and it's equally wrong, is to *condemn* himself. He sins over and over in the same area, guilt sets in, and then he begins the self-condemnation trip.

Satan loves to get his hands on one of these "sensitive" Christians. With no trouble at all, he can get them to feel like no-good worms before God. He'll convince them they couldn't possibly expect God to hear them when they pray, and surely He wouldn't answer their prayers even if He did hear. He gets their eyes so focused on their shabby Christian lives that they're sure God couldn't possibly use them.

Satan just sits back and relaxes when he gets us going on self-condemnation. We're out of the ball game as far as he's concerned.

At this point you may ask, is there any kind of bona fide guilt in the life of a believer in Christ?

There is what I call *"legal"* guilt. This is every man's curse as he comes into the world. It is his inherited culpability for sin, and this is what Christ removed as a barrier between God and man when He went to the cross for us. I have a lot more to say about this a little later.

Then there is the *"emotion"* of guilt. This is what Satan delights in heaping upon believers who feel they have failed God. This kind of guilt is Satan's tool and has no place in the life of a child of God.

Finally, there is a convicting ministry of the Holy Spirit described by the Apostle Paul in Second Corinthians 7:8-9 as *"sorrow"* which leads to repentance. If the *"godly sorrow"* caused by the Spirit's conviction doesn't lead to a repentance, or a turning around, then it well may go into the second kind of guilt, the *emotion of guilt*, which is deadly to a Christian's walk with God.

There is a need to acknowledge to God when we are guilty of sinning, and we freely can if we know for sure that God will keep on loving and accepting us. When we continue to feel unforgiven after we have acknowledged or confessed our sin, it's an indication that we have turned our focus away from God's forgiveness to ourselves. Then we're saying that our sinful weaknesses are more powerful than God's forgiving power. Either He isn't big enough to forgive us or He doesn't want to forgive us.

In either case, when there is unresolved guilt in the life of a person, he will feel estranged from God. He will not trust God to work in his life through the Holy Spirit and deliver him from the temptations of the flesh and the cunning wiles of Satan. He just won't come to God for help if he believes He is angry with him.

A Christian caught in the guilt trip will begin to seek to do things for God in the energy of the flesh to appease Him for his sense of guilt. This results in more frustration because, as the Bible says, ". . . the mind set on the flesh is hostile toward God; for it does not subject itself to the Law of God, for it is not even able to do so" (Romans 8:7).

King David of Israel certainly understood this progression. He knew quite a bit about sinning and its repercussions. Not only was he guilty of adultery with another man's wife, Bathsheba, but later he plotted her husband's death to cover up his sin.

In his later life David wrote Psalm 130, which shows us what he had learned from his rugged experiences. Listen to this particularly: "If Thou, Lord, shouldst mark iniquities, O Lord, who could stand? But there is forgiveness with Thee, that Thou mayest be feared" (Psalm 130:3-4).

In the original Hebrew the word "mark" meant to keep an itemized account of something—to write it out. David is saying here, "Lord, if You were a celestial bookkeeper keeping an itemized account of my sins, I'd be in big trouble!"

What did David learn from God's dealings with him? He learned that "there is forgiveness with (God) that (He) may be feared." That word "fear" in Hebrew means to be able to *reverently trust* someone.

David put his finger on a fantastic truth here, one of the most important things we can ever know about God. If we think God is keeping an itemized account of our sins and holding them against us, we can't really trust Him; it's impossible to have a dynamic, bold faith in Him. Why? Because you can only trust someone whom you believe really loves and accepts you *completely* in spite of all your faults.

Learning what Christ accomplished at the cross is the most important truth you will ever absorb in your lifetime. It should saturate your mind every day.

Counting as true the absolute forgiveness which Christ accomplished at the cross is the foundation of having a power-packed faith. You can't really respond to God in faith unless you know He has accepted you just as you are, unless you know what it means to be accepted in the Beloved (Ephesians 1:6). *The Beloved* is the title for God's dear Son, Jesus. God sees us all wrapped up in Jesus. The acceptance He has for Him, the Son of His love, the Beloved One, is the acceptance He keeps on having for us.

To fail to be accepted completely by God for even one second would mean that somehow we had gotten out of Christ, and that just isn't possible. He won't let go of us! Isn't that great news?

Satan Blinds Us to the Cross

Satan would like to blind us to all this wonderful truth. In fact, he keeps trying to blind us every day. We may not even realize it, but the number one reason the power of God is short-circuited in our lives is that we have never really learned what the cross of Christ means on a day-by-day basis. The cross is the continuing basis of God accepting and forgiving us.

We've all had experiences that we consider "mountaintoppers"—times when we experienced the Holy Spirit's working in our lives in a fresh way. For a while everything was going great and then, without even really knowing why, things began to drag. Spiritual flabbiness began to weaken us, and we wondered what was wrong.

I've gone down this painful road before, and each time I've discovered the real problem: I've started off on a "guilt trip." I've failed to believe that from God's perspective I'm already forgiven for disappointing Him; I only need to claim a forgiveness that is already a fact, not beg God as if forgiveness were in doubt.

The Believer's Defense Attorney

It's the Lord's desire that His children live godly lives and not sin, but our omniscient Father, knowing our nature, made provision for His erring children.

The Apostle John, in writing to the new believers of his day, said, "My little children, I am writing these things to you that you may not sin. And if any one sins, we have an Advocate with the Father, Jesus Christ the righteous; and He Himself is the propitiation for our sins; and not for ours only, but also for those of the whole world" (1 John 2:1-2).

An advocate means a defense attorney. Why would we need a defense attorney in the presence of God, our Father? Most of us think that it means Jesus defends us against the Father so that He won't judge us. Is that true? Absolutely not. Because of what Jesus did at the cross, the Father will never condemn us again.

The word "propitiation" means to turn away deserved wrath by the satisfaction of justice. What Christ did on the cross was to bear the compounded wrath of a Holy God on every sin that would ever be committed by every man who would ever live. The big theological word "propitiation" simply means, "God isn't mad at me anymore."

He poured out all His anger that He would have against our sins onto Jesus as He hung on the cross. Now He has set Himself free on a perfectly just basis to keep on dealing with us in love, even when He disciplines us.

God Doesn't Get Even

Are you ready for this?

God does not punish. Punishment means to "get even," and God doesn't do that. He's already "gotten even" with Jesus for all our sins. God "disciplines" His children, but it's always in love—never in anger. The words "discipline" and "training" are interchangeable words. God's disciplining always has a forward look to it (Hebrews 12:5-13).

When God sees a child of His who continually refuses to depend upon the Holy Spirit to deliver him from his temptations, then out of deep concern for that child's well-being and happiness God will begin to train him so that he will come to depend upon Him in the future. God knows we are only happy when we are living holy lives. This is true discipline and it has no resemblance to punishment.

Sometimes this discipline may seem grievous, but if we are learning to see everything that comes our way as being permitted by the loving hand of our Heavenly Father, then we can give thanks even for the discipline.

Unfortunately, at this point Satan has taken his toll with many believers. They live in constant fear of punishment for their sins.

Most of us have a few especially gross sins we committed in our past that spook us like the proverbial skeleton in the closet. Whenever some difficulty or calamity hits our lives, we trot the skeleton out and say, "Oh yes, God is getting even with me for 'that sin'."

Some live with the gnawing fear that lightning is going to strike them or God is going to kill one of their children to get even with them for some sin they committed long ago or are involved in at the moment.

God does not deal with us that way. To be sure, adversities are permitted in the believer's life, but they are designed to teach us to trust God, not to destroy us with vengeance.

But What About . . .

Now some of you may be saying, "All right, Hal, if God never punishes us for our sins, what about Galatians 6:7 which says, 'Do not be deceived, God is not mocked; for whatever a man sows, this he will also reap'?"

This verse is jerked out of context by so many Christians that it's incredible. The verse just before this one says, "And let the one who is taught the Word share all good things with him who teaches" (Galatians 6:6). This context is talking about supporting financially the one who gives himself to studying and teaching the Bible.

This same idea of sowing money for God's work is contained in Second Corinthians 9:6, "Now this I say, he who *sows* sparingly shall also reap sparingly; and he who sows bountifully shall also reap bountifully."

This concept of "whatsoever a man sows, he shall also reap" is concerned with investing our money in God's work and the reward or lack of reward for our stewardship.

To apply this passage to God's method of discipline is to contradict the whole principle of grace with which God now deals with His children.

Satan, the Old Guilt Tripper

If you still feel guilty after you acknowledge your sin and have remembered that you are forgiven, guess who is laying it on you. It's the old guilt-tripper himself, Satan.

Satan does not want you to remember that God did away with your sin at the cross. That's why you need a defense attorney before the Father. Satan's name means "The Accuser."

Christ doesn't have to defend you against the Father; He defends you against Satan, before the Father.

Here's a scene which has probably taken place in heaven in the presence of God today. We can thank Job for this bit of insight into Satan's tactics.

Satan's been up there today with a portfolio on each one of God's children. He brought a dossier on Buzz and Tom and Karin and an especially large file on Hal. He charges in and points, "Ah ha! There's Hal. He's one of Your children, huh? Did you see what he just did?"

And Satan begins to accuse.

Then Jesus steps up and says, "Father, Hal believed in Me in 1956. The forgiveness I paid for at the cross was then applied to him. This is our only plea."

And the Father says, "Case dismissed!"

God will not let anyone discipline His children but Himself. He'll do it in love because He has set Himself free to deal with us in grace. God, on the basis of His indwelling Spirit whom He trusts and has put into the life of every believer, is conforming us daily into the image of Jesus.

Old Testament Pictures

There's a wonderful picture in the Old Testament of Christ's intercessory work for believers. He bears our names upon His heart as He continually represents us before the Father.

We're taught this in the Old Testament from the practice of the high priest. He would go into the Tabernacle before the Presence of the Lord, before the Ark, as it was called, and he would burn incense, which was a picture of prayer.

Bound over his heart was a special vest with precious stones upon it, and on each stone were the names of the children of Israel.

God said, "And Aaron shall carry the names of the sons of Israel . . . over his heart when he enters the holy place, for a memorial before the Lord continually" (Exodus 28:29).

This is a beautiful picture of how Jesus Christ continually is before the throne of God with your name on His heart.

That's why in Hebrews 7:24-25 we have these encouraging words: "but He, on the other hand, because He abides forever, holds His priesthood permanently. Hence also He is able to save forever those who draw near to God through Him, since He always lives to make intercession for them."

According to this fantastic promise of assurance, once we have believed in Christ as Savior, it is impossible to be lost again or unforgiven. For a child of God to become lost, Christ would have to stop interceding for him. The promise is that "He is able to save *forever* those who draw near to God through Him." "Forever" is a very long time.

Jesus Himself promised, "I will never desert you, nor will I ever forsake you" (Hebrews 13:5). Thank God that "He always lives to make intercession for us," and because of that we can "draw near with confidence to the throne of grace, that we may receive mercy and find grace to help in time of need" (Hebrews 4:16).

Satan: Accuser Before God and Conscience

After Satan accuses us before God and doesn't make any headway there, he begins to accuse our consciences. He'll get us into a hopeless treadmill: sinning, vowing we won't do it again, trying not to sin, and then sinning again.

Here's the way it works:

First, he'll start working on an area of weakness. Every Christian has at least one area where he is especially vulnerable. We still have the old sin nature in us which can tempt us, and when we don't depend upon the indwelling Holy Spirit to overcome temptations, we will sin.

Seeking to be a good Christian we might say, "God, I know I've been wrong: thank You for forgiving me." Our burden is lifted and everything goes along fine for awhile. Then Satan gets us to fall down again in the same area. We hate ourselves for being such an awful Christian, but we accept His forgiveness and keep moving—only we're feeling a little guilty about having so little will power to live for God.

Pretty soon Satan will get us to sin again in the same area, and this time we're feeling so unworthy that we promise, "Oh God, if You'll just forgive me one more time, I vow I won't do this again."

At this piece of news, Satan and his demon hordes let out a rousing cheer of victory. He has us right where he wants us—on the sin treadmill.

We try so hard to please God, only we do it in the power of the flesh. The harder we try, the more we fail. The more we fail, the more we vow not to do it again.

Then Satan steps in and says accusingly, "Too bad! God won't forgive you this time. You've had it. There's no more grace for you." Or if he sees that we're too smart to fall for that extreme line of reasoning, he'll say, "God may forgive you, but He can't forget how unreliable you are. You'll never be able to be used by God as fully as before."

It's that old "bird with the broken wing will never fly so high again" routine.

Wham! You're wiped out! You forget that the issue is not *will* God forgive you, but will you believe that He *has* forgiven you and trust Him for the inner strengthening to turn from sin.

I'm not trying to teach that we can go out and sin and have no conscience about it, so don't get all uptight about that. The Holy Spirit will faithfully convict a believer of sin, not so he can confess in order to get forgiven, but so that he can claim forgiveness and believe Him again.

God does not want us to dwell on our sins, but rather on our forgiveness. If your focus is continually on yourself, then you cannot be "Looking away [from all that will distract] to Jesus" (Hebrews 12:2, *Amplified Bible*).

When you finally understand what Jesus Christ accomplished at the cross, you realize that God never stops forgiving you, even while you're in the process of sinning, although you yourself cannot appreciate the comfort of the forgiveness while you're sinning.

When Christ died on the cross, how many of your sins were future? Every last one of them.

I used to think that when I accepted Christ it meant that Christ had died for my sins up to that point, but from that point on I'd just have to confess them as I did them or else I wasn't forgiven. That's a perilous position to be in because you're never quite sure if you've confessed all your sins, and there just might be one or two that God is holding against you.

One day I realized what the *all* in Colossians 2:13 meant: "And when you were dead in your transgressions and the uncircumcision of your flesh, He made you alive together with Him, having forgiven us *all* our transgressions."

We were dead before we accepted Jesus, dead spiritually, unable to know God as a living reality, as a Person.

Then the Bible says, "He made you *alive* together with Him." This is talking about the new birth, the experience of being given spiritual life the moment you believe in Christ. Why is this possible? "Having forgiven us *all* our transgressions."

The verb translated "having forgiven" means something which happens at a point of time that doesn't have to be repeated. A final act. In God's mind, how many does that *all* mean? How many of our sins did God see when He judged them in Jesus on the cross?

The answer is *all*!

God Sees the Whole Parade of Life

God is looking at our lives as a helicopter pilot would look down at a parade. If we're standing on a corner watching a parade, we see the beginning of the parade, each segment passing by, and then we see the end of it. We see consecutively. But God, like the pilot, sees the whole parade at one time. That's the way God sees your life: your past, present, and future is all in the *now* with Him.

When you place faith in Jesus as your Savior, God has already seen (back in A.D. 33) your life go by like a parade. He took your whole life and the sin and guilt of it and put it all on Jesus Christ.

So when you believe in Christ as Savior, how many sins has God forgiven you? Not just those you have committed up to that point, but those from your whole lifetime. He couldn't accept you into a relationship with Himself at all unless He could forgive you for the whole thing.

This doesn't mean that God condones sinning in the life of a believer—far from it. It means He has set Himself free to be ready to work in us the moment we see that we've sinned and acknowledge it and accept His forgiveness.

First John 1:9 says, "If we keep on confessing our sins, He is faithful and righteous, to have forgiven us our sins and to have cleansed us from all unrighteousness" (literal translation of the Greek verb tenses). The Word never tells a believer *after the cross* to ask forgiveness. It's already a settled fact with God, and He just wants us to claim what is already true.

In First John 1:9 the word "confess" means to agree with someone about something; in this case to agree with God about our sins. But I can't agree with God about His attitude toward my sins until I see clearly what His attitude is.

Agree With God

First of all, God wants us to see our sin as He sees it—it is sin. But He doesn't want us to stop there. If we really agree with God about our sin, then we also have to see it as already forgiven. That's the way God sees it.

Finally, He wants us to turn from the sin and begin to trust Him to empower us to have victory over it in the future.

If we don't judge our sin in this way, accepting His forgiveness and turning from the sin in His power, Satan is going to come in and grab hold of that handle of guilt. He will get us to try to make up for our sins, and we'll end up punishing ourselves or someone else to try to relieve the guilt.

Someone Has to Pay

Every time we sin, we instinctively know someone has to pay for it. We don't have to be taught that; it's part of our very make-up. When I sin, either I've got to pay for it, or I make someone else pay (usually those dearest to me), or I look to Jesus as already having paid for it.

In the years I have been a believer I have had many counseling experiences in this area. I remember a beautiful young girl whose husband had to go on a long trip abroad. While he was gone, she committed adultery. That was a sin, no question about it.

After this happened she realized it was a sin and acknowledged this to God. But she didn't believe what God said, that it was already forgiven. She did not count His forgiveness as being true in her case. She was in much worse shape than she realized, because unresolved guilt is one of the most destructive forces on earth.

Her husband returned. Deeply implanted in that girl's mind was the sin and the unresolved guilt from it—not because God still held her guilty, but because she didn't believe what God said and therefore she didn't forgive herself.

A few years after her husband returned, they had their first child. Satan began to put his hand into her subconscious mind and grab hold of that guilt. Pretty soon she was having serious mental problems. She told her husband what had happened, thinking that maybe this would clear her conscience. He forgave her, but she still couldn't forgive herself.

Do you know what she wound up doing? One day her husband came in and found her trying to strangle their child. Why? Because she loved that child more than anything in the world. Killing him was a way of inflicting maximum punishment upon herself for the sense of guilt. What a needless tragedy!

She didn't understand all this at first until it was unraveled in counseling. Deep down inside was this unresolved guilt. Instead of relating this to the cross of Jesus Christ and saying, "Thank You for forgiving me," she had tried to punish herself for what she had done. She instinctively knew that someone had to pay, and she was making herself pay.

Guilt is the most crippling disease in the world today!

A friend of mine was in a doctor's office when he looked across the street at a hotel and saw a woman about ready to jump from the tenth floor. He rushed across the street, went up in the elevator, and got there just in time to say, "Wait, don't jump. Let me just talk to you."

Slowly and distinctly he said, "God loves you."

The girl turned and looked at him with a horrible expression of guilt and despair, then turned and jumped. She was killed immediately.

Psychiatrists and doctors say that unresolved guilt is the number one cause of mental illness and suicide. Over half of all hospital beds are filled with people who have emotional illnesses. The greatest therapy they could possibly have would be to find out that God loves them and has made an all-encompassing forgiveness available to them in Christ.

God didn't have to wait until Freud came along to have an answer for mental illness. We don't have to go to a psychiatrist to get the answer for guilt. Jesus provided the only real answer to guilt some two thousand years ago. If we believe what God has said, there's an answer that cleanses us in our conscience and sets us free from dead works to serve the living God.

I don't want you to suffer from crippling guilt like this. I want you to be able to release the power of God in your life day by day, moment by moment—to be set free from a guilt complex and be able to acknowledge to God, "Yes, Lord, I'm guilty, but I thank You that I've been forgiven."

Then turn and believe that the Spirit of God will work in your life right now. You don't have to wait until you are worthy for it or earn it.

Here's a passage that thrills me every time I read it—it never gets old. "Having canceled out the certificate of debt, consisting of decrees against us and which was hostile to us; and He has taken it out of the way, having nailed it to the cross" (Colossians 2:14).

Out of Debt

This is a powerful word picture. In the day in which this was written the word translated as "certificate of debt" was widely known. Whenever a person would be convicted in a Roman court, a "certificate of debt" or bond would be prepared. The scribe of the court would itemize and write down every crime for which the person had been convicted. This certificate meant that the prisoner owed Caesar a prescribed payment for those crimes. It would then be taken with the prisoner to wherever he would be imprisoned and nailed to the door of his cell.

What an illustration the Apostle Paul used to show how God has dealt with our sins. When Jesus hung on the cross nineteen centuries ago, the "certificate of debt" of every man who would ever live was nailed to the cross with Him.

Our certificate of debt lists every time that we fall short of God's perfect law in thought, word, or deed. Just as that certificate would have been nailed to the cell of the criminal, Jesus took our certificate of debt and nailed it to the cross.

Why? Because He intended to pay for it.

According to Roman law, when a person was put in prison and the certificate of debt was nailed to the door, it would remain there until the sentence was carried out. Then they would take this certificate and write across it the word meaning "It is finished." They would roll it up, give it to the prisoner, and he could never be punished for those crimes again.

Did you know that was one of the last things Jesus shouted from the cross?

Just before He bowed His head and said, "Father, into Your hands I commit my spirit," He gave a cry of victory. He called from the cross "It is finished." The Greek word for this is "tetelestai," meaning "paid in full" (John 19:30).

Paid in Full

Jesus took our certificate of debt and wrote across it in His own blood, "Paid in full." We can never be tried for our sins again after we receive the pardon. It's settled forever in heaven by the blood of the only begotten Son of God.

That's why it says in Colossians 2:14, "He has taken it (our certificate of debt) out of the way, having nailed it to the cross." I owe God perfect obedience to His law, but God will never grade my law-keeping on the curve. It's perfection or nothing—and I can't pay.

That's what the word "redemption" means: to purchase out of slavery and set free by paying the price of a ransom. The ransom that Christ had to pay to set us free was the price of our owing God perfect obedience to His law, and Christ paid the sentence of debt in full. ". . . knowing that you were not redeemed with perishable things like silver or gold from your futile way of life inherited from your forefathers, but with precious blood, as of a lamb unblemished and spotless, the blood of Christ" (1 Peter 1:18-19).

That's why it says in Colossians 2:15: "When He had disarmed the rulers and authorities, He made a public display of them, having triumphed over them through Him."

The "rulers and authorities" are Satan and all his armies.

And Christ disarmed them! They have no legal basis to put their hands on a child of God any more. *Satan has no legal grounds to work in a Christian's life.* We can give him the legal ground, if we don't want to believe in God, but we certainly don't have to. God wants us to take our Magna Charta of freedom, which is the perfect forgiveness of Jesus Christ, and to realize that when we sin we should come to Him immediately with the heart attitude, "Oh, Lord, I agree with You that I have sinned." This is not in order to be forgiven, however. It's just to realize a forgiveness which is already a fact.

When Christ died on the cross, He took care of the sin problem forever. Another sacrifice will never be necessary. Why? Because of the value of the life of the One who was sacrificed. It's not like the blood of the goats and the bulls in the Old Testament, which merely covered sin. When Christ died for sin, He took it away as an issue.

"And not through the blood of goats and calves, but through His own blood, He entered the holy place once for all, *having obtained eternal redemption*" (Hebrews 9:12).

How long is eternal? God doesn't offer anything less. It is based upon the value of the sacrifice of Jesus Christ.

"For if the blood of goats and bulls and the ashes of a heifer sprinkling those who have been defiled, sanctify for the cleansing of the flesh, how much more will the blood of Christ, who through the eternal Spirit offered Himself without blemish to God, *cleanse your conscience from dead works to serve the living God?*" (Hebrews 9:13-14).

License to Serve

This is the most powerful message the Holy Spirit ever brought home to me. It was a license to serve, not to sin. The motivation which comes from knowing a perfect acceptance with God is so much greater than walking in fear that you're going to lose the relationship that there's just no comparison.

God wants us to serve not out of duty, but out of thanksgiving for what He has done in Jesus Christ.

"Cleanse your conscience"—that's where guilt becomes imbedded—"from dead works to serve the living God."

A "dead work" is anything which you and I do to try to help God forgive us for our sin. It is trying to add to what Christ has fully accomplished on the cross.

A dead work is when we don't believe we're really forgiven and we try to do something to make up for what we've done.

What does God want us to do when we sin?

We need Him at that moment more than at any other time in our lives. It's not a time for running from God, as Adam did. When Adam sinned, God appeared in the Garden and said, "Adam, where are you?" Did God really need to ask? Don't you think He knew where Adam was?

Adam hid himself because he was afraid. He should have known that God still loved him or He wouldn't have been looking for him. Then Adam committed the first dead work of history! He tried to hide his sense of guilt with fig leaves. He tried to cover his sin and guilt by the work of his own hands, and in doing that he committed the first "religious" act. That's really what "religion" is, if you understand it correctly.

Christianity isn't a religion; Christianity is a personal relationship with God through Jesus Christ and His finished work. It's not our trying to gain God's approbation by what we do.

In God's Family

Think of it!

We have an access into the presence of God. "Let us draw near with a sincere heart in full assurance of faith, having our hearts sprinkled clean from an evil conscience and our body washed with pure water" (Hebrews 10:22).

When we knowingly sin, God wants us to draw near to Him "with a sincere heart," to be honest "in full assurance of faith" (i.e., in what Christ has done). "By this will we have been sanctified through the offering of the body of Jesus Christ once for all" (Hebrews 10:10).

God loves us and accepts us. We're forgiven. He wants us to own up to what we've done and thank Him for His forgiveness. If we don't do this, we will have an evil conscience.

I know one heart-breaking story after another of people who have gone into mental illness because of unresolved guilt; others remain reasonably sane but have no power in their lives. They try to draw upon some experience they have had in their past and wonder why they don't have the same power any more.

How absolutely fantastic to know there is a forgiveness which is guaranteed to us through the once-and-for-all offering of Jesus Christ on our behalf. That's why it says, "Therefore He is able also to save to the uttermost—completely, perfectly, finally and for all time and eternity—those who come to God through Him, since He is always living to make petition to God *and* intercede with Him *and* intervene for them" (Hebrews 7:25, *Amplified Bible*).

I'm sure that some of you reading this have allowed guilt to tie you in knots for years. You've just been waiting for God to lower the boom on you for some secret sin or for a life lived in open rebellion against His will for you. That very guilt has produced an estrangement from the one Person you need to be closest to right now—your loving Heavenly Father. Can't you see how wonderful it would be to have Him fold His great, strong arms of love around you and comfort and reassure you of His love and acceptance?

Let Him do it now. He isn't angry with you—no matter how much you've let Him down. He has utterly forgiven you for any offenses toward Him. The only thing that grieves God now is for His children to feel alienated toward Him when He cares for them so much.

13 ○ Weapons of Warfare

"Finally, be strong in the Lord, and in the strength of His might. Put on the full armor of God, that you may be able to stand firm against the schemes of the devil. For our struggle is not against flesh and blood, but against the rulers, against the powers, against the world-forces of this darkness, against the spiritual forces of wickedness in the heavenly places. Therefore take up the full armor of God, that you may be able to resist in the evil day, and having done everything, to stand firm." EPHESIANS 6:10-13

WHENEVER NATIONS HAVE fought wars, covering the battlefields of history with broken lives, there have been some countries which have remained neutral in spite of the conflict surrounding them.

In this book we have seen that we are in a war where we can't be neutral! The battle lines are clearly drawn. There are no conscientious objectors in this war, no draft dodgers, no armchair generals, no advocates of peace at any price.

This is a time when every Christian must stand for Christ, covered to the hilt with the full armor of God. It doesn't make any difference if you are old or weak physically; the Lord Jesus will be your strength. It doesn't make any difference if you are young and don't understand all the battle strategy of your adversary, the Devil; God's armor will protect you.

But you can't be a do-it-yourself expert. You cannot assemble a self-made armor from bits and pieces of determination, grit, resolve, intelligence, or basic goodness. Satan can and will find every hole in a suit with a hand-made label in it.

Our only defense against the "prince of darkness" who works in the world system, distorting for his own purposes everything that is good and beautiful, is to put on the full armor of God. It is our only protection against the temptations that bombard the body, soul, and spirit.

Be Strong in the Lord

We cannot live the Christian life in our own strength. You've probably already discovered that. It is imperative that we allow the Lord to give us His strength. Without it, we don't stand a chance against the incredible power of Satan. Human strength is totally useless against the attacks of the Devil and his ingenious "schemes."

Paul's command to "be strong in the Lord" is even more powerful in the original text. The command is in the passive voice, which means that we receive the action that the verb is describing. It is actually saying that we are to be "constantly allowing ourselves to be strengthened by the Lord." In other words, He does the strengthening and we enjoy the results in our lives.

What does it mean to be strengthened with "His might"? Luke gives us the answer to that question: "And Jesus, *full of the Holy Spirit*, returned from the Jordan and was led about by the Spirit in the wilderness" (Luke 4:1).

Perhaps you're thinking, "Of course Jesus was full of the Holy Spirit, but how does that affect me?"

The writer of Hebrews tells us that Jesus was the author and the perfecter of our faith. That means that Jesus thought up the whole plan of the Holy Spirit living through man, but He didn't just sit up in heaven and say, "Now you guys, go live it." He came down into the arena and lived by faith Himself and showed that the whole plan worked beautifully.

He Laid Aside the Use of His Deity

In the second chapter of Philippians we're told that when Jesus came into this world, He chose to temporarily leave the *use* of His divine powers behind and live here on this planet just as any other man would have to do. Had He chosen to do otherwise, He would not have been a true man and would not have qualified as a substitute to bear the penalty for our sins in our place.

Also, if He had met and handled life's problems using part human and part divine strength, He wouldn't have set any kind of example we could follow. We would have been licked before we got started because we aren't part divine.

The great truth that Jesus wants us to know is that He chose to live His life as He expects us to live, in a moment-by-moment reliance upon the Father who worked through Him by the Holy Spirit. That fantastic life that the world knew as the life of Jesus was actually lived not *by* Jesus, but *in* Him by the Holy Spirit.

I remember one day when a friend asked me who I thought was the only person who had ever lived the Christian life just the way God wanted it lived. After thinking for a minute I replied, "Well, Jesus, of course."

I was shocked when he said, "No, Jesus didn't live the Christian life; it was lived in Him by the Holy Spirit."

After I thought about that for awhile, it really made sense and shed some light on a few Bible verses—one in particular, John 14:12, where Jesus said, "... the works that I do shall he do also; and greater works than these shall he do; because I go to the Father."

While Jesus was here on earth, the specific residence of the Holy Spirit was in Him. When He went to the Father, He sent the Holy Spirit back to fill His followers, just as He had been filled. The life which had been produced in Jesus by the Holy Spirit was produced in His followers as they relied upon the Spirit as Jesus had.

This makes the Christian life an exciting possibility. If I thought I had to duplicate a life like Jesus lived with my own strength or even with some of the Holy Spirit's strength mixed in, I would be discouraged before I started. But it's great to know that is not God's plan for doing His work on earth.

Jesus' Temptation

Jesus gave us a tremendous pattern for walking in the Spirit. In Luke 4:23, we read that the Holy Spirit *led* Jesus out into the desert to be tempted by the Devil.

"And He ate nothing during those days; and when they had ended, He became hungry. And the Devil said to Him, 'If You are the Son of God, tell this stone to become bread.'"

Here you see one of Satan's clever tactics: how he capitalizes on situations in our lives trying to get us to sin. Satan is a master strategist; he knows our pattern of weakness. Jesus had not eaten for forty days, and He was hungry. The Devil said sarcastically, "If you are the Son of God, tell this stone to become bread."

Don't you think Satan knew this was the Son of God? Of course he did. Satan isn't stupid. He wouldn't have been wasting all that time on Jesus if he hadn't believed that He was the Son of God.

In reality he was saying, "Now look, Jesus, *since* You're the all-powerful Son of God, why don't You fix Yourself a little lunch here; make these stones into bread."

As a matter of fact, this temptation is a great proof of the deity of Christ. If we hadn't eaten for forty days and forty nights and the Devil came to us and said, "Since you're a child of God, why don't you make these stones become bread?" it wouldn't be a temptation to us—because we couldn't do it!

Jesus could have snapped His fingers and there would have been a bagel on every bush!

Satan's Real Purpose

Do you see Satan's sinister plan? Jesus was being tempted to stop living in total dependence upon the Holy Spirit to provide His needs, as any man would have to do, and to use His own deity to meet those needs. Satan knew that Jesus was both God and man and that He had chosen never to use His own divine power while here on earth. Satan would have done anything to get Jesus to step outside the Father's will and use His own divinity to meet His needs.

Jesus flatly rejected Satan's offer and allowed the Father to sustain Him through the Holy Spirit. One reason He did this was so that you and I might have a pattern to follow and might know what a great and powerful God we have available to meet our every need.

He took all the guff this world and Satan had to offer, and He did it all as a man, depending upon the inner strengthening and power of the same Holy Spirit who lives in us.

Christ's Walk, Our Example

Christ's whole life was lived in dependence upon the Father who worked in Him by the Spirit. He related every circumstance He faced to the Father's ability to handle it through His humanity. He could have handled any one of them in His own divine strength, but for the sake of the example He wanted to leave us, He didn't.

John said of Jesus, "The one who says he abides in Him ought himself to walk in the same manner as He (Jesus) walked" (1 John 2:6).

Jesus Christ walked with His focus on the Father, and the Father worked through Him by the indwelling Holy Spirit.

We are to walk with our focus on Jesus, and He will work through us by the same Holy Spirit who indwells us.

Be Filled With the Spirit

This pattern of living is called "the filling of the Spirit" in Ephesians 5:18, where it says, "And do not get drunk with wine, for that is dissipation, but be filled with the Spirit."

The command to every Christian, "be filled with the Spirit," is in a verb tense in the original Greek which means to be *continually* filled with the Spirit. It is to be a moment-by-moment experience in the life of the believer.

Many people have the idea that being filled with the Spirit is like screwing the lid off one's head and pouring Holy Spirit in until one is full.

This is not what it means. You don't get more of Him; He gets more of you.

What exactly does it mean, then, to be filled with the Spirit?

Paul uses a good illustration in Ephesians 5:18 when he compares the filling of the Spirit with the experience of being drunk. When you are drunk, it means that another force has taken over your mind and dominates your personality. You have voluntarily yielded control of your life to the stimulant alcohol.

When Paul commands all Christians to be filled with the Spirit, he means to voluntarily yield control of yourself to another person, the Holy Spirit. Let Him empower your personality.

How Can We Do This?

We must first know that the Holy Spirit has taken up permanent residence in us the moment we received Christ. Romans 8:9 says that not to have the Holy Spirit in you is tantamount to not being a Christian. The Holy Spirit who indwells us is a person who is co-equal and co-eternal with the Father and the Son.

Secondly, we should know that sin grieves the Holy Spirit but doesn't cause Him to leave us (Ephesians 4:30). Jesus promised, "I will never desert you, nor will I ever forsake you" (Hebrews 13:5).

The third thing we should know is that it is one thing for the Holy Spirit to dwell in us, but quite another thing for Him to fill or control us.

God wants us to be continually *filled* with the Spirit. The only way we can have this happen is to decide who runs the show in our lives. We need to make a once-and-for-all decision to give the title deed of our lives to God. This does not mean that we are always going to do what God wants us to do. It does mean that we have come to a point in life where we have soberly assessed what God has done for us in Christ. We reason that if He has given us eternal life, put us into His forever family, given us an inheritance with His Son, and made us kings and priests forever, then we can say with confidence, "I can trust a God like that. If I give my life totally into His keeping, He will know how to handle it and do the best with it that can be done."

Present Your Body to Him

When we get to that point—and for some of us it's after we've hit bottom spiritually—then we can really appreciate the Apostle Paul's words: "I urge you therefore, brethren, by the mercies of God, to present your bodies

a living and holy sacrifice, acceptable to God, which is your spiritual service of worship" (Romans 12:1).

When Paul uses the word "present" in this verse, it is in the aorist tense
in the original language, and it means to do it once and for all time. It's
something which doesn't need to be done over and over again.

Maybe you've come to a place in your Christian life when you think, "I've
had it. So much is stacked against me; I can't run my life the way it ought
to go. I'm worn out trying. I give up."

Believe me, that's a great place to get as a Christian. When you hit bottom spiritually, there's no place to go but up. God lets us exhaust every
trick we have for living a victorious life. When we're finally hanging on
the ropes, He steps in and says, "Will you throw in the towel now and let
Me take over?"

I remember when I made the decision to do this myself. I'd been a believer for several years and had enthusiastically worked for God. What had
been easy at first began to get to be work after awhile. I found myself on a
spiritual roller coaster, and the Christian life was getting to be a drag.

In an effort to get myself back in shape, I began following various people's
advice on how to be a victorious Christian. I tried giving up all my bad
habits and found that some of them had a tight grip on me. One friend urged
me to begin memorizing Bible verses. I did, but that didn't produce the con-
sistency for which I was looking.

I went through one gimmick after another, most of them good things in
themselves such as witnessing, Bible study, prayer, and confession, but none
of these helped for long.

Finally one day as I was driving around in my car, desperately asking
God for the solution to my problem, He seemed to say, "Stop struggling,
child. Just give Me your life right now, and you won't have the headache
of running yourself from this point on."

I don't really know what happened, except that I stopped struggling and
gave myself to Him unreservedly. The peace of God flooded my soul. I felt
a tremendous burden lift from me and John 7:38-39 became a living reality.
"'. . . From his innermost being shall flow rivers of living water.' Now this
He said about the Spirit. . . ."

Starting that day, I began to experience what it meant to walk in the Spirit.
I saw God remake me emotionally and psychologically. He took some
impossible situations in my life and worked them out fantastically to His
glory and my good.

I Know Who Holds the Future

Since that time I've had this attitude: I don't know what the future holds, but I know who holds the future.

This is the attitude that God wants of us if we are going to have a life continually filled with the Spirit. However, let me warn you: Be sure that you mean it when you give your life to God this way, because He will be serious about taking it. You will be saying, "Lord, I want Your will, even though I don't know now what it will be."

As you get to know God in this intimate way, you'll discover you haven't made a risky deal. His will for your life will go far beyond your wildest dreams. All He's been waiting for is a blank check from you so He could begin to fill in His marvelous plan and purpose.

There have been times when I've said, "Okay, Lord, things have been going all right, but I'd like to try running my life for awhile." I was in the process of running it into the ground when suddenly I was reined up short and the Lord said, "You're not going that way, pal."

There have been times when I have had tears in my eyes from the Lord pulling me away from the direction I was going, but I have never regretted the fact that I gave Him the right to hold those reins.

God wants you to decide who is master of your life. When you accept Jesus Christ, you receive eternal life and become a member of God's family. After that He urges you to present Him the title deed to your life, although He will not force you. But it does make sense to do it. After all, who really would know better how to run you than the One who put you together, atom by atom, molecule by molecule?

"Do Not Be Conformed to This World" (Romans 12:2)

What did Paul mean by "this world"? He meant the world system of thinking and doing which excludes God. I like the way J. B. Phillips puts it in his modern translation of the New Testament: "Don't let the world around you squeeze you into its own mold, but let God remold your minds from within . . ." (Romans 12:2).

The only way we can escape conformity to the world's mold is to come to that place where we present ourselves to God and say, "Here is my life. You run it, God. Make me over from the inside by giving me a new mind, a new outlook on You, on myself, and on the world."

If we by faith depend upon Him to do this and simply live our lives daily expecting Him to control and fill us with the Holy Spirit, He will do it.

You don't have to have any ecstatic emotional experience to be filled with the Spirit. You don't get zapped by some mysterious force which indicates that you've arrived in the Christian life. Sorry, it just doesn't work that way.

God has a plan that's even better. He has promised to meet the circumstances of life which we encounter moment by moment and handle them for us if we let Him. He can overcome fear, timidity, hostility, anxiety, pride, lust, jealousy, and any other emotions we can't handle. All He wants us to do is back away from the problem and let Him at it.

And He doesn't want *any* help from us. Either He does it all for us and through us, or He lets us tackle it alone. Don't patronize God by asking for His help. *He doesn't help those who help themselves. On the contrary, He helps those who admit they are helpless.* That really goes against the grain of the world's thinking, but that is God's plan of action.

I remember the first time I ever tried to give a speech in public. It was in a college speech course, and as I stood there in front of the class I became more and more flustered. Finally I said, "Oh phooey! I quit," and turned around and walked out. That was the end of my speech-making days.

A few years later I became a Christian. One Sunday at church I was asked to teach an adult Sunday school class. I nearly fainted when they asked me, but I had been learning the principle of walking in the Spirit, so I decided to see if it would work in this needy area of my life. I stood up in front of the class that morning and literally let the Holy Spirit pour His message through my yielded vocal cords. It went quite well, too, but I can't take any credit for it. It was God's show all the way.

Walking in the Spirit

Sometimes it gets a bit confusing as to just how we're to live the Christian life. First you read that you're to be *filled* with the Spirit and that will give you the power you need. Then someone comes along and speaks of *walking* in the Spirit and tells you that will keep you from sinning. Someone else has found that walking by *faith* is the secret of victorious Christian living. Currently, many are claiming that we must be *baptized* with the Spirit to overcome the temptations of life.

Just what is the formula anyway? Is there some point in our Christian lives where we must have a special encounter with the Holy Spirit which will alter the course of our lives and the way we live?

Let me share with you what I feel the Word teaches about this. Paul's exhortations to the believers to be *filled with the Spirit* (Ephesians 5:18), to *walk in the Spirit* (Galatians 5:16), and to *walk by faith* (2 Corinthians 5:7; Hebrews 11) all refer to the same principle of the believer coming to the conclusion that he can't live *for* God. He must trust the Holy Spirit to live the Christian life in and through him.

For many Christians the realization that the Holy Spirit wants to and is able to live the Christian life through them is such welcome news that when they begin to experience victory instead of defeat, they are literally overwhelmed.

For many, this entering into the Spirit-filled life is a crisis experience. If for years you've been wallowing in defeat in your Christian life and suddenly the indwelling Christ becomes magnificently alive to you, you may feel like you've been zapped!

God doesn't want to give us a one-shot exposure to His power, however. He wants to give us a new pattern of living where He fills us moment by moment with new life and spiritual energy. Any encounter with the Holy Spirit which doesn't produce a whole new life isn't the walk in the Spirit or filling of the Spirit that the New Testament teaches.

Baptism of the Spirit

The baptism of the Spirit is mentioned many times in the New Testament, but it is only defined in one place, 1 Corinthians 12:13: "For by one Spirit we were all baptized into one body, whether Jews or Greeks, whether slaves or free, and we were all made to drink of one Spirit."

This verse simply tells us that the baptism of the Spirit is that particular ministry of the Holy Spirit which joins us into a living union with Christ and His body, the Church. This happens to each person the moment he places faith in Jesus Christ as Savior.

The baptism of the Spirit is *not* the ministry of the Holy Spirit which is designed to give the believer power in his daily life. That is the *filling* ministry of the Spirit. *Walking* in the Spirit, being *filled* with the Spirit, and walking by *faith* are synonymous terms.

Nowhere in the New Testament epistles are we commanded to be baptized with the Spirit. If that were the means of power in the Christian life, Paul's teachings would be full of it.

The baptism of the Spirit is a valid biblical teaching, but it must be carefully related to all the New Testament scriptures. (For a more complete treatment of this subject, see the appendix to this chapter.)

Satan's Domain

Naturally Satan is livid with rage when a believer finds out about the Spirit-filled life and begins to walk in the Spirit. A Christian who begins to live in this new realm will find himself exposed to such open hostility from Satan that sometimes it's overwhelming. Areas of our old sinful life that have laid dormant for years begin to give us trouble.

Why? Because the Holy Spirit is not the only one who dwells in the realm of the spirit. Satan lives there too, and when we begin to traverse his home base, we're in enemy territory.

To go into this battlefield without being filled with the Spirit and clothed with His armor is utter folly. Satan will make mincemeat out of us. Don't forget, he's had thousands of years of practice fouling up God's children. We're no match for him.

But praise God, Jesus is! As we walk in the Spirit, we will not fulfill the lusts of the flesh. That's what Paul promised in Galatians 5:16.

As he states in another passage, ". . . we are more than conquerors *and* gain a surpassing victory through Him Who loved us" (Romans 8:37, *Amplified Bible*).

If the filling of the Spirit sounds like just what you've been needing in your Christian life, why not make a decision right now to begin to let the Holy Spirit control your life? He is more than willing, and He's certainly able to answer your faith, however small, and begin to duplicate Jesus' life in and through you.

Short-Circuiting God's Power

What happens to us if we don't walk by faith? Paul says, "Whatever is not from faith is sin" (Romans 14:23).

If we don't walk in the Spirit, then we are walking according to the flesh, and that is sin (Romans 8:4-5). That means that we are seeking to handle our lives and problems with our own human wisdom. We are living in the realm of the five senses and concluding that what we feel, see, and think is what is really true, instead of relating the problem to God's wisdom and ability to handle it.

If we walk in the energy of the flesh, we are prime candidates to end up on a class-A guilt trip or get caught in the sin syndrome. We cannot knowingly be walking in the flesh and walking in dependence upon the Holy Spirit at the same time.

When we stop trusting the Holy Spirit to deliver us from temptations and seek to handle them ourselves, we are guaranteeing a spiritual nose dive. The inevitable result of the activity of the flesh is sin, and sin will short-circuit the power of God in the life of a believer.

It isn't that God stops loving us and accepting us. It's simply that we've stopped believing in that love and acceptance, and our focus is off the problem-solver and onto the problem—us!

The moment a child of God recognizes the futility of living this way and acknowledges to God that he's walking in the flesh, he is restored into God's fellowship in his own mind. God never stopped "fellowshiping" with him, but he stopped fellowshiping with God.

Don't let the world, the flesh, or the Devil spook you. We are the victors in all three of these areas as we walk in the Spirit and wear the full armor of God.

Let's Take a Look at the Armor

"Put on the full armor of God, that you may be able to stand firm against the schemes of the devil" (Ephesians 6:11).

The Devil exploits our personality quirks, the lusts of the flesh, and our natural physical drives to conspire against us.

There are times when I have a message to prepare or studying to do. I gather my materials and settle down in my study. Then they hit me—hunger pains! Now I know I shouldn't be hungry—I probably had breakfast less than an hour before—but a built-in excuse has been offered me to get away from the Word of God.

I wish I always said, "Satan, be gone," but I don't. I begin prowling around, getting something to eat, and before I know it I've killed an hour—an hour of valuable time. I didn't really need that food, but Satan can use any natural drives we have if they are not being controlled by the Holy Spirit.

Another drive which Satan uses is our natural need for sex. Once you are married, that need has the potential of being met, but even in marriage it can get out of control. Satan can use that normal drive to break up a marriage or produce such hostility that there's no communication at all. He can get a man too intense in his desire at the expense of not meeting his wife's emotional needs.

Satan uses another natural drive in his campaign on young people: the need for a mate. This is an area where the girls are especially vulnerable. If they think they need a mate, and if they don't trust the Lord with this area of their lives, Satan can come in and get them so anxious about finding the right man that he has them in a tailspin.

I have seen so many great Christians get fouled up because they don't trust the Lord to provide them with a mate. Satan gets a grip on them, and in some cases they become involved sexually because they feel this is the only way they can hold their boyfriend or girlfriend. Others don't trust the Lord to provide them with a mate, and they marry the wrong person. Perhaps they marry a non-Christian or a Christian who is really out of it spiritually.

Satan uses these natural needs when they are not under the Spirit's control. This is why we need the armor of God.

"For our struggle is not against flesh and blood. . . ."

What is really behind these drives when they get out of control? Our own flesh or sin nature starts rumbling in us for satisfaction, and then along come the "rulers . . . the powers . . . the world-forces of this darkness . . . the spiritual forces of wickedness in the heavenly places" who energize our flesh with unnatural cravings (Ephesians 6:12).

Satan is on constant guard, watching every believer and waiting for his armor to slip, even slightly, so he can fling in his fiery darts.

"Therefore take up the full armor of God, that you may be able to resist in the evil day, and having done everything, to stand firm" (Ephesians 6:13).

The Belt

When the Apostle Paul wrote this letter to the Ephesians, he had been closely guarded by a Roman soldier for several months. He must have had a good opportunity to observe pieces of the soldier's armor at close range.

"Stand firm therefore, having girded your loins with truth, and having put on the breastplate of righteousness" (Ephesians 6:14).

The Roman army had the finest armor of the ancient world, and Paul used it as an illustration of the armor God has for the Christian to use against Satan.

In the Roman's armor the girdle was the belt, six to eight inches wide, which went around his waist. It was one of his most important pieces of equipment because everything else was fastened to his belt. If the belt wasn't in place, then the armor wouldn't be secure.

Paul says that the Christian's foundation piece of armor is *the truth*: a growing knowledge and understanding of the Scriptures and how they apply to life. God wants us to have defensive armor against the wiles of Satan. A soldier does not put on his armor after going *into* battle, but in preparation *for* battle. The belt of truth must be secure or everything else will fall off!

Breastplate

In the Roman armor there was a breastplate which was made of bronze backed with tough pieces of hide. This protected one of the most vital areas of the body, the heart.

The breastplate of our armor which protects our heart from attacks of Satan is *righteousness*. This refers to the righteousness of Christ. In his second letter to the Corinthians Paul describes what Christ has done for us: "He made Him who knew no sin to be sin on our behalf, that we might become the righteousness of God in Him" (2 Corinthians 5:21).

This is not talking about *our* righteousness; when we believe in Jesus Christ, *His* righteousness is given to us. We are not only forgiven for all our sins, but we are clothed with the very righteousness of Christ. From that point on, as far as our relationship with God is concerned, He sees us as righteous as Christ.

What Satan likes to do is to come in when we have failed God and say, "Aha, you are not going to be acceptable to God now. Look what you did!" At that time, if we have on the breastplate of righteousness, we can say, "Phase out, Satan. I don't appear to God in my own righteousness, and I never did. It's Christ's righteousness which has always made me acceptable, and it hasn't changed."

Boots

"And having shod your feet with the preparation of the gospel of peace" (Ephesians 6:15).

Anyone who has ever fought in any kind of hand-to-hand combat knows that sure footing is most important. I used to box, and I remember how we put resin on the bottom of our shoes. More than once I was floored because I lost my footing just at the time I was throwing a punch. In fighting with a sword as they did at the time of the Roman legions, losing your footing could mean death. So the G.I. issue in footgear at that time was the hobnail sandal. When they were fighting in face-to-face combat, their feet were planted solid; their footing was sure.

In the Christian life we need solid footing, too, if we are going to walk and resist Satan. That solid footing is provided by the *gospel of peace*. This is not the same as the Gospel of salvation. "Gospel" means "good news," and it is certainly great news that we have forgiveness through believing in Jesus Christ, but there is some more good news for us. There is a place of rest and peace of mind for every Christian; it is God's hiding place for every believer in Jesus Christ. Hebrews 4 tells us about entering God's rest. It is a rest for here and now, not the "sweet by and by." That is good news!

God has peace of mind and a resting place available to every believer in Jesus Christ. If we do not learn how to depend upon the *promises* of God for peace, then we will not have the sure footing to be able to stand against the wiles of Satan. He will knock us off balance and have us on the ground before we know it.

Satan uses worry, anxiety, and tension to really keep us off balance. The gospel of peace is concerned with meeting worry with the promises of God.

Are you afraid? Then claim this promise: "Do not fear, for I am with you; Do not anxiously look about you, for I am your God. I will strengthen you, surely I will help you, surely, I will uphold you with My righteous right hand" (Isaiah 41:10).

Are you worried about your needs? Bills stacking up? Pressures of business closing in? Children or parents presenting problems which seem impossible to handle? Look at these promises and claim them: "Be anxious for nothing, but in everything by prayer and supplication with thanksgiving let your requests be made known to God. And the peace of God, which surpasses all comprehension, shall guard your hearts and your minds in Christ Jesus" (Philippians 4:6-7).

These promises are real. One of the few things God tells us to fear is that we will fail to claim His promises (Hebrews 4:1).

When we get up in the morning, we should check out our armor. Do we have on the belt of truth? Do we have on the breastplate of righteousness? Are we beginning to slip into a performance-based relationship with God? Are we collecting merit badges for our good deeds, church work, and charitable contributions? If Satan gets us on that trip, we are in for a lethal blow.

Make sure you are resting on the promises of God.

Shield

"In addition to all, taking up the shield of faith with which you will be able to extinguish all the flaming missiles of the evil one" (Ephesians 6:16).

A Roman soldier's shield was about two feet wide by four feet long. He used it to ward off the blows of the enemy and also to hide behind when the enemy archers would let go a volley of arrows. The Romans could kneel down on the ground and erect a wall of shields around them to block out the flaming missiles.

Satan is always firing his hot darts at us; he is always trying to get inside of us with guilt or with some accusation. If you have the shield of *faith* protecting you, that simple, implicit faith in the fact that Christ is more than able to meet your needs, you have adequate protection right there.

Helmet

"And take the helmet of salvation . . ." (Ephesians 6:17).

The helmet, of course, protected the head, another area which needed to be guarded from a fatal blow. This was a vital piece in the Roman armor, just as it is in ours.

Satan loves to pervert the Word of God. This is what he did with Jesus. When Jesus was tempted in the wilderness, He repeated to Satan, "It is written" and "It is said." In the last temptation that Satan fired at Jesus, he quoted the Word to Jesus. Satan knows the Bible by heart; the Word is no stranger to him. If he finds a Christian who is standing on the Word, he will try to distort it. That is when we need the helmet of *salvation.*

I have met too many people who are virtually on the brink of mental illness because they think they have lost their salvation—that eternal life is no longer theirs. They believe they have committed some terrible sin, and the enemy comes in and says, "You have committed the unpardonable sin." Or, "You've committed some sin that God won't forgive you for this time." Back on the old guilt trip!

The helmet of salvation is knowing that your salvation is absolutely secure and complete. Once you believe in Jesus Christ you are forgiven for your sins— past, present, and future. Once you have believed in Him you can never be taken out of His family. "And I give eternal life to them; and they shall never perish, and no one shall snatch them out of My hand. My Father, who has given them to Me, is greater than all; and no one is able to snatch them out of the Father's hand. I and the Father are one (essence)" (John 10:28-30).

However, Satan will take some obscure verse and try to undo all of the clear teaching in the rest of the Bible and have you thinking you have lost your salvation. He will take some of these verses and twist them to undo the teaching of the entire Book of Romans which clearly declares that salvation is a once-and-for-all matter through faith alone.

Salvation does not depend upon performance; it never has and never will. It depends upon what Christ did for us. If you do not have that helmet or assurance of salvation, you cannot have a vitally strong faith.

Sword

"And the sword of the Spirit, which is the word of God" (Ephesians 6:17).

The sword is an offensive weapon; the Roman sword was the atomic bomb of ancient warfare. It had a blade about twenty-four inches long which was sharp on both edges and pointed on the end.

The design of this sword was important. A trained legionnaire could thrust and cut from any position so that he was never caught off balance. Opposing soldiers with larger swords had to get into a certain position to swing. The Roman soldier would duck, catch his opponent off balance, and finish him off before he could crawl back for another swing.

The Word of God is like that. It is "living and active, and sharper than any two-edged sword . . ." (Hebrews 4:12).

When we are trusting the Holy Spirit to teach us the Bible and help us use it against Satan's temptations, we are never out of position or knocked off balance by the attacks of Satan.

When Satan tempted Jesus (Luke 4), Jesus quoted verses of Scripture to him that expressed God's viewpoint regarding each temptation. There is no greater example from whom we can learn than Jesus, is there? This is why whenever I sense I am being attacked by Satan I begin to quote *out loud* verses of Scripture addressed to him.

I'll never forget the thrill of the first time I tried this. I had been plagued with a certain temptation for hours. Nothing made it subside. I had claimed promises, depended on the Holy Spirit, prayed and asked the Lord to take it away—nothing worked.

Then I recalled what Jesus had done in His hour of trial, so I found a verse of Scripture which directly expressed God's viewpoint about the temptation. Then, feeling a little silly, I said, "Satan, leave me alone, for it is written . . ." and I quoted the verse out loud. Pow! The temptation was gone—and so was Satan.

I believe this is how we are to "resist the Devil." When we do, God's promise is, "he (Satan) will flee from you" (James 4:7).

The believer needs a combat knowledge of the Word of God.

Prayer

"With all prayer and petition pray at all times in the Spirit, and with this in view, be on the alert with all perseverance and petition for all the saints" (Ephesians 6:18).

The sword of the Spirit and prayer are the Christian's offensive weapons. Once we have Satan on the run, we can keep him from a counterattack by using these weapons. But remember, God answers prayer because we believe Him, not because we bombard Him with profound and lengthy phrases.

Check List

In view of the deluge of Satan's attacks today, we need to check out our armor, keeping it polished and oiled at all times, ready for active duty. If our sword is getting rusty because we haven't been studying the Word, we'd better sharpen it. If our breastplate is slipping out of place because we are getting on the performance-kick, we'd better adjust it. If our helmet is off because we are not sure about our salvation, then we'd better get into the Word of God or go to someone who knows the Word and make sure it is in place.

We cannot afford to be tin soldiers: we do not dare play games with Satan. He is capturing men right and left, using all his arsenal of weapons to do it.

"For our struggle is not against flesh and blood, but against the rulers, against the powers, against the world-forces of this darkness, against the spiritual forces of wickedness in the heavenly places" (Ephesians 6:12).

Real spiritual beings are beginning to come out in the open to such an extent that people are willing to worship Satan, and he is still practicing his subtle ways on the people who do not believe he exists—in fact, he is having a field day with them!

Whistle a happy tune, if you wish, but be sure your armor is in place while you are whistling.

To the armory, troops!

14 ○ On a Note
of Triumph

DID YOU BEGIN this book with a feeling of apprehension? Was the subject matter intriguing but frightening?

The magnitude of forces arrayed against us may overwhelm some; the reality and power of Satan and his hordes, the steady pull of the flesh, and the subtle attractiveness of the world system could easily get our focus off Christ's super provisions for victory.

Nothing would delight Satan more!

Satan's strategy has always been to blind men's minds to the truth of God's forgiveness in Christ. When that doesn't succeed and a person is rescued from the kingdom of darkness and born into the kingdom of light, then Satan commands all of his efforts to keep the believer unaware of the miraculous provisions God has made for his daily victory.

Satan will use every clever and insidious device of the world and the flesh to focus attention on ourselves and our problems instead of on Christ.

Satan will magnify our natural human weaknesses in our own minds, causing us to feel inferior with God and with man. He will stir up our pride to make us think that we're not getting the recognition from other believers that we feel we deserve. He will let jealousy bring division between brothers in Christ. He loves to get Christians so off-balance on doctrinal issues that we forget to love and accept those real brothers who differ with us.

If we spend much time dwelling on our weaknesses and sins, it won't be long before we become discouraged and defeated.

Spiritual Myopia

God knew that this "spiritual myopia" would be our biggest problem. I think that's why Jesus went to all the trouble to give us a classic example of the folly of focusing on ourselves and our circumstances rather than on Him.

In Matthew 14:22-33 we read how Jesus deliberately sent his disciples out in their boats on the Sea of Galilee, even though He knew that a storm was coming. He knew that they had more confidence in their seamanship than they did in anything else because of their long years of being fishermen.

When the storm hit, it was more violent than anything they had experienced, and the disciples were terrified. For the first time in their lives they could not rely on their own abilities to handle a problem.

God will test His children in areas where they are most confident of their human ability in order to show them their complete need to depend upon Him.

When the disciples began to despair, Jesus came to them walking upon the water. Peter said boldly, "Lord, if it is really You, command me to come to You on the water." He had enough faith to believe that if Jesus commanded him to come to Him on the water, He would also enable him, somehow, to do it.

At this point Peter had no confidence in his own ability to walk on water, but he did have confidence in Jesus. He took what little faith he had and put it on the right object.

This is an important principle to remember. Christ will *empower* us to do whatever He *commands* us to do. "For it is God who is at work in you, both to will and to work for His good pleasure" (Philippians 2:13).

Peter gingerly stepped out of the boat onto the stormy sea. He was actually walking on the water and moving toward Jesus with his trusting eye fixed on Him and His ability to miraculously support him.

Everything was going fine until we read, ". . . but *seeing* the wind, he became afraid, and beginning to sink he cried out, saying, 'Lord, save me!'"

Peter's Lesson Learned

What happened? Peter was doing great until he did what you and I do frequently. He got his eyes onto the problem, in his case the stormy seas, and off of the Problem-Solver, Jesus. When he did, down he went.

Praise the Lord for His faithfulness in spite of our lack of it. He caught Peter just before he went under; just in time for him to have learned his lesson, but not be overwhelmed by it.

Peter isn't the only one this lesson was designed for. As you and I walk through our particular storms, we must keep our eye of faith focused on Jesus and His ability to handle us in the midst of the storm.

What is your "storm" right now? Are you out of a job and getting desperate financially? As the bills pile up, do your spirits go down? You're no fool. You know you've got to have food and a roof. And there's Satan, always around to take advantage of the situation, saying, "Look at the condition things are in. Can't you see what a failure you are in providing for your family? Where do you think the money is coming from to get you out of this mess?" On and on he accuses, with the purpose of taking your eyes off your loving, powerful, all-providing Heavenly Father and onto yourself and your problems.

Remember what happened to Peter when he did that? The same thing will happen to us unless we sink our teeth into His promises to meet our needs.

"And my God shall supply all your needs according to His riches in glory in Christ Jesus" (Philippians 4:19).

"Behold, I am the Lord, the God of all flesh; is anything too difficult for Me?" (Jeremiah 32:27).

If we take our eye of trust off Christ and put our focus onto the problems, even with the good intention of trying to deal with them ourselves, we will begin to sink into despair and defeat.

Faith, the Key

You may be saying to yourself, "That sounds great, Hal—now all I need is enough faith to believe it would work for me."

You're right! Faith is really the key to appropriating everything the Lord has already provided for us. For this reason, Satan will try to confuse us about what faith is and how it works.

When we begin to learn about all our spiritual assets and armor with which to live for God, Satan will come in and whisper what you were just thinking: "All of God's provisions are wonderful! Wouldn't it be great if I just had enough faith to use them!"

How Much Is Enough?

Once Satan gets us thinking about faith in a quantitative way, we're sunk. To say, "I wish I had more faith" is to reflect a basic misconception of what faith is.

Faith is responsibility: *my response to God's ability*. It's just that simple!

In biblical faith, it's the *object* of faith that gives it its power. Jesus said that if we have as little as a mustard seed of faith, if it's placed in Him, we can move mountains. There is *no* power in faith. The power is in Jesus.

Faith is similar to eyesight. There must be an object in order for sight to occur. Faith must have an object in order for power to occur, and that object is Christ and what He provided for us at the Cross.

It's so sad to hear Christians begging God for more faith. Every believer already has 20/20 faith. To be sure, some see God more clearly than others, but that is because some have moved closer to Him, the object of their faith.

If you're standing a hundred miles away from a mountain, it will be obscure and indistinct to you. You may know a lot of facts about that mountain, but it will never grow in size until you move closer to it.

We just can't respond to God's great ability to meet our needs until we get to know Him in a closer way and find out about all the provisions He's made for His children to live in this world today.

The Leap of Faith

Suppose you are on the fifth floor of a burning building. There is no way to escape, and you are trapped out on a ledge. You can't see the ground because of the smoke, but suddenly you hear a voice cry out, "Jump, we have a net ready to catch you!"

Fear grips your heart. You find yourself thinking of all the sadistic people in the world; it might be some splatter-happy lunatic down below hollering at you. You don't have any confidence in that person because you don't know anything about him.

Suddenly you hear another voice. This one is familiar to you. It calls, "Son, it's Dad. Jump, there's a net down here." On the strength of your confidence in your dad and your knowledge of his love for you, you commit yourself to him and jump. And what do you find as you fall through the darkness? "Underneath are the everlasting arms" (Deuteronomy 33:27).

Keep Your Eyes on Christ

Have you ever had anyone tell you that all you need to do is just look to Jesus when you have a problem and that will solve it? I remember the first time someone told me that. I was having a problem in my life, so I tried to conjure up a mental image of Jesus in my mind, picturing my favorite painting of Him. I just kept thinking about this picture. You know, that didn't seem to help me at all with my problem.

I decided right then that there must be something else I was supposed to focus on about Jesus other than His physical image. I'm glad that situation happened to me because it forced me to sit down and think through just what it is that I'm supposed to look at when I focus on Jesus.

First, I must see that God loves me unconditionally. Second, I must believe that God's forgiveness of my sins covers *all* of them, past, present, and future, and He is not holding any of them against me. Third, I must realize that God has a plan for my life and He will take everything that happens to me, whether seemingly good or evil, and work it all together for my good (Romans 8:28). And last, I must see that God is utterly faithful and able to keep every promise He has made to me in the Bible.

Triumph in Trials

When you know and count upon these facts, then you can properly relate to the trials that God permits to come into your life. You can see that they are all planned as a means of blessing, not cursing, in your life. When a trial hits, you can say, "I know that God loves me so much that He could not allow one thing to touch my life that is not consistent with that great love."

Because you have come to know that God judged Christ for all your sins, you know that this testing is not to get even with you for some secret sin or to punish you for any reason. God has already punished Christ for all your sins.

Whenever a trial or a real tragedy should enter your life, if you know that God has an overall plan and He is fitting this situation into a pattern of good for you, then you can praise Him for the trial. You may not see one ounce of good in the difficulty itself, and there may be none, but God has unalterably committed Himself to work it into the greatest possible blessing in your life. For it not to have happened to you would have cheated you of a rare privilege of God's special blessing.

Is Your God Too Small?

As we grow in our understanding of all these marvelous provisions God has made for our needs, we begin to see God as being bigger than our problems. If the difficulties in our lives still seem too much for God to handle, then our God is too small for us.

Once we see that the issue is not how much faith we have, but rather how faithful, trustworthy, and powerful Jesus is, then we are ready for the major leagues in the Christian life. When we take whatever faith we have at the moment, whether little or great, and put it in the Lord Jesus Christ, it releases His power to work through us and in our behalf.

If God's provisions for me were always just a little bit beyond the grasp of my faith, what good would all these spiritual assets be to me? How could I ever grow? It would be like dangling a carrot in front of a donkey to make him move. It might result in some semblance of progress, but at the expense of utter frustration.

Far from God's rich blessings always being just beyond our faith, the Scripture says, "Blessed be the God and Father of our Lord Jesus Christ, who *has blessed us* with every spiritual blessing in the heavenly places in Christ . . ." (Ephesians 1:3). Victory over the flesh, the world, and the Devil is ours—*now*.

Power Versus Authority

Much has been said in this book about the *power* that works within the believer through the Holy Spirit. But until now, nothing has really been set forth about the *authority* that is available to us. In fact, little seems to be said anywhere in the Christian world about this critical truth. Yet when it comes to dealing with attacks from demons and Satan, no other spiritual asset is more important to understand and appropriate.

You may be saying, "What's the difference between power and authority in the Christian life?"

There is a great deal of difference. In the Greek of the New Testament two words are consistently used for the two concepts. The word "dunamis" is used to describe the power of the Holy Spirit which operates within the Christian. The word "exousia" is used to describe authority. Unfortunately the translators are not always consistent in translating "exousia" into the English word, authority.

"Exousia," or authority, means delegated power.

Dr. F. Huegel, a great Christian theologian and friend, told me a story that illustrates the difference in these two concepts. We were sitting near the great boulevard of Mexico City, the Avenue Reforma, and discussing the believer's authority over the demonic world when he related this story.

He told of a group of young Mexican boy scouts who were trying to cross the Avenue Reforma during the wild rush-hour traffic. They made it halfway across the broad street and took refuge on the esplanade in the street's center. At the corner of the esplanade there was a special pedestal where the traffic officer stood to direct traffic. The boys watched as the traffic officer would raise his right arm and all the powerful speeding automobiles would screech to a halt.

In Mexico City that pedestal is a place of authority, and all the motorists know it.

About this time a slight accident occurred nearby and the officer left his place to investigate. While the officer was arguing with the motorists, one of the boy scouts stepped up on the pedestal and raised his right hand. Instantly cars began to grind to a halt. You see, the motorists recognized that the boy was standing in the place of authority and that all the power of the Mexican government backed up the one who stood upon the pedestal.

Suppose the boy had tried to physically stop one of those powerful automobiles. That would have been a case of pitting his power against the car's power, and you can guess who would be the loser. This is what happens when we try to deal with the Devil in our own power. We get steam-rolled!

But the motorists had to stop, even when a small boy stood in the place of authority because all of the power of the government of Mexico was invoked with just the wave of his right hand.

The same principle applies to us when we realize our place of authority and step into it. Only in our case, all of the power of God is behind us, and even Satan has to respect that and back off.

To exercise authority is to operate in the realm of delegated power. The greatness of the authority is proportionate to the greatness of the power of the one who delegated it.

In the case of the believer's authority, there is the greatest power in the universe standing behind it, Jesus Christ Himself. He said, "All authority has been given to Me in heaven and on earth" (Matthew 28:18).

Christ's Authority

Most Christians have some vague concept of the power and authority that are Christ's, but most cannot put their finger on just how He got His authority or how it relates to them.

I can't think of another truth that has been more foundational to my whole understanding of God's working in my life than the truth of Christ's victorious defeat of Satan. It's impossible to appreciate your position of victory in Christ until you know how He won His victory over your three great enemies, the world, the flesh, and the Devil.

In numerous places in the New Testament Paul makes crystal clear God's plan for subjecting all hostile powers to Christ and those who believe in Him.

There are three words that summarize Christ's acquisition of authority for Himself and us: *crucified*, *resurrected*, and *ascended*.

If you understood no other concepts of the Bible than these three words, you would know enough to live a victorious Christian life daily.

Crucified

When Christ hung on the cross with our sins on Him, He was not only bearing our sin and its consequence of death, but we were actually hanging there on the cross with Him. This complete union with Christ is the incredible truth Paul wants us to fathom in the sixth chapter of Romans.

When God poured out His unleashed wrath and judgment upon our sins, He not only judged *Christ* with the guilt of our sins, but He judged us too. When Christ experienced the final sting of sin, *death*, we died too.

I have often imagined the hysterical joy that must have swept across hell as news of the death of the Son of God was spread. Not realizing that Christ's death was the final nail in his coffin, Satan mistakenly cheered His crucifixion.

You see, many times in Jesus' life Satan tried to get Jesus to sin so He would be vulnerable to sin's consequence, death. When he saw Jesus assume the sins of mankind and then voluntarily die because of those sins, Satan thought he had finally won in his conflict with God. He had cleverly gotten God's first perfect man, Adam, to sin and now God's second "Adam," Jesus Christ, the Perfect One, was also bearing sin and death.

There must have been a wild celebration among Satan and his demon hordes for those three days and nights—a real lost weekend. But then a sobering and deadly hush fell over Satan's forces as these astonished beings observed the greatest display of power ever unleashed from the hand of Almighty God.

The Son of God was resurrected from the dead!

And so were we!

Resurrection Power

"O death, where is thy sting? O grave, where is thy victory?" (1 Corinthians 15:55, KJV).

The defeat of Satan was sealed! With the resurrection of Jesus, Satan forever lost his authority over the humanity of Jesus and over everyone who claims union with Him.

Just picture the chagrin that Satan must have had before his rebel followers. Far from being the victor, he became the vanquished; he and his hordes were the captives in the victory train of the triumphant Jesus.

Paul tells us that "He (Christ) had disarmed the *rulers* and *authorities*, He made a public display of them, having triumphed over them through Him" (Colossians 2:15).

When Jesus stripped Satan and his demons of their authority, that victory was ours. In Satan's mind, not only is Jesus his conqueror, but so are those who are *in* Christ.

Satan knows that he has no legal right to any ground in the life of a believer, but if he can keep us from finding out this truth, he will have a field day in our lives.

We are told that Jesus "disarmed" those hostile powers. That's just exactly what it means. Satan is like a toothless bulldog. He can growl and intimidate, but he has no authority to back up his threats in the life of a believer. If we don't know this or believe it, though, we will allow him to intimidate us, and he is a master at that. He loves to get Christians to cower or run from him in fear.

Many people think that God and Satan are opposites, but equal in power and authority. Nothing could be farther from the truth. Satan is a vanquished enemy. But he is alive and well and a master of bluff, threat, intimidation, accusation, and temptation.

The believer who does not know and count upon his complete identification with Christ in His crucifixion and resurrection is a prime target for these clever attacks of Satan.

Ascended With Christ

I said that there are three words that comprise Christ's position of authority over Satan. We've briefly seen what Jesus' crucifixion and resurrection have done to the hosts of hell.

The culmination of God's whole redemptive plan was to place Christ on the throne at His right hand, forever putting Christ's enemies under His feet. Any enemy of Christ's is an enemy of ours, and anyone put under Christ's feet is put under ours also because "we are members of His body" (Ephesians 5:30).

Because of my total identification with Christ in the mind of God, whatever is true of Christ is true of me.

Christ is now seated on His throne in heaven at the right hand of God, the center of the greatest power and authority in the whole universe. And we are seated there with Him. He has delegated to us the use of the same authority He has and the power to use it over our mutual enemies while we are here on earth.

Isn't that fantastic? God has so completely dealt with me, the sinner, and my sins that He has *already* seated me in the heavenlies with Christ. I may be standing in the state of California right now, but I am also seated in the heavenlies. I don't have to wait until I die and go to heaven before this becomes true of me.

Claiming Our Legal Rights

These truths that I have set forth here are the "legal" rights of every child of God. These legal facts were forever settled in the "Divine Courtroom of the Godhead" in ages past. Nothing can annul them, and the only thing that can keep a believer from exercising his power and authority in Christ is his ignorance of these truths or his refusal to believe them.

In Ephesians 1:18-23 and 2:4-7 Paul earnestly pleads with us to see what our tremendous inheritance is as a child of God. God isn't offering us "pie in the sky, by and by" either. Every tense of every verb that Paul uses emphasizes our divine position *now*.

"I pray that the eyes of your heart may be enlightened, so that you may know what is the hope of His calling, what are the riches of the glory of His inheritance in the saints, and what is the surpassing greatness of His power toward us who believe. These are in accordance with the working of the strength of His might which He brought about in Christ, when He raised Him from the dead, and seated Him at His right hand in the heavenly places, far above all *rule* and *authority* and *power* and *dominion* (these refer to Satan's powers), and every name that is named, not only in this age, but also in the one to come. And He put all things in subjection under His feet, and gave Him as head over all things to the church, which is His body. . . .

"But God, being rich in mercy, because of His great love with which He loved us, even when we were dead in our transgressions, made us alive together with Christ (by grace you have been saved), and raised us up with Him, and seated us with Him in the heavenly places, in Christ Jesus, in order that in the ages to come He might show the surpassing riches of His grace in kindness toward us in Christ Jesus."

The Wonderful Name of Jesus

"Therefore also God highly exalted Him, and bestowed on Him the name which is above every name, that at the name of Jesus every knee should bow, of those who are in heaven, and on earth, and under the earth, and that every tongue should confess that Jesus Christ is Lord, to the glory of God the Father" (Philippians 2:9-11).

There is more power in the name "Jesus" than in any other word ever uttered from the lips of God or man.

When we use His name in prayer, God the Father knows all that that name encompasses and the riches it has made available to the one who uses it in faith.

When we declare that wonderful name in telling the good news of salvation to people today, and when they come to believe what that name has done for them, they are turned from darkness to light.

But there is a realm of spiritual existence that is more aware of the power in that name than any other sphere, and that is Satan's domain.

When a believer, knowing he is seated in the position of authority in Christ in the heavenlies, uses that name on Satan or demons, they *must* back off. They are terrified of His name because it represents to them their humiliating defeat at Jesus' resurrection.

A Word to the Wise

Using Jesus' name also reminds the believer that the conquest of Satan was Christ's victory; we are only conquerors *because of Him*. If we dare to step out from behind the cross of Christ and try to battle Satan in our own strength, we've had it.

I've seen zealous believers get hold of this new authority in Christ and go along great for awhile. Then they begin to get heady with power, and before long they are ordering Satan around and naively dismissing demons from Christians' lives. Satan will "roll over and play dead" the first few times we try this just to get us overwhelmed with *our* great new power. But he'll lay in wait for us, and once we've become convinced that *we're* his conquerors, it's just a matter of time before we're flat on our backs looking up and wondering what hit us.

Jesus is the victor, and as we abide in Him and draw upon *His* power and count upon *His* victory, He delegates it to us. If we dare to draw upon our own power and authority, we'll be no match for Satan.

The only place of safety is the heavenly throne itself. It is located "far above" the enemy camp, and as long as we are mentally abiding there, we can't be touched.

Satan will employ every possible trick to get us to step down from the heavenlies and deal with him ourselves. But if we are walking in the Spirit, our normal daily lives will be lived with the awareness that we are seated with Christ in His position of authority and power.

Alive and Well

The world is groaning with its problems. Hearts are crying with their needs. How can anyone bear to live today without Christ?

If you know Him, does your very being ache for those who do not? If you know Him, are you living on a note of triumph?

Each morning as we awaken to the new day which God has given to us, we need to put on our armor and take our seat with Christ. We need to remind ourselves that we have victory over the world, the flesh, and the Devil through the work of Christ on our behalf. Personally, I reaffirm my life commitment to Jesus and authorize the Holy Spirit to control me moment by moment.

As the day progresses and the world begins to press in, if I blow it spiritually I talk it over with my understanding Heavenly Father, admitting freely what I've done. He then reassures me of His love and acceptance of me. If I've harmed someone else, I seek to set it right with them.

One of the greatest blessings I've continually experienced is to allow Jesus to carry my burden of "self-condemnation" and guilt. This truth alone has done more to free me from Satan's grasp than any other concept God has taught me.

What a time for *us* to be alive! We can see the "rulers, the powers, the world-forces of this darkness" engulfing Planet Earth, but we can have Christ's authority, Christ's power to bring about victory.

Tell it to the world!

May God use these liberating truths to bring new freedom to your life, new hope for the future. Remember our victory cry which Jesus shouted from the cross—"It is finished!"

Tetelestai!

BAPTISM OF THE HOLY SPIRIT

Appendix (To Chapter 13)

WE HEAR MANY believers talking about the "baptism of the Spirit," and its proponents make many claims for it. Some are seeking to show, mostly from the Book of Acts, that this experience ushers a Christian into a dynamic, power-packed life. Some say it is the actual point at which the Holy Spirit indwells one who is already a believer.

Most adherents, however, believe that this is a crisis point in a Christian's life when he initially comes into contact with the Spirit's filling power. In fact, they often use the phrase "filling of the Spirit" and "baptism of the Spirit" interchangeably. The charismatic and Pentecostal brethren believe this "baptism" will be evidenced by speaking in tongues.

The question we must raise is: was the baptism of the Spirit the means designed by God to give power to impotent believers?

Without emotional bias, let's look at what the Word teaches on this subject. I'm going to limit myself to two aspects of this question: what the baptism of the Spirit is and the transitional nature of the Book of Acts.

The baptism of the Spirit is defined in only one place in the Word, First Corinthians 12:13. "For by one Spirit we were all baptized into one body, whether Jews or Greeks, whether slaves or free, and we were all made to drink of one Spirit."

The word "baptism" is from the Greek word "baptizo," and it means *to totally identify one thing with another.* When a person is baptized in water, it is a public testimony of his faith that he was taken by the Holy Spirit at salvation and joined into living union with Jesus. This identifies him with Christ in His death, burial, and resurrection (Romans 6).

In the baptism of the Spirit, each believer, at the moment of his conversion, is totally identified with Christ in His death, burial, and resurrection and with that one body which is Christ's body here on earth, of which He is the head (1 Corinthians 12). The ritual of water baptism is a symbol of the inner baptism of the Spirit which has already taken place at the moment the person was born again.

The Transitional Nature of Acts

The Book of Acts is a book which shows us the transitional problems of believers who were living under the law of Moses. With the giving of the Holy Spirit they were taken from under that law and placed under grace.

The first Jewish believers had been raised under the Mosaic system of worship and teaching. In that teaching the Holy Spirit only came upon certain people for special ministries. Before the Cross, not all believers had the Holy Spirit dwelling in them. Also, they had no teachings of a union with each other and with God that would make them into one body. This was the mystery, hidden from the world, which Paul revealed in Ephesians 3. This was part of the New Covenant which Christ was instituting.

In the Book of Acts an unusual situation is present. Hundreds of Jesus' followers and believers were not even aware that He was going to change their way of relating to God by joining them into union with His own body. This He was going to do by baptizing and indwelling *each* believer with the Holy Spirit.

God first revealed this new truth on the day of Pentecost when the Holy Spirit was poured out on the 120 Jewish believers who were present in the upper room in Jerusalem (Acts 2). After this initial giving of the Spirit to the Jewish nation, whenever a Jew believed in Christ, he simultaneously received the Holy Spirit and was baptized by Him into living union with the body of Christ.

In Acts 8, the half-Jew, half-Gentile Samaritan believers were introduced into this new indwelling and empowering ministry of the Holy Spirit. They were brought into union with the Jewish believers through their new union with Christ. After that, whenever Samaritans became believers, they were baptized with the Holy Spirit at the same time.

In Acts 10 the Roman centurion, Cornelius, and his friends were Gentiles who experienced the initiation into the body of Christ, the Church. The Jewish believers who were present were astonished to realize that this new relationship to the Holy Spirit was the privilege of Gentile believers, too.

In Acts 19 there was a group of devout believers who had been converted through John the Baptist's ministry. Although they were already true believers in all that he had taught them about Jesus, they hadn't heard that there was a Holy Spirit. When Paul got to Ephesus, he asked them, "Did you receive the Holy Spirit *when* you believed?" If they said "yes," then he would have known that they had become believers *since* Pentecost (all new believers received the Holy Spirit simultaneously with conversion after the transition took place at Pentecost—Acts 2, 8, 10).

When he found out that they did not have the Holy Spirit yet, but had been true believers before Pentecost, then he knew they were in need of an initial giving of the Holy Spirit. So Paul laid hands on them and they received the Holy Spirit the same as the 120 *Jews* in Acts 2, the *Samaritans* in Acts 8, and the *Gentiles* in Acts 10.

All the different ethnic groups of believers were now initiated into the New Testament way of relating to God through His indwelling Spirit and through union with Him. From that point on, all believers have been baptized with the Spirit *at the moment of their conversion*. This is the pattern set forth in the Epistles. They assume the *transition* as complete.

Union With Christ

The clear teaching of the Word is that the baptism of the Spirit is that ministry whereby a new believer is joined into a living union with Christ and His body, the Church, here on earth.

This happens to every person the moment he believes in Christ for personal salvation. You don't need to ask for it or seek it; it is done *to* you by the Holy Spirit as a part of salvation.

It does not need to be evidenced by speaking in tongues because there is no biblical or historical evidence that tongues were the *required* manifestation of this baptism.

I believe that confusion has arisen regarding this term "baptism of the Spirit" because in the Book of Acts each time a group was initially introduced into the new relationship with the Holy Spirit there was a manifestation of new power, and in several, *but not all*, cases they spoke in tongues.

However, we cannot use the pattern of the baptism of the Spirit in the Book of Acts as the pattern for our relating to the Holy Spirit today unless we understand the fact that the whole book is dealing with a transition from the Old Covenant to the New Covenant, from law to grace.

It is in the epistles of the New Testament that we find our pattern for relating to the Holy Spirit today. Over and over again we are given the imperative of being *filled* with the Spirit, of *walking* in the Spirit, and of walking by *faith*. We are NEVER told to be baptized with the Spirit because Paul knew that all true believers had already been baptized by the Spirit at the moment of their conversion.

Let me say it again. The *filling* of the Spirit is the means God has given for living the Christian life with power. It isn't optional. It is a command.

"And do not get drunk with wine, for that is dissipation, *but be filled with the Spirit*" (Ephesians 5:18).

I know that the people who urge others to be baptized with the Spirit are sincerely seeking to meet a legitimate need for power in the church today. The church has become weakened through the centuries, and there is a great need for revitalization.

However, we must be doctrinally correct in what we teach. Many Christians who are desperately in need of the Spirit's power won't buy the *message* intended by the term "baptism of the Spirit" because they know that term is a misapplication of a valid biblical doctrine.

Unfortunately, the whole concept of being filled with the Spirit has been brought into disrepute and confusion for some because of those who have applied excessive and unscriptural claims to what they term the "baptism of the Spirit." This has closed the minds of many who critically need to be *filled* with the Spirit and experience what it is to walk in Him moment by moment.

There is only one person who wins in this kind of confusion—Satan!

NOTES

CHAPTER 1

1. Arthur Lyons, *The Second Coming: Satanism in America* (New York: Dodd, Mead & Co., 1970).

2. Robert Somerlott, *Here, Mr. Splitfoot* (New York: Viking Press, 1971).

3. Lyons, *The Second Coming*.

4. *Santa Monica Evening Outlook*, 24 June 1971.

5. *Life*, 11 November 1964.

6. *Los Angeles Times*, 7 March 1971.

7. *Commonweal*, 6 November 1970.

8. *Los Angeles Times*, 7 March 1971.

9. *Los Angeles Times*, 21 April 1972.

10. *Los Angeles Times*, 28 January 1972.

11. Somerlott, *Splitfoot*.

12. *Life*, 9 January 1970.

13. *Los Angeles Times*, 4 May 1970.

14. *Los Angeles Times*, 5 May 1970.

15. *Los Angeles Times*, 10 May 1970.

16. *Life*, 11 November 1964.

17. *Ibid.*

18. *New York Times*, 1 June 1969.

19. *Los Angeles Times*, 22 March 1971.

20. *Time*, 19 June 1972.

CHAPTER 2

1. *Los Angeles Times*, 18 April 1972.

2. Merrill Unger, *The Haunting of Bishop Pike* (Wheaton, Ill.: Tyndale House, 1968).

3. *Chicago Tribune*, 17 April 1972.

4. *Saturday Review of Literature*, 7 February 1970.

5. *Los Angeles Times*, 8 November 1970.

6. Eden Gray, *The Tarot Revealed* (New York: Crown Publishers, Inc., 1970).

7. Eden Gray, *A Complete Guide to the Tarot* (New York: Crown Publishers, Inc., 1970).

8. *Los Angeles Times*, 31 October 1971.

9. *Los Angeles Times,* 25 April 1972.

10. *Life,* 9 January 1970.

11. *Los Angeles Times,* 31 October 1971.

12. McCandlish Phillips, *The Bible, The Supernatural and The Jews* (New York: World Publishing Co., 1970).

13. Advanced Organization of Los Angeles, *Advance,* Issue 4, Volume 1.

14. The Church of Scientology of California, *The Auditor,* No. 61.

15. *Ibid.*

16. *Life,* 15 November 1969.

17. *Ibid.*

18. *West,* supplement of *Los Angeles Times,* 25 April 1971.

19. Raphael Gasson, *The Challenging Counterfeit* (Plainfield, N.J.: Logos International, 1966).

20. Ostrander and Schroeder, *Psychic Discoveries Behind the Iron Curtain* (Englewood Cliffs, N.J.: Prentice-Hall, 1971).

21. *Ibid.*

22. *Today's Health,* November 1970.

CHAPTER 3

1. Merrill F. Unger, *Introductory Guide to the Old Testament* (Grand Rapids, Mich.: Zondervan Publishing House, 1956).

2. *New York Times Magazine,* 1 June 1969.

3. Hal Lindsey with C. C. Carlson, *The Late Great Planet Earth* (Grand Rapids, Mich.: Zondervan Publishing House, 1970).

CHAPTER 4

1. Donald Barnhouse, *The Invisible War* (Grand Rapids, Mich.: Zondervan Publishing House, 1965).

2. *Ibid.*

CHAPTER 5

1. Albert C. Wedemeyer, *Wedemeyer Reports* (Henry Holt and Co., 1958).

2. William Arndt and F. Wilbur Gingrich, *A Greek-English Lexicon of the New Testament* (Chicago: University of Chicago Press, 1959).

3. Barnhouse, *The Invisible War.*

4. Francis Schaeffer, *The God Who Is There* (Chicago: Inter-Varsity Press, 1968).

CHAPTER 6

1. *Los Angeles Times*, 8 November 1971.

2. Maurice Merleau-Ponty, *The Structure of Behavior* (Boston: Beacon Press, 1963).

3. *Lincoln Library* (The Frontier Press Co., 1970).

4. Soren Kierkegaard, *Fear and Trembling* (1843).

5. Cleon Skousen, *The Naked Communist* (Salt Lake City, Utah: Ensign Publishing Co., 1961).

6. J. Edgar Hoover, *Masters of Deceit* (New York: Holt, Rinehart and Winston, Inc., 1958).

7. *Lincoln Library*.

8. Desmond Morris, *The Naked Ape* (New York: McGraw-Hill, 1969).

9. Dr. A. A. Brill, *The Basic Writings of Sigmund Freud* (New York: Random House, 1938).

10. Franz Alexander, *Fundamentals of Psychoanalysis* (New York: W. W. Norton & Co., 1948).

11. Sigmund Freud, *A General Introduction to Psychoanalysis* (Garden City, N.Y.: Garden City Publishing Co., 1943).

12. Boris Sokoloff, *The Permissive Society* (New Rochelle, N.Y.: Arlington House, 1971).

13. *Ibid.*

14. *Time*, 24 April 1972.

15. *U.S. News and World Report*, 24 April 1972.

16. *Ibid.*

17. James Kilpatrick, *Los Angeles Times*, 21 April 1972.

18. William L. Shirer, *The Rise and Fall of the Third Reich* (New York: Simon and Schuster, 1960).

19. *Ibid.*

CHAPTER 7

1. *Time*, 30 September 1971.

2. *Ibid.*

3. Prof. Dennis L. Meadows, *A Report for the Club of Rome Project on the Predicament of Mankind* (New York: Universe Books, 1972).

4. Sokoloff, *The Permissive Society*.

5. Lewis Alesen, *Mental Robots* (Carton Printers, Ltd., 1957).

6. *International Socialist Review*, Winter, 1960.

7. Erich Fromm, from the foreword to A. S. Neill's *Summerhill* (New York: Hart Publishing Co., 1960).

8. *Ibid.*

9. *Ibid.*

10. Bertrand Russell, *New Hopes for a Changing World* (New York: Simon and Schuster, 1951).

11. H. G. Wells, *The New World Order* (New York: Alfred Knopf, 1940).

12. D. Talbot Rice, *Teach Yourself to Study Art* (London: The English Universities, Ltd.).

13. Calvin Tomkins, *The Bride and the Bachelors* (New York: Viking Press, 1965) .

14. H. R. Rookmaaker, *Modern Art and the Death of Culture* (London: Intervarsity Press, 1970).

15. *Los Angeles Times*, 7 January 1972.

16. *Time*, 20 September 1971.

17. *Santa Ana Register*, 27 March 1968.

18. *U.S. News and World Report*, 22 May 1967.

19. *U.S. News and World Report*, 3 February 1969.

20. H. G. Wells, *New World Order*.

CHAPTER 8

1. Jeane Dixon, *The Call to Glory* (New York: William Morrow & Company, 1972), p. 42.

2. *Ibid.*, p. 43.

3. *Ibid.*, p. 175.

4. *Ibid.*, p. 24.

5. *Ibid.*, p. 23.

6. Jeane Dixon, *My Life and Prophecies* (New York: William Morrow & Company, 1969), p. 10.

7. *Ibid.*, p. 54.

8. *Ibid.*, p. 62.

9. Kurt Koch, *Between Christ and Satan* (Grand Rapids, Mich.: Kregel Publications, 1970).

10. Dixon, *My Life and Prophecies*, p. 26.

CHAPTER 9

1. Delphine Lyons, *Everyday Witchcraft* (New York: Dell Publishing Co., 1972).

2. Koch, *Between Christ and Satan*.

3. Jesse Penn Lewis, *War on the Saints* (Bournemouth, England: The Overcomer Book Room, 1912).

CHAPTER 10

1. Merrill F. Unger, *Demons in the World Today* (Wheaton, Ill.: Tyndale House, 1971).
2. *Ibid.*
3. *Ibid.*
4. *Ibid.*
5. Jesse Penn Lewis, *War on the Saints.*

CHAPTER 11

1. *Los Angeles Times*, 14 April 1972.
2. *Ibid.*

CHAPTER 14

References: 1 Corinthians 12:13; Romans 6; Colossians 3:1-15; Ephesians 1:15; 2:10; 3:14-21; Galatians 2:20; 3:26-27.

THE

LIBERATION

OF

PLANET EARTH

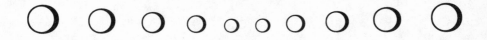

I dedicate this book to three very special gals in my life, my daughters Robin, Jenny, and Heidi. They've cheerfully given up overnight guests and parties, trips to Disneyland and the beach, and have spent many quiet hours playing because Daddy and Mom were working on "the book." Without this loving cooperation, The Liberation of Planet Earth might not have come into existence. Whatever blessing God may give as a result of this book, it's theirs to share for all eternity.

CONTENTS

INTRODUCTION

Y OU CAN BUY transparent, ouchless, polkadotted and happy-faced Band-Aids in every size for every kind of hurt, except the kind of hurt that men have in their souls—a hurt that has spilled over to make an aching, wounded world.

That's not to say attempts haven't been made to put giant-sized bandages on the ills of mankind. One trip to a bookstore will reveal thousands of titles that promise a cure for loneliness, depression, sexual hangups, marital problems, mental illness, crime, wars, alcoholism, and myriads of other desperate ailments that afflict men today.

All these volumes have one thing in common. They agree that humanity is in trouble. But after that point, there's no accord as to what can be done about repairing these damaged lives.

My feeling is that you can't begin to prescribe an effective cure until you have an accurate diagnosis of the real nature of the problem. But how can we know where to look amid the books and voices spouting their "proven" cures for an accurate assessment of what ails men and women in our world today? We don't want to be taken in by promises of cheap remedies and halfway healings. Life is too short for that.

Somewhere in the midst of all this human chaos and confusion we've forgotten a very fundamental fact. All of creation seems to have a great unity, design, and purpose, and it's inconceivable to me that man should be an exception to this. There must have been an original meaning and purpose for him that got lost somewhere along the way and resulted in a morass of alienation, frustration, and hopelessness.

I've written this book to share how I was rescued from my own personal alienation from God, myself, and society and how I found the reason for why I had been put on this earth. My sincere hope is that any kindred souls who need forgiveness, encouragement, and hope will read these pages and find God's solution for their own lives.

1 ○ A Candidate
for a Miracle

A FOURTH-CENTURY philosopher, Augustine, said, "God, You have made us for Yourself, and our hearts are restless until they find their rest in You." I believe he was accurately describing the first twenty-five years of my life.

When I was a ten-year-old, living in Houston, Texas, I first began to ask the big question, "Is there really a God that a guy could know personally?" I was a normal kid with more than the usual amount of spunk. I gave my folks a lot of worries and headaches, and although our family life had its ups and downs we got along pretty well.

My folks weren't what you'd call regular churchgoers. My mom periodically went and took me along with great reluctance on my part. I halfheartedly listened to the sermons, sort of hoping to find out if there was any way to feel closer to God (if He was real).

Misfire No. 1

At age twelve, seriously wanting to know God, I impulsively responded to a call to walk down to the front of the church and make a religious commitment. When I talked with the counselor he said, "Of course, you want to join the church."

I answered, "Well, if that's what you're supposed to do, I guess so."

He said, "Naturally, you'll want to be baptized."

"Well, yeah, I guess so," I replied.

Inside I thought, "Come on, tell me what this is all about." But nobody explained to me what a real commitment to Jesus was all about, at least not so I could understand it.

And so I went through the ritual of joining the church. I was baptized. But somehow all that got through to me was that I had now made a sort of New Year's resolution with God that I was going to try to do the best I could the rest of my life. And if my good deeds by the end of my life outweighed my bad deeds, somehow I'd make it.

Well, I really tried to stick with this new commitment and find some meaning in it. Yet after a few months I realized that if there was a God, I still didn't know Him. There was no reality of God or Jesus in my life. I kept going to church periodically, listening and trying to find out where I'd missed the boat.

Misfire No. 2

By the time I was fifteen I was extremely frustrated. There was conflict in my home and in my personal life, and I was becoming a very hostile young man. But I still had a deep sense of need to get on the right track with God, so I responded that year, in another church, to another invitation for those who wanted to know God to come to the front. It was a long walk down the aisle and I surely hoped it would work this time.

I wound up being told to join the church and be baptized again. So I was baptized a second time, and after a few more months of stumbling around with no new reality of Jesus in my life, I said to myself, "You know, there must be something wrong with this whole business of walking to the front of a church, because it didn't take this time either."

In the particular churches I had attended, they emphasized that if you're a Christian, you don't drink, you don't smoke, you don't go to movies, and you don't dance. I had honestly tried to play the "Christian" game by their rules, so I didn't do any of these things. I was an athlete, and the coach didn't want us to drink or smoke anyway.

I soon began to realize that all the other guys my age were beginning to explore sex and booze and seemed to be having a great time while all I had to show for my "Christianity" was that I wished I could do what they were doing, but couldn't. I began to think, "I've got all the liabilities and none of the assets of this business of being a Christian." I was tired of God cramping my style so I began to stray away from the whole church scene.

Misfire No. 3

By the time I was seventeen though, I began to fight a great battle inside me. I started doing a lot of things everyone else was doing, but I gradually developed a deep sense of guilt. I was sure that if there was a God, He surely must be angry with me and probably wanted nothing to do with me.

In desperation I decided I'd give God one more chance because I really felt as if I needed to have my life cleaned up. I remember going to yet another church at the urging of a friend, and when the call was given to go forward, I headed for the front again, much to my friend's embarrassment. The personal worker who knelt to pray with me was no doubt very sincere and eager to get me into the fold, but he had no idea how to communicate with a high-geared teenager and I never did understand what it was all about. He finally got around to asking me to join the church and be baptized, so I went through the whole process a third time.

The Hardening Process Starts

Well, trip No. 3 didn't last very long. One thing I'd found out for certain was that simply going to the front of a church during an altar call and being baptized won't get your heart right with God. All these false starts eventually brought me to the point where I said, "I've got to be honest; I don't know if there is a God because I've gone looking for Him and haven't found Him. All religion has done is cramp my style. I'm just going to kiss it all off and live the way I want to."

And I did!

Systematically I began to harden my mind against God. I knew what I was doing, but I'd become very bitter and figured that I'd given God a chance at me and He'd muffed it. Now it was my turn to run my own life. And how I did run it! I pulled out all the stops. I started in big with booze and sex, and although my conscience did bother me at first, I finally got to where I could do those things with no conscious sense of guilt at all.

I entered the University of Houston, but partied my way out two years in a row. Uncle Sam wasn't impressed with my academic career and decided my talents could be put to better use in the army. I beat him to the punch, though, and joined the U.S. Coast Guard where I figured I'd never see much of the action in Korea.

I played every angle I could and wound up going to school the whole first year in special classes at the Coast Guard training school in Connecticut. During this time I really thought I'd reached the apex of living because I'd luckily taken up with some friends who had connections in New York City. I was running around with a guy whose father was vice-president of one of the largest corporations in America. He kept a suite of rooms at all times at a swank hotel in New York City, and he let us use them any time we went into town. Naturally I tried to pull liberty every weekend in New York City.

Would You Believe—Times Square?

One Saturday, after blowing my paycheck at a wild party the night before, I was standing on Times Square with another sailor and we were looking for someone to touch for a loan so we could eat. About three o'clock in the afternoon we finally decided no one was coming.

I looked across the street from Times Square and saw this sign that said "Free Food" in big letters. And in small letters underneath, it said "Jesus Saves." I nudged my buddy and said, "Let's go over and make those Holy Joes feed us—they ought to be good for something."

You see, by this time the contempt I had for God and religion was deeply ingrained in my behavior. But I figured I could swallow my antagonism long enough to get something to eat. We had finished our meal and were about to make a strategic withdrawal when a worker blocked our way and said to me, "Young man, are you a Christian?"

I didn't want to get into a hassle with the guy so I looked him straight in the eye and muttered through clenched teeth "Well, I hope so." I thought that would get him off my back. But it didn't.

He said, "I can tell by your answer that you're not a Christian."

I shot back sarcastically, "How can you know that about somebody else? If there's anything I've found out about this whole religion business, it's that you can't be sure of anything."

But the man wasn't scared off, and he looked at me with real compassion and concern—and that got to me. He said, "I think I can understand why you might feel that way. Obviously you've never had it made clear to you why Jesus had to come into the world and what it is that He really offers you."

I nodded and said wryly, "That's for sure."

"You see, sailor," he went on, "you look as if you've lived a pretty rough life. But with God it's not a matter of how bad you've been or even how good you've been. The only issue with God is whether you've come to see that when Jesus hung on that cross, God put all those sins of yours onto Him, and then Jesus took the punishment of death for those sins which should have fallen on you. Now He can offer you a gift of His love and forgiveness instead of His holy wrath. If you'll accept that forgiveness, it'll bring you to God and make Him real to you."

That was more than twenty years ago, but what he said to me that day was so clear and startling I can still remember essentially what it was.

Yet I had built such a wall around my heart that I wasn't ready to believe what he'd said. So I shoved the guy out of the way and walked out with a cynical laugh. As I left he fired a final statement at me that I never forgot: "Young man, you may reject me, but if you reject the gift of God's love, then His wrath will fall on you for all eternity."

That "shot" hit below the belt!

Off to the Mardi Gras

That was my only brush with spiritual things for the next five years. From Connecticut I was transferred to New Orleans, which I came to think was the swingingest place on earth. I was stationed there for about two years. I liked New Orleans so much that when I was discharged from the Coast Guard I decided to stay there. I lived near the French Quarter.

With the experience I'd gained in the Coast Guard, I got a job as a tugboat captain on the Mississippi. For almost four years I worked on the river. During this time I'd work a week, then have a week off. I hit New Orleans every other week with a full paycheck and a week in which to spend it. Every other week I'd drag back to the boat half dead and broke. Wow! I really thought I was living!

But in giving myself devoutly to wine, women, and song, I began to find there were diminishing returns. The more I experimented with first one thing and then another, the less I was satisfied. Finally I got to the point in life where I began to ask, "What do you do for an encore?"

By now I was almost twenty-six years old. I began desperately grasping for something that might give some meaning to my life. Being the life of the party and the one no one ever took seriously was a role I increasingly hated. I started talking to people about their philosophies of life. I realized then how shallow I was. My playboy philosophy was to "live fast, play hard, die young, and leave a good-looking corpse."

I even began to be interested in talking to people about their ideas on religion. Everyone's ideas were so different, yet they all thought they were right. But they couldn't all be right. I came to the conclusion that everyone else was as mixed up as I was about religion.

Too Close for Comfort

One night while I was aboard ship, I had to make a crossing in a dense fog to take several oil drilling crews across the river. The fog was so thick you couldn't see the bow of the boat. I attempted to start up the generator and it wouldn't go. Without the generator you don't have radar, and without radar you don't know where you are on that river in the fog.

"We don't care what the risks are," the men said.

"Okay," I told them. "It's your neck." I pulled out a stopwatch and a compass and took off across the river.

All of a sudden my blood ran cold as I heard a steamship whistle just to my left. A big ship was coming right at us. I throttled. I couldn't see anything, but I could hear those big engines bearing down on me. Instinctively, and for no navigational reason, I whipped the wheel to the right and felt my boat just graze the side of the steamship. We slid along the side of it all the way back.

To this day I don't know how we made it. God was really with me. Had we been hit broadside, it would have cut our craft in two and sent it to the bottom within seconds.

After that close call I started doing a lot of thinking about death. Like a lot of people, I'd had thoughts of taking my own life on several occasions, but the nagging fear of what might lie beyond the grave kept me from it. I saw that night, however, that we all stand just a breath away from death and it can find us even if we're not looking for it.

That experience did a lot to sober me, and I can see now that it was an important turning point in my life.

More Than Good Luck

Everything came to a head one night a few months later. I tossed and turned on my bed; my head was spinning with doubts and fears and questions. I had to get some answers.

I remembered that I had a Bible in the bottom of my seabag. I'd carried it for years as a good-luck charm—like a rabbit's foot—but I'd never read it. I pulled it out and began thumbing through it, and I found myself really interested as I read a few things about the life of Jesus. I decided right then that I would try to forget everything I'd heard about Jesus from men and just try to see what He said about Himself. I began reading at the beginning of the New Testament—in the gospel of Matthew.

To my surprise I ran into the Sermon on the Mount in chapters five through seven. I'd never been too excited about what I'd heard this Sermon contained. The only part I remembered hearing was that if you looked at a woman with lust in your mind, you'd already committed adultery with her in your heart.

There it was again, those same words, right in front of me. I stopped and thought, "Man, who's got a chance with a rule like that? And I haven't just been lusting either!"

As I read on and saw all the other commandments Jesus gave, I thought to myself, "Forget it, Lindsey. You haven't got a chance. You've broken every rule in the Book."

The New Beginning

Despondently I flipped over to another part of the New Testament—John, Chapter Three. As I glanced down the page I was intrigued by a conversation Jesus had with a man who was looking for answers about God, just as I had been for years. The man's name was Nicodemus, and Jesus told him that unless he was born again, he could never understand the kingdom of God or enter it.

"What's all this about being 'born again'?" I asked myself. "If there's anything I need, it's to be born all over again. I was surely born wrong the first time."

And you know, at that point the Spirit of God really began to work on me because my whole life seemed to flash before me. I remembered how I'd grown up grappling for the meaning of life, struggling to find God, with heartaches, emotional stresses, and a terrible self-image. I recalled my high school years and how I knew I basically had plenty of ability, but because I was so messed up emotionally I never finished anything I started. It seemed as if I just couldn't succeed. When I finished high school, I'm sure the senior class thought of me as the guy most likely to fail.

I saw that my whole life was the pattern of a loser, a guy with more than enough talent who never seemed to get it together. And I thought, "Man, it would be so wonderful to be able to start all over again—to wipe the slate clean and have a new life."

That's what being born again suggested to me—having a new life! Maybe the second time around I could get it all together. And yet, as Jesus talked about being born again, I couldn't see how something like that could ever happen to me. I figured I was too far gone.

As I read that third chapter of John over and over, it finally dawned on me that all I had to do to be born again was to *believe* that what Jesus did on the cross was done for *me* personally.

Not the Praying Type

I really felt as if I wanted to pray, but I honestly didn't know how. I simply said out loud, "God, if this is real, then show me how to believe. I don't have any faith. I don't even know if You're there."

The New Testament I had was one of those distributed by the Gideons to public school children. In the back it said, "If you want to make a decision to believe in Jesus as your Savior, this is the way you do it." It quoted the words of Jesus from Revelation 3:20, "Behold, I stand at the door and knock; if anyone hears My voice and opens the door, I will come in to him, and will dine with him and he with Me." It explained that the "door" is our will and we can choose to invite Jesus Christ into our lives and accept the forgiveness for our sins that His death made available.

So I said, "God, if all this is real, then I want Jesus Christ to come into my life. I really need to be forgiven. If He can do that, then I accept Him right now. God, please show me the truth."

The next morning, to my amazement, the first thing I wanted to do when I awoke was read that Bible—and that was something new! For the first time it really began to make sense.

I returned to New Orleans after a couple of days and went on my usual wild week-long tear. The only thing was, this time it wasn't as big a kick as it had always been.

That Fantastic Fanatic!

When I got back on board ship the next week, a deckhand came up to me and said, "Skipper, there's a new boat-driver that tied up here and, man, is he crazy. He's been down in the barroom every day—preaching."

"What in the world is he preaching about?" I said.

"About Jesus," he replied.

"Well, you tell him I'd like him to come aboard," I said. "I'd like to get some of his ideas about Jesus."

My deckhand looked at me as if *I'd* lost my mind.

The next day he brought the preacher aboard. The guy had heard about me and was a little uncomfortable. But I began to talk and he eased up.

"You know, a week ago something happened that I'd just like to get your opinion about. I understand you're a preacher."

He nodded and started rambling a bit. "This has been the wildest tour of duty I've ever had," he said. "I've got a wife and six kids over in Alabama and I couldn't get a job anywhere but here. I've been wondering what I'm doing here in this God-forsaken place."

I began to tell him my story. I told him about what I'd read in the Bible and how I'd prayed. This guy's mouth dropped open, then it got a little wider and a little wider, and I'll never forget what he first said to me.

"So *you're* the reason I couldn't get a job anywhere else."

"What do you mean by that?" I asked.

"Well, God wanted us to meet. He obviously sent me here to talk to you and let you know that you've done the right thing."

It turned out that he was an Assemblies of God preacher. He took the Bible and went through many parts that basically gave me the assurance that what I'd done was right. He talked to me about the importance of reading the Bible daily. By the time he was through, I knew Christ was in my life and that I had truly been born again. A couple of days later he left and I never saw him again.

That New Life Begins

I didn't start going to any church because I didn't know which one to go to, but I progressively began to notice changes taking place in my life. I became intensely interested in reading the Bible, and without my trying to reform myself, my inner desires about many things began to change. I would slip down into my cabin to read the Bible because I didn't want my crew to think I'd flipped-out over religion. A lot of my friends began to notice the change in my lifestyle and really began to worry about me. They even brought a minister to talk with me one day; he told me not to get all worked up about the Bible.

Six months passed. I decided that the New Orleans scene was not the most conducive to my living a Christian life, so I returned to my hometown of Houston. I remember saying to myself, "Maybe I can find someone here who can tell me more about what the Bible means." I knew I was on the right track, but I'd gotten a late start and had to learn a lot in a hurry.

I worked at several different jobs, and I usually ate my lunch alone and read the Bible. One day a fellow worker noticed me and asked me if I wanted to come to his church and hear a scholar speak on the Middle East conflict (the Suez Crisis). He said the minister was going to explain how the Bible had predicted much of what was happening in the Middle East.

This really intrigued me, so I went with my friend. The man spoke for two and a half hours, and I was so excited I couldn't sleep that night. I literally stayed up all night checking out what he had said, and by morning all those fulfilled prophecies had convinced me that the Bible was really the inspired Word of God.

I began to go to this church and study under this man's teaching. Without realizing what was happening, I was studying the Bible about six to eight hours every day and holding a full-time job at the same time. My folks began to get a little worried about me becoming overly zealous.

And a Child Shall Lead Them

Finally my dad came to me and said, "Hal, I remember that when you were living in New Orleans, I came over to visit you and you took me on a wild tour of the French Quarter. I was shocked to see the way you were living. Now a year later you come home with a Bible under your arm and you're completely different. I don't know what's happened to you, but I'd surely like to."

I sat down and explained as best I could what had happened to me. To my amazement, tears came to his eyes. He said, "I'd like to know Jesus Christ like that."

We got on our knees in the front room, and he asked Christ to come into his life and be his Savior. My dad at age fifty-two became a new-born child of God, just like I had become. My mom still wasn't too sure about what was going on. She was a true believer in Jesus, but had never been taught anything about how to make the Christian life work day by day for her. Within a few months Jesus began to be real to her also.

Called to the Ministry

After about a year and a half of intensive Bible study in my church, God used a story from the Book of Exodus to show me the plan He had outlined for my life. He wanted me to teach His Word to others.

You can't imagine how shocked I was as I read the story of Moses at the burning bush and in no uncertain terms God said to me, "You're going to be another bush through which I'm going to speak."

The reason for my amazement was that I was scared to death to get up in front of people and speak. I'd quit a speech class at the university because I was terrified to open my mouth.

I told the Lord, "If You want to make a preacher out of me, You've got to perform a miracle on me first."

"That's no problem for Me," He said. "Look at the conversation I had with Moses in Exodus four. When I called Moses to go before Pharaoh and tell him to let My people go from their bondage in Egypt, look what he said to Me:

"'Please, Lord, I have never been eloquent, neither recently nor in time past, nor since You have spoken to Your servant; for I am slow of speech and slow of tongue.'

"And this is what I, the God of the impossible, said to Moses: 'Who has made man's mouth? Or who makes him dumb or deaf, or seeing or blind? Is it not I, the Lord? Now then go, and I, even I, will be with your mouth and teach you what you are to say.'"

As I looked at those verses of Scripture and recalled the mighty way in which God had used Moses *after* this incident, I said, "Lord, You can do *anything*. If You made my mouth and You're calling me to use it for You, then You can put the words into it just as You did for Moses."

Trial Run

Shortly after this I was asked to teach an adult Bible class one Sunday. I almost said No when they asked me, but then I decided this was a good chance to give God an opportunity to put some of those words of His into my mouth.

I studied for days, and when I got up before the class it was with trembling knees but a bold heart that was putting all its confidence in God! To my amazement (Oh, me of *much* faith!) the people were really hit by what I said, and furthermore it was a terrific experience for me. Now and then during my lesson I'd start to remember where I was, and the old panic would begin inside me. Then I'd remember what God told Moses about putting His words into our mouths, and my heart would calm down.

After the class a woman came up to talk. I'd noticed her in the back of the room and she looked as if someone had been tromping on her toes all during my talk. She said, "Young man, I believe God has singled you out to teach His Word far and wide someday, but your grammar is so offensive that nobody is going to want to listen to you."

I knew she was right. I really murdered the King's English!

The World's Oldest Third Grader

"I'm an English teacher," she said. "If you'll come twice a week to my home, I'll teach you proper grammar."

I asked her why she was willing to do this.

"Because God told me to," she replied.

So I began to learn. She had to start back with third grade grammar; she brought me up to college level in a year. During this same period of my life I was really beginning to thrill at an expanded understanding of the Scriptures.

Hungry for the Word

As my knowledge of Scripture broadened, and the calling of God became clearer, I sensed more than ever my need to really *learn* God's Word. One night I said, "Lord, You know what I really want to do is go to seminary."

But how could I get accepted? Besides my sordid past and lack of any "religious credentials" whatever, I had never finished college. The school I wanted to attend was a four-year *graduate* school of theology, one of the toughest in the country.

God's answer came as He directed me to read one day in Psalm 71. I knew that these verses of Scripture, penned so many years ago by David, were God's mantle thrown upon me; for reasons known only to God, I was to be one of those who would somehow declare His power to my generation.

"O God, You have taught me from my youth; and I still declare Your wondrous deeds. And even when I am old and gray, *O God, do not forsake me, until I declare Your strength to this generation*, Your power to all who are to come.

"For Your righteousness, O God, reaches to the heavens, You who have done great things; O God, who is like You? You, who have showed me many troubles and distresses, will revive me again, and will bring me up again from the depths of the earth" (Psalm 71:17-20).

Since God was calling me to speak for Him; it only made sense that He would have to open the doors to seminary for me. When I realized this, I stopped worrying about how it was all going to come about and I just started trusting Him and making my plans to go.

Faithful Is He Who Calls You

I submitted my application for seminary and I'm sure that when they received it, it took them two or three days just to stop laughing. There was virtually nothing on the form that would recommend me as a candidate for Dallas Theological Seminary.

Unknown to me, my pastor had made a special trip to the seminary to talk to the admissions director. "On paper this guy doesn't look like much," he told him, "but he's taught himself Greek on his own initiative, and he has a fire burning in his heart for God."

So they sent me an IQ test, and I knew my acceptance depended on my performance. I said, "Lord, I don't know what my IQ is (I knew my IQ score must have been low when I went into the service, because I'd taken the test with a terrible hangover), but I believe You can give me supernatural wisdom."

It was as though my mind had become a computer! I knew the hand of the Lord was on me, and I thought to myself as I whizzed through that test, "If I could think like this all the time, I'd be a genius." I finished way before the time limit. I went over the test again, correcting a few places, sealed it up, and sent it in.

In—By the Grace of God

I received an immediate reply: "You're accepted!" That miracle I'd been expecting had happened.

Here I was, accepted. But I was also flat broke! I'd been out of a job, laid off because of the 1958 recession.

I was sitting at home one afternoon. My mother came in and said, "Hal, you've got to write the seminary and tell them you can't come. We wish we had the money to help you, but right now it's just impossible for your dad and me to spare the money."

"Mom, God has called me to go to seminary and He's led those at Dallas to accept me. Now, *somehow* He's going to provide the money."

I remember going into my bedroom, closing the door, getting down on my face on the floor, and saying, "Okay, Lord. I said those words. Now You back me up!" While I was praying, my mother came into my room with some mail that had just arrived. "There are several letters here for you," she said.

Keep Those Cards and Letters Comin', Lord!

I opened the envelopes, and every one of them contained a check. I had not made my need known, yet many people said later that God had strangely placed within their hearts an urge to send money to help toward my seminary education. Letters began coming in nearly every day. By the time I left for Dallas I had enough money to go through the entire first year.

That's the way the Lord took me through four years of seminary. I never had any guaranteed income, but all my bills were paid by the time I graduated. That living by faith was good preparation for the ministry God was preparing me for.

Further Preparation for My Ministry

One of the greatest needs I'd begun to feel was for someone to share my life with. I'd had a heartbreaking experience with marriage when I was an unbeliever in New Orleans, and my wife had found someone she liked better and divorced me. I knew I needed a woman's love and companionship, but I was scared to death that it might blow up on me again. For this reason, although I was in my late twenties, I didn't date much during seminary. I really believed God had a woman of His choice somewhere for me and if I would simply wait for His best, He'd give her to me.

I knew that whoever He gave me would have to be someone very special to put up with me. She'd have to be mature and deeply committed to serving the Lord. I also thought it wouldn't hurt if she were pretty.

During the last part of my junior year at seminary, this very gal, Jan Houghton, walked quite unexpectedly into my life. We knew each other only five days before we both recognized we were the ones God had saved each other for.

Those five days were all we had together, for then she had to return to her ministry with Campus Crusade for Christ at Smith College in Northampton, Massachusetts. Three weeks later God unmistakably led me to call her and ask her to marry me. She'd already committed this to the Lord, and He gave her an immediate Yes.

Two months later, without our having seen each other once in between, Jan flew to Houston and married me. In the flesh we were total strangers, but we had the unmistakable mandate from God that we belonged to each other, and He had already given us a spiritual oneness.

Through the years that we've been married God has vindicated over and over the reasons He brought us together. We served Him as a team in Campus Crusade for many years after my seminary days, and now we work together in teaching and speaking around the country and in writing.

Summing It All Up

I hope by now you can see why I've exposed so much of my personal life to you. I've wanted you to see how God delights in taking very ordinary and sometimes messed-up lives and doing extraordinary things through them. Never in a thousand years would I have dreamed God would use me to write books that have sold in the millions and have brought life and hope to so many. Me, who lived so hopelessly for so many years of my own life.

But that's God's peculiar delight—turning Simons into Peters, Sauls into Pauls, and messed-up men into vessels that can bring honor to Him.

In the chapters that follow I want with all my heart to help you see what it is that's done this to my life. I'm certainly no "finished product," and I'm daily being pruned by God to become more of what He wants me to be. But that too is an exciting process and one that's going on in all of us. Getting a better look at how God is refining us and how He's equipped us to live *above* our circumstances in this life makes the future something to look forward to rather than to dread.

If you want to move from the ranks of the ordinary into the world of unlimited possibilities, I challenge you to read on with an open heart and mind and you'll become a candidate for a miracle.

2 ∘ What in the World is Wrong with Man?

ANY MEDICAL DOCTOR worth his salt knows he can't bring about a cure for a disease unless he first diagnoses the problem correctly. Politicians and statesmen must carefully and accurately assess the underlying causes of problems in their town or state or country before they can pass effective legislation to correct matters.

The same is true when seeking to understand the most perplexing and challenging question of all time: "Why does man think and behave as he does?"

There's no shortage of diagnoses for why we do the things we do. Whole fields of scientific study are devoted to this question. Psychology tries to find out why *individuals* think and act the way they do. Sociology specializes in the dynamics of *group* behavior.

But whether you've got one man alone or a whole group together, almost all rational thinkers today are trying to come to grips with what's wrong with human behavior, what's wrong with our institutions and what's wrong with the world.

Man Seen as a Quirk of Evolution

One suggested answer to this problem was set forth by Arthur Koestler in a talk given at the fourteenth Nobel Symposium in Stockholm in 1969. He said, "There have been many diagnostic attempts made to explain man's abnormal behavior, from the Hebrew prophets to contemporary ethologists [scientists who study animal behavior]. But none of them started with the premise that man is an aberrant [abnormal] species, suffering from a *biological* malfunction."

He asked the question, "Is our aggressiveness towards our fellowmen socially acquired, or is it biologically built in, part of our genetic makeup and evolutionary heritage?"

Koestler pointed out that from the dawn of consciousness until the middle of the twentieth century, man had to live with the prospect of his death as an *individual*. But since the incredible forces of atomic power were unlocked three decades ago, man now has to live with the prospect of his death as a *species*.

Faced with this threat of self-extinction, one would have expected man's aggressiveness to have become tempered by reason.

"But," Koestler wrote, "appeals to reasonableness have always fallen on deaf ears, for the simple reason that man is not a reasonable being; nor are there any indications that he is in the process of becoming one.

"On the contrary, the evidence seems to indicate that at some point during the last explosive stages of the evolution of Homo sapiens, something has gone wrong. There is a flaw, some subtle engineering mistake built into our native equipment which would account for the paranoid streak running through our history."[1]

While one may not agree with all of Arthur Koestler's conclusions, the fact remains that he too has sought to give an explanation of man's deviant behavior and has concluded that we are stuck with a genetical quirk of nature for which there is no hope of remedy.

Are We Ready to Go "Beyond Freedom and Dignity"?

B. F. Skinner, the author of the controversial book *Beyond Freedom and Dignity* and the man who is thought by many to be the most influential living American psychologist, has his theories about the nature of man and how he functions best, yet they are diametrically opposed to Arthur Koestler's. Koestler felt man's *internal* mechanism was defective and the cause of his malfunction, while Skinner feels the entire problem of man's errant behavior lies in the *external* influences that affect him daily.

Skinner's solution to self-centered behavior is to place sufficient control over a man's external conduct and culture until he no longer has any inner freedom or free will. In this tightly controlled environmental state, men will refrain from polluting, overpopulating, rioting, making war, being selfish, greedy, unloving and arrogant—*not* because of the disastrous results of these, but because he has been conditioned to want what serves the group interests.

This may sound a little like the supposed utopia of George Orwell's *1984*, but this thinking is no joke to Dr. Skinner. Because of his many experiments with the controlled behavior of animals (and to a lesser degree with humans)

[1] *Los Angeles Times*, June 7, 1970.

there are many reputable thinkers who have bought all or parts of this philosophy of behavioral control.

Although Skinner is strongly opposed by most humanists, religionists, and Freudian psychoanalysts, he steadfastly maintains that behavior is determined completely from without, *not* from within. He insists that any idea of a soul or inner man is a superstition that originated, like belief in God, from man's inability to understand his world and his own actions.

Two Opposing Camps

If we were to follow B. F. Skinner's philosophy to its inevitable conclusions, we would be forced to admit that no man is responsible for his failure to behave correctly. He could simply plead that he was never "conditioned" to do the right thing. This would perhaps result in removing all sense of personal guilt from man but it would also create civil and moral anarchy.

What we're really dealing with here in these two men's representative views are two completely opposing views of man and of why he behaves the way he does. They both agree that man has a behavioral problem, but one view says it's an inner problem and the other says it's external. Nevertheless, in both camps *no* appreciable solution to the dilemma of how to start man behaving in an unselfish, loving, peaceful, generous, kind, patient and concerned manner has been discovered.

Whatever Happened to "Sin"?

For years most psychiatrists and psychologists have dismissed the old-fashioned religious idea of "sin" as irrelevant at best and downright dangerous at its worst. They've accused religion of producing guilt in its followers and have counseled patients to cast off their guilt feelings and do what they want.

But now, one of the sacred inner circle of psychiatry has defected from his previously held views of why man behaves improperly. Dr. Karl Menninger, world-renowned psychiatrist, says in his new book *Whatever Became of Sin?* that mental health and moral health are identical and the only way our suffering, struggling, anxious society can hope to prevent mental ills is by recognizing the reality of sin.

"If the concept of personal responsibility and answerability for ourselves and for others were to return to common acceptance," he says, "and man once again would feel guilt for sins and repent and establish a conscience that would act as a deterrent for further sin, then hope would return to the world."

Tragically, Menninger says he was prompted to write his new book after speaking to a group of young liberal theologians and hearing them express their frustration and inadequacy to deal with the problems of their parishioners or compete with the evil forces attracting their young people.

"It came to me," Menninger said, "that our clergymen have become shaken reeds, smoking lamps, earthen vessels . . . spent arrows."

His solution is to stand up and tell the world what its problem is. "Preach it! Tell it like it is. Say it from the pulpits. Cry it from the housetops!" says Dr. Menninger, psychiatrist, *not* evangelist!

A Viable Alternative

Dr. Karl Menninger has not traded in his psychiatrist's couch for a pulpit, and certainly many people will find things in Menninger's views that they can't go along with completely, but he has done something many ministers have failed to do in our times. He's offered a diagnosis for man's problem which is the same one the Bible has taught. Man is a sinner and needs reconciliation with God, with his fellowman, and with himself.

Sin Has Caused a Barrier
Between God and Man

I would like to assume that anyone reading this book has come with an open mind and wants to understand the Bible's diagnosis of the human dilemma.

From the first book of the Old Testament to the last book of the New Testament, there is one consistent theme and that is that God and man experience an alienation—a barrier, if you please—that man cannot remove and God says He already has.

Every error ever taught regarding man's relationship to God has historically begun with an improper understanding of sin and its devastating effect on man. There's no use talking about who Jesus was or why He came until we first understand the nature of the barrier that exists between man and his God.

If a couple came to me who were alienated from each other and had erected an insurmountable barrier between them, I could begin to help them resolve their conflict only when I got them to see how the barrier between them had come about.

The Universal Barrier—Its
Causes and Results

Picture if you will the first record we have of man's relationship with God. It was in a beautiful environment, and there was true fellowship and communication between God and man. Man was free to do as he wanted in all areas, but he was asked, as a free expression of love and obedience toward God, not to do one simple thing; don't eat of a certain tree in the garden.

Now that doesn't seem like much for God to ask. I often ask my children not to do certain things and I know that whether they obey me or not, to a certain degree, represents their love and trust of me. Because I love them I don't force their obedience, but I do desire it as a recognition that they respect my judgment above theirs—that what I've asked is only something for their best interest.

When Adam and Eve decided to take a bite of that forbidden fruit in defiance of God's command, their disobedience erected a barrier between themselves and God, and the fellowship they had been experiencing with their Creator was broken.

That story is recorded in the first book of the Bible, the Book of Genesis; in the other thirty-eight books of the Old Testament and the twenty-seven books of the New, we have the continuing story of what God has done to reconcile man to Himself by removing the barriers of separation.

The Fourfold Barrier

We can condense into four categories the blocks that we've erected one on top of the other in the barricade that separates man from God. This wall is so impenetrable that all the religions, philosophies, idealisms, good works, and ingenuity of men can't pull it down.

The compelling reason that made me write this book is to pass on the best news I have ever heard and that is that God Himself *has* torn down the barrier.

Let's look at the barrier first and then we can fully appreciate what it cost God to abolish it!

3 ∘ Barrier Number One: God's Holy Character

MANY OF US know someone whose life is so pure and exemplary, who has such a goodness about him, that we're just a little uncomfortable in his presence. Especially if we have any idea that he knows about some of *our* grosser habits. We don't feel that way around most of our friends, though, because we know *they* live just like we do.

What do you suppose it is that makes us feel such a difference, almost an invisible barrier between that person and ourselves?

It's his saintly character.

We know we don't measure up to his standard of conduct, and we feel he might be inclined to be judgmental of us. So we feel an alienation of sorts.

To a much greater degree, that's the problem between God and man. The character of God is so flawless and the nature of man is so full of flaws that the very holiness of God becomes a barrier to man.

Now, before you say to yourself, "Well, it's God's fault, then, that man is alienated from Him. God needs to lower His standards if He wants to reconcile with man," we need to take a look at what the character of God is really like.

We're talking about a standard of character that's way out of our league. Most of us can pick out ten people we know and measure ourselves up against their lives and not come off too badly. There's only one small problem when it comes to measuring ourselves against the character of God—it's perfect. There's no grading on the curve with God! If we want to be accepted by Him and brought back into reconciliation with Him, we must become as perfect as He is.

Impossible, you say?

Not so!

The story of how God went about making man acceptable again, after he lost his fellowship with God in the Garden of Eden, is the story we tell in this book. The first thing we must thoroughly understand is

The Character of God

These are the component parts of the character of God as He has revealed Himself in His Word and His history of dealing with men.

GOD IS

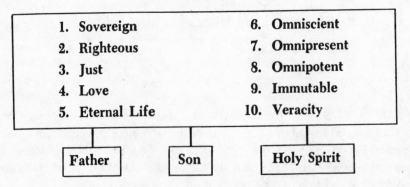

1. Sovereign	6. Omniscient
2. Righteous	7. Omnipresent
3. Just	8. Omnipotent
4. Love	9. Immutable
5. Eternal Life	10. Veracity

Father   Son   Holy Spirit

All these characteristics are found in the Father, Son, and Holy Spirit.

1. *Sovereign.* God has a will. By Himself and with assistance from no one He makes decisions and policies and sets up principles. He has the right to do as He pleases. He always acts in accordance with all the other attributes of His character, and He will never express one attribute at the expense of another.

   For example, a mother may tell a child he will receive a spanking if he plays with matches. But then, when the child plays with the matches and burns himself, she may forgo the spanking and, instead, hold him in her lap and love him. In that case she has expressed her love at the expense of her justice.

   Not so with God. He knows how to express His love without compromising His justice (Deuteronomy 4:39; 1 Chronicles 29:12; Psalms 47:2; 83:18; 93:1; 135:6; Daniel 4:35; Acts 17:24).

2. *Righteous.* God is absolute rightness and perfection. It's impossible for Him to do or cause anything that is wrong. He is the standard of all that is right. He is morally perfect without a shadow of deviousness (Ezra 9:15; Psalms 48:10; 119:137; 145:17; Jeremiah 23:6; 1 John 2:29).

3. *Just.* God is absolutely just. It's impossible for Him to do anything that's unfair either to Himself or to man. He executes perfect justice in accordance with His attribute of righteousness. All that is unrighteous must be judged and separated from a relationship with Him (see Romans 1:18; Deuteronomy 32:4; Isaiah 45:21).

4. *Love.* God is perfect, infinite love. It's given freely and without any consideration to the loveliness or merit of the object. It includes His enemies as well as His friends (Matthew 5:44; John 3:16; 16:27; Romans 5:8; Ephesians 2:4; 1 John 3:1; 4:9, 16).

5. *Eternal Life.* There has never been a time when God did not exist, and there never will be a time when He ceases to exist. He is the unmoved Mover, the ground of all being. His existence has no beginning and no end. He is the answer to the question men have grappled with since the dawn of history, "What is the power, the force, the Person who created everything that exists?" He is the self-existent fount of both physical and spiritual life (Exodus 15:18; Deuteronomy 32:40; 33:27; Job 36:26; Psalms 9:7; 135:13; Lamentations 5:19; 1 Timothy 1:17; Revelation 1:8).

6. *Omniscient.* God possesses all the knowledge there is to have. He always has and always will know everything that has happened, is happening, or will happen. Nothing ever takes Him by surprise (Job 26:6; 31:4; 34:21; Psalm 147:5; Proverbs 15:3; Hebrews 4:13; 1 John 3:20).

7. *Omnipresent.* God is infinitely and everywhere personally present, through all of time and space (Genesis 28:15; 31:3; Deuteronomy 4:39; 31:6; Joshua 1:9; Psalm 139:8; Proverbs 15:3; Isaiah 66:1; Jeremiah 23:24; Acts 17:27; Hebrews 13:5).

8. *Omnipotent.* God is all powerful, having more than enough strength to do the sum total of all things. A question often asked by skeptics is, "Could God make a rock so big that He couldn't lift it?" The answer is, "Yes, He could, but to do so would be to express the attribute of omnipotence at the expense of omniscience, and He would never do that." In other words, He would know better than to do it (Job 42:2; 26:7; Psalm 115:3; Matthew 19:26; Mark 14:36; Luke 1:37; Hebrews 3:6; Revelation 19:6).

9. *Immutable.* God never changes in His nature or attributes. Therefore we can believe that when He says He will do something, He'll do it. There are more than 7,000 things God has promised to do for those who belong to Him. He can be trusted to keep His word (Numbers 23:19; Psalm 33:11; Hebrews 1:12; 13:8).

10. *Veracity.* God is absolute truth. Anything in word or deed that doesn't conform to what He's revealed in His Word is *not* the truth. To know Him is to know reality (Deuteronomy 32:4; 2 Samuel 7:28; Psalms 33:4; 146:6; Isaiah 65:16).

The Infinite Gap

There's not a person who's ever lived who could stack his life up against the character of God that we've just looked at and then say, "That's just the kind of person I am."

No, the Bible makes a sober statement about what man is like: "The heart of man is deceitful about all things, and desperately wicked" and "All our righteousnesses are as filthy rags" (Jeremiah 17:9; Isaiah 64:6 KJV).

It isn't very flattering, is it? Isaiah isn't saying that it's just our *bad* habits and deeds that are offensive to God. It's what we would consider our *good* human acts that offend God as well. He describes them as *filthy* because by comparison with God's holy character they fall so far short.

I know this is hard to swallow, especially for people who have always prided themselves on the good things they do for God and their fellow-man. But listen to what the Apostle James says: "Whoever keeps the whole law and yet stumbles in *one* point, he has become guilty of all [breaking the whole law]" James 2:10).

The Apostle Paul says virtually the same thing: "Cursed is every one who does not abide by *all things* written in the book of the Law, to perform them" (Galatians 3:10b).

What is the Law?

The Law of God, which is summarized in the ten commandments and the Sermon on the Mount, expresses the overwhelming purity of God's holy character. All the laws that God has ever given to men tell us what we'd have to be like if we were to try to approach God on the basis of our own merit.

But according to James and Paul, we could keep every single point of the law and yet stumble in just *one small area* and that would be enough to disqualify us from enjoying fellowship with God for even a moment.

What a commentary on the magnitude of God's holiness.

The reason it's so difficult for us to accept the absoluteness of this concept is because of all the relativistic thinking that predominates our lives. We just can't fathom a holiness that won't bend "just a little" to accommodate our human weaknesses. And none of us can believe that those "little" sins we commit could be so offensive to God.

Statistics Don't Lie!

Of course, once we start trying to decide if one of our sins is a little or a big one, we've got a delicate job on our hands. What we call "little" might not seem that way to God at all.

But suppose that an average person sinned only one "little" sin a day from the age of five, until he was sixty-five years old. By that time he would have on his hands (or should I say "conscience") 21,915 sins.

That means that at least 21,915 times the person fell short of measuring up to the character of God which is the perfect standard that God measures man against.

But, you say, suppose for every sin that man committed he did five good deeds. Wouldn't that offset his sins and balance the scorecard?

Let me answer that with an illustration.

Sink or Swim

The State of Hawaii boasts of one of the most comfortable climates in the entire world. Say that you and I want to take a trip there, but neither of us can afford to go by commercial means. So we decide to swim.

Our plan is to meet at 6:00 A.M. one day and leave from Long Beach, California. Our families come down to the ocean to see us off, someone offers up a prayer for divine guidance (we'll need it!), another man fires a pistol with blanks, and away we go.

By midmorning we're exhausted, and by noon we begin to sink. There is no way we can make it. It is simply beyond human ability. Maybe you go fifteen miles, I go ten, but we still fall hopelessly short of the 2,400-mile distance.

Perhaps the greatest swimmer of our times, Olympic seven-Gold-Medalist Mark Spitz, could get in shape for marathon swimming and go two hundred or three hundred miles, but even he would fail, because the standard, in this case, is all the way to Hawaii.

People tend to compare themselves with each other and see who comes the closest to a given mark. But "closeness" doesn't count with God. Closeness counts in darts, horseshoes, and hand grenades, but not in holiness.

What I'm trying to get across is that there is no possible way to achieve right standing with God by our own human efforts. The standard is too tough! There has to be some divine intervention by which man has supernaturally credited to him God's own righteousness.

The Divine Dilemma

We've seen that a major barrier between God and man is the holy character of God. By man's failing to measure up to that he has incurred the just sentencing of God, the "death penalty" (Romans 1:18).

Our first parents, Adam and Eve, were told by God that there would be the awesome consequence of spiritual death immediately, and physical death eventually, if they disobeyed Him. When they flaunted God's command and broke His divine law, they incurred a DEBT OF SIN with God.

When any law is broken, a "debt to the law" is incurred and justice demands retribution of some kind. So it was that when man broke God's law, the *justice* of God (which is one of His character traits) had to demand full payment from man of the threatened penalty of death. This was tantamount to man's banishment from free access to the intimate presence of his loving Creator.

Now, here was God's dilemma (if there could be such a thing). Whereas the *justice* of God burned in wrath against man for outraging God's holiness, God's *love* equally yearned to find a way to justly forgive him and bring him back into fellowship with Himself.

But how could God express His *love*, His *righteousness*, and His *justice* toward man all at the same time and still require that the justly deserved DEBT OF SIN be paid? There was no greater challenge ever to confront God than how He could remain *just* and yet declare sinners forgiven and righteous. How could God satisfy the requirements of His absolute righteousness which could not allow anyone less than that into His presence?

Justice and love both had to be vindicated. But how could they be when the justifiable demand against rebellious man was to banish him forever from the presence of a holy God?

Can a judge whose son has broken the law do away with the law in order to free his son?

The answer to these questions is the most important information you will ever learn and that's what this book is all about.

4 ○ Barrier Number Two: A Debt of Sin

To UNDERSTAND THE nature of this DEBT OF SIN, we have to reach back into the practices of the criminal courts of the Roman Empire.

In the days of the great dominion of Rome, it was assumed by Caesar that every Roman citizen owed him perfect allegiance and obedience to his laws. Justice was swift to enforce this assumption, and if any citizen broke any law of the land, he soon found himself standing before the courts or Caesar himself.

Nailed to the Prison Door

If the man were found guilty of breaking the law and sentenced to prison, an itemized list was made of each infraction and its corresponding penalty. This list was, in essence, a record of how the man had failed to live up to the laws of Caesar. It was called a "Certificate of Debt."

When the man was taken to his prison cell, this Certificate of Debt was nailed to his cell door so that anyone passing by could tell that the man had been justly condemned and could also see the limitations of his punishment. For instance, if he were guilty of three crimes and the total time of imprisonment were twenty years, then it would be illegal to keep him there twenty-five years, and all could see that.

When the man had served his time and was released, he would be handed the yellowed, tattered Certificate of Debt with the words "Paid in Full" written across it. He could never again be imprisoned for those crimes as long as he could produce his canceled Certificate of Debt.

But until the sentence was paid, that Certificate of Debt stood between him and freedom. It continued to witness to the fact that the imprisoned man had failed to live according to the laws of Rome and was, in essence, an offense to Caesar.

Mankind's "Certificate of Debt"

As we saw in the last chapter, man owes God perfect obedience to His holy laws as summarized in the Ten Commandments and the Sermon on the Mount. By his failure to live up to this standard of perfection, man has become an offense to the very character of God, and the eternal court of justice has pronounced the death sentence upon man.

A Certificate of Debt was prepared against every person who would ever live, listing his failure to live in thought, word, and deed in accordance with the law of God. This death sentence has become a DEBT OF SIN which has to be paid, either by man or, if possible, someone qualified to take his place (Colossians 2:14).

And this DEBT OF SIN has become another piece of the barrier that separates God and man.

Now, the subject of "sin" isn't too popular. You can tell a person that he's failed to measure up to the holy character of God, and if he's even halfway honest he'll have to agree to that, because that doesn't make him sound too bad.

But somehow people don't like to be told that they're sinners, even though they know they commit "little" sins all the time. It's all part of the relativistic thinking that's become a part of our society and has helped us rationalize all our actions.

It's Not the Fault of the Environment

One look at the morning newspaper is all we need to confirm the mess that men have made of their lives. We don't have to have a degree in psychology, either, to figure out what makes them do what they do. All we have to do is look inside ourselves and we'll see all kinds of emotions, lusts, drives, and temptations that overpower us from time to time and cause us to do things we know are wrong.

Those actions are what God calls "sins," and they *aren't* caused by our environment. They are caused by our "reaction" to our environment, and that's an *internal* problem which man has.

Listen to how Jesus described man and his sinning: "That which comes *out* of the man is what defiles him. For from *inside*, out of the heart of men comes the evil thoughts and fornications, thefts, murders, adulteries, deeds of coveting, and wickedness, as well as deceit, lust, envy, slander, pride and foolishness. All these evil things proceed from *within* and defile man" (Mark 7:20-23).

These words of Jesus blow most of secular psychology right out of the ballpark because they show that man's wrong actions don't come primarily from *without*, they come from *within*. Misbehavior is not primarily the result of our environment; it's a problem of the heart.

The Sin Nature

In using the word "heart," Jesus is talking about that inner part of man's being which has in it the "sin nature," or a disposition toward rebellion against God.

Have you ever done something which was totally stupid and senseless and you said to yourself afterwards, "What on earth made me do that?" Your better judgment *knew* it was wrong, but you went ahead anyway. Well, it was your "sin nature" which prompted you to do it.

The Bible uses the terms "flesh" and "sin" (in the singular) to describe that force within us that is in total rebellion against God. This "nature" was not in man when God created him. It entered Adam and Eve the moment they disobeyed God and He withdrew His spiritual life from them.

Stranger Than Fiction

I saw a science-fiction movie once that made me think of how the sin nature works in us. Men from outer space landed on earth and captured a number of people. They implanted tiny electrodes in the back of their heads through which they could completely control the actions of their victims.

After the spaceships left the earth, their victims remained here and from all appearances seemed to be just like they'd always been. However, anytime the spacemen wanted them to kill someone or follow any other command, they simply transmitted this to their victims, who were forced to obey.

Our sin natures work a lot like that. Satan, either directly or through some subtle temptation that appeals to one of our senses, gets our sin nature to start rebelling against the known will of God for us (as expressed in His laws) and the first thing you know, we've given in to it and sinned.[1]

Do We Sin Because We're Sinners?

Sooner or later most of us get around to wondering, "Do I sin because I'm a sinner, or am I a sinner because I sin?"

Now that isn't a silly question like "Which came first, the chicken or the egg?" It's very important to know whether my sinning stems from a nature

---

[1] For a full explanation of how this principle of rebellion to the Law works, see the author's book, *Satan Is Alive and Well on Planet Earth*, chapter 12, "The Guilt Trip" (Grand Rapids: Zondervan Publishing House, 1972).

that I'm born with or whether it's just something I start doing because everyone else does it and it's "catching," like some disease.

The Bible teaches that when Adam and Eve disobeyed God in the Garden of Eden, they didn't just lose their sense of fellowship with God and become unlike Him in their character; they actually had something *added* to them—a sin nature. And that made them sinners. Since that awful day of infamy, all men have been born with that same sinful nature, and that is the source of our sins.

I know it's hard to believe that a tiny, innocent baby cooing sweetly in our arms has in it a sin nature that will soon begin committing sins, but that's what the Bible teaches from start to finish.

When Is Sin, Sin?

Is it a sin to be tempted?

The answer to that is No. If a girl in a short miniskirt stoops down to pick a flower and I'm standing right behind her, there's no way I can stop a tempting thought from passing through my mind. But if I continue to look and start to toy with the idea of getting into the sack with her, then it becomes a sin.

The sin is not the temptation; the sin is in not saying No to the temptation and in not handing the matter over to Christ for Him to deal with on the spot.

It's What's Inside That Counts

To me, the greatest thing that true Christianity has to offer the world in general and individuals specifically is that God will go to work on the *inside* and clean us up and make us brand-new people. He'll give a new motivation, new hope, and new power for living. Most religions simply offer an external program or code of ethics that seeks to change a man's outer behavior. That would be all right if that was where the problem is, but it's not. This sort of outer renovation usually blinds men to the real problem which is on the inside.

I heard once of a girl who was having terrible stomach pains and went to the doctor for some medicine. He gave her a bottle of green-colored liquid and told her to take two tablespoons internally every three hours. Well, she took one whiff of the medicine and nearly vomited. So she hit upon another plan. She decided to *rub* the two tablespoons *on* her stomach every three hours.

The medicine smelled as bad as it looked and strangely enough, although she was saturated with the medicine, she didn't get any better. Of course, when she went back to the doctor, he quickly convinced her that all the medicine in the world rubbed on the *outside* of her stomach wasn't going to get her well. The problem was on the *inside* and that's where the remedy needed to get.

Now, you know, of course, that was only a silly story, but I hope you got the point. The problem that men have is called "sin," and it's down *inside* us. No amount of "medicine" applied to the outside can ever soak through to where this problem of sin is.

Because men can't stand to admit that they have this *internal* weakness called sin, they've invented "religion" and "philosophy." Both these studies more or less admit that mankind has a problem, but generally speaking, they believe it's external in nature and can be solved through rituals or reason.

I personally believe it's another case of the old "ointment on the stomach" routine, and although for many a "patient" the operation appears to be successful, unfortunately the patient dies.

Summing It Up

In summarizing this barrier to God, man's DEBT OF SIN, we can see that man's problem is really twofold.

First is the fact that when Adam and Eve sinned, they lost their relationship and fellowship with God, and a nature of sin and rebellion against God was introduced into them and through them into all their descendants. This nature is the source of all of our "acts" of sin and is a major reason why we are unacceptable for a relationship with God.

Secondly, a DEBT OF SIN was incurred by them and all mankind which must be paid. The penalty for that debt is death, and it must be paid either by us or by someone qualified to take our place.

Adam Wasn't the Only Culprit

It makes a lot of people angry to hear that something which some far-off ancestor did implicates them with such grievous consequences. And I can sympathize with how they feel.

But in God's mind, Adam was representative man—the federal head of the human race. What he did judicially implicated all his fellowmen. If the President of the United States and our Congress declared war on some country today, I would be at war too, even though I might not personally be in favor of it. It makes no difference whether I voted for them or not. What they did would implicate me because they act as my federal head.

A story I have heard illustrates this very well.

In the days of slavery, old Mose grew weary of working out in the cotton fields and chopping wood day after day and year after year. One day Mose got to thinkin' about whose fault it was that his lot in life was so tough. After finding legitimate excuses for everyone he could think of, he finally decided it was all really Adam's fault for eating that apple in the first place. That drove man out of his lush, comfortable garden home and into the fields to toil by the sweat of his brow.

The more he thought about this, the angrier Mose got with Adam. As he swung his axe into each block of wood, he'd mutter, "Old Adam, old Adam," whacking a little harder with each utterance.

One day his master came along and overheard this tirade. He went up to Mose and asked him what he meant by "Old Adam."

"Well," said Mose, "if it hadn't been for Adam, I wouldn't be stuck out here in this woodpile, slavin' away all day long. I'd be in the house restin' and sippin' lemonade."

The master thought for a minute and then he said to Mose, "You come into the house, Mose. From now on you don't have to do any more hard work. You can lay around all day long, doing whatever you like. There is just one thing, though. See the little box here on the table? I don't want you to open it. Okay? Enjoy yourself now."

Well, for the next few weeks Mose couldn't get over his good fortune. He wandered around the house enjoying his leisure and lemonade.

Then he noticed the box the master had spoken about. At first all he did was look at it. But as the days went by, the temptation grew stronger and stronger to touch it. After a few days of only feeling it and carrying it around, it finally got too much for him and he couldn't imagine what harm there'd be in just a little peek into it.

As he cautiously opened one corner of it, a white piece of paper inside caught his eye. His curiosity wouldn't be satisfied until he'd taken out the paper and read it. This is what it said:

"Mose, you old rascal. I don't ever want you blaming Adam anymore. If you'd been there in the garden, you'd have done the same thing Adam did. Now, you hightail it back out to the woodpile and get to chopping again."

The point of the story is evident. If we'd been in Adam's shoes, the chances are very good we'd have done the same thing he did. God in His great foreknowledge (His omniscience) could see that all men would, indeed, ratify Adam's rebellion in their own behavior.

If God had left it there and never done anything to reconcile man to Himself, then He might be considered unfair.

But the good news of the "Gospel" is that God so loved the world that, at infinite cost to Himself, He provided a means of removing man's DEBT OF SIN and of dealing with the nature of sin in men.

5 ○ Barrier Number Three: Slavery to Satan

UP TO NOW we have dealt with two of the basic problems that help form the barrier that exists between God and man. We've seen how man's sin was an affront to the holy CHARACTER OF GOD, and how his failure to keep God's laws resulted in a DEBT OF SIN.

Now let's take a look at the third barrier separating God and man, the fact that man is in SLAVERY TO SATAN.

I know this assertion will raise bristles with many people because Jesus got the same reaction when He told some of *His* generation that Satan was their father.

The Truth is Often Unpopular

During the early part of His ministry Jesus got into frequent hassles with some of His fellow Jews. On one occasion He was talking with a group of militant Jews who maintained that because they were born of the stock of Abraham, they were "in," and that they had it made with God as their Father.

Jesus told them that if God were their Father, they would have loved Him (Jesus) for He had come from the Father and had in fact been sent by Him to the earth.

"Why don't you understand what I'm saying?" He queried.

And then answering His own question, He said with an air of authority, "It is because you cannot hear My word. You are of your *father* the devil, and you want to do the desires of your father. He was a murderer from the beginning, and does not stand in the truth, because there is no truth in him. Whenever he speaks a lie, he speaks from his own nature; for he is a liar, and the father of lies" (John 8:43, 44).

Needless to say, the reaction Jesus got to this scathing indictment wasn't too favorable. In fact, after calling Him the two dirtiest names they could think of—*Samaritan* (a hated half-breed Jew) and *demon-possessed*—they eventually tried to stone Him, but He slipped out of their hands.

The Two "Fatherhoods" of Mankind

What were the grounds Jesus had for telling His fellow Jews that they were children of Satan?

There were two prime factors.

First, the Jews prided themselves on being children of Abraham by physical descent and therefore children of God as a result. Jesus didn't dispute their claim to physical relationship with Abraham, but He emphatically denied that it made them children of *God*. He told them that unless they had the same faith in Him, as Messiah, which Abraham had had, then Abraham's God wasn't their father, Satan was.

The second point Jesus sought to hammer home was that there are only *two* fatherhoods of mankind, the fatherhood of God and the fatherhood of Satan. So, if they weren't God's children, then they must have been Satan's.

That statement made the Jews furious, and it still affects people that way today. But there's a reason why there's such a violent reaction to this truth. It's because one of Satan's chief tactics down through the history of mankind has been to blur and confuse people on this very issue. It makes it much easier for him to maintain control over his "children" if they don't fully comprehend who their father really is.

How successful Satan has been in this area is evidenced by the number of churches of all religions, including Christianity, which have as a basic tenet of their religion that God is the father of all mankind and therefore we're all brothers.

As admirable as it is to want to practice brotherhood, and without my impugning the need for it, the truth of the matter is that God is the *creator* of all men, but only the *father* of those who have His *spiritual life* in them.

When man was created, he *did* have God's spiritual life resident within him, but when he sinned and turned his back on God, he lost that spiritual life. Now every man is born without it, and if he wants God to be his father for now and through eternity, he must have God's life put back into him sometime before he dies physically on this earth.

A Powerful Adversary

How did Satan get to be the powerful authority he seems to be? That he does have power, there is no doubt. History is strewn with the wreckage he's made of individuals and nations.

A classic example of the evil that just one man could do when brought under Satan's *direct* control is the story of Adolf Hitler. There is ample evidence that he was either demon-possessed or possessed by Satan himself.

But damage as great as that is caused every day in this world by a system of thinking and acting which is subtly controlled by Satan to exclude the need for God. The toll in human suffering, physically, emotionally, and spiritually from a lack of a true relationship with God, is incalculable. Broken homes, suicides, murders, rape, greed, hate—all these and more are mute testimony to the fact that this world couldn't possibly be the way God had originally planned for it to be.

What went wrong?

Adam's Power-of-Attorney

In the Book of Genesis we're told that God put man on earth and entrusted him with authority over himself and all of God's creation. Man was told by God to be fruitful and multiply and replenish, subdue and have dominion over every living thing that moved on the earth (Genesis 1:28).

In other words, God put man in charge of this planet and its inhabitants. And aside from the one restraint that God gave them, not to eat of the Tree of the Knowledge of Good and Evil, no other stipulations were laid down as to how they were to govern God's creation.

I'm sure that's because Adam was a loved and trusted friend of God. And on this basis God gave him the power-of-attorney to govern this planet in God's stead.

A Wolf in Snake's Clothing!

But there was another personage already there in the garden with Adam when God put him in charge. That person was one who had already made known to God and all His angelic hosts that he wanted to usurp the place of Number One from his creator God.[1]

The name of this being was Lucifer (later known as Satan or the Devil). He was power mad! More than anything else he wanted to control what God had created.

---

[1] For a fuller understanding of Satan, his origin, and his fall, read the author's book, *Satan Is Alive and Well on Planet Earth* (Grand Rapids: Zondervan Publishing House, 1972).

So there he was in the garden. And through his subtle lies and innuendos about God, he convinced Adam and Eve that God was holding out on them by not wanting them to eat of that tree. He told them that God didn't want to share His power with them and that since that tree would make them as wise as God, that's why He had forbidden them to eat of it.

We look back at that scene now and see the paradise they were enjoying. Then we look at the mess the world is in today and we say, "Wow! They didn't know how good they had it. How on earth could they have blown it so badly and felt that God was holding out on them when they'd already been given such fantastic power and authority?"

Mankind's Benedict Arnold!

If only Adam and Eve had realized the devastating consequences that would result from their disobedience to God's one prohibition.

Not only did they lose their spiritual life and ability to have free access into the presence and fellowship of God, but in capitulating to Satan's temptation they unwittingly turned over their God-given power and authority to Satan's control. He became the legal controller of all men who would ever be born from Adam's seed. He also took control of the planet itself and all creation on it, animal and vegetable.

"But," you may be saying, "how could God permit such a terrible thing to happen? Couldn't He have taken the power away from Satan once he'd gotten it from Adam?"

No, He couldn't. You see, God is so just in His nature that He couldn't even be unjust to Satan. A legal transference of property and power had taken place, and a legal means of reversing it would have to be found.

The Slave Market of Sin

This sellout of Adam to Satan is how the world got into the mess it's in today. With Satan as the legal ruler of this planet, it became one great big slave market and everyone born into it of Adam's seed is born a slave of Satan.

This was clearly taught by Jesus and His disciples.

The Apostle John wrote, "The whole world lies in the power of the evil one" (1 John 5:19b). The word "world" in that verse is the Greek word, *cosmos*, which means an orderly system. This is what is meant when we say that Satan calls the shots over this present world system.

The great defender of the faith, Paul, called Satan "the god of this world" and said he had "blinded the minds of the unbelieving, that they might not see the light of the gospel of the glory of Christ, who is the image of God" (2 Corinthians 4:4).

In another place in the New Testament Paul spoke of Satan as "the prince of the power of the air" and called him "the spirit that is now working in the sons of disobedience" (Ephesians 2:1-4).

When the Apostle Paul stood on trial before the great King Agrippa to defend the message he had been preaching, he clearly declared man's need of being set free from SLAVERY TO SATAN when he said, "[Jesus sent me] to open their eyes so that they may turn from darkness to light and *from the dominion of Satan to God*" (Act 26:18).

Jesus' Temptations

The most arrogant display of Satan's authority is seen in his attempt to get Jesus to sin.

You see, Jesus is the only person ever born into this world who was not born under Satan's dominion. The reason is that Jesus did not have a human father, and therefore the curse of SLAVERY TO SATAN which was passed from Adam to all his descendants didn't affect Him.

Jesus was called the "second Adam" because He was the second man who was brought into this world perfect (1 Corinthians 15:4-5). He could have sinned, just as the first Adam had done, but had He done so He would have been brought under Satan's dominion, just as Adam had been.

Because He was the only person ever born into this world who wasn't a slave to Satan, He became the special object of Satan's hatred. He sought continually either to kill Jesus before He could go to the cross, or to get Him to sin so He would be brought under Satan's authority as all unredeemed sinners are.

That's why on one occasion when Satan was tempting Jesus, he showed Him all the kingdoms of the world and their glory and then he said to Him, "I will give you all this domain and its glory; for it has been handed over to me, and I can give it to whomever I wish. Therefore if You worship before me, it shall all be Yours" (Luke 4:6, 7).

No Crown Without a Cross

Jesus didn't dispute Satan's claim for a moment. He knew that the world and mankind had been legally transferred by Adam into Satan's control. He also knew He could take it back from Satan anytime He chose to. But had He done so, it would have meant bypassing the cross because it was there God intended that the ransom price be paid to free enslaved mankind and restore the rightful rulership of the world to God.

For Him to have chosen the easy way and taken the crown of dominion from Satan when He offered it would have been sin. And the minute He had sinned, He, too, would have entered into the slave market of sin and come under Satan's control.

Consequently there would have been no "free man" in the world who could pay the ransom price and set men free from their bondage to Satan. All would have been in the slave market together, and none could have qualified to buy anyone else's freedom.

Satan Is "Some" Father!

At the beginning of this chapter we talked about a conversation Jesus had with some unbelieving Jews and how He had told them that Satan was their father.

When you think of someone as being a "father," you usually picture some kindly, concerned, and tenderhearted person who has his children's best interests at heart.

But, though Satan knows how to masquerade as an "angel of light," his heart is black and evil, full of hate and bitter revenge against God and men. This is no normal father. This is an evil, sadistic creature who has imprisoned his children in a slave camp, caring nothing for them as human beings. He uses them for his purposes and then throws them on a junk heap when he's finished with them.

His only worry is that someday they might find out that a ransom has been paid for their freedom and there is no longer any reason for them to be held in bondage.

But until they find this out, man's SLAVERY TO SATAN is a barrier to a restored fellowship with God, the heavenly Father.

6 ○ Barrier Number Four: Spiritual Death

A FRIEND TOLD me a story once that's a pretty clear illustration of what it's like to be spiritually dead.

He said his son had gotten an electric train for Christmas and together the two of them got it all set up. They spent hours playing with it, and the train raced up and down the tracks through the tunnels and in and out of the depot.

One day when he came home from work, his son met him at the door and was really upset: the train wouldn't run. Together they took the electrical mechanisms apart, but they all checked out fine. They checked the connections between all the cars, and they were all in place.

After hours of trying to get the train running it was just no use. There was no power getting through to the train. For all practical purposes it was dead.

Then, by chance, my friend spotted a small metal crossing sign that had fallen across the tracks and was obscured by some buildings along the rails. As he picked up the crossing sign from the tracks, the train began to roll.

What had happened was that the metal on the tracks had caused a short circuit. All the power of the City of Los Angeles was kept from entering that train because of a tiny piece of seemingly insignificant metal.

Mankind Is "Short-Circuited"

As we've looked at in previous chapters, there was a time when God and man experienced an unbroken fellowship and things were fine between them. Then something happened that short-circuited the relationship between God and man. Something fell across mankind's "tracks," and all the divine power and spiritual life of the omnipotent Creator God were cut off from His special creation, man, and he became dead spiritually.

That "something" was sin!

It's not as though this awful consequence took Adam and Eve by surprise. God had told them that if they ate of the Tree of the Knowledge of Good and Evil, they would die (Genesis 2:17). But since they had never seen anything die before this, they didn't fully comprehend what "death" meant.

The Three Faces of Death

Adam and Eve had no idea how utterly disastrous it would be to be *spiritually dead* in relationship to their wonderful Creator. Likewise they didn't comprehend the horror of eventually being cut off from each other and their loved ones by *physical death*. And finally, they failed completely to realize the implications of *eternal death*, that condition of separation from God for eternity.

Although all three aspects of this death sentence imposed upon them went into effect immediately, only one was instantly evident to man himself. He knew that something irreparable had happened to his rapport with God. That "something" was SPIRITUAL DEATH.

Adam and Eve immediately felt an alienation from God and even went so far as to hide themselves from Him. But even though God went looking for them and, by His gracious words and actions to them, reassured them of His love, He nevertheless had to execute the sentence of death and separate man from fellowship with Himself. Hence Adam was banished from the garden and free access to God.

The "Sin" Infection

Sin and death had entered the human race through one man's disobedience (Romans 5:12). When Adam sinned he *became* a sinner, and that one sin infected the whole human race, still in his loins, with the sickness of sin and death. Since then, all men are *born* sinners with the sentence of death upon them.

A Look at Man from God's Viewpoint

There's no way even to begin to understand how that event in the garden affected mankind down through the centuries and even today, until we get a look at God as He really is, and ourselves as He sees us.

In creating man, God anticipated every physical and mental faculty that man would ever need to relate to the beautiful material world into which He placed him.

However, God also equipped man to function in relation to the nonphysical or spiritual realm which was also a reality. He did so by giving man a soul and spirit.

The following diagram gives you a picture of how the three parts of man's make-up work together. When seeking to express divine truth, no human illustration is perfect, but this diagram suffices to give us the framework we need for looking at the interwoven and sometimes separate functions of the body, soul, and spirit of man.

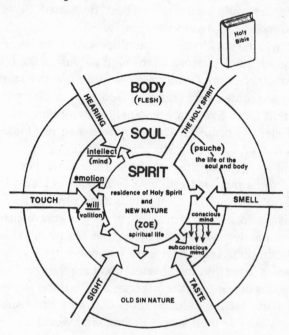

BORN AGAIN BELIEVER

The Body

The body is the *material* part of man, that part which enables him to function in and relate to the physical world around him. The body contains physical life. This is an illusive, indefinable force which keeps the heart beating. Despite the various efforts to create human life in test tubes, no one has succeeded in creating and sustaining the kind of life necessary to cause a human body to function as designed.

When the body dies, it returns to the dust it was taken from. But that's not the end of it. Eventually it will be brought back together again and have an eternal existence, either with God or separated from Him.

The Soul

The soul is the immaterial part of man. When God formed man, He breathed into man's nostrils the breath of *lives* and man became a living soul (Genesis 2:7). The Hebrew word translated "life" in most English versions of the Bible should actually have been translated "lives" because it's a plural word in the original Hebrew Bible.

I believe it was no accident that the Bible says God breathed into man "lives" instead of "life," because all through the rest of the Bible two kinds of life are spoken of in relation to man—soulish life and spiritual life.

The soulish life contains the image of God in man. Being in the image of God means that man, like God, has intellect, emotion, moral reasoning, volition, and eternity of being. It does not refer to us "looking" like God physically, however, or having His *spiritual* life in us.

Physical life and soulish life are one and the same. For, if you take the physical life from a man, his soul also departs from his body. And if you take the soul out of a man, it means he is dead physically. Even though a person may live for many years in a state of deep unconsciousness, it doesn't mean his soul has left him. It's simply that his physical body will not respond to the impulses sent to it from his soul.

The five senses located in the physical body are the windows of the soul. They're the means of bringing the information about the physical world into the mind of man. But their limitation is that they can't substantiate any reality which is outside their scope, the material world.

For instance, the rationality that much of the world has is that if it can't be seen, tasted, touched, smelled, or heard, it isn't real. This approach to life is usually called "materialistic" or "empiricist." The problem with this philosophy is that it shuts out a whole realm of existence that's outside the world of the senses.

This is the realm of the spirit.

The Spirit

When God breathed into man the breath of lives, not only did He give him soulish or physical life, but He also gave man God's own kind of life—spiritual life.

You see, God is spirit and in order to worship Him the way He has ordained or fellowship with Him on a personal basis, we must also be spiritual creatures (John 4:24).

That's why God created man with a human spirit. It was to be the part of man to contain God's life, spiritual life. Adam and Eve had soulish life *and* spiritual life. With their soulish life they comprehended the beauty of their physical surroundings and each other. With their spiritual life they experienced communication with God who was present in the garden as a spirit.

You might say that man was originally created with *six* senses instead of five. Five of them plugged him in to the physical world and operated on *soulish* power, but the sixth sense, which is called "faith," operated on *spiritual* power. It enabled him to establish reality in the spiritual realm and experience uninhibited communication with God.

The Tragedy of the Fall

Aside from all the other disastrous consequences of man's disobedience to God, perhaps the worst is that God withdrew from man His spiritual life and left man with a dead spirit, a spiritual vacuum if you please. No longer did man have the internal spiritual equipment to experience a relationship with God who is a spirit. Within a few generations of Adam, men had so lost their concept of the one true God that they wandered hopelessly in spiritual darkness.

You can see the dilemma that arose between God and man. Whereas God had made man in such a way that it would be possible for communication with him through his spirit, now that man no longer had spiritual life, God had to communicate with men in ways that their five senses could comprehend.

That's the whole story of the Bible: God seeking ways to make fallen man aware of His existence, His love, and His judgment against sin. But always God had to take the initiative and reach out to man in ways that he could understand by sight, hearing, taste, touch, or smell.

The Barrier Is Complete

So here we have the complete picture of the universal barrier which separates man from God. Man can't tear the barrier down and he can't climb over it by his own efforts. In fact, he can't even climb over with God's help. The barrier must come down, and God alone can do that.

You will meet people every day who say they have no need for God and don't feel any of the barriers we've looked at. But the crucial issue is that

God says they have a need whether they are aware of that need or not. And His Word shows very clearly what the need is.

I may visit the doctor, and he could say to me, "Hal, you have a severe illness which proper treatment can completely cure."

"But, Doc, I don't *feel* sick."

"No matter. Tests show conclusively that you're ill."

Since he's an expert in his field, I really have little choice but to take his word for it. After all, effective cure depends completely on accurate diagnosis. But after the diagnosis is made, I've got to submit myself to the cure.

God says we have a problem. That problem is called sin. It's a fatal disease with only one known cure. Let's take a look now at what that remedy is.

7 ∘ Why God Had to Become a Man

HAVE YOU EVER stopped to wonder what the main factor is that divides true Christianity and most other religions?

Christians accept the same God of the Old Testament that Jews and several other religions do. But where they part company with other creeds is in the Christian teaching that the God of the Old Testament actually put on a human body for thirty-three years, and without ceasing to be God, He lived on this earth as a man.

To many religions, and Jews especially, this concept is blasphemy. But in true Christianity, this conviction that God took on human form is so central that unless it's true, there is no adequate explanation as to how the barriers that separate God and man could be torn down.

Furthermore, Christians believe that the Old Testament gave ample testimony to the fact that God would one day take on humanity in His plan to redeem mankind and bring about a reconciliation between God and man.

But before we look at who this God-man might be, let's see why it would have been necessary for God to have become a man.

The Communication Problem

We're very conscious of this problem in our modern world. Marriage counselors tell us that the failure to communicate is one of the main factors in couples not being able to reconcile differences. Parents and children grow apart because of this problem.

But as bad as these communication failures are, the worst breakdown that man has in this area is between himself and God.

We've already seen why this is. It's because God is a spirit and can be understood in the deepest sense only by one who also has spiritual life. Men are born with soulish life which gives them a world-consciousness, but they lack spiritual life whereby they can communicate with God.

Therefore, since the fall of man, God has had to take into account man's inability to comprehend spiritual truth by spiritual means. He has been forced to reveal Himself to men in ways that they could understand with their soulish life and their five senses, but it was always with a view to bringing them to a point of submission to Him.

His problem was similar to that of the naturalist who had a special concern for a certain ant hill which he had been observing for months. Each day the man spent hours watching the intricate maneuverings of these ants and had come to the place where he felt a very special affinity for them.

One day the naturalist saw a huge bulldozer in the distance and immediately realized that this ant hill lay right in the path of the construction of a new road.

The man panicked. He desperately searched his mind for a way to remove the ants. He scooped up handfuls of them, but they only bit him. He thought of building a fence around the ant pile, but realized the bulldozer would only tear it down.

In his frenzied mind he thought to himself, "If only I could speak to them and tell them about the danger ahead of them. If only I could make them see that I'm their friend and only want to save them from destruction."

But despite his great concern, he could think of no way to communicate to them in a way they would understand. To be able to do that, he'd have to become an ant himself, and yet retain the nature of a man so he could continue to clearly assess the problem and make it known to the ants.

God's "Ant Hill," the World!

Down through the long history of the human race, God has spared no effort to reveal Himself to man in terms of natural and material phenomena which man could comprehend.

David, the Psalmist, tells us that the whole world is God's "kindergarten" to teach us the ABCs of the reality of God and the spiritual realm.

> The heavens are telling of the glory of God; and the earth is declaring the work of His hands.
> Day to Day pours forth speech, and night to night reveals knowledge.
> There is no speech, nor are there words; their voice is not heard. Their *sound* has gone out through all the earth, and their utterances to the end of the world (Psalm 19:1-4a).

This is one of the most profound things ever said in the Bible. It tells us that the great majesty and marvel of the universe with its heavenly bodies, and the beauty, the wonder, the incredible balance of design and function of all the creation of God on the earth, are the actual *verbalization* of the fact that God's hands created them.

The fact that day follows day with such certainty and night after night appears like clockwork is the same as God actually *speaking* to man about His reality and trustworthiness.

David said, "They aren't *actually* speaking nor can you listen intently and hear any words as such, but nevertheless, their *sound* has gone out to all the earth."

Why the Sound?

What's the purpose of this grandiose demonstration in nature of the reality of God?

The Apostle Paul in the New Testament gives us the answer to that question.

"That which is known about God is evident within [men]; for God made it evident to them. For since the creation of the world His invisible attributes, His eternal power and divine nature, have been clearly seen, being understood through what has been made, *so that they are without excuse*" (Romans 1:19, 20).

Paul says the true nature of the invisible God has been openly revealed by His material creation so that the soulish intellects of men could put two and two together and come up with the realization that God exists.

But not only to recognize that He exists. They also are without excuse for not knowing that He will eventually judge ungodliness and the suppression of the truth that He is the sovereign authority over men (Romans 1:18).

Nature's Lesson Ignored

It's fairly obvious to a fair-minded thinker that most people down through the history of mankind did not conclude from nature's lesson that there was only one God and He was knowable and worthy of their praise.

There's no question but what all civilizations had a concept of some supreme force that wasn't completely controllable by them. And there is abundant evidence in archaeology that men had gods and worshiped them.

But the Apostle Paul tells us what the problem was with this. He says that even though men knew from nature that there was a creator God, they didn't honor Him in their own lives as sovereign, but went about their daily lives as though He had no say-so over them.

Then they would sit around and make futile speculations about what He looked like, where He lived, was He married, did He have children, was He kind and benevolent or harsh and cruel, and eventually they ended up making some kind of an image or statue of one of God's creations and worshiped it (see Romans 1:21-25).

You see, since they were men who were spiritually dead, they could not have understood fully what God was like, but they had enough light given to them through nature to reach out to the one true God and submit themselves to Him. Had they done so, He would have imparted spiritual life to their dead human spirits and they could have become children of God. Acts 17:26, 27 says that if men had even so much as "blindly groped" for God, they would have found Him.

Into the Arena of Humanity

As powerful as God's nature lesson has been, it was never intended as God's ultimate revelation of Himself to man. The only way for a spirit God to really be able to do and say what He wanted to, was to actually leave His eternal residence and enter the arena of humanity.

Even then He wouldn't be able to communicate with man who is strictly a physical creature unless He, God, also took on physical form and life. It would also be necessary for Him to retain His divine nature and intellect, or He wouldn't be able to accomplish what He'd come to earth to say and do.

The Barriers Have to Go!

But what was the *main* necessity for God to come to earth?

It was to tear down the barriers that man had erected between himself and God. No one but God Himself was capable of doing that job. Man couldn't eradicate the obstacles that separated him from God because of the consequences of sin which crippled him spiritually and made him unacceptable to God.

Some have felt that God could have stayed in heaven but directed men as to how to remove the barriers. This is the "God helps those who help themselves" philosophy. Unfortunately none of man's efforts alone or with God will work because in neither case is any provision made to remove sin which caused the barrier in the first place. Also it would leave man's sentence of death unpaid, and the justice of God would be compromised.

No! For a holy God who had an unquenchable love for man and a divine necessity to vindicate His justice, the only solution was to leave the glory of heaven, take on flesh and blood, and enter the human race. Since He is the supreme sovereign of the universe, this in no way tainted His deity. God could take on any form He wanted to, and it wouldn't have affected who He intrinsically was.

God's Provision for Forgiveness

You'll remember that in the account of the temptation of Adam and Eve, after they had sewn fig leaves together in an effort to hide their shame of transgression from God, God rejected that clothing and took the skins of some animals and clothed them. If you think about it for a minute, you'll realize that the death of those animals is the first record of any creature dying physically.

The animals themselves had done nothing worthy of death, but in their dying a pattern was established by God—an innocent substitute of God's choosing had to shed its blood and thereby provide a *temporary* forgiveness and covering for man's sin.

Several hundred years later when God's law was given through Moses, He instructed him to write, "Without the shedding of blood there is no remission of sin" (Hebrews 9:22 paraphrased).

That was the basis of the whole Jewish system of animal sacrifice—an innocent substitute could bear the sin and death penalty due man if the sacrifice were offered to God in accordance with His ordained system of sacrifice and with expectant faith in His forgiveness.

But Why Become a Man?

The animal sacrifice system couldn't go on forever because it provided only a temporary covering of man's sin from God's eyes.

The New Testament writer of the letter to the Hebrews said, "It is impossible for the blood of bulls and goats to take away sins." And then he added, "Every priest stands daily ministering and offering time after time the same sacrifices, which can never take away sins" (Hebrews 10:4,11). You see, animal sacrifice never took sins away; it merely covered them temporarily from God's judgment.

The whole picture God wanted people to understand from the animal sacrifices was that God's justice demanded that someone had to take the penalty of death which was due man because of his sin. The fact that God would not exact the penalty from man and would allow a substitute to die in man's place was designed to show man the depths of God's love.

But God never planned that His forgiveness would go on being temporary and conditional. From the moment of man's fall in the garden God had in mind a plan that would provide a *permanent* forgiveness of sin and removal of the barriers separating God and man.

God's Plan for a Man

Since it was human beings who had sinned and incurred the penalty of spiritual and physical death, another true human being would have to be God's final and permanent substitute for man. It would have to be someone of God's choosing who could *qualify* to step in as a substitute and take the compounded wrath of God against *all sin* that would ever be committed. The covering for sin provided by the animal sacrifices never included *all* the sins of a man. And, of course, it made no provision for men who didn't participate in this ritual.

But in order for a man to qualify to take man's place of judgment and be his sin-bearer, there are five things that would have to be true of him:

1. He would have to be a true human being, born into this world the same way other men are. He would have to live and die in the same manner all humans do.

2. He would have to be without any personal sin of his own for which he would already be under God's condemnation. He would have to be born without a sin nature just as Adam was created without one. At no time in his life could he have ever committed even one sin, and yet, he would have to be subjected to real temptations just as Adam had been.

3. He would have to live under God's law and keep it perfectly. He would have to be absolutely righteous in his nature and in all actions so that God's holy character would be satisfied that here was a man who never broke God's law even once in motive, act, or word.

4. He would have to have full knowledge of what he was doing.

5. He would have to be willing to take mankind's guilt and be judged and put to death for that guilt in the place of and for the sake of mankind.

What a Man!

The whole reason for the writing of this book is to set forth the fact that just such a person came into the world, according to promise, nineteen hundred years ago. He perfectly fulfilled each qualification to be the savior of men.

That man was called Jesus Christ.

8 ○ The Man
That God Became

ONE OF THE things that has made the Old Testament scriptures so enduring and always relevant is its prophetic emphasis. Not only was history accurately recorded for us, but hundreds of predictions of future things were made.

Many of these had to do with the appearance in Israel of a great personage who was prophesied to bring a kingdom of peace on earth and rule it with righteousness and justice.

This man was referred to as the "Messiah."

There were perhaps hundreds of zealous reformers who appeared on the pages of Israel's history seeking to fulfill the messianic commission of establishing a kingdom of God on earth. Most of them passed from the scene with little notice or remembrance.

But one man didn't!

It can be clearly demonstrated that nearly three hundred of the prophecies about the Messiah actually found a literal fulfillment in the birth, life, and death of Jesus of Nazareth. The chances of this happening by mere coincidence are mathematically of such magnitude that it's impossible to calculate.

The Witness of Prophecy

As you put together the pieces of prophecy in the Old Testament concerning the Messiah, it becomes clear that in some way this promised Messiah would be both God and man. This is evident from the number of times the prophecies referred to Him as a "child" or "son" who would be born. Then, often in the same context it spoke of Him as being eternal and God.

Let's look at some of these well-known Old Testament prophecies.

Isaiah 7:14 says, "Therefore the Lord Himself will give you a sign: Behold, a virgin will be with child and bear a son, and she will call His name Immanuel." The word "Immanuel" in Hebrew means "God with us."

I'm aware of the efforts of some Bible interpreters to dismiss this as a prophecy that found its fulfillment in Jesus' virgin birth. They point out that the Hebrew word *alma* used for "virgin" can also be translated "young woman."

It's true that it can be. But the biggest textual argument *against* translating it as "young woman" is that at least 160 years before Jesus was born, a translation of the Old Testament was made into Greek and the brilliant Hebrew scholars who made that translation, which is called "The Septuagint," translated the Hebrew word *alma* into the Greek word *parthenos*. And that Greek word can *only* mean "virgin."

So, many years before Jesus was born, it was clearly understood that a virgin would bear a son whose name would mean "God is with us."

In another part of the Book of Isaiah, he writes, "For a child will be born to us, a son will be given to us; and the government will rest on His shoulders; and His name will be Wonderful Counselor, *Mighty God, Eternal Father*, Prince of Peace.

"There will be no end to the increase of His government or of peace, on the throne of David and over his kingdom, to establish it and to uphold it with justice and righteousness from then on and *forevermore*" (Isaiah 9:6, 7).

Isaiah spoke here of one who would sit on the throne of David forever. He called him the "Mighty God" and the "Eternal Father."

In using these names, there can be no question but that he was speaking of the God of Israel who would one day assume a human body and allow Himself to be brought into this world like any other man, through the means of a human birth.

Micah the prophet, seven hundred years before Jesus was born, prophesied that the Messiah would be born in a small town in Judah called Bethlehem. He said of this town, "From you One will go forth for Me to be ruler in Israel. His goings forth are from long ago, from the *days of eternity*" (Micah 5:2).

There's no doubt that this prophecy was understood to be concerning the promised Messiah, because at the time of Jesus' birth when the wisemen came from the East with their gifts, they asked the religious leaders of the nation of Israel where their Messiah-king would be born. The Jewish priests consulted their scriptures, found the prophecy of Micah 5:2, and then sent the wisemen down to Bethlehem.

If the priests had only been "wise men," they would have gone to worship their Messiah too!

The Son of God

Any honest investigation of these and the hundreds of other prophecies concerning Messiah will bring you to the conclusion that no one but Jesus of Nazareth could have fulfilled them.

Jesus was called by many names. The name "Christ" was the Greek word for "Messiah." "Jesus of Nazareth" denoted His hometown. He loved to be called "the Son of Man" because it reminded Him of His kinship with humanity whom He loved so dearly.

But I suspect His favorite name was "the Son of God" because it let the whole world know who His Father was.

The angel in announcing the conception of Jesus to Mary said, "And behold, you will conceive in your womb, and bear a son and you shall name Him Jesus. . . . The Holy Spirit will come upon you and the power of the Most High will overshadow you; and for that reason *the holy offspring* shall be called the Son of God" (Luke 1:31, 35).

The "Most High" who overpowered Mary was none other than God Himself. In some miraculous way, the ovum in the womb of Mary was impregnated with life apart from a human father. God simply put the spark of life into it, and one by one the cells began to divide and multiply and in nine months the baby Jesus was born.

God was the father of the *humanity* of Jesus. The deity of Jesus is not the focus of the title "Son of God," for His divinity needed no father. He's called the Son of God because in His *human* nature He *is* the Son of God. It's so simple it's profound.

Hypostatic Union

This big phrase, "hypostatic union," is a theological term which describes the twofold nature of Jesus. Here's what it means: In the one Person of Jesus Christ there were two natures—*undiminished deity* and *true humanity*. These two natures are never confused in essence or function, and Jesus will have this double nature from the day He assumed it in the manger in Bethlehem, throughout all eternity.

I mention the hypostatic union because it's often the key to understanding why He said what He did in the gospels. He sometimes spoke with reference to His deity as when He said, "I and the Father are one [essence]" (John 10:30). But most of the time He spoke from His humanity, "If you loved Me, you would have rejoiced, because I go to the Father; for the Father is greater than I" (John 14:28).

In Jesus' humanity, He is subject to the Father because the Father is greater than His humanity. But in His deity, He is coequal with God the Father because He is of one essence with Him.

Out of Eternity into Time

Jesus Christ who, as God, always existed in the Godhead with the Father and the Holy Spirit, some two thousand years ago left the Throne of God to come to earth and become a man. Considering the repugnance that this must have meant for One who had never known anything but the sinlessness of heaven, we should consider carefully why He did it.

Let's enumerate seven reasons why God found it necessary to take on visible form and become the man Jesus Christ.

1. *God became a man in order to be the Savior of men*. In writing about the origin of Jesus, the Apostle John calls Him a unique name, "the Word." He says the Word existed before the beginning of all things. He was there face to face with God and was, in fact, God (John 1:1).

Then John says, "And the Word became flesh, and dwelt among us, and we beheld His glory, glory as of the only begotten from the Father, full of grace and truth" (John 1:14).

There's no possible way to misunderstand what John is saying. You may disagree with it, but his statement is clear. This One, called the Word, who was present in the beginning of time and who was God, took on flesh and dwelt down here on earth among men.

Why do you suppose Jesus was called "the Word"? It's because He was the personification of all that the Father wanted to *say* to men.

Two Conditions Contrasted

On several occasions in the New Testament, Jesus is referred to as "the second Adam." It's because as a man He perfectly fulfilled all the dreams and aspirations that God had originally had for the first Adam.

The two conditions of mankind are often contrasted by what Adam brought down on man and what Jesus did to reverse it. Let's look at several of these contrasts.

"For since by a man [*Adam*] came death, by a man [*Jesus*] also came the resurrection of the dead. For as in Adam all die, so also in Christ all shall be made alive" (1 Corinthians 15:21, 22).

"For if by the transgression of the one [*Adam*], death reigned through the one, much more those who receive the abundance of grace and of the gift of righteousness will reign in life through the One, Jesus Christ.

"So then as through one transgression [Adam's] there resulted condemnation to all men; even so through one act of righteousness [Christ's death] there resulted justification of life to all men.

"For as through the one man's disobedience [Adam's] the many [mankind] were made sinners, even so through the obedience of the One [Jesus] the many will be made righteous" (Romans 5:17-19).

The point of all these verses is that the first man got mankind into all its trouble, but God sent another Man into the world and He undid it.

In order to qualify as a true human being who could undo sin's damage, Jesus did not use His divine power while He was on earth. Paul tells us that "although He existed in the form of God, [He] did not regard equality with God a thing to be clung to, but He laid aside His divine privileges, taking the form of a bond-servant, and being made in the likeness of men" (Philippians 2:6, 7 paraphrased).

Jesus' whole life was lived in total dependence upon the Father who worked through Him by the Holy Spirit who indwelt Him. That's the exact way that God intended for all men to live. If Jesus had ever withstood one temptation or performed one miracle using His own divine power, He would not have been behaving as a true man and He would have disqualified Himself from being the Savior of men. (See John 5:19, 30.)

Now, let's look at another reason why God had to become man.

2. *He had to be someone who could and would die for men.*

What is sin's penalty? Death. Can God die? Obviously not. Therefore the One who would take the penalty for man had to be a true human being as well as truly God.

The writer of Hebrews said that by the grace of God, Jesus came so He might taste death for everyone (Hebrews 2:9).

Philippians 2:8 states, "And being found in appearance as a man, He [Jesus] humbled Himself by becoming obedient to the point of death, even death on a cross."

Not only *could* Jesus die for men, but He was willing to do so. It's one thing to have a friend who *could* give His life for you, but it's quite another thing to find one who *would!*

Jesus was born to die!

We all have death ahead of us as a consequence of our fallen natures. But Jesus knew when He came into the world that His main mission in life was to die for men (Hebrews 10:5-10). What a thing to have hanging over your head all your life! Yet the Bible tells us, it was because of the joy that was set before Him that He endured the shame and pain of the cross (Hebrews 12:2). That joy was the anticipation of removing all the barriers between God and man and bringing about a reconciliation.

3. *God became a man to be a mediator.* A mediator is one who effects a reconciliation between estranged parties. Paul wrote to Timothy, "For there is one God, and one mediator also between God and men, the man Christ Jesus" (1 Timothy 2:5).

Back in the Book of Job the "daysman" or "mediator" showed us that in order to be a go-between, it was necessary to be equal to both persons involved in the mediation (Job 9). The One who could bring man and God back together had to be equal to both.

This qualification narrows it down quickly to only One in the history of the universe—Jesus Christ, the God-man.

This mediator had to be the sinless Son of God in order to have the quality of righteousness acceptable to a holy God in the mediation. Jesus had that kind of personal perfection, and as a confirmation of that fact, when He was being baptized in the River Jordan, a voice out of heaven spoke saying, "This is My beloved Son, in whom I am well pleased" (Matthew 3:17).

The mediator also had to be able to sympathize with the predicament of man, and thus he had to also be a true man, but a man who never sinned. Jesus was this man.

4. *God had to become a man to be a priest.* A priest is a man who represents humanity's cause before God. He has to experience all the temptations and trials of men in order to be a sympathetic and knowledgeable intercessor for men.

Six chapters in the Book of Hebrews are devoted to a discussion of the priesthood of Jesus (Hebrews 4, 5, 7, 8, 9, 10). But six verses sum up the work of Jesus as mankind's high priest.

"And the former priests [*those who lived in Israel's past history*], on the one hand, existed in greater numbers, because they were prevented by death from continuing [in office], but He [*Jesus*], on the other hand, because He abides forever, holds His priesthood permanently.

"Hence also He is able to save forever those who draw near to God through Him, since He always lives to make intercession for them.

"For it was fitting that we should have such a high priest [*as Jesus*], holy, innocent, undefiled, separated from sinners and exalted above the heavens;

who does not need daily, like those high priests [of old], to offer up sacrifices, first for His own sins, and then for the sins of the people, because this He did once for all when He offered up Himself.

"For the Law appoints men as high priests who are weak, but the word of the oath, which came after the Law, appoints a Son, made perfect forever" (Hebrews 7:23-28).

Jesus is a high priest who's been in our shoes. He knows what it's like to live under the pressures and temptations of this world. "For we do not have a high priest who cannot sympathize with our weaknesses, but one who has been tempted in all things as we are, yet without sin. Let us therefore draw near with confidence to the throne of grace, that we may receive mercy and may find grace to help in time of need" (Hebrews 4;15, 16).

5. *He had to become man to be the revealer of God.* Man, in his spiritual death, had lost any accurate concept of God. God had to become visible to us in terms that our soulish life could grasp, and Jesus is God made real in human form.

Jesus said of Himself, "He who has seen Me has seen the Father. I and the Father are one" (John 14:9; 10:30). In a very real sense, Jesus is a living photograph of the Father. All that God wanted revealed of Himself, He revealed in the Person of His Son, Jesus.

But Jesus is not only the revealer of the Father to man, He's also the revealer of the Father's plan to redeem mankind (Hebrews 1:1-3).

6. *He had to be a man to occupy King David's throne.* Long ago God promised David He would have a greater son who would reign on his throne over Israel forever (see 1 Chronicles 17:11-15 and Isaiah 9:6, 7). So Jesus had to be born as a direct blood descendant of David in order to fulfill that prophecy.

When the angel spoke to Mary about the miraculous conception which was to take place in her womb, he said, concerning the child, "He will be great, and will be called the Son of the Most High; and the Lord God will give Him the throne of his father David; and He will reign over the house of Jacob forever; and His kingdom will have no end" (Luke 1:32, 33).

Both Mary and her husband Joseph were direct descendants of King David. Through Mary, Jesus received the blood right to the throne of David, and through Mary's husband, Joseph, who acted as Jesus' earthly father, He received the legal right.

7. *God had to become a man in order to be a "kinsman redeemer."* This is a concept taught in the Old Testament, especially in the Book of Ruth. In the Law

of Moses, whenever a Jewish person was put into slavery, the only one who could pay the ransom price to release him was someone "near of kin" (Leviticus 25:25). This was to establish the principle that whoever would be the one to free mankind from its slavery to Satan would have to be a "near of kin" to the ones being freed, in this case the human race. In taking on humanity, Jesus became a "kinsman" of men and qualified to be the "kinsman redeemer." This is one of the reasons that Jesus loved to call Himself the Son of Man.

Jesus, the God-Man

In the last two chapters we've examined many lines of evidence that clearly shows why it was necessary for God to come into this world, clothed with a human body. We've also seen that the complete humanity which was prepared for Him to live in while here on earth for thirty-three years was none other than Jesus of Nazareth.

Jesus firmly believed he was God, Incarnate (*in the flesh*). He said that He had come from God (John 6:38, 15; 16:27, 28; 17:5) and that He actually was God (John 10:30; John 20:26-29; Mark 14:61, 62). He accepted worship (Matthew 8:2, 3; 9:18; 14:33) and told people that He forgave them of their sins, which only God had the power to do (Mark 2:5-12; Matthew 9:1-8).

He predicted He would rise from the dead (Matthew 27:62-66; Mark 8:31, 32; 9:31), which He did. He said He was going back to the Father's house to prepare dwelling places for His children and He would return personally to the earth and take them with Him into heaven (John 14:1-3; Acts 1:10, 11).

Was He Telling the Truth?

Now, what do you do with a man who said all those things about Himself? You can't dismiss it simply because you don't want to make a judgment as to His truthfulness or sanity. You must come to some conclusion in your own mind about Jesus.

As C.S. Lewis, the brilliant British scholar said of Jesus, in his wonderful book, *Mere Christianity*, "I'm trying here to prevent anyone saying the really foolish thing that people often say about Jesus: *'I'm ready to accept Jesus as a great moral teacher, but I don't accept His claim to be God.'* That is the one thing we must not say. A man who was *merely* a man and said the sort of things Jesus said would not be a great moral teacher. He would either be a lunatic—on the level with the man who says he is a poached egg—or else he would be the Devil of Hell. You must make your choice. Either this man was, and is, the Son of God, or else a madman or something worse. You can shut Him up for a fool, you can spit at Him and kill Him as a demon, or you can fall at His feet and call Him Lord and God. But let us not come up with any patronising nonsense about His being just a great human teacher. He has not left that open to us. He did not intend to."[1]

[1] C. S. Lewis, *Mere Christianity* (New York: The Macmillan Company, 1943).

9 ○ Propitiation

IN THE LAST two chapters we've looked at why God had to become a man and why it could have been no other man but Jesus.

Now I want to show why Jesus had to go to the cross; why there was no other way for God to reconcile men to Himself.

I've shown that the first work of Christ on the cross is called "propitiation." Don't be scared by this word. It's a beautiful word which means to "turn away wrath by the *satisfaction* of violated justice." Webster's dictionary defines the word similarly as "to appease and render favorable; to conciliate and reconcile."

Christ's act of propitiation has removed the barrier of God's offended character. It's because when Jesus hung on the cross, He bore the compounded fury of God's just wrath against the sins of mankind. Now God has no more wrath to pour out on men. His justice is satisfied that all sin has been paid for.

Propitiation removed God's wrath.

Is God's Wrath Real?

It's amazing to me that there are so many theologians around who are saying, "Oh, if you teach propitiation as a removal of God's wrath, you're contributing to the idea of a petty God who simply has to be appeased in order to be happy."

So, because they only want to think about a God of love, they try to do away with the fact that the Bible deals in depth with the truth of God's just wrath against sin. In the Old Testament alone, God's wrath against sin is mentioned 585 times.[1]

God's wrath is also a very important reality in the New Testament, but there the emphasis is on the propitiation of Christ which has removed God's wrath from mankind. (See John 3:36; Romans 9:22; Ephesians 5:6; Colossians 3:6.)

---

[1] For a good Bible study tool both in this area and in general, let me recommend *Young's Analytical Concordance*. If you look up the word "wrath" in this volume, for example, it will show you every place it is used in the Bible and how it is used. It will categorize the English translation with the word in the original language it was written in.

Because we're human we don't always look at everything in terms of black and white. We let our sympathy blur our judgment at times.

But God, as the sovereign and righteous judge of the universe, must direct His wrath against sin, wherever it's found and in whomever it's found. He can't let His love for man cause Him to compromise His just condemnation of man's sin.

For instance, I know a judge who is a very warm and loving person with real empathy for human needs. He has certainly overlooked and dismissed wrongs done to him in the sphere of his family and friends. But when he is officially in the role of a judge, even though a member of his family has broken the law, he can't sweep the facts under the table and not execute the penalty. If he did, he'd no longer be qualified to judge. A judge who shows partiality and inequity in the administration of the law is unacceptable in any society.

How much more so in the case of God. He's not only our creator, but also the judge of the universe. As such, He doesn't have the liberty of breaking the very laws which inherently emanate from His character. If He did, the universe would be in chaos. There would be no absolute standards at all that anyone could count on.

No! God's wrath is real, but so is His solution—Christ's propitiatory death on the cross.

Propitiation Propounded

Since this concept of propitiation is so new to many, let's look at it more in depth. The central verses in the New Testament that teach the doctrine of propitiation are Romans 3:25, 26.

There are two important points I want to emphasize about propitiation. First, when the Bible says Christ died to satisfy the offended righteousness and justice of God, and to turn away wrath from those who believe in Him, this even included believers in the Old Testament who lived *before* the cross! That's what it means when it says in that passage, "God passed over the sins previously committed." God put the sins of those Old Testament saints on a charge account which was guaranteed to be paid by the promise of a coming Savior. (See Isaiah 53; Jeremiah 31:31-34.)

But the second emphasis of this passage in Romans 3 is that Jesus was displayed "publicly" as a propitiation. God did this so that the whole world would know that His offended character had been conciliated by Jesus' death and now God had a perfect right to declare righteous all who would believe in His Son's substitutionary death on their behalf.

The Tent in the Wilderness

Perhaps the clearest example in the Bible as to what propitiation means is found in its Old Testament counterpart. The Greek word for "propitiation" is *hilasterion*. This is the same word for the Old Testament Hebrew word, "mercy seat."

The "mercy seat" was part of the furniture God told Moses to build and set in a special place of worship in the wilderness. This special worship building was a portable tentlike affair which served the Hebrews in their worship of their God while they traveled in the Sinai Wilderness for forty years. It was called the"Tabernacle."

This was the place where God came down to meet with men through the intercession of their high priest, and it was the place where men came to meet God and have their sins forgiven through the system of animal sacrifices which God had instructed Moses to institute.

Everything about this Tabernacle and its articles of furniture was intended to portray in a temporal way what God would one day do permanently. The animal sacrifices were valid until God would one day provide the lamb of His choosing.

That "Lamb" was His Son, Jesus. As John the Baptist said of Jesus when He saw Him coming toward him, "Look! Here comes the Lamb of God who will take away the sins of the world" (John 1:29).

Levi and Sons' Furniture

There were a number of pieces of important furniture in the two rooms in the Tabernacle which the priestly tribe of Levi used in their daily intercessions for the people.

But the most important article in the entire Tabernacle was located in the inner room called the "Holy of Holies." This was the room where God's presence dwelt on earth, and it was the place of "propitiation" for God. The central object in the room was a rather small acacia wood box, covered with gold. God had given Moses exact instructions on how to make this "Ark of the Covenant." You can learn the details of its construction in Exodus 25.

Everything about this focal piece of furniture was symbolic of the Person and work of God's coming Lamb, Jesus Christ. The wood represented His humanity, the gold His deity. The top, or lid, of this ark was solid gold and became known as the "mercy seat," which the New Testament word *hilasterion* describes as the place of propitiation.

God left nothing to chance in His detailed blueprint to Moses as to how this Ark of the Covenant was to be constructed. Each tiny part of it held unbelievable symbolic significance in God's eternal plan to redeem fallen mankind.

Extremely significant were the replicas of two angels called "cherubim" made facing each other with outstretched wings, looking down upon the mercy seat. And under this mercy seat, in the ark itself, were three peculiar items described for us in Hebrews 9:1-6.

Manna for all Seasons

First, God told Moses to place inside the ark a pot of manna. You'll remember that manna was a food God provided for the Israelites during their forty-year stint in the wilderness. At first the people had welcomed this miraculous provision, but soon they began griping about it and asked for some variety in their diet.

"Boy, we wish we had some of those delicious foods we had back in Egypt," they murmured.

Their attitude really angered God. After all, no one had gotten sick in those forty years, so it must have been plenty nutritious.

So God said, "Put the manna in the pot and put it in the ark." This became a symbol of man's rejection of God's material provisions.

A Rod to Remember

The second item for the Ark originated from a rebellion within the camp of Israel against Moses' and Aaron's leadership (Numbers 16, 17). After God had dealt with the rebel instigators, He called the tribal leaders to come before Moses. The symbol of leadership was a rod, or wooden staff. Moses took a rod from each tribe and deposited all twelve in the Tabernacle overnight. The man whose rod sprouted leaves was the one God wanted as the leader.

When the rods were taken from the Tabernacle the next day, Aaron's was budded with leaves. But the Israelites disobeyed Aaron's and Moses' leadership anyway, and his rod was placed inside the ark as a reminder of man's refusal of God's leadership.

Stones That Speak

The third item in the ark was the stones upon which the Ten Commandments were inscribed. After Moses had received the two tablets of the Law written by the finger of God, he came down the mountain, only to find the people in rebellion and idolatry. The gross sins of the crowd angered Moses so much, he flung the tablets onto the ground and they smashed into pieces. Later God rewrote them on stone and had them placed inside the ark as the symbol of man's rejection of God's holiness.

The ark, therefore, contained the physical representations of the total sinfulness of man—

the manna, man's rejection of God's earthly provisions;

Aaron's rod, man's rejection of God's leadership;

the tablets of the law, man's rejection of God's holiness.

The Day of Atonement

The Ark of the Covenant was located in the Holy of Holies, the inner chamber of the Tabernacle. Only one man in all the world was allowed in that chamber, the high priest of Israel, and he, only once a year on the Day of Atonement. On that day he would take the blood of an animal sacrifice and sprinkle it over the top of the mercy seat.

Cherubs in the Bible are always associated with the holiness of God, as His guardians and personal servants (Ezekiel 1; Genesis 3:24). It appears that one of the cherubim hovering over the mercy seat represented the absolute righteousness of God; the other, His perfect justice.

When the cherub of righteousness looked down on the symbols in the ark, it saw all the evidences of man's rejection of God. The cherub of justice saw that man was no longer like God's righteousness, and pronounced the penalty of death upon man.

How Wrath Becomes Mercy

But on the Day of Atonement, what did the angels see?

The symbols of sin?

No. They saw the *blood* of a divinely ordained innocent sacrifice covering the symbols of sin. Justice could now say, "I'm satisfied, because the death penalty has been paid." Righteousness said, "I'm no longer offended because the evidence of man's sin has been covered from my eyes and I see only the blood of an innocent substitute who paid the required penalty of death."

One more thing is very important here symbolically. The golden lid (mercy seat) was comparable to being God's throne on earth, because He said He dwelt between the cherubim.

"And there I will meet with you, and from above the mercy seat, from between the two cherubim which are upon the ark of the testimony . . ." (Exodus 25:22).

Until the blood of the animal was sprinkled on the mercy seat, this throne
of God depicted a place of judgment. But, covered by the blood once a year,
it became a throne of mercy, or mercy seat. God could now sit upon this
throne and show the facet of His character called "mercy" because His righteousness and justice were completely satisfied by the blood sacrifice which
He had ordained!

"I will appear in the cloud over the mercy seat," God said in Leviticus
16:2. Here was the place where estranged man could now meet God through
the mediation of the sacrifice.

The symbolism represented in the sacrificial system and the worship in
the Tabernacle is really beautiful. Through this picture the Old Testament
believers learned more of the nature of God and His Messiah, and how God
would one day perfect His work of salvation.

A Shadow of Things to Come

I've gone into some detail about the Tabernacle, and particularly the Ark
of the Covenant, because it's written about them that they are "a copy and
shadow of the *heavenly* things." In fact, that's why Moses was warned by
God when he was about to build the Tabernacle that he should make everything about it *exactly* according to the pattern God showed him while He
was up on Mount Sinai. It was to be a copy and picture of things which
actually exist in heaven (Hebrews 8:5).

This command of God takes on great importance when we start analyzing the various functions of the Tabernacle and attempting to see the deeper
truths that they were "foreshadowing." We have to keep in mind that whatever was enacted in symbol and type in the *earthly* tabernacle where God
dwelt, was either being enacted, or would be in the future, in the *heavenly*
tabernacle where God dwells now.

Jesus Is the Real Thing

One reason why I usually get bogged down and spend months teaching
the lessons of the Tabernacle when I teach Old Testament classes is that
every function and symbol of the tabernacle worship found its deeper fulfillment in the life, death, and resurrection of Jesus Christ. Only God could
have so perfectly planned such a detailed and minute correlation between
the "shadow" and its ultimate reality.

If you want a fascinating and rewarding study of all the ways in which

Jesus fulfilled the types pictured in the Tabernacle, I suggest you read Dr. J. Vernon McGee's book, *Tabernacle, God's Portrait of Christ*.[2]

I also suggest a thorough reading of the Book of Hebrews, since it's in this book that much of this typology is unraveled for us.

The New Testament writer who wrote the Book of Hebrews had as his main audience hundreds of Hebrews who had accepted Jesus as the promised Messiah. He himself must have been Jewish since he had such a perfect understanding of the correlation of the Old Testament symbols of worship and Christ's fulfillment of them.

The Only Perfect High Priest

Because our particular interest in this chapter deals with Christ's propitiatory work for man, I want to center on His role as high priest.

In the tabernacle worship, it was the role of the high priest to enter the Holy of Holies once a year and place the blood of an innocent sacrifice onto the mercy seat and thereby obtain God's mercy for the people for another year.

Listen to what the writer of Hebrews says of Jesus,

But when Christ appeared as a high priest of the good things to come, He entered through the greater and more perfect tabernacle, not made with hands, that is to say, not of this creation; and not through the blood of goats and calves, but through His own blood, He entered the holy place once for all, having obtained eternal redemption (Hebrews 9:11, 12).

The importance of this statement is overwhelming! Jesus, as our high priest, actually entered the Holy of Holies in heaven with the blood of an innocent sacrifice, HIS OWN BLOOD. There He sprinkled it on the mercy seat of the heavenly tabernacle and obtained, not just a temporary, year-long forgiveness for men, but an *eternal* redemption. And it says He did it "once for all," which means it never has to be done again and again as the former priests had to do.

Think of it!

This one act of Jesus, the High Priest and Lamb, has forever satisfied God's justice and righteousness. His infinitely efficacious blood has been put on record at the throne of God so that it will *forever* remind the Father that His wrath has already been fully poured out upon man's sin.

[2] J. Vernon McGee, *Tabernacle, God's Portrait of Christ* (Thru the Bible Books).

The blood of Jesus is our guarantee that God will never again be angry with anyone who believes in Jesus as his personal Savior. Jesus' blood has turned God's throne from one of judgment to one of mercy.

The substitutionary death of Christ has removed the barrier of God's offended character for all men—the whole world. God's wrath has been conciliated, and He is now free to deal with every man individually on the basis of grace. If a person spends eternity separated from God, it won't be because of God's wrath. It will be because he hasn't availed Himself of God's mercy made available through Jesus' death on the cross.

10 ∘ Redemption

IN THE LAST chapter we saw the first barrier between God and man, GOD'S HOLY CHARACTER, being torn down by the propitiation of Christ. That was the work of Christ in presenting His blood at the mercy seat in heaven and obtaining *permanent* forgiveness for men by satisfying the outraged holiness of God.

Redemption is the work of Jesus Christ on our behalf to (1) cancel out the DEBT OF SIN, and (2) release us from SLAVERY TO SATAN and the sin nature. All barriers have been torn down by the redemptive work of Christ on the cross.

The Certificate of Debt

In chapter four, when we were discussing how man had incurred his DEBT OF SIN, we saw that the Apostle Paul, in describing this indebtedness, had used a scene right out of the Roman law courts.

Every time a Roman citizen was convicted of a crime, the jurisprudence of the day demanded that a "Certificate of Debt" be prepared. On this certificate the criminal's unlawful deeds were listed, one by one, and the exact penalty he owed. He would be sent to jail and the Certificate of Debt was nailed on the outside of his cell door. And it hung there until the man had served his time and thereby paid the penalty for those crimes enumerated on the certificate.

Listen to the powerful way Paul convinces his hearers that they have been set free from their sinful indebtedness to God. "And when you were dead in your transgressions and the uncircumcision of your flesh, He made you alive together with Him, having forgiven us all our transgressions, having cancelled out the certificate of debt consisting of decrees against us and which was hostile to us; and He has taken it out of the way, having nailed it to the cross" (Colossians 2:13, 14).

Our Certificate of Debt consists of decrees—God's laws which we've broken—and they stand against us. They're "hostile" to us because *we can't keep them*, without breaking some of them. There's nothing wrong with God's laws; they're perfect. The problem lies with our inability to keep them.

Paul gives us a fantastic picture here of Jesus taking your Certificate of Debt and mine and nailing it to the cross. In doing this, it was tantamount to saying He was guilty of every sin listed on every certificate of every man who would ever be born. Not only was He volunteering to take our certificates, but also their penalty which was death.

The Day the Planet was Liberated

Let's take a brief glance at that day in history that forever altered God and man's relationship—the day Jesus died.

Here's how it happened. Jesus was nailed to the cross at about 9:00 in the morning. He prayed for those who had nailed Him there. Then He made provision for His mother, turning her over to the keeping of His disciple, John. Just before noon He began His dialog with the two criminals on each side of Him, and one of them turned in repentance to the Lord. He was promised a place in paradise, beginning at the moment of his death.

At noonday God drew a veil of darkness over the whole earth. It was pitch black. I believe God did this so that no one would be able to witness visually the horror of what was happening to Jesus as He hung there—because in that moment, the entire wrath of God was engulfing Him as He allowed the sins of all mankind to be put on Him.

Until then Jesus hadn't uttered even a whimper.

But then, all of a sudden, the silence was broken and Jesus cried out in His humanity, *"Eloi, Eloi, lama sabachthani,"* which means, "My God, My God, why have You forsaken Me?"

In that instant God had taken the Certificates of Debt of every human being from the beginning of mankind until the close of history, and nailed them to the cross, making Jesus responsible and guilty for each one!

And God had to turn His back on His own Son in His greatest hour of need, because Christ had voluntarily allowed Himself to be made a sinner on our behalf and God could have no fellowship with sinners of *any* kind until redemption was completed.

When I get to heaven I want to ask Jesus, "Lord, what really happened in that awful hour of blackness?"

Even after He explains it to me, I know I won't be able to comprehend what it must have been like for the poured-out fury of a holy God to fall like an atomic blast on Jesus.

His scream was out of deep agony of soul because, for the first and last time for all eternity, the Second Person of the Godhead, Jesus, was separated from the other two members of the Godhead, the Father and the Spirit.

No one will ever be as alone as Jesus was there on the cross. He was separated from every person He'd ever loved and trusted. Forsaken by His closest friends, forsaken by God the Father and God the Holy Spirit, forsaken by all, He hung there in an aloneness that nobody will ever be able to fathom.

Do you know why He did it?

So that you and I would never have to be alone again. So He could tell those who believed in Him, "I will never desert you, nor will I ever forsake you" (Hebrews 13:5).

The Cry That Shook the World

But that's not the end of the story.

Just before Jesus gave up His earthly life and commended His Spirit to the Father, He shouted a word which is the Magna Carta of all true believers.

That victorious cry was *"Tetelestai!"*

Let that word burn like a firebrand into your mind, because that's the *exact same word* that a Roman judge would write across a released criminal's Certificate of Debt to show that all his penalty had been paid and he was free at last. The word used in this way means "paid in full" and is translated in many Bibles as "It is finished."

In the mind of God, "Paid in Full" has been written across the Certificate of Debt of every man who will ever live because His debt to God has been fully paid by Jesus.

But if a man would be so foolish as to insist on staying imprisoned by his sins, even though their debt has been paid, then the Certificate of Debt assuring his freedom is of no benefit to him. And when he comes to the end of his life, he will have to pay the penalty of death and separation from God himself, even though it's totally unnecessary.

The Other Side of Redemption

Having our DEBT OF SIN canceled is the first benefit of Christ's redemptive work on the cross. But equal to that is the fact that it also released us from SLAVERY TO SATAN and the power of the indwelling sin nature.

The word "redemption" was a very familiar word in the first century since nearly half the world was involved in slavery in one way or another. The sweetest word a slave could hope to hear was the word "redemption."

Since one of the major barriers between God and man is man's SLAVERY TO SATAN, the New Testament writers have freely used the concept of redemption to describe the work of Christ on the cross which has reclaimed man from Satan's clutches.

In the Greek language there are several different words for "redemption" which emphasize different aspects of it. These have all been translated into our one English word "redemption." In order to appreciate fully the scope of freedom from SLAVERY TO SATAN which Christ has purchased for us, let's look at four different emphases of the word "redemption."

Emphasis on Freedom

The first word is a verb, *lutroo*. Its root meaning is "to set free," and its inherent emphasis is the *state of being free*. Since the word means to be set free from slavery by the payment of a ransom, it's translated "redemption."

The word *lutroo* is used in 1 Peter 1:18, 19 as follows: "Knowing that you were not *redeemed* with perishable things like silver or gold from your futile way of life inherited from your forefathers, but with precious blood, as of a lamb unblemished and spotless, the blood of Christ."

Emphasis on Being God's Possession

Another verb is *peripoieo*, which means "redeemed" but is translated "purchased" in Acts 20:28: ". . . shepherd the church of God which He [Jesus] *purchased* [literally: "gained possession of"] with His own blood." Here the emphasis is not on freedom as such, but *on the means to freedom*: the act of buying or gaining possession of something so that it becomes yours to own. Thus, through redemption we've become God's personal property.

Emphasis on the Place of Slavery

A third word is *agorazo*, coming from the root noun, *agora*, meaning the actual slave market itself. This derived word came to mean "being set free from the *slave market* by paying a ransom." It emphasizes the awfulness of the place from which we're purchased and is used in Revelation 5:9: "Worthy are You [Jesus] . . . for You are slain, and *purchased* for God with Your blood men from every tribe and tongue and people and nation."

Emphasis on Permanence of Freedom

Then there's a final verb, which is the intensive form of *agorazo*; it's *exagorazo*. The prefix *ex* is added which means "out of" ("ex" as in "exit") and emphasizes being purchased *out of* the slave market, never to be sold as a slave again.

The implication here is obvious, as the word is used in Galatians 3:13: "Christ *redeemed* us from the curse of the Law, having become a curse for us." The Law is a "curse" to us because we can't keep it, and that has brought us under SLAVERY TO SATAN and to sin. But Jesus redeemed us from this curse, having taken the curse of sin and death for us. Yet in His resurrection, He once and for all defeated Satan and threw off his temporary dominion over His humanity.

This Little "Slave" Went to Market

The Word of God graphically pictures mankind as being, not only sinful, but also, as a result, in SLAVERY TO SATAN in a slave market of sin. The Scriptures are very clear that there's only one way out of the dilemma. A redeemer, who is not himself in the slave market, must redeem all mankind out of it.

That redeemer is Jesus. Here's the picture.

THE SITUATION	THE INTERPRETATION	BIBLE REFERENCE
The Slave Market	The World System	1 John 5:19
The Slave Master	Satan	John 12:31
The Slaves	Humanity	Eph. 2:2, 3
The Problem	Sin	Col. 2:14
The Highest Bidder	Jesus (Redeemer)	Heb. 2:14, 15
The Ransom Price	Blood of Christ	1 Pet. 1:18, 19

Jesus said, "Every one who commits sin is the slave of sin" (John 8:34). Since everyone commits sin (if you ever run into somebody who says he doesn't, check around with his friends!), we're all slaves. It's a condition we're born into with Satan as the father and head of the fallen race of mankind (John 8:44). He energizes the unbelievers (Ephesians 2:1-4), and He empowers the whole world system as well (1 John 5:19).

Have you ever wondered why the world's in the mess it's in?

Consider the source!

The evil in the world is not just some impersonal force. We're dealing with the reality of a personal being so influential that the whole world has fallen prey to his devices. "For our struggle is not against flesh and blood, but against the rulers, against the powers, against the world-forces of this darkness, against spiritual forces of wickedness in the heavenly [atmospheric] places" (Ephesians 6:12).[1]

Jesus, the Liberator!

Into this insane "slave market of sin" God sent a redeemer to "open [men's] eyes so that they may turn from darkness to light and from the dominion of Satan to God" (Acts 26:18). But Jesus didn't just "happen along"; it was by careful design in the plan of God. God couldn't select just anyone to be the liberator of mankind; he had to meet the qualifications of a redeemer.

And Jesus perfectly did!

In the Roman system of slavery, every citizen of the empire knew that a slave couldn't free himself, nor could he be freed by another slave. It took a free man with an authentic and proper ransom to do it.

In the same way, no human being can free another because we're all in the slave market together. The services of a qualified outsider—One chosen by God—are required, as we discussed in chapters seven and eight.

Let's briefly review the qualifications of Jesus as the redeemer of mankind.

Sinless Redeemer

First of all, the one who would redeem men from Satan's slavery had to be without sin himself. After warning His listeners of their slavery to sin, Jesus says, "The slave does not remain in the house forever; the son does remain forever" (John 8:35).

In other words, the son is a permanent part of the household, the slave is not. And since the son is above the slave, he has authority over the slave and could even set him free if he chose to.

And then Jesus pulls a fantastic play on words. He says, in the very next verse, "If therefore the Son shall make *you* free, you shall be free indeed." In saying this to them, He is equating them with being slaves and is, in essence, telling them that He is the Son and He alone has the power to set them, the sin-slaves, free.

As we've seen already, Christ is the only man to be born on this earth since Adam who was not Himself a slave to sin. That's because of His unique conception. God was the father of His humanity, and Jesus' mother was a

---

[1] See author's book, *Satan Is Alive and Well on Planet Earth,* for more details (Zondervan Publishing House, 1972).

virgin. Since the culpability for sin is passed from human father to child, Jesus by-passed inherited sin because His "family tree" on His Father's side was not human, but divine. Jesus also lived a life that was completely sinless.

Thus Jesus met the first qualification for being a redeemer. He Himself was a free man and the only one capable of paying the ransom price.

Kinsman Redeemer

Secondly, the redeemer had to be "next of kin" to the human race. Hebrews 2:14, 15 explains why this was so: "Since then the children [mankind] share in flesh and blood, He Himself likewise also partook of the same [flesh and blood], that through death He might render powerless him who had the power of death, that is, the devil; and might deliver those who through fear of death were subject to slavery all their lives."

You see, the price of redemption for man has always been the shed blood of an innocent substitute. Moses taught in the Law, "Without the shedding of blood, there is no remission of sin" (Hebrews 9:22). However, the blood of animals could never take the sin away; it only atoned for, or covered it, temporarily until God provided a complete remission of sins through His ultimate sacrifice of Jesus (Hebrews 10:11-14).

But, since the redemption price had to be the shed *blood* of an *innocent* sacrifice, the redeemer had to be someone with blood in his veins who could actually experience death. In other words, a man, but one who was completely innocent of any sins.

That's why we read about Christ's death in 1 Peter 1:19, that it accomplished redemption "with precious blood, as of a lamb *unblemished* and *spotless*, the blood of Christ."

Mediating Redeemer

Third, the redeemer had to be a mediator, one who was equal to both parties in the mediation—those in the slave market, and the One seeking to release the slaves. In other words, the redeemer needed to be both God and man. "For there is one God, and one mediator also between God and men, the man Christ Jesus, who gave Himself as a *ransom* for all" (1 Timothy 2:5, 6).

Willing Redeemer

Finally, in order for a person to become a redeemer, he must do so voluntarily. Certainly a slave was in no position to order a free man to liberate him. The free man would have to be motivated somehow to come and pay the ransom.

When speaking of the life He was to give as a sacrifice for sin, Jesus told the Pharisees in John 10:17, 18, "I lay down My life that I may take it again. No one takes it away from Me, but I lay it down on My own initiative."

The reason why?

His love for you and me!

That love is what sent Him to the cross, canceling our DEBT OF SIN and purchasing us out of SLAVERY TO SATAN. These are no longer barriers between God and man:

Unless we let them be!

From Jesus, With Love!

The redemption that Jesus made available to men at the cross is a love gift with no strings attached. We're not used to receiving things without someone wanting something in return, so it's hard to really grasp the nature of this fantastic offer of a free salvation. In the back of many peoples' minds is the thought that there must be a hidden gimmick somewhere. No one gives something for nothing!

But let me assure you, there's no fine print in the contract of salvation. It doesn't even say that we have to give Him ourselves. All we're asked to do is to *take* the pardon He's graciously offered us and then begin to enjoy our freedom.

Jesus said, "Come to Me all you who labor and are heavily burdened, and *I will give you rest*" (Matthew 11:28 Modern Language Bible). All we have to do is come to Him, give Him our burdens, and take the gift of rest from Him.

John wrote, "As many as received Him [Jesus], *to them God gave the power* to become the children of God, even to those who believe in His name" (John 1:12). Here again we're asked only to believe in what Jesus did for us in providing our liberation at the cross, and then God gives us the power to become His children.

The Tragedy of the "Might-Have-Been"

As much as I hate to, I must add this final note to this chapter on redemption. Just because Christ has redeemed all mankind from Satan's slave market of sin, unfortunately not everyone has chosen to avail himself of the ransom and go free.

The story is told of a young man who was convicted of murder in an eastern state many years ago. His parents, being influential and wealthy, finally obtained a stay of execution from the governor, and eventually the convict was granted a pardon.

This man, still sitting on death row, was given the news that he had been given his freedom. But when he was handed the pardon, he rejected it. He said, "I'm guilty and I want to die."

Try as they could, his family and lawyers couldn't persuade him to change his mind. In an effort to keep him from being executed, the family took the case all the way to the highest court in the state. And the court ruled that a pardon is not a pardon until it is accepted by the one for whom it was intended.

So the man went to his death, not because he had no alternative, but because he refused to accept the pardon.

So it is with men. Those who spend eternity separated from God in bitter anguish of soul and body will do so, not because there isn't an alternative, but because they won't accept the pardon that has already been made available.

But once a man accepts the pardon, he's forever free. And not just after he dies, either. He's free in this life, in the here-and-now as well as the sweet-by-and-by.

If you've never done so before, why not right this moment thank Jesus Christ for dying for *you*, personally, and accept His gracious pardon and forgiveness. You'll be eternally glad you did!

11 ○ Substitutionary Death

BILLY GRAHAM, IN an address at Yale University, told the story of how he was driving through a small town in the South one evening and was picked up by radar in a speed trap. He was clocked at several miles over the limit.

A squad car pulled him over and instructed him to follow the car to the local justice of the peace. The justice happened to be a barber, and the office was right there in the barber shop.

Graham tells how he walked into the place and the justice was busy shaving a man. He took his time and finished the job. Then he turned to Graham and quickly reviewed his case. "How do you plead?" the justice asked.

"Guilty, your honor," Graham said.

"That'll be $15," replied the justice.

Graham reached for his wallet to pay the fine.

The justice shot him a second glance and said, "Say, aren't you Billy Graham, the evangelist?"

"I regret to say, sir, that I am," Graham responded, hopefully tucking the wallet back into his pocket.

"That'll be $15," the man said again with a smile.

"But I'll tell you what I'm going to do," said the justice after a moment's hesitation. "I'm going to pay the fine for you."

He reached into his back pocket for his billfold, took it out, removed a five and a ten-dollar bill, slipped them underneath the cash box in the till, and closed the drawer.

"You've been a big help to me and my family, and this is something I want to do," he said.

Justice Isn't Blind

The law had been broken, the penalty assessed, and the fine *had* to be paid.

But in this case, as in the case of God versus mankind, a substitute came forward and volunteered to pay the fine. It didn't cost Billy Graham's "savior" much to pay Billy's fine, but the cost to God to provide a savior to pay our "fine" of death, was the death of His Son, Jesus, in our place.

Substitutionary death is the subject of this chapter. This is the work of Christ on the cross that removed forever the barrier of SPIRITUAL DEATH which hangs over the head of every man who's ever been born. It not only has removed our death penalty, but it's made it possible for God to *restore* His life to every man who will accept it.

Just to review briefly:

Propitiation is toward God, satisfying His absolute righteousness and holiness. Christ's death did that for us.

Redemption is toward *sin*, providing payment of the sin-debt through Jesus' blood. As a result, man has also been set free from the slave market of sin and brought out from under Satan's authority. Christ's death did that for us.

Substitutionary death is toward *death*, through Christ's dying in our place. This is the work of Christ we want to look at in depth now.

Sin's Inescapable Penalty

The penalty for sin has always been death. One of the first principles Adam and Eve ever learned from God was that in the day they ate of the forbidden fruit, they would die (Genesis 2:17). They didn't fully understand that "death" meant a spiritual separation from God.

Then on that sad day when Adam and Eve stood over the lifeless body of their dead son, Abel, they were all too aware of what it meant to die physically.

The final aspect of death is still future and is called "the second death" or eternal death. This will be the final eternal state of all who die on this earth without ever having their spiritual lives restored. This is *not* a state of eternal unconsciousness, but rather one of very real torment and remorse for ever and ever (Revelation 20:14, 15; Matthew 8:12; Luke 16:19-31).

The Concept of Sacrifice

In each layer of civilization which the archaeologists' spades have uncovered, there have been evidences of sacrifices made to gods. Since many of these scholars have *not* been prone to accept the Biblical concept of divine creation and the subsequent fall of man, they've used the presence of these numerous artifacts of sacrifice to ridicule and discredit the biblical claim of the efficacy of animal sacrifice.

They would claim that the Hebrews were only one race out of many who evolved a system of sacrifice to appease a god they couldn't fathom. And they would point to sacrificial evidence that predated the appearance of the Hebrew race in their effort to disprove any merit in the biblical concept of animal sacrifice for sins.

But how you interpret the relics in the archaeologist's shovel is entirely dependent on the basic premise you have as to the origin of things. If you believe that man is in a process of evolution from a one-celled organism to some glorious superhuman creature of the future, then you would tend to discount the biblical claim of the fall of man and a subsequent *downward* devolution or degeneration.

But if you accept the biblical claim that God created man full grown, in His own image, and that man distorted that image in himself by disobeying God and thereby incurring a penalty of death, then you'll see that the concept of substitutionary sacrifice was a necessary *immediate* intervention of God to reestablish fellowship with man.

It would then be understandable also as to why every stage of human history has its record of animal and human sacrifices. It's because there was an original prototype at the very beginning of human history from which all the other patterns developed, some staying close to the original type and others evolving into bizarre perversions.

The Biblical History of Sacrifice

The account of animal sacrifice found in the Old Testament Book of Genesis occurred long before God gave the command to Moses to institute a system of worship which included animal sacrifices.

The first time an innocent animal had to die because of man's sin was when God killed at least one animal, and possibly several, in the Garden of Eden, to provide a covering for Adam and Eve's nakedness. They had attempted to cover themselves with leaves, but in God's rejecting their feeble effort to hide their guilt from Him, He established a principle that an innocent substitute must die to provide a temporary covering of man's sinfulness.

Although this is not spelled out in detail by Moses in his writing of the Book of Genesis, it's obvious from succeeding records of animal sacrifice that God must have explained this substitutionary-death concept to Adam, and then Adam to his children.

Genesis records the fact that Abel, Noah, Abraham, Isaac, Job, and Jacob all offered sacrifices to God before the time of Moses and the institution of the tabernacle worship (Genesis 4:4; 8:20; 12:7; 26:25; 33:20; Exodus 12:3-11; Job 1:5; 42:7-9).

So the necessity of seeking God's forgiveness of sins through the sacrifice of an innocent substitute was a familiar practice from the very beginning of man's history on this earth. And it was a symbolism instituted by God Himself.

It's also thrilling to me to see how God developed the concept of the substitutionary death of *one lamb for one man* to the ultimate goal of *one lamb for the whole world*.

One Lamb for One Man

God initially authorized the slaying of one animal to atone for the sins of one man. This is pictured for us in the story of Adam's son, Abel's sacrificial offering to God. His brother, Cain, brought an offering of fruit to God, but it was rejected. Obviously, God had previously given instructions through Adam that blood must be shed in order to provide a covering for sins. Abel brought the right sacrifice, and it so angered his brother Cain that he killed him (see Genesis 3, 4; Hebrews 11:4).

One Lamb for One Family

In the story of the Passover experience of the Hebrews in Egypt we see that God ordained that one lamb could suffice as a sacrifice for one family (Exodus 12:3-14).

The Passover referred to the night when God had Moses tell Pharaoh that if he didn't let the Hebrews go out of their slavery in Egypt, the first-born of all animals and families in the land (both Hebrew and Egyptian) would die as the death angel passed over Egypt.

In order to spare the Hebrews the death of their first-born, God made the provision that they could kill a lamb and sprinkle its blood over the door and on the two doorposts. Then when the death angel passed over the land of Egypt that night, wherever he saw the blood, he would *pass over* that house and those inside would be spared God's judgment.

God commanded that this Passover day be celebrated yearly as a reminder of God's provision for the salvation of those who sacrificed their lamb for their family.

One Lamb for a Nation

After the Jews left their servitude in Egypt and were on their way to the promised land, God met Moses on Mount Sinai and gave him the ten commandments and many other laws by which the people were to regulate their lives and their worship.

Principally Moses was commanded to construct a portable building which was to be used in their worship and sacrificing to God. This was called the "Tabernacle."

It was made up of an outside court in which there was an altar for the animal sacrifices. There were two rooms on the inside. The first room was called the "Holy Place" and had several articles of furniture that were involved in the worship of God. The innermost room was the most important spot in the Tabernacle. It was called the "Holy of Holies," and it was where the Ark of the Covenant was kept and where the presence of God dwelt above the ark in a blaze of light called "Shekinah Glory."

It was in this Holy of Holies that God ordained that the blood of one sacrificial lamb could atone for the sins of the whole nation of Israel from year to year. It was the job of the high priest to select a perfect animal once a year and take the blood of it into the Holy of Holies and sprinkle it on the mercy seat. In so doing, it conciliated God's wrath against the nation for another year by atoning for the sins of the people. This day came to be called the "Day of Atonement."

One Lamb for the World

Jesus' cousin, John the Baptist, was the first person to call Jesus by the name "Lamb of God." When he saw Jesus coming toward him one day, he said, "Behold, the Lamb of God who takes away the sin of the world" (John 1:29).

Now, where do you suppose John got that mental picture of Jesus as a lamb, taking away the sins of the world?

No doubt in his knowledge of the Old Testament scriptures and his experience with animal sacrifice in the Temple in Jerusalem, he had come to realize that the continual shedding of the blood of substitutionary animals did *not* take away sins or the guilt they produced. He must have sensed that God had made some other provision for forgiveness and cleansing. I'm sure also that God must have supernaturally revealed to him that here was the One who would be that permanent provision for sin.

A few years after this incident with John and Jesus, the writer of the Book of Hebrews explained the whole reason why Jesus was called the "Lamb of God" who takes away the world's sins. I'm going to let him tell you in his own words, because he was obviously Jewish and had experienced some of the frustration of the empty religious treadmill of a sacrificial worship system that didn't really deal with the problem of sin.

You'll notice the number of times he contrasts the old way of doing things with a new one which Jesus instituted. He makes very clear that the old

system of approaching God through the blood of animals was never satisfactory to man or God. And then he convincingly sets forth the fact that
Jesus was the permanent sacrifice that God had in mind all the time.

The old system of Jewish laws gave only a dim foretaste of the good things Christ
would do for us. The sacrifices under the old system were repeated again and again,
year after year, but even so they could never save those who lived under their rules. If
they could have, one offering would have been enough; the worshipers would have
been cleansed once for all, and their feelings of guilt would be gone.

But just the opposite happened: those yearly sacrifices reminded them of their
disobedience and guilt instead of relieving their minds. For it is not possible for the
blood of bulls and goats really to take away sins.

That is why Christ said, as He came into the world, "O, God, the blood of bulls and
goats cannot satisfy you, so you have made ready this body of mine for me to lay as a
sacrifice upon your altar. You were not satisfied with the animal sacrifices, slain and
burnt before you as offerings for sin. Then I said, 'See, I have come to do your will, to
lay down my life, just as the Scriptures said that I would.'"

After Christ said this, about not being satisfied with the various sacrifices and
offerings required under the old system, he then added "Here I am. I have come to give
my life."

He cancels the first system in favor of a far better one. Under this new plan we have
been forgiven and made clean by Christ's dying for us once and for all. Under the old
agreement the priests stood before the altar day after day offering sacrifices that could
never take away our sins.

But Christ gave himself to God for our sins as one sacrifice for all time, and then sat
down in the place of highest honor at God's right hand, waiting for his enemies to be
laid under his feet. For by that one offering he made forever perfect in the sight of God
all those whom he is making holy (Hebrews 10:1-14, Living Bible).

Jesus Died Twice

When Jesus was hanging on the cross as our substitute, the writer of
Hebrews tells us, it was that "He might taste death for every one" (Hebrews
2:9). Since man's penalty for being a sinner is both spiritual and physical
death, Jesus had to taste both kinds of death.

When He shouted out, "My God, My God, why have You forsaken Me?"
at that moment, there on the cross, He was actually made sin for us, and in
His human spirit He died spiritually.

The Apostle Paul referred to this when he said, "He made Him [Jesus]
who knew no sin *to be sin on our behalf*, that we might become the righteousness of God in Him" (2 Corinthians 5:21).

This doesn't mean Jesus was actually sinful in Himself. It means He was
treated by the Father as if He were actually sinful. Since Jesus was bearing

our sins, God had to judge Him just as He would have had to judge us because of our sins.

In dying spiritually and physically as our substitute, God looked at Jesus' death and credited it to the account of fallen humanity. His spiritual death means God can give spiritual life to all men who will receive it; and His physical death, and defeat of it in the resurrection, means God can ultimately raise our physical bodies and give them immortality.

God's Ultimate Lamb

There's little more that can be said to amplify this vivid picture of Jesus' substitutionary death on our behalf. The only thing to add is that in becoming a Lamb for the world's sins, Jesus *fulfilled the need* for one lamb for a man, one lamb for a family, and one lamb for a nation.

It was no mere coincidence that His crucifixion took place on the day of Passover. He was destined by God to be the world's Passover Lamb whose blood, when applied to the doorposts of our hearts, would cause God to "pass over" us in judgment.

He was also the fulfillment of the lamb on the Day of Atonement upon whom the sins of the people were laid and who was slain in their behalf.

Why?

The only question that might come to mind is, "Why did He do it?"

Jesus gave us the answer to that question when He told His disciples, "Greater love has no one than this, that one lay down his life for his friends" (John 15:13).

Jesus died for us because He loved us!

12 ○ Reconciliation

To ME, ONE of the happiest words in the English language is "reconciliation." I immediately picture two people being restored into a new relationship.

It's one of God's favorite words too, because it means He can now restore man into fellowship with Himself because of the sum total of the threefold work of Christ on the cross:

1. *Propitiation* brings man out from under the wrath of God through satisfying His righteousness and justice.

2. *Redemption* brings man out from slavery to sin and Satan through the payment of a ransom.

3. *Substitutionary Death* brings man out from under the penalty of death through the death of Christ in our place.

The above three have torn down the barrier that man's sin has built up against God. But even with the *barrier* gone, the *relationship* between God and man must be reestablished. This is the work of reconciliation.

You see, God hasn't changed; He's always loved man and still does. The world hasn't changed either; it's still in rebellion against God. But what has changed is that judicially the barrier is now down, and when anyone sees this and *believes* it, at that moment he becomes personally reconciled to God.

Reconciliation brings man out from under his mental attitude of alienation from God. With the barrier taken out of the way through the work of Christ on the cross, reconciliation means that, through Christ, man may now be brought from alienation to fellowship with God. In fact, it's when man really begins to see how Christ has so completely removed the barrier so that He's no longer angry, that he begins to open up toward God and want to be reconciled to Him.

The Greeks Have a Word for It!

You've heard the statement, "The Greeks have a word for it." The Greek language has many words to every one in the English. It was the most explicit language ever devised in the history of the human race. I'm sure it's no mere accident that this was the language God chose for the writing of the New Testament.

There are three words in the Greek language expressing the idea of reconciliation, and all are translated by the one English word "reconciliation."

Word No. 1

The word *daillassomai* means to change two people to friendship who are *both* at odds with each other. It's used that way in Matthew 5:24. ". . . first be reconciled to your brother, and then come and present your offering." Here the parties or "brothers" have turned their backs on each other; both are angry and need to be reconciled.

This word is *never* used with reference to God, because it's we who have turned our backs on God, not He on us!

Word No. 2

The second word for reconciliation is *apokatallasso*. It's closely aligned with the main verb we want to consider, and it means a change completely from enmity to fellowship. When this word is used it means that only one person has been at enmity and that person has been completely restored to fellowship with another.

Word No. 3

The word we'll spend the most time considering is the third word, *katallasso*. This word, meaning to change from enmity to fellowship, is used several places in the New Testament. It's used throughout 2 Corinthians 5:17-21, the key passage on reconciliation.

Katallasso (reconciliation) views it this way: here is God; here is man. Man is at odds with God; he's turned his back on God. God never had to be reconciled; it was man who needed to be. *Katallasso* means only one person in a relationship has turned away and needs to be brought back—just one.

Hosea and the Hooker

The perfect example of the story of reconciliation is the Old Testament Book of Hosea, especially the first few chapters. I call the book the "Romance of Reconciliation." Here's why.

God told Hosea to marry a certain woman He had picked out for him. The woman God chose was a prostitute. Hosea married her and treated her with love and respect. She bore his children.

Then one day she ran off from him and returned to being a prostitute. God told Hosea to go and find her and bring her back.

He finally found his wife on the block at a slave auction. She stood there at the mercy of the bidders, stripped naked—the custom of the day for the auctioning of female slaves—waiting to be sold into slavery. Hosea bought back his own wife, clothed her, brought her back home, and kept right on loving her with no retribution at all.

What a picture! Hosea learned experientially just how God felt about Israel, how Israel's love affairs with pagan gods hurt Him, and how He would stop at nothing to bring these people back.

But this is also a picture of what man has done to God and of what God has done to bring us back. It's a picture of *real* love. You see, Hosea never stopped loving his wife; it was she who turned from him. And the idea is given that Hosea's great love absolutely overwhelmed his wife. She couldn't get over the fact that he still loved her.

As a picture of reconciliation, the Book of Hosea is a Rembrandt!

God never had to be reconciled! He's like Hosea. But it's man who has to be brought back and reconciled, and that's what this word *katallasso* means.

Like Hosea, God knew we would never be brought back to Him unless (a) God took the initiative and (b) God took us "just as we are" in our condition of sin. Hosea didn't try to clean up his wife before he brought her home, nor did she try to clean herself up. She came just as she was and the clean-up took place later.

I'm sure Gomer, Hosea's wife, must have been filled with guilt and shame when she heard Hosea bidding for her at the slave auction. After he got her home, her sense of unworthiness and guilt probably produced an attitude of suspicion and alienation toward Hosea, wondering when he was going to get even with her.

But as the days went by and all that Gomer got from Hosea was love and acceptance, her hostility turned to love and gratitude and she became a love-slave of his.

Reconciliation Neutralizes Hostility

True reconciliation always does away with hostility. That's what the Apostle Paul was speaking of when he said, "And although you were *formerly* alienated and hostile in mind, engaged in evil deeds, yet He has now reconciled you in His fleshly body through death" (Colossians 1:21, 22).

If we think someone is holding something against us, then we'll feel alienated and hostile toward them, simply out of self-defense. It's even more true when it comes to God. If we feel our sins are still an issue between us and God, then we won't feel like coming to Him because we know how He feels about sin.

But listen to this terrific good news from the pen of the Apostle Paul: "God was in Christ reconciling the world to Himself, *not counting their trespasses against them*, and He has committed to us the word of reconciliation" (2 Corinthians 5:19).

Did you get it? God isn't holding our sins against us anymore. The reconciliation He made available to us through the cross has neutralized His just anger at our sins.

That's why the "cross" must always be the central message of the Gospel, because it's what Christ did there that makes reconciliation with God possible. And without reconciliation there's no way to remove the alienation and hostility that we have in our minds toward God.

When we find out how totally God has done away with the barrier that separated us from Him, and that He isn't mad at us, then we're going to want to "come home" like Hosea's wife did. And when we "come home," we're so grateful for the lack of recrimination and the complete acceptance, that all we want to do is serve our Master.

The Wayward Son Comes Home

Another beautiful illustration of reconciliation is the parable that Jesus told about the prodigal son (Luke 15).

It's important to get the setting of this incident or a great deal of its meaning is lost. Jesus was teaching, and the biggest part of His audience were tax-gatherers and self-admitted sinners. Interspersed among them were some of the pious super-religious Pharisees and scribes, and they began to make snide remarks about Jesus' friendship with sinners.

Jesus tells three parables to this group, the purpose of which is to teach what God's attitude is toward those who recognize that they are sinners. You see, the Pharisees were sinners, but they didn't think they were. So Jesus was trying to show them that it's better to admit you're a sinner and place yourself under God's grace, than to bravely defend your self-righteousness and miss out on God's blessing.

In this particular parable of the prodigal or wayward son, there was a father with two sons. The younger one decided he wanted his inheritance so he could leave home and live it up (He represents the publicans and sinners). The older son (representing the self-righteous Pharisees) stayed at home and continued to work for his father (who represents God in this story).

The younger son went into a far-off country and squandered all his inheritance with wild living. A severe famine came in that land, and he found himself in real need. So he hired out to a certain citizen and found himself out in the fields feeding pigs (this citizen was Satan).

Finally the kid said to himself, "This is ridiculous! I'm here starving and my father's slaves have better food than this. I'll go to my father and tell him, 'Father, I know I've sinned against heaven and you by the stupid way I've blown my inheritance, and I'm not even worthy to be a son of yours. But if you'll let me come home, I'll be glad just to be one of your servants.'"

You can tell by what he said that he expected his father to want to have nothing to do with him after the way he'd disappointed him. But he was in for a big surprise!

While he was still a long way from his father's house, his dad caught sight of him. It's obvious the father must have been hopefully keeping an eye out for him ever since he left. And when he saw him, he ran to the son and threw his arms around him and kissed him.

Then the boy gave him the speech he'd planned about not being worthy, and being willing to come home as a hired man.

But the father never heard a word he said, for he was already giving instructions to the servants to get a big welcome-home party ready. There was no resentment or wrath in the father toward that boy, even though there was plenty of reason for him to be upset.

The father's attitude was expressed in his statement to everyone, "This son of mine was dead and has come to life again. He was lost and has been found."

Reconciliation Isn't "Reasonable"

This parable is such a terrific illustration of reconciliation. Obviously this father dearly loved this boy all his life or he never would have given him his inheritance before it was due, as he had asked. During all those long months and possibly years, the father kept on loving the boy and yearning for him to come home and be reconciled to him.

When the boy recognized how foolish he'd been, he expected there to be stern barriers between him and his father if he wanted to come home. But when he got to the place of willingness to come back to his dad, he found that instead of being barriers there, there was nothing but love and complete acceptance.

Don't Miss the Point

There are certain very important truths which this parable teaches, but there are also some very strong things it *doesn't* teach.

First of all, keep in mind that it is a parable. This was one of Jesus' favorite teaching devices. In a parable, each character generally represented some true person or situation.

In this parable of the prodigal son, the most important thing it doesn't teach is that we're all sons of God, some of whom have simply gone astray. The persons represented by the wayward son were the self-admitted sinners, and these were people who still needed to get right with God.

All men are *creatures* of God and, as such, the objects of His love. Man was once in a relationship of intimacy with God, but has been in a position of straying and rebellion since Adam's fall. And the fact that the father says of his son that he was "dead and is now alive, was lost and is now found" shows that a very radical change had taken place in the relationship of these two.

The change that had taken place is called "reconciliation."

Be Ye Reconciled! ! !

But reconciliation is worth nothing unless the barriers that caused it in the first place are torn down, and then the one who is alienated decides to become reconciled. The prodigal son had to decide to renounce the rebellious life he'd chosen and to go home. That's simply called "repenting," which means to "change your mind and your direction."

Hosea's wife had run from him, but when he came to get her, she had to be willing to go back home with him.

By these four mighty works of Christ on the cross,

propitiation (1 John 2:2),
redemption (1 Timothy 2:5, 6),
substitutionary death (Hebrews 2:9),
reconciliation (2 Corinthians 5:19),

God has made all men "reconcilable," but the effect of these truths becomes a reality only when a person believes them. 1 Timothy 4:10 says, "We have fixed our hope on the living God, who is the Savior of all men, *especially of believers.*"

Just how a person becomes personally reconciled to God is a matter of the greatest importance. Our whole eternal destiny depends upon the right decision in this matter. The next chapter will carefully discuss this most important question we must answer: "Have I personally been reconciled to God?"

13 ○ A Decision
of Destiny

IN THE LAST four chapters we saw the wonders of God's love by which He has removed all the barriers between Himself and man.

But the really incredible thing is that God has accomplished a total provision of salvation for even those human beings whom He knew would reject it.

God so loved the "world" that He gave His son (John 3:16). It wasn't just for the part of the world that He knew would receive His salvation that He died. It was for all of those who would ridicule His name, ignore His salvation, despise His Word, and reject His authority.

Whether they want to be or not, the whole world has been made "savable" because of the death of Christ on the cross.

But being "savable" and being "saved" are two different things.

If someone has put $100,000 in a bank account for you, it won't do you any good unless, first of all, you know about it, and secondly, you draw upon it.

The four great doctrines of Christ's death in man's behalf are for the whole world, but applicable only to those who draw upon it personally.

Propitiation

"He Himself [Jesus] is the propitiation for our sins; and not for ours only, but also *for those of the whole world*" (1 John 2:2).

Redemption

"For there is one God, and one mediator also between God and men, the man Christ Jesus, who gave Himself *a ransom for all*" (1 Timothy 2:5, 6) .

Substitutionary Death

"But we do see Him who has been made for a little while lower than the angels, namely, Jesus, because of the suffering of death crowned with glory and honor, that by the grace of God, He might *taste death for every one*" (Hebrews 2:9).

Reconciliation

"God was in Christ *reconciling the world to Himself,* not counting their trespasses against them . . ." (2 Corinthians 5:19).

I once heard a speaker liken God's worldwide offer of salvation to a petstore owner who puts a free kitten in the window of his shop. It's available to everyone, but it only becomes the possession of the one who goes in and takes it.

God has put His offer of "free forgiveness" in His window and it's *available* to everyone, but only the possession of those who come in and take it.

Don't Get the Cart Before the Horse!

Now, in light of the fact that the barriers have been removed from between God and man, and God freely offers a new relationship with Himself, what must a man do to receive the results of this and have it be a reality in his own life?

At no other point is it more important to distinguish between the *means* of coming into God's salvation and the *effects* of it. It's of utmost importance that we don't get the cart before the horse in the matter of *how* to appropriate all that Christ accomplished for us on the cross.

If we make something which the Bible calls a *result* of salvation part of the *means* by which it's obtained, then we insert human merit into the picture of God's redemptive plan. And human merit nullifies the whole concept of a *free* salvation.

Now let's take a look at some of the things that men have tried to add to "faith" as an additional means of salvation.

Faith, Plus Works?

The Apostle Paul, knowing that all men have an insatiable selfcenteredness that makes them want to boast of their spiritual or moral prowess, wrote to the believers in Ephesus, "For by *grace* you have been saved through faith; and *that not of yourselves,* it is the gift of God; *not as a result of works,* that no one should boast" (Ephesians 2:8, 9).

It's a real commentary on the nature of the human heart that at the very outset of Christianity, Paul has to admonish people that salvation is a free gift from God and there's no possible way to do anything to merit it, or else human pride and boasting would come in.

You see, if there were anything God required of man in the way of good deeds or human effort in order to receive God's salvation, then there would be good reason for some people to boast about how they'd helped themselves get into God's family. Because, obviously some people would work much harder than others to obtain God's favor and it follows that it would only be fair that He give them more love and acceptance than the ones who didn't work too hard at it.

Grace: God's Riches At Christ's Expense

But over and over we keep running into a word in the New Testament that tells us the true basis on which God accepts us. That word is "grace."

If we could have only a half-dozen words in our human vocabulary, that word should be one of them. It's one of those words that's so loaded with meaning, you feel as if you need fifty words just to begin to explain it.

But simply put, it means to *freely give something to someone which he can in no possible way deserve or merit or earn.*

The minute there's even a shadow of a hint of someone trying to merit or earn the thing being given, then it's not grace any longer (see Romans 11:6).

Now, what is it that God has given to us that we can't in any way merit?

His love, forgiveness, righteousness, acceptance, mercy, redemption, and eternal life—all of which are wrapped up in one package called "salvation." This is what He's given to us, if we'll take it, and it's given completely on the basis of "grace."

My first brush, on the human level, with the concept of grace was when I got my first health insurance policy. After paying ten hard-earned bucks a month for a couple of years on this policy, I came to a place where I just couldn't scrape together ten dollars one month. I hated to let the policy lapse, because I'd paid so much on it already and I'd never used it once.

But when the payment date arrived, I just didn't send them anything and I sadly figured that would be the last I'd hear of them. Yet, after a couple of weeks I got a letter from them telling me that my policy hadn't been canceled and I was in a thirty-day "grace" period.

I didn't deserve that thirty extra days of coverage, and I hadn't paid for it, but I found out that I was fully covered anyway in case any sickness or accident had happened to me.

That was only human grace, so you can imagine what divine grace must be like.

Grace Is God's Part: Faith Is Man's!

If you had a present for someone you loved and he kept trying to do something to earn it, you'd feel rebuffed in your effort to show your unreserved affection. If you wanted him to work for the present, then it wouldn't really be a gift—it would be a wage.

That's what Paul says about man's efforts to work for God's favor: "Now to the one who works, his wage is not reckoned according to grace, but according to what is due. But to the one who does not work, but *believes* in Him [Jesus] who declares righteous the ungodly, his *faith* is reckoned as righteousness" (Romans 4:4, 5 paraphrased).

Nothing could be more clear.

A man's *faith* in what Jesus freely made available to him at the cross by *grace* is what God credits to his account as righteousness. I put my faith in Jesus, and He puts His righteousness into me.

Yeah, But . . . !

The "cart-before-the-horse-crowd" is probably bursting right now with "Yeah, but what about the Book of James that says that 'faith without works is dead'?"

There's one thing for sure: if James means that faith and works *together* constitute salvation (as some believe he means), then his teaching is in diametric opposition to everything Paul taught. Now, since I don't believe the Bible can contradict itself, let's take a good look at what James was really emphasizing in the second chapter of his book.

The Man from Missouri

In chapter two, James is addressing a group of people who claim to be true believers in Jesus but don't manifest any evidence of this fact in their lives. So James takes the position that faith can only be seen *by men*, through what it produces in a life. He gives two completely different biblical case histories to prove this point and to show that *true* faith always produces evidence of its genuineness.

Case No. 1: Abraham

The first case James mentions is that of Abraham when God called upon him to be willing to offer up his dearly loved and only son, Isaac, as a sacrifice to the Lord. In complete obedience and trust that God knew what He was doing, Abraham actually went so far as to place Isaac onto an altar and raise a knife above him to plunge it into his heart. But God told Abraham to stop, just in time. God saw what He wanted to see, and it was that Abraham was still a man who would trust God no matter what the case might be and that he was the kind of man God could use to be the father of a race of people called the "Hebrews."

You see, it's very important to note that this testing in Abraham's life, recorded in Genesis 22, happened forty years *after* God had already declared Abraham righteous on the basis of his faith alone. Genesis 15:6 records the conversation that God initially had with Abraham when He told him that he would have many descendants. Abraham was about seventy-five years old then, and he was childless. Even though he couldn't figure out how he could be the father of so many nations, he simply believed that if God said he would, then he would.

And it was this simple faith in God that, alone, caused God to count Abraham as righteous. From that day, until the day that he actually took his son to Mount Moriah to offer him as a sacrifice, nearly forty years transpired, and many times during that period Abraham failed God. But one thing stood sure in all those years: he was still considered a righteous man by God on the basis of his believing faith at the beginning.

After giving this illustration of Abraham's faith in offering up Isaac, James says about this, "*You see* that a man is justified by works, and not by faith alone" (2:24).

It's true that *man* sees the works. But it's also true that *God saw* Abraham's faith forty years before and on that basis pronounced him unconditionally righteous (Genesis 15; Romans 4:1-5).

The point is that after forty years of being righteous one should expect Abraham to show some evidence of his faith—and he did. But faith was the *means* of his salvation, and works were simply the *evidence* of the genuineness of it.

True faith will always produce works as evidence. But works will never produce true faith. Get the point?

Case No. 2: Rahab the Harlot

Lest we get the idea that in order to be declared righteous by God we must have some enormous demonstration of faith as Abraham did, James gives another case history to show how little a thing is evidence enough to show true faith.

At a time in Israel's history when she was seeking to enter the promised land, spies were sent from the wandering nation of Israel into Jericho to see what kind of opposition they would encounter if they tried to enter. Two Hebrew spies entered the home of a harlot named Rahab, and although she was a gentile and didn't know these two men, she hid them from her fellow countrymen when they came looking for the spies (Joshua 2:1-7).

After their pursuers were gone, Rahab told the Hebrew spies that her whole nation had heard about the Red Sea opening up for them forty years earlier. And how all the people of Jericho had lived in fear of the nation of Israel because of the great things their God had done for them in bringing them out of captivity in Egypt.

Then this gentile prostitute said, ". . . for the LORD your God, He is God in heaven above and on earth beneath. Now therefore, please swear to me by the LORD, since I have dealt kindly with you, that you also will deal kindly with my father's household" when you come in to conquer the land (Joshua 2:11, 12).

Now, this doesn't seem like much of a work, but it was enough to show that she had come to believe in the God of Israel and that *belief* prompted her *act* of hiding Israel's spies.

From both these illustrations of James it can be seen that faith is only as good as its object, and the object must be God and confidence in His power and His word. When whatever faith we have, whether it be great like Abraham's or small like Rahab's, is placed in God then there will be the resulting evidence in our lives.

If there are never any righteous works in a person's life, then it well may be that there is no true faith. But if there is true faith, I guarantee you there will be good deeds eventually.

Faith, Plus Repentance?

Anytime anything is added to the one necessary ingredient of "faith" in order to receive God's salvation, then we're in danger of getting that cart in front of the horse again. Some people put a big stress on repentance as a necessary condition for receiving reconciliation. To be sure, repentance is definitely involved in becoming a child of God, but it must be carefully defined.

There are those who, in their zeal to get people to turn from their sinful ways and receive the Lord, almost put repentance on a par with believing. Repentance is defined by them as a deep sorrow over sin, usually evidenced by weeping and much emotion.

This is a faulty understanding of the word "repentance." It's certainly all right to have a deep emotional sorrow about having spent a life rejecting Christ, but that's not all that's involved in repentance.

Judas Iscariot felt such sorrow about betraying Jesus that he wept uncontrollably and even returned the money he'd received for turning Him over to His enemies. But he never repented or believed. Instead, he hung himself as a result of utter despair from guilt (see Matthew 27:3-5).

When we're talking with someone about his need for Christ, we need to find out where his head is about the matter of sin. If he doesn't realize that he's a sinner, then he won't know that he needs a Savior. So in a case like that it might be necessary to emphasize God's view of sin and seek to show the person that according to the Bible's definition, he qualifies as a sinner.

But generally speaking, the emphasis should *not* be upon the man's personal sins—such as lying, cheating, adultery, dope, or what have you—with an effort to try to get him to feel bad for doing those things. The emphasis should be upon what God has done to remove *all* the barriers that separate God and man, including the barrier of sin. Jesus should be made the issue.

To Change, or Not to Change!
That's the Question!

The word repentance, *metanoeo* in the Greek, means to have a *change of mind* toward something or someone. It means a turning around from one attitude to another which produces a change in direction. It's a word related to our reason, rather than to our emotions, although whatever deeply affects our reason will also touch our emotions.

Repentance, as it relates to Christ, means to change our minds about Him, who He is and what He's done to provide forgiveness and deliverance from our sins. When we place faith in Jesus as having taken our place personally on the cross and borne the penalty due our sins, then we're automatically repenting, because we couldn't accept Him in this way without having had to change our minds in some way concerning Him.

The essence of the issue is this: you can repent and not believe; but you can't believe and not repent. This is why in the gospel of John, which was expressly written to bring people to new life in Christ, the condition "believe in Christ" is stated ninety-nine times. But the word "repent" isn't used at all in the book.

You may wonder why I've made an issue of this. It's because I've seen people sit in a meeting or read a book about Christ's work of salvation for them, and they've said to themselves, "This is really true and I believe it," but then because they didn't have some deep emotional experience of repenting and getting all worked up, they haven't been sure whether their belief was sincere enough to save them.

Let me tell you right now, if while you've been reading this book, you've said to yourself, "This is true and I believe it. I don't understand it all, but I believe what I do understand," then I guarantee you that you've become a child of God. Whether your faith is strong like Abraham's or weak like Rahab's, it makes no difference. You've placed it in the right object by putting it in Christ.

Faith, Plus the Lordship of Christ?

This is a very subtle form of human merit which some add to "faith" as a condition of salvation. It's another "cart before the horse" and this one presents a tremendous problem, because it's an open-ended, indefinable condition.

For instance, who can say at this moment, no matter how long he's been a believer, that he has *everything* in his life under the lordship of Jesus? Most believers would like to have that be true, but as long as we're still in this world, with our unreformed sin natures, and the world, the flesh, and the devil are still out to get us, there's not much chance that there'll be a time in our lives when *everything* is under Christ's lordship at the same time.

If even mature believers are conscious of areas of their lives that aren't always in total submission to Christ, how can we make an unbeliever responsible to do something as a condition of salvation that we're still not able to do?

Those who say, "If Christ is not Lord of all, He's not Lord at all" have an admirable slogan, but they're laying a burden on the potential believer that's impossible to bear. But worse than that, they're subtly adding "works" to faith which nullifies grace and makes salvation, if not impossible, then very much of an albatross around the prospective believer's neck.

The scriptural teaching on this issue is that we must recognize Jesus as Lord in the sense that He's not a mere man, but the Lord from heaven who became a man to die for our sins. Yet even this understanding doesn't fully come until we've believed in Him as Savior and received new spiritual life so that we have the facility for understanding spiritual truth.

There's nothing wrong with telling an interested seeker that Christ wants to be his Lord once He comes to live within him, but unless that information is coupled with the teaching regarding the Holy Spirit's indwelling power to progressively make Jesus Lord of your life, then it's better not to bring it up. Once the person is saved, the Holy Spirit Himself will bring up the issue of Christ's Lordship.

In Romans 10:9, 10 Paul says this about what's involved in being saved, "If you confess with your mouth Jesus as Lord, and believe in your heart that God raised Him from the dead, you shall be saved; for with the heart man believes, resulting in righteousness, and with the mouth he confesses, resulting in salvation."

Two ingredients of salvation are mentioned in these verses. One is a *cause* and the other is an *effect*. One has to do with the heart or mind, and the other has to do with the mouth.

Look at the verses carefully. Paul says that what a man believes with his heart about Christ's resurrection and what it means will result in God giving him Christ's righteousness. That's another way of saying that the man has just become a child of God.

Then it says that with the mouth he is to confess or tell the world that Christ is the Lord and now his own personal Savior as well.

The believing is the *cause* of salvation, and the *effect* is the confession of Jesus as the Lord.

Faith, Plus Baptism?

The adding of a God-ordained ritual to faith as a condition of salvation down through the dark history of God's dealing with man has been one of the most subtle errors. The issue of water baptism has been the most confusing, since Jesus himself commanded this ritual (Matthew 28:19, 20) and the Book of Acts shows that this was the common practice of believers.

There's no question but that a believer who's had the real meaning of water baptism explained to him will want to be baptized after receiving Christ as Savior. The rite of baptism is the believer's testimony to the world that he believes he's been totally identified with Christ in His death and burial, and he's now raised with Jesus into a new life where sin has no right to rule over him.

It's been particularly thrilling to me to see the way thousands of people today have desired to express in this dramatic, tangible way the fact that they have come to believe in Christ as their Savior. No one has laid any big trip on these people about the necessity of being baptized, but strangely enough, once they've been joined to Christ they just seem to want to jump into the nearest ocean, lake, or swimming pool and publicly announce that they belong to Christ.

But as beautiful and as meaningful as this necessary symbol is, it still must be seen as a *result* of salvation, not a *cause* of it, or even a partial cause of it. If we add baptism as a condition of being saved, then it becomes a work and an act of human merit which nullifies pure grace that says that nothing is needed from man, but faith.

An Old Error, Revived

The Jews at the time of Jesus, for the most part, made the same error as some believers do today. The ritual of circumcision given to them through Abraham corresponded to the ritual of water baptism today.

This teaching of the necessity of adding circumcision to faith was the source of a great controversy in the early church (see Acts 15:1-11). The Apostle Paul, in demonstrating that salvation has always been by faith alone, selected two of the greatest men in the Old Testament as an illustration of that fact: Abraham and David.

Read carefully what Paul says of Abraham: "If Abraham was justified by works, he has something to boast about; but not before God. For what does the Scripture say? 'And Abraham *believed* God, and it was reckoned to him as righteousness'" (Romans 4:2, 3).

Then Paul shows that Abraham's being declared righteous before God on the basis of faith was apart from any ritual: "Is this blessing then upon the circumcised, or upon the uncircumcised also? For we say, 'Faith was reckoned to Abraham as righteousness.'

"How then was it reckoned? While he was circumcised, or uncircumcised?" And then Paul answers his own question, "Not while circumcised, but while uncircumcised; and he received the sign of circumcision, a seal of the righteousness of the faith which he had while uncircumcised" (Romans 4:9-11).

Paul argues relentlessly on this point, because any ritual, be it circumcision, Communion, or baptism, added to faith as a condition of salvation becomes a work of human merit, and that's incompatible with grace.

Paul Wasn't Sent to Baptize

Paul shows that baptism clearly isn't a condition of salvation when he says, "I thank God that I baptized none of you, except Crispus and Gaius, that no man should say you were baptized in my name."

And then he suddenly remembers some others he'd baptized and so he adds, "Now I did baptize also the household of Stephanas; beyond that, I do not know whether I baptized any other. For Christ did not send me to baptize, but to preach the gospel, not in cleverness of speech, that the cross of Christ should not be made void" (1 Corinthians 1:14-17).

Though Paul had led most of the Corinthian church to Christ, he couldn't remember too well whom he had baptized. Then he makes a colossal statement, "Christ didn't send me to baptize, but to preach the gospel." Paul's mission in life was to bring people into the salvation of Jesus Christ. If baptism were an integral part of the qualification for salvation, then he could never have made the above statement. Paul would have practically pulled a portable baptistry around behind him if baptism was a condition of the Gospel he was commissioned by Christ to preach.

Instead Paul concentrated on the one thing, preaching the Gospel. Because when men believe it, it's the power of God that brings salvation (see Romans 1:16, 17).

The Real Issue Is Faith, Plus Nothing!

God has always had only one way of saving men, and that's been on the principle of "grace, through faith, not as a result of works, lest any one should have a reason to boast" about how he helped God save him (see Ephesians 2:8, 9).

Even in the Old Testament, salvation was by "Grace, through faith." There was no man who could say he deserved God's forgiveness. All men deserved His condemnation, but before Christ came, God graciously provided the animal sacrifices to picture the coming Lamb of God who would take away the world's sins.

However, simply offering sacrifices didn't save a man. He had to come in faith, believing that this was God's provision at that time to atone for his sins, and he had to trust in God to graciously withhold his judgment from him as long as he brought his offerings in faith.

The New Testament also clearly teaches that faith is the *means* of salvation. There are many *results*. Among them will be good deeds, repentance, Christ progressively becoming the Lord of your life, baptism, obedience, service, the fruits of the Spirit, spiritual gifts, and on and on.

But the issue that must remain central is that faith alone is all that's necessary for salvation. Remember the thief on the cross beside Jesus. He believed in Christ while hanging there in the process of dying. He couldn't come down from the cross and do any good deeds, he couldn't be baptized, and he couldn't go out and manifest the Christian life to the world by holy living.

Nevertheless, Jesus told him that that very day he would be in paradise with him because he had believed on Jesus.

I'm aware of the fact that some teach that God has had different ways of saving man at different times in human history. But if God ever compromised and made an exceptional case out of even one man's salvation, He would be honorbound by His own character to do it for all.

God's attribute of justice demands that He be equitable and fair with everyone, for as Paul points out in Romans 2:11, "there is no partiality with God." If God could save a thief by faith alone—and He did—then He must do it the same way for everyone.

Besides all this, if there had been some other way for man to be reconciled to God without God's having to put to death His dear Son, don't you think God would have done it? But that death was necessary to remove every barrier that stood between God and man so that God could deal with us in grace. Having done that, God isn't going to impose conditions on us for salvation which involve any human merit, thus nullifying what cost Him an infinite price to make a free gift to us.

Making Our "Withdrawal"

I said at the beginning of this chapter that if someone had put $100,000 in a bank account for you, it would do you no good unless you knew about it and then withdrew it from the bank.

Now you know what it is that God has done for you on the cross and how to draw upon it by faith alone.

The next move is up to you!

14 ∘ Justification

THERE'S A STORY in the New Testament which so beautifully illustrates justification that I'm going to begin with it and wait a few pages even to define the word. By the time you've digested this "Saga of Justification," little definition will be necessary.

A Clergyman and a Tax Collector (Luke 18:9-14)

Two men went over to the Temple to pray. One was a super-religious do-gooder called a Pharisee, and the other a tax collector, called a Publican.

A tax man in those days was considered by the Pharisees, the religious crowd, to be the most wicked sinner in the world. He was a man who betrayed his own countrymen by collecting more taxes than were assigned by the government. This dishonest profit was the only payment for services he received; he didn't get a salary. He was told to keep everything "over and above." A Publican, then, made his money by extortion from his fellow citizens.

A Pharisee was a member of a Jewish religious order that went to the Temple three times a day and prayed on his own seven times daily. Talk about trying to pile up brownie points with God, in Luke 18:11 it says, "The Pharisee stood and was praying thus to himself, 'God, I thank Thee that I am not like other people, swindlers, unjust, adulterers, or even like this [*ugh!*] tax-gatherer.'" Then you can just hear him ticking all his good deeds off to the Lord—fasting, tithing, praying, sacrificing.

Do you think this guy was kidding?

No! He did all these things. Why, in the average church today he'd be considered a real pillar, wouldn't he? People would applaud him: "Look at this great saint of God." Everything he did in the public eye was beyond reproach.

Then in verse 13, the other man prayed, "God, be merciful to me, the sinner." It says he was unwilling even to lift his eyes to heaven, but instead was beating his breast. This "beating of the breast" was a sign of sorrow and unworthiness. He counted himself unworthy to come to God. His prayer reflected that.

Let's look more carefully at this prayer for mercy.

The Greek word *hilastheti* used here should *never* have been translated into the English word "merciful" because it actually means "to be propitious." I'm sure that the translators felt the word "merciful" was a more familiar word to the English reader than the word "propitious," but theologically it does not connote the true meaning of the word or the passage.

You see, God has never had to be persuaded to be merciful. It was His mercy that caused Him to find a way to satisfy His outraged holiness so that He could act toward us in grace. When the tax-collector prayed to God and asked Him to be "propitious" toward him, he was actually saying, "I know you're not satisfied with *me*. I'm nothing but a no-good sinner who only deserves Your righteous wrath. But please receive me in the light of the atoning blood of sacrifice on the mercy seat which has satisfied your judgment against me."

He may not have used those words, but when he asked God to be propitious toward him, that's exactly what he meant.

Jesus Looks at the Heart

What did Jesus say about this tax-collecting sinner?

"I tell you, this man went down to his house *justified* rather than the other; for everyone who exalts himself shall be humbled, but he who humbles himself shall be exalted."

To be humble means to have a true estimation of yourself and where you stand with God. To recognize there's nothing you can do to gain acceptance in God's sight, but to merely allow Him to make you acceptable.

By contrast, look at how the Pharisee approached God. He was full of pride about all the things he was *doing* to gain God's approbation. His deeds in themselves were not wrong, only his motives. His pride gave away the fact that he didn't understand the real meaning of God's propitiation through sacrifice.

Justification Defined

A simple definition which I've often heard defining "justification" is *"just-as-if-I'd* never sinned." It makes a clever-sounding phrase, but unfortunately it isn't correct.

You see, even in light of the fact that Christ has taken all my sins away, that only leaves me in a *neutral* status with God. Just having no sin will never make me acceptable in God's sight.

In order to be acceptable to God, I need more than just the *subtraction* of my sins. I need the *addition* of Christ's righteousness.

The Apostle Paul tells us how God arranged for this exchange. "God made Christ who knew no sin to be sin on our behalf, that we might become the righteousness of God in Him" (2 Corinthians 5:21). In other words, God took our sins and put them on Christ and then took Christ's righteousness and gave it to us in exchange.

That's what it means to be justified.

Because of the propitiation accomplished by Christ, God is now set free to instantly and irrevocably "declare righteous" any man, woman, or child who places faith in Christ as Savior. God declares that person to be just as righteous in *His* sight as His Son, Jesus Christ. This is our new "standing" with God.

The "Misinterpretation" That Split the Church

It's very important however, that the meaning of the word "justify" as used in the New Testament be precisely understood. There's a vast difference between being "declared" righteous by God and actually "becoming" righteous in my daily behavior. The first happens instantly the moment I believe in Christ and forever settles my acceptance and standing in the eyes of God. He can never again see me in any way except as having the righteousness of His Son.

However, my "becoming" righteous in my daily behavior is a life-long process which begins with my becoming a child of God, and it is culminated with my becoming just like Jesus the day I enter His eternal presence. But, whether I'm making good progress in my daily perfecting or not, it doesn't alter the fact that God continues to view me as absolutely righteous because of my union with Christ.

The biggest rift that ever developed in Christianity grew out of a confusion of this very issue of the difference between being "declared" righteous and actually "being" righteous in behavior. This rift became known as the "Reformation" and it forced a re-focus on two greatly abused truths: *first*, that justification is exclusively a work of God whereby He imparts to a believing soul the irrevocable righteousness of Christ; and *second*, Christ's righteousness is received by man at the *moment* of salvation on the basis of faith alone.

Luther and the Reformation of the Church

The German monk, Martin Luther, was the catalyst that brought about the Reformation. The theology of his day taught that justification meant that when one professed belief in Christ, God declared all his *past* sins forgiven. But he must then enter into a life-long process of obtaining continued forgiveness and righteousness by his own religious performance. This included the necessity of such things as good works, self-denial, penance in the form of self-inflicted punishment and pain, prayers, confession, giving of money, worship, and so forth.

In spite of careful performance of all these things, Luther wrestled continually with a sense of spiritual inadequacy. Finally, in desperation he determined to go to Rome, the center of the Christian faith, and perform an act of penance and pain which might ease his troubled conscience. While crawling on his knees up the steps of a church in Rome, and wondering if all this would bring him the sense of spiritual peace which he sought, a verse from the Book of Romans kept flashing across his mind: "The just shall live by *faith*" (Romans 1:17 KJV).

There was no way Luther could equate what he was doing at that moment with living by faith. He was living by "works" and seeking to improve his righteousness in God's eyes by all these human merits.

In that instant the Reformation, which had been in a long incubation period, was born. Luther got up from his knees and with pen and preaching began to liberate hundreds of thousands of sincere believers in God who had never heard that Christ's death secured for them a *permanent* and *total* forgiveness and righteous standing with God which was obtainable *in toto* by faith in Christ alone.

Justification by Faith: A Neglected Doctrine

Down through the dark history of the church, this fact of "justification by faith" has been the most maligned, misunderstood, and neglected truth of the Christian faith. A failure to properly understand and accept the reality of having been declared irrevocably righteous by God has stripped believers of the assurance of their standing with God and has crippled them into thinking they must be on an endless treadmill of works in order to maintain their acceptance with God.

It's hard to see how this vital truth could be missed by anyone who's seeking to carefully examine and teach the Word, since it's the heart of the message of the Apostle Paul. What Jesus had introduced in numerous parables in the gospels concerning justification, Paul amplified doctrinally in the epistles, particularly in Romans and Galatians.

Obviously the reason Paul made such an emphasis upon this truth is because of the impact that this doctrine had upon his own life. He makes this clear in his word of caution to the Philippians. In that letter to this young church, Paul seeks to undo some of the erroneous teaching that a group of super-religious Pharisaical Jews had sown behind his back and which subtly contradicted his previous teaching.

These Judaizers were Jews who in some ways accepted Jesus as the Messiah, but believed it was still imperative to keep all the old Mosaic laws, as well as being circumcised, if they truly wanted to be acceptable to God. This was diametrically opposed to what Paul had taught. His emphasis was upon faith alone as being sufficient to bring about salvation.

In his admonishment to the church in Philippians 3:1-9, Paul argues that the truly circumcised person is the one who worships God in the Spirit and puts *no* confidence in fleshly rituals or deeds. He then cites his own admirable testimony of how blameless he was in his keeping of the Jewish laws and his zealous persecution of the church, prior to his conversion.

Here's what he says: "If anyone else has a mind to put confidence in the flesh, I far more: circumcised the eighth day, of the nation of Israel, of the tribe of Benjamin, a Hebrew of Hebrews; as to the Law, a Pharisee; as to zeal, a persecutor of the church; . . ."

Now, notice what he says about his "law-keeping": ". . . as to the righteousness which is in the Law, *found blameless*" (Philippians 3:4b-6).

Two Kinds of Righteousness

You can see from what Paul just said that there are *two* kinds of righteousness. We've already discussed the first one, that which belongs exclusively to Christ and is imputed or credited to the one who does nothing more than place faith in Christ's atoning death. But the second kind of righteousness is that which comes out of an attempt to keep God's laws. This is strictly relative. In other words, God's perfect righteousness might be looked at as a standard representing 100 percent. All human efforts to keep God's laws measure somewhere from zero to one hundred, with *no one* reaching 100 percent.

As men look at our law-keeping, they applaud enthusiastically the closer we get to 100 percent, and usually we pat ourselves on the back. But from God's perspective, *anything* less than 100 percent perfect law-keeping flunks. That's what Isaiah meant when he said, "All *our* righteousnesses are as filthy rags in God's sight" (see Isaiah 64:6).

You've heard the saying, "The enemy of the best is the good." Nowhere is that more true than in this matter of righteousness. Although Paul could brag more than any Pharisee about how righteous he was in relation to keeping the Mosaic law, look at his estimation of the value of his own righteousness as over against that which he received from Christ. He says, "I count all things [all those humanly produced good deeds] to be *loss* in view of the surpassing value of knowing Christ Jesus my Lord, for whom I have suffered the loss of all things, and count them but rubbish in order that I may gain Christ, and may be found in Him, *not having a righteousness of my own derived from the Law, but that which is through faith in Christ, the righteousness which comes from God on the basis of faith*" (Philippians 3:8, 9).

The point of all Paul's trying to say here is that he was willing to compare his life with anyone who said his personal righteousness was enough to gain him God's acceptance, but if Paul's righteousness didn't save him, then no one else's lawkeeping would save them either.

Why Israel "Missed the Ball"

In his letter to the Romans, Paul tells why the majority of the nation of Israel stubbornly clung to the wrong kind of righteousness and thereby missed out on God's salvation. "But Israel, pursuing a law of righteousness, did not arrive at that law. Why? Because they did not pursue it by *faith*, but as though it were by *works*. They stumbled over THE STUMBLING-STONE [*Jesus*]" (Romans 9:31, 32).

He further comments, "For I bear them witness that they have a zeal for God, but not in accordance with knowledge. For not knowing about God's righteousness, and seeking to establish their own, they did not subject themselves to the righteousness of God. For Christ is the end of the law for righteousness to everyone who believes" (Romans 10:2-4).

Paul wasn't just picking on his fellow Jews here. His heart's desire and constant prayer to God were for their eyes to be opened to see the mistake they were making by rejecting God's way to be made righteous and trusting in their own righteousness instead.

I'm Justified—So What?

I've used a lot of pages so far in this chapter to say two things over and over.

First, on the basis of Christ's propitiatory work on the cross, God's offended character has been satisfied and God is now free to impart a new dimension to all who receive His Son as Savior. This new dimension is the *righteousness of Christ* and it's like a cloak placed around a person, completely covering what he is in his own humanness, giving him a completely new standing in the eyes of God. This imputed righteousness means that every time God looks at me, now that I'm His child, He doesn't see my own righteousness (which falls far short of His perfection anyway); He sees me through the grid of Jesus' righteousness, and therefore I'm as acceptable to Him as His Son Jesus is, regardless of my daily performance.

The *second* point I've stressed is that this righteousness is given to a person, free and complete, the moment he places faith in Christ as Savior. It can't be added to, improved upon by God or man or ever revoked. It's given strictly on the basis of faith alone.

The ramifications in the life of the believer of "justification by faith" are incredible. We'll focus on the three major benefits: peace with God, a standing in grace, and no more condemnation.

Peace with God

In Romans 5:1 the Apostle Paul says, "Therefore having been justified by faith, we have *peace with God* through our Lord Jesus Christ."

"Having been justified" is in the aorist verb tense in the original Greek New Testament. This means it happened at a point of time in the past, and the implication here is that it never need be repeated because its effects go on forever.

It's imperative that once and for all we get straight in our minds the fact that we *have been* justified. If we don't, it's impossible to experience "peace with God." If I think my relationship with God is in constant jeopardy because of my failure to always live the Christian life correctly, then I'll be a nervous wreck, wondering whether God is upset with my performance. I can never experience peace with God until I begin to count as true the fact that I have been given Christ's righteousness and that makes me acceptable with God.

In their book, *Guilt and Freedom*,[1] Bruce Narramore and Bill Counts point out the hidden dangers of not seeing ourselves as God sees us. They correctly show that sin erected very real barriers between God and man and that although Christ has torn down the barriers and enabled God to reconcile men to Himself, there remain psychological barriers on the part of man. Man's knowledge of his failure to please God has brought fear of punishment, fear of rejection, and a loss of self-esteem.

There is absolutely no way to have these psychological barriers removed between ourselves and God until we accept as true the fact that God is now at peace with us because He has justified us once and for all. If I'm the least bit fuzzy in my thinking about this, then in spite of myself, I'm going to live with fear of punishment and rejection by God each time I fail Him. Eventually my sense of guilt will pile up so heavy on my head that I'll look at myself as a worm and of absolutely no worth to God.

Maybe you've never thought of it this way, but to have those kinds of feelings about yourself is like a slap in the face to Jesus. In essence, what you're saying when you fail to believe that you're totally acceptable to Him, just like you are, because of Christ's righteousness in you, is that you have higher standards for yourself than God does. And that attitude is both conceited and false.

If God says He is at peace with *us* on the basis of our justification, then what right do we have not to be at peace with God?

Peace with Ourselves and Others

One thing that's sure. If you don't have peace with God, then it will be impossible to be at peace consistently with yourself. You'll be constantly condemning yourself for your failures, and that self-condemnation will keep your focus on yourself instead of on Jesus and what He's done to remove God's wrath from you.

It's also impossible to be at peace with others if you haven't first settled in your mind that God is at peace with you. The last great commandment Jesus gave to His disciples was "Love one another, in the same way as I have loved you" (John 13:34). If you're not convinced that God's love for you is unconditional on the basis of His justification of you, then your love for others won't be unconditional either. You'll accept them in the same way

[1] Bruce Narramore and Bill Counts, *Guilt and Freedom* (Santa Ana, Calif.: Vision House Publishers, 1974).

that you see yourself accepted by God. That is, when you perform up to God's expectations, He accepts you; when you don't perform, He doesn't.

That's the way you'll respond to those around you. When they meet your expectations, you'll give them unconditional acceptance. When they let you down, you'll withdraw your full acceptance of them until they shape up and start performing up to your standards again.

All this fouled-up thinking is straightened out by simply believing that what God says is true of us, is true. We *have been* justified and now God is at peace with us and nothing will ever cause Him to stop being at peace with us.

The only issue is, will we believe what He says about our justification and be at peace with him?

A Standing in Grace

A second great benefit which has come to the believer through justification by faith is a new standing in grace.

"Therefore having been justified by faith, we have peace with God through our Lord Jesus Christ, through whom also we have obtained our introduction by faith into this *grace in which we stand*" (Romans 5;1, 2).

Remember that we defined grace as being "all that God has set Himself free to give us and do for us completely apart from any human merit." If we can earn it in any way, then it can't be given to us on the basis of grace.

Paul tells us in this passage in Romans that we have a standing in grace. This means God can treat us in no other way than by grace because that's our new standing with Him. There'll never be a time in our lives when God will require us to deserve or earn any blessing or favor from Him.

I don't know why it's so hard for people to really believe this. They can accept the fact that they could do nothing to deserve or earn their initial salvation, but somehow they've gotten the idea they must earn the right to be used by God or have His blessings once they've become His child.

I found myself subtly slipping into this thinking only recently. Jan and I were given a chance for a week's vacation on a cruise to Mexico. It was like a dream come true. We were waited-on hand and foot, the food was sensational, and best of all, there were no telephones ringing or appointments to keep. But about the third day out, I began to feel guilty about having such a good time. Jan sensed something was wrong and she asked me what it was. I told her I was feeling guilty because I felt I didn't really deserve to have the Lord give me such a bountiful display of His love.

Whereupon, Jan reminded me, "When did you ever *deserve* any of the blessings God has given you?"

That's really the truth! When did any of us ever deserve anything from a holy and righteous God except His wrath? And yet, because He has declared us as righteous as His Son, Jesus, God is able to give us His gracious blessings at any time, quite apart from any merit in us. It's because of our standing in grace with Him.

Relax, Believer!

One of the marvelous things about being in an atmosphere of grace is that you don't have to walk around on eggshells worrying about offending someone or getting someone uptight with you. I'm sure we've all known people who create anything but an atmosphere of grace, and the whole time we're around them we're watching our Ps and Qs to be sure we perform just right. It isn't long before that kind of relationship gets to be a drag and we don't want to be around the person.

This often becomes one of the major factors in marital problems. One of the partners has the other on such a performance-based relationship that if the other one doesn't always come across as the model mate, they really let them know that they've been displeased. Instead of freeing the offensive partner to become the ideal mate, it simply tightens him up worrying about whether he's just done something wrong or not. It definitely *isn't* an atmosphere of grace.

But with God we don't have to walk around on eggshells because we have a standing in grace with Him, and He just doesn't get bugged with us when we fail to perform the way He might want. You see, our acceptance with Him is based on one key factor only: we are in His Son and His Son's righteousness is in us.

That's what it means to be "accepted in the beloved" (Ephesians 1:6 KJV). Jesus is the Beloved, and since I'm in Him, and He's in me, I'm accepted by the Father in the same way He is.

No More Condemnation

The third, and yet perhaps least understood, benefit of justification is that God doesn't condemn us anymore. That's what Paul was talking about when he wrote, "There is therefore *now* no condemnation for those who are in Christ Jesus" (Romans 8:1).

Boy, do I ever remember the day that truth hit me. It exploded in my life like a bombshell. I was under such a pile of self-condemnation, and what I thought was God's condemnation, that I could hardly see out from under the pile.

I was just reading that verse one day, and all of a sudden I discovered the word "now." I don't know where it had been all that time, but I saw it for the first time and did it ever speak to me! I realized right then that on the basis of everything Paul had said in the first seven chapters of Romans about Jesus' death and resurrection, I wasn't under God's condemnation now and never could be again. That set the stage for me to stop condemning myself and stop believing others who tried to make me feel guilty because I wasn't living up to their ideas of what a Christian ought to be.

The sheer magnitude of this "no condemnation" concept has obviously been hard for the church to handle all down through its history. You can't find much written about it in early church writings because it wasn't clearly taught or understood. Part of that reason has to do with an incorrect addition to the text of Romans 8:1. Let's take a look at it.

The Naked Truth of "No Condemnation"

In the first verse of Romans 8, where Paul makes the summary statement that "there is therefore now no condemnation for those who are in Christ Jesus," you'll notice that the King James Version of the Bible adds a further statement, "who walk not after the flesh, but after the Spirit." This phrase is not in any of the earliest Greek manuscripts dating before the fourth century and was obviously added by someone or a group of people sometime during the middle centuries of the church. None of the most recent Bible translations include it.

It has been thought that the addition of this seemingly innocent and supposedly correct statement was the mistake of some scribe who glanced at the end of Romans 8:4, where this same phrase ends the verse, and accidentally copied it onto verse one.

I personally don't see how that could have happened because it's inconceivable to me that any one man could have had such unsupervised liberty in copying the most sacred document in the possession of the church.

My personal opinion is that the naked truth of the statement that Paul made—"there is therefore now *no condemnation* for those who are in Christ Jesus"—was simply more than some of the early church fathers could handle. They were willing to grant that if we walked in the Spirit we couldn't be condemned, but they couldn't accept the fact that just being in Christ and His righteousness being in us could make us free of all condemnation.

But, praise God, that's exactly what Paul meant to say because that's the truth!

If we'll just accept the statement for what it says and not bring our own religious bias to it, we can soon discover that Paul had good grounds on which to tell us that there's no more condemnation for us.

But before we look at those grounds, we need to define just what it means to no longer be condemned.

Condemned by Whom and for What?

There are two facets to the concept of "condemnation." First, there's the genuine reality of the fact that unless a person believes in the redemptive work of Christ on the cross, he *is* condemned to an eternal separation from God in a very real place called hell.

But once that person has believed in Christ's substitutionary death in his place, Jesus Himself promised, "Truly, truly, I say to you, he who hears My word, and believes Him who sent Me, has eternal life, and *does not come into condemnation*, but has passed out of death into life" (John 5:24).

So the issue of *eternal* condemnation is a settled matter in the life of a true believer in Jesus. That's the very essence of what Jesus was saying. If we've passed from death into life, we can't go back into death again unless God undid His whole work of justification, and there's NO chance of that happening.

However, what's at stake in the misunderstanding of Romans 8:1 is whether, having been delivered from *eternal* condemnation, a believer can come back under any form of condemnation by God because of his behavior.

The answer to that is an absolute NO.

The very reason that verse is located where it is, is meant to establish the finality of the fact that we can never again be condemned by God from the minute we believe in Jesus as Savior. In Romans 7 we see the picture of the believer, Paul, going through the most despairing period of his Christian life. It seems to Paul like everything is condemning him—the Law of God, his own conscience, and possibly, even God Himself.

But one chapter later in Romans 8, Paul is joyously writing of the fact that "If God be for us, who can be against us" (verse 31 KJV). This is no longer a defeated and despairing believer.

Now, what do you think it was that brought him out of the despair of Romans 7 and into the victory of Romans 8?

One great fact!

He realized there was no more condemnation from the Law, from God, and consequently no legitimate condemnation from his own conscience, because he was *in* Christ Jesus. And the realization of that set him free to begin to allow the indwelling Holy Spirit to make him holy in his daily living and to actually live in, and out through him, the very righteousness of Christ.

Realizing that he didn't have to live *for* God in order not to be condemned, he began to relax and trust the Holy Spirit to live the Christian life *through* him. That's what he meant when he said God rejected the method of using laws to try to make people behave the right way, because it never worked (Romans 8:3). But the same result of righteousness was achieved by walking in dependence upon the indwelling Holy Spirit and letting Him produce the righteousness of God *in* him (Romans 8:4).

The Grounds of "No Condemnation"

Now let's look at just a couple of the arguments Paul calls upon to substantiate the fact that God will *never* be the source of any condemnation of one of His children.

The first argument has a basis in the laws of jurisprudence which govern the courtrooms of America and other countries as well. There's a law called "the Law of Double Jeopardy." This law states that an individual cannot be subjected to a second trial and penalty for the same offense.

This has a perfect application in the case of God against man. God has already condemned Jesus *in our place* for every sin we will ever commit. For that reason, and true to the law of double jeopardy, He cannot and will not condemn the one who believes in Jesus as his substitute and Savior. One person has already taken our penalty. Now we don't have to.

Peter explains Jesus' taking our place in this way: "For Christ also died for sins once for all, the *just for the unjust,* in order that He might bring us to God" (1 Peter 3:18a). He was the "just" One and we were the "unjust."

God Is on Our Side

Paul's second argument as to why we can never be condemned by God, once we become His children, reaches deep into the very character of God Himself. Two great facets of God's character, His sovereignty and His immutability (unchangeableness), are called upon to witness to the fact that God is unalterably "for us" and could never condemn us again.

In Romans 8:31-35 Paul sums up this second argument by posing five penetrating questions, the answers of which form a powerful argument for God never again condemning us and why neither we nor anyone else can legitimately condemn us either.

The first question: "If God is for us, who is against us?" (verse 31). The very nature of the question implies that "whoever" might be against us, they don't amount to anything because the Almighty, Sovereign God of the Universe is for us.

That fact can be mighty comforting when you've made your stand for the Lord in a hostile situation and you feel a little like the Lone Ranger. Joshua, the prophet of old, quoted God, "Have I not commanded you? Be strong and courageous! Do not tremble or be dismayed, for the LORD your God is with you wherever you go" (Joshua 1:9).

The second question: "He who did not spare His own Son, but delivered Him up for us all, how will He not also with Him freely give us all things?" (Romans 8:32). The point here is that if, when we were still enemies of God, He gave up the most precious thing He had in our behalf, now that we're His children, will He give us less? Of course not!

The "all things" He's promised to freely give us refer to the thousands of privileges and blessings outlined in the promises of God throughout the entire Bible. They're like a treasure storehouse just waiting to be entered.

You can see, on the basis of this unequivocal statement, that there's no need to beg at the back door of heaven for any of your needs. Paul wrote to the Philippians, "My God shall supply all your needs according to His riches in glory in Christ Jesus" (Philippians 4:19).

Part of the blessing of knowing we can never be condemned again is the certainty that when we go to the Lord in prayer, we'll find a gracious and loving acceptance no matter how we've been behaving in our Christian lives. You see, when we were His bitter enemies, He did the most for us, and He won't do less now that we're His children.

The third question: "Who can (*is qualified to*) bring a charge against God's elect?" (Romans 8:33). Who has a right to bring accusations or condemnations against a person who has been declared righteous by the sovereign Judge of the universe? The answer is, "Only the Judge Himself!" But will the Almighty Judge of Heaven do this? Paul doesn't even bother to answer the question with a No because the answer is so obvious. God is the One who justified man, so He's not about to declare man unjust and condemned again.

What it boils down to is that God can't reverse a sovereign, immutable declaration which He's already made, even if He wanted to. And since it cost God the most incredible price that He could pay to justify man, why would He now want to throw all that out and say it was all for nothing? There's no remote chance that He would. The cost was too great!

The fourth question: "Who was the one who condemns?" (Romans 8:34). There's a saying, "Don't count your critics: weigh them!" That really applies here. There may be ever so many people, including yourself, who will condemn you, but there's only One who has the *right* to, and that's Jesus Himself.

John tells us, "For not even the Father judges any one, but He has given all judgment to the Son, in order that all may honor the Son, even as they honor the Father" (John 5:22, 23).

Now, the question is, will Jesus condemn the one whom the Father has already declared righteous? We must again answer with a resounding NO! To do so would contradict four of His mightiest works in our behalf.

The *first* was that "He died for us." The *second*, "He was raised from the dead" to prove the Father's acceptance of His atonement for us. *Thirdly*, "He sits at God's right hand" as a glorified man assuring the fact that we'll also be there one day. The *fourth* is that He is continually "interceding for us" as our high priest (see Romans 8:34).

The fifth question: "Who shall separate us from the love of Christ?" (Romans 8:35). The question really is, "Is there anything or anyone, anywhere in this world or the spiritual realm, who can, by its condemnation, cause God's unchangeable love to stop flowing toward us?" The point of all that Paul's said in Romans 8 is that there isn't.

Now, that's not to say there won't be those who *will* condemn us and accuse us of having "fallen from God's grace" because of some behavior which they've judged as being wrong, and perhaps, really was wrong. But nothing, not even wrong behavior, can ever cause God to condemn one of His children again.

Because so few believers really understand the depths of this truth, they mistake the condemnation of Satan, fellow believers, and their own consciences as being from God. Satan is called "the accuser of the Brethren" by the Apostle John in Revelation 12:10. He accuses believers because he knows he won't get anywhere trying to accuse us before God. But if we aren't anchored in the bedrock truth of the fact that God can't and won't ever condemn us again, we may fall for Satan's accusations and actually think they're from God.

Since God No Longer Condemns, Do You?

Since God has gone to such great lengths to prove He doesn't condemn us anymore, then do we have a right to condemn ourselves? No one can have a bold faith when he's walking around condemning himself for his miserable performance as a child of God.

True faith comes from focusing on Christ and what He's done for you through justification. But if you don't concentrate on that and instead focus on your behavior as a believer, you'll soon end up being discouraged and condemning yourself for your failure to live up to what you know God requires of you.

It's also true that if you condemn yourself for a shabby Christian life, you're bound also to have a critical view of others. We hate most in others what we hate about ourselves. Yet if Christ doesn't condemn a brother, but accepts Him on the basis of having declared him righteous in Christ, then what right do I have to condemn him? As the Scriptures say, "Who are you to judge the servant of another? To his own master he stands or falls; and stand he will, for the Lord is able to make him stand" (Romans 14:4).

What an incredible promise! Don't we all know some Christian friend who hasn't been living very close to God and we've taken all kinds of "spiritual" potshots at him? This verse of Scripture should give great encouragement to us because it says he is God's servant and the Lord is able to make him stand. And stand he will!

It may be that *our* condemnation of him is the very thing keeping him from seeing that God is not condemning him for having strayed. Nobody wants to snuggle up to a porcupine, and if an erring believer thinks God is still angry with him and just waiting to condemn him, he'll never want to come back into fellowship with the Lord.

Our loving and accepting attitude may be his path back.

Justification Is the Name of the Game

I realize that this chapter has been the longest one in the book, but how could I have hurried through this most critical truth of justification by faith? If we aren't straight in our thinking on this subject, nothing else will work right in our Christian lives.

In summing it up, let me just say that justification is the work of God whereby He declares righteous, on the basis of faith alone, that one who simply believes in Jesus as Savior. This righteousness is something which is added to the believer when he believes and can never be taken away. It assures him of three great realities: peace with God, a standing in grace, and no more condemnation.

15 ∘ Forgiveness

IN BEGINNING THIS chapter, let me say that some of you who have read my book, *Satan Is Alive and Well on Planet Earth*, will recognize some of this material from the chapter entitled "The Guilt Trip." In that volume I presented the subject of forgiveness from the standpoint of seeing more clearly our victory over Satan. Here I want to demonstrate the power of forgiveness from the standpoint of the total Christian life.

Not long ago I was speaking to a group of young married couples on the truths of the total forgiveness in Jesus Christ. A young gal stayed around until everyone else had gone and then walked up and said, "I have a question."

"All right," I said. "What can I do to help?"

She told me she and her husband were both believers, but they'd only been married about three months and were already having problems.

"I know this may sound stupid," she said, "but I can't forgive him because of something he did. And it was really as much my fault, I guess, as it was his."

She went on to tell me that they'd slept together before they were married, at his insistence, and now every time he wanted to make love, she really resented him and couldn't forgive him for taking away her virginity.

The guilt on her face was apparent. And to make matters worse, her husband was sitting at the back of the room, waiting for us to finish talking. I had no idea what his attitude was about our conversation.

"I've got some great news for you," I began. "Do you know what Christ did with sin when He died for us?" I asked.

"Yes, He forgave it," she replied.

"How much of it?" I asked.

"Everything."

"How many of yours and your husband's sins did Jesus forgive?" I said.

"All of them," she answered.

"Well then," I said, "if God has forgiven you and your husband, don't you think you should forgive yourself and him too?"

"I'd never really thought about it that way before," she said. "Praise the Lord, I really *do* forgive him."

She thanked me and was about to turn around and head over to where her husband was waiting.

"I hate to hold you up," I said. "But there's one more thing you ought to know."

The expression on her face looked as if she thought I was going to withdraw some of the good news I had told her and recant on it.

"The other thing is that God has not only forgiven you two, but *He has forgotten it's ever happened*! Because Hebrews 10:17 says, 'Their sins and their lawless deeds I will remember no more.' Not only has He forgiven you, but He's chosen not to remember it. Because of Christ's death on the cross, it's covered. Now, since He's forgotten all about it, you two forget it too. Okay?"

"Wow! Thank you," she said. "This is the greatest thing I've ever heard."

She took off like a bullet, ran across the room, and hugged her hubby so hard it almost knocked him off his chair. Needless to say, that marriage was going to be different from then on because all unforgiveness ever produces is a sense of estrangement.

Redemption Is the Ground of Forgiveness

Now, before anyone is tempted to protest that my counsel to her made a light thing out of a serious sin, let's see just how extensive God's forgiveness for sin really is.

As you have already seen, forgiveness is one of the results of Christ's redemptive work on the cross. As we'll see in the next chapter, freedom is another. Man's debt of sin was canceled out by Christ's redemption, making it possible for God to totally forgive us all our sins. Then He purchased us out of the slave market of sin and gave us freedom.

In this chapter we concentrate on what it means to be forgiven by God.

In Colossians 2:13 Paul sets forth the extent of God's forgiveness in the clearest possible way. He speaks here to the young believers in the church at Colossae: "And when you were dead in your sins and the uncircumcision of your flesh, He made you alive together with Him, having forgiven us all our sins."

Three things are emphasized here. First, God says we were all dead in our sins at one time. This is the state of all of us before we came to Christ. We learned this in the chapter on spiritual death.

Second, God has made us alive in Christ. This is a fantastic truth, and we'll look at it carefully in chapter seventeen on regeneration.

Third—and this is the facet of this passage that we want to concentrate on here—"God has forgiven us all our sins." The verb "having forgiven" in Colossians 2:13 is in the aorist tense in the Greek, meaning it happened at a point of time in the past. In other words, once God dealt with sin at the cross, it was a closed case.

I want us to lock in on one particular phrase in this verse, "forgiven us *all* our sin."

Have you ever stopped to consider how much "all" really is? A lawyer friend of mine told me that in a legal decision stemming from a case in Pennsylvania, the word "all" was defined this way: "*All* includes everything and excludes nothing."

All Isn't Always All, to All

But you know, in the mind of the average Christian, when he reads the words "having forgiven us all our sins," he thinks it refers to all the sins he committed *before* he accepted Jesus. I used to think this.

Say that this diagram represents my life—

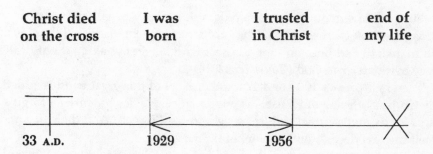

| Christ died on the cross | I was born | I trusted in Christ | end of my life |

33 A.D.   1929   1956

Up here to the left, Christ died for my sins in A.D. 33. Further on in history, a guy named Hal Lindsey was born in 1929. Then in 1956, he accepted Jesus Christ.

Okay—born, 1929, received Christ, 1956. I used to think that when I believed in Jesus Christ as my personal Savior, He forgave me all my sins from the day I was born up until 1956, as a result of His death in A.D. 33. I don't know what I thought His provision was for the rest of my life! I guess I felt I had to somehow get forgiveness for all my future sins by confessing each one right after I did it.

But how many of my sins were future when Christ died? ALL OF THEM! Do you know that the sins I committed from 1956 until the day I go to be with Christ are just as much paid for as the previous ones? They were all so offensive to a holy God, that in A.D. 33 He *had* to deal with *everything* I would ever do wrong. In order for God to have forgiven me in 1956, He had to have forgiven me for all future sins *or He could not have accepted me in the first place*! You see, my future sins were as real and repugnant to God as my past ones.

Half a Cross Isn't Enough for Salvation

Many people have a concept of a cross that only looks to the rear of their lives, but never looks ahead. That's only half of a cross and that's really no cross at all. When God says He forgave us *all* our sins, that's a cross with two arms, one stretching back into our past and one reaching into our entire future. Anything less than an all-inclusive forgiveness on the timeline of history falls pathetically short of God's infinite provision for sin.

The Two Most Important Truths About Forgiveness

First, we saw in our chapter on redemption that when Christ went to the cross, He took there with Him the certificates of debt, listing *all* the sins of all mankind, and once and for all dealt with all sin by taking it out of the way as a barrier to God (Colossians 2:14).

Then in Hebrews 10:14 and 17 another facet of this great truth is added. By Christ's offering of Himself as our sacrifice, He has procured a forgiveness for us that's *eternal* and *irreversible*. Verse 17 says, "And their sins and their lawless deeds I will remember no more."

Isaiah the prophet quoted the Lord as saying the same thing: "I, even I, am the one who blots out your transgressions for My own sake; and I will not remember your sins" (Isaiah 43:25).

These two truths form the bedrock foundation that you must build on in order to experience the reality of God's forgiveness in your daily life.

First, all your sins—past, present, and future—were forgiven when you believed in Jesus. There are none He hasn't already forgiven.

Second, not only has He forgiven you *all* your sins, but He's blotted them out from His own memory forever. They'll never be brought up against you again.

Can We Forgive as God Has?

If God has forgiven us all our sins and isn't holding them against us anymore, then what should our attitude be about sins in ourselves and others? Thousands of hospital beds, mental institutions, and jails are filled with people who have never forgiven themselves or others for wrongdoings. This kind of poison eats away at a person until real illness or damaging hostility results.

One of the key factors in unhappy marriages is the fact that two people living in such intimate proximity to each other see the worst there is in the other one. In this kind of emotionally charged relationship, while the rough edges are being worn off each other, things are often said and done that are unkind or cruel. If these things are allowed to fester and are never forgiven, bitterness and resentment can build up inside the two partners to the point where complete estrangement takes place.

More and more people take what they consider the easy "out" when this kind of alienation occurs: they get a divorce. But that hasn't really solved the problem of the lack of forgiveness in the person's heart. All they do is take it with them into their next marriages, and the new partners get punished with the inner hostility.

In many cases, marriages that appear to be fairly normal on the outside also suffer because there's unforgiveness on the part of one or both partners. They punish each other by sexual neglect, sloppy housekeeping and personal grooming, failure to achieve in their jobs, attention to others of the opposite sex, fighting, frigidity, constant criticism and nagging, and on and on. Both they and their children suffer from the lack of forgiveness.

There are also many people who have never been able to forgive themselves for their past sins. Maybe they've had a secret habit which they've felt was sin, and because they can't forgive themselves, they get a terrible self-image. They feel they're no good, and they develop a self-consciousness and inferiority complex.

Or, a knowledge of their inner sin-life causes some people to develop a defensiveness that makes them hostile and argumentative. It's as though they have the attitude that no matter how little they really think of themselves, they're going to be very sure no one else sees how raunchy they are inside.

Is All This Bitterness Necessary?

There's only one basis on which we can fully forgive ourselves and others for sins and shortcomings. We have to know and continually count on the reality of the complete forgiveness by God for those very same sins we've developed the bitterness over. If God isn't holding those things against us and He's forgiven and forgotten, then we can too!

Now, you might be thinking to yourself, "Yes, but if you only knew what he did to me, you'd see why I can't forgive him."

But you know, God could say that to us about what our sins did to His only, and dearly beloved Son, Jesus. They sent Him to the cross to suffer in a way that none of us could ever imagine. And yet, God has forgiven us, for Christ's sake.

For me to fail to forgive myself or anyone else who has offended me is to say that I have a higher standard of forgiveness than God, because whatever it is that has so hurt me that I can't forgive it, God already has.

The Sin Syndrome: Sin, Guilt, Estrangement

A failure to understand properly the full extent of God's forgiveness is always going to hamper our spiritual lives. It's because there's an inevitable cycle involved with sinning, even after we've become children of God.

When we sin, the Holy Spirit convicts us and we experience a bonafide conviction which is referred to in 2 Corinthians 7:8-11 as "godly sorrow." However, if that "sorrow" is not properly related to the forgiveness God procured at the cross, it will lead to guilt and that will lead to estrangement from God. This estrangement doesn't mean we don't belong to God anymore. But it can cause us to live in fear of God's punishment or rejecting us, and that leads to a sense of inferiority before God.

Now, how can this "sin syndrome" of sin, guilt, and estrangement be broken? We know we don't stop committing sins even though we're believers. So how can we keep from developing guilt which leads to estrangement from God?

Here's the solution. When I knowingly sin, I must confess my sin to the Lord (1 John 1:9). The word "confess" is a combination of two Greek words, *homo* and *logeo*. These two words together mean "to say the same thing about something that someone else says about it." In this case, when I've sinned, I must say the same thing about my sin that God says about it.

Now, what does God say about my sin?

First of all, He says it *is* sin. So I agree with God that what I just did was sin. I don't try to make excuses for myself or cover it up; I openly admit that I sinned. And if I know that I'm already forgiven, then I'm not afraid to come to God and be honest with Him about my sin.

Secondly, God says He *has* forgiven all my sins, including that one I just committed. So I look to the cross of Jesus and there remind myself of the great fact of my forever forgiveness which He purchased there. Then I thank Him that in His sight my sin has *already been* forgiven. Jesus has already suffered and died for the penalty of that sin.

And *thirdly*, out of appreciation for that great forgiveness, I accept it gratefully, turn from my sin, and begin to focus consciously upon the Lord Jesus again, drawing upon His Holy Spirit, who is indwelling me and who alone can empower me not to sin.

The Consequences of Not Relating Sin to the Cross

When a believer sins, he's immediately convicted by the Spirit. Even if he's hardened his heart through many ignorings of the Spirit's conviction, the Spirit can always be counted on to get through in that still, small voice. If the believer doesn't immediately relate that sin to the cross and the forgiveness that's already his because of it, then it will eventually produce a sense of guilt which is not from God. And that guilt will lead into a temporal estrangement from God.

Now, when we sin, a strange phenomenon sets in. We instinctively know that someone has to pay. Even if we don't recognize this on the conscious level, it occurs in our subconscious minds.

Since we can't cope with this unresolved inner conviction, we'll handle it in one of three ways. Either we'll punish ourselves in some way in an effort to make up for the sin, or we'll punish someone else. Or we'll look to the cross of Jesus and believe that He's already borne the punishment in such a permanent way that we have no need for personal recriminations or taking it out on anyone else.

Sin Is No Longer the Issue

What I've been trying to say through this whole chapter is that there's no longer any reason to focus on sin in our lives. The work of Christ in redemption has so completely dealt with our sins that they can never be brought up against us again after we come to know Jesus as our personal Savior.

Now, you may be wondering: if sin is no longer an issue with God, what should my attitude be toward sin as I find it coming into my daily life?

First of all, as I already discussed, it should be confessed and God's forgiveness appropriated. But if there's some insensitivity to the Spirit's convicting, and we fail to agree with God that what we did was sin, then He'll keep putting His finger on the sin and make an issue of it until we admit it was sin and claim His forgiveness. If we fail to readily agree with God that we've sinned, when He's convicted us of it, then He may be forced to discipline us—but even that's always done in love, not anger (Hebrews 12:5-13).

The words "discipline" and "training" are interchangeable. God's disciplining is always forward looking, and that's why it's comparable to training.

When God sees a child of His who continually refuses to depend upon the Holy Spirit to deliver him from his temptations, out of deep concern for the child's well-being and happiness God will begin to train and discipline him so that he will come to depend upon Him in the future. God knows we're happy only when we're living holy lives.

But even when God has to discipline us, His focus is not so much on our sins as it is on the lessons He's teaching us about walking in dependence upon His indwelling Spirit.

I know it worries some people to hear that our sins are no longer an issue with God, because they wonder what will motivate people to keep in line if they aren't worried about God coming down on them for their sins.

Well, I can't find any verses of Scripture that ever sanction a child of God "worrying about his sins" as a proper motivation for serving and loving God. But there are abundant verses that teach us that God isn't alienated from us anymore now that we're His children and all He requires of us is to walk by faith so we won't fulfill the lusts of our sinful natures (Galatians 5:16).

It's easy to walk by faith when you *know* you're forgiven. You're not afraid to be honest with God if you *know* He isn't carrying a club, just waiting for you to sin so He can get even with you. You can't wait to love and serve a God whose *only* attitude toward you is one of love and complete acceptance.

Isn't it great to know you're forgiven?

Now, let the realization of this cause you to forgive yourself for that thing which you've been holding in your conscience. And let it also lead you to forgive those toward whom you've been harboring bitterness and unforgiveness.

That's the pathway to real freedom!

16 ○ Freedom

IF THERE'S ONE word that expresses the battle cry of the decade of the 1960s, it's FREEDOM.

Those ten years witnessed the often frenzied efforts of millions to throw off their feeling of being shackled. Students wanted freedom in determining the courses they should be required to take, and who their teachers should be. Minorities wanted freedom from the exploitation and racism they had felt for centuries. Children wanted to be free from parental supervision and authority. Workers wanted more freedom in determining their working conditions. Churchgoers wanted freedom from the stifling and rigid form of institutional churches. Millions of Americans wanted our military forces to be free of involvement in Vietnam and any other war games.

In short, the 1960s saw the emergence of millions of "freedom freaks."

But I have an idea that long before the '60s the word "freedom" was the most cherished word in every language known to man. For if a man lost his freedom, it made little difference what other possessions he might have.

And yet, undoubtedly, for much of the world's history, most of its population has experienced slavery in one way or another, that of either the body, the mind, or the spirit.

Slavery has Many Faces

You don't have to have irons around your legs to be a slave. The crowd to whom Jesus said, "If the Son shall make you free, you shall be free indeed" (John 8:36), were not standing there in shackles. In fact they were the ruling elite of the nation of Israel. Their response to this straightforward rebuke showed how little they really realized their inner condition of heart: "We are Abraham's offspring, and have never yet been enslaved to any one; how is it that You say, 'You shall become free'?" (John 8:33).

Jesus went on to explain to them that their bondage was an inner one. They belonged to Satan.

In chapter five we saw that one of the barriers separating God and man was man's slavery to Satan. But man was also a slave to two other forces, the old sin nature and the Law, and he just as desperately needed to be set free from them as from Satan himself.

This chapter shows how the redemptive work of Christ on the cross unshackled mankind and allowed God to give us freedom from (1) the tyranny of our inborn natures of sin, (2) the principle of law with its demands for obedience or death, and (3) that sadistic slave master of men, Satan.

Twentieth-Century Allegory

There's a story the Apostle Paul tells in the first four verses of Romans 7 that more than anything else has helped me understand *how* I was set free from bondage to the sin nature, the Law, and Satan. Although the story, as I'm going to tell it, will be an "amplified" version of what Paul wrote, still, I believe, this is what he was really trying to say. This will be a twentieth-century interpretation.

Once upon a time there was a lovely, gentle woman who found herself married to a demanding, tyrannical perfectionist. All he did, from the day they were married, was lay down the law to her about how he wanted her to behave as his wife. Nothing was ever good enough for him no matter how she tried to please him, and he never once offered to help her become the kind of woman he demanded that she be.

Year after year went by, and I don't need to tell you that they had anything but an ideal relationship. She spent most of her time worrying about whether she had upset him, and alternately feeling guilty about it, then hostile and resentful.

Now, I don't mean to give the impression that this husband was not a good man, in the truest sense of that word. He was not only good, he was perfect. But there, you see, was the very problem in their relationship. She wasn't.

Well, not being able to live with the sense of failure that was now a daily part of her thought-life, she began to wish secretly that somehow he would leave her, even if it meant he would have to die. But, alas, he was in perfect health and so very moral that divorce would be out of the question for him entirely.

As if matters weren't already bad enough, about this time she met another man. And what a man! He was everything her husband was in the way of perfection, but he had a gentleness and love about him that was definitely missing in her husband.

And then he began to woo her! And the promise of what he would be like as a husband was so tantalizing to her that in spite of her present status she could feel herself falling deeply in love with this wonderful man.

And then the day came when he put the anticipated question to her, "Will you become mine?"

Of course he knew of her present marital state, and so he came to her with a plan. Since her husband would not leave her or die, thus breaking her relationship to him, the only other solution would be for *her* to die. Then there would be a legal severance of relationship, and she would be free to marry the new husband.

Voila! What an ingenious plan.

But wait a minute!

If she were now dead, how could she be married to *anybody*, let alone this wonderful suitor?

You're way ahead of me! Right! She would have to be raised from the dead and become alive again.

AND THAT'S JUST WHAT HAPPENED TO YOU! "For since we have become united with Him in the likeness of His *death*, certainly we shall be also in the likeness of His *resurrection*. . . . Now since we have *died* with Christ, we believe that we shall also *live* with Him. . . . Even so consider yourselves to be *dead* to sin, but *alive* to God in Christ Jesus" (Romans 6:5, 8, 11).

The Characters of the Allegory

I'm sure by now you've pretty well figured out who the characters are in this allegory. You, the believer, are the wife, pictured in a before-and-after relationship with the wonderful Suitor, Jesus. The tyrannical, perfectionist husband is the Law of God. In the broader sense he also represents the sin nature and Satan himself.

These three hostile masters will never die as far as their relationship to us is concerned. So the simple solution which God arrived at was to crucify us with Jesus, thus legally breaking our relationship to these tyrants. But then, when Jesus rose from the dead—since in God's mind we were there in the grave with Him—we rose into newness of life too, and were joined into union with our beloved Suitor and Savior, Jesus.

On the basis of this legal transaction, the authority of the *old sin nature*, the *Law*, and *Satan* have been forever broken over us, Christ's bride. As far as they're concerned, we're dead to them. They can't legally touch us for a second unless we fail to realize and claim our freedom in Christ.

Just What Is It That's Dead?

It's extremely important to get straight in our minds just what or who it is that's dead. I've seen people going around trying to crucify themselves and thereby trying to get rid of the power of sin and Satan. But Paul says in Romans 6:6 (paraphrased), ". . . that our old self *was* crucified with Jesus, that our body of sin [sin nature] might be rendered powerless, so that we should no longer be slaves to sin [that which the sin nature produces]."

Your "old self" is all that you were—with your appetites, drives, desires, sins, self-centeredness, and rebellion toward God—*before* you believed in Jesus and were given a "new self." At the moment you received Christ, your "old self," sometimes called the "old man," was judicially declared to be dead.

But there's nothing so great in just being dead. Being "alive" is where the action is! And that's why Jesus raised us up with Him from the dead into a whole new realm of life. This "new self" which came out of the grave could no longer be legally dominated by any of those powers which had so easily dominated the "old man."

Now, when we were raised with Christ into this new dimension of life, our "old self" was left behind in the grave. The three times it's referred to in the Bible, it's spoken of as being dead. In Romans 6:6 it specifically says that "our old self *was crucified* with Christ." In the other two passages that speak of the "old man" (Ephesians 4:22-24; Colossians 3:9, 10), the fact that he *has been* put off forever is made the basis of an appeal for a holy manner of life.

So, as far as I can see, the only enemy believers have which is really dead is their "old self" or "old man." All the other foes dedicated to the destruction of God's children are still very much alive. But the whole basis of our freedom over them is that *we* have died in our relationship to them. The authority of these adversaries—the *sin nature*, the *Law*, and *Satan*—has forever been broken in regard to the believers.

Freedom from the Power as Well as the Penalty

There are *two* aspects to the freedom which the redemptive work of Christ has made available to men. First, we've been set free from the *penalty* of sin by the death of Christ *for* us (1 Corinthians 15:3). That took care of removing the barriers that separated us from a holy and righteous God.

But secondly, His death also has provided for a daily deliverance of believers from the *power* of sin. To make this possible, Christ died, not only *for* sin, but to *sin* (Romans 6:10). This means that He forever put away from Himself the enemies of men's souls, and so Paul tells us on that basis we should "consider ourselves to be dead to sin, but alive to God in Christ Jesus" (Romans 6:11).

A Closer Look at Our Freedom

What I'd like to do now is to consider in some depth the extent of the freedom from the sin nature, the principle of law, and Satan's authority which Christ's redemption has made possible. To understand fully the far-reaching implications of this new liberty, however, it must be kept in mind that at the instant we believed in Christ, the *actual* and *legal* authority of these three great enemies of the believer was judicially severed. But whether their control and power has, in fact, ceased over us depends *entirely* upon whether we've claimed our victory and depended on the indwelling Holy Spirit to deal with their attempts at illegal access to us again.

For we must realize that these are vicious and adamant enemies who are relentless in their efforts to regain the dominion they had over us. As long as we're still alive they'll be constantly at us, so we can never relax around them and let down our guard.

But God has a provision for all of our needs, and this case is no different. God never intended for *us* to have to deal with the pull and lure of these tempters. So into the "new self" which He made us to be in our resurrection with Him, He put the third person of the Godhead, the Holy Spirit. It then became the job of this indwelling Holy Spirit to deal with the temptations of the old sin nature, the Law, and Satan. We'll look at the work of the Holy Spirit in greater detail in the next chapter.

In chapter four I discussed in depth what the sin nature is and how it operates in man, so I only want to briefly review that here, and then look at the extent of our freedom from it.

The Old Sin Nature

The old sin nature is that predisposition toward rebellion against God with which we're all born. It's the old sinful Adamic nature that we inherited from Adam. That's what Paul meant in Romans 5:12: "Through one man [*Adam*] sin [*the sin nature and its product, sin*] entered into the world."

This nature is sometimes referred to as "sin" in the singular. That's the way Paul uses it in the principle passages of Scripture which teach about this sinful nature, Romans 6, 7, and 8. It's also spoken of as "the flesh" in some passages, although "the flesh" is not always meant to refer to that "fallenness" in us which is generally connoted by the use of the word "flesh." It occasionally has a neutral or even holy meaning, but that's almost always evident by the immediate context.

In chapter four I told about the science-fiction movie where men from outer space planted tiny receiving sets in the back of the heads of their victims here on earth. Then when they went back into space, they transmitted instructions to their robotlike victims, who were programmed to obey.

That's much the way the old sin nature works in us. It's the "enemy agent" inside us that's constantly being energized by tactics of Satan to keep us from living holy and victorious lives. It's not a hopeless situation, though, and in this and the next chapter we'll see clearly what God has done to set us free from our spiritual enemies.

Satan Gets at us Through the Law

One of the favorite tactics of Satan in trying to keep believers enslaved is to get them on the treadmill of trying to live for God by keeping all His laws. In chapter eleven of my book, *Satan Is Alive and Well on Planet Earth,*[1] I show what the Law is, how it works on man, and why it's completely impotent as an instrument for helping us live holy lives. I'm going to reemphasize some of that material here and show that the Law has no more legal jurisdiction over us. We've been set free from it.

First of all, I need to deal with the subject of what makes us sin in our daily lives as believers. Sometimes when we sin we like to say, "The Devil made me do it," and there's usually a twinkle in our eye when we say it. It may help us get off the hook in our own minds, but we can't blame Satan for all our sinning.

There are two ingredients necessary for a person to sin. In Romans 7:5 Paul says, "For while we were in the flesh [before we became believers], the *sinful passions*, which were *aroused by the Law*, were at work in the members of our body to bear fruit for death."

Here Paul indicates there are two things at work within a non-believer to make him sin: his sinful passions, or sin nature as it's sometimes called, and the Law. When the Law stirs up the sinful passions, rebellion against the Law occurs and that's what the Bible calls "sin."

This principle of law works exactly the same way in us after we've become a child of God, for Paul says, "I would not have come to know sin except through the Law; for I would not have known about coveting if the Law had not said, 'You shall not covet.' But sin, taking opportunity through the

---

[1] *Satan Is Alive and Well on Planet Earth* (Grand Rapids: Zondervan Publishing House, 1972).

commandment, produced in me coveting of every kind; for apart from the Law sin is dead" (Romans 7:7, 8).

Psychology has noticed this same tendency in man to do just the opposite of what he's commanded to do. We call it the "law of reverse psychology." If you want someone to do something, tell him to do just the opposite. Most parents have figured this out before their children get very old.

The Law Is Not the Culprit

I know that all this tends to put the law in a bad light, whether God's law or man's law. But the law isn't the real problem. Those sinful passions or sin natures that get stirred up by the Law are the problem.

Now, you might be wondering why God gave the Law if He knew it would work against us rather than for us. Well, first of all, God knew that ultimately the Law *would* work for us when it had brought us to the place God intended for it to. We'll look at that in a minute, but first let's see why God gave the Law.

The first reason is to show man what sin is. Law is a principle which guides our behavior by setting up standards of conduct and threatening certain consequences if the standards aren't met.

There are several kinds of law set forth in the Bible. There's the "law of conscience" referred to in Romans 2:14, 15: "For when Gentiles who do not have the Law [of Moses] do instinctively the things of the Law, these, not having the Law, are a law to themselves, in that they show the work of the Law written in their hearts, their conscience bearing witness, and their thoughts alternately accusing or else defending themselves."

This law of conscience means that even people who've never heard of the Law of Moses, which is God's law, still have an innate law of good and evil and are responsible to live in the light of that.

God rejected the law of conscience as a means for man to know Him because the conscience was too easily seared. About the time that Moses came along, the people had so little consciousness of what sin was that God saw their need for an objective standard or law that would forever nail down what He considered to be sin.

This law was what we've referred to as "the Law of Moses." This was not only the Ten Commandments, but also hundreds of other laws which regulated how people were to live their daily lives.

Then when Jesus came and preached the Sermon on the Mount and gave all His other admonitions during His teaching, and later the Apostle amplified these and added more rules and regulations, this was still another kind of law called "the law of the New Testament."

All these kinds of law were given for the purpose of defining and showing man what sin was. That's the first reason for God giving the Law.

The second reason these laws were given was to provoke man's sin nature to sin more. Paul said in Romans 5:20, "And the Law came in that the transgression might increase." God wants the unbeliever to get so loaded with sin that there's no way he can fail to see how utterly sinful he is and how much he needs a Savior.

Paul's pitiful story of his tangle with the Law in Romans 7 shows that the Law provokes even the believer to sin more. He said in verses 7-9 that the Law told him he shouldn't covet, but his sin nature, aroused by that law, produced all the more coveting. He said he was once a fruitful, alive believer, with his tendency to covet, well under control. Then all of a sudden he got to dwelling on the fact that the Law said not to covet and then this commandment, activating the sin nature into rebelling, caused him to die. He didn't mean to die physically or to die spiritually. The word "die" here means to cease walking in dependence upon the Holy Spirit and so *fellowship* with God dies, not relationship.

The third reason God gave the law was to drive us to despair of self-effort. It seems God is working against Himself to get us to sin more, but this is His way of bringing us to total despair of self-effort in seeking to live for Him. You see, the harder we try to live for God by trying to keep His laws, the more we fail and that's what He intended. And the more we fail, the more we have to admit our helplessness and human inadequacy. When we finally get to that place of despair, we're ready for the fourth reason God gave the Law.

The fourth reason God gave the Law was to bring the unbeliever to Christ for salvation and the believer to the Holy Spirit for His empowering. Paul uses a good illustration of this fact in Galatians 3:24, 25, where he says, "The Law has become our tutor to lead us to Christ, that we may be justified by faith. But now that faith has come, we are no longer under a tutor."

A tutor was a specially chosen slave whose job it was to take a Roman child by the hand every morning and lead him to the school. He would wait there until the lessons were done and then lead the child home again. Once the child's school days were over, he no longer needed his "tutor."

That's exactly what the Law does, and it was the ultimate purpose of God's giving the Law. The Law takes the unbeliever by the hand and leads him to Christ for salvation. But the Law also takes the believer by the hand and leads him to the Holy Spirit who is the only source of power to be and do what the Law demands.

The Law Has Done its Job

The job of the Law was to show us what sin was and actually make us sin more. Then it was meant to drive us to despair of our self-efforts in trying to live for God and ultimately to bring us to Christ for salvation and for the moment-by-moment power to live a godly and victorious life. When this progression is finished, then the Law is finally done with the believer. Its purpose is finished and we have no more need for it, because it's been replaced by the giving of the Holy Spirit to dwell in us and actually produce the results of the law in and through us.

But, even though the law is through with us, we won't let go of it. In place of the Law of God, we've substituted man-made rules and taboos for how to live the Christian life. Instead of teaching people how to walk in the Spirit, it's been easier to pass a few rules prohibiting this behavior and that. All this has served to do is stimulate the sin natures of the believers. It has *never* produced holy living and it never will.

Anarchy is Not Freedom

However, it would be folly to go around telling believers that they're no longer responsible to keep God's law unless you also told them about the grounds of their deliverance from it. Those grounds are twofold.

First, if you'll recall the allegory I started this chapter with, you'll remember that the husband in that story was the Law. When the woman could no longer bear the condemnation she lived under for her failure to perform to his satisfaction, she allowed herself to be put to death and then raised into a whole new life, legally free and severed from her old husband's authority.

Now, that's just what's happened to each of us in our relationship to the Law. It will never die, but that shouldn't bother us in the least since we've died to it. Knowing this as a fact is paramount in actually experiencing freedom from the Law. If you don't "reckon" on this deadness, as Paul says in Romans 6, then you'll find yourself being intimidated by law of every kind. Someone will tell a story of how he witnessed to five waitresses and they all received Christ, and before long you'll feel so guilty about going into a restaurant without witnessing to the waitresses that you'll probably never eat out again.

I often hear people accuse others of putting them under the Law, and it's true that some people do wrongly emphasize that as a means of living a Christian life. But if you allow yourself to be put under Law, that's your own fault because God has provided your freedom from it and it's up to you to reckon on that deliverance.

The Spirit Replaced the Law

I said there are two reasons why we can tell believers they are no longer responsible to live under the law. I've just explained the first, and the second is, "If you are led by the Spirit, you are not under the Law" (Galatians 5:18). The Spirit is our replacement for the Law. He wrote it, and He's perfectly able to keep it in us as we walk by faith, trusting Him to do so.

In this same context Paul says, "Walk by the Spirit, and you will not carry out the desire of the flesh [sin nature]" (Galatians 5:16).

So you can see that freedom from the Law and the sin nature doesn't mean you have no one over you in authority at all. That's anarchy and it's anything but freedom. Real freedom comes when we submit ourselves to the moment-by-moment control of the indwelling Holy Spirit and allow Him to empower us to live for God.

Freedom from Satan's Domination

So far we've looked at two enemies from which we've been set free by Christ's redemptive work on the cross, our sin natures and the principle of living by law instead of grace. Now we'll look at the third area in which we've been given our freedom: the area of Satan's dominion and authority.

One of the great effects of the death of Christ, and your death with Him, is that in it you were set free from Satan's and demons' authority and control. They can no longer use that illegal lie on you, "You must give in to this temptation, because I'm still the master of your life."

The key passage which amplifies this truth is Acts 26:18, in which God has said He has opened people's eyes, "so that they may turn from darkness to light and from the dominion of Satan to God." The word "dominion" here means "authority"; Satan doesn't hold any authority or legal right to tell you what to do anymore. Your sin debt was paid by Jesus at the cross, and when He rose from the dead, "He made you alive together with Him, having forgiven us all our transgressions" (Colossians 2:13).

The resurrection of Christ proved to be Satan's final undoing. Paul tells us that when Jesus rose from the dead, He disarmed the rulers and authorities—referring to Satan and demons—and made a public spectacle of them in showing His triumph over them. He's now the head over all these rulers and authorities (see Colossians 2:15, 10).

But there's a critical truth here that's generally not understood by believers. Since we were crucified with Christ and rose with Him, His victory over Satan and demons is our victory too. Their legal right to touch us is forever gone.

A clear illustration of this truth is the story that follows. It's a case on record from many years back.

The Case of the "Deposed Captain"

A ship at sea had a captain so ruthless and brutal to his men that they became desperate and fearful for their individual safety.

In maritime law, the captain of a ship is the absolute master until officially relieved from command by the country with which the ship is registered.

The first mate aboard the vessel was an understanding and humanly sympathetic man, respected by all hands. After much personal consideration and real insistence on the part of the entire crew, he radioed the home port, reporting the atrocities of the captain against his men, and requested permission to assume command at once.

A message was flashed back commissioning him to take official command. The former captain was to be relieved of all authority effective immediately and would be brought home aboard the ship to stand trial. He was allowed freedom to move about on deck, but it was made clear to the entire crew that he had been relieved of his position of authority.

Not long after that, the former captain decided to test his power. A seaman was busy at work, happily enjoying the leadership of the new commander. The old captain came by, jerked the man aside, and began issuing stern orders. The seaman had been so accustomed to following his commands that he instinctively buckled under. And as soon as he started to obey, the old captain proceeded to lay it on all the more.

Amidst the verbal barrage, the seaman came to his senses and realized the man no longer had authority over him to bark out these insulting commands. He began to resist—and got the beating of his life. Bruised and battered, he told his rightful commander of the incident.

He left, reminded by the new captain that the next time a confrontation developed, the former commander held absolutely no authority over him or any of the crew. There was no reason even to listen to the old man. And should another incident arise, the men were to subdue him, on the direct orders of the new ship's captain, and he would be held in the brig.

Set Free to Serve

Let's face it. We're at war. But God wants us to know that we no longer have to give in to the demands of our sin natures, that we're no longer under the law, and that we've been liberated from the authority and dominion of Satan. The ransom was paid by Jesus, and we've been set free from the slave market of sin. The only slavery for us now is our willing slavery to Jesus out of love and gratitude.

A wonderful story illustrates this.

In the days of slavery in ancient Rome, a notorious and cruel slaveholder was in the Roman slave market to purchase some additional slaves. That particular day there was a stranger there also, a kindly man who was new at the market. He bought slaves in order to set them free.

A slave was put up on the dock, and the bidding started. The cruel man opened the bid, and the good man immediately set forth a competitive bid. The prices offered began to soar to dizzy heights as the men bid back and forth.

Finally the good man named a price so high that the wicked slaveholder couldn't match it.

As the new owner walked up to the proprietor of the slave market to make payment of the ransom, the slave marched over behind his new master and prepared to follow him.

The good man who had bought the slave turned around and said, "You're free to go. I bought you to set you free." And he started to walk away.

"Wait a minute," the slave answered. "If I'm a free man, then I'm free to follow you. My desire is to serve you out of gratitude for what you've done for me."

What this slave experienced is just what Christ has done for us. He's set us free from the impossible demands of the Law. He's taken us out of Satan's slave market by stripping him of his authority over us. And He's delivered us from the tyranny of our sin natures by giving us a new nature and the indwelling Holy Spirit to empower it.

But not only has Jesus Christ set our *spirits* free through His redemption, He's also provided for the ultimate redemption of our *bodies* (Romans 8:23). Inasmuch as He's already paid the ransom price for our physical redemption, this refers to the resurrection of our physical bodies that's yet to come—and in the near future, I believe.

When a believer dies, his soul and spirit go immediately to be with the Lord in heaven, but his body goes into the grave and back to dust (2 Corinthians 5:8). But the day is coming when all God's children who are in the graves will hear His trumpet and shout and come out of the graves with the same bodies they went in with—only now they'll be made whole and immortal. Then those believers who are alive will be instantly changed into immortal bodies and they'll go to be with Jesus also, without having to go through physical death.[1]

This physical redemption—as well as our freedom from Satan, the Law, and sin—is what Paul refers to as God's "mercies" toward us who believe. On the basis of these, he urges us who are believers to "present your bodies a living and holy sacrifice, acceptable to God, which is your spiritual service of worship" (Romans 12:1).

God doesn't demand that we become His servants, but Paul says it's the only reasonable thing to do in light of all God's done for us.

[1] For a fuller treatment of this subject of the ultimate redemption of believers' bodies, see chapter 4 of the author's book, *There's a New World Coming* (Vision House Publishers: Santa Ana, California, 1973).

17 ∘ Regeneration

EVERY SPRING THE whole earth gives testimony to the truth of regeneration as it emerges from its wintry slumber and comes forth with fresh, green vegetation from the soil. Plant life is thus reborn or given new life. What has been dead for a time now comes back to life.

But as great a phenomenon as it is to put a kernel of corn into the ground and then watch new life spring forth from the dead kernel, the greater miracle of regeneration of the human spirit has been made possible because of Christ's substitutionary death on the cross. The moment we place our trust in that death in our behalf, the Holy Spirit of God impregnates our dead human spirits with the eternal life of God and we're reborn spiritually.

One of the clearest declarations of man's need to be born again, or "from above," is a conversation Jesus had with the leading religious teacher of Israel, Nicodemus. This was a sincere and humanly righteous man, and the fact that he sought Jesus out to try to get an understanding of who He really was, shows he was a true seeker after God and His kingdom.

In this conversation Jesus revealed one of the most important truths He ever taught. Man must have a spiritual rebirth in order to comprehend God and His kingdom.

"Now there was a man of the Pharisees, named Nicodemus, a ruler of the Jews; this man came to Jesus by night, and said to Him, 'Rabbi, we know that You have come from God as a teacher; for no one can do these signs that You do unless God is with him.'

"Jesus answered and said to him, 'Truly, truly, I say to you, unless one is born again [*from above*], he cannot see the kingdom of God.'

"Nicodemus said to Him, 'How can a man be born when he is old? He cannot enter a second time into his mother's womb and be born, can he?'

"Jesus answered, 'Truly, truly, I say to you, unless one is born of water and the Spirit, he cannot enter into the kingdom of God. That which is born of the flesh is flesh; and that which is born of the Spirit is spirit.

"'Do not marvel that I said to you, "You must be born again."

"'The wind blows where it wishes and you hear the sound of it, but do not know where it comes from and where it is going; so is every one who is born of the Spirit'" (John 3:1-8). Or, "You can see the effect on their lives, even though you can't see what caused it."

The Re-education of Nicodemus

Nicodemus's response to what Jesus said was simple and straightforward: "How can these things be?"

Jesus answered and said to him, "Are you *the* teacher of Israel, and do not understand these things" (John 3:9, 10)? "You mean to say, Nicodemus, that you're the leading religious teacher of Israel and you've never realized that there was a spiritual dimension of man that was missing?"

You see, Nicodemus prided himself on the fact that he was born into the race of God's chosen people. He was banking his eventual salvation too heavily on his physical heritage. That's why Jesus went right to the real issue and pulled the rug out from under him. In essence, what he told Nicodemus was that "he wasn't all there."

Mankind "Isn't All There!"

I'm sure you've already noticed that something's desperately wrong with people in this world. A casual glance at the morning news is enough to put you under a gloom cloud all day. Nothing but murders, scandal, war, crooked politicians, divorces, and so forth.

The thing that's wrong with people is, they aren't all there. The most important dimension of their being is nonfunctioning, their human spirit. Without it, nothing else seems to go right for very long in a life.

In chapter six on Spiritual Death, we saw a diagram of the three parts of man—spirit, soul, and body. We briefly looked at what these were, but now in this chapter I want to show how they work in a believer. It's absolutely imperative to have a clear understanding of the functions of these three parts of our being, or we can't put our finger on the source of the problem when things go haywire and don't work right.

The Creation of Man's Two Kinds of Life

When God decided to make man, He picked up a handful of dust and shaped it into a man. Then He breathed into this creation's nose the breath of lives, and man became a living soul (Genesis 2:7).

Two kinds of life were born that day, *soulish life* (*psuche*) which started the heart beating and blood flowing and created the soul and personality of man. And *spiritual life* (*zoe*) which became the human spirit in man and enabled him to communicate with God who is spirit. These two kinds of life found their home in the physical body of man, and there was harmony in their interworkings.

The Bible says man became a "living soul" (KJV). The soul was to stand in the center, between the spirit and body, and be the merging place of these two. It was to be the part of man through which the spirit and body expressed themselves. It stood between these two worlds, yet it belonged integrally to both. Since the soul has free will, it was to decide which would dominate the life, the spirit or the body.

Before Adam sinned, the spirit dominated his soul and body, but with the free will he was given as part of his soul, Adam made the decision to disobey God; and when he did, the spirit of man underwent a violent change. Its capacity to communicate with God ceased, and a deadness developed in man's relationship with God. The tragic result of this was that the soul and body of men were now left without a spiritual monitor and their whole development *excluded* the enlightening and restraining power of God. Instead of being "God" centered, man became "self" centered. Instead of being a "flower" out of the Creator's hand, he became a "weed" growing wild, with no cultivation or grooming.

Let's look at each one of these functions of man separately now, using the diagram on the next page to help visualize these critical truths.

The Spirit

The obvious first step in spiritual growth is regeneration. This is where the human spirit of man plays its most important role. When Adam and Eve were created, they were given a human spirit that enabled them to commune with God. Their spirit did *not* contain the uncreated eternal life of God, however. As long as they were in the garden they had God Himself there, and that was all they needed for then.

Right in the middle of the garden, where it couldn't be overlooked, was the Tree of Life. This was available for man to eat of anytime he wanted to, and I believe this would have given him the eternal life of God if he had eaten of it.

But there was another tree there also, the Tree of Knowledge of Good and Evil. We've already seen in past chapters that this tree was the "test" tree. Man was forbidden to eat of it. To do so meant he was vaunting his will over God's, and the consequence of that was going to be a loss of spiritual life and communion with God (Genesis 2:17).

As soon as he had eaten, however, God said, "'Behold, the man has become like one of Us, knowing good and evil; and now, lest he stretch out

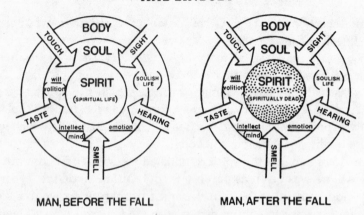

MAN, BEFORE THE FALL   MAN, AFTER THE FALL

his hand, and take also from the Tree of Life, and eat, and live forever,' he must be sent out of the Garden and his way back to the Tree of Life prohibited" (Genesis 3:22-24). God couldn't let spiritually dead men be given eternal life without all the necessary renovations inside them that would fit them for eternity with God. And those renovations were going to be the most costly thing God ever undertook. They wouldn't come cheaply.

The Renovation of the Spirit

The renovation of your spirit begins the day you believe in Jesus' substitutionary death for you and thank Him for dying in your place. Some people like to use the concept of inviting Jesus to come into their heart. That's based on Jesus' statement in Revelation 3:20, "Behold, I stand at the door and knock; if any one hears My voice and opens the door, I will come in to him, and will dine [fellowship] with him, and he with Me." The *door* referred to in this verse is likened to the door of their will.

But whatever your mental picture is at the moment you receive Christ as your personal Savior, the important thing is that your nonfunctioning, dormant human spirit is finally revived and given a new source of spiritual life, the Holy Spirit.

Sometimes it's been mistakenly thought that the human spirit doesn't exist in us until we've been reborn, but there are too many verses of Scripture that refer to the spirit in unregenerate men for us to be dogmatic about this. I believe the spirit has continued to exist in men right from the day Adam sinned, but what we inherit from him is a spirit void of its ability to communicate with God or be the recipient of God's communication to us. So in every real sense it's dead, because it isn't working the way it was intended. The great French philosopher and theologian, Pascal, called this spiritual void in man a "God-shaped vacuum which only Christ could fill."

Actually it's much like a lamp to which the electricity is turned off. The lamp is good for nothing but ornamentation until it's connected to its source of power and life. But it doesn't cease being a lamp just because it isn't functioning the way it should.

The Dead Spirit does Serve a Function

Even though the human spirit is void of any spiritual life in the one who's not been born again, still its very inactive presence in the unbeliever plays an important role. It serves as a constant reminder that something very basic is missing from our inner beings. It's as Augustine said, "You have made us for yourself, O God, and our hearts are restless until they find their rest in You."

Until the One who made us comes to dwell in His rightful place in our spirits, we'll never feel complete. There'll always be a sense of something missing. This accounts for the many things that people give themselves too hedonistically in an effort to find inner fulfillment and peace. An overemphasis in the use of sex, money, fame, power, beauty, pleasure, religion, and good deeds is often symptomatic of an effort to fill the inner void in the spirit which only Christ can fill.

The Light in Men Comes Back On

The Bible pictures the unregenerate man as "walking in darkness." That's why he can't see that all the things he tries to substitute for Jesus in his life are only delusive counterfeits. When Adam sinned, his spirit became darkened without God's inner illumination. His spiritual light went out.

But at the heart of God's plan to regenerate men was His intention of restoring the light to the darkened spirits of men. Listen to how the Apostle John pictured Jesus as the One who would bring the light back to men. "In Him [Jesus] was life; and the life was the *light* of men ... [He] was the true light which, coming into the world, enlightens every man" (John 1:4, 9).

Peter said the same thing of Jesus when he wrote of Him as the One who has "called you out of darkness into His marvelous light" (1 Peter 2:9b).

But the greatest authority on the subject of "light" was Jesus Himself. He called Himself "the Light of the World." "He who follows Me shall not walk in the darkness," He said, "but shall have the light of life" (John 8:12).

So when a person is born again, the light really goes on inside him. For the first time he's able to understand the things of God and the spiritual realm. He prays and knows for certain that he's getting through because he now has God's life and light in him. And God begins to shine that new light onto his path and show him what His will for his life is.

Walk as "Children of Light"

It's because we've been given this inner light that Paul admonishes us in the way he does in Ephesians 5:1-8. There he talks about a number of sins that unregenerate men freely participate in: greed, immorality, silly and dirty talk, coveting, and so forth. Then he says, "Do not be partakers with them, for you were formerly darkness, but now you are light in the Lord; walk as children of light." (verses 7, 8).

I think that's a terrific description of born-again believers—"Children of Light." If there's anything this dark old world needs, it's light. You can see that by the fantastic rise in popularity of psychics, astrologers, prophets, and others trying to find out what's going on. But the only true source of light as to where the world's going, and how to be prepared to live at peace in the world, are the "Children of Light." That's why Jesus said, "Let your light shine before men in such a way that they may see your good works, and glorify your Father who is in heaven" (Matthew 5:16).

Let's take a look now at the main function of the regenerated spirit.

The Sixth Sense: Faith

When a man is born again, life is restored to his spirit and there, in the "inner man," he's able to understand, love, and worship God in the deep way in which the new nature longs to. And the things of the spiritual realm are no longer unreal and alien. The Holy Spirit comes to take up residence in his recreated spirit and begins to reveal the mind and heart of God to him.

This restoration of spiritual life gives back to man what Adam lost. It's called the "sixth sense," *faith*. Faith is the eyesight of the spirit. It causes us to reach out to God to know Him. Faith enables us to believe that when God says He'll do something for us, He will! The body has its five senses that make the material world real, and the knowledge man gains through them is called the "human viewpoint" of life (HVP for short). But the intimate knowledge of God can only be known through the sixth sense, faith, and it's called the "divine viewpoint" of life (DVP for short).

Only the person who's been born again has a sixth sense and thus both these viewpoints in him. The unregenerate person has only the human viewpoint.

These two viewpoints of life are very often in conflict with each other. The five senses continually pour into the mind the world's view on everything, and this is a viewpoint that says man determines his own destiny and God is not a relevant force. It says, "If you wanna' make it, kid, *you've* got what it takes. Get in there and pitch!"

On the other hand, the sixth sense says, "Look, God made you. He put you together atom by atom and then after you'd turned your back on Him, He provided a redemption for you. Now don't you think you can trust a God like that to be able to handle whatever this problem is you're trying to cope with on your own?"

And so, both the recreated human spirit (*the sixth sense*) and the flesh (*the five senses*) bombard the soul (*mind*) with their viewpoints, and these two are almost always opposed to one another.

For example, Paul promises the believers that "God causes all things to work together for good to those who love God" (Romans 8:28). Now, suppose when you walked into work this morning, your boss met you and said you were fired. Through the senses of sight and hearing, this (*humanly speaking*) very bad information came into your mind. At the same time, through your sixth sense, faith, God reminded you of His promise that this will all work together for your good.

At this point *you* must decide which viewpoint of life is going to dominate you. If the HVP dominates, you'll probably panic and grab air! But if you choose to deliberately shut out the five senses and only listen to the sixth sense, you'll experience the calm and peace of God, because you'll be assured that the problem is in His able hands.

Faith Depends on God's Faithfulness

Now, this is really all that faith is. It's our response to God's ability to handle our lives. If I really believe He's able, then I'll automatically have faith. If I don't know how trustworthy He is, then no amount of spiritual gimmicks is going to make me trust Him at a time when I need faith.

Faith is such a misunderstood concept. I often hear people praying for more faith, but strictly speaking, that's a wrong prayer. Once you've been born again and had your sixth sense restored to your spirit, you now have all the faith you can ever get.

You see, faith operates in your re-created spirit just as the five senses operate in your body. Take the sense of sight, for example. You can have 20/20 vision and yet look at a mountain fifty miles away and not see it very clearly. In that case you don't need better eyesight; you need to get closer to the mountain so that it will come into better focus.

That's the way faith works. We're all given 20/20 faith when we're born again. But faith needs an object in order for it to function, and Jesus is that object, revealed to us through His Word.

If Jesus has not seemed as real to you as you might want, and you've felt that you needed more faith to bring Him closer, I hope you can see from this that what you really need is to get a closer view of this wonderful Object. You do this by getting into His Word and starting to see just who He is and what He's done for you and promises still to give you. Your faith won't grow, but your concept of Jesus will, and the end result will be the same in your life. You'll start to believe Him more, and you'll find yourself loving and responding to Him in a way you've never done before.

The Soul

Whereas the spirit is that part of man which makes him conscious of God and relates him to Him, the soul is that part of us which relates us to ourselves and gives us self-consciousness. Then through the various functions of the soul—namely *mind, emotion,* and *will*—we're able to give expression to our inner selves.

The soul allows us to reveal our personalities. It draws upon both the conscious and subconscious minds which are part of it. It's the part of man where the spirit and body find their external expression.

In the Bible people are occasionally referred to as "souls." This is because God views the soul as the man himself. A man without a soul is a dead man because the soul is the actual life in us. The Hebrew word for soul, *nephesh*, is often translated "life" in the Old Testament. The New Testament uses the Greek word *psuche* for both "soul" and "soul life" and it's often translated as "life."

"The *life* [soul] of the flesh is in the blood" (Leviticus 17:11).

"I do not consider my life [soul] of any account. . ." (Acts 20:24).

"The good shepherd lays down His life [soul] for the sheep" (John 10:11).

Adam "Blew It," But He Was No Dummy!

When we're born into this world, the only kind of life we have is soulish life (*psuche*). That's what we educate, train, discipline, pamper, and eagerly protect. The power in a human soul is not unlimited, but it's certainly very great.

When you stop to think about the fantastic degree of intelligence Adam had in his soul, it makes you believe a little bit more in the *downward* spiral of men's minds, not the upward climb.

Adam was given the dominion over the whole earth and everything in it (Genesis 1:27, 28). It took tremendous organizational skill and know-how to accomplish just that task. But that wasn't all he had to do; he was given the job of naming all the animals. You and I could take a dictionary and write out the names of all the hundreds of animals and birds, but trying to memorize them would be another job. Yet Adam thought up those names.

Adam was also a skilled gardener because he was given the job of keeping the Garden of Eden in shape. I know what a job it is just to try to keep my own small garden fertilized, pruned, and groomed. But the size of the Garden of Eden must have been staggering. Yet, evidently it was no problem for Adam, because he never even knew what it was to sweat until he was driven from the Garden and his soul began to deteriorate in its great power (see Genesis 3:19).

Man's Self-Centeredness Begins

From the pattern of what Adam's soul was capable of, we can see what God had in mind for man originally in his soulish life. Unfortunately, when Adam sinned, the soul was no longer under the control of the spirit, and so all it could do was become more and more *self*-conscious and *self*-centered. Men began to think only about themselves, of meeting their own needs and having their own fleshly desires fulfilled. The soul—which had been intended by God to be the place of the balanced expression of the complete man, *body, soul,* and *spirit*—now became the center of the fallen "ego" or "self." The spirit of man was dead as far as its influence over the soul was concerned.

The Apostle Paul coined a name for man in this condition. He called him, "the soulish man" (1 Corinthians 2:14). That's because the soul, with its mind, emotions, will, and capitulation to the desires of the flesh, was what dominated the man. In this same verse of Scripture Paul speaks of the limitations of the soulish man; "But a natural man [soulish man] does not accept the things of the Spirit of God; for they are foolishness to him, and he cannot understand them, because they are spiritually appraised." The point is, if a man were spiritually dead, he could train his mind to the level of Ph.D. but still have no spiritual discernment.

Body (Flesh)

So far we've seen briefly the makeup of the spirit and soul in man. But before we can look at how God has transformed them by the new birth, we've got to get a look at the body, or flesh, of men and see its role in the whole man.

The body is the part of us that's world-conscious. It's the house of the soul and spirit. But it's intimately united with the soul because the life of the soul (*psuche*) is what keeps the physical body alive. After the fall of man, the soul and body tended to merge into one, with one or the other being dominant. If it was the soul, then the person was artistic or intellectual. If the body dominated, then the person was more sensuous or athletic.

The five senses located in the physical body are the mechanisms which bring the reality of the material world into the consciousness of the person. They're like windows of the soul. In order for the senses to operate, however, they must have an external stimulus of some kind. For example, there has to be an object in order for sight to function. Likewise, there has to be a sound in order for hearing to occur, and so forth.

One of the basic principles that many psychologists teach is that man is a product of his environment. What that means is simply that we're the sum total of all the things that have touched our lives. All these experiences and forces that have molded our lives have come into us through the agency of the five senses. Of course, the way we've handled this information once it's come into our minds is influenced greatly by our inherited temperaments and traits. And once we become believers, the indwelling Holy Spirit influences our reactions to the things that happen to us.

The Flesh Is No Friend of God

The actual substance of the flesh is not what's usually meant by the references to it in the Bible. It generally refers to a principle of rebellion against God that's permeated all that we are in the Old Man. It's so unreformable that God didn't even try to salvage it in the new creation. He simply pronounced it hopelessly rebellious and then proceeded to lay down the principles for how we could live in victory over it.

Whatever is wrapped up in the concept of the flesh, all men have it. But it's the *only* realm that unregenerate men can operate in, since soulish life is the only kind of life they have. The born-again person still has the flesh, but he doesn't have to live and operate in that realm because he's also alive in the realm of the spirit by virtue of his spiritual rebirth.

Listen to how the Apostle Paul viewed the matter of the flesh as he wrote to the believers at Ephesus. "And you were dead in your trespasses and sins, in which you formerly walked according to the course of this world, according to the prince of the power of the air, of the spirit that is now working in the sons of disobedience.

"Among them we too all formerly lived in the *lusts of our flesh*, indulging the *desires of the flesh* and of the mind, and were by nature children of wrath, even as the rest" (Ephesians 2:1-3).

As much as some people might not like to think about it, God has a very dim view of the flesh whether it's in a believer or an unbeliever. That's because the flesh has a very dim view of God. In fact, Paul says, it's hostile to God and anyone who operates consistently in the realm of the flesh can't please God (Romans 8:7, 8). He even says that the mind that's habitually controlled by the flesh is evidence that the person is still spiritually dead (Romans 8:6). In Romans 7:18 in which Paul is speaking about the problem which he, as a believer, still had with the flesh, he said, "For I know that nothing good dwells in me, that is, in my flesh."

It's obvious from these verses and many more that there is a "fallenness" about us that's inherent in the flesh. This rebellious streak is sometimes spoken of as "sin," as in 1 John 1:8: "If we say that we have no sin, we are deceiving ourselves and the truth is not in us." The flesh is also synonymous with the Old Sin Nature which as we've already seen is that force in us which is dedicated to resisting God in our lives. All men are born with this curse, and it's *not* removed from us when we're born again, although victory over it is made available to us.

The Two Sides of the Flesh

At the Fall, the body and soul merged together to comprise this spiritual foe we know as the flesh. It includes the "*attitudes* of the flesh" as well as the "*works* of the flesh." These two sides of the flesh will continue to manifest themselves through the life of the believer to the degree that he allows his soul to dominate him, rather than his spirit.

The "attitudes of the flesh" are all the ideas, plans, schemes, imaginations, and good works which proceed out of the human mind without the Holy Spirit being the source of them. They can be either good or bad, as the world views such things, but in God's estimation they're all unacceptable because the flesh is the source of them, not the spirit. These "attitudes of the flesh" are sometimes hard to detect because they deal in the realm of ideas and thoughts and often seem so noble. However, these soulish activities *always* have self somewhere at the center.

Self-confidence and *self*-reliance are two notable traits of the soul. The world applauds these and they seem like such admirable qualities, but God says they indicate a reliance on the flesh rather than on the indwelling Holy Spirit.

The "works of the flesh" are often referred to as the "lusts of the flesh," and these refer to the sins which are stimulated by the fleshy drives and passions. These are fairly easy to spot in a life because they're usually pretty gross and overt. Paul lists some of them in Galatians 5:19-21: "Now the *deeds of the flesh* are evident, which are: immorality, impurity, sensuality, idolatry, sorcery, enmities, strife, jealousy, outbursts of anger, disputes, dissensions, factions, envyings, drunkenness, carousings, and things like these."

The Flesh Is Tricky

Where believers get tripped up is in not realizing that the flesh is not only the *sin* tendency, but also the *self* tendency. It's easier to spot the overt sins that originate out of the desires and demands of the flesh. But the "attitude" sins of the flesh are much more subtle and more acceptable in the Christian community. That's because, like Lady Clairol, "only the Lord knows for sure" what the source of the attitude is.

For instance, as a kid growing up I used to be preached at all the time, by preachers and Sunday school teachers, that drinking, smoking, and going to movies were sinful. But I never heard any sermons about the evils of teaching a Sunday school class if you weren't filled with the Spirit, or of preaching a message when the preacher and his wife had problems between them which they needed to reconcile.

You see, these are works of the flesh of which only God and you know whether He's the source. But if He isn't, then these good deeds are every bit as unacceptable in His sight as those overt sins of the flesh.

The Renovation of Regeneration

One of my favorite songs has the first line, "I believe in miracles, I've seen a soul set free."

To me, in this age of miracles, the greatest one of all is the marvel of God undoing the internal damage to man's spirit, soul, and body and bringing the harmony and balance He originally designed us for.

Paul amplifies this when he says in 2 Corinthians 5:17, "Therefore if any man is in Christ, he is a new creature; the old things passed away; behold, new things have come."

What were those old things that passed away?

Basically, your "Old Man" passed away. (*May he rest in peace!*) That's everything you were in Adam: spiritually dead, hostile to God, under the Law, headed for eternity in hell, obliged to serve Satan, dominated by your soulish life and the flesh, not indwelt by the Holy Spirit, unrighteous, condemned, and self-centered.

The Apostle Paul named this fact of the "Old Man" having been crucified as the basis for all those things we were in Adam losing their power over us. "Knowing this, that our old man *was crucified* with Christ, that our body of sin *might be made powerless*, that we should no longer be slaves to sin; for he who has died is acquitted of sin" (Romans 6:6, 7 paraphrased).

But as I said in the last chapter, there's no particular power in simply being dead. We went into the grave as the "Old Man," but we came out in our resurrection with Christ as a "New Man." Paul stresses that in Colossians 3:2-10. Here he tells the believers to set their minds on things above, not on the things of earth, for they *have* died to those things and are simply to consider it as a fact. Then he urges them to put aside things like anger, wrath, ill-will, dirty language, and lies, because they *have* laid aside the Old Man (*self*) with its evil practices and *have* already put on the New Man (*self*) who is in the process of being renovated into the image of God.

Off With the Old Man—On With the New

Not only did old things pass away when you were born again, but all things became new in your relationship with God and inside of you. Everything that's true of you now that you're in Christ—whether you're actually experiencing it or not—is the New Man that you've become. This is the real you that God looks at.

Now, in actual behavior, all things haven't become new yet. We still have many of the same old hangups and soul-kinks we had before we were born again. But the reason God calls us New Men is that He always looks at us in the light of the finished product He's making us into. And this attitude of God toward man has a creative power in it that actually brings our behavior into line with the way God sees us.

Paul talks about this New Man in Romans 7. He calls it "I," which is the translation of the word Greek *ego*. Freudian psychology has made the word "ego" familiar to us and it generally has the connotation of "self-centeredness." In the unregenerate man, the "ego" *is* totally self-centered because self is the primary thing that man is interested in.

But Paul uses the word *ego* in Romans 7 to refer to the man that God says he now is, the New Man in Christ. He says this New Man hates to sin, but unfortunately he still finds himself sinning. He laments that his New Man wants to do good, but somehow doesn't seem to have the power to perform the good it wants to do.

He finally concludes that even though he's a New Man in Christ and God will always look at him that way, he's still got the old rebellious flesh with him and it still wants to control him and often does. It expresses itself through Paul's attitudes as well as his actions; sins of the flesh as well as the soul (*self*).

But Paul's despair in Romans 7 leads to his biggest discovery, one that could come only by personal experience. That is, the New Man has no power in itself to overcome sin and live for God; it has desire, but no ability to do what it desires.

Then he writes the whole eighth chapter of Romans to show what all of his defeat had taught him. And that is that the power of the New Man is in the indwelling Holy Spirit and *He* must be depended on by the believer in order to overcome sin and live for God.

He Won Our Victory—Now We Must Claim It

Regeneration takes place in the human spirit because that's the part of us that needs new life. But the repercussions take place throughout our whole being as our souls and bodies come under the rightful domination of the spirit again. This is the whole purpose in regeneration, to bring the original unity and harmony back into the relationship between the body, soul, and spirit of man.

From the moment we're born again, our spirits are indwelt by the Holy Spirit of God, because He's the actual agent of our new life. In fact, Paul says that if anyone doesn't have the Spirit in him, he doesn't belong to Christ (Romans 8:9). But whether the Holy Spirit is allowed to fill (control) our soul and flesh is a matter of our personal decision. The soul still has free will, and it must decide moment by moment what will dominate the life— the Holy Spirit, living through our reborn spirit, or the flesh (sin).

It's to the free will in the souls of men that Paul makes his plea in Romans 6:11-13: "*Reckon yourselves* to be dead to sin. . . . *Do not* let sin reign in your mortal body. . . . *Do not go on presenting* the members of your body to sin as instruments of unrighteousness."

These are commands which can be ignored or followed whichever the mind decides. Our responsibility is to *decide* to obey, and then the Spirit goes into action in us and pours the power into us to *do* what we've decided. We're never relieved of the responsibility of *deciding* to follow the Father's will, but the actual power *to do it* comes from the Holy Spirit. That's what Paul meant when he said, "For it is God who is at work in you, both to will and to do" (Philippians 2:13). The *willing* part comes from the presence of the New Nature within us, and the *doing* comes from the power of the indwelling Holy Spirit.

Obedience and the Spirit's Power

A lot of believers want the *power* to come before they move out in response to the commands of the Word. They want to see, feel, and experience the victory before they follow the command to get into the battle. That really amounts to walking by sight and not by faith, because faith only needs the *promise* that God has already gone before us and is in control of the situation. The flesh demands visible proof before it can believe.

This truth is often confusing to believers who are just beginning to learn to walk by faith. They don't want to run ahead of the Lord. So, when they read certain commands in the Word of what God says should be true in the life of believers, they wait for some strong motivation and almost physical "shove" from the Holy Spirit before they move into action.

As far as I can see, you can't steer a car unless it's moving, and the Holy Spirit can't force us into action unless we've already made the decision to step out into whatever we've had revealed to us as God's will. For instance, we know it's God's will that we love one another because His Word teaches that (John 13:34). He doesn't tell us to have the "emotion" of love for one another. He tells us to "love" one another, and that's a verb, something that you *do*, not something that you necessarily *feel*.

So how do we handle a situation where we find ourselves disliking someone? Do we ask the Spirit to give us the emotion of love for him or her and then keep on hating him until we suddenly have some divine spurt of love come to us?

No! I believe we already know it's God's will to *demonstrate* love to this person, not necessarily feel it. And we know that if God wills something, then He's already promised to back that up with His enabling power. So trusting Him to empower us to *show* him love, whether we "feel" it or not, we begin to demonstrate love to him in the same ways we do to those we really love. We don't bad-mouth him to others. We begin to be sensitive to his needs and try to look at things from his point of view. We take time to show him kindnesses, and we simply accept him in the same way that God has accepted us, His former enemies.

Now, as we do these things, our attitude is that since we're doing what Jesus has commanded us, then He must also take care of the consequences of our actions and turn our "demonstration" of love into a true "feeling" of love.

There's a three-step progression that's involved in this example and in how we relate to the hundreds of other commands in the Word: *trust, obey, expect.*

First, we simply *trust* that what God has called us to do, or cease doing, represents His best and highest plan for us, because He loves us so much.

Secondly, in the light of that knowledge, and with the promise that what He's called us to do He'll give us the power to, we *obey* His will.

Thirdly, we *expect* Him to keep His end of the bargain and empower us to do that which we've moved into by faith.

The Two Kinds of Believers

Now, you'd think that once a man was born again, he'd be so thankful to have his relationship with God restored that he would gladly and consistently allow the Holy Spirit to dominate his whole being, and would walk by faith, moment by moment.

But such is not the case with a great many believers. The soul (*self*) has held sway over us for so many years, that there's a lot of unlearning and relearning to do. Our minds must be renewed, as Paul tells us in Romans

12:2, in order that we might be transformed in our behavior. We've already been transformed on the inside because of the new birth. So now what we need to do is bring our behavior in line with what God says He's already made us. And that's where the need for the power of the Holy Spirit comes in. *We* can't transform ourselves, but the Holy Spirit can as He applies the cleansing and renewing power of the Word of God to our lives.

This, of course, necessitates that we spend time reading and studying the Bible. For as the Psalmist prayed, "Thy Word I have treasured in my heart, that I may not sin against Thee" (Psalm 119:11).

A believer who's consistently allowing himself to be renewed in his mind and has his human spirit in the dominant role in his life, allowing the Holy Spirit to work in him through it, is said by Paul to be a "spiritual man" (1 Corinthians 3:1). This doesn't mean that he's a perfect, sinless man. But it does mean that the thing which generally characterizes him is a preoccupation with the things of God and the spirit. When he sins, he confesses it to God and quickly relates it to His forgiveness on the cross. Then he turns again to walking by faith and being available to the Lord for whatever He might have in mind for him.

But in 1 Corinthians 3, Paul describes another kind of believer. This one is still a babe in Christ, even though he may have been a true believer for years. He's all caught up with the things of this world, and he's still living like the old soulish man he used to be. The flesh is the dominant factor in his life, so Paul calls him "carnal," which means "fleshly."

Throughout the New Testament epistles, a picture comes together of the things that characterize a carnal believer. It would do us all good to check this list and see if too many of these things apply to us too consistently. All believers will have some of these things in their lives occasionally and yet they couldn't honestly be categorized as "carnal." But if *many* of these things are true of you, I sincerely urge you to consider the possibility that you may be a carnal believer and in need of confessing your sins and claiming the power of the Holy Spirit to cleanse and renew you.

Carnal Believers:

... argue and reason about most things
... are self-righteous and defensive about their actions
... can't concentrate on spiritual things for long
... are up and down emotionally
... are overly sensitive

... don't give thanks in all things

... are worriers

... are talkative, always having to be at the center of each conversation and usually dominate it

... give in to lust of the eyes; are always buying things

... have an unbalanced emphasis on sex

... have a poor prayer life

... are undisciplined

... are easily discouraged

... when it comes to preaching, can't rely wholly on God, but fill up their sermons with illustrations, stories, and jokes

... are proud, because self is their center

... thrive on the sensational, because they're not sure people will be duly impressed with them if they don't

... are critical of fellow believers

... have a poor family life

... are braggers

... engage in frivolous and suggestive jesting

... are intemperate in eating and drinking

... indulge in swearing and dirty talk

... have no desire for the Word

... give in to jealousy and strife

Paul sums up the carnal believer's problem by saying, "You're walking like mere men" (1 Corinthians 3:3b).

And there's the tragedy, because believers aren't like "mere men." "Mere men" aren't all there. They have only a body and a soul; their spirits are nonfunctioning—dead. They're not *normal* human beings, but they don't realize it because everyone else they know is just like them.

Except true believers who walk by faith, allowing their spirits to have the rightful role of dominance in their lives. These are the "normal" people of the world because that's how God made man to function in the first place, and neither man nor God is truly happy until he does.

Summing It All Up

When the subject of regeneration is taught, it's usually related just to the work of God in giving new life to our dead human spirits and imparting the Holy Spirit to dwell in us. I hope you've been able to see from this chapter that there's much more than this involved in the complete work of regeneration. It's actually the work of God giving balance and harmony to the whole man once again. The spirit of man is put back into its rightful place of dominance in us, and the soul and flesh, that had gotten so out of hand with no inner restraint, are gradually brought back under the authority of the Holy Spirit, who dwells in our human spirit.

So regeneration means God has made us whole people again and by virtue of that fact has equipped us to live victoriously in this life and gloriously with Him for eternity.

18 ○ New Position

WE'VE COME NOW to the last chapter of the book, and it seems right that we should close this study of what Jesus Christ has done for man by looking at the incredible NEW POSITION that His reconciliation has given us. I'm convinced this subject is understood by few believers and that's why the church today as a whole doesn't have the vitality and power of the first-century church.

In the last hundred years a number of books have appeared which have dealt with this concept in one way or another. The believer's new position in Christ has made possible an intimate relationship with Him which has been called by many names: the Deeper Life, the Abiding Life, the Higher Life, the Crucified Life, the Exchanged Life, the Spirit-filled Life, the Victorious Life, the Faith-Rest Life, the Baptism of the Spirit, Identification With Christ, and Union With Christ.

Such writers as Jesse Penn Lewis, Ruth Paxson, Fritz Huegel, Charles Trumbull, E. W. Kenyon, Watchman Nee, Major Ian Thomas, L. S. Chafer, Miles Stanford, and Andrew Murray are among those many whose pens have given great clarity and insight into the liberating results of the believer's new position in Christ.

No matter what name we choose to call it, however, there can be little doubt that there is a life of great spiritual depth, power, and victory available to all believers, yet actually experienced by only a few. We want to examine in this final chapter just what our new position is in Christ and why it's the basis for consistent and victorious Christian living.

The Search for the "Deeper" Life

You don't have to be a believer for long before you discover by personal experience that *being* a Christian and *living* like one are often different things. Like the Apostle Paul in Romans 7, we find that we want to do the right thing but too often end up doing the very thing we hate.

When the realization of this conflict in our dual nature hits many believers, they simply don't feel like fighting it, and they give in to the up-and-down Christian life and settle into spiritual mediocrity. Others who are fighters by nature set out to find the solution to living above the pull of the world, the flesh, and the devil.

Many of these sincere souls have been led on strange pilgrimages by well-meaning friends, looking for this "deeper" life, only to come away with no lasting answers and more frustration. That's because what they're looking for isn't located in some higher or deeper *place* or some *experience*. It's located in a person, Jesus Christ.

The *deeper, higher, victorious, abiding, exchanged, and Spirit-filled* life is not an elusive, wishful aspiration. It's simply a matter of living with the moment-by-moment awareness that because of my absolute oneness with Jesus in the eyes of God, all that He is, *I am*. His victory over sin *is mine*. He's holy and blameless in the eyes of the Father and *so am I*. Satan no longer has any authority over Him, *and he doesn't over me either*. He's more than conqueror, and Paul tells me that *I am too*. Christ was crucified, buried, raised from the dead, and is now seated at God's right hand. In the mind of God, *each true believer went through these same experiences* with Christ *and is now seated in the heavenlies* in Christ, regardless of where his actual physical body may be located here on earth at the moment.

In other words, my new position in Christ gives me a *total* identification with Jesus in God's eyes. As He looks at the Son, He looks at me in the same way because He sees me *in* the Son and the Son *in* me. If I took a grimy piece of paper and inserted it into the pages of a book and closed it, that paper would be totally identified with the book and we could no longer see it, only the book. Because Christ removed the barriers separating God and man, the one who places faith in that as having been done for him personally is "inserted" into Christ and Christ into Him. What becomes true of the One becomes true of the other.

Why Don't I Live Like What I Am?

If you're an honest believer you're probably saying to yourself about now, "Well, God may say I'm holy and blameless, and victorious over sin and Satan because of my union with Christ, but it doesn't come out that way in my daily experience. There's something wrong somewhere!"

More than likely there is something wrong, and it probably has to do with a failure to understand the difference between your new eternal *position* in Christ and your daily *experience* of living the Christian life. One is what you are in God's estimation and the other is what you are in practice.

A clear distinction must be made between these two relationships which each believer has with Christ. Our new position or union with Christ is a *legal* status which we have with God, and it becomes absolutely true of us the instant we place saving faith in Christ and never changes. But our day-to-day living of the Christian life here in this world is the *experiential* side of redemption, and it varies from moment-to-moment, depending on whether we walk with the Spirit of God in control of us or let our flesh dominate us.

Our New Possessions and Blessings

Believers are the richest people in town! They're spiritual billionaires, if they only knew it. Paul tells us in Ephesians 1:3 that God "has blessed us with every spiritual blessing in the heavenly places in Christ." Now that's something to get excited about, but many believers don't. They'd rather have some *"physical* blessings down here in *earthly* places." That would be more realistic and practical, they feel. But this attitude is only indicative of the fact that they've never really seen that our "treasures are laid up in heaven" because that's where we actually are in God's mind. What we have down here is only temporary and will benefit us only for our threescore and ten and then someone else gets it.

Once we've been born again, we're citizens of heaven and eternal beings. We're only passing through here on earth and God doesn't want us to settle down and get too comfortable and complacent.

Dr. Lewis Chafer, founder of Dallas Theological Seminary, went through the Bible and counted thirty-three different spiritual blessings that become legally true of us the moment we believe.[1] These new possessions and positions are instantaneously and simultaneously declared to be ours at that moment.

In the previous chapters in this book we looked at some of those spiritual blessings; justification, forgiveness, freedom, regeneration, new nature, acceptance with God, new righteousness, reconciliation, no more condemnation, peace with God, a standing in grace, and redemption. There are at least twenty-one more eternal possessions that were given to us in the one package of salvation, and the thrill of the Christian life is finding out what these are and beginning to enjoy them here and now, not by and by.

Our Two Relationships With Christ

I think the chart on the next page will help to give us a better perspective of the two relationships a believer has with Christ; his *positional* and his *experiential*. Another way of saying it is the *eternal* and the *temporal (related to the believer's earthly life)*. I want you particularly to notice the different

[1] Lewis Sperry Chafer, *Systematic Theology* vol. III (Dallas. Tex.: Dallas Seminary Press, 1948).

characteristics of these two relationships. Our eternal position is credited to us *in toto* at the moment of salvation. It can't be improved on and it can't be diminished in any way. It's eternal.

In case it isn't perfectly clear to you yet, what the Bible is saying is that once you've been born again you can *never* lose your salvation because this eternal position will never cease to be true of you. Your temporal experience may change from day to day as sin comes into your life, but your eternal position is a forever fact. What happens *to* you or *in* you in your daily walk with Christ can never change, in the slightest degree, your eternal relationship with Christ.

When you're born into your earthly family, you may be a winner or a loser in your behavior, but you're still a member of that family. There's no way to be unborn just because you don't measure up to the standards of your family. It's just the same when you're born into God's family. You may be disciplined for wrong behavior, but you won't be disowned.

Look at the chart carefully. The cross represents that moment when you believe in Christ's death on your behalf and are born again. At that instant the Holy Spirit puts you into a family relationship with Christ which has two aspects to it, the eternal, invisible one in the heavenlies (where Christ sits) and the temporal (earthly) one while you're still alive here on earth.

The act of placing you into Christ is called the "baptism of the Spirit" in 1 Corinthians 12:13: "For by one Spirit we were all baptized into one body, whether Jews or Greeks, whether slaves or free, and we were all made to drink of one Spirit."[2] Paul also says that when we believe in Christ we're made "of his flesh, and of His bones" (Ephesians 5:30 KJV). This is our union with Christ, and Paul likens it to the oneness that a man and woman enter in marriage. In God's eyes it's a fact even though it takes a lot of tears and prayers to bring about an actual oneness in experience.

Temporal Fellowship

By our temporal fellowship with God I don't in any way mean "temporary." Temporal simply means that which relates to time and space and in this case refers to the daily fellowship we experience with Christ. At the moment we're born again, not only are we placed into *Christ*, but He is

---

[2] For a fuller study of the baptism of the Holy Spirit see the appendix of the author's book, *Satan Is Alive and Well on Planet Earth* (Grand Rapids: Zondervan Publishing House, 1972).

ETERNAL POSITION AND POSSESSIONS

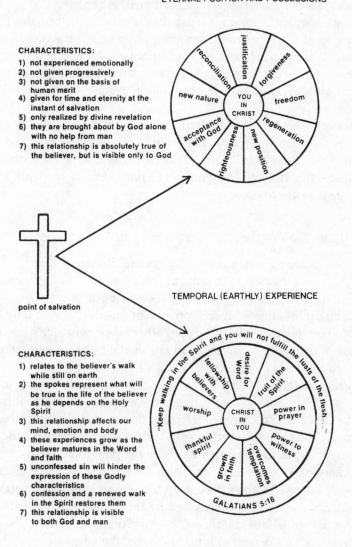

CHARACTERISTICS:

1) not experienced emotionally
2) not given progressively
3) not given on the basis of human merit
4) given for time and eternity at the instant of salvation
5) only realized by divine revelation
6) they are brought about by God alone with no help from man
7) this relationship is absolutely true of the believer, but is visible only to God

point of salvation

TEMPORAL (EARTHLY) EXPERIENCE

CHARACTERISTICS:

1) relates to the believer's walk while still on earth
2) the spokes represent what will be true in the life of the believer as he depends on the Holy Spirit
3) this relationship affects our mind, emotion and body
4) these experiences grow as the believer matures in the Word and faith
5) unconfessed sin will hinder the expression of these Godly characteristics
6) confession and a renewed walk in the Spirit restores them
7) this relationship is visible to both God and man

placed into *us*, into our revived human spirits, and we come alive spiritually. His dwelling in us is to equip us to live here in this life until He comes to get us or we go home by death. He puts the Holy Spirit in us to empower us to live the kind of life He wants for us.

In the lower circle of the chart I've shown just a few of the new characteristics that can be expected in the life of a believer who submits to the

empowering of Christ through the Holy Spirit. When we yield to temptation and subsequently to sin, Christ doesn't leave us, but the flesh or
old self replaces Christ as the controlling influence in the life. If we stay
in this condition for any length of time without judging it as sin and turning from it, we become carnal believers. But confessing our sin and
once again authorizing Christ to take control restore our fellowship with
Him.

With these things in mind, take time now to examine the chart. Notice
particularly the eternal, permanent nature of our position in Christ. You'll
see also that while we're still here on earth, Christ is to be the center of our
lives, but it's the Holy Spirit who puts Him there as we walk in total
dependence on Him to do so.

How Do I Make My "Position" My "Experience"?

When God planned man's reconciliation, He obviously didn't mean for
us to be holy and victorious in our "position" and weak and defeated in
our "experience." His plan has always been that our position and experience be brought into line with each other. But this can happen only by our
finding out how fantastic our heavenly Father is and what He's made us to
be because of our union with Christ in His death, burial, resurrection, and
ascension to the Father's right hand.

In this regard I always think of a story I heard once, similar to Mark
Twain's *The Prince and the Pauper*, which beautifully illustrates this point.

One day the King and Queen of a far-off country were bringing their new
little Prince home from the royal hospital when their carriage collided with
a poor pauper's cart. In this humble vehicle the poor man was bringing his
wife and new baby home from the midwife's house. In the confusion of
the moment, the two couples picked up the wrong babies by mistake and
the little Prince went home to be raised by the pauper and his wife.

As this baby grew into childhood, he was forced to go into the streets
and beg for food. Unknown to him, of course, the very streets he begged
on belonged to him because they were the property of his true father. Day
after day he would go to the palace and look through the iron fence at the
little boy playing there and he would say to himself, "Oh, if only *I* were a
Prince." Which, of course, he was, but he wasn't aware of it.

All his life he lived in poverty and want because he didn't know who he
really was since he didn't know "who" his father was.

Believers Live Like Spiritual Paupers

But do you know that millions of true believers are doing the same thing? They've never taken the time to find out "who" their real Father is, the King of Kings and Lord of Lords. They don't realize they're royal heirs to a royal throne. They're living in self-imposed spiritual poverty and cheating themselves of the experience of the riches of God's grace. I say the "experience" of them, because the riches are theirs whether they enjoy them or not.

I read not long ago about a man who lived like a bum for many years. He had been left a huge sum of money, but the authorities couldn't locate him. They traced him from flophouse to flophouse and finally found him asleep on a fifty-cents-a-night cot in a mission. He was then informed of His inheritance. He'd been rich for years but never knew it. He had lived needlessly as a tramp.

When I read that I thought, "What a waste of all those years." And that's just how I feel when I think of all the wasted years of happiness and spiritual service that go down the drain because "believers" are "unbelievers" when it comes to taking God at His word when He tells them *who* they are because of *whose* they are.

When we fail to live in the reality of our new position, daily experiencing the forgiveness, freedom, acceptance, and empowering of the Spirit (*just to name a few of our spiritual riches*), we short-change not only God, but ourselves and those whose lives we touch who so desperately need to see the reality of God in a human life.

Our "Position" Is the Basis of All Victory

I said at the beginning of this chapter that knowing and counting on our new position in Christ is the basis of all victorious and consistent Christian living. Why do I say that?

It's because there's no other way to be set free from the *power* of the Law, the sin nature, and Satan. In Romans 1-5, Paul lays out the *redemptive* work of Christ and shows us that it's our remedy for the *penalty* of sins. But in chapters 6-8 of Romans we see our complete identification with Christ in His death, burial, and resurrection and discover that that's the remedy for overcoming the *power* of sin.

Without the *power* of sin being dealt with in our lives, we'd be helpless victims of Satan's wiles and our own fleshly lusts even though we are born again. There'd be no hope of deliverance from depression, defeat, discouragement, failure, and doubt.

But praise God, His plan for our *complete* salvation includes a means of victory over sin's power, and that's our co-crucifixion and resurrection with Jesus Christ.

The "Old Man" Is Dead! Good Riddance!

In chapter sixteen, the chapter on Freedom, I told an amplified version of the allegory Paul uses in Romans 7:1-4. This was about a woman, who was married to a perfectionist tyrant and who could never satisfy his demands for perfection. Therefore she lived under constant condemnation. She finally met someone who was everything her husband was in the way of being perfect, but he was filled with love and concern for her. She wanted to be joined to him, but the law said she would be an adulteress if she left her husband. She could be rid of her domineering mate if he would die, but he was in perfect health; so the only other solution was for *her* to die, thereby effecting a legal separation from her husband. Then she would be free to marry anyone she chose. So she allowed her new lover to put her to death and then raise her back to life again and was joined in marriage to him.

This allegory is a fantastic application of the truths taught in Romans 6, 7, and 8. When you understand what the people in the allegory represent, the picture of your union with Christ in His death, burial, and resurrection will begin to unfold, and you'll be able to see how the cross has set you free.

The tyrannical husband represents the Law, but by application includes the sin nature and Satan. The woman is you, the believer. The "other man" is Jesus.

The Law, sin, and Satan will never die as far as their relationship to us is concerned here in this life. So the solution which God arrived at was to crucify us with Jesus, thus legally breaking our relationship to these tyrants. Then when Jesus rose from the dead, since in God's mind we were there in the grave with Him, we rose into a new life too, the same life that Jesus now lives, a life of total victory over the enemies of our soul.

On the basis of this legal severance of relationship, the authority of the old sin nature, the Law, and Satan have been forever broken over us, Christ's bride. As far as these things are concerned, we're dead to them. They can't legally touch us for a second unless we fail to realize and claim our freedom in Christ.

Out of Adam, Into Christ

To be in complete union with Christ is to have been legally taken out of our relationship to the first Adam and his ruin and placed into the Last Adam, Jesus, and thus made a partaker of all that He is. Both Adam and Christ demonstrate the principle that many can be affected for good or evil by one person's deed.

In Romans 5:12-21 Paul shows this analogy between Adam and Christ—the mess that Adam got mankind into and the means by which Christ got us out of it. He says sin entered the race through Adam, but we were forgiven our sins through Christ. Death came by Adam's transgression, but life came to us by Christ's obedience. Our relationship to the first Adam made us dead *in* sin, but our crucifixion with Christ made us dead *to* sin. Our identification with Christ completely removes the effect of our identification with Adam.

When we're born again, the baptism of the Holy Spirit is that ministry of the Spirit which takes us out of Adam and puts us into union with Christ. In fact, the word *baptism* means to totally identify one thing with another. It's the Greek word, *baptizo*, and it was never even translated into English from the original Greek; it was transliterated (which means to take the phonetics of a foreign word and make it a word in English). If we were to translate the word *baptizo* into its English equivalent, it would be the word "identification." So every time you read the word *baptized* in the Bible, you can mentally substitute the words *identified with* and you'll have a better understanding of the true meaning of this sometimes misunderstood word.

He Died For What I "Am" and What I've "Done"

We learned in the early chapters of this book that Christ bore our sins while He hung on the cross. In doing that He judged our sinful *deeds* and removed them as a barrier to God. But now we see that not only were our *sins* on Christ while He was on the cross, but because we have been so totally identified (baptized) with Christ in the mind of God, *we ourselves* were also hanging there on the cross with Jesus.

By taking *us* to the cross with Him and then into the grave, He forever put to death not only our sinful *deeds*, but our sinful *selves*, thus removing not only what we did, but what we *were* (hostile to God, unrighteous, etc.) as a barrier between ourselves and God. He's provided *forgiveness* for what we've *done* and *deliverance* from what we *are*.

Now, not only are my sins not offensive to God, but I'm not either. I'm so accepted by the Father, because of my union with Christ, that in His mind He sees me as actually being seated in heaven in Christ. Paul emphasized this when he wrote, "But God, being rich in mercy, because of His great love with which He loved us, even when we were dead in our transgressions, made us alive together with Christ . . . and raised us up with Him, and seated us with Him in the heavenly places in Christ Jesus" (Ephesians 2:4-6).

Identified with Christ from the Cross to the Throne

The key that unlocks the hidden truth of our release from Satan and the sin nature's power is the little preposition "with." We died *with* Christ, were buried *with* Him, resurrected *with* Him, are seated *with* Him, and will eventually reign *with* Him (Romans 6:1-13; Colossians 3:1-3; Revelation 20:6). Our entire ground for victory as a believer is wrapped up in the death-dealing blow that the death, burial, resurrection, and ascension of Jesus gave to the authority and power of Satan and sin.[3] If you understood no other truths in the Bible than these and fully grasped your total identification with Christ in this victory, you'd be equipped to live victoriously over Satan and over the constant lure and pull of the flesh.

No Need to be Crucified Daily: Once Was Enough!

In one beautiful, all-inclusive statement in Galatians 2:20 Paul sums up the finality and the purpose of our crucifixion with Christ: "I *have been* crucified with Christ; and it is no longer I who live, but Christ lives in me; and the life which I now live in the flesh I live by faith in the Son of God, who loved me, and delivered Himself up for me."

Notice that Paul is careful to point out that our crucifixion with Christ is already a fact, not something which I must do to myself daily or try to get Christ to do to me at some point in my Christian life. In Romans 6, each time Paul speaks of our identification with Christ in His death, he uses the past tense of the verb: "we *have been* buried with Him (verse 4); "we *have become* united with Him in the likeness of His death" (verse 5); "our old self *was crucified* with Him" (verse 6); "we *have died* with Christ" (verse 8).

---

[3] For a fuller understanding of this subject, see chapter fourteen of the author's book, *Satan Is Alive and Well on Planet Earth*.

Then Paul makes the powerful statement in Romans 6:9-11 that on the basis of our *having been* crucified with Christ, we ourselves are actually as dead to sin's power as Jesus is, since His victory over it is ours also. Obviously it goes without saying that if we haven't let it become a reality to us that we've been identified with Christ in His death and resurrection, then we won't see Christ's victory as ours and consequently won't reckon ourselves dead to sin's power in our daily lives. We'll valiantly struggle against temptation out of a genuine desire not to sin; but without knowing that we have legitimate grounds for claiming complete immunity to its power, we'll eventually wear down in our defenses and give in and sin.

We Died in Order to Live!

Knowing that we've been made dead to sin is only half the necessary information that leads to daily victorious Christian living. The other half of the co-crucifixion fact is that we've been made alive with Christ in order to experience the same newness of life that's His. This is called "resurrection life," and it's totally free from any domination of Satan, sin, self, the flesh, and the Law of God.

In Romans 6:11 Paul urges believers to "consider yourselves to be dead to sin, but alive to God in Christ Jesus." Couple this with his statement in Galatians 2:20 that he had been "crucified with Christ," nevertheless was still alive, and it looks like a contradiction. How can you be both dead and alive at the same time? The answer to that is found in that same verse: "It is no longer I who live, but Christ lives in me; and the life which I now live in the flesh I live by faith in the Son of God." We're judicially declared dead to sin's power, but it only becomes a reality in our lives as we consider it to be a fact and by faith count on Christ to live His life in and through us.

Why Are These "Co-Crucifixion" Truths Hard to Grasp!

I'm under no illusions that everyone who has read the words in this last vital chapter has understood the depth of them. For 2,000 years these liberating truths have been prominent in Paul's teachings, particularly in Romans 6, 7, 8 and Galatians and Colossians, yet few believers have grasped their reality in the daily experience of coping with temptation and the lusts of the flesh.

Why is this so?

I believe there are several reasons. First of all, as much as some believers would like it, there are no shortcuts to spiritual maturity just as there are no shortcuts to emotional and physical maturity. Time and the experience of trial and error go into preparing us for an acceptance of these deeper life truths. If we have any notion that there's even the least little thing we can do in ourselves to improve our status with God and strengthen ourselves against the power of sin, then we'll miss God's solution. I can't begin to tell you of the countless believers I've known, including myself, who, not know-ing of our co-crucifixion with Christ, set out on rigorous programs of Bible study, prayer, seeking to walk in the Spirit, witnessing, Scripture memori-zation, and a variety of other good, religious activities in an effort to fortify themselves against sin and Satan's power.

In nearly every case the results have been the same. At first, it seemed to help, but gradually what had been done with a sense of joy and enthusi-asm began to be a drag and legalistic ritual. When all these good spiritual deeds failed to keep us from yielding to sin's power, we were driven to frustration. And that's where far too many believers spend most of their Christian lives, with conscious or subconscious frustration and discourage-ment because they know they've tried the formulas that sincere ministers and friends have suggested and they haven't worked.

If you've come to the point where you haven't any more tricks left up your sleeve for living victoriously over sin and your old self, then there's one of three things you can do: settle down in your defeat and live openly in the flesh with no pretense of trying to be godly or spiritual; or reluctantly come to the conclusion that there isn't any real victory available but try to keep up a spiritual front so as not to be a bad testimony to others; or thank God that He's finally revealed the path to victorious Christian living to you, the path of your co-crucifixion with Christ to sin's power, and begin to reckon it daily to be a fact in your life. Only then can the resurrected life of Christ—the Spirit-filled life—be consistently manifest through you. And only then can you say No to temptation and yield your new self to God and fully expect to be delivered from sin's power.

Believers Need to Be "Son" Conscious

Another reason why believers fail to grasp the reality of their emancipa-tion from sin's power is because so much preaching and teaching today is centered around our sinfulness and not around Christ's forgiveness of it. If we're "sin" conscious continually, then we can't be "Son" conscious. Sin-consciousness only leads us to self-condemnation and self-effort to overcome the sin. But Son-consciousness continually reminds us of God's love and acceptance of us and the forgiveness which He purchased at the cross.

Let's take a practical look at this concept. Nearly every believer has some area of his life where he feels God would like him to change. It may be a habit that isn't consistent with a Christian testimony or it may be an inner attitude of bitterness, jealousy, or lust. Much time is spent in self-recrimination and anger at our inability to give up this sin. In fact, we're so absorbed in our problem that we have little time to focus on the problem-solver, Jesus. And because we're consumed with the consciousness of how sinful and unfaithful we are, we fail to appreciate the forgiveness and faithfulness of God toward us. Our sin-consciousness will always lead us to some kind of *human* effort to change our behavior and that path is doomed to failure since that's simply the flesh trying to change itself.

What's the solution, then, to applying the work of the cross to our daily lives? How can we be consistently reminded to reckon ourselves dead to sin and alive to God? And what are the practical results that we can expect in our lives as we walk by faith, with the resurrection life of Christ manifesting itself through our emotions and behavior?

Only a Renewed Mind Can Grasp These Co-Crucifixion Truths

When you come into the family of God by your rebirth, you bring with you the accumulation of attitudes, behavior, outlook, complexes, and experiences of perhaps years of living without Christ and His influence. All these have combined to make you the person you are. Now suddenly the Bible tells you that you're a "new creation" in Christ. "The old has passed away, behold, the new has come." God also says He now sees you as "holy and blameless" in His eyes because you're "hidden in Christ" and all He sees is Him (2 Corinthians 5:17; Colossians 1:22; 3:3).

The question now is, how do you make what God says is true of you to be more real in your mind than what you know yourself to be on the basis of your past performance? You know you've been anything but holy and blameless, and there are probably a number of things in your life you haven't been able to forgive yourself for, let alone accept God's forgiveness for.

There's only one answer. You must have your mind flushed of the lingering consciousness of the old self-life and a whole new viewpoint of yourself put in its place. You must have your mind renewed before your behavior can change.

How does this take place?

Paul says in Romans 12:2 that the only way to be transformed and not conform to the old way you used to behave is to have your mind renewed. Then the psalmist tells us how this is done: "How can a young man keep his way pure? By keeping it according to Thy word. . . . Thy word I have treasured in my heart that I may not sin against Thee" (Psalm 119:9, 11).

There's no way to have our minds renewed apart from the cleansing and nurturing power of God's Word. The writer of Hebrews calls the Word "milk" and "meat" because it's that which gives us growth and understanding (Hebrews 5:12-14 KJV). Countless believers are struggling along trying to keep their heads above water spiritually, and in almost every case with which I've had to counsel, they had no regular intake of the Word or Christian literature or tapes. There's just no way to find out about the incredible new person you've been made to be apart from the revelation of it in God's Word. You won't be consistently reminded to reckon yourself dead to the flesh and Satan's temptings unless you saturate your mind with God's viewpoint of you.

Your "New Self" Means That You Can Have a New Self-Image

The world, the flesh, and the devil don't let up on you just because you've been born again. In fact, that's when they really go to work trying to keep you from finding out your new authority over them so you won't give them a hard time. They'll particularly conspire together to keep you conscious of all your faults and failures so you'll never come to see the brand new creation God has made you into. If you're full of a sense of inferiority before God, you'll never be greatly used by Him because you won't believe He can use someone like you conceive yourself to be.

In the new science of psycho-cybernetics, the study of self-image, it's been conclusively demonstrated that you can't act consistently contrary to your own self-image—that which you conceive yourself to be. Every person has developed an image of himself over his years of growing up, and unless there is a radical intervention at some point which changes him in some way, physically, emotionally or spiritually, he'll be able to act only in accordance with what he believes he is.

Dr. Maxwell Maltz, a plastic surgeon who had years of experience at observing people's preoperative and postoperative self-images, said in his book *Psycho-cybernetics* that even after dramatic surgery which erased ugly disfigurements, some people still behaved as though they looked the same. They simply could not stop believing they weren't the same old ugly person. Their self-image was so deeply ingrained that they had built their whole life out of it, and it was virtually impossible for them to conceive of themselves as being or looking any different.

Yet he observed a definite phenomenon in other patients. Within several weeks after the plastic surgery had removed an ugly scar, large nose, or similarly unattractive feature, some patients began to experience a change in their whole personalities and behavior. Those who had previously let their disfigurement give them an inferiority complex began to be very self-confident and outgoing. Others who had been failures in one thing or another began to see themselves as winners, and when they did, they actually became more successful in their endeavors.

From twenty years of observing this, Dr. Maltz rightly concluded that it's impossible to behave consistently differently from what you see yourself to be.

But as startling as this discovery was to the field of science, it's a principle as old as the Bible. This is the heart of what it means to be a "new creation" in Christ. When I began to live with the intimate awareness of my new position in Christ, seated far above this old corrupt earth at the right hand of God and viewed as holy and blameless in His eyes, then I'll begin to behave like the royal heir to the royal throne which God says I am. As I let the Holy Spirit renew my mind through God's Word to really see my union with Christ in His defeat of Satan, demons, sin, the world, and my old corrupted self, then and only then will I begin to be transformed into His image and likeness while I'm still here on this earth.

My *self*-image can be permanently improved only when I realize that I've got a whole new *self* inside of me. That new self is beautiful to God because He created it. I don't need to be afraid to have men or God look deeply into me because I know what they'll see. They'll see God's handiwork, not in its finished form, but nevertheless perfect in His eyes. It's a great feeling to like your "self" and not be afraid to be transparent.

A Closing Word of Personal Testimony

I began this book with my personal story of the miracle of God's finding me and putting me into His forever family. One of my main purposes in writing this book has been to show God's great Father's-heart in providing a way to reconcile all of mankind back to Himself.

But I have wanted to show Christ not only as our reconciler, but also as the healer of broken hearts and damaged lives. No one could have been more fouled up in his personal life than I was. My self-image was so rotten that I often contemplated suicide because I felt the world would be better off without someone like me. Even after I became a true believer in Christ I was often inhibited from being available for God's use because I felt so unworthy. I even felt it was spiritual to feel unworthy of God's love and acceptance.

It wasn't until I began to learn about my new exalted position in Christ and the thirty-three new possessions and eternal endowments He had conferred upon me that I began to feel like a different person. No one else had ever thought so highly of me. As I began to find out more and more about this great God who had loved me so much that He put me into union with His Son, I had a greater and greater appreciation of *who* I was because of *whose* I was. My Father was a King, so that made me a royal prince.

As you've read this book, my sincere hope has been that you've seen Jesus and yourself in a whole new light. If you've needed to be reconciled to God, I pray that you have been. If you've needed to be liberated from a quagmire of self-life and defeat, I trust you've seen the provision God has made for your liberation at the cross.

You were made to soar, not crawl. In Christ you're lifted above the stain and fetters of sin on the "wings of eagles." Settle back now and begin to enjoy this "so great salvation."